SERIAL AND PARALLEL ROBOT MANIPULATORS – KINEMATICS, DYNAMICS, CONTROL AND OPTIMIZATION

Edited by **Serdar Küçük**

Serial and Parallel Robot Manipulators – Kinematics, Dynamics, Control and Optimization
Edited by Serdar Küçük

Published by InTech

Janeza Trdine 9, 51000 Rijeka, Croatia

Publishing Process Manager Molly Kaliman

Technical Editor Teodora Smiljanic

Cover Designer InTech Design Team

Additional hard copies can be obtained from orders@intechopen.com

Serial and Parallel Robot Manipulators – Kinematics, Dynamics, Control and Optimization,
Edited by Serdar Küçük
p. cm.
ISBN 978-953-51-0437-7

For EU product safety concerns:
IN TECH d.o.o., Prolaz Marije Krucifikse Kozulić 3, 51000 Rijeka, Croatia,
info@intechopen.com or visit our website at intechopen.com.

Meet the editor

Dr. Serdar Kucuk was born in the eastern region (Mus) of Turkey in 1970. He received the BA and MSc degree in Electronics & Computer Department from Marmara University (1995) and in Electronic & Telecommunication Department from Marmara University (1998), Istanbul, Turkey, respectively, and the Ph.D. degree in Electrical Education Department of Kocaeli University (2004) in Turkey. He became an assistant professor in 2005 and associate professor in 2011 at the Kocaeli University. He has several scientific publications including international conference papers, journal papers, books and book chapters. He currently serves as an Editorial Board Member of the International Journal of Advanced Robotic Systems. His research interests are optimization, control, kinematics and dynamics modeling of serial and parallel robotic manipulators.

Contents

Preface

The interest in robotics has been steadily increasing during the last decades. This concern has directly impacted the development of the novel theoretical research areas and products. Some of the fundamental issues that have emerged in serial and especially parallel robotics manipulators are kinematics & dynamics modeling, optimization, control algorithms and design strategies. In this new book, we have highlighted the latest topics about the serial and parallel robotic manipulators in the sections of kinematics & dynamics, control and optimization. I would like to thank all authors who have contributed the book chapters with their valuable novel ideas and current developments.

Assoc. Prof. PhD. Serdar Küçük
Kocaeli University, Electronics and Computer Department, Kocaeli
Turkey

Part 1

Kinematics and Dynamics

1

Inverse Dynamics of RRR Fully Planar Parallel Manipulator Using DH Method

Serdar Küçük
Kocaeli University
Turkey

1. Introduction

Parallel manipulators are mechanisms where all the links are connected to the ground and the moving platform at the same time. They possess high rigidity, load capacity, precision, structural stiffness, velocity and acceleration since the end-effector is linked to the movable plate in several points (Kang et al., 2001; Kang & Mills, 2001; Merlet, J. P. 2000; Tsai, L., 1999; Uchiyama, M., 1994). Parallel manipulators can be classified into two fundamental categories, namely spatial and planar manipulators. The first category composes of the spatial parallel manipulators that can translate and rotate in the three dimensional space. Gough-Stewart platform, one of the most popular spatial manipulator, is extensively preferred in flight simulators. The planar parallel manipulators which composes of second category, translate along the x and y-axes, and rotate around the z-axis, only. Although planar parallel manipulators are increasingly being used in industry for micro-or nano-positioning applications, (Hubbard et al., 2001), the kinematics, especially dynamics analysis of planar parallel manipulators is more difficult than their serial counterparts. Therefore selection of an efficient kinematic modeling convention is very important for simplifying the complexity of the dynamics problems in planar parallel manipulators. In this chapter, the inverse dynamics problem of three-**D**egrees **O**f **F**reedom (**DOF**) RRR **F**ully **P**lanar **P**arallel **M**anipulator (**FPPM**) is derived using DH method (Denavit & Hartenberg, 1955) which is based on 4x4 homogenous transformation matrices. The easy physical interpretation of the rigid body structures of the robotic manipulators is the main benefit of DH method. The inverse dynamics of 3-DOF RRR FPPM is derived using the virtual work principle (Zhang, & Song, 1993; Wu et al., 2010; Wu et al., 2011). In the first step, the inverse kinematics model and Jacobian matrix of 3-DOF RRR FPPM are derived by using DH method. To obtain the inverse dynamics, the partial linear velocity and partial angular velocity matrices are computed in the second step. A pivotal point is selected in order to determine the partial linear velocity matrices. The inertial force and moment of each moving part are obtained in the next step. As a last step, the inverse dynamic equation of 3-DOF RRR FPPM in explicit form is derived. To demonstrate the active joints torques, a butterfly shape Cartesian trajectory is used as a desired end-effector's trajectory.

2. Inverse kinematics and dynamics model of the 3-DOF RRR FPPM

In this section, geometric description, inverse kinematics, Jacobian matrix & Jacobian inversion and inverse dynamics model of the 3-DOF RRR FPPM in explicit form are obtained by applying DH method.

2.1 Geometric descriptions of 3-DOF RRR FPPM

The 3-DOF RRR FPPM shown in Figure 1 has a moving platform linked to the ground by three independent kinematics chains including one active joint each. The symbols θ_i and α_i illustrate the active and passive revolute joints, respectively where i=1, 2 and 3. The link lengths and the orientation of the moving platform are denoted by l_j and ϕ, respectively, j=1, 2, ··· ,6. The points B_1, B_2, B_3 and M_1, M_2, M_3 define the geometry of the base and the moving (Figure 2) platform, respectively. The {XYZ} and {xyz} coordinate systems are attached to the base and the moving platform of the manipulator, respectively. O and M_1 are the origins of the base and moving platforms, respectively. $P(X_B, Y_B)$ and ϕ illustrate the position of the end-effector in terms of the base coordinate system {XYZ} and orientation of the moving platform, respectively.

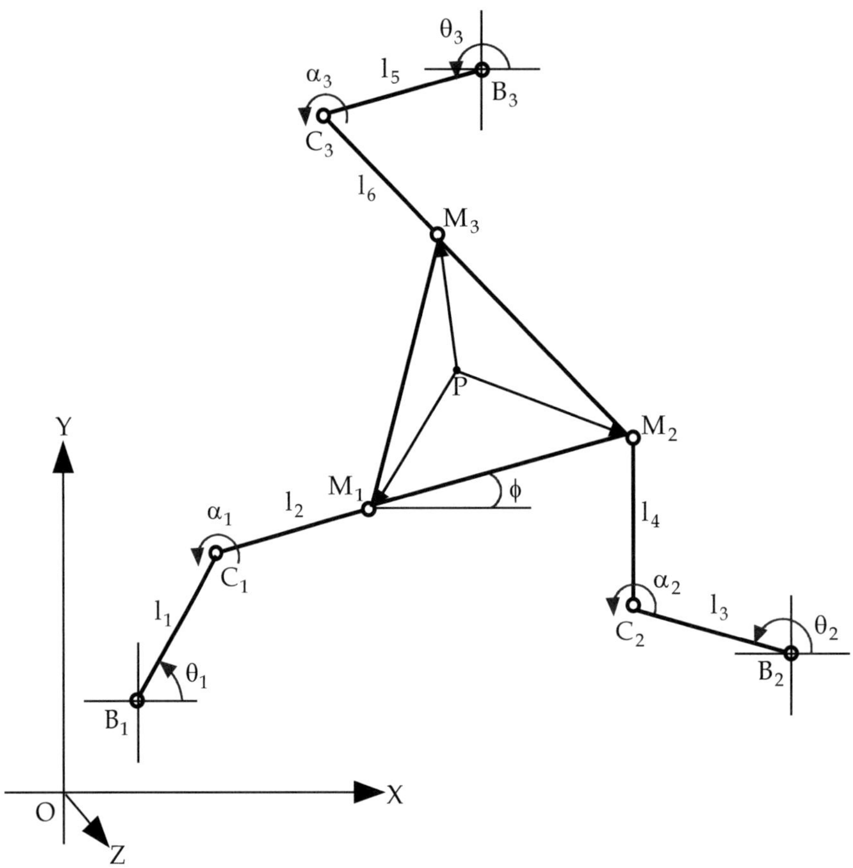

Fig. 1. The 3-DOF RRR FPPM

The lines M_1P, M_2P and M_3P are regarded as n_1, n_2 and n_3, respectively. The γ_1, γ_2 and γ_3 illustrate the angles $B\hat{P}M_1$, $M_2\hat{P}B$, and $B\hat{P}M_3$, respectively. Since two lines AB and M_1M_2 are parallel, the angles $P\hat{M}_1M_2$ and $P\hat{M}_2M_1$ are equal to the angles $A\hat{P}M_1$ and $M_2\hat{P}B$, respectively. $P(x_m, y_m)$ denotes the position of end-effector in terms of {xyz} coordinate systems.

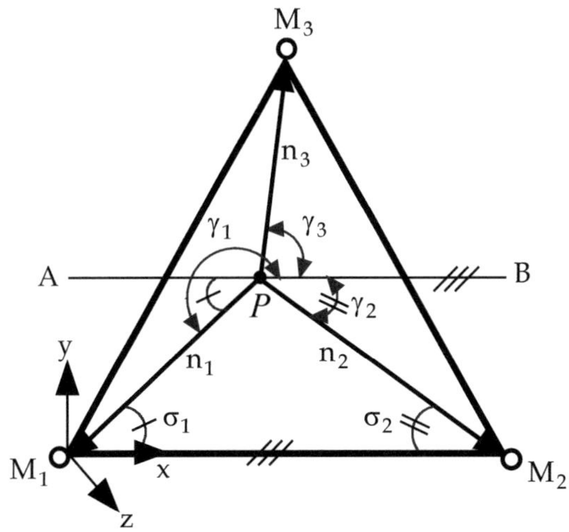

Fig. 2. The moving platform

2.2 Inverse kinematics

The inverse kinematic equations of 3-DOF RRR FPPM are derived using the DH (Denavit & Hartenberg, 1955) method which is based on 4x4 homogenous transformation matrices. The easy physical interpretation of the rigid body structures of the robotic manipulators is the main benefit of DH method which uses a set of parameters ($\alpha_{i-1}, a_{i-1}, \theta_i$ and d_i) to describe the spatial transformation between two consecutive links. To find the inverse kinematics problem, the following equation can be written using the geometric identities on Figure 1.

$$OB_i + B_iM_i = OP + PM_i \tag{1}$$

where i=1, 2 and 3. If the equation 1 is adapted to the manipulator in Figure 1, the ${}^{O_i}_{M_i}T^1$ and ${}^{O_i}_{M_i}T^2$ transformation matrices can be determined as

$$
{}^{O_i}_{M_i}T^1 = \begin{bmatrix} 1 & 0 & 0 & o_{x_i} \\ 0 & 1 & 0 & o_{y_i} \\ 0 & 0 & 1 & 0 \\ 0 & 0 & 0 & 1 \end{bmatrix} \begin{bmatrix} \cos\theta_i & -\sin\theta_i & 0 & 0 \\ \sin\theta_i & \cos\theta_i & 0 & 0 \\ 0 & 0 & 1 & 0 \\ 0 & 0 & 0 & 1 \end{bmatrix} \begin{bmatrix} \cos\alpha_i & -\sin\alpha_i & 0 & l_{2i-1} \\ \sin\alpha_i & \cos\alpha_i & 0 & 0 \\ 0 & 0 & 1 & 0 \\ 0 & 0 & 0 & 1 \end{bmatrix} \begin{bmatrix} 1 & 0 & 0 & l_{2i} \\ 0 & 1 & 0 & 0 \\ 0 & 0 & 1 & 0 \\ 0 & 0 & 0 & 1 \end{bmatrix}
$$

$$
= \begin{bmatrix} \cos(\theta_i + \alpha_i) & -\sin(\theta_i + \alpha_i) & 0 & o_{x_i} + l_{2i}\cos(\theta_i + \alpha_i) + l_{2i-1}\cos\theta_i \\ \sin(\theta_i + \alpha_i) & \cos(\theta_i + \alpha_i) & 0 & o_{y_i} + l_{2i}\sin(\theta_i + \alpha_i) + l_{2i-1}\sin\theta_i \\ 0 & 0 & 1 & 0 \\ 0 & 0 & 0 & 1 \end{bmatrix} \tag{2}
$$

$$
{}^{O_i}_{M_i}T^2 = \begin{bmatrix} 1 & 0 & 0 & P_{X_B} \\ 0 & 1 & 0 & P_{Y_B} \\ 0 & 0 & 1 & 0 \\ 0 & 0 & 0 & 1 \end{bmatrix} \begin{bmatrix} \cos(\gamma_i + \phi) & -\sin(\gamma_i + \phi) & 0 & 0 \\ \sin(\gamma_i + \phi) & \cos(\gamma_i + \phi) & 0 & 0 \\ 0 & 0 & 1 & 0 \\ 0 & 0 & 0 & 1 \end{bmatrix} \begin{bmatrix} 1 & 0 & 0 & n_i \\ 0 & 1 & 0 & 0 \\ 0 & 0 & 1 & 0 \\ 0 & 0 & 0 & 1 \end{bmatrix}
$$

$$= \begin{bmatrix} \cos(\gamma_i + \phi) & -\sin(\gamma_i + \phi) & 0 & P_{X_B} + n_i\cos\gamma_i\cos\phi - n_i\sin\gamma_i\sin\phi \\ \sin(\gamma_i + \phi) & \cos(\gamma_i + \phi) & 0 & P_{Y_B} + n_i\cos\gamma_i\sin\phi + n_i\sin\gamma_i\cos\phi \\ 0 & 0 & 1 & 0 \\ 0 & 0 & 0 & 1 \end{bmatrix} \quad (3)$$

where (P_{X_B}, P_{Y_B}) corresponds the position of the end-effector in terms of the base {XYZ} coordinate systems, $\gamma_1 = \pi + \sigma_1$ and $\gamma_2 = -\sigma_2$. Since the position vectors of ${}^{O_i}_{M_i}T^1$ and ${}^{O_i}_{M_i}T^2$ matrices are equal, the following equation can be obtained easily.

$$\begin{bmatrix} l_{2i}\cos(\theta_i + \alpha_i) \\ l_{2i}\sin(\theta_i + \alpha_i) \end{bmatrix} = \begin{bmatrix} P_{X_B} + b_{x_i}\cos\phi - b_{y_i}\sin\phi - o_{x_i} - l_{2i-1}\cos\theta_i \\ P_{Y_B} + b_{x_i}\sin\phi + b_{y_i}\cos\phi - o_{y_i} - l_{2i-1}\sin\theta_i \end{bmatrix} \quad (4)$$

where $b_{x_i} = n_i\cos\gamma_i$ and $b_{y_i} = n_i\sin\gamma_i$. Summing the squares of the both sides in equation 4, we obtain, after simplification,

$$l_{2i-1}^2 - 2P_{Y_B}o_{y_i} - 2P_{X_B}o_{x_i} + b_{x_i}^2 + b_{y_i}^2 + o_{x_i}^2 + o_{y_i}^2 + P_{X_B}^2 + P_{Y_B}^2$$

$$+2l_{2i-1}b_{y_i}[\sin(\phi - \theta_i) - \cos(\phi - \theta_i)] + 2\cos\phi\left(P_{X_B}b_{x_i} + P_{Y_B}b_{y_i} - b_{x_i}o_{x_i} - b_{y_i}o_{y_i}\right)$$

$$+2\sin\phi\left(P_{Y_B}b_{x_i} - P_{X_B}b_{y_i} - b_{x_i}o_{y_i} + b_{y_i}o_{x_i}\right) + 2l_{2i-1}\cos\theta_i(o_{x_i} - P_{X_B})$$

$$+2l_{2i-1}\sin\theta_i\left(o_{y_i} - P_{Y_B}\right) - l_{2i}^2 = 0 \quad (5)$$

To compute the inverse kinematics, the equation 5 can be rewritten as follows

$$A_i\sin\theta_i + B_i\cos\theta_i = C_i \quad (6)$$

where

$$A_i = 2l_{2i-1}\left(o_{y_i} - b_{x_i}\sin\phi - b_{y_i}\cos\phi - P_{Y_B}\right)$$

$$B_i = 2l_{2i-1}\left(o_{x_i} + b_{y_i}\sin\phi - b_{x_i}\cos\phi - P_{X_B}\right)$$

$$C_i = -\left[l_{2i-1}^2 - 2P_{Y_B}o_{y_i} - 2P_{X_B}o_{x_i} + b_{x_i}^2 + b_{y_i}^2 + o_{x_i}^2 + o_{y_i}^2 + P_{X_B}^2 + P_{Y_B}^2 - l_{2i}^2\right.$$

$$\left.+2\cos\phi\left(P_{X_B}b_{x_i} + P_{Y_B}b_{y_i} - b_{x_i}o_{x_i} - b_{y_i}o_{y_i}\right) + 2\sin\phi\left(P_{Y_B}b_{x_i} - P_{X_B}b_{y_i} - b_{x_i}o_{y_i} + b_{y_i}o_{x_i}\right)\right]$$

The inverse kinematics solution for equation 6 is

$$\theta_i = \mathrm{Atan2}(A_i, B_i) \mp \mathrm{Atan2}\left(\sqrt{A_i^2 + B_i^2 - C_i^2}, C_i\right) \quad (7a)$$

Once the active joint variables are determined, the passive joint variables can be computed by using equation 4 as follows.

$$\alpha_i = \mathrm{Atan2}(D_i, E_i) \mp \mathrm{Atan2}\left(\sqrt{D_i^2 + E_i^2 - G_i^2}, G_i\right) \quad (7b)$$

where

$$D_i = -\sin\theta_i, \; E_i = \cos\theta_i$$

and

$$G_i = \left(P_{X_B} + b_{x_i}\cos\phi - b_{y_i}\sin\phi - o_{x_i} - l_{2i-1}\cos\theta_i\right)/l_{2i}$$

Since the equation 7 produce two possible solutions for each kinematic chain according to the selection of plus '+' or mines '-' signs, there are eight possible inverse kinematics solutions for 3-DOF RRR FPPM.

2.3 Jacobian matrix and Jacobian inversion

Differentiating the equation 5 with respect to the time, one can obtain the Jacobian matrices.

$$B\dot{\mathbf{q}} = A\dot{\chi}$$

$$\begin{bmatrix} d_1 & 0 & 0 \\ 0 & d_2 & 0 \\ 0 & 0 & d_3 \end{bmatrix} \begin{bmatrix} \dot{\theta}_1 \\ \dot{\theta}_2 \\ \dot{\theta}_3 \end{bmatrix} = \begin{bmatrix} a_1 & b_1 & c_1 \\ a_2 & b_2 & c_2 \\ a_3 & b_3 & c_3 \end{bmatrix} \begin{bmatrix} \dot{P}_{X_B} \\ \dot{P}_{Y_B} \\ \dot{\phi} \end{bmatrix} \tag{8}$$

where

$$a_i = -2\left(P_{X_B} - o_{x_i} + b_{x_i}\cos\phi - l_{2i-1}\cos\theta_i - b_{y_i}\sin\phi\right)$$

$$b_i = -2\left(P_{Y_B} - o_{y_i} + b_{y_i}\cos\phi - l_{2i-1}\sin\theta_i + b_{x_i}\sin\phi\right)$$

$$c_i = -2\big[l_{2i-1}b_{y_i}\cos(\phi-\theta_i) + l_{2i-1}b_{x_i}\sin(\phi-\theta_i) + \cos\phi\left(P_{Y_B}b_{x_i} - P_{X_B}b_{y_i} - b_{x_i}o_{y_i} + b_{y_i}o_{x_i}\right) + \sin\phi\left(b_{x_i}o_{x_i} + b_{y_i}o_{y_i} - P_{X_B}b_{x_i} - P_{Y_B}b_{y_i}\right)\big]$$

$$d_i = 2\big[l_{2i-1}\cos\theta_i\left(o_{y_i} - P_{Y_B}\right) + l_{2i-1}\sin\theta_i\left(P_{X_B} - o_{x_i}\right) - l_{2i-1}b_{y_i}\cos(\phi-\theta_i) - l_{2i-1}b_{x_i}\sin(\phi-\theta_i)\big]$$

The A and B terms in equation 8 denote two separate Jacobian matrices. Thus the overall Jacobian matrix can be obtained as

$$J = B^{-1}A = \begin{bmatrix} \frac{a_1}{d_1} & \frac{b_1}{d_1} & \frac{c_1}{d_1} \\ \frac{a_2}{d_2} & \frac{b_2}{d_2} & \frac{c_2}{d_2} \\ \frac{a_3}{d_3} & \frac{b_3}{d_3} & \frac{c_3}{d_3} \end{bmatrix} \tag{9}$$

The manipulator Jacobian is used for mapping the velocities from the joint space to the Cartesian space

$$\dot{\theta} = J\dot{\chi} \tag{10}$$

where $\dot{\chi} = [\dot{P}_{X_B} \quad \dot{P}_{Y_B} \quad \dot{\phi}]^T$and $\dot{\theta} = [\dot{\theta}_1 \quad \dot{\theta}_2 \quad \dot{\theta}_3]^T$ are the vectors of velocity in the Cartesian and joint spaces, respectively.

To compute the inverse dynamics of the manipulator, the acceleration of the end-effector is used as the input signal. Therefore, the relationship between the joint and Cartesian accelerations can be extracted by differentiation of equation 10 with respect to the time.

$$\ddot{\theta} = J\ddot{\chi} + \dot{J}\dot{\chi} \tag{11}$$

where $\ddot{\chi} = [\ddot{P}_{X_B} \quad \ddot{P}_{Y_B} \quad \ddot{\phi}]^T$ and $\ddot{\theta} = [\ddot{\theta}_1 \quad \ddot{\theta}_2 \quad \ddot{\theta}_3]^T$ are the vectors of acceleration in the Cartesian and joint spaces, respectively. In equation 11, the other quantities are assumed to be known from the velocity inversion and the only matrix that has not been defined yet is the time derivative of the Jacobian matrix. Differentiation of equation 9 yields to

$$\dot{J} = \begin{bmatrix} K_1 & L_1 & R_1 \\ K_2 & L_2 & R_2 \\ K_3 & L_3 & R_3 \end{bmatrix} \tag{12}$$

K_i, L_i and R_i in equation 12 can be written as follows.

$$K_i = \frac{\dot{a}_i d_i - a_i \dot{d}_i}{d_i^2} \tag{13}$$

$$L_i = \frac{\dot{b}_i d_i - b_i \dot{d}_i}{d_i^2} \tag{14}$$

$$R_i = \frac{\dot{c}_i d_i - c_i \dot{d}_i}{d_i^2} \tag{15}$$

where

$$\dot{a}_i = -2\left(\dot{P}_{X_B} - \dot{\phi} b_{x_i} \sin\phi + \dot{\theta}_i l_{2i-1} \sin\theta_i - \dot{\phi} b_{y_i} \cos\phi\right)$$

$$\dot{b}_i = -2\left(\dot{P}_{Y_B} - \dot{\phi} b_{y_i} \sin\phi - \dot{\theta}_i l_{2i-1} \cos\theta_i + \dot{\phi} b_{x_i} \cos\phi\right)$$

$$\begin{aligned} \dot{c}_i = -2\big[& -l_{2i-1} b_{y_i}(\dot{\phi} - \dot{\theta}_i)\sin(\phi - \theta_i) + (\dot{\phi} - \dot{\theta}_i) l_{2i-1} b_{x_i} \cos(\phi - \theta_i) \\ & -\dot{\phi}\sin\phi\left(P_{Y_B} b_{x_i} - P_{X_B} b_{y_i} - b_{x_i} o_{y_i} + b_{y_i} o_{x_i}\right) + \cos\phi\left(\dot{P}_{Y_B} b_{x_i} - \dot{P}_{X_B} b_{y_i}\right) \\ & +\dot{\phi}\cos\phi\left(b_{x_i} o_{x_i} + b_{y_i} o_{y_i} - P_{X_B} b_{x_i} - P_{Y_B} b_{y_i}\right) - \sin\phi\left(\dot{P}_{X_B} b_{x_i} + \dot{P}_{Y_B} b_{y_i}\right)\big] \end{aligned}$$

$$\begin{aligned} \dot{d}_i = 2\big[& -l_{2i-1}\dot{\theta}_i \sin\theta_i\left(o_{y_i} - P_{Y_B}\right) - l_{2i-1}\cos\theta_i \dot{P}_{Y_B} + l_{2i-1}\dot{\theta}_i \cos\theta_i\left(P_{X_B} - o_{x_i}\right) + l_{2i-1}\sin\theta_i \dot{P}_{X_B} \\ & + l_{2i-1} b_{y_i}(\dot{\phi} - \dot{\theta}_i)\sin(\phi - \theta_i) - l_{2i-1} b_{x_i}(\dot{\phi} - \dot{\theta}_i)\cos(\phi - \theta_i)\big] \end{aligned}$$

2.4 Inverse dynamics model

The virtual work principle is used to obtain the inverse dynamics model of 3-DOF RRR FPPM. Firstly, the partial linear velocity and partial angular velocity matrices are computed by using homogenous transformation matrices derived in Section 2.2. To find the partial linear velocity matrix, B_{2i-1}, C_{2i-1} and M_3 points are selected as pivotal points of links l_{2i-1}, l_{2i} and moving platform, respectively in the second step. The inertial force and moment of each moving part are determined in the next step. As a last step, the inverse dynamic equations of 3-DOF RRR FPPM in explicit form are derived.

2.4.1 The partial linear velocity and partial angular velocity matrices

Considering the manipulator Jacobian matrix in equation 10, the joint velocities for the link l_{2i-1} can be expressed in terms of Cartesian velocities as follows.

$$\dot{\theta}_i = \begin{bmatrix} \frac{a_i}{d_i} & \frac{b_i}{d_i} & \frac{c_i}{d_i} \end{bmatrix} \begin{bmatrix} \dot{P}_{X_B} \\ \dot{P}_{Y_B} \\ \dot{\phi} \end{bmatrix}, \quad i = 1,2 \text{ and } 3. \tag{16}$$

The partial angular velocity matrix of the link l_{2i-1} can be derived from the equation 16 as

$$\boldsymbol{\omega}_{2i-1} = \begin{bmatrix} \frac{a_i}{d_i} & \frac{b_i}{d_i} & \frac{c_i}{d_i} \end{bmatrix}, \quad i = 1,2 \text{ and } 3. \tag{17}$$

Since the linear velocity on point B_i is zero, the partial linear velocity matrix of the point B_i is given by

$$\boldsymbol{\upsilon}_{2i-1} = \begin{bmatrix} 0 & 0 & 0 \\ 0 & 0 & 0 \end{bmatrix}, \quad i = 1,2 \text{ and } 3. \tag{18}$$

To find the partial angular velocity matrix of the link l_{2i}, the equation 19 can be written easily using the equality of the position vectors of ${}^{O_i}_{M_i}T^1$ and ${}^{O_i}_{M_i}T^2$ matrices.

$$\begin{bmatrix} o_{x_i} + l_{2i}\cos(\theta_i + \alpha_i) + l_{2i-1}\cos\theta_i \\ o_{y_i} + l_{2i}\sin(\theta_i + \alpha_i) + l_{2i-1}\sin\theta_i \end{bmatrix} = \begin{bmatrix} P_{X_B} + b_{x_i}\cos\phi - b_{y_i}\sin\phi \\ P_{Y_B} + b_{x_i}\sin\phi + b_{y_i}\cos\phi \end{bmatrix} \tag{19}$$

The equation 19 can be rearranged as in equation 20 since the link l_{2i} moves with $\delta_i = \theta_i + \alpha_i$ angular velocity.

$$\begin{bmatrix} o_{x_i} + l_{2i}\cos\delta_i + l_{2i-1}\cos\theta_i \\ o_{y_i} + l_{2i}\sin\delta_i + l_{2i-1}\sin\theta_i \end{bmatrix} = \begin{bmatrix} P_{X_B} + b_{x_i}\cos\phi - b_{y_i}\sin\phi \\ P_{Y_B} + b_{x_i}\sin\phi + b_{y_i}\cos\phi \end{bmatrix} \tag{20}$$

Taking the time derivative of equation 20 yields the following equation.

$$\begin{bmatrix} -l_{2i}\dot{\delta}_i\sin\delta_i - l_{2i-1}\dot{\theta}_i\sin\theta_i \\ l_{2i}\dot{\delta}_i\cos\delta_i + l_{2i-1}\dot{\theta}_i\cos\theta_i \end{bmatrix} = \begin{bmatrix} \dot{P}_{X_B} - \dot{\phi}b_{x_i}\sin\phi - \dot{\phi}b_{y_i}\cos\phi \\ \dot{P}_{Y_B} + \dot{\phi}b_{x_i}\cos\phi - \dot{\phi}b_{y_i}\sin\phi \end{bmatrix} \tag{21}$$

Equation 21 can also be stated as follows.

$$\begin{bmatrix} -\sin\delta_i \\ \cos\delta_i \end{bmatrix} l_{2i}\dot{\delta}_i + \begin{bmatrix} -l_{2i-1}\sin\theta_i \\ l_{2i-1}\cos\theta_i \end{bmatrix} \dot{\theta}_i = \begin{bmatrix} 1 & 0 & -b_{x_i}\sin\phi - b_{y_i}\cos\phi \\ 0 & 1 & b_{x_i}\cos\phi - b_{y_i}\sin\phi \end{bmatrix} \begin{bmatrix} \dot{P}_{X_B} \\ \dot{P}_{Y_B} \\ \dot{\phi} \end{bmatrix} \tag{22}$$

If $\dot{\theta}$ in equation 16 is substituted in equation 22, the following equation will be obtained.

$$\begin{bmatrix} -\sin\delta_i \\ \cos\delta_i \end{bmatrix} l_{2i}\dot{\delta}_i = \left(\begin{bmatrix} 1 & 0 & -b_{x_i}\sin\phi - b_{y_i}\cos\phi \\ 0 & 1 & b_{x_i}\cos\phi - b_{y_i}\sin\phi \end{bmatrix} - \begin{bmatrix} -l_{2i-1}\sin\theta_i \\ l_{2i-1}\cos\theta_i \end{bmatrix} \begin{bmatrix} \frac{a_i}{d_i} & \frac{b_i}{d_i} & \frac{c_i}{d_i} \end{bmatrix} \right) \begin{bmatrix} \dot{P}_{X_B} \\ \dot{P}_{Y_B} \\ \dot{\phi} \end{bmatrix} \tag{23}$$

If the both sides of equation 23 premultiplied by $[-\sin\delta_i \quad \cos\delta_i]$, angular velocity of link l_{2i} is obtained as.

$$\dot{\delta}_i = \begin{bmatrix} -\frac{\sin\delta_i}{l_{2i}} & \frac{\cos\delta_i}{l_{2i}} \end{bmatrix} \left(\begin{bmatrix} 1 & 0 & -b_{x_i}\sin\phi - b_{y_i}\cos\phi \\ 0 & 1 & b_{x_i}\cos\phi - b_{y_i}\sin\phi \end{bmatrix} - \begin{bmatrix} -l_{2i-1}\sin\theta_i \\ l_{2i-1}\cos\theta_i \end{bmatrix} \begin{bmatrix} \frac{a_i}{d_i} & \frac{b_i}{d_i} & \frac{c_i}{d_i} \end{bmatrix} \right) \begin{bmatrix} \dot{P}_{X_B} \\ \dot{P}_{Y_B} \\ \dot{\phi} \end{bmatrix} \tag{24}$$

Finally the angular velocity matrix of l_{2i} is derived from the equation 24 as follows.

$$\omega_{2i} = \begin{bmatrix} -\frac{\sin\delta_i}{l_{2i}} & \frac{\cos\delta_i}{l_{2i}} \end{bmatrix} \left(\begin{bmatrix} 1 & 0 & -b_{x_i}\sin\phi - b_{y_i}\cos\phi \\ 0 & 1 & b_{x_i}\cos\phi - b_{y_i}\sin\phi \end{bmatrix} - \begin{bmatrix} -l_{2i-1}\sin\theta_i \\ l_{2i-1}\cos\theta_i \end{bmatrix} \begin{bmatrix} \frac{a_i}{d_i} & \frac{b_i}{d_i} & \frac{c_i}{d_i} \end{bmatrix} \right) \quad (25)$$

The angular acceleration of the link l_{2i} is found by taking the time derivative of equation 21.

$$\begin{bmatrix} -l_{2i}(\ddot{\delta}_i\sin\delta_i + \dot{\delta}_i^2\cos\delta_i) - l_{2i-1}(\ddot{\theta}_i\sin\theta_i + \dot{\theta}_i^2\cos\theta_i) \\ l_{2i}(\ddot{\delta}_i\cos\delta_i - \dot{\delta}_i^2\sin\delta_i) + l_{2i-1}(\ddot{\theta}_i\cos\theta_i - \dot{\theta}_i^2\sin\theta_i) \end{bmatrix}$$

$$= \begin{bmatrix} \ddot{P}_{X_B} - (\ddot{\phi}b_{x_i}\sin\phi + \dot{\phi}^2 b_{x_i}\cos\phi) - (\ddot{\phi}b_{y_i}\cos\phi - \dot{\phi}^2 b_{y_i}\sin\phi) \\ \ddot{P}_{Y_B} + (\ddot{\phi}b_{x_i}\cos\phi - \dot{\phi}^2 b_{x_i}\sin\phi) - (\ddot{\phi}b_{y_i}\sin\phi + \dot{\phi}^2 b_{y_i}\cos\phi) \end{bmatrix} \quad (26)$$

Equation 26 can be expressed as

$$\begin{bmatrix} -\sin\delta_i \\ \cos\delta_i \end{bmatrix} l_{2i}\ddot{\delta}_i = \begin{bmatrix} s_{i1} \\ s_{i2} \end{bmatrix} \quad (27)$$

where

$$s_{i1} = \ddot{P}_{X_B} - (\ddot{\phi}b_{x_i}\sin\phi + \dot{\phi}^2 b_{x_i}\cos\phi) - (\ddot{\phi}b_{y_i}\cos\phi - \dot{\phi}^2 b_{y_i}\sin\phi) + l_{2i}\dot{\delta}_i^2\cos\delta_i$$

$$+l_{2i-1}(\ddot{\theta}_i\sin\theta_i + \dot{\theta}_i^2\cos\theta_i)$$

$$s_{i2} = \ddot{P}_{Y_B} + (\ddot{\phi}b_{x_i}\cos\phi - \dot{\phi}^2 b_{x_i}\sin\phi) - (\ddot{\phi}b_{y_i}\sin\phi + \dot{\phi}^2 b_{y_i}\cos\phi) + l_{2i}\dot{\delta}_i^2\sin\delta_i$$

$$-l_{2i-1}(\ddot{\theta}_i\cos\theta_i - \dot{\theta}_i^2\sin\theta_i)$$

If the both sides of equation 27 premultiplied by $[-\sin\delta_i \quad \cos\delta_i]$, angular acceleration of link l_{2i} is obtained as.

$$\ddot{\delta}_i = \begin{bmatrix} -\frac{\sin\delta_i}{l_{2i}} & \frac{\cos\delta_i}{l_{2i}} \end{bmatrix} \begin{bmatrix} s_{i1} \\ s_{i2} \end{bmatrix} \quad (28)$$

where i=1,2 and 3. To find the partial linear velocity matrix of the point C_i, the position vector of ${}^{O_i}_{C_i}T^1$ is obtained in the first step.

$${}^{O_i}_{C_i}T^1 = \begin{bmatrix} 1 & 0 & 0 & o_{x_i} \\ 0 & 1 & 0 & o_{y_i} \\ 0 & 0 & 1 & 0 \\ 0 & 0 & 0 & 1 \end{bmatrix} \begin{bmatrix} \cos\theta_i & -\sin\theta_i & 0 & 0 \\ \sin\theta_i & \cos\theta_i & 0 & 0 \\ 0 & 0 & 1 & 0 \\ 0 & 0 & 0 & 1 \end{bmatrix} \begin{bmatrix} 1 & 0 & 0 & l_{2i-1} \\ 0 & 1 & 0 & 0 \\ 0 & 0 & 1 & 0 \\ 0 & 0 & 0 & 1 \end{bmatrix}$$

$$= \begin{bmatrix} \cos\theta_i & -\sin\theta_i & 0 & o_{x_i} + l_{2i-1}\cos\theta_i \\ \sin\theta_i & \cos\theta_i & 0 & o_{y_i} + l_{2i-1}\sin\theta_i \\ 0 & 0 & 1 & 0 \\ 0 & 0 & 0 & 1 \end{bmatrix} \quad (29)$$

The position vector of ${}^{O_i}_{C_i}T^1$ is obtained from the fourth column of the equation 29 as

$${}^{O_i}_{C_i}T^1_{P(x,y)} = \begin{bmatrix} o_{x_i} + l_{2i-1}\cos\theta_i \\ o_{y_i} + l_{2i-1}\sin\theta_i \end{bmatrix} \quad (30)$$

Taking the time derivative of equation 30 produces the linear velocity of the point C_i.

$$v_{C_i} = \frac{d}{dt}\left({}^{O_i}_{C_i}T^{1}_{P(x,y)}\right) = \begin{bmatrix} -l_{2i-1}\sin\theta_i \\ l_{2i-1}\cos\theta_i \end{bmatrix}\dot{\theta}_i \tag{31}$$

If $\dot{\theta}$ in equation 16 is substituted in equation 31, the linear velocity of the point C_i will be expressed in terms of Cartesian velocities.

$$v_{C_i} = \begin{bmatrix} -l_{2i-1}\sin\theta_i \\ l_{2i-1}\cos\theta_i \end{bmatrix}\begin{bmatrix} \frac{a_i}{d_i} & \frac{b_i}{d_i} & \frac{c_i}{d_i} \end{bmatrix}\begin{bmatrix} \dot{P}_{X_B} \\ \dot{P}_{Y_B} \\ \dot{\phi} \end{bmatrix}$$

$$= \frac{l_{2i-1}}{d_i}\begin{bmatrix} -a_i\sin\theta_i & -b_i\sin\theta_i & -c_i\sin\theta_i \\ a_i\cos\theta_i & b_i\cos\theta_i & c_i\cos\theta_i \end{bmatrix}\begin{bmatrix} \dot{P}_{X_B} \\ \dot{P}_{Y_B} \\ \dot{\phi} \end{bmatrix} \tag{32}$$

Finally the partial linear velocity matrix of l_{2i} is derived from the equation 32 as

$$\mathbf{v_{2i}} = \frac{l_{2i-1}}{d_i}\begin{bmatrix} -a_i\sin\theta_i & -b_i\sin\theta_i & -c_i\sin\theta_i \\ a_i\cos\theta_i & b_i\cos\theta_i & c_i\cos\theta_i \end{bmatrix} \tag{33}$$

The angular velocity of the moving platform is given by

$$a_{mp} = \begin{bmatrix} 0 & 0 & 1 \end{bmatrix}\begin{bmatrix} \dot{P}_{X_B} \\ \dot{P}_{Y_B} \\ \dot{\phi} \end{bmatrix} \tag{34}$$

The partial angular velocity matrix of the moving platform is

$$\boldsymbol{\omega_{mp}} = \begin{bmatrix} 0 & 0 & 1 \end{bmatrix} \tag{35}$$

The linear velocity ($l_{v_{mp}}$) of the moving platform is equal to right hand side of the equation 22. Since point M_3 is selected as pivotal point of the moving platform, the b_{x_i} is equal to b_{x_3}.

$$l_{v_{mp}} = \begin{bmatrix} 1 & 0 & -b_{x_3}\sin\phi - b_{y_3}\cos\phi \\ 0 & 1 & b_{x_3}\cos\phi - b_{y_3}\sin\phi \end{bmatrix}\begin{bmatrix} \dot{P}_{X_B} \\ \dot{P}_{Y_B} \\ \dot{\phi} \end{bmatrix} \tag{36}$$

The partial linear velocity matrix of the moving platform is derived from the equation 36 as

$$\boldsymbol{v_{mp}} = \begin{bmatrix} 1 & 0 & -b_{x_3}\sin\phi - b_{y_3}\cos\phi \\ 0 & 1 & b_{x_3}\cos\phi - b_{y_3}\sin\phi \end{bmatrix} \tag{37}$$

2.4.2 The inertia forces and moments of the mobile parts of the manipulator

The Newton-Euler formulation is applied for deriving the inertia forces and moments of links and mobile platform about their mass centers. The m_{2i-1}, m_{2i} and m_{mp} denote the masses of links l_{2i-1} , l_{2i} and moving platform, respectively where i=1,2 and 3. The c_{2i-1} c_{2i} and c_{mp} are the mass centers of the links l_{2i-1}, l_{2i} and moving platform, respectively. Figure 3 denotes dynamics model of 3-DOF RRR FPPM.

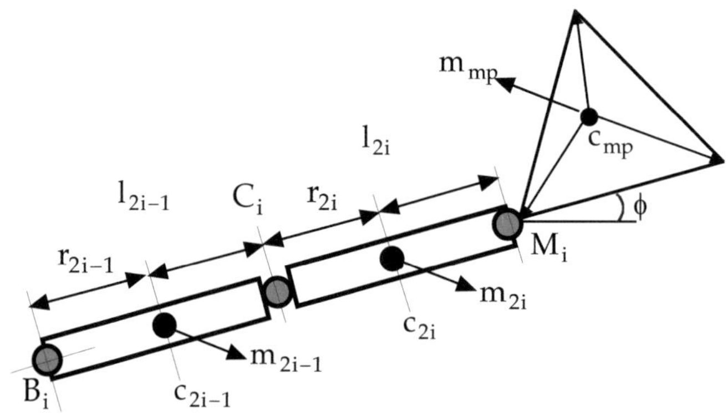

Fig. 3. The dynamics model of 3-DOF RRR FPPM

To find the inertia force of the mass m_{2i-1}, one should determine the acceleration of the link l_{2i-1} about its mass center first. The position vector of the link l_{2i-1} has already been obtained in equation 30. To find the position vector of the center of the link l_{2i-1}, the length r_{2i-1} is used instead of l_{2i-1} in equation 30 as follows

$$ {}^{O_i}_{C_i}T^1_{Pc_{2i-1}} = \begin{bmatrix} o_{x_i} + r_{2i-1}\cos\theta_i \\ o_{y_i} + r_{2i-1}\sin\theta_i \end{bmatrix} \tag{38} $$

The second derivative of the equation 30 with respect to the time yields the acceleration of the link l_{2i-1} about its mass center.

$$ a_{c_{2i-1}} = \frac{d}{dt}\left(\frac{d}{dt}\begin{bmatrix} o_{x_i} + r_{2i-1}\cos\theta_i \\ o_{y_i} + r_{2i-1}\sin\theta_i \end{bmatrix}\right) = r_{2i-1}\begin{bmatrix} -\ddot{\theta}_i\sin\theta_i - \dot{\theta}_i^2\cos\theta_i \\ \ddot{\theta}_i\cos\theta_i - \dot{\theta}_i^2\sin\theta_i \end{bmatrix} \tag{39} $$

The inertia force of the mass m_{2i-1} can be found as

$$ \boldsymbol{F_{2i-1}} = -m_{2i-1}\left(a_{c_{2i-1}} - g\right) $$

$$ = m_{2i-1}r_{2i-1}\begin{bmatrix} \ddot{\theta}_i\sin\theta_i + \dot{\theta}_i^2\cos\theta_i \\ -\ddot{\theta}_i\cos\theta_i + \dot{\theta}_i^2\sin\theta_i \end{bmatrix} \tag{40} $$

where g is the acceleration of the gravity and $\mathbf{g} = [0 \quad 0]^T$ since the manipulator operates in the horizontal plane. The moment of the link l_{2i-1} about pivotal point B_i is

$$ \boldsymbol{M_{2i-1}} = -\left[\ddot{\theta}_i I_{2i-1} + m_{2i-1}\left(\frac{d}{d\theta_i}\,{}^{O_i}_{C_i}T^1_{Pc_{2i-1}}\right)^T a_{B_i}\right] $$

$$ = \ddot{\theta}_i I_{2i-1} \tag{41} $$

where I_{2i-1}, ${}^{O_i}_{C_i}T^1_{Pc_{2i-1}}$ and a_{B_i}, denote the moment of inertia of the link l_{2i-1}, the position vector of the center of the link l_{2i-1} and the acceleration of the point B_i, respectively. It is noted that $a_{B_i} = 0$.

The acceleration of the link l_{2i} about its mass center is obtained first to find the inertia force of the mass m_{2i}. The position vector of the link l_{2i} has already been given in the left side of the equation 20 in terms of δ_i and θ_i angles. To find the position vector of the center of the link l_{2i} $\left({}^{O_i}_{M_i}T^1_{Pc_{2i}}\right)$, the length r_{2i} is used instead of l_{2i} in left side of the equation 20.

$$ {}^{O_i}_{M_i}T^1_{Pc_{2i}} = \begin{bmatrix} o_{x_i} + r_{2i}\cos\delta_i + l_{2i-1}\cos\theta_i \\ o_{y_i} + r_{2i}\sin\delta_i + l_{2i-1}\sin\theta_i \end{bmatrix} \tag{42} $$

The second derivative of the equation 42 with respect to the time produces the acceleration of the link l_{2i} about its mass center.

$$ a_{C_{2i}} = \frac{d}{dt}\left(\frac{d}{dt}\begin{bmatrix} o_{x_i} + r_{2i}\cos\delta_i + l_{2i-1}\cos\theta_i \\ o_{y_i} + r_{2i}\sin\delta_i + l_{2i-1}\sin\theta_i \end{bmatrix}\right) $$

$$ = \begin{bmatrix} -r_{2i}\left(\ddot{\delta}_i\sin\delta_i + \dot{\delta}_i^2\cos\delta_i\right) - l_{2i-1}\left(\ddot{\theta}_i\sin\theta_i + \dot{\theta}_i^2\cos\theta_i\right) \\ r_{2i}\left(\ddot{\delta}_i\cos\delta_i - \dot{\delta}_i^2\sin\delta_i\right) + l_{2i-1}\left(\ddot{\theta}_i\cos\theta_i - \dot{\theta}_i^2\sin\theta_i\right) \end{bmatrix} \tag{43} $$

The inertia force of the mass m_{2i} can be found as

$$ \boldsymbol{F_{2i}} = -m_{2i}\left(a_{c_{2i}} - g\right) $$

$$ = -m_{2i}\begin{bmatrix} -r_{2i}\left(\ddot{\delta}_i\sin\delta_i + \dot{\delta}_i^2\cos\delta_i\right) - l_{2i-1}\left(\ddot{\theta}_i\sin\theta_i + \dot{\theta}_i^2\cos\theta_i\right) \\ r_{2i}\left(\ddot{\delta}_i\cos\delta_i - \dot{\delta}_i^2\sin\delta_i\right) + l_{2i-1}\left(\ddot{\theta}_i\cos\theta_i - \dot{\theta}_i^2\sin\theta_i\right) \end{bmatrix} \tag{44} $$

where $\mathbf{g} = [0 \quad 0]^T$. The moment of the link l_{2i} about pivotal point C_i is

$$ \boldsymbol{M_{2i}} = -\left[\ddot{\delta}_i I_{2i} + m_{2i}\left(\frac{d}{d\delta_i}\,{}^{O_i}_{M_i}T^1_{Pc_{2i}}\right)^T a_{C_i}\right] $$

$$ = -\left(\ddot{\delta}_i I_{2i} + m_{2i}r_{2i}l_{2i-1}\left[\sin\delta_i\left(\ddot{\theta}_i\sin\theta_i + \dot{\theta}_i^2\cos\theta_i\right) \quad \cos\delta_i\left(\ddot{\theta}_i\cos\theta_i - \dot{\theta}_i^2\sin\theta_i\right)\right]\right) \tag{45} $$

where I_{2i}, ${}^{O_i}_{M_i}T^1_{Pc_{2i}}$ and a_{C_i}, denote the moment of inertia of the link l_{2i}, the position vector of the center of the link l_{2i} in terms of the base coordinate system {XYZ} and the acceleration of the point C_i, respectively. The terms $\frac{d}{d\delta_i}\,{}^{O_i}_{M_i}T^1_{Pc_{2i}}$ and a_{C_i} are computed as

$$ \frac{d}{d\delta_i}\,{}^{O_i}_{M_i}T^1_{Pc_{2i}} = \frac{d}{d\delta_i}\begin{bmatrix} o_{x_i} + r_{2i}\cos\delta_i + l_{2i-1}\cos\theta_i \\ o_{y_i} + r_{2i}\sin\delta_i + l_{2i-1}\sin\theta_i \end{bmatrix} = r_{2i}\begin{bmatrix} -\sin\delta_i \\ \cos\delta_i \end{bmatrix} \tag{46} $$

$$ a_{C_i} = \frac{d}{dt}\left(\frac{d}{dt}\begin{bmatrix} o_{x_i} + l_{2i-1}\cos\theta_i \\ o_{y_i} + l_{2i-1}\sin\theta_i \end{bmatrix}\right) = -l_{2i-1}\begin{bmatrix} \ddot{\theta}_i\sin\theta_i + \dot{\theta}_i^2\cos\theta_i \\ -\ddot{\theta}_i\cos\theta_i + \dot{\theta}_i^2\sin\theta_i \end{bmatrix} \tag{47} $$

The acceleration of the moving platform about its mass center is obtained in order to find the inertia force of the mass m_{mp}. The position vector of the moving platform has already been given in the right side of the equation 20.

$$ {}^{O_i}_{M_i}T^2 = \begin{bmatrix} P_{X_B} + b_{x_i}\cos\phi - b_{y_i}\sin\phi \\ P_{Y_B} + b_{x_i}\sin\phi + b_{y_i}\cos\phi \end{bmatrix} \tag{48} $$

The second derivative of the equation 48 with respect to the time produces the acceleration of the moving platform about its mass center (c_{mp}).

$$ a_{c_{mp}} = \frac{d}{dt}\left(\frac{d}{dt}\begin{bmatrix} P_{X_B} + b_{x_i}\cos\phi - b_{y_i}\sin\phi \\ P_{Y_B} + b_{x_i}\sin\phi + b_{y_i}\cos\phi \end{bmatrix}\right) $$

$$ = \begin{bmatrix} \ddot{P}_{X_B} - \ddot{\phi}(b_{x_3}\sin\phi + b_{y_3}\cos\phi) - \dot{\phi}^2(b_{x_3}\cos\phi - b_{y_3}\sin\phi) \\ \ddot{P}_{Y_B} + \ddot{\phi}(b_{x_3}\cos\phi - b_{y_3}\sin\phi) - \dot{\phi}^2(b_{x_3}\sin\phi + b_{y_3}\cos\phi) \end{bmatrix} \tag{49} $$

The inertia force of the mass m_{mp} can be found as

$$ \boldsymbol{F_{mp}} = -m_{mp}\left(a_{c_{mp}} - g\right) $$

$$ = -m_{mp}\begin{bmatrix} \ddot{P}_{X_B} - \ddot{\phi}(b_{x_3}\sin\phi + b_{y_3}\cos\phi) - \dot{\phi}^2(b_{x_3}\cos\phi - b_{y_3}\sin\phi) \\ \ddot{P}_{Y_B} + \ddot{\phi}(b_{x_3}\cos\phi - b_{y_3}\sin\phi) - \dot{\phi}^2(b_{x_3}\sin\phi + b_{y_3}\cos\phi) \end{bmatrix} \tag{50} $$

where $\mathbf{g} = [0 \quad 0]^T$. The moment of the moving platform about pivotal point M_3 is

$$ \boldsymbol{M_{mp}} = -\left[\ddot{\phi}I_{mp} + m_{mp}\left(\frac{d}{d\phi}{}^{O_i}_{M_3}T^2_{P(x,y)}\right)^T a_{c_{mp}}\right] $$

$$ = -\left(\ddot{\phi}I_{mp} + m_{mp}\left[\ddot{P}_{X_B}(-b_{x_3}\sin\phi - b_{y_3}\cos\phi) + \ddot{P}_{Y_B}(b_{x_3}\cos\phi - b_{y_3}\sin\phi)\right]\right) \tag{51} $$

where I_{mp}, ${}^{O_i}_{M_3}T^2_{P(x,y)}$ and $a_{c_{mp}}$, denote the moment of inertia of the moving platform, the position vector of the moving platform in terms of {XYZ} coordinate system and the acceleration of the point c_{mp}, respectively. The terms $\frac{d}{d\phi}{}^{O_i}_{M_3}T^2_{P(x,y)}$ and $a_{c_{mp}}$ are computed as

$$ \frac{d}{d\phi}{}^{O_i}_{M_3}T^2_{P(x,y)} = \frac{d}{d\phi}\begin{bmatrix} P_{X_B} + b_{x_3}\cos\phi - b_{y_3}\sin\phi \\ P_{Y_B} + b_{x_3}\sin\phi + b_{y_3}\cos\phi \end{bmatrix} = \begin{bmatrix} -b_{x_3}\sin\phi - b_{y_3}\cos\phi \\ b_{x_3}\cos\phi - b_{y_3}\sin\phi \end{bmatrix} \tag{52} $$

$$ a_{c_{mp}} = \begin{bmatrix} \ddot{P}_{X_B} \\ \ddot{P}_{Y_B} \end{bmatrix} \tag{53} $$

The inverse dynamics of the 3-DOF RRR FPPM based on the virtual work principle is given by

$$ J^T\tau + F = 0 \tag{54} $$

where

$$ F = \sum_{i=1}^{3}\left(\begin{bmatrix}\boldsymbol{v}_{2i-1}^T & \boldsymbol{\omega}_{2i-1}^T\end{bmatrix}\begin{bmatrix}\boldsymbol{F}_{2i-1} \\ \boldsymbol{M}_{2i-1}\end{bmatrix}\right) + \sum_{i=1}^{3}\left(\begin{bmatrix}\boldsymbol{v}_{2i}^T & \boldsymbol{\omega}_{2i}^T\end{bmatrix}\begin{bmatrix}\boldsymbol{F}_{2i} \\ \boldsymbol{M}_{2i}\end{bmatrix}\right) + \begin{bmatrix}\boldsymbol{v}_{mp}^T & \boldsymbol{\omega}_{mp}^T\end{bmatrix}\begin{bmatrix}\boldsymbol{F}_{mp} \\ \boldsymbol{M}_{mp}\end{bmatrix} \tag{55} $$

The driving torques ($\tau_1 \quad \tau_2 \quad \tau_3$) of the 3-DOF RRR FPPM are obtained from equation 54 as

$$ \tau = -(J^T)^{-1}F \tag{56} $$

where $\tau = [\tau_1 \quad \tau_2 \quad \tau_3]^T$.

3. Case study

In this section to demonstrate the active joints torques, a butterfly shape Cartesian trajectory with constant orientation ($\phi = 30^o$) is used as a desired end-effector's trajectory. The time dependent Cartesian trajectory is

$$P_{X_B} = P_{X_0} + a_m \cos(\omega_c \pi t) \quad 0 \le t \le 5 \text{ seconds} \tag{57}$$

$$P_{Y_B} = P_{Y_0} + a_m \sin(\omega_s \pi t) \quad 0 \le t \le 5 \text{ seconds} \tag{58}$$

A safe Cartesian trajectory is planned such that the manipulator operates a trajectory without any singularity in 5 seconds. The parameters of the trajectory given by 57 and 58 are as follows: $P_{X_{B0}} = P_{Y_{B0}} = 15$, $a_m = 0.5$, $\omega_c = 0.4$ and $\omega_s = 0.8$. The Cartesian trajectory based on the data given above is given by on Figure 4a (position), 4b (velocity) and 4c (acceleration). On Figure 4, the symbols VPBX, VPBY, APBX and APBY illustrate the velocity and acceleration of the moving platform along the X and Y-axes. The first inverse kinematics solution is used for kinematics and dynamics operations. The moving platform is an equilateral triangle with side length of 10. The position of end-effector in terms of {xyz} coordinate systems is $P(x_m, y_m)=(5, 2.8868)$ that is the center of the equilateral triangle moving platform. The kinematics and dynamics parameters for 3-DOF RRR FPPM are illustrated in Table 1. Figure 5 illustrates the driving torques ($\tau_1 \quad \tau_2 \quad \tau_3$) of the 3-DOF RRR FPPM based on the given data in Table 1.

Link lengths		Base coordinates		Masses		Inertias	
l_1	10	o_{x_1}	0	m_1	10	I_1	10
l_2	10	o_{y_1}	0	m_2	10	I_2	10
l_3	10	o_{x_2}	20	m_3	10	I_3	10
l_4	10	o_{y_2}	0	m_4	10	I_4	10
l_5	10	o_{x_3}	10	m_5	10	I_5	10
l_6	10	o_{y_3}	32	m_6, m_{mp}	10	I_6, I_{mp}	10

Table 1. The kinematics and dynamics parameters for 3-DOF RRR FPPM

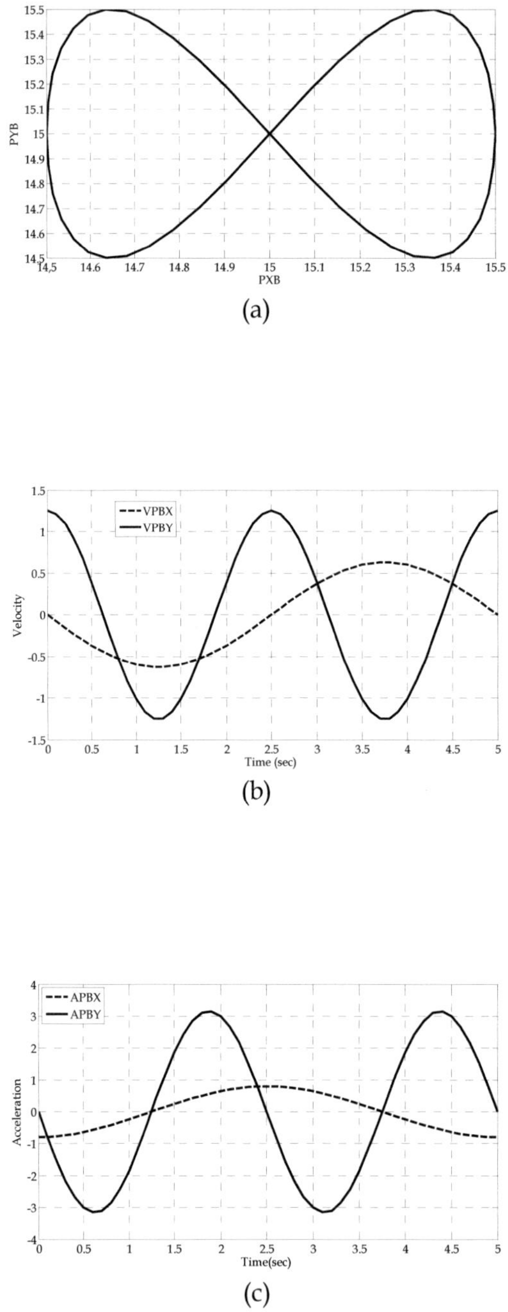

Fig. 4. a) Position, b) velocity and c) acceleration of the moving platform

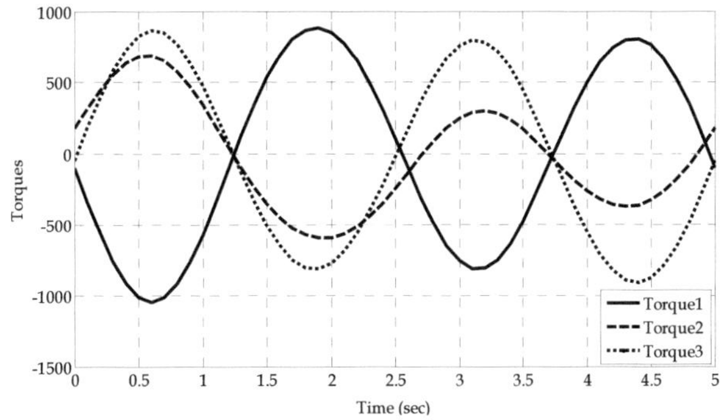

Fig. 5. The driving torques (τ_1 τ_2 τ_3) of the 3-DOF RRR FPPM

4. Conclusion

In this chapter, the inverse dynamics problem of 3-DOF RRR FPPM is derived using virtual work principle. Firstly, the inverse kinematics model and Jacobian matrix of 3-DOF RRR FPPM are determined using DH method. Secondly, the partial linear velocity and partial angular velocity matrices are computed. Pivotal points are selected in order to determine the partial linear velocity matrices. Thirdly, the inertial force and moment of each moving part are obtained. Consequently, the inverse dynamic equations of 3-DOF RRR FPPM in explicit form are derived. A butterfly shape Cartesian trajectory is used as a desired end-effector's trajectory to demonstrate the active joints torques.

5. References

Denavit, J. & Hartenberg, R. S., (1955). A kinematic notation for lower-pair mechanisms based on matrices. Journal of Applied Mechanics, Vol., 22, 1955, pp. 215–221

Hubbard, T.; Kujath, M. R. & Fetting, H. (2001). MicroJoints, Actuators, Grippers, and Mechanisms, CCToMM Symposium on Mechanisms, Machines and Mechatronics, Montreal, Canada

Kang, B.; Chu, J. & Mills, J. K. (2001). Design of high speed planar parallel manipulator and multiple simultaneous specification control, Proceedings of IEEE International Conference on Robotics and Automation, pp. 2723-2728, South Korea

Kang, B. & Mills, J. K. (2001). Dynamic modeling and vibration control of high speed planar parallel manipulator, In Proceedings of IEEE/RJS International Conference on Intelligent Robots and Systems, pp. 1287-1292, Hawaii

Merlet, J. P. (2000) Parallel robots, Kluwer Academic Publishers

Tsai, L. W. (1999). Robot analysis: The mechanics of serial and parallel manipulators, A Wiley-Interscience Publication

Uchiyama, M. (1994). Structures and characteristics of parallel manipulators, Advanced robotics, Vol. 8, no. 6. pp. 545-557

Wu, J.; Wang J.; You, Z. (2011). A comparison study on the dynamics of planar 3-DOF 4-RRR, 3-RRR and 2-RRR parallel manipulators, Robotics and computer-integrated manufacturing, Vol.27, pp. 150–156

Wu, J.; Wang L.; You, Z. (2010). A new method for optimum design of parallel manipulatorbased on kinematics and dynamics, Nonlinear Dyn, Vol. 61, pp. 717-727

Zhang, C. D. & Song, S. M. (1993). An efficient method for inverse dynamics of manipulators based on the virtual work principle, J. Robot. Syst., Vol.10, no.5, pp. 605-627

2

Dynamic Modeling and Simulation of Stewart Platform

Zafer Bingul and Oguzhan Karahan
Mechatronics Engineering, Kocaeli University
Turkey

1. Introduction

Since a parallel structure is a closed kinematics chain, all legs are connected from the origin of the tool point by a parallel connection. This connection allows a higher precision and a higher velocity. Parallel kinematic manipulators have better performance compared to serial kinematic manipulators in terms of a high degree of accuracy, high speeds or accelerations and high stiffness. Therefore, they seem perfectly suitable for industrial high-speed applications, such as pick-and-place or micro and high-speed machining. They are used in many fields such as flight simulation systems, manufacturing and medical applications.
One of the most popular parallel manipulators is the general purpose 6 degree of freedom (DOF) Stewart Platform (SP) proposed by Stewart in 1965 as a flight simulator (Stewart, 1965). It consists of a top plate (moving platform), a base plate (fixed base), and six extensible legs connecting the top plate to the bottom plate. SP employing the same architecture of the Gough mechanism (Merlet, 1999) is the most studied type of parallel manipulators. This is also known as Gough–Stewart platforms in literature.
Complex kinematics and dynamics often lead to model simplifications decreasing the accuracy. In order to overcome this problem, accurate kinematic and dynamic identification is needed. The kinematic and dynamic modeling of SP is extremely complicated in comparison with serial robots. Typically, the robot kinematics can be divided into forward kinematics and inverse kinematics. For a parallel manipulator, inverse kinematics is straight forward and there is no complexity deriving the equations. However, forward kinematics of SP is very complicated and difficult to solve since it requires the solution of many non-linear equations. Moreover, the forward kinematic problem generally has more than one solution. As a result, most research papers concentrated on the forward kinematics of the parallel manipulators (Bonev and Ryu, 2000; Merlet, 2004; Harib and Srinivasan, 2003; Wang, 2007).
For the design and the control of the SP manipulators, the accurate dynamic model is very essential. The dynamic modeling of parallel manipulators is quite complicated because of their closed-loop structure, coupled relationship between system parameters, high nonlinearity in system dynamics and kinematic constraints. Robot dynamic modeling can be also divided into two topics: inverse and forward dynamic model. The inverse dynamic model is important for system control while the forward model is used for system simulation. To obtain the dynamic model of parallel manipulators, there are many valuable studies published by many researches in the literature. The dynamic analysis of parallel manipulators has been traditionally performed through several different methods such as

the Newton-Euler method, the Lagrange formulation, the principle of virtual work and the screw theory.

The Newton–Euler approach requires computation of all constraint forces and moments between the links. One of the important studies was presented by Dasgupta and Mruthyunjaya (1998) on dynamic formulation of the SP manipulator. In their study, the closed-form dynamic equations of the 6-UPS SP in the task-space and joint-space were derived using the Newton-Euler approach. The derived dynamic equations were implemented for inverse and forward dynamics of the Stewart Platform manipulator, and the simulation results showed that this formulation provided a complete modeling of the dynamics of SP. Moreover, it demonstrated the strength of the Newton-Euler approach as applied to parallel manipulators and pointed out an efficient way of deriving the dynamic equations through this formulation. This method was also used by Khalil and Ibrahim (2007). They presented a simple and general closed form solution for the inverse and forward dynamic models of parallel robots. The proposed method was applied on two parallel robots with different structures. Harib and Srinivasan (2003) performed kinematic and dynamic analysis of SP based machine structures with inverse and forward kinematics, singularity, inverse and forward dynamics including joint friction and actuator dynamics. The Newton-Euler formulation was used to derive the rigid body dynamic equations. Do and Yang (1988) and Reboulet and Berthomieu, (1991) presented the dynamic modeling of SP using Newton–Euler approach. They introduced some simplifications on the legs models. In addition to these works, others (Guo and Li, 2006; Carvalho and Ceccarelli, 2001; Riebe and Ulbrich, 2003) also used the Newton-Euler approach.

Another method of deriving the dynamics of the SP manipulator is the Lagrange formulation. This method is used to describe the dynamics of a mechanical system from the concepts of work and energy. Abdellatif and Heimann (2009) derived the explicit and detailed six-dimensional set of differential equations describing the inverse dynamics of non-redundant parallel kinematic manipulators with the 6 DOF. They demonstrated that the derivation of the explicit model was possible by using the Lagrangian formalism in a computationally efficient manner and without simplifications. Lee and Shah (1988) derived the inverse dynamic model in joint space of a 3-DOF in parallel actuated manipulator using Lagrangian approach. Moreover, they gave a numerical example of tracing a helical path to demonstrate the influence of the link dynamics on the actuating force required. Guo and Li (2006) derived the explicit compact closed-form dynamic equations of six DOF SP manipulators with prismatic actuators on the basic of the combination of the Newton-Euler method with the Lagrange formulation. In order to validate the proposed formulation, they studied numerical examples used in other references. The simulation results showed that it could be derived explicit dynamic equations in the task space for Stewart Platform manipulators by applying the combination of the Newton-Euler with the Lagrange formulation. Lebret and co-authors (1993) studied the dynamic equations of the Stewart Platform manipulator. The dynamics was given in step by step algorithm. Lin and Chen presented an efficient procedure for computer generation of symbolic modeling equations for the Stewart Platform manipulator. They used the Lagrange formulation for derivation of dynamic equations (Lin and Chen, 2008). The objective of the study was to develop a MATLAB-based efficient algorithm for computation of parallel link robot manipulator dynamic equations. Also, they proposed computer-torque control in order to verify the effectiveness of the dynamic equations. Lagrange's method was also used by others (Gregório and Parenti-Castelli, 2004; Beji and Pascal 1999; Liu et al., 1993).

For dynamic modeling of parallel manipulators, many approaches have been developed such as the principle of virtual work (Tsai, 2000, Wang and Gosselin, 1998; Geike and McPhee, 2003), screw teory (Gallardo et al., 2003), Kane's method (Liu et al., 2000; Meng et al., 2010) and recursive matrix method (Staicu and Zhang, 2008). Although the derived equations for the dynamics of parallel manipulators present different levels of complexity and computational loads, the results of the actuated forces/torques computed by different approaches are equivalent. The main goal of recent proposed approaches is to minimize the number of operations involved in the computation of the manipulator dynamics. It can be concluded that the dynamic equations of parallel manipulators theoretically have no trouble. Moreover, in fact, the focus of attention should be on the accuracy and computation efficiency of the model.

The aim of this paper is to present the work on dynamic formulation of a 6 DOF SP manipulator. The dynamical equations of the manipulator have been formulated by means of the Lagrangian method. The dynamic model included the rigid body dynamics of the mechanism as well as the dynamics of the actuators. The Jacobian matrix was derived in two different ways. Obtaining the accurate Jacobian matrix is very essential for accurate simulation model. Finally, the dynamic equations including rigid body and actuator dynamics were simulated in MATLAB-Simulink and verified on physical system.

This chapter is organized in the following manner. In Section 2, the kinematic analysis and Jacobian matrices are introduced. In Section 3, the dynamic equations of a 6 DOF SP manipulator are presented. In Section 4, dynamic simulations and the experimental results are given in detail. Finally, conclusions of this study are summarized.

2. Structure description and kinematic analysis

2.1 Structure description

The SP manipulator used in this study (Figure 1), is a six DOF parallel mechanism that consists of a rigid body moving plate, connected to a fixed base plate through six independent kinematics legs. These legs are identical kinematics chains, couple the moveable upper and the fixed lower platform by universal joints. Each leg contains a precision ball-screw assembly and a DC- motor. Thus, length of the legs is variable and they can be controlled separately to perform the motion of the moving platform.

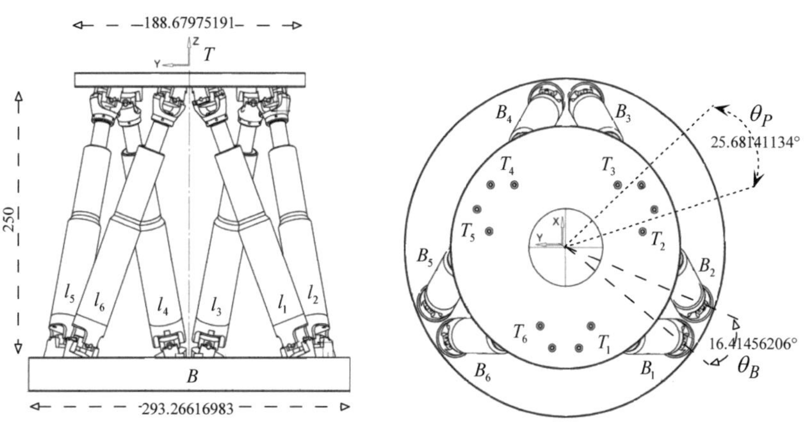

Fig. 1. Solid model of the SP manipulator

2.2 Inverse kinematics

To clearly describe the motion of the moving platform, the coordinate systems are illustrated in Figure 2. The coordinate system (B_{XYZ}) is attached to the fixed base and other coordinate system (T_{xyz}) is located at the center of mass of the moving platform. Points (B_i and T_i) are the connecting points to the base and moving platforms, respectively. These points are placed on fixed and moving platforms (Figure 2.a). Also, the separation angles between points (T_2 and T_3, T_4 and T_5, T_1 and T_6) are denoted by θ_p as shown in Figure 2.b. In a similar way, the separation angles between points (B_1 and B_2, B_3 and B_4, B_5 and B_6) are denoted by θ_b.

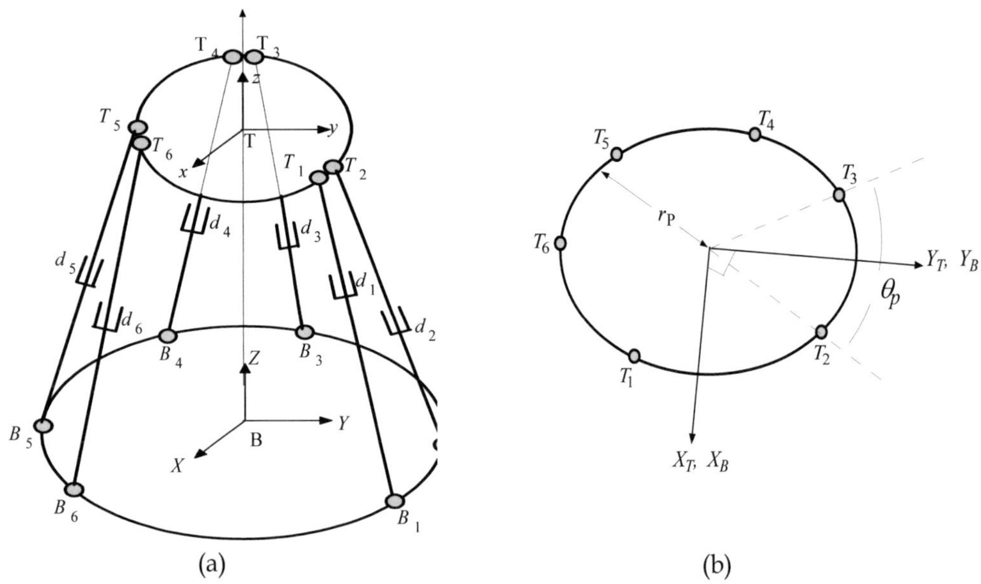

Fig. 2. The schematic diagram of the SP manipulator

From Figure 2.b, the location of the ith attachment point (T_i) on the moving platform can be found (Equation 1). r_p and r_{base} are the radius of the moving platform and fixed base, respectively. By the using the same approach, the location of the ith attachment point (B_i) on the base platform can be also obtained from Equation 2.

$$GT_i = \begin{bmatrix} GT_{xi} \\ GT_{yi} \\ GT_{zi} \end{bmatrix} = \begin{bmatrix} r_p \cos(\lambda_i) \\ r_p \sin(\lambda_i) \\ 0 \end{bmatrix}, \quad \begin{matrix} \lambda_i = \dfrac{i\pi}{3} - \dfrac{\theta_p}{2} & i = 1,3,5 \\ \lambda_i = \lambda_{i-1} + \theta_p & i = 2,4,6 \end{matrix} \tag{1}$$

$$B_i = \begin{bmatrix} B_{xi} \\ B_{yi} \\ B_{zi} \end{bmatrix} = \begin{bmatrix} r_{base} \cos(\upsilon_i) \\ r_{base} \sin(\upsilon_i) \\ 0 \end{bmatrix}, \quad \begin{matrix} \upsilon_i = \dfrac{i\pi}{3} - \dfrac{\theta_b}{2} & i = 1,3,5 \\ \upsilon_i = \upsilon_{i-1} + \theta_b & i = 2,4,6 \end{matrix} \tag{2}$$

The pose of the moving platform can be described by a position vector, P and a rotation matrix, ${}^{B}R_T$. The rotation matrix is defined by the roll, pitch and yaw angles, namely, a rotation of α about the fixed *x-axis*, $R_X(\alpha)$, followed by a rotaion of β about the fixed *y-axis*, $R_Y(\beta)$ and a rotaion of γ about the fixed *z-axis*, $R_Z(\gamma)$. In this way, the rotation matrix of the moving platform with respect to the base platform coordinate system is obtained. The position vector *P* denotes the translation vector of the origin of the moving platform with respect to the base platform. Thus, the rotation matrix and the position vector are given as the following.

$$\begin{aligned} {}^{B}R_T = R_Z(\gamma)R_Y(\beta)R_X(\alpha) = \begin{bmatrix} r_{11} & r_{12} & r_{13} \\ r_{21} & r_{22} & r_{23} \\ r_{31} & r_{32} & r_{33} \end{bmatrix} \\ = \begin{bmatrix} \cos\beta\cos\gamma & \cos\gamma\sin\alpha\sin\beta - \cos\alpha\sin\gamma & \sin\alpha\sin\gamma + \cos\alpha\cos\gamma\sin\beta \\ \cos\beta\sin\gamma & \cos\alpha\cos\gamma + \sin\alpha\sin\beta\sin\gamma & \cos\alpha\sin\beta\sin\gamma - \cos\gamma\sin\alpha \\ -\sin\beta & \cos\beta\sin\alpha & \cos\alpha\cos\beta \end{bmatrix} \end{aligned} \tag{3}$$

$$P = \begin{bmatrix} P_x & P_y & P_z \end{bmatrix}^T \tag{4}$$

Referring back to Figure 2, the above vectors GT_i and B_i are chosen as the position vector. The vector L_i of the link *i* is simply obtained as

$$L_i = R_{XYZ}GT_i + P - B_i \qquad \text{i=1,2, … ,6.} \tag{5}$$

When the position and orientation of the moving platform $X_{p-o} = \begin{bmatrix} P_x & P_y & P_z & \alpha & \beta & \gamma \end{bmatrix}^T$ are given, the length of each leg is computed as the following.

$$\begin{aligned} l_i^2 = \left(P_x - B_{xi} + GT_{xi}r_{11} + GT_{yi}r_{12}\right)^2 \\ + \left(P_y - B_{yi} + GT_{xi}r_{21} + GT_{yi}r_{22}\right)^2 + \left(P_z + GT_{xi}r_{31} + GT_{yi}r_{32}\right)^2 \end{aligned} \tag{6}$$

The actuator length is $l_i = \|L_i\|$.

2.3 Jacobian matrix

The Jacobian matrix relates the velocities of the active joints (actuators) to the generalized velocity of the moving platform. For the parallel manipulators, the commonly used expression of the Jacobian matrix is given as the following.

$$\dot{L} = J\dot{X} \tag{7}$$

where $\dot{L}$ and $\dot{X}$ are the velocities of the leg and the moving platform, respectively. In this work, two different derivations of the Jacobian matrix are developed. The first derivation is made using the general expression of the Jacobian matrix given in Equation 7. It can be rewritten to see the relationship between the actuator velocities, $\dot{L}$ and the generalized velocity of the moving platform ($\dot{X}_{p-0}$) as the following

$$\dot{L} = J_A\,\dot{X}_{p-0} = J_{IA}\,\vec{V}_{T_J} \tag{8}$$

The generalized velocity of the moving platform is below:

$$\vec{V}_{T_j} = J_{IIA}\,\dot{X}_{p-o} \qquad (9)$$

where $\vec{V}_{T_j}$ is the velocity of the platform connection point of the leg. Figure 3 shows a schematic view of one of the six legs of the SP manipulator.

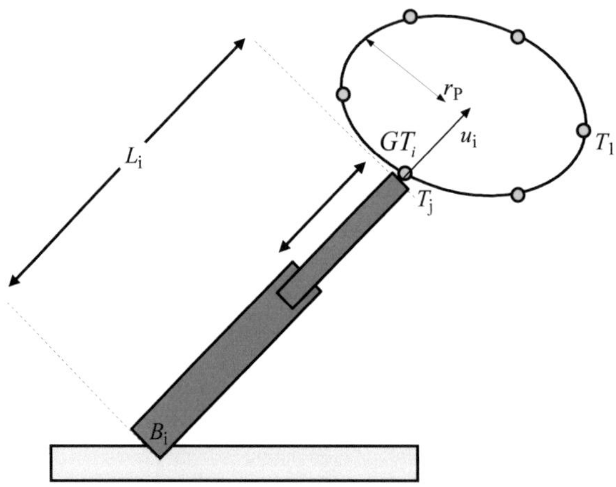

Fig. 3. Schematic view of the ith leg of the parallel manipulator

Now combining Equation 8 and Equation 9 gives

$$\dot{L} = J_A\,\dot{X}_{p-o} = J_{IA}\,J_{IIA}\,\dot{X}_{p-o} \qquad (10)$$

The first Jacobian matrix in the equation above is

$$J_{IA} = \begin{bmatrix} \vec{u}_1^T & \cdots & \cdots & \cdots & \cdots & 0 \\ 0 & \vec{u}_2^T & \cdots & \cdots & \cdots & 0 \\ 0 & \cdots & \vec{u}_3^T & \cdots & \cdots & 0 \\ 0 & \cdots & \cdots & \vec{u}_4^T & \cdots & 0 \\ 0 & \cdots & \cdots & \cdots & \vec{u}_5^T & 0 \\ 0 & \cdots & \cdots & \cdots & \cdots & \vec{u}_6^T \end{bmatrix}_{6x18} \qquad (11)$$

where u_i is the unit vector along the axis of the prismatic joint of link i (Figure 3). It can be obtained as follows

$$\vec{u}_i = \frac{B_iT_j}{|L_i|} = \frac{L_i}{l_i}, \begin{cases} j = \dfrac{i+1}{2} & if\ i\ is\ odd \\ j = \dfrac{i}{2} & if\ i\ is\ even \end{cases} \qquad (12)$$

The second Jacobian matrix in Equation 10 is calculated as the following.

$$J_{IIA} = \begin{bmatrix} I_{3x3} & R_Y(\beta)S(X)R_X(\alpha)R_Z(\gamma)GT_1 & S(Y)R_Y(\beta)R_X(\alpha)R_Z(\gamma)GT_1 & R_Y(\beta)R_X(\alpha)S(Z)R_Z(\gamma)GT_1 \\ \vdots & \vdots & \vdots & \vdots \\ \vdots & \vdots & \vdots & \vdots \\ \vdots & \vdots & \vdots & \vdots \\ \vdots & \vdots & \vdots & \vdots \\ I_{3x3} & R_Y(\beta)S(X)R_X(\alpha)R_Z(\gamma)GT_6 & S(Y)R_Y(\beta)R_X(\alpha)R_Z(\gamma)GT_6 & R_Y(\beta)R_X(\alpha)S(Z)R_Z(\gamma)GT_6 \end{bmatrix}_{18x6} \quad (13)$$

where I_{3x3} denotes the 3x3 identity matrix and S designates the 3x3 screw symmetric matrix associated with the vector $a = \begin{bmatrix} a_x & a_y & a_z \end{bmatrix}^T$,

$$S = \begin{bmatrix} 0 & -a_z & a_y \\ a_z & 0 & -a_x \\ -a_y & a_x & 0 \end{bmatrix} \quad (14)$$

The first proposed Jacobian matrix of the SP manipulator is defined as

$$J_A = J_{IA} \, J_{IIA} \quad (15)$$

The second proposed Jacobian matrix of the SP manipulator is defined as

$$J_B = J_{IB} \, J_{IIB} \quad (16)$$

Given $GT_i = \begin{bmatrix} GT_{xi} & GT_{yi} & GT_{zi} \end{bmatrix}^T$, T_j on the moving platform with reference to the base coordinate system (B_{XYZ}) is obtained as

$$T_j = \begin{bmatrix} P_x & P_y & P_z \end{bmatrix}^T + {}^{B}R_T GT_i = x + {}^{B}R_T GT_i \quad (17)$$

The velocity of the attachment point T_j is obtained by differentiating Equation 17 with respect to time

$$\vec{V}_{T_j} = \begin{bmatrix} \dot{P}_x & \dot{P}_y & \dot{P}_z \end{bmatrix}^T + \omega \times {}^{B}R_T GT_i = \dot{x} + \omega \times {}^{B}R_T GT_i \quad (18)$$

where $\omega = \left(\omega_x, \omega_y, \omega_z\right)$ is angular velocity of the moving platform with reference to the base platform.

$$\omega = \begin{bmatrix} \omega_x \\ \omega_y \\ \omega_z \end{bmatrix} = \begin{bmatrix} \cos\beta & 0 & 0 \\ 0 & 1 & -\sin\alpha \\ -\sin\beta & 0 & \cos\alpha \end{bmatrix} \begin{bmatrix} \dot{\alpha} \\ \dot{\beta} \\ \dot{\gamma} \end{bmatrix} \quad (19)$$

Since the projection of the velocity vector ($\dot{T}_j$) on the axis of the prismatic joint of link i produces the extension rate of link i, the velocity of the active joint ($\dot{L}_i$) is computed from

$$\dot{L}_i = \vec{V}_{T_j} \vec{u}_i = \begin{bmatrix} \dot{P}_x & \dot{P}_y & \dot{P}_z \end{bmatrix}^T \cdot \vec{u}_i + \omega \times \left({}^{B}R_T \, GT_i\right) \cdot \vec{u}_i = \dot{x} \cdot \vec{u}_i + \omega \times \left({}^{B}R_T \, GT_i\right) \cdot \vec{u}_i \quad (20)$$

Equation 20 is rewritten in matrix format as follows.

$$\dot{L}_i = J_B \begin{bmatrix} \dot{x} \\ \omega \end{bmatrix} = J_B \, \dot{X}_{p-o} = J_{IB} \, J_{IIB} \, \dot{X}_{p-o} \tag{21}$$

The first Jacobian matrix is

$$J_{IB} = \begin{bmatrix} u_{x1} & u_{y1} & u_{z1} & \left({}^{B}R_T G T_1 \, x \, \vec{u}_1 \right)^T \\ \vdots & \vdots & \vdots & \vdots \\ u_{x6} & u_{y6} & u_{z6} & \left({}^{B}R_T G T_6 \, x \, \vec{u}_6 \right)^T \end{bmatrix}_{6x6} \tag{22}$$

The second Jacobian matrix is

$$J_{IIB} = \begin{bmatrix} 1 & 0 & 0 & 0 & 0 & 0 \\ 0 & 1 & 0 & 0 & 0 & 0 \\ 0 & 0 & 1 & 0 & 0 & 0 \\ 0 & 0 & 0 & \cos\beta & 0 & 0 \\ 0 & 0 & 0 & 0 & 1 & -\sin\alpha \\ 0 & 0 & 0 & -\sin\beta & 0 & \cos\alpha \end{bmatrix}_{6x6} \tag{23}$$

3. Dynamic modeling

The dynamic analysis of the SP manipulator is always difficult in comparison with the serial manipulator because of the existence of several kinematic chains all connected by the moving platform. Several methods were used to describe the problem and obtain the dynamic modeling of the manipulator. In the literature, there is still no consensus on which formulation is the best to describe the dynamics of the manipulator. Lagrange formulation was used in this work since it provides a well analytical and orderly structure.

In order to derive the dynamic equations of the SP manipulator, the whole system is separated into two parts: the moving platform and the legs. The kinetic and potential energies for both of these parts are computed and then the dynamic equations are derived using these energies.

3.1 Kinetic and potential energies of the moving platform

The kinetic energy of the moving platform is a summation of two motion energies since the moving platform has translation and rotation about three orthogonal axes, *(XYZ)*. The first one is translation energy occurring because of the translation motion of the center of mass of the moving platform. The translation energy is defined by

$$K_{up(trans)} = \frac{1}{2} m_{up} \left(\dot{P}_X^2 + \dot{P}_Y^2 + \dot{P}_Z^2 \right) \tag{24}$$

where m_{up} is the moving platform mass. For rotational motion of the moving platform around its center of mass, rotational kinetic energy can be written as

$$K_{up(rot)} = \frac{1}{2}\vec{\Omega}_{up(mf)}^{T} I_{(mf)} \vec{\Omega}_{up(mf)} \tag{25}$$

where $I_{(mf)}$ and $\vec{\Omega}_{up(mf)}$ are the rotational inertia mass and the angular velocity of the moving platform, respectively. They are given as

$$I_{(mf)} = \begin{bmatrix} I_X & 0 & 0 \\ 0 & I_Y & 0 \\ 0 & 0 & I_Z \end{bmatrix} \tag{26}$$

$$\vec{\Omega}_{up(mf)} = R_Z(\gamma)^T R_X(\alpha)^T R_Y(\beta)^T \vec{\Omega}_{up(ff)} \tag{27}$$

where $\vec{\Omega}_{up(ff)}$ denotes the angular velocity of the moving platform with respect to the base frame. Given the definition of the angles α, β and γ, the angular velocity, $\vec{\Omega}_{up(ff)}$ is

$$\begin{aligned} \vec{\Omega}_{up(ff)} &= \dot{\alpha} R_Y(\beta)\vec{X} + \dot{\beta}\vec{Y} + \dot{\gamma} R_X(\alpha) R_Z(\gamma)\vec{Z} \\ &= \left(\begin{bmatrix} \cos\beta & 0 & \sin\beta \\ 0 & 1 & 0 \\ -\sin\beta & 0 & \cos\beta \end{bmatrix} \begin{bmatrix} 1 & 0 & 0 \\ 0 & 0 & 0 \\ 0 & 0 & 0 \end{bmatrix} + \begin{bmatrix} 0 & 0 & 0 \\ 0 & 1 & 0 \\ 0 & 0 & 0 \end{bmatrix} \right. \\ &\left. + \begin{bmatrix} 1 & 0 & 0 \\ 0 & \cos\alpha & -\sin\alpha \\ 0 & \sin\alpha & \cos\alpha \end{bmatrix} \begin{bmatrix} \cos\gamma & -\sin\gamma & 0 \\ \sin\gamma & \cos\gamma & 0 \\ 0 & 0 & 1 \end{bmatrix} \begin{bmatrix} 0 & 0 & 0 \\ 0 & 0 & 0 \\ 0 & 0 & 1 \end{bmatrix} \right) \begin{bmatrix} \dot{\alpha} \\ \dot{\beta} \\ \dot{\gamma} \end{bmatrix} = \begin{bmatrix} \cos\beta & 0 & 0 \\ 0 & 1 & -\sin\alpha \\ -\sin\beta & 0 & \cos\alpha \end{bmatrix} \begin{bmatrix} \dot{\alpha} \\ \dot{\beta} \\ \dot{\gamma} \end{bmatrix} \end{aligned} \tag{28}$$

In the moving platform coordinate system, the angular velocity of the moving platform given in Equation 27 is calculated as

$$\vec{\Omega}_{up(mf)} = \begin{bmatrix} c\gamma & c\alpha s\gamma & -c\alpha c\gamma s\beta - c\alpha s\alpha s\gamma + c\alpha c\beta s\alpha s\gamma \\ -s\gamma & c\alpha c\gamma & -c\alpha c\gamma s\alpha + c\alpha s\beta s\gamma + c\alpha c\beta s\alpha c\gamma \\ 0 & -s\alpha & s^2\alpha + c^2\alpha c\beta \end{bmatrix} \begin{bmatrix} \dot{\alpha} \\ \dot{\beta} \\ \dot{\gamma} \end{bmatrix} \tag{29}$$

where $s(\cdot) = \sin(\cdot)$ and $c(\cdot) = \cos(\cdot)$. As a result, the total kinetic energy of the moving platform in a compact form is given by

$$\begin{aligned} K_{up} &= K_{up(trans)} + K_{up(rot)} = \frac{1}{2} m_{up}\left(\dot{P}_X^2 + \dot{P}_Y^2 + \dot{P}_Z^2\right) + \frac{1}{2}\vec{\Omega}_{up(mf)}^{T} I_{(mf)} \vec{\Omega}_{up(mf)} \\ &= \frac{1}{2}\dot{X}_{P-O}^{T} \cdot M_{up}\left(X_{P-O}\right) \cdot \dot{X}_{P-O} = \frac{1}{2}\begin{bmatrix} \dot{P}_X & \dot{P}_Y & \dot{P}_Z & \dot{\alpha} & \dot{\beta} & \dot{\gamma} \end{bmatrix} M_{up} \begin{bmatrix} \dot{P}_X \\ \dot{P}_Y \\ \dot{P}_Z \\ \dot{\alpha} \\ \dot{\beta} \\ \dot{\gamma} \end{bmatrix} \end{aligned} \tag{30}$$

where M_{up} is the 6x6 mass diagonal matrix of the moving platform. Also, potential energy of the moving platform is

$$P_{up} = m_{up} g P_Z X_{P-O} = \begin{bmatrix} 0 & 0 & m_{up} g & 0 & 0 & 0 \end{bmatrix} \begin{bmatrix} P_X \\ P_Y \\ P_Z \\ \alpha \\ \beta \\ \gamma \end{bmatrix} \tag{31}$$

where g is the gravity.

3.2 Kinetic and potential energies of the legs

Each leg consists of two parts: the moving part and the fixed part (Figure 4). The lower fixed part of the leg is connected to the base platform through a universal joint, whereas the upper moving part is connected to the moving platform through a universal joint.

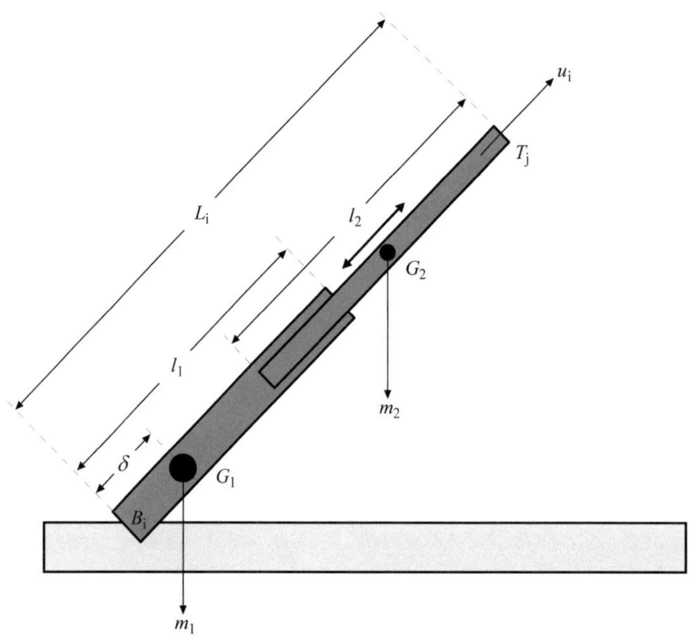

Fig. 4. Leg of the SP manipulator

As shown in the figure above, the center of mass, G_i for each part of the leg ($Leg_i\, i = 1...6$) is considered. G_{1i} denotes the center of mass of the fixed part. l_1 and m_1 are the length and the mass of the fixed part, respectively and δ is the distance between B_i and G_i. For the moving part of the leg, G_{2i} denotes its center of mass. l_2 and m_2 are the length and mass of the part, respectively.

The length of the leg is assumed to be constant. The rotational kinetic energy caused by the rotation around the fixed point B_i as shown in Figure 4 is given by

$$K_{Li(rot)} = \frac{1}{2}(m_1 + m_2)\left[h_i\left(\vec{V}_{T_j}^T\vec{V}_{T_j} - \vec{V}_{T_j}^T\vec{u}_i\vec{u}_i^T\vec{V}_{T_j}\right)\right], \begin{cases} j = \frac{i+1}{2} & if\ i\ is\ odd \\ j = \frac{i}{2} & if\ i\ is\ even \end{cases} \tag{32}$$

where

$$h_i = \left(\frac{\hat{I}}{L_i} + \frac{m_2}{m_1 + m_2}\right)^2, \hat{I} = \frac{1}{m_1 + m_2}\left(\delta m_1 l_1 - \frac{1}{2}m_2 l_2\right) \tag{33}$$

Moreover, the translation kinetic energy due to the translation motion of the leg is computed from

$$K_{Li(trans)} = \frac{1}{2}(m_1 + m_2)\left[\left(\frac{m_2}{m_1 + m_2}\right)^2 \vec{V}_{T_j}^T\vec{u}_i\vec{u}_i^T\vec{V}_{T_j}\right] \tag{34}$$

Therefore, the total kinetic energy of the leg L_i is calculated as the following.

$$K_{Li} = K_{Li(rot)} + K_{Li(trans)} = \frac{1}{2}(m_1 + m_2)\left[\vec{V}_{T_j}^T h_i \vec{V}_{T_j} - \dot{L}_i k_i \dot{L}_i\right] \tag{35}$$

where

$$k_i = \frac{\hat{I}}{L_i}\left(\frac{\hat{I}}{L_i} + \frac{m_2}{m_1 + m_2}\right) = h_i - \left(\frac{m_2}{m_1 + m_2}\right)^2 \tag{36}$$

Remember that $\vec{u}_i$ is the unit vector along the axis of the leg (L_i). By using this vector, the velocity of the leg can be calculated by $\dot{L}_i = \vec{V}_{T_j}\vec{u}_i$.

As a result, the compact expression for the kinetic energy of the six legs can be written as

$$K_{Legs} = \sum_{i=1}^{6} K_{Li} = \frac{1}{2}\dot{X}_{P-O}^T \cdot M_{Legs}\left(X_{P-O}\right) \cdot \dot{X}_{P-O} \tag{37}$$

Total potential energy of the legs can be defined as

$$P_{Legs} = \left(m_1 + m_2\right) g \sum_{i=1}^{3}\left[\hat{I}\left(\frac{1}{L_{2i}} + \frac{1}{L_{2i-1}}\right) + \frac{2m_2}{m_1 + m_2}\right]\left(p_z + Z_{T_j}\right) \tag{38}$$

where

$$Z_{T_j} = \begin{bmatrix} 0 \\ 0 \\ 1 \end{bmatrix}^T R_Z(\gamma)^T R_X(\alpha)^T R_Y(\beta)^T GT_j, \begin{cases} j = \frac{i+1}{2} & if\ i\ is\ odd \\ j = \frac{i}{2} & if\ i\ is\ even \end{cases} \tag{39}$$

3.3 Dynamic equations

In this subsection, the Lagrange formulation is used to derive the dynamic modeling of the SP manipulator. Considering q and τ as the corresponding generalized coordinates and generalized forces, respectively, the general classical equations of the motion can be obtained from the Lagrange formulation:

$$\frac{d}{dt}\frac{dL}{d\dot{q}}-\frac{\partial L}{\partial q}=\frac{d}{dt}\left(\frac{\partial K(q,\dot{q})}{\partial \dot{q}}\right)-\frac{\partial K(q,\dot{q})}{\partial q}+\frac{\partial P(q)}{\partial q}=\tau \tag{40}$$

where $K(q,\dot{q})$ is the kinetic energy, and $P(q)$ is the potential energy.

Generalized coordinates q is replaced with Cartesian coordinates (X_{p-o}). The dynamic equation derived from Equation 40 can be written as

$$J^T(X_{P-O})F=M(X_{P-O})\ddot{X}_{P-O}+V_m(X_{P-O},\dot{X}_{P-O})\dot{X}_{P-O}+G(X_{P-O}) \tag{41}$$

where $F=[f_1\ \ f_2\ \ f_3\ \ f_4\ \ f_5\ \ f_6]$, f_i is the force applied by the actuator of leg i in the direction $\vec{u}_i$ and J is the Jacobian matrix. Since the platform is divided into two parts (the moving platform and the legs), inertia, Coriolis-Centrifugal and gravity matrix in Equation 41 are summation of two matrix. Each of these matrices is computed using by two different Jacobian matrices.

$${}^AM(X_{p-o})=M_{up}+{}^AM_{Legs},\qquad {}^BM(X_{p-o})=M_{up}+{}^BM_{Legs} \tag{42}$$

$${}^AV_m(X_{p-o},\dot{X}_{p-o})=V_{mup}+{}^AV_{mLegs},\qquad {}^BV_m(X_{p-o},\dot{X}_{p-o})=V_{mup}+{}^BV_{mLegs} \tag{43}$$

$${}^AG(X_{p-o})=G_{up}+{}^AG_{Legs},\qquad {}^BG(X_{p-o})=G_{up}+{}^BG_{Legs} \tag{44}$$

where M_{up} obtained from Equation 30, ${}^AM_{Legs}$ and ${}^BM_{Legs}$ obtained from Equation 37 are the inertia matrix of the moving platform and legs, respectively. V_{mup}, ${}^AV_{mLegs}$ and ${}^BV_{mLegs}$ are Coriolis-Centrifugal matrix of the moving platform and legs, respectively. G_{up}, ${}^AG_{Legs}$ and ${}^BG_{Legs}$ are the gravity matrix of the moving platform and legs, respectively. V_{mup}, ${}^AV_{mLegs}$ and ${}^BV_{mLegs}$ are defined as follows:

$$V_{mup(i,j)}=\frac{1}{2}\sum_{k=1}^{6}\left(\frac{\partial M_{up}(k,j)}{\partial X_{p-o}(i)}+\frac{\partial M_{up}(k,i)}{\partial X_{p-o}(j)}-\frac{\partial M_{up}(i,j)}{\partial X_{p-o}(k)}\right)\dot{X}_{p-o}(k) \tag{45}$$

$${}^AV_{Legs(i,j)}=\frac{1}{2}\sum_{k=1}^{6}\left(\frac{\partial {}^AM_{Legs}(k,j)}{\partial X_{p-o}(i)}+\frac{\partial {}^AM_{Legs}(k,i)}{\partial X_{p-o}(j)}-\frac{\partial {}^AM_{Legs}(i,j)}{\partial X_{p-o}(k)}\right)\dot{X}_{p-o}(k) \tag{46}$$

$${}^BV_{Legs(i,j)}=\frac{1}{2}\sum_{k=1}^{6}\left(\frac{\partial {}^BM_{Legs}(k,j)}{\partial X_{p-o}(i)}+\frac{\partial {}^BM_{Legs}(k,i)}{\partial X_{p-o}(j)}-\frac{\partial {}^BM_{Legs}(i,j)}{\partial X_{p-o}(k)}\right)\dot{X}_{p-o}(k) \tag{47}$$

Finally, the gravity matrix can be obtained from the equations below.

$$G_{up}(k)=\frac{\partial P_{up}(X_{p-o})}{\partial X_{p-o}(k)} \tag{48}$$

$$\begin{aligned}
{}^{A}G_{Legs}(k)&=\frac{\partial\,{}^{A}P_{Legs}(X_{p-o})}{\partial X_{p-o}(k)}\\
&=(m_1+m_2)g\sum_{i=1}^{3}\left[\hat{I}\left[\frac{1}{{}^{A}L_{2i}^{2}}\left(\frac{\partial\,{}^{A}L_{2i}}{\partial X_{p-o}(k)}\right)+\frac{1}{{}^{A}L_{2i-1}^{2}}\left(\frac{\partial\,{}^{A}L_{2i-1}}{\partial X_{p-o}(k)}\right)\right]\right]\left(p_z+Z_{T_i}\right)\\
&+(m_1+m_2)g\sum_{i=1}^{3}\left[\hat{I}\left(\frac{1}{{}^{A}L_{2i}}+\frac{1}{{}^{A}L_{2i-1}}\right)+\frac{2m_2}{(m_1+m_2)}\right]\left(p_z+Z_{T_i}\right)
\end{aligned} \tag{49}$$

$$\begin{aligned}
{}^{B}G_{Legs}(k)&=\frac{\partial\,{}^{B}P_{Legs}(X_{p-o})}{\partial X_{p-o}(k)}\\
&=(m_1+m_2)g\sum_{i=1}^{3}\left[\hat{I}\left[\frac{1}{{}^{B}L_{2i}^{2}}\left(\frac{\partial\,{}^{B}L_{2i}}{\partial X_{p-o}(k)}\right)+\frac{1}{{}^{B}L_{2i-1}^{2}}\left(\frac{\partial\,{}^{B}L_{2i-1}}{\partial X_{p-o}(k)}\right)\right]\right]\left(p_z+Z_{T_i}\right)\\
&+(m_1+m_2)g\sum_{i=1}^{3}\left[\hat{I}\left(\frac{1}{{}^{B}L_{2i}}+\frac{1}{{}^{B}L_{2i-1}}\right)+\frac{2m_2}{(m_1+m_2)}\right]\left(p_z+Z_{T_i}\right)
\end{aligned} \tag{50}$$

In equation 49 and 50, the expression of $\left(\frac{\partial L_n}{\partial X_{p-o}(k)}\right)$ is needed to compute. This can be obtained using with the Jacobian matrices (J_A and J_B) as follows:

$$\frac{\partial\,{}^{A}L_n}{\partial X_{p-o}(k)}=\sum_{m=1}^{9}J_{IA_{nm}}\,J_{IIA_{mk}},\qquad \frac{\partial\,{}^{B}L_n}{\partial X_{p-o}(k)}=\sum_{m=1}^{9}J_{IB_{nm}}\,J_{IIB_{mk}} \tag{51}$$

3.4 Actuator dynamics

6 identical motor-ball-screw drives are used in SP. Dynamic equation of SP with actuator dynamics can be written in matrix form as

$$\tau_m=M_a\ddot{L}+N_a\dot{L}+K_aF \tag{52}$$

$$M_a=\frac{2\pi}{np}\left(J_s+n^2J_m\right)I_{6x6} \tag{53}$$

$$N_a=\frac{2\pi}{np}\left(b_s+n^2b_m\right)I_{6x6} \tag{54}$$

$$K_a=\frac{p}{n2\pi}I_{6x6} \tag{55}$$

where M_a, N_a and K_a are the inertia matrix, viscous damping coefficient matrix and gain matrix of the actuator, respectively. Also, J_s and J_m are the mass moment of inertia of the ball-screw and motor, b_s and b_m are the viscous damping coefficient of the ball-screw and motor, p and n are the pitch of the ball-screw and the gear ratio. τ_m and F are the vectors of motor torques and the forces applied by the actuators.
The electrical dynamics of the actuator can be described by the following equations.

$$\tau_m = K_t i \tag{56}$$

$$V = L\frac{di}{dt} + Ri + K_b \dot{\theta}_m \tag{57}$$

where K_t, L, R and K_b are the torque constant, the rotor inductance, terminal resistance and back-emf constant of the actuators, respectively. V and i are the motor voltage and motor current , respectively. The angular velocity of the motor is given as

$$\dot{\theta}_m = \frac{2\pi n}{p}\dot{L} \tag{58}$$

Since the dynamics of the platform is derived in the moving platform coordinates (Cartesian space, X_{p-o}), Equation 52 can be generally expressed in Cartesian space as the follows.

$$\tau_m = \bar{M}_c(X)\ddot{X} + \bar{N}_c(X)\dot{X} + \bar{G}_c(X) \tag{59}$$

The terms in the equation above are obtained from joint space terms and the Jacobian matrix.

$${}^{A}\bar{M}_c(X) = K_a \left(J_A\right)^{-T}\, {}^{A}M(X_{p-o}) + M_a J_A \tag{60}$$

$${}^{B}\bar{M}_c(X) = K_a \left(J_B\right)^{-T}\, {}^{B}M(X_{p-o}) + M_a J_B \tag{61}$$

$${}^{A}\bar{N}_c(X) = K_a \left(J_A\right)^{-T}\, {}^{A}N(X_{p-o}, \dot{X}_{p-o}) + N_a J_A + M_a \dot{J}_A \tag{62}$$

$${}^{B}\bar{N}_c(X) = K_a \left(J_B\right)^{-T}\, {}^{B}N(X_{p-o}, \dot{X}_{p-o}) + N_a J_B + M_a \dot{J}_B \tag{63}$$

$${}^{A}\bar{G}_c(X) = K_a \left(J_A\right)^{-T}\, {}^{A}G(X_{p-o}) \tag{64}$$

$${}^{B}\bar{G}_c(X) = K_a \left(J_B\right)^{-T}\, {}^{B}G(X_{p-o}) \tag{65}$$

Figure 5 shows the simulation block diagram of the Stewart Platform manipulator including the actuator dynamics (Equation 56, 57, 58 and 59). In order to model the platform dynamics without using forward kinematics, the block diagram is developed below.

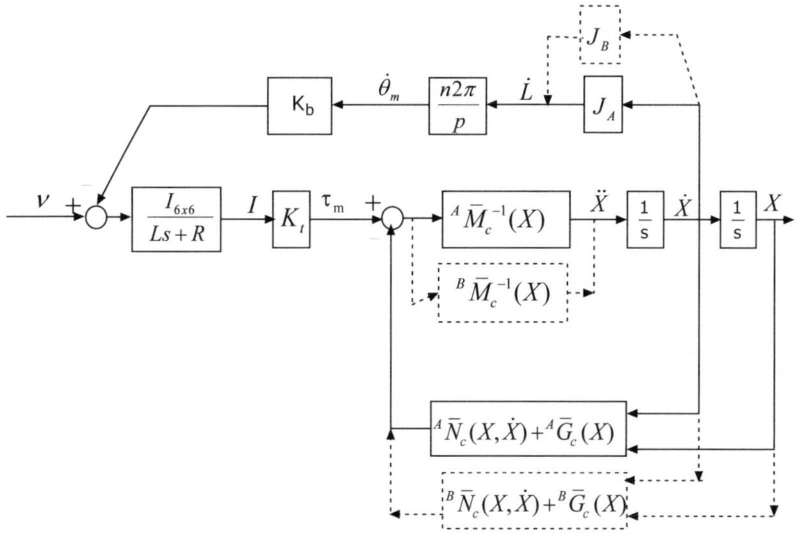

Fig. 5. Simulation block diagram for SP dynamics

4. Results

4.1 Experimental setup and simulation blocks

Figure 6 shows the Stewart Platform manipulator used in the experiments. It is constructed from two main bodies (top and base plates), six linear motors, controller, space mouse, accelerometer, gyroscope, force/torque sensor, power supply, emergency stop circuit and interface board as shown in the figure. Inverse kinematics and control algorithm of SP are embedded in MATLAB/Simulink module. Moreover, controller board like the space DS1103owning real-time interface implementation software to generate and then download the real time code to specific space board is used, and it is fully programmable from MATLAB/Simulink environment. Thus, it is possible for the user to observe the real process and collect the data from encoders for each leg while the experiment is in progress.

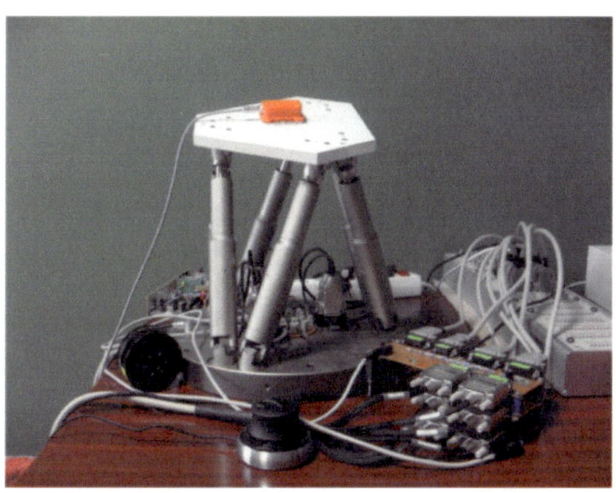

Fig. 6. SP manipulator used in experiments

To demonstrate the effectiveness and the validation of the two dynamic models of the SP manipulator including the actuator dynamics, experimental tests are performed on the manipulator.

The first Simulink model ("*Desired*" block) as shown in Figure 7 is used for the inverse kinematic solution for a given $X_{p-o} = \begin{bmatrix} P_x & P_y & P_z & \alpha & \beta & \gamma \end{bmatrix}^T$. Thus, the reference lengths of the legs are obtained from this block. Figure 8 shows the forward dynamics Simulink block (Jacobian matrix and its derivative, motor torques, the position and velocity of the moving platform, etc.). Figure 9 shows the developed Simulink model for the actual lengths of the legs. This block is designed using the following equation.

$$\ddot{L}_i = \dot{J}\,\dot{X}_{P-O} + J\,\ddot{X}_{P-O} \tag{66}$$

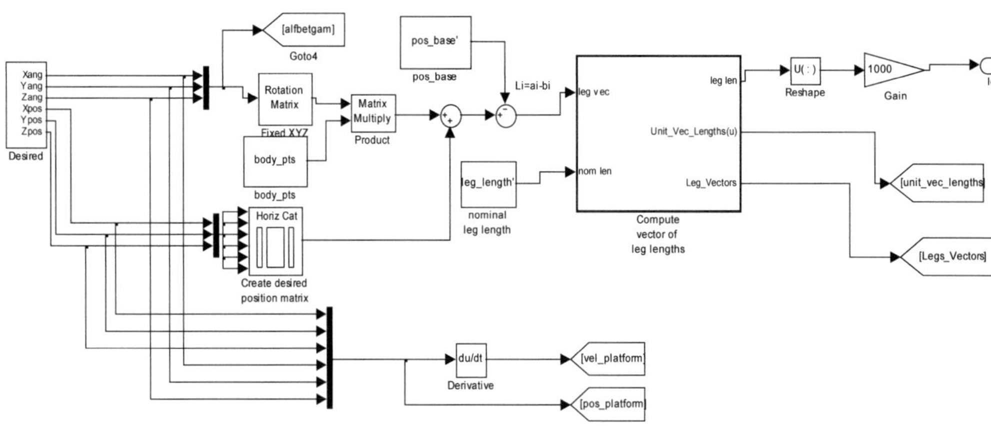

Fig. 7. Inverse kinematic solution Simulink model, "*Leg_Trajectory*"block

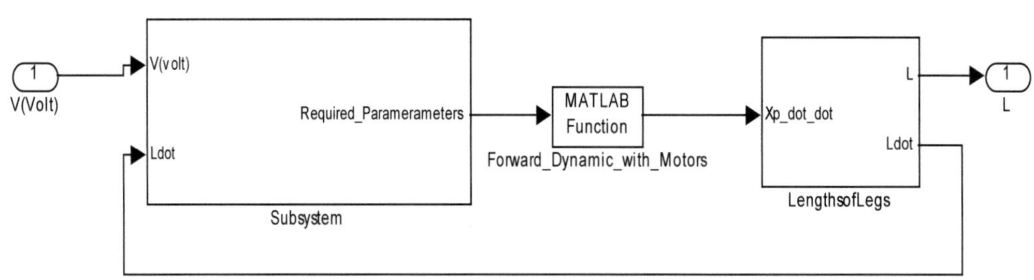

Fig. 8. The Simulink model of the forward dynamics, "*Stewart_Platform_Dynamics*" block

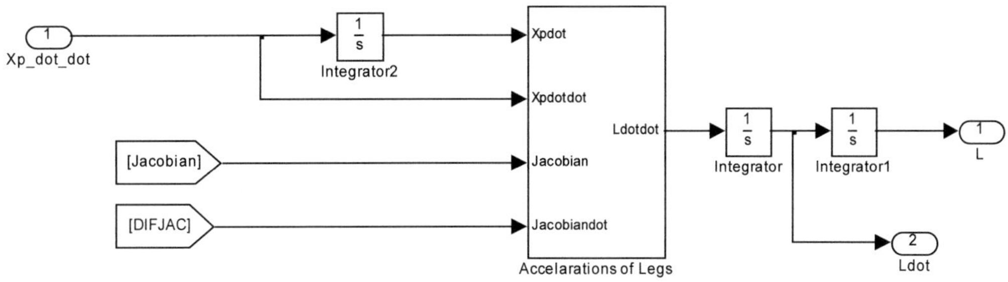

Fig. 9. The leg Simulink model, *"LengthofLegs"*block

To examine trajectory tracking performance of the SP dynamic model, a Simulink model shown in Figure 10 is developed.

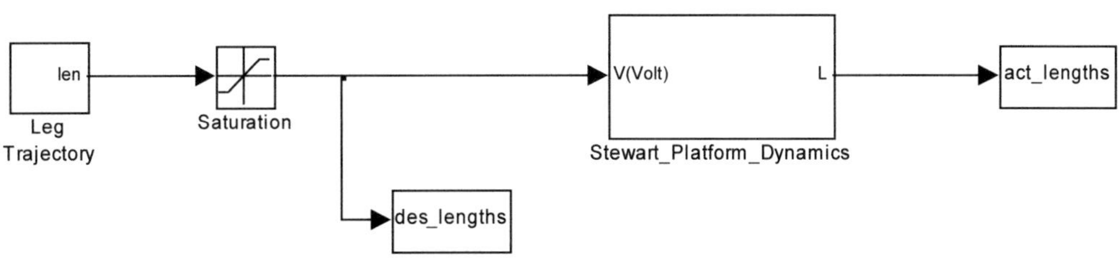

Fig. 10. Simulink model of the SP manipulator

In the figure, the reference lengths of the legs are limited between -25 mm and 25 mm with saturation block. The*"Stewart_Platform_Dynamics"* block computes the dynamic equations of the SP manipulator and outputs the actual lengths of the legs.
The attachment points GT_i and B_i on the moving and base platform, respectively are given in Table 1 and Table 2.

	GT_1 (m)	GT_2 (m)	GT_3 (m)	GT_4 (m)	GT_5 (m)	GT_6 (m)
X	0.0641	0.0641	0.0278	-0.0919	-0.0919	0.0278
Y	-0.0691	0.0691	0.0901	0.0209	-0.0209	-0.0901
Z	0	0	0	0	0	0

Table 1. Attachment point on the moving platform

	B_1 (m)	B_2 (m)	B_3 (m)	B_4 (m)	B_5 (m)	B_6 (m)
x	0.1451	0.1451	-0.0544	-0.0906	-0.0906	-0.0544
y	-0.0209	0.0209	0.1361	0.1152	-0.1152	-0.1361
z	0	0	0	0	0	0

Table 2. Attachment point on the base platform

Also, the system constants are given in Table 3.

Parameter	Value
m_{up}	1.1324 (Kg)
m_1	0.4279 (Kg)
m_2	0.1228 (Kg)
l_1	0.22 (m)
l_2	0.05 (m)
r_p	0.18867975191 (m)
r_{base}	0.29326616983 (m)
$I_{(mf)}$	$\begin{bmatrix} 0.0025 & 0 & 0 \\ 0 & 0.0025 & 0 \\ 0 & 0 & 0.005 \end{bmatrix} Kg.m^2$

Table 3. SP constants

The constants of the motor used in the SP manipulator are given in Table 4.

Parameter	Value
R	7.10 (ohm)
L	265e-6 (H)
K_b	2.730e-3 (V/rpm)
K_t	26.10e-3 (Nm/A)
n	1 (Rad/rad)
J_m	0.58e-6 (Kg.m^2)
J_s	0.002091e-3 (Kg.m^2)
b_m	0.0016430e-3 (N.s/rad)
b_s	0.11796e-3 (N.s/rad)
P	0.001 (m)

Table 4. SP motor constants

4.2 Dynamic simulations and experimental results

In this subsection, the effectiveness and the validation of the dynamic models of the SP manipulator with the actuator dynamics were investigated. In order to compare the experimental results with the simulation results, three trajectory tracking experiments were conducted. Also, the dynamic models obtained with two different Jacobian matrices (J_A and J_B) are examined. In all experiments, SP was worked in open-loop. In the first experiments, the translation motion along z-axis was applied to the SP system.

$$x(t) = 0 \qquad \alpha(t) = 0$$
$$y(t) = 0 \qquad \beta(t) = 0 \qquad (67)$$
$$z(t) = 0.25 + 10\sin(\pi t) \qquad \gamma(t) = 0$$

Figure 11 shows the reference lengths of the legs, the actual lengths from the encoder and the lengths predicted by the dynamic equations of the SP manipulator with two different Jacobian J_A (Sim-A) and J_B (Sim-B).

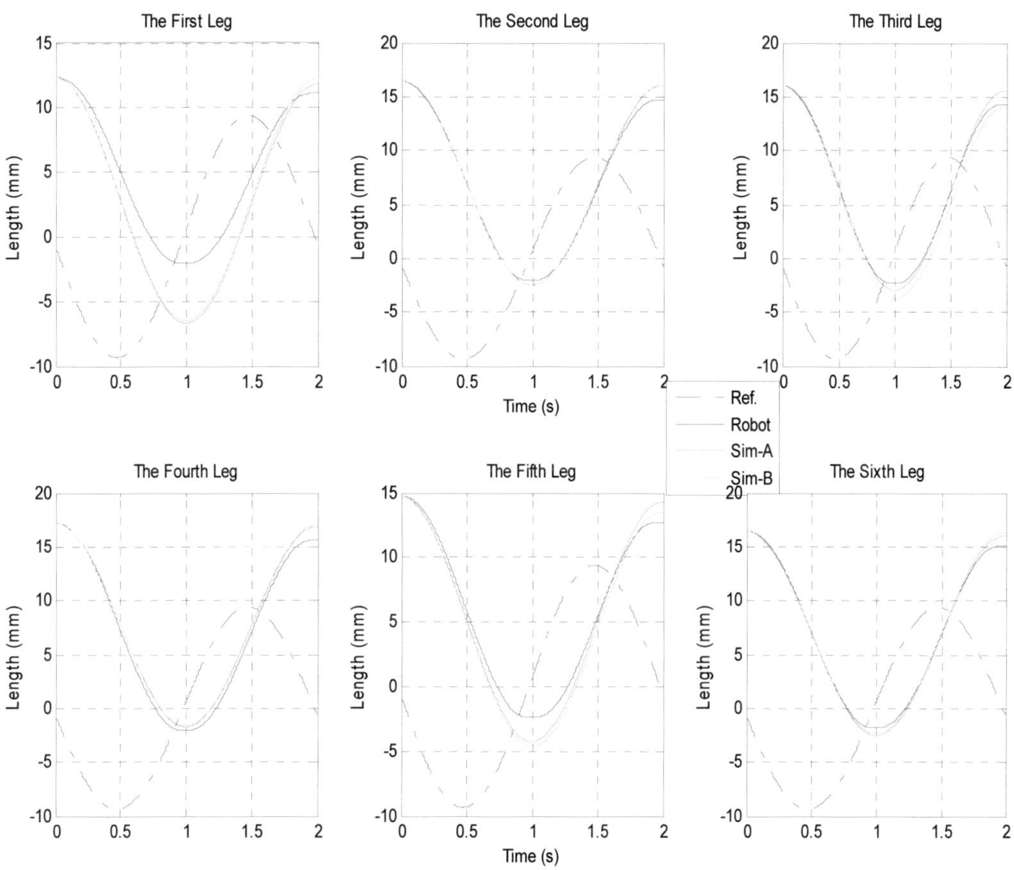

Fig. 11. Comparison of simulation results (red and blue) and experimental results (black) for the first experiment

Response of two dynamic simulation models (Sim-A and Sim-B) is almost same. But, it is observed that the *Sim-A* shows better performance than the *Sim-B* for this trajectory. Also, simulation and experimental results are very close to each other.
The second experiment, both translational and rotational motion along all axes (x,y,z) was applied to the SP system. The trajectory is defined in Equation 68. The experimental and simulation results for this trajectory are shown in Figure 12.

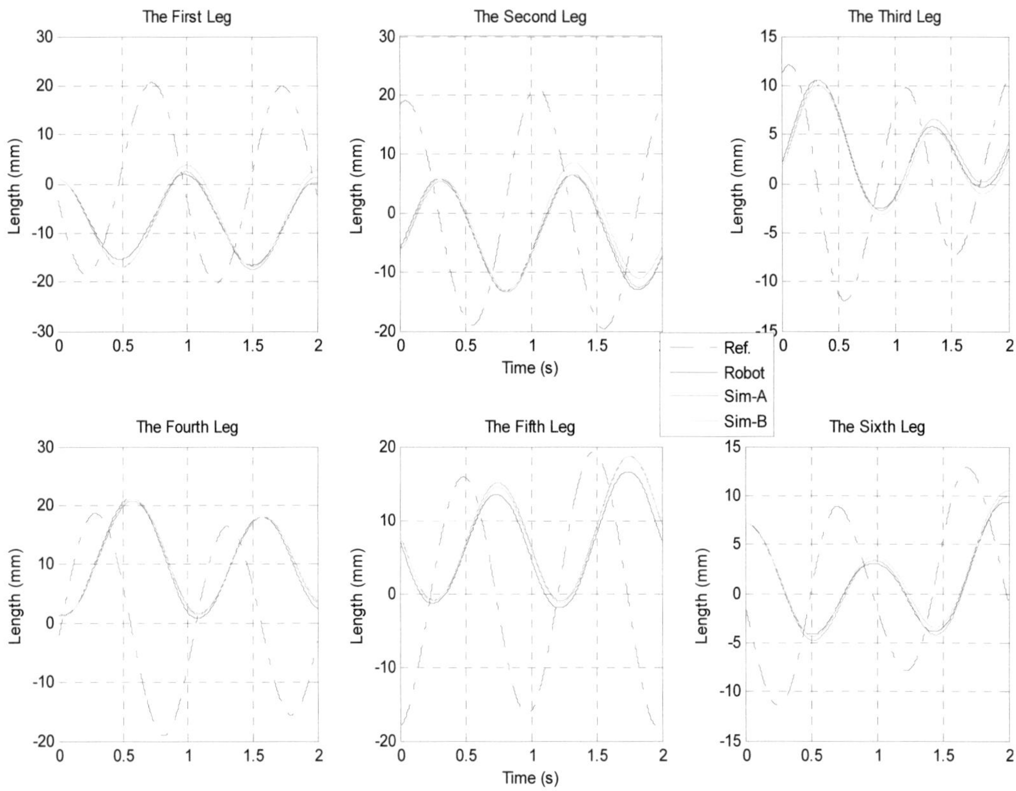

Fig. 12. Comparison of simulation results (red and blue) and experimental results (black) for the second experiment

$$x(t) = 5\sin(\pi t) \qquad \alpha(t) = 10\cos(2\pi t)$$

$$y(t) = 5\cos(\pi t) \qquad \beta(t) = 10\sin(2\pi t) \tag{68}$$

$$z(t) = 0.25 + \sin(\pi t) \qquad \gamma(t) = 10\cos(2\pi t)$$

As can be shown in the figure, the dynamic model (red) has better performance compared to other (blue). There is good match between the simulation and experimental results.

In the last experiment, the fast translational and rotational motion along all axes (x,y,z) was conducted. The trajectory is given below.

$$x(t) = 10\sin(2\pi t) \qquad \alpha(t) = 5\cos(4\pi t)$$

$$y(t) = 10\cos(3\pi t) \qquad \beta(t) = 5\sin(5\pi t) \tag{69}$$

$$z(t) = 0.25 + 3\sin(\pi t) \qquad \gamma(t) = 5\cos(3\pi t)$$

Figure 13 illustrates the results obtained from dynamic models and experimental results for this trajectory. In accordance with the results shown in Figure 13, the relative small deviations between the models and the experimental data are occurred. However, the obtained dynamic models can track the high frequency reference trajectory.

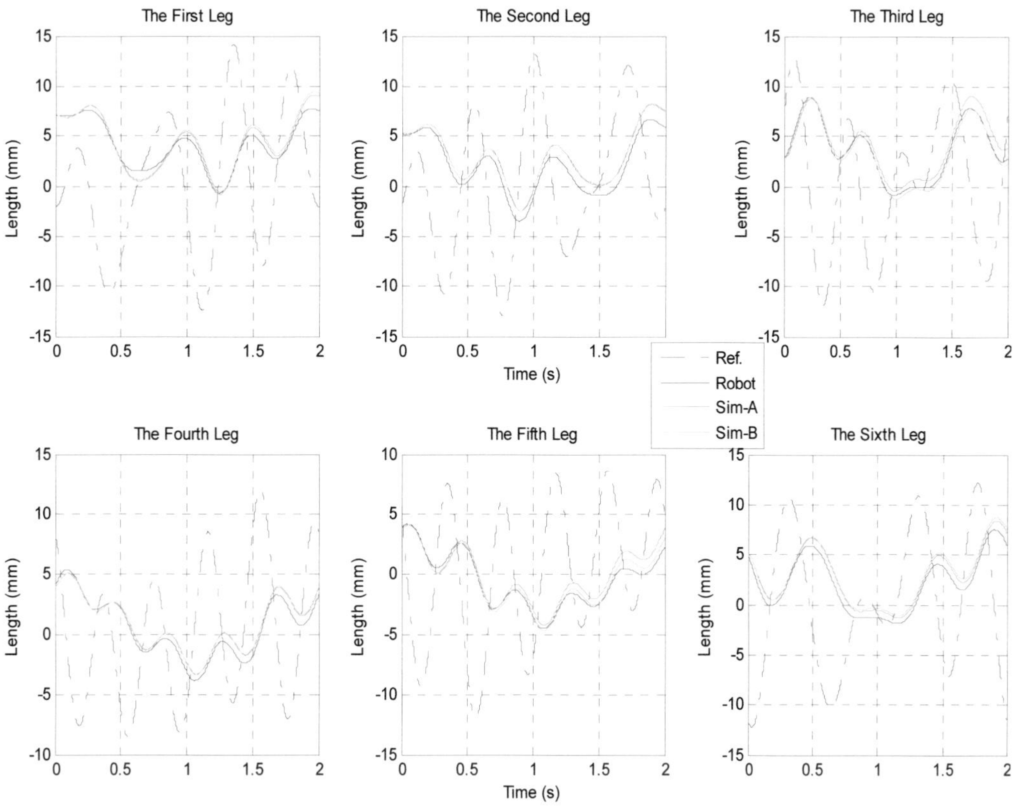

Fig. 13. Comparison of simulation results (red and blue) and experimental results (black) for the third experiment

The errors between simulation and experimental results were computed for all experiments. The cost function for the modeling error is defined as

$$E = \frac{1}{N}\sum_{i=1}^{N} \left|e_1(i)\right| + \left|e_2(i)\right| + \left|e_3(i)\right| + \left|e_4(i)\right| + \left|e_5(i)\right| + \left|e_6(i)\right| \tag{70}$$

where $e_1(i)...e_6(i)$ are the trajectory errors of ith sample obtained from difference between the experimental and the simulation results and N is the number of sample.

Table 5 gives the cost function values obtained from the two different dynamic models.

The two dynamic models of the SP manipulator using J_A and J_B exhibit very good performance in terms of model accuracy. Performance of the dynamic model using J_A is better than which of other model.

Experiment	Sim-A	Sim-B
1-EXP(z)	4.4337	5.0121
2-EXP(x,y,z,α,β,γ)	4.5389	4.5877
3-EXP(x,y,z,α,β,γ)	3.6470	3.3697

Table 5. The cost function values for the two different dynamic models

5. Conclusion

In this paper, closed-form dynamic equations of the SP manipulator with the actuator dynamics were derived using Lagrangian method. A computational highly efficient method was developed for the explicit dynamic equations. Besides, two simple methods for the calculation of the Jacobian matrix of SP were proposed. Two dynamic models of the SP were obtained using these Jacobian matrices. Two SP models were simulated in a MATLAB-Simulink. In order to verify the simulation results, three experiments were conducted. Considering all of the results, there is very good agreement between the experiments and the simulations. Modeling errors for each experiment were computed. Based on the modeling error, modeling accuracy of the developed models is very high. Thus, the verified model of the SP can be used for control and design purposes. Especially, a model based controller needs the verified model.

6. Acknowledgment

This work is supported by The Scientific and Technological Research Council of Turkey (TUBITAK) under the Grant No. 107M148.

7. References

Abdellatif, H. & Heimann, B. (2009). Computational efficient inverse dynamics of 6-DOF fully parallel manipulators by using the Lagrangian formalism. *Mechanism and Machine Theory*, 44, pp. (192-207)

Beji, L. & Pascal, M. (1999). The Kinematics and the Full Minimal Dynamic Model of a 6-DOF Parallel Robot Manipulator. *Nonlinear Dynamics*, 18, pp. (339-356)

Bonev, I. A., & Ryu, J. A. (2000). New method for solving the direct kinematics of general 6-6 Stewart platforms using three linear extra sensors. *Mechanism and Machine Theory*, 35, pp. (423–436)

Carvalho, J. & Ceccarelli, M. (2001). A Closed-Form Formulation for the Inverse Dynamics of a Cassino Parallel Manipulator. *Multibody System Dynamics*, Vol. 5, pp. (185–210)

Dasgupta, B. & Mruthyunjaya, T. S. (1998). Closed-Form Dynamic Equations Of The General Stewart Platform Through The Newton-Euler. *Mechanism and Machine Theory*, 33 (7), pp. (993-1012)

Do, W. & Yang, D. (1988). Inverse Dynamic Analysis and Simulation of a Platform Type of Robot.*Journal of Robotic Systems*, Vol. 5, pp. (209-227)

Gallardo, J.; Rico, J.M.; Frisoli, A.; Checcacci, D.; Bergamasco, M. (2003). Dynamics of parallel manipulators by means of screw theory. *Mechanism and Machine Theory*, 38, pp. (1113-1131)

Geike, T. & McPhee J. (2003). Inverse dynamic analysis of parallel manipulators with full mobility. *Mechanism andMachine Theory*, 38, pp. (549-562)

Gregório, R. & Parenti-Castelli, V. (2004). Dynamics of a Class of Parallel Wrists. *Journal of Mechanical Design*, Vol. 126, pp. (436-441)

Guo, H. & Li, H. (2006). Dynamic analysis and simulation of a six degree of freedom Stewart platform manipulator. Proceedings of the Institution of Mechanical Engineers, Part C: *Journal of Mechanical Engineering Science*, Vol. 220, pp. (61-72)

Harib , K.; Srinivasan, K. (2003). Kinematic and dynamic analysis of Stewart platform-based machine tool structures, *Robotica*, 21(5), pp. (541-554)

Khalil W, Ibrahim O. (2007). General solution for the dynamic modelling of parallel robots.*J Intell Robot Systems*, 49, pp. (19-37)

Lebret G.; Liu K.; Lewis F. L. (1993). Dynamic analysis and control of a Stewart platform manipulator. *Journal of Robotic System*, 10, pp. (629-655)

Lee, K & Shah, D.K. (1988). Dynamical Analysis of a Three-Degrees-of-Freedom In-Parallel Actuated Manipulator. *IEEE Journal of Robotics and Automation*, 4(3).

Lin, J. & Chen, C.W. (2008). Computer-aided-symbolic dynamic modeling for Stewart-platform manipulator.*Robitica*, 27 (3), pp. (331-341)

Liu, K.; Lewis, F. L.; Lebret, G.; Taylor, D. (1993). The singularities and dynamics of a Stewart platform manipulator. *J. Intell. Robot.* Syst., 8, pp. (287-308)

Liu, M.J.; Li, C.X.; Li, C.N., 2000. Dynamics analysis of the Gough-Stewart platform manipulator. *IEEE Trans. Robot. Automat.*, 16 (1), pp. (94-98)

Meng, Q.; Zhang, T.; He, J-F.; Song, J-Y.; Han, J-W.(2010). Dynamic modeling of a 6-degree-of-freedom Stewart platform driven by a permanent magnet synchronous motor. *Journal of Zhejiang University-SCIENCE C (Computers & Electronics)*, 11(10), pp. (751-761)

Merlet, J.P. (1999). *Parallel Robots*, Kluwer Academic Publishers.

Merlet, J. P. (2004). Solving the forward kinematics of a Gough-type parallel manipulator with internal analysis. *International Journal of Robotics Research*, 23(3), pp. (221-235)

Reboulet, C. & Berthomieu, T. (1991). Dynamic Models of a Six Degree of Freedom Parallel Manipulators. *Proceedings of the IEEE International Conference on Robotics and Automation*, pp. (1153-1157)

Riebe, S. & Ulbrich, H. (2003). Modelling and online computation of the dynamics of a parallel kinematic with six degrees-of-freedom. *Arch ApplMech*, 72, pp. (817-29)

Staicu, S. & Zhang, D. (2008). A novel dynamic modelling approach for parallel mechanisms analysis. *Robot ComputIntegrManufact*, 24, pp. (167-172)

Stewart, D. (1965). A Platform with Six Degrees of Freedom, *Proceedings of the Institute of Mechanical Engineering*, Vol. 180, Part 1, No. 5, pp. (371-386)

Tsai L-W. (2000). Solving the inverse dynamics of Stewart-Gough manipulator by the principle of virtual work. *J Mech Des*, 122, pp. (3-9)

Wang, J. & Gosselin, C. (1998). A New Approach for the Dynamic Analysis of Parallel Manipulators. *Multibody System Dynamics*, 2, pp. (317-334)

Wang , Y. (2007). A direct numerical solution to forward kinematics of general Stewart-Gough platforms, *Robotica*, 25(1), pp. (121-128)

3

Exploiting Higher Kinematic Performance – Using a 4-Legged Redundant PM Rather than Gough-Stewart Platforms

Mohammad H. Abedinnasab[1], Yong-Jin Yoon[2] and Hassan Zohoor[3]
[1]Door To Door Company, Sharif University of Technology
[2]Nanyang Technological University
[3]Sharif University of Technology,
The Academy of Sciences of IR Iran
[1,3]Iran
[2]Singapore

1. Introduction

It is believed that Gough and Whitehall (1962) first introduced parallel robots with an application in tire-testing equipments, followed by Stewart (1965) , who designed a parallel mechanism to be used in a flight simulator. With ever-increasing demand on the robot's rigidity, redundant mechanisms, which are stiffer than their non-redundant counterparts, are attracting more attention.

Actuation redundancy eliminates singularity, and greatly improves dexterity and manipulability. Redundant actuation increases the dynamical capability of a PM by increasing the load-carrying capacity and acceleration of motion, optimizing the load distribution among the actuators and reducing the energy consumption of the drivers. Moreover, it enhances the transmission characteristics by increasing the homogeneity of the force transmission and the manipulator stiffness (Yi et al., 1989). From a kinematic viewpoint, redundant actuation eliminates singularities (Ropponen & Nakamura, 1990) which enlarge the usable workspace, as well. The kinematic analysis on general redundantly actuated parallel mechanisms was investigated by Müller (2005).

A number of redundantly full-actuated mechanisms have been proposed over the years and some of them which are more significant are listed in this section. The spatial octopod, which is a hexapod with 2 additional struts, is one of them (Tsai, 1999). A 5-DOF 3-legged mechanism was proposed by Lu et al. (2008), who studied its kinematics, statics, and workspace. Staicu (2009) introduced a new 3-DOF symmetric spherical 3-UPS/S parallel mechanism having three prismatic actuators. As another work of Lu et al. (2009), they introduced and used 2(SP+SPR+SPU) serial–parallel manipulators. Wang and Gosselin (2004) addressed an issue of singularity and designed three new types of kinematically redundant parallel mechanisms, including a new redundant 7-DOF Stewart platform. They concluded that such manipulators can be used to avoid singularities inside the workspace of non-redundant manipulators.

Choi et al. (2010) developed a new 4-DOF parallel mechanism with three translational and one rotational movements and found this mechanism to be ideal for high-speed machining.

Gao et al. (2010) proposed a novel 3DOF parallel manipulator and they increased the stiffness of their system, using an optimization technique. Lopes (2010) introduced a new 6-DOF moving base platform, which is capable of being used in micro robotic applications after processing serial combination with another industrial manipulator. It is in fact a non-redundant parallel mechanism with 6 linear actuators.
Deidda et al. (2010) presented a 3-DOF 3-leeged spherical robotic wrist. They analyzed mobility and singularity. Tale Masouleh et al. (2011) investigated the kinematic problem of a 5-DOF 5-RPUR mechanism with two different approaches, which differ by their concepts of eliminating passive variables. Zhao and Gao (2010) investigated the kinematic and dynamic properties of a 6-DOF 8-PSS redundant manipulator. They presented a series of new joint-capability indices, which are general and can be used for other types of parallel manipulators.
Li et al. (2007) worked on the singularity-free workspace analysis of the general Gough–Stewart platform. In a similar line of work, Jiang and Gosselin (Jiang & Gosselin, 2009a;b;c) determined the maximal singularity-free orientation workspace at a prescribed position of the Gough–Stewart platform. Alp and Ozkol (2008) described how to extend the workspace of the 6-3 and 6-4 Stewart platforms in a chosen direction by finding the optimal combination of leg lengths and joint angles. They showed that the workspace of the 6-3 Stewart platform is smaller than that of the 6-4 one.
Mayer and Gosselin (2000) developed a mathematical technique to analytically derive the singularity loci of the Gough-Stewart platform. Their method is based on deriving an explicit expression for the determinant of the jacobian matrix of the manipulator.
To demonstrate the redundancy effects, Wu et al. (2010) compared a planar 2-DOF redundant mechanism with its non-redundant counterpart. Arata et al. (2011) proposed a new 3-DOF redundant parallel mechanism entitled as Delta-R, based on its famous non-redundant counterpart, Delta, which was developed by Vischer & Clavel (1998).
Sadjadian and Taghirad (2006) compared a 3-DOF redundant mechanism, hydraulic shoulder, to its non-redundant counterpart. They concluded that the actuator redundancy in the mechanism is the major element to improve the Cartesian stiffness and hence the dexterity of the hydraulic shoulder. They also found that losing one limb reduces the stiffness of the manipulator significantly.
The rest of the chapter is organized as follows. In Section 2, in addition to introduction and comparison of non-redundant 3-legged and redundant 4-legged UPS PMs, four different architectures of the Gough-Stewart platforms are depicted. The kinematics of the abovementioned mechanisms are reviewed in Section 3. The jacobian matrices using the screw theory is derived in Section 4. In Sections 5 and 6, the performances of the redundant and non-redundant mechanisms are studied and compared with four well-known architectures of hexapods. Finally we conclude in Section 7.

2. Mechanisms description

The schematics of the 6-DOF non-redundant,3-legged and redundant 4-legged mechanisms are shown in Figs. 1 and 2, respectively.
The non-redundant 3-legged mechanism was first introduced by Beji & Pascal (1999). The redundant 4-legged mechanism has the similar structure, with a single leg added to the 3-legged system, which keeps symmetry. Each leg is composed of three joints; universal,

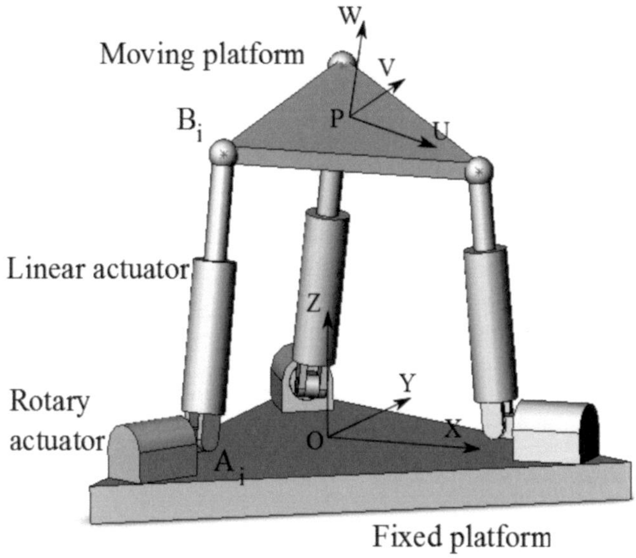

Fig. 1. Schematic of the non-redundant mechanism.

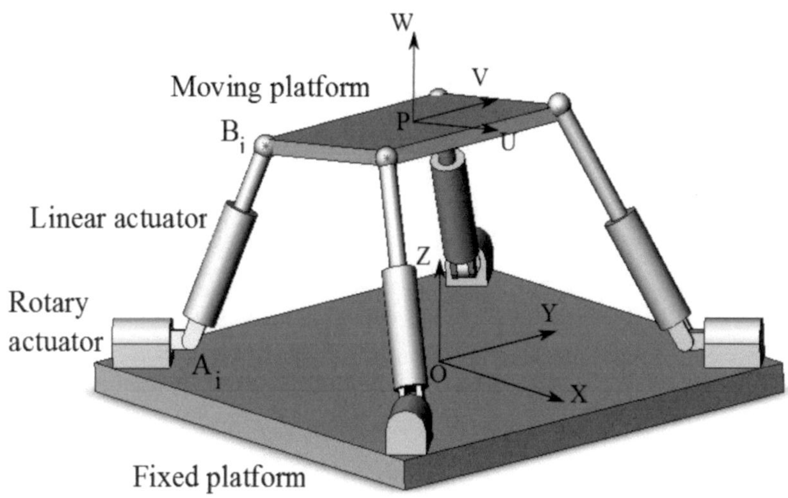

Fig. 2. Schematic of the redundant mechanism.

prismatic, and spherical (Fig. 3). A rotary actuator and a linear actuator are used to actuate each leg. The rotary actuators, whose shafts are attached to the lower parts of the linear actuators through the universal joints, are placed on the corners of the fixed platform (Abedinnasab & Vossoughi, 2009; Aghababai, 2005). The spherical joints connect the upper parts of the linear actuators to the moving platform.

Rotary actuators are situated on the corners A_i (for $i=1, 2, 3, 4$) of the base platform and each shaft is connected to the lower part of linear actuators through a universal joint (Figs. 1 and 2). The upper parts of linear actuators are connected to the corners of the moving platform, B_i points, through spherical joints (Fig. 3).

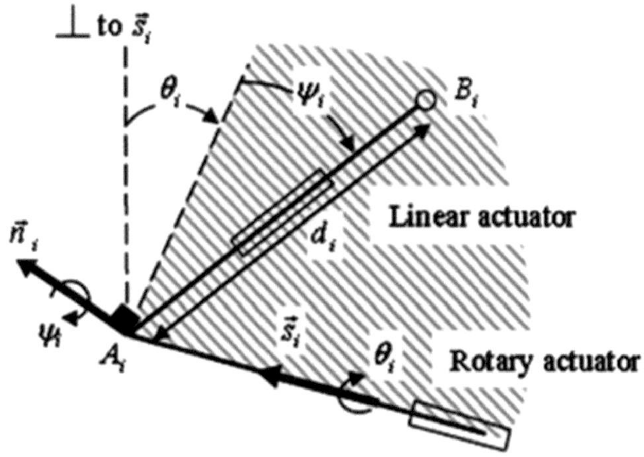

Fig. 3. Schematic of the universal joint, and the joints variables.

Cartesian coordinates A (O, x, y, z) and B (P, u, v, w) represented by {A} and {B} are connected to the base and moving platforms, respectively. In Fig.3, $\vec{s}_i$ represents the unit vector along the axes of ith rotary actuator and $\vec{d}_i$ is the vector along $\overrightarrow{A_iB_i}$ with the length of d_i. Assuming that each limb is connected to the fixed base by a universal joint, the orientation of ith limb with respect to the fixed base can be described by two Euler angles, rotation θ_i around the axis $\vec{s}_i$, followed by rotation ψ_i around $\vec{n}_i$, which is perpendicular to $\vec{d}_i$ and $\vec{s}_i$ (Fig. 3). It is to be noted that θ_i and d_i are active joints actuated by the rotary and linear actuators, respectively. However, ψ_i is inactive.
By replacing the passive universal joints in the Stewart mechanism with active joints in the above mentioned mechanisms, the number of legs could be reduced from 6 to 3 or 4. This

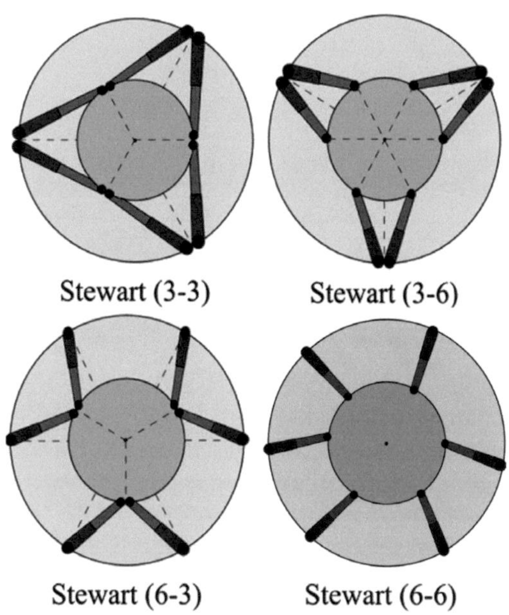

Fig. 4. Schematics of well-known Stewart platforms.

change makes the mechanism to be lighter, since the rotary actuators are resting on the fixed platform, which causes higher accelerations to be available due to smaller inertial effects.
The applications of this type of robots can be found in flight simulators, high precision surgical tools, positioning devices, motion generators, ultra-fast pick and place robots, haptic devices, entertainment, multi-axis machine tools, micro manipulators, rehabilitation devices, etc.
Advantages of high rigidity and low inertia make these PMs ideal for force feedback control, assembly, manufacturing, underground projects, space technologies, and biology projects.

3. Kinematic analysis

One of the most important issues in the study of parallel mechanisms is the kinematic analysis, where the generated results form the base for the application of the mechanism. $\vec{a}_i$ represents the vector $\overrightarrow{OA_i}$ (Fig. 1). $\vec{a}_i = g[\cos\gamma_i \quad \sin\gamma_i \quad 0]^T$, in which,

$$\gamma_1^{\text{Red.}} = -45^\circ,\ \gamma_2^{\text{Red.}} = 45^\circ,\ \gamma_3^{\text{Red.}} = 135^\circ,\ and\ \gamma_4^{\text{Red.}} = -135^\circ,$$

and

$$\gamma_1^{Non-Red.} = 0^\circ,\ \gamma_2^{Non-Red.} = 120^\circ,\ and\ \gamma_3^{Non-Red.} = -120^\circ,$$

where g and r are the radius of the fixed and moving platforms, respectively. $\overrightarrow{^B b_i}$ represents the position of the ith joint on the platform in the moving frame {B}, $\overrightarrow{^B b_i} = \overrightarrow{PB_i}\Big)_B$. $\overrightarrow{^B b_i}$ is constant and is equal to $\overrightarrow{^B b_i} = h[\cos\gamma_i \quad \sin\gamma_i \quad 0]^T$. We can represent ${}^A_BR = \left[r_{ij}\right]$, the rotation matrix from $\{B\}$ to $\{A\}$, using Euler angles as

$$ {}^A_BR = \begin{bmatrix} c\alpha_2 c\alpha_3 & c\alpha_3 s\alpha_2 s\alpha_1 - s\alpha_3 c\alpha_1 & c\alpha_3 s\alpha_2 c\alpha_1 + s\alpha_3 s\alpha_1 \\ c\alpha_2 s\alpha_3 & s\alpha_3 s\alpha_2 s\alpha_1 + c\alpha_3 c\alpha_1 & s\alpha_3 s\alpha_2 c\alpha_1 - c\alpha_3 s\alpha_1 \\ -s\alpha_2 & c\alpha_2 s\alpha_1 & c\alpha_2 c\alpha_1 \end{bmatrix}, \quad (1)$$

where $s\alpha_1 = \sin\alpha_1$ and $c\alpha_1 = \cos\alpha_1$, and so on. α_1, α_2, and α_3 are three Euler angles defined according to the $z-y-x$ convention. Thus, the vector $\overrightarrow{^B b_i}$ would be expressed in the fixed frame {A} as

$$\vec{b}_i = {}^A_BR\,\overrightarrow{PB_i}\Big)_B. \quad (2)$$

Let $\vec{p}$ and $\vec{r}_i$ denote the position vectors for P and B_i in the reference frame $\{A\}$, respectively. From the geometry, it is obvious that

$$\vec{r}_i = \vec{p} + \vec{b}_i. \quad (3)$$

Subtracting vector $\vec{a}_i$ from both sides of (3) one obtains

$$\vec{r}_i - \vec{a}_i = \vec{p} + \vec{b}_i - \vec{a}_i. \quad (4)$$

Left hand side of (4) is the definition of $\vec{d_i}$, therefore

$$d_i^2 = (\vec{p} + \vec{b}_i - \vec{a}_i) \cdot (\vec{p} + \vec{b}_i - \vec{a}_i) . \tag{5}$$

Using Euclidean norm, d_i can be expressed as:

$$d_i = \sqrt{\left((x - x_i)^2 + (y - y_i)^2 + (z - z_i)^2\right)} , \tag{6}$$

where,

$$\begin{cases} x_i = -h\left(\cos\gamma_i r_{11} + \sin\gamma_i r_{21}\right) + g\cos\gamma_i \\ y_i = -h\left(\cos\gamma_i r_{12} + \sin\gamma_i r_{22}\right) + g\sin\gamma_i \\ z_i = -h\left(\cos\gamma_i r_{13} + \sin\gamma_i r_{23}\right) \end{cases} . \tag{7}$$

Coordinates $C_i(A_i, x_i, y_i, z_i)$ are connected to the base platform with their x_i axes aligned with the rotary actuators in the $\vec{s}_i$ directions, with their z_i axes perpendicular to the fixed platform. Thus, one can express vector $\vec{d_i}$ in $\{C_i\}$ as

$${}^{C_i}\vec{d_i} = d_i \begin{bmatrix} \sin\psi_i \\ -\sin\theta_i \cos\psi_i \\ \cos\theta_i \cos\psi_i \end{bmatrix} , \tag{8}$$

and from the geometry is clear that

$$\vec{r}_i = \vec{a}_i + {}^{A}_{C_i}R\, {}^{C_i}\vec{d_i} , \tag{9}$$

where ${}^{A}_{C_i}R$ is the rotation matrix from $\{C_i\}$ to $\{A\}$,

$${}^{A}_{C_i}R = \begin{bmatrix} \cos\gamma_i & -\sin\gamma_i & 0 \\ \sin\gamma_i & \cos\gamma_i & 0 \\ 0 & 0 & 1 \end{bmatrix} . \tag{10}$$

By equating the right sides of (3) and (4), and solving the obtained equation, ψ_i and θ_i can be calculated as follows:

$$\psi_i = \sin^{-1}\left(\frac{\cos\gamma_i (x - x_i) + \sin\gamma_i (y - y_i)}{d_i} \right) , \tag{11}$$

$$\theta_i = \sin^{-1}\left(\frac{\sin\gamma_i (x - x_i) - \cos\gamma_i (y - y_i)}{d_i \cos\psi_i} \right) . \tag{12}$$

4. Jacobian analysis using screw theory

Singularities of a PM pose substantially more complicated problems, compared to a serial manipulator. One of the first attempts to provide a general framework and classification may be traced back to Gosselin and Angeles (1990) ,who derived the input-output velocity map for a generic mechanism by differentiating the implicit equation relating the input and output configuration variables. In this way, distinct jacobian matrices are obtained for the inverse and the direct kinematics, and different roles played by the corresponding singularities are clearly shown.

For singularity analysis other methods rather than dealing with jacobian matrix are also available. Pendar et al. (2011) introduced a geometrical method, namely *constraint plane method,* where one can obtain the singular configurations in many parallel manipulators with their mathematical technique. Lu et al. (2010) proposed a novel analytic approach for determining the singularities of some 4-DOF parallel manipulators by using *translational/rotational jacobian matrices.* Piipponen (2009) studied kinematic singularities of planar mechanisms by means of *computational algebraic geometry* method. Zhao et al. (2005) have proposed *terminal constraint* method for analyzing the singularities based on the physical meaning of reciprocal screws.

Gosselin & Angeles (1990) have based their works on deriving the jacobian matrix. They performed this by defining three possible conditions. In these conditions the determinant of forward jacobian matrix or inverse jacobian matrix is investigated. They have shown that having dependent Plücker vectors in a parallel manipulator is equivalent to zero determinant of the forward jacobian matrix and then a platform singularity arises.

In this section the jacobian analysis of the proposed PMs are approached by using the theory of screws. Zhao et al. (2011) proposed a new approach using the screw theory for force analysis, and implemented it on a 3-DOF 3-RPS parallel mechanism. Gallardo-Alvarado et al. (2010) presented a new 5-DOF redundant parallel manipulator with two moving platforms, where the active limbs are attached to the fixed platform. They find the jacobian matrix by means of the screw theory.

A class of series-parallel manipulators known as 2(3-RPS) manipulators was studied by Gallardo-Alvarado et al. (2008) by means of the screw theory and the principle of virtual work. Gan et al. (2010) used the screw theory to obtain the kinematic solution of a new 6-DOF 3CCC parallel mechanism. Gallardo-Alvarado et al. (2006) analyzed singularity of a 4-DOF PM by means of the screw theory.

Hereafter we derive the jacobian matrices of the proposed mechanisms using screw theory. Joint velocity vector in the redundant mechanism, $\dot{\vec{q}}^{\mathrm{Red.}}$, is an 8×1 vector:

$$\dot{\vec{q}}^{\mathrm{Red.}} = [\,\dot{\theta}_1 \quad \dot{\theta}_2 \quad \dot{\theta}_3 \quad \dot{\theta}_4 \quad \dot{d}_1 \quad \dot{d}_2 \quad \dot{d}_3 \quad \dot{d}_4]^T \tag{13}$$

where $\dot{\theta}_i$ and $\dot{d}_i$ are the angular and linear velocities of the rotary and linear actuators, respectively. However, joint velocity vector in the non-redundant mechanism, $\dot{\vec{q}}^{Non-\mathrm{Red.}}$, is a 6×1 vector:

$$\dot{\vec{q}}^{Non-\mathrm{Red.}} = [\dot{\theta}_1 \quad \dot{\theta}_2 \quad \dot{\theta}_3 \quad \dot{d}_1 \quad \dot{d}_2 \quad \dot{d}_3]^T\,. \tag{14}$$

The linear and angular velocities of the moving platform are defined to be $\vec{v}$ and $\vec{\omega}$, respectively. Thus, $\dot{\vec{x}}$ can be written as a 6×1 velocity vector;

$$\dot{\vec{x}} = [\vec{v}^T \quad \vec{\omega}^T]. \tag{15}$$

Jacobian matrices relate $\dot{\vec{q}}$ and $\dot{\vec{x}}$ as follow;

$$J_x\dot{\vec{x}} = J_q\dot{\vec{q}}, \tag{16}$$

where J_x and J_q are forward and inverse jacobian matrices, respectively. If one defines J as follows;

$$J = J_q^{-1}J_x. \tag{17}$$

Thus $\dot{\vec{q}}$,and $\dot{\vec{x}}$ can be simply related as;

$$\dot{\vec{q}} = J\,\dot{\vec{x}}. \tag{18}$$

The concept of reciprocal screws is applied to derive J_x and J_q (Tsai, 1998; 1999). The reference frame of the screws is point P of the moving platform. Fig. 5 shows the kinematic chain of each leg, where universal joints are replaced by intersection of two unit screws, $\hat{\$}_1$ and $\hat{\$}_2$. $\hat{\$}_1 = \begin{bmatrix} \vec{s}_{1,i} \\ (\vec{b}_i - \vec{d}_i)\times\vec{s}_{1,i} \end{bmatrix}$ and $\hat{\$}_2 = \begin{bmatrix} \vec{s}_{2,i} \\ (\vec{b}_i - \vec{d}_i)_i\times\vec{s}_{2,i} \end{bmatrix}$ where $\vec{s}_{1,i}$ and $\vec{s}_{2,i}$ are unit vectors along the inactive and active joints of each universal joint, respectively. Spherical joints in each leg are replaced by intersection of three unit screws, $\hat{\$}_4$, $\hat{\$}_5$, and $\hat{\$}_6$. $\hat{\$}_4 = \begin{bmatrix} \vec{s}_{4,i} \\ \vec{b}_i\times\vec{s}_{4,i} \end{bmatrix}$, $\hat{\$}_5 = \begin{bmatrix} \vec{s}_{5,i} \\ \vec{b}_i\times\vec{s}_{5,i} \end{bmatrix}$, and $\hat{\$}_6 = \begin{bmatrix} \vec{s}_{6,i} \\ \vec{b}_i\times\vec{s}_{6,i} \end{bmatrix}$, where $\vec{s}_{4,i} = \vec{s}_{1,i}$, $\vec{s}_{6,i}$ is the unit vector along the linear actuator, and $\vec{s}_{5,i} = \vec{s}_{6,i}\times\vec{s}_{4,i}$. $\hat{\$}_3 = \begin{bmatrix} 0 \\ \vec{s}_{3,i} \end{bmatrix}$ explains the prismatic joint, as well. It is to be noted that $\vec{s}_{3,i} = \vec{s}_{6,i}$. Each leg can be assumed as an open-loop chain to express the instant twist of the moving platform by means of the joint screws:

$$\begin{aligned} \hat{\$}_P = \dot{\psi}_i\hat{\$}_{1,i} + \dot{\theta}_i\hat{\$}_{2,i} + \dot{d}_i\hat{\$}_{3,i} + \dot{\phi}_{1,i}\hat{\$}_{4,i} \\ + \dot{\phi}_{2,i}\hat{\$}_{5,i} + \dot{\phi}_{3,i}\hat{\$}_{6,i} \end{aligned}. \tag{19}$$

By taking the orthogonal product of both sides of (19) with reciprocal screw $\hat{\$}_{r1,i} = \begin{bmatrix} \vec{s}_{3,i} \\ \vec{b}_i\times\vec{s}_{3,i} \end{bmatrix}$, one can eliminate the inactive joints and rotary actuator which yields to

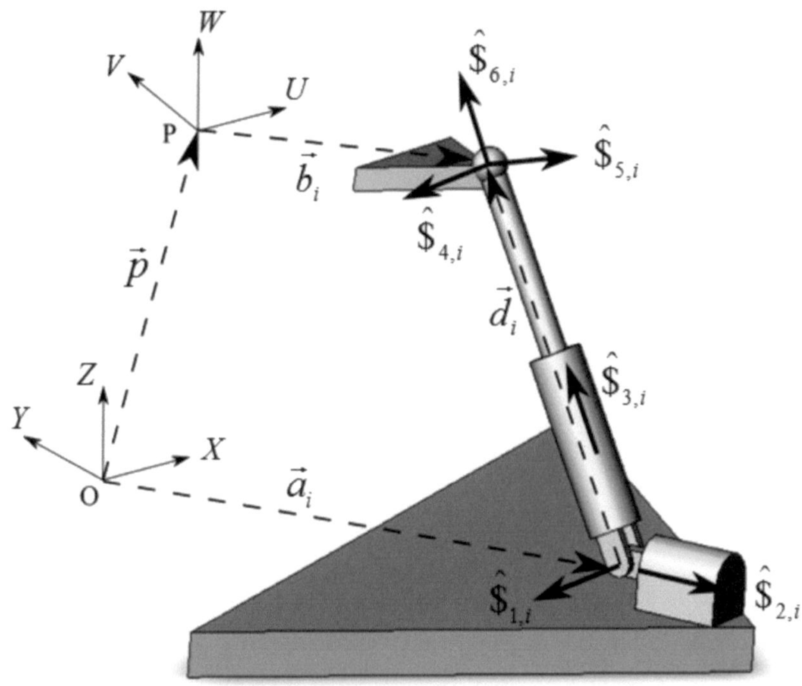

Fig. 5. Infinitesimal screws.

$$\begin{bmatrix} \frac{\vec{d}_i^{\,T}}{d_i} & \frac{(\vec{b}_i \times \vec{d}_i)^T}{d_i} \end{bmatrix} \dot{\vec{x}}_P = \dot{d}_i\,,\ i = 1,2,3,4\,. \tag{20}$$

Similarly, if one takes the orthogonal product of both sides of (19) with reciprocal screw $\hat{\$}_{r6,i} = \begin{bmatrix} \frac{\vec{s}_i \times \vec{d}_i}{d_i \cos\psi_i} \\ \vec{b}_i \times \frac{\vec{s}_i \times \vec{d}_i}{d_i \cos\psi_i} \end{bmatrix}$ the resultant is as follows;

$$\begin{bmatrix} (\frac{\vec{s}_i \times \vec{d}_i}{d_i \cos\psi_i})^T & (\vec{b}_i \times \frac{\vec{s}_i \times \vec{d}_i}{d_i \cos\psi_i})^T \end{bmatrix} \dot{\vec{x}}_P = d_i \cos\psi_i \dot{\theta}_i\,. \tag{21}$$

Note that in (21), $\left|\vec{s}_i \times \vec{d}_i\right| = d_i \cos\psi_i$.

Finally, using (20) and (21), jacobian matrices $J_x^{\mathrm{Red.}}$ and $J_q^{\mathrm{Red.}}$ are expressed as;

$$J_x^{\mathrm{Red.}} = \begin{bmatrix} (\vec{s}_1 \times \overrightarrow{d_1})^T & (\vec{b}_1 \times (\vec{s}_1 \times \overrightarrow{d_1}))^T \\ (\vec{s}_2 \times \overrightarrow{d_2})^T & (\vec{b}_2 \times (\vec{s}_2 \times \overrightarrow{d_2}))^T \\ (\vec{s}_3 \times \overrightarrow{d_3})^T & (\vec{b}_3 \times (\vec{s}_3 \times \overrightarrow{d_3}))^T \\ (\vec{s}_4 \times \overrightarrow{d_4})^T & (\vec{b}_4 \times (\vec{s}_4 \times \overrightarrow{d_4}))^T \\ \overrightarrow{d_1}^T & (\vec{b}_1 \times \overrightarrow{d_1})^T \\ \overrightarrow{d_2}^T & (\vec{b}_2 \times \overrightarrow{d_2})^T \\ \overrightarrow{d_3}^T & (\vec{b}_3 \times \overrightarrow{d_3})^T \\ \overrightarrow{d_4}^T & (\vec{b}_4 \times \overrightarrow{d_4})^T \end{bmatrix}, \tag{22}$$

and

$$J_q^{\mathrm{Red.}} = diag(d_1^2 \cos^2 \psi_1, d_2^2 \cos^2 \psi_2, d_3^2 \cos^2 \psi_3, d_4^2 \cos^2 \psi_4, d_1, d_2, d_3, d_4). \tag{23}$$

Similarly, jacobian matrices of non-redundant mechanism ($J_x^{Non-\mathrm{Red.}}$ and $J_q^{Non-\mathrm{Red.}}$) can be expressed as;

$$J_x^{Non-\mathrm{Red.}} = \begin{bmatrix} (\vec{s}_1 \times \overrightarrow{d_1})^T & (\vec{b}_1 \times (\vec{s}_1 \times \overrightarrow{d_1}))^T \\ (\vec{s}_2 \times \overrightarrow{d_2})^T & (\vec{b}_2 \times (\vec{s}_2 \times \overrightarrow{d_2}))^T \\ (\vec{s}_3 \times \overrightarrow{d_3})^T & (\vec{b}_3 \times (\vec{s}_3 \times \overrightarrow{d_3}))^T \\ \overrightarrow{d_1}^T & (\vec{b}_1 \times \overrightarrow{d_1})^T \\ \overrightarrow{d_2}^T & (\vec{b}_2 \times \overrightarrow{d_2})^T \\ \overrightarrow{d_3}^T & (\vec{b}_3 \times \overrightarrow{d_3})^T \end{bmatrix}, \tag{24}$$

and

$$J_q^{Non-\mathrm{Red.}} = diag(d_1^2 \cos^2 \psi_1, d_2^2 \cos^2 \psi_2, d_3^2 \cos^2 \psi_3, d_1, d_2, d_3). \tag{25}$$

And for the Stewart platform one can have

$$J_x^{Stewart} = \begin{bmatrix} \overrightarrow{d_1}^T & (\vec{b}_1 \times \overrightarrow{d_1})^T \\ \overrightarrow{d_2}^T & (\vec{b}_2 \times \overrightarrow{d_2})^T \\ \overrightarrow{d_3}^T & (\vec{b}_3 \times \overrightarrow{d_3})^T \\ \overrightarrow{d_4}^T & (\vec{b}_4 \times \overrightarrow{d_4})^T \\ \overrightarrow{d_5}^T & (\vec{b}_5 \times \overrightarrow{d_5})^T \\ \overrightarrow{d_6}^T & (\vec{b}_6 \times \overrightarrow{d_6})^T \end{bmatrix}, \tag{26}$$

and

$$J_q^{Stewart} = diag(d_1, d_2, d_3, d_4, d_5, d_6). \tag{27}$$

Note that the joint velocity vector in stewart mechanism, $\dot{q}^{Stewart}$, is the following 6×1 vector:

$$\dot{q}^{Stewart} = [\dot{d}_1 \quad \dot{d}_2 \quad \dot{d}_3 \quad \dot{d}_4 \quad \dot{d}_5 \quad \dot{d}_6]^T . \tag{28}$$

Based on the existence of the two jacobian matrices above, the mechanism is at a singular configuration when either the determinant of J_x or J_q is either zero or infinity (Beji & Pascal, 1999).

Inverse kinematic singularity occurs when the determinant of J_q vanishes, namely;

$$\det(J_q) = 0 . \tag{29}$$

As it is clear from (25) and (27), the determinant of J_q in the workspace of this mechanism cannot be vanished. Therefore we do not have this type of singularity.

Forward kinematic singularity occurs when the rank of J_x is less than 6, namely;

$$rank(J_x) \le 5 . \tag{30}$$

If (30) holds, the moving platform gains 1 or more degrees of freedom. In other words, at a forward kinematic singular configuration, the manipulator cannot resist forces or moments in some directions. As it can be seen, the redundancy can help us to avoid this kind of singularity, which is common in nearly all parallel mechanisms.

5. Performance indices

With the increasing demand for precise manipulators, search for a new manipulator with better performance has been intensive. Several indices have been proposed to evaluate the performance of a manipulator. Merlet reviewed the merits and weaknesses of these indices (Merlet, 2006). The dexterity indices have been commonly used in determining the dexterous regions of a manipulator workspace. The condition number of the jacobian matrix is known to be used as a measuring criterion of kinematic accuracy of manipulators. Salisbury & Craig (1982) used this criterion for the determination of the optimal dimensions for the fingers of an articulated hand. The condition number of the jacobian matrix has also been applied for designing a spatial manipulator (Angeles & Rojas, 1987).

The most performance indices are pose-dependant. For design, optimization and comparison purpose, Gosselin & Angeles (1991) proposed a global performance index, which is the integration of the local index over the workspace.

The performance indices are usually formed based on the evaluation of the determinant, norms, singular values and eigenvalues of the jacobian matrix. These indices have physical interpretation and useful application for control and optimization just when the elements of the jacobian matrix have the same units (Kucuk & Bingul, 2006). Otherwise, the stability of control systems, which are formed based on these jacobian matrices, will depend on the physical units of parameters chosen (Schwartz et al., 2002). Thus, different indices for rotations and translations should be defined (Cardou et al., 2010).

5.1 Manipulability

For evaluation of kinematic transmissibility of a manipulator, Yoshikawa (1984) defined the manipulator index,

$$\mu = \sqrt{\det(J^T J)} . \tag{31}$$

The manipulability can geometrically be interpreted as the volume of the ellipsoid obtained by mapping a unit n-dimensional sphere of joint space onto the Cartesian space (Cardou et al., 2010). It also can be interpreted as a measure of manipulator capability for transmitting a certain velocity to its end-effector (Mansouri & Ouali, 2011). To have a better performance for a manipulator, It is more suitable to have isotropic manipulability ellipsoid (Angeles & Lopez-Cajun, 1992). The isotropy index for manipulability can be defined as:

$$\mu_{iso} = \frac{\sigma_{Min}}{\sigma_{Max}} , \tag{32}$$

where σ_{Max} and σ_{Min} are maximum and minimum of singular values of jacobian matrix (*J*), respectively. The isotropy index is limited between 0 and 1. When the isotropy index is equal to 1, it indicates the ability of manipulator to transmit velocity uniformly from actuators to the end-effector along all directions. Inversely, when the isotropy index is equal to zero, the manipulator is at a singular configuration and cannot transmit velocity to the end-effector.

5.2 Dexterity

The accuracy of a mechanism is dependent on the condition number of the jacobian matrix, which is defined as follows:

$$k = ||J||.||J^{-1}||, \tag{33}$$

where *J* is the jacobian matrix and $\|J\|$ denotes the norm of it and is defined as follows:

$$||J|| = \sqrt{tr(\frac{1}{n} JJ^T)} , \tag{34}$$

where n is the dimension of the square matrix *J* that is 3 for the manipulator under study. Gosselin (1992) defined the local dexterity (υ) as a criterion for measuring the kinematics accuracy of a manipulator,

$$\upsilon = \frac{1}{||J||.||J^{-1}||} . \tag{35}$$

The local dexterity can be changed between zero and one. The higher values indicate more accurate motion generated at given instance. When the local dexterity is equal to one, it denotes that the manipulator is isotropic at the given pose. Otherwise, it implies that the manipulator has reached a singular configuration pose.

To evaluate the dexterity of a manipulator over the entire workspace (*W* Gosselin & Angeles (1991) have introduced the global dexterity index (GDI) as:

$$GDI = \frac{\int_W \upsilon \; dW}{\int_W dW}, \qquad (36)$$

which is the average value of local dexterity over the workspace. This global dexterity index can be used as design factor for the optimal design of manipulators (Bai, 2010; Li et al., 2010; Liu et al., 2010; Unal et al., 2008). Having a uniform dexterity is a desirable goal for almost all robotic systems. Uniformity of dexterity can be defined as another global performance index. It can be defined as the ratio of the minimum and maximum values of the dexterity index over the entire workspace,

$$\upsilon_{iso} = \frac{\upsilon_{Min}}{\upsilon_{Max}}. \qquad (37)$$

5.3 Sensitivity

Evaluating of the kinematic sensitivity is another desirable concept in the performance analysis of a manipulator. The kinematic sensitivity of a manipulator can be interpreted as the effect of actuator displacements on the displacement of the end-effector. Cardou et al. (2010) defined two indices (τ_r , τ_p) for measuring the rotation and displacement sensitivity of a manipulator. They assumed the maximum-magnitude rotation and the displacement of the end-effector under a unit-norm actuator displacement as indices for calculating the sensitivity of a manipulator. The sensitivity indices can be defined as:

$$\tau_r = || J_r ||, \qquad (38)$$

and

$$\tau_p = || J_p ||, \qquad (39)$$

where J_r and J_p are rotation and translation jacobian martices (Cardou et al., 2010), respectively, where $|| \; ||$ stands for a *p*-norm of the matrix. Cardou et al. (2010) suggested to use 2-norm and ∞-norm for calculating the sensitivity.

6. Comparison between 4-legged mechanism and other mechanisms

In order to investigate the kinematic performance of 4-legged mechanism, the response of the mechanisms are compared in several different aspects; reachable points, performance indices, and singularity analysis.

6.1 Reachable points and workspace comparison

Consider the 3-legged and the 4-legged mechanisms with g=1 m and h=0.5 m, respectively; g and h are the radii of the fixed and moving platforms, respectively.

By assuming a cubic with 1m length, 1 m width and 1 m height located 0.25 m above the base platform, we are interested in determining the reachability percentage in which each mechanism can successfully reach to the locations within this cubic space.

Table 1 shows that adding one leg to the 3-legged mechanism reduces the *R.P.* (Reachable points Percentage) by 5.03%. However, it should be noted that, although the non-redundant mechanism has a wider workspace, it has much more singular points than the redundant mechanism, and actuator forces and torques are also less in the redundant mechanism. As it can be seen from Table 1, *RP*s in the Stewart platforms are smaller than 3-legged and 4-legged mechanisms. In the 6-legged Stewart-like UPS mechanisms (Stewart, 1965), the workspace is constructed by intersecting of 6 spheres. On the other hand, in the proposed 4-legged UPS mechanism, the workspace is constructed by intersecting of only 4 spheres.

Mechanism	% RP
Stewart (6-6)	76.35
Stewart (3-6)	74.21
Stewart (6-3)	73.70
Stewart (3-3)	63.46
3-legged mechanism	84.75
4-legged mechanism	79.72

Table 1. Reachable points

Assuming similar dimensions for the two mechanisms result in a larger workspace for the 4-legged mechanism.

To compare the workspace of the proposed 4-legged mechanism with the 3-legged mechanism and Steward platforms, the reachable points for them were calculated and obtained results are shown in Fig. 6 It is appear that the 3-legged mechanism has the largest workspace followed by 4-legged mechanism, 3-6 and 3-3 Steward Platforms.

6.2 Performance comparison

To compare the kinematic performance of the proposed 4-legged mechanism with the 3-legged mechanism and Steward platform, abovementioned performance indices were used. The results obtained are shown in Figs. 7 to 10. These figures show how performance indices vary on a plate ($Z=0.75$) within the workspace.

Fig. 7 depicts the Stewart 3-3 has the higher isotropy index for manipulability comparing with Stewart 3-6, 3-legged and 4-legged mechanisms. After Stewart 3-3, the 4-legged mechanism presents the better performance. This figure illustrates that adding a leg to a 3-legged mechanism can significantly improve the manipulability of the mechanism. Furthermore, a 4-legged mechanism can have a performance comparable with the Stewart platforms or even better.

Fig. 8 depicts the Stewart 3-3 compared with the other mechanisms under study has the higher dexterity index. After Stewart 3-3, again, the 4-legged mechanism presents the better performance. This figure also illustrates significant enhancement of the dexterity of the mechanism due to the additional leg. Also it shows that, in terms of dexterity, the 4-legged mechanism can have a comparable performance against the Stewart platforms or even better.

In the next step of performance comparison of manipulators, displacement and rotation sensitivities for mechanisms of our interest are compared. Fig. 9 shows the amount of displacement sensitivity indices of the abovementioned mechanisms on the selected plane

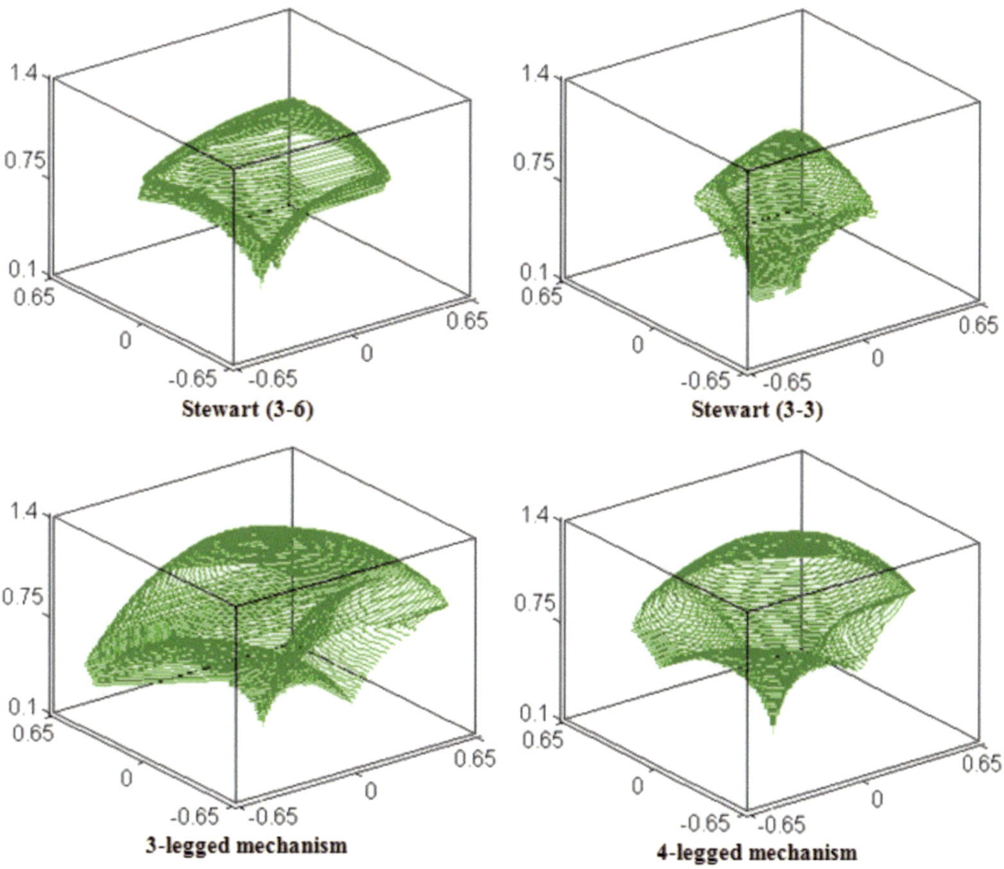

Fig. 6. Workspaces of Stewart (3-6), Stewart (3-3), 3-legged and 4-legged mechanisms.

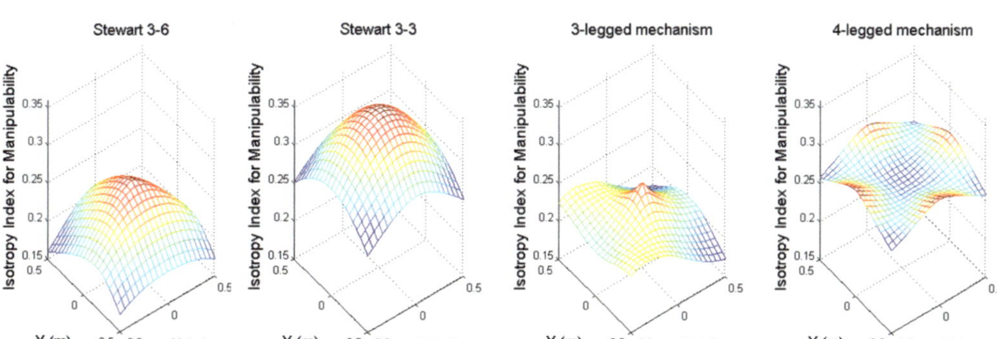

Fig. 7. Isotropy index for manipulability of Stewart 6-6, Stewart 3-6, 3 Legged mechanism and 4 legged mechanism on the plane z= 0.75 m

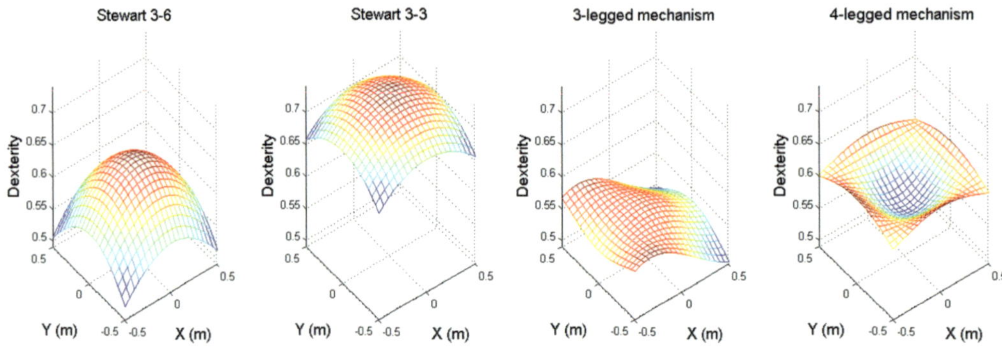

Fig. 8. Dexterity index of Stewart 6-6, Stewart 3-6, 3-Legged mechanism and 4-legged mechanism on the plane z= 0.75 m.

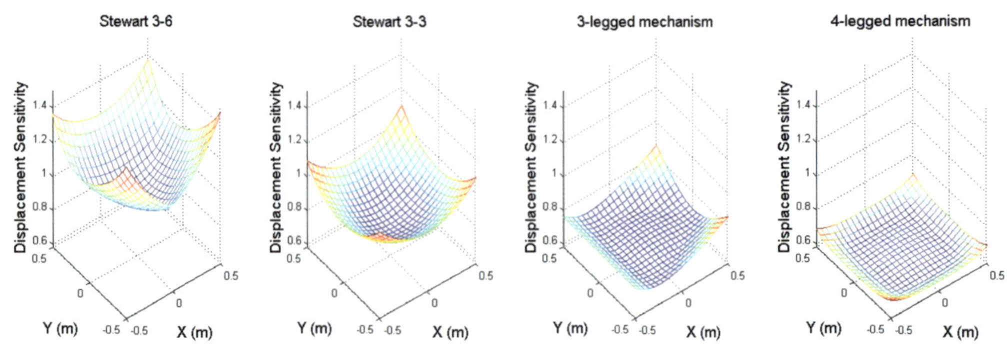

Fig. 9. Displacement Sensitivity index of Stewart 6-6, Stewart 3-6, 3-Legged mechanism and 4-legged mechanism on the plane z= 0.75 m.

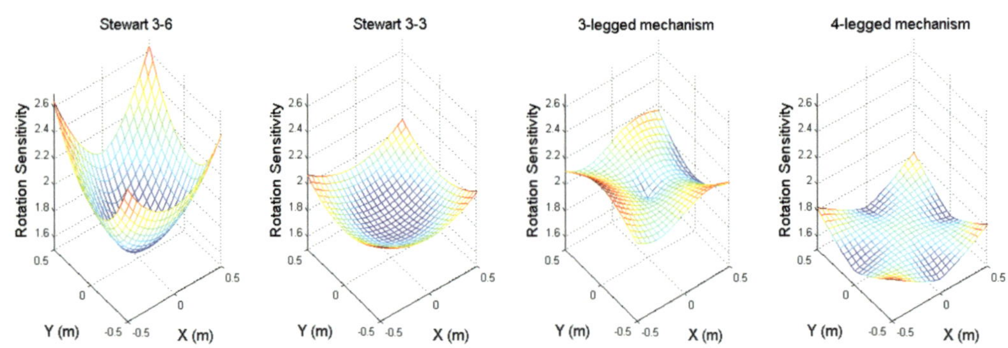

Fig. 10. Rotation Sensitivity index of Stewart 6-6, Stewart 3-6, 3-Legged mechanism and 4-legged mechanism on the plane z= 0.75 m.

(*Z=0.75*). It clearly shows that the 4-legged mechanism has less displacement sensitivity index by far. Fig. 10 depicts the 4-legged mechanism has also less rotation sensitivity compared with other mechanisms.

So far from Figs. 7 to 10, the amounts of performance indices are shown on the planes. To compare the kinetics performance of manipulators over the entire workspace, the global performance Index (GPI) can be evalueated as:

$$GPI = \frac{\int_W PI \ dW}{\int_W dW}, \tag{40}$$

which is the average value of local performance index (*PI*) over the workspace (*W*).

The amounts of GPI for Isotropy Index for Manipulability (*IIM*), Dexterity (*DX*), Displacement Sensitivity (*DS*) and Rotation Sensitivity (*RS*) were calculated and obtained results were listed in Table 2.

Table 2 shows that the 4-legged mechanism has a better *IIM* within the selected workspace, which explicitly indicates a better ability for transmitting a certain velocity to its end-effector.

As it is seen from Table 2, the Stewart 3-3 platform has the biggest global *DX* compared with other mechanisms and the 4-legged mechanism has the second (i.e. difference in *DX* is only 5.71% less). It represents that the Stewart 3-3 platform and the proposed 4-legged mechanism have the better kinematics accuracy.

Having the lower sensitivity is a demand for industrial mechanisms. By comparing the values of *DS* and *RS*, which are listed in Table 2, it is obvious the 4-legged mechanism is an appropriate candidate.

Based on the results shown in Table 2, the 4-legged mechanism is recommended for better kinematic performances

	The higher, the better		The lower, the better	
Mechaniasm	*IIM*	*DX*	*DS*	*RS*
Stewart (6-6)	0.0429	0.1589	1.3249	3.5791
Stewart (3-6)	0.1296	0.3969	1.2070	2.5725
Stewart (6-3)	0.1020	0.3449	1.2113	2.8991
Stewart (3-3)	0.1978	0.5284	1.0485	2.6077
3-legged mechanism	0.1136	0.3423	0.8538	2.3861
4-legged mechanism	0.2140	0.4982	0.7279	1.8441

Table 2. Performance comparison between 3-legged mechanism, 4-legged mechanism, Stewart 6-6, and Stewart 3-6

6.3 Singularity analysis of 3-legged and 4-legged mechanisms

Several types of workspace can be considered. For example, the 3D constant orientation workspace, which describes all possible locations of an arbitrary point P in the moving system with a constant orientation of the moving platform, the reachable workspace (all the locations that can be reached by P), the orientation workspace (all possible orientations of the end-effector around P for a given position) or the inclusive orientation workspace (all the locations that can be reached by the origin of the end-effector with every orientation in a given set) (Abedinnasab & Vossoughi, 2009).

Out of those types, we have used the inclusive orientation workspace, where for every position in a fixed surface, the moving platform is rotated in every possible orientation to determine if that configuration is singular or not. After trials and errors, we figured out that for a better determination of the singular configurations, the roll-pitch-yaw rotation about the global coordinate is the most critical set of rotations compared to the other rotations such as the reduced Euler rotations.

To illustrate the positive effects of redundancy on eliminating singular configurations, we have done jacobian analysis in planes in different orientations of the workspace as shown in Fig. 11. The results are shown in Figs. 12 and 13. In Figs. 12 and 13, the jacobian determinant of center of the moving platforms of 3-legged and 4-legged mechanisms has been calculated. The platform is rotated simultaneously in three different directions according to the roll-pitch-yaw Euler angles discussed above. Each angle is free to rotate up to ±20°. After the rotations in each position, if the mechanism did not encounter any singular configuration, the color of that position is represented by light gray. If there was any singular configuration inside ±20° region and beyond ±10° region, the color is dark gray. At last, if the singular configuration was encountered in ±10° rotations, the color is black.

As seen from Fig. 12, in the 3-legged mechanism, there exist singular configurations in the most of the X-Y, X-Z and Y-Z planes (black and dark gray regions). However, in the 4-legged mechanism, the singular points do not exist at the most of the plane. Figure 13 shows the same patterns as in the other planes. Figures 12 and 13 simply illustrate the great effect of a simple redundancy; namely, the addition of a leg to the 3-legged mechanism can remove vast singular configurations.

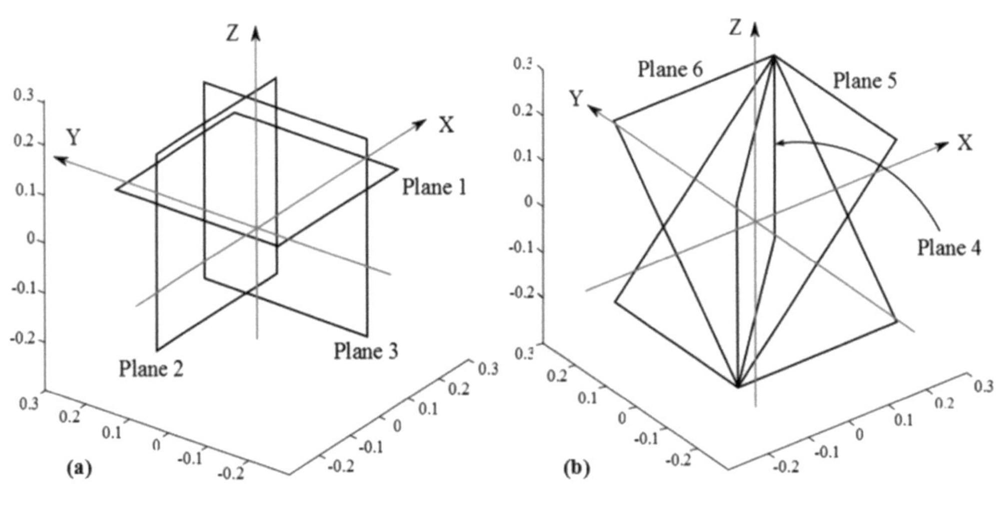

Fig. 11. (a) Schematic view of planes 1, 2, and 3. (b) Schematic view of planes 4, 5, and 6.

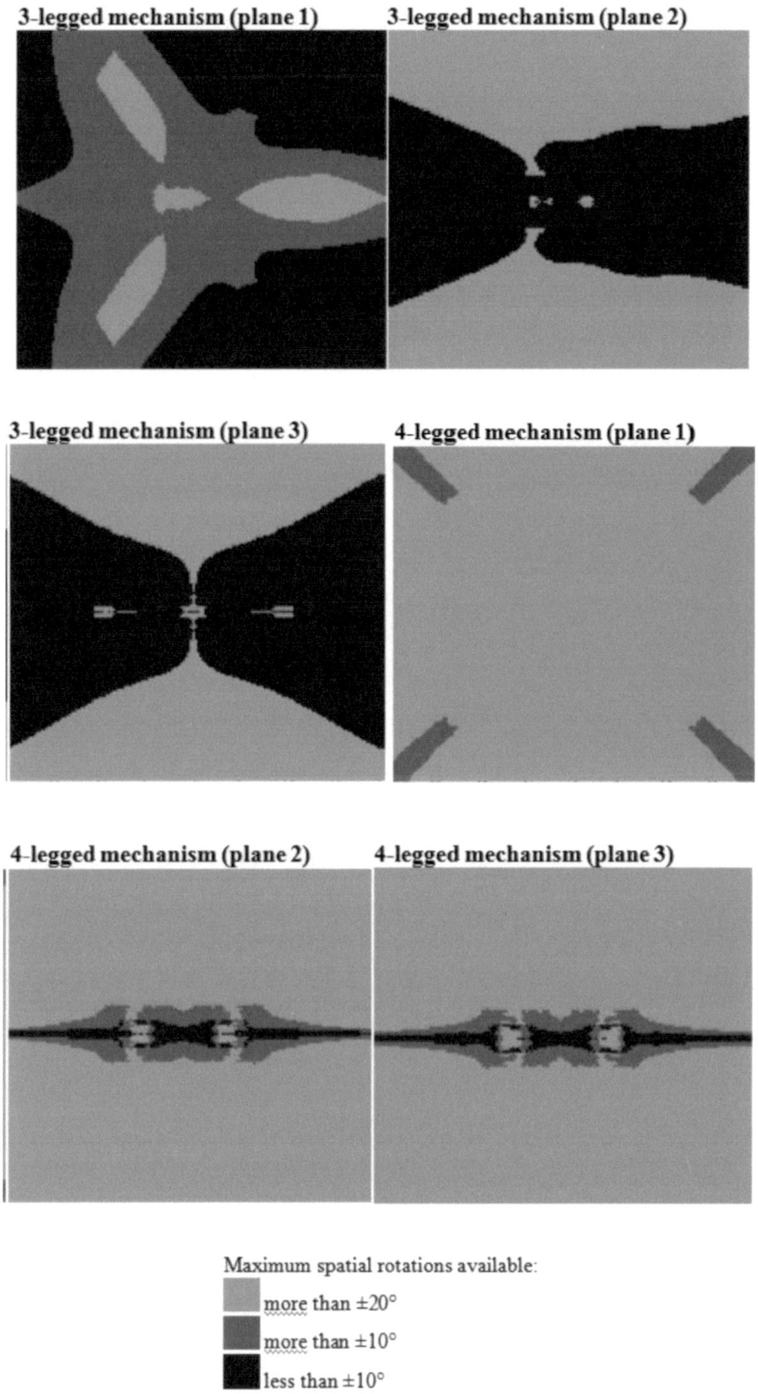

Fig. 12. Singularity analysis in planes 1, 2 and 3 for both 3-legged (non-redundant) and 4-legged (redundant) mechanisms.

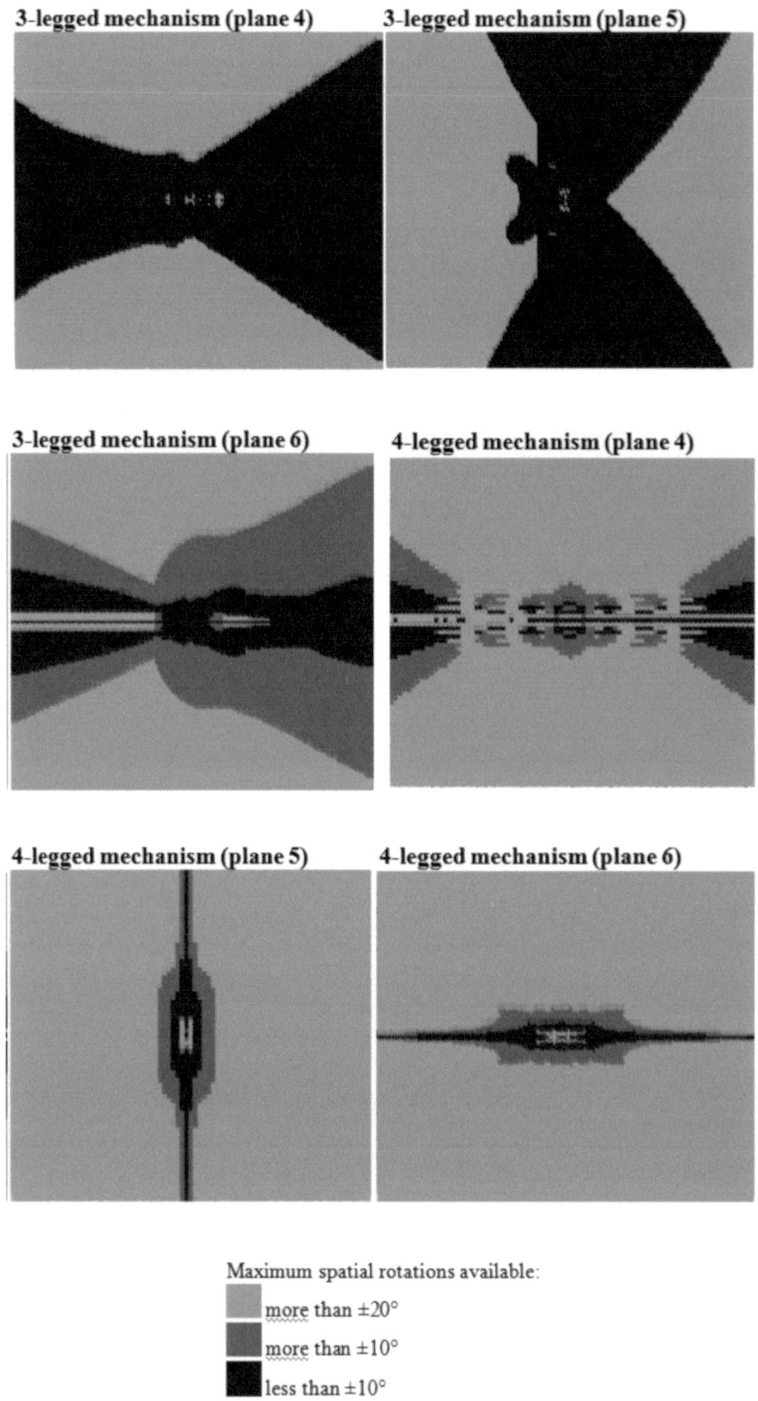

Fig. 13. Singularity analysis in planes 4, 5 and 6 for both 3-legged (non-redundant) and 4-legged (redundant) mechanisms.

7. Conclusion

The effects of redundant actuation are studied. The redundant 4-legged and non-redundant 3-legged parallel mechanisms are compared with 4 well-known architectures of Gough-Stewart platforms. It is shown that the inverse kinematics of the proposed 3-legged and 4-legged mechanisms have a closed-form solution. Also the Jacobian matrix has been determined using the concept of reciprocal screws.

From the design point of view, by replacing the passive universal joints in the Stewart platforms with active joints in the above mentioned mechanisms, the number of legs could be reduced from 6 to 3 or 4. It makes the mechanism to be lighter, since the rotary actuators are resting on the fixed platform, which allows higher accelerations to be available due to smaller inertial effects.

It is illustrated that redundancy improves the ability and performance of the non-redundant parallel manipulator. The redundancy brings some advantages for parallel manipulators such as avoiding kinematic singularities, increasing workspace, improving performance indices, such as dexterity, manipulability, and sensitivity. Finally, we conclude that the redundancy is a key choice to remove singular points, which are common in nearly all parallel mechanisms.

It is worthy to state that the applications of these robots can be found in flight simulators, high precision surgical tools, positioning devices, motion generators, ultra-fast pick-and-place robots, haptic devices, entertainment, multi-axis machine tools, micro manipulators, rehabilitation devices, etc.

8. References

Abedinnasab, M. H. & Vossoughi, G. R. (2009). Analysis of a 6-dof redundantly actuated 4-legged parallel mechanism, Nonlinear Dyn. 58(4): 611–622.

Aghababai, O. (2005). Design, Kinematic and Dynamic Analysis and Optimization of a 6 DOF Redundantly Actuated Parallel Mechanism for Use in Haptic Systems, MSc Thesis, Sharif University of Technology, Tehran, Iran.

Alp, H. & Özkol, I. (2008). Extending the workspace of parallel working mechanisms, Proc. Inst. Mech. Eng., Part C: J. Mech. Eng. Sci. 222(7): 1305–1313.

Angeles, J. & Lopez-Cajun, C. S. (1992). Kinematic isotropy and the conditioning index of serial robotic manipulators, Int. J. Rob. Res. 11(6): 560–571.

Angeles, J. & Rojas, A. A. (1987). Manipulator inverse kinematics via condition-number minimization and continuation, Int. J. Rob. Autom. 2: 61–69.

Arata, J., Kondo, J., Ikedo, N. & Fujimoto, H. (2011). Haptic device using a newly developed redundant parallel mechanism, IEEE Trans. Rob. 27(2): 201–214.

Bai, S. (2010). Optimum design of spherical parallel manipulators for a prescribed workspace, Mech. Mach. Theory 45(2): 200–211.

Beji, L. & Pascal, M. (1999). Kinematics and the full minimal dynamic model of a 6-dof parallel robot manipulator, Nonlinear Dyn. 18: 339–356.

Cardou, P., Bouchard, S. & Gosselin, C. (2010). Kinematic-sensitivity indices for dimensionally nonhomogeneous jacobian matrices, IEEE Trans. Rob. 26(1): 166–173.

Choi, H. B., Konno, A. & Uchiyama, M. (2010). Design, implementation, and performance evaluation of a 4-DOF parallel robot, Robotica 28(1): 107–118.

Deidda, R., Mariani, A. & Ruggiu, M. (2010). On the kinematics of the 3-RRUR spherical parallel manipulator, Robotica 28(6): 821–832.

Gallardo-Alvarado, J., Aguilar-Nájera, C. R., Casique-Rosas, L., Rico-Martínez, J. M. & Islam, M. N. (2008). Kinematics and dynamics of 2(3-RPS) manipulators by means of screw theory and the principle of virtual work, Mech. Mach. Theory 43(10): 1281–1294.

Gallardo-Alvarado, J., Orozco-Mendoza, H. & Rico-Martínez, J. M. (2010). A novel five-degrees-of-freedom decoupled robot, Robotica 28(6): 909–917.

Gallardo-Alvarado, J., Rico-Martínez, J. M. & Alici, G. (2006). Kinematics and singularity analyses of a 4-dof parallel manipulator using screw theory, Mech. Mach. Theory 41(9): 1048–1061.

Gan, D., Liao, Q., Dai, J. & Wei, S. (2010). Design and kinematics analysis of a new 3CCC parallel mechanism, Robotica 28: 1065–1072.

Gao, Z., Zhang, D., Hu, X. & Ge, Y. (2010). Design, analysis, and stiffness optimization of a three degree of freedom parallel manipulator, Robotica 28(3): 349–357.

Gosselin, C. & Angeles, J. (1990). Singularity analysis of closed-loop kinematic chains, IEEE Trans. Rob. Autom. 6(3): 281–290.

Gosselin, C. & Angeles, J. (1991). Global performance index for the kinematic optimization of robotic manipulators, J. Mech. Transm. Autom. Des. 113(3): 220–226.

Gosselin, C. M. (1992). The optimum design of robotic manipulators using dexterity indices, Rob. Autom. Syst. 9(4): 213–226.

Gough, V. E. & Whitehall, S. G. (1962). Universal tyre test machine, in Proc 9th Int. Tech. Congress FISITA pp. 117–137.

Jiang, Q. & Gosselin, C. M. (2009a). Determination of the maximal singularity-free orientation workspace for the gough-stewart platform, Mech. Mach. Theory 44(6): 1281–1293.

Jiang, Q. & Gosselin, C. M. (2009b). Evaluation and Representation of the Theoretical Orientation Workspace of the Gough-Stewart Platform, J. Mech. Rob., Trans. ASME 1(2): 1–9.

Jiang, Q. & Gosselin, C. M. (2009c). Maximal Singularity-Free Total Orientation Workspace of the Gough-Stewart Platform, J. Mech. Rob., Trans. ASME 1(3): 1–4.

Kucuk, S. & Bingul, Z. (2006). Comparative study of performance indices for fundamental robot manipulators, Rob. Autom. Syst. 54(7): 567–573.

Li, H., Gosselin, C. M. & Richard, M. J. (2007). Determination of the maximal singularity-free zones in the six-dimensional workspace of the general, Mech. Mach. Theory 42(4): 497–511.

Li, J.,Wang, S.,Wang, X. & He, C. (2010). Optimization of a novel mechanism for a minimally invasive surgery robot, Int. J. Med. Rob. Comput. Assisted Surg. 6(1): 83–90.

Liu, X., Xie, F., Wang, L. & Wang, J. (2010). Optimal design and development of a decoupled A/B-axis tool head with parallel kinematics, Adv. Mech. Eng. 2010: 1–14.

Lopes, A. M. (2010). Complete dynamic modelling of a moving base 6-dof parallel manipulator, Robotica 28(5): 781–793.

Lu, Y., Hu, B., Li, S.-H. & Tian, X. B. (2008). Kinematics/statics analysis of a novel 2SPS + PRRPR parallel manipulator, Mech. Mach. Theory 43(9): 1099–1111.

Lu, Y., Hu, B. & Yu, J. (2009). Analysis of kinematicsstatics and workspace of a 2(SP+SPR+SPU) serial-parallel manipulator, Multibody Sys. Dyn. 21(4): 361–374.

Lu, Y., Shi, Y. & Yu, J. (2010). Determination of singularities of some 4-dof parallel manipulators by translational/rotational jacobian matrices, Robotica 28(6): 811-819.

Mansouri, I. & Ouali, M. (2011). The power manipulability a new homogeneous performance index of robot manipulators, Rob. Comput. Integr. Manuf. 27(2): 434-449.

Masouleh, M. T., Gosselin, C., Husty, M. & Walter, D. R. (2011). Forward kinematic problem of 5-RPUR parallel mechanisms (3T2R) with identical limb structures, Mech. Mach. Theory 46(7): 945-959.

Merlet, J. P. (2006). Jacobian, manipulability, condition number, and accuracy of parallel robots, J. Mech. Des., Trans. ASME 128(1): 199-206.

Müller, A. (2005). Internal preload control of redundantly actuated parallel manipulators - its application to backlash avoiding control, IEEE Trans. Rob. 21(4): 668-677.

Pendar, H., Mahnama, M. & Zohoor, H. (2011). Singularity analysis of parallel manipulators using constraint plane method, Mech. Mach. Theory 46(1): 33-43.

Piipponen, S. (2009). Singularity analysis of planar linkages, Multibody Sys. Dyn. 22(3): 223-243.

Ropponen, T. & Nakamura, Y. (1990). Singularity-free parameterization and performance analysis of actuation redundancy, Proc. IEEE Int. Conf. Robot. Autom. 2: 806-811.

Sadjadian, H. & Taghirad, H. D. (2006). Kinematic, singularity and stiffness analysis of the hydraulic shoulder: A 3-dof redundant parallel manipulator, Adv. Rob. 20(7): 763-781.

Salisbury, J. K. & Craig, J. J. (1982). Articulated hands - force control and kinematic issues, Int. J. Rob. Res. 1(1): 4-17.

Schwartz, E., Manseur, R. & Doty, K. (2002). Noncommensurate systems in robotics, Int. J. Rob. Autom. 17(2): 86-92.

St-Onge, B. M. & Gosselin, C. M. (2000). Singularity analysis and representation of the general gough-stewart platform, Int. J. Rob. Res. 19(3): 271-288.

Staicu, S. (2009). Dynamics of the spherical 3-U-PS/S parallel mechanism with prismatic actuators, Multibody Sys. Dyn. 22(2): 115-132.

Stewart, D. (1965). A platform with six degrees of freedom, Proc. Inst. Mech. Eng. 180: 371-386.

Tsai, L.-W. (1998). The jacobian analysis of a parallel manipulator using reciprocal screws in Advances in Robot Kinematics: Analysis and Control, J. Lenarcic and M. L. Husty, Eds., Kluwer Academic.

Tsai, L.-W. (1999). Robot analysis: the mechanics of serial and parallel manipulators, Wiley.

Unal, R., Kizltas, G. & Patoglu, V. (2008). A multi-criteria design optimization framework for haptic interfaces, Symp. Haptic Interfaces Virtual Environ. Teleoperator Syst. pp. 231-238.

Vischer, P. & Clavel, R. (1998). Kinematic calibration of the parallel delta robot, Robotica 16(2): 207-218.

Wang, J. & Gosselin, C. M. (2004). Kinematic analysis and design of kinematically redundant parallel mechanisms, J. Mech. Des., Trans. ASME 126(1): 109-118.

Wu, J., Wang, J. & wang, L. (2010). A comparison study of two planar 2-DOF parallel mechanisms : one with 2-RRR and the other with 3-RRR structures, Robotica 28(6): 937-942.

Yi, B.-J., Freeman, R. A. & Tesar, D. (1989). Open-loop stiffness control of overconstrained mechanisms/robotic linkage systems, Proc. IEEE Int. Conf. Robot. Autom. 3: 1340 - 1345.

Yoshikawa, T. (1984). Analysis and control of robot manipulators with redundancy, Int. Symp. Rob. Res. pp. 735–747.

Zhao, J., Feng, Z., Zhou, K. & Dong, J. (2005). Analysis of the singularity of spatial parallel manipulator with terminal constraints, Mech. Mach. Theory 40(3): 275–284.

Zhao, Y. & Gao, F. (2010). The joint velocity, torque, and power capability evaluation of a redundant parallel manipulator. accepted in Robotica.

Zhao, Y., Liu, J. F. & Huang, Z. (2011). A force analysis of a 3-rps parallel mechanism by using screw theory. accepted in Robotica.

4

Kinematic and Dynamic Modelling of Serial Robotic Manipulators Using Dual Number Algebra

R. Tapia Herrera, Samuel M. Alcántara,
J.A. Meda-Campaña and Alejandro S. Velázquez
Instituto Politécnico Nacional
México

1. Introduction

The kinematic and dynamic modelling of robotic manipulators has, as a specific field of robotics, represented a complex problem. To deal with this, the researchers have based their works on a great variety of mathematical theories (Seiling, 1999). One of these tools is the Dual Algebra, which is a concept originally introduced in 1893 by William Kingdon Clifford (Fisher, 1998; Funda, 1988). A dual number is a compact form that can be used to represent the rigid body motion in the space (Keller, 2000; Pennestrí & Stefanelli, 2007), it has therefore, a natural application in the analysis of spatial mechanisms specifically mechanical manipulators (Bandyopadhyay, 2004, 2006; Bayro-Corrochano & Kähler, 2000, 2001).

Several works related to dual-number in kinematics, dynamics and synthesis of mechanisms have been developed (Cheng, 1994; Fisher, 1998, 1995, 2003) in (Moon & Kota, 2001) is presented a methodology for combining basic building blocks to generate alternative mechanism concepts. The methodology is based on a mathematical framework for carrying out systematic conceptual design of mechanisms using dual vector algebra. The dual vector representation enables separation of kinematic function from mechanism topology, allowing a decomposition of a desired task into subtask, in order to meet either kinematic function or spatial constraints. (Ying et al, 2004) use dual angles as an alternative approach to quantify general spatial human joint motion. Ying proposes that dual Euler angles method provides a way to combine rotational and translational joint motions in Cartesian Coordinate systems, which can avoid the problems caused by the use of the joint coordinate system due to non-orthogonality. Hence the dual angles method is suitable for analyzing the motion characteristics of the ankle joint. The motion at the ankle joint complex involves rotations about and translations along three axes. In the same field of biomechanics (KiatTeu et al, 2006) present a method that provides a convenient assessment of golf-swing effectiveness. The method can also be applied to other sports to examine segmental rotations. In general, this method facilitates the study of human motion with relative ease. The use of a biomechanical model, in conjunction with dual-number coordinate transformation for motion analysis, was shown to provide accurate and reliable results. In particular, the advantage of using the dual Euler angles based on the dual-number coordinate transformation approach, is that it allows, for a complete 3D motion, to use only six parameters for each anatomical joint. KiatTeu infers that the method has proved to be an effective means to examine high-speed movement in 3D space. It also provides an option in assessing the contributions of the individual segmental rotations in production of the relevant velocity of the end-effector.

(Page et al, 2007) present the location of the instantaneous screw axis (ISA) in order to obtain useful kinematic models of the human body for applications such as prosthesis and orthoses design or even to help in disease diagnosis techniques. Dual vectors are used to represent and operate with kinematic screws with the purpose of locating the instantaneous screw axes which characterize this instantaneous motion. A photogrammetry system based on markers is used to obtain the experimental data from which the kinematic magnitudes are obtained. A comprehensive analysis of the errors in the measurement of kinematic parameters was developed, obtaining explicit expressions for them based on the number of markers and their distribution.

1.1 Dual-number representation in robotics

The dual-number representation has been extended to other fields of mechanics; rigid body mechanics is an area where the dual number formulation has been applied, especially in the kinematics and dynamics of mechanisms.

The homogeneous transformation is a point transformation; in contrast, a line transformation can also naturally be defined in 3D Cartesian space, in which the transformed element is a line in 3D space instead of a point. In robotic kinematics and dynamics, the velocity and acceleration vectors are often the direct targets of analysis. The line transformation will have advantages over the ordinary point transformation, since the combination of the linear and angular quantities can be represented by lines in 3D space. Since a line in 3D space is determined by four independent parameters. (Gu, 1988) presents a procedure that, offers an algorithm which deals with the symbolic analysis for both rotation and translation. In particular, the aforementioned is effective for the direct determination of Jacobian matrices and their derivatives. The dual-number transformation procedure, based on these properties and the principle of transference, can be used for finding Jacobian matrices in robotic kinematics and their derivatives in robotic dynamics and control modeling. A related work was performed in (Pennock & Mattson, 1996) where the forward position problem of two PUMA robots manipulating a planar four bar linkage payload is solved using closed-form solutions for the remaining unknown angular displacements based in orthogonal transformation matrices with dual-number. (Brosky & Shoham, 1998; Sai-Kai, 2000) introduce the generalized Jacobian matrix which consists of the complete dual transformation matrices. The generalized Jacobian matrix relates force and moment at the end-effector to force and moment at the joints for each axe. Furthermore, the generalized Jacobian matrix also relates motion in all directions at the joints to the motion of the end-effector, an essential relation required at the design stage of robot manipulators. An extension of these kinematics and statics schemes into dynamics is possible by applying the dual inertia operator. (Brodsky, 1999) formulated the representation of rigid body dynamic equations introducing the dual inertia operator. Brodsky gives a general expression for the three-dimensional dynamic equation of a rigid body with respect to an arbitrary point. Then the dual Lagrange equation is established by developing derivative rules of a real function with respect to dual variables.

(Bandyopadhyay & Ghosal, 2004) performs a study in order to determinate principal twist of the end-effector of a multi-degree of freedom manipulator, which plays a central role in the analysis, design, motion planning and determination of singularities.
(Yang & Wang, 2010) solve the direct and inverse kinematics of a SCARA robot. They proved that the dual number allows compact formulations considerably facilitating the analysis of robot kinematics. To deal with coordinate transformation in three dimensional Cartesian space, the homogeneous transformation is usually applied. It is defined in the four-dimensional space and its matrix multiplication performs the simultaneous rotation and translation.

2. Mathematical preliminaries

Let us consider a transformation of coordinates between the Cartesian Coordinate system (x,y) and the oblique coordinate system (u,v) given by the equations:

$$x = au + bv; \quad y = 0u + av \tag{1}$$

With a, b real numbers. The geometry is depicted in Figure 1.
It is well known that the point (u,v) is localized by the vector $\vec{r} = x\hat{\imath} + y$ from the origin of the Cartesian coordinate. From the transformation (1):

$$\vec{r} = (au + bv)\hat{\imath} + avj \tag{2}$$

The tangent vectors to u and v are:

$$\frac{\partial \vec{r}}{\partial u} = ai; \quad \frac{\partial \vec{r}}{\partial v} = bi + aj \tag{3}$$

From the obvious $\hat{e}_u \cdot \hat{e}_v = \frac{b}{\sqrt{b^2 + a^2}}$ it is clear that the coordinates (u, v) are not orthogonal.

The unit vectors of the Cartesian frame can be written in the form of column vectors:

$$i = \begin{pmatrix} 1 \\ 0 \end{pmatrix}; \quad j = \begin{pmatrix} 0 \\ 1 \end{pmatrix} \tag{4}$$

We can describe the oblique frame (u,v) in terms of the tangent vectors ai and bi+aj written as a column vectors:

$$ai = \begin{pmatrix} a \\ 0 \end{pmatrix} \quad ; \quad bi + aj = \begin{pmatrix} b \\ a \end{pmatrix} \tag{5}$$

The column vectors $\begin{bmatrix} 1 & 0 \end{bmatrix}^T$, $\begin{bmatrix} 0 & 1 \end{bmatrix}^T$ can be combined into a single matrix describing the Cartesian Frame:

$$\text{Cartesian Frame: } \begin{pmatrix} 1 & 0 \\ 0 & 1 \end{pmatrix}$$

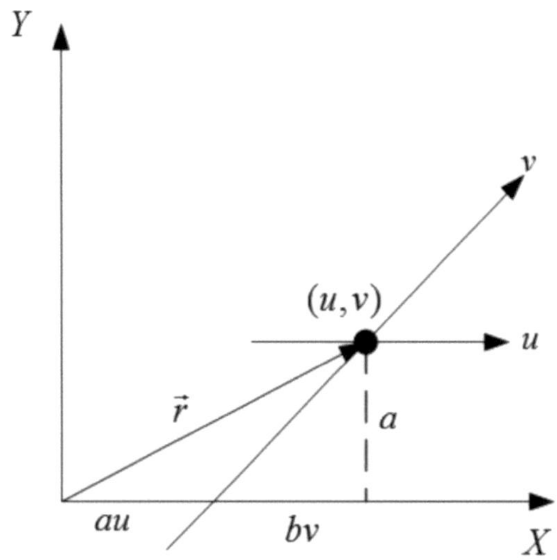

Fig. 1. Oblique plane

The column vectors $\begin{bmatrix} a & 0 \end{bmatrix}^T \begin{bmatrix} b & a \end{bmatrix}^T$ can be combined into a single matrix describing the oblique frame:

$$\text{Oblique Frame: } \begin{pmatrix} a & b \\ 0 & a \end{pmatrix}$$

The matrix $\begin{pmatrix} a & b \\ a & a \end{pmatrix}$ is the transformation matrix that describes the Oblique Frame relative to the Cartesian Frame.

The matrix $\begin{pmatrix} a & b \\ a & a \end{pmatrix}$ can be decomposed as:

$$\begin{pmatrix} a & b \\ 0 & a \end{pmatrix} = \begin{pmatrix} 1 & 0 \\ 0 & 1 \end{pmatrix} a + b \begin{pmatrix} 0 & 1 \\ 0 & 0 \end{pmatrix} \tag{6}$$

Where $\begin{pmatrix} 1 & 0 \\ 0 & 1 \end{pmatrix} = 1$ is the unitary matrix and $\begin{pmatrix} 0 & 1 \\ 0 & 0 \end{pmatrix} = \varepsilon$ is a matrix with the following properties:

a. ε is nilpotent:

$$\varepsilon^2 = \begin{pmatrix} 0 & 1 \\ 0 & 0 \end{pmatrix}^2 = \begin{pmatrix} 0 & 1 \\ 0 & 0 \end{pmatrix}\begin{pmatrix} 0 & 1 \\ 0 & 0 \end{pmatrix} = \begin{pmatrix} 0 & 0 \\ 0 & 0 \end{pmatrix} = 0$$

b. ε is a ninety degree rotation operator

$$\varepsilon j = \begin{pmatrix} 0 & 1 \\ 0 & 0 \end{pmatrix}\begin{pmatrix} 1 \\ 0 \end{pmatrix} = i$$

Finally expression (6) is written in the form:

$$\begin{pmatrix} a & b \\ 0 & a \end{pmatrix} = a + \varepsilon b \tag{7}$$

Equation (7) is easily extended to 3D:

$$1 = \begin{pmatrix} 1 & 0 & 0 \\ 0 & 1 & 0 \\ 0 & 0 & 1 \end{pmatrix}; \quad \varepsilon = \begin{pmatrix} 0 & 0 & 1 \\ 0 & 0 & 0 \\ 0 & 0 & 0 \end{pmatrix}$$

Study in 1903 called the expression $a + \varepsilon b$ "dual number" because it is constructed from the pair of real numbers (a, b). A dual number is usually denoted in the form:

$$\hat{a} = a + \varepsilon b \tag{8}$$

The algebra of dual numbers has been originally conceived by William Kingdon Clifford. Elementary operation of addition is defined as: $\left(\hat{a} = a + \varepsilon a_0; \quad \hat{b} = b + \varepsilon b_0\right)$

$$\hat{a} + \hat{b} = (a + b) + \varepsilon(a_0 + b_0) \tag{9}$$

Multiplication is defined as:

$$\hat{a}\hat{b} = (a + \varepsilon a_0)(b + \varepsilon b_0) = ab + \varepsilon(ab_0 + a_0 b) \tag{10}$$

Division is defined as:

$$\frac{\hat{a}}{\hat{b}} = \frac{a + \varepsilon a_0}{b + \varepsilon b_0} = \left(\frac{a + \varepsilon a_0}{b + \varepsilon b_0}\right)\left(\frac{b + \varepsilon b_0}{b + \varepsilon b_0}\right) = \frac{a}{b} + \varepsilon \frac{a_0 b - ab_0}{b^2} \tag{11}$$

Division by a pure dual number (εa_0) is no defined. It immediately follows that:

$$\hat{a}^n = (a + \varepsilon a_0)^n = a^n + \varepsilon n a_0 a^{n-1} \tag{12}$$

$$\sqrt{\hat{a}} = \sqrt{a} + \varepsilon \frac{a_0}{a\sqrt{a}} \tag{13}$$

A function F of a dual variable $\hat{x} = x + \varepsilon x_0$ can be represented in the form:

$$F(\hat{x}) = f(x, x_0) + \varepsilon g(x, x_0) \tag{14}$$

Where f and g are real functions of real variables x & x_0. The necessary and sufficient conditions in order that F be analytic are:

$$\frac{\partial f}{\partial x_0} = 0; \quad \frac{\partial f}{\partial x} = \frac{\partial g}{\partial x_0} \tag{15}$$

From these it immediately follows the Taylor Series expansion:

$$f(\hat{x}) = f(x + \varepsilon x_0) = f(x) + \varepsilon x_0 \frac{\partial f(x)}{\partial x} \tag{16}$$

Because $\varepsilon^2 = 0$, $\varepsilon^3 = 0$, $\varepsilon^4 = 0$ and so on, all formal operation of dual number are the same as those of ordinary algebra.

2.1 The dual angle

The dual angle represents the relative displacement and orientation between two lines L_1 and L_2 in the 3D space (Figure 2).

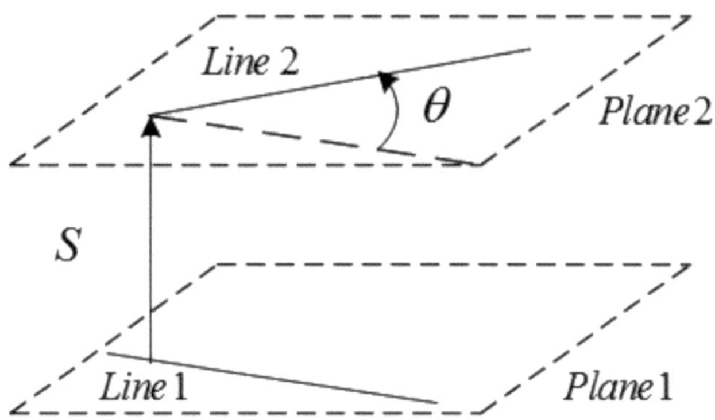

Fig. 2. Geometric representation of a dual angle.

The dual angle is defined as:

$$\hat{\theta} = \theta + \varepsilon S \tag{17}$$

This concept was introduced by Study in 1903. θ the primary component of $\hat{\theta}$ is the projected angle between L_1 and L_2. S the dual component of $\hat{\theta}$ is the shortest distance between lines L_1 & L_2 (as is obvious S is the length of common perpendicular to plane 1 and plane 2. Table 1 summarizes some properties:

$\hat{c} = \hat{a} + \hat{b}$	$\hat{c} = (a+b) + \varepsilon(a_0 + b_0)$
$\hat{c} = \hat{a}\hat{b}$	$\hat{a}\hat{b} = (a + \varepsilon a_0)(b + \varepsilon b_0)$
$\hat{a}^n$	$\hat{a}^n = a^n + \varepsilon n a_0 a^{n-1}$
$\sqrt{\hat{a}}$	$\sqrt{\hat{a}} = \sqrt{a} + \varepsilon \frac{a_0}{2\sqrt{a}}$
$\hat{a}/\hat{b}$	$\hat{c} = \frac{a}{b} + \varepsilon \frac{a_0 b - a b_0}{b^2}$
$f(\hat{a})$	$f(\hat{a}) = f(a) + \varepsilon a_0 \frac{df(a)}{da}$

Table 1. Basic dual algebra operations

In particular a dual angle is an advantageous tool to represent the coordinates of a rigid body in the space relative to other rigid body, if two planes are parallel and exists a line in each plane, dual angle will be the distance between the planes and the angle produced by the projection of one of the lines onto plane, thus a dual angle is used to describe each one of a robot's joints as a cylindrical one, which means that the entire topology is formulated as a set of dual angles (Fisher, 1995; Cecchini et al, 2004).

2.2 Dual vectors

A dual vector $\hat{V} = \vec{V} + \varepsilon(\vec{r} \times \vec{V})$ is a vector constrained to lie upon a given line L in 3D space. The primary component $\vec{V}$ is called the "resultant vector" and comprises the magnitude and direction of dual vector $\hat{V}$. It is independent of the location frame origin. The dual component $\vec{r} \times \vec{V}$ is called the "moment vector". The vector $\vec{r}$ is the position vector from the frame origin to any point on the line L of dual vector $\vec{V}$. $\vec{r} \times \vec{V}$ is invariant for any choice of point on line L, it depends on the choice of the frame origin. (Figure 3).

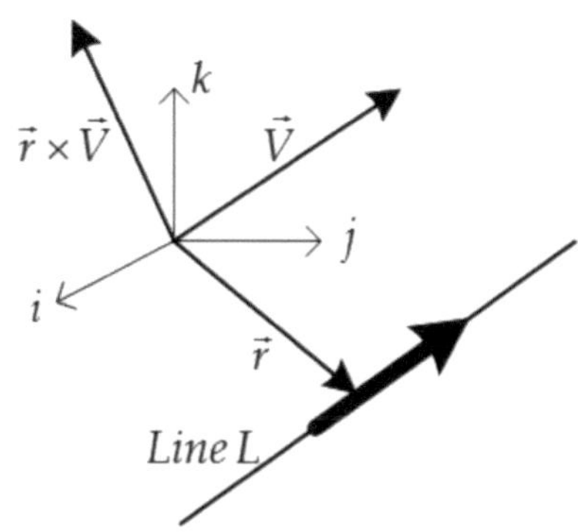

Fig. 3. Dual vector

Among the important dual vectors are:

1. Velocity defined as: $\hat{V} = (\omega + \varepsilon v)\hat{u}$
2. Linear momentum: $\hat{p} = \vec{p} + \varepsilon \vec{r} \times \vec{p}$
3. Force: $\hat{F} = \vec{F} + \varepsilon \vec{r} \times \vec{F}$
4. Angular momentum: $\hat{L} = \vec{L} + \varepsilon \vec{r} \times \vec{L}$

Important dual rotations around and along z, y, x axis are (Figure 4):

$$\hat{R}_{x,\hat{\alpha}} = \begin{bmatrix} 1 & 0 & 0 \\ 0 & \cos\hat{\alpha} & -\sin\hat{\alpha} \\ 0 & \sin\hat{\alpha} & \cos\hat{\alpha} \end{bmatrix}$$

$$\hat{R}_{y,\hat{\phi}} = \begin{bmatrix} \cos\hat{\phi} & 0 & sen\hat{\phi} \\ 0 & 1 & 0 \\ -sen\hat{\phi} & 0 & \cos\hat{\phi} \end{bmatrix} \qquad \hat{R}_{z,\hat{\theta}} = \begin{bmatrix} \cos\hat{\theta} & -\sin\hat{\theta} & 0 \\ sen\hat{\theta} & \cos\hat{\theta} & 0 \\ 0 & 0 & 1 \end{bmatrix}$$

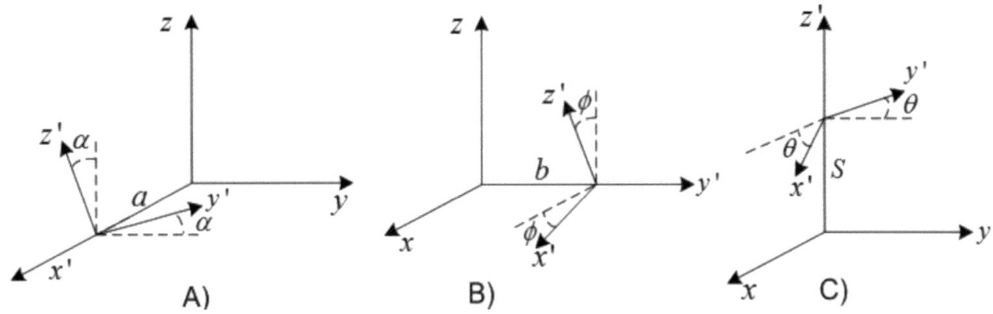

Fig. 4. Dual rotations: A) around and along x, B) around and along y, C) around and along z.

2.3 Algebra of dual vectors and matrices

Let: $\hat{A} = \vec{a} + \varepsilon(\vec{r}_1 \times \vec{a})$ and $\hat{B} = \vec{b} + \varepsilon(\vec{r}_2 \times \vec{b})$:

$$\hat{A} + \vec{B} = \vec{a} + \vec{b} + \varepsilon(\vec{r}_1 \times \vec{a} + \vec{r}_2 \times \vec{b})$$

Definition of dot and cross products are:

$$\hat{A} \cdot \hat{B} = ab\cos\hat{\theta}; \quad \hat{A} \times \hat{B} = ab\sin\hat{\theta}\hat{S}$$

Product of two dual matrices:

Let $\left[\hat{A}\right] = [A] + \varepsilon[A_0]$ & $\left[\hat{B}\right] = [B] + \varepsilon[B_0]$, the definition of their dual product is:

$$\left[\hat{A}\right]\left[\hat{B}\right] = [A][B] + \varepsilon\{[A][B_0] + [A_0][B]\}$$

It is similar with the multiplication rule for dual numbers. The inverse of a square matrix is defined as:

$$\left[\hat{A}\right]\left[\hat{A}\right]^{-1} = [I]$$

$$\left[\hat{A}\right]^{-1} = [A]^{-1} - \varepsilon\left\{[A]^{-1}[A_0][A]^{-1}\right\}$$

3. Denavit – Hartenberg parameters

Mechanisms analysis is facilitated by fixing a coordinate system on each link in a specific manner. With reference to Figure 5, a coordinate frame $\{i+1\}$ is fixed on the distal end of a link i joining joints i and $i+1$ such that:

$\hat{k}_{i+1}$ axis coincident with axis of joint $i+1$

i_{i+1} axis coincident with shortest distance between axes $\hat{k}_i$ & $\hat{k}_{i+1}$

i_{i+1} axis perpendicular to both axes i_{i+1} & $\hat{k}_{i+1}$

The origin of frame $\{i+1\}$ is located at the intersection of axes $\hat{k}_{i+1}$ and i_{i+1}. Frame $\{i\}$ is fixed on the previous link $i-1$. Translation S_i is the distance from point i, the origin of frame $\{i\}$ to the line segment whose length a_i is the shortest distance between joint axes $\hat{k}_i$ and $\hat{k}_{i+1}$. That line segment of shortest distance between join axes intersects axis $\hat{k}_{i+1}$ at point $i+1$, the origin of frame $\{i+1\}$ fixed on the distal end of link i. The projected angle between axes $\hat{k}_i$ and $\hat{k}_{i+1}$ represent the twist α_i of link i. The values α, θ, a, S are the well-known Denavit-Hartenberg parameters.

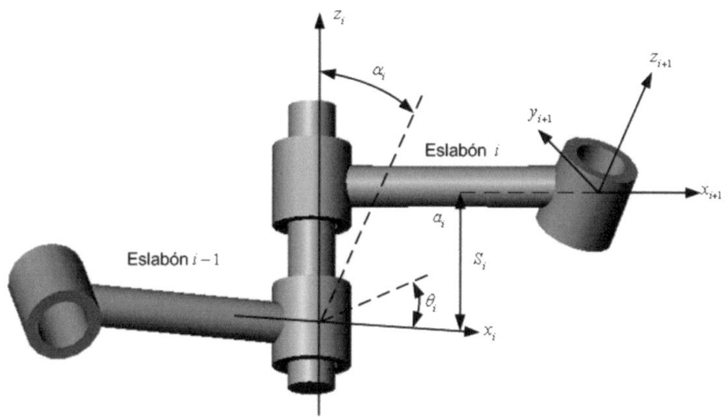

Fig. 5. Denavit and Hartenberg parameters (Pennestrí & Stefanelli, 2007)

A dual matrix rotation that represent the necessary motions of frame $\{i\}$ in terms of an attached $\{i-1\}$ frame is the composition of rotation $R_x(\hat{\alpha}_i)$ and rotation $R_z(\hat{\theta}_i)$, i.e.

$$^{i-1}\hat{M}_i = \left(\hat{R}_{z,\hat{\theta}}\right)\left(\hat{R}_{x,\hat{\alpha}}\right) = \begin{bmatrix} \cos\hat{\theta}_i & -\cos\hat{\alpha}_i \sin\hat{\theta}_i & \sin\hat{\alpha}_i \sin\hat{\theta}_i \\ \sin\hat{\theta}_i & \cos\hat{\alpha}_i \cos\hat{\theta}_i & -\sin\hat{\alpha}_i \cos\hat{\theta}_i \\ 0 & \sin\hat{\alpha}_i & \cos\hat{\alpha}_i \end{bmatrix} \tag{18}$$

So the open chain dual equation is:

$$^{0}\hat{M}_n = \prod_{i=1}^{n} {}^{i-1}\hat{M}_i \tag{19}$$

According with Funda the dual rotation matrix $^{0}\hat{M}_n = {}^{0}T_n + \varepsilon\, {}^{0}D_n$

The above expression is useful for modeling prismatic, rotational and cylindrical joints, this represents a main advantage respecting to real numbers, to represent the relative position of a point respecting an inertia frame an alternative is establishing the representation of Denavit and Hartenberg trough the dual angles θ, α :

4. Dual Jacobian matrix

If a point P on a body j is moving with respect to a body I (Fig. 6), the velocity can be expressed in terms of inertial frame R $\left({}^{R}\hat{V}^{P}_{j,i}\right)$.

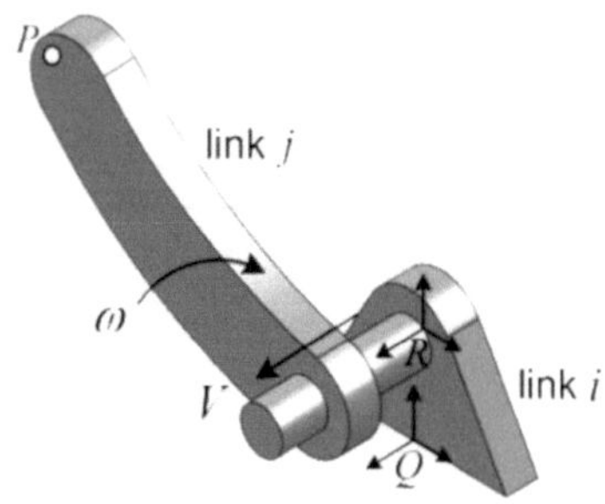

Fig. 6. Dual velocity scheme.

When the dual velocity needs to be represented in terms of frame Q, a rotation from frame R is done:

$$^{Q}\hat{V}_{j,i}^{P} = {}^{Q}T_{p}\,{}^{P}\hat{V}_{j,i}^{P} \tag{20}$$

The relative velocity of a link k with respect to link i $\left(\hat{V}_{k,i}\right)$ in dual form is established as:

$$\hat{V}_{k,i} = \hat{V}_{j,i} + \hat{V}_{k,j} \tag{21}$$

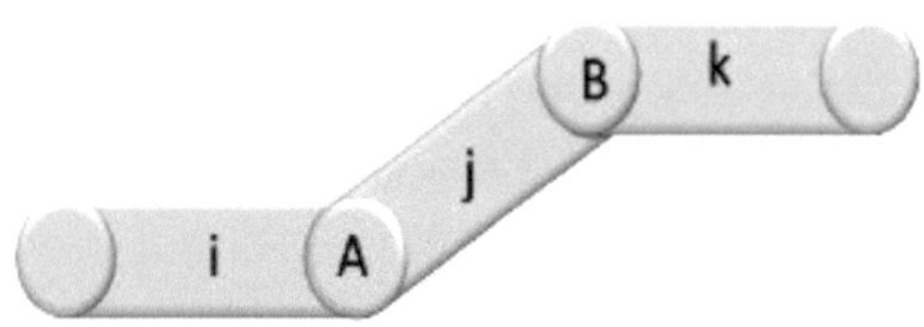

Fig. 7. Relative dual velocity theorem in a kinematic chain.

From dual velocities theorem, the vector of dual velocities in the end of n link in terms of the n frame can be found as:

$$^{0}\hat{V}_{n,0}^{n} = {}^{0}T_{n}\sum_{i=1}^{n}{}^{n}\hat{M}_{i-1}\,{}^{i-1}\hat{V}_{i,i-1}^{i-1} \tag{22}$$

Where $^{0}T_{n}$ is the primary component of the dual matrix(19).
The generalized dual Jacobian matrix is obtained by applying the relative velocity theorem in dual form. The differential motions, whether axial or radial, are expressed in a matrix formed by the dual homogenous matrices, in contrast with the conventional Jacobian matrix that is obtained from specific columns of homogeneous transformation matrix (Sai-Kai, 2000).

$$^{0}\hat{V}_{n,0}^{n} = \begin{bmatrix} \omega_x + \varepsilon V_x \\ \omega_y + \varepsilon V_y \\ \omega_z + \varepsilon V_z \end{bmatrix} = \left[{}^{0}T_{n}\right]\left[{}^{n}\hat{M}_{0} \quad {}^{n}\hat{M}_{1} \quad {}^{n}\hat{M}_{2} \ldots \quad {}^{n}\hat{M}_{n-1}\right] \begin{bmatrix} {}^{0}\hat{V}_{1,0}^{0} \\ \hline {}^{1}\hat{V}_{2,1}^{1} \\ \hline \vdots \\ {}^{n-1}\hat{V}_{n,n-1}^{n-1} \end{bmatrix} \tag{23}$$

The block matrix $\left[{}^n\hat{M}_0 \quad {}^n\hat{M}_1 \quad {}^n\hat{M}_2 ... \quad {}^n\hat{M}_{n-1} \right]$ is called Dual Jacobian matrix (Brodsky).

5. Dynamic analysis: Dual force

One of the most important features of dual number formulation is the capability of generalization for a great variety of robot topologies, without modifying the main program, this is an advantage when compared to typical homogenous matrices wherein is required to specify in dynamical model whether a joint is rotational or prismatic.

In dual algebra, if a force and a momentum act with respect a coordinate system, they can be represented in an expression called dual force:

$$\hat{F} = \vec{F} + \varepsilon\vec{\tau} \tag{24}$$

A clear example would be a screwdriver where is necessary to apply a force axially and around to screw.

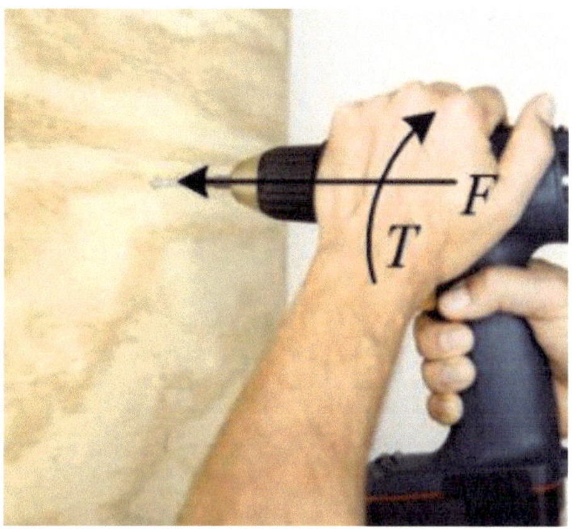

Fig. 8. Example of dual force

If a dual force is applied on a point "B" different to the origin point "A", the effect on the point "B" will be determined by a coordinate transformation. Then a dual force applied on "A" in terms of the frame "B" is given by:

$$ {}^B\hat{F}_A = {}^BT_A\,{}^A\vec{F}_A + \varepsilon\,{}^BT_A\,{}^A\vec{\tau}_A \tag{25}$$

5.1 Dual momentum

Dual momentum concept is introduced due to the acceleration is a dual pseudo-vector, that means that it can not be established as a dual vector.

$$ {}^B\hat{H}_A = \int_A \left({}^B\vec{P}_p + \varepsilon\,{}^B\vec{H}_p \right) \tag{26}$$

The terms ${}^B\vec{P}_p$ & ${}^B\vec{H}_p$ are the linear and angular momentum of a particle "p" on a body "A" respectively, in terms of frame "B".

$$^{B}P_{A} = m_{A}\left[{}^{B}V_{A}^{B}\right] - \left[{}^{B}S_{A}^{B}\right]\left[{}^{B}\omega_{A}^{B}\right]$$

$$^{B}H_{A} = \left[{}^{B}S_{A}^{B}\right]\left[{}^{B}V_{A}^{B}\right] + \left[{}^{B}J_{A}^{B}\right]\left[{}^{B}\omega_{A}^{B}\right]$$

5.2 Dual inertial force

According with (Pennock & Meehan, 2000) the dual inertial forces on a rigid body are the derivative of the dual momentum:

$$^{B}\hat{f}_{A} = \frac{d}{dt}\left({}^{B}\hat{H}_{A}\right) \tag{27}$$

$$^{B}\hat{f}_{A} = \begin{bmatrix} {}^{B}\dot{\hat{H}}_{Ai} \\ {}^{B}\dot{\hat{H}}_{Aj} \\ {}^{B}\dot{\hat{H}}_{Ak} \end{bmatrix} + \begin{bmatrix} 0 & -{}^{B}\hat{V}_{Ak}^{B} & {}^{B}\hat{V}_{Aj}^{B} \\ {}^{B}\hat{V}_{Ak}^{B} & 0 & -{}^{B}\hat{V}_{Ai}^{B} \\ -{}^{B}\hat{V}_{Aj}^{B} & {}^{B}\hat{V}_{Ai}^{B} & 0 \end{bmatrix} \begin{bmatrix} {}^{B}\hat{H}_{Ai} \\ {}^{B}\hat{H}_{Aj} \\ {}^{B}\hat{H}_{Ak} \end{bmatrix}$$

$$\begin{bmatrix} {}^{B}\hat{f}_{Ai} \\ {}^{B}\hat{f}_{Aj} \\ {}^{B}\hat{f}_{Ak} \end{bmatrix} = \begin{bmatrix} {}^{B}\dot{\hat{H}}_{Ai} - {}^{B}\hat{V}_{Ak}^{B}\,{}^{B}\hat{H}_{Aj} + {}^{B}\hat{V}_{Aj}^{B}\,{}^{B}\hat{H}_{Ak} \\ {}^{B}\dot{\hat{H}}_{Aj} - {}^{B}\hat{V}_{Ai}^{B}\,{}^{B}\hat{H}_{Ak} + {}^{B}\hat{V}_{Ak}^{B}\,{}^{B}\hat{H}_{Ai} \\ {}^{B}\dot{\hat{H}}_{Ak} - {}^{B}\hat{V}_{Aj}^{B}\,{}^{B}\hat{H}_{Ai} + {}^{B}\hat{V}_{Ai}^{B}\,{}^{B}\hat{H}_{Aj} \end{bmatrix}$$

5.3 Dynamic equilibrium

Extending the D'Alembert principle to dual numbers for dynamic equilibrium

$$^{B}\hat{M}_{A}\,{}^{A}\hat{F}_{A} - {}^{B}F_{B} = {}^{B}\hat{f}_{A} \tag{28}$$

6. Example: Robot with cylindrical joints

The robot shown in the Figure 9 is a clear example where the dual numbers can be employed:

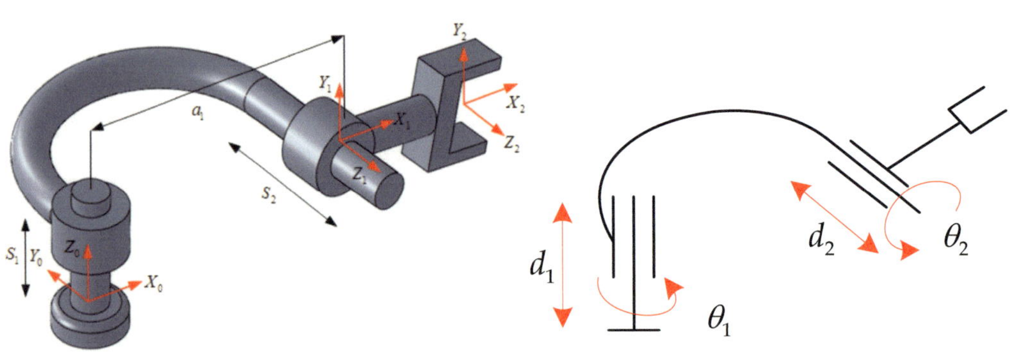

Fig. 9. Assignment of reference systems and Denavit-Hartenberg parameters.

i	θ_i	S_i	a_i	α_i
1	θ_1	d_1	l_1	90°
2	θ_2	d_2	l_2	0°

Table 2. Denavith and Hartemberg parameters of 2C robotic arm.

From Table 2, the dual angles $\hat{\theta}$ & $\hat{\alpha}$ are constructed as:

$$\hat{\theta}_1 = \theta_1 + \varepsilon d_1 \qquad \hat{\theta}_2 = \theta_2 + \varepsilon d_2 \qquad \hat{\alpha}_1 = \alpha_1 + \varepsilon a_1 \qquad \hat{\alpha}_2 = \alpha_2 + \varepsilon a_2$$

It is observed that different topologies can be solved from the assigned values to θ_1, d_1, θ_2, d_2; for example if θ_1 is 0 the robot will change the original topology CC to PC then nine different robots can be solved from the same aforementioned equations.

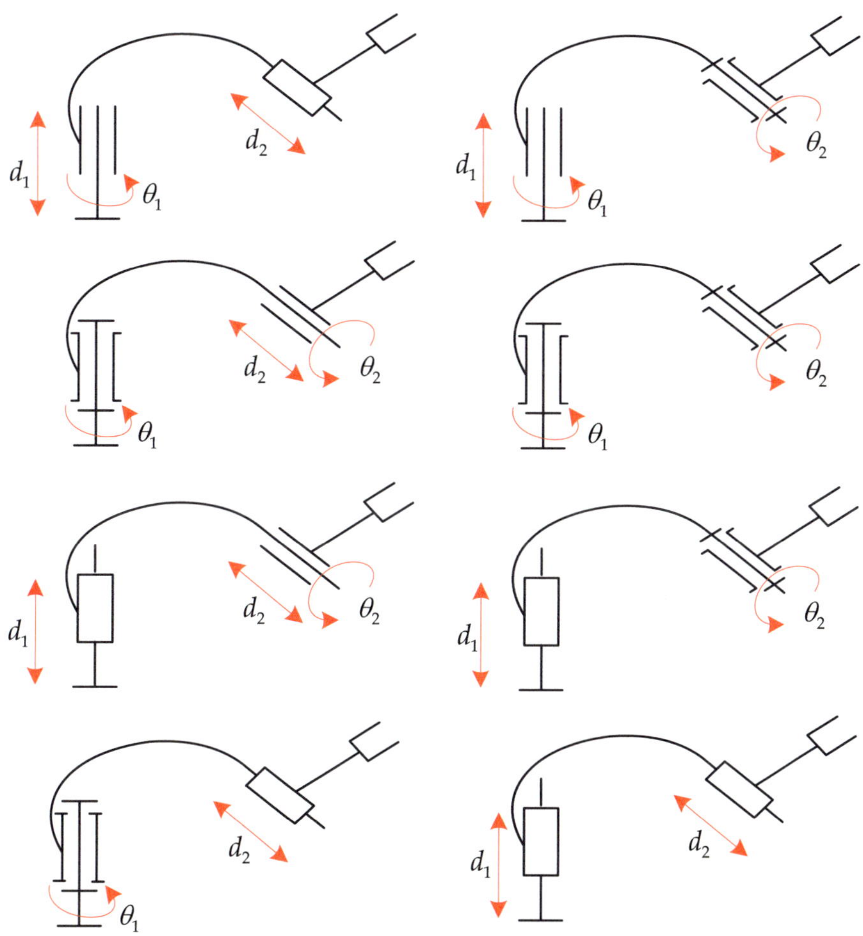

Fig. 10. Possible topologies for different values of θ_1 & θ_2.

$$^{0}\hat{M}_2=\begin{bmatrix}\cos\hat{\theta}_1 & -\cos\hat{\alpha}_1\sin\hat{\theta}_1 & \sin\hat{\alpha}_1\sin\hat{\theta}_1\\ \sin\hat{\theta}_1 & \cos\hat{\alpha}_1\cos\hat{\theta}_1 & -\sin\hat{\alpha}_1\cos\hat{\theta}_1\\ 0 & \sin\hat{\alpha}_1 & \cos\hat{\alpha}_1\end{bmatrix}\begin{bmatrix}\cos\hat{\theta}_2 & -\cos\hat{\alpha}_2\sin\hat{\theta}_2 & \sin\hat{\alpha}_2\sin\hat{\theta}_2\\ \sin\hat{\theta}_2 & \cos\hat{\alpha}_2\cos\hat{\theta}_2 & -\sin\hat{\alpha}_2\cos\hat{\theta}_2\\ 0 & \sin\hat{\alpha}_2 & \cos\hat{\alpha}_2\end{bmatrix}$$

For the inverse solution:

$$^{0}\hat{M}_2=\begin{bmatrix}n_x & o_x & a_x\\ n_y & o_y & a_y\\ n_z & o_z & a_z\end{bmatrix}$$

$$+\varepsilon\begin{bmatrix}-p_z n_y+p_y n_z & -p_z o_y+p_y o_z & -p_z a_y+p_y a_z\\ p_z n_x-p_x n_z & p_z o_x-p_x o_z & p_z a_x-p_x a_z\\ -p_y n_x+p_x n_y & -p_y o_x+p_x o_y & -p_y a_x+p_x a_y\end{bmatrix}$$

$$^{0}\hat{M}_2=\begin{bmatrix}c_1c_2 & -c_1s_2 & s_1\\ s_1c_2 & -s_1s_2 & -c_1\\ s_2 & c_2 & 0\end{bmatrix}$$

$$+\varepsilon\begin{bmatrix}100.5\mathrm{s}_1\mathrm{s}_2-d_1\mathrm{s}_1\mathrm{c}_2-d_2\mathrm{c}_1\mathrm{s}_2 & 70\mathrm{s}_1+100.5\mathrm{s}_1\mathrm{c}_2-d_2\mathrm{c}_1\mathrm{c}_2+d_1\mathrm{s}_1\mathrm{s}_2 & \mathrm{c}_1\left(d_1+70\mathrm{s}_2\right)\\ 100.5\mathrm{c}_1\mathrm{s}_2+d_1\mathrm{c}_1\mathrm{c}_2-d_2\mathrm{s}_1\mathrm{s}_2 & 70\mathrm{c}_1-100.5\mathrm{c}_1\mathrm{c}_2-d_1\mathrm{c}_1\mathrm{s}_2-d_2\mathrm{s}_1\mathrm{c}_2 & \mathrm{s}_1\left(d_1+70\mathrm{s}_2\right)\\ d_2\mathrm{c}_2 & -d_2\mathrm{s}_2 & -70\mathrm{c}_2-100.5\end{bmatrix}$$

Dividing elements (2,1) and (1,1) in both matrices:

$$\theta_1=tg^{-1}\left(\frac{n_y}{n_x}\right)\ ;\ \theta_2=tg^{-1}\left(\frac{\pm\sqrt{1-o_z^2}}{o_z^2}\right)$$

The velocities in the cylindrical joints are given by:

$$^{0}\hat{V}_{1,0}^{0}=\begin{bmatrix}0\\0\\\omega_1\end{bmatrix}+\varepsilon\begin{bmatrix}0\\0\\v_1\end{bmatrix}\qquad ^{1}\hat{V}_{2,1}^{1}=\begin{bmatrix}0\\0\\\omega_2\end{bmatrix}+\varepsilon\begin{bmatrix}0\\0\\v_2\end{bmatrix}$$

Computing the velocities on the end-effector:

$$^{0}\hat{V}_{2,0}^{2}={}^{0}T_2\left\{{}^{2}\hat{M}_0\,{}^{0}\hat{V}_{1,0}^{0}+{}^{2}\hat{M}_1\,{}^{1}\hat{V}_{2,1}^{1}\right\}$$

The above expression can be rewritten in terms of dual Jacobian matrix.

$$^{0}\hat{V}_{2,0}^{2}=\begin{bmatrix}\omega_x+\varepsilon V_x\\ \omega_y+\varepsilon V_y\\ \omega_z+\varepsilon V_z\end{bmatrix}=\left[{}^{0}T_2\right]\left[{}^{2}\hat{M}_0\quad\Big|\quad{}^{2}\hat{M}_1\right]\begin{bmatrix}{}^{0}\hat{V}_{1,0}^{0}\\ \hline {}^{1}\hat{V}_{2,1}^{1}\end{bmatrix}$$

$$
{}^0\hat{V}_{2,0}^2 = \begin{bmatrix} c_1c_2 & -c_1s_2 & s_1 \\ s_1c_2 & -s_1s_2 & -c_1 \\ s_2 & c_2 & 0 \end{bmatrix} \begin{bmatrix} {}^0\hat{M}_2^T & {}^1\hat{M}_2^T \end{bmatrix} \begin{bmatrix} 0 \\ 0 \\ \omega_1 + \varepsilon v_1 \\ 0 \\ 0 \\ \omega_2 + \varepsilon v_2 \end{bmatrix}
$$

Dual velocities:

$$
{}^1\hat{V}_{1,0}^1 = {}^1\hat{M}_0\, {}^0\hat{V}_{1,0}^0 = \begin{bmatrix} 0 \\ \sin\hat{\alpha}_1(\omega_1 + \varepsilon v_1) \\ \cos\hat{\alpha}_1(\omega_1 + \varepsilon v_1) \end{bmatrix} \qquad {}^2\hat{V}_{2,0}^2 = {}^2\hat{M}_1\, {}^1\hat{V}_{2,0}^1 = \begin{bmatrix} 0 \\ \sin\hat{\alpha}_2(\omega_2 + \varepsilon v_2) \\ \cos\hat{\alpha}_2(\omega_2 + \varepsilon v_2) \end{bmatrix}
$$

6.1 Dynamic analysis

Once obtained the velocities, the next step for solving the dynamic equations is, according with Fisher, to compute the dual momentum, being for each link:

$$
{}^1\hat{H}_0 = m_1\left[{}^1\vec{V}_{1,0}^1\right] - \left[{}^1S_1\right]\left[{}^1\vec{\omega}_{1,0}^1\right] + \varepsilon\left\{\left[{}^1S_1\right]\left[{}^1\vec{V}_{1,0}^1\right] + \left[{}^1I_1\right]\left[{}^1\vec{\omega}_{1,0}^1\right]\right\}
$$

$$
{}^2\hat{H}_1 = m_2\left[{}^2\vec{V}_{2,0}^2\right] - \left[{}^2S_2\right]\left[{}^2\vec{\omega}_{2,0}^2\right] + \varepsilon\left\{\left[{}^2S_2\right]\left[{}^2\vec{V}_{2,0}^2\right] + \left[{}^2I_2\right]\left[{}^2\vec{\omega}_{2,0}^2\right]\right\}
$$

Derivating the above expressions:

$$
{}^1\dot{\hat{H}}_0 = m_1\left[\frac{d}{dt}\left({}^1\vec{V}_{1,0}^1\right)\right] - \left[{}^1S_1\right]\left[\frac{d}{dt}\left({}^1\vec{\omega}_{1,0}^1\right)\right]
$$

$$
+\varepsilon\left\{\left[{}^1S_1\right]\left[\frac{d}{dt}\left({}^1\vec{V}_{1,0}^1\right)\right] + \left[{}^1I_1\right]\left[\frac{d}{dt}\left({}^1\vec{\omega}_{1,0}^1\right)\right]\right\}
$$

$$
\begin{bmatrix} {}^1f_{0i} + \varepsilon\, {}^1t_{0i} \\ {}^1f_{0j} + \varepsilon\, {}^1t_{0j} \\ {}^1f_{0k} + \varepsilon\, {}^1t_{0k} \end{bmatrix}
= \begin{bmatrix} {}^1\dot{P}_{0i} - {}^1\omega_{1,0k}^1\, {}^1P_{0j} + {}^1\omega_{1,0j}^1\, {}^1P_{0k} \\ {}^1\dot{P}_{0j} - {}^1\omega_{1,0i}^1\, {}^1P_{0k} + {}^1\omega_{1,0k}^1\, {}^1P_{0i} \\ {}^1\dot{P}_{0k} - {}^1\omega_{1,0j}^1\, {}^1P_{0i} + {}^1\omega_{1,0i}^1\, {}^1P_{0j} \end{bmatrix}
+\varepsilon \begin{bmatrix} {}^1\dot{H}_{0i} - {}^1\omega_{1,0k}^1\, {}^1H_{0j} - {}^1V_{1,0k}^1\, {}^1P_{0j} + {}^1\omega_{1,0j}^1\, {}^1H_{0k} + {}^1V_{1,0j}^1\, {}^1P_{0k} \\ {}^1\dot{H}_{0j} - {}^1\omega_{1,0i}^1\, {}^1H_{0k} - {}^1V_{1,0i}^1\, {}^1P_{0k} + {}^1\omega_{1,0k}^1\, {}^1H_{0i} + {}^1V_{1,0k}^1\, {}^1P_{0i} \\ {}^1\dot{H}_{0k} - {}^1\omega_{1,0j}^1\, {}^1H_{0i} - {}^1V_{1,0j}^1\, {}^1P_{0i} + {}^1\omega_{1,0i}^1\, {}^1H_{0j} + {}^1V_{1,0i}^1\, {}^1P_{0j} \end{bmatrix}
$$

$$\begin{bmatrix} {}^2f_{1i} + \varepsilon\, {}^2t_{1i} \\ {}^2f_{1j} + \varepsilon\, {}^2t_{1j} \\ {}^2f_{1k} + \varepsilon\, {}^2t_{1k} \end{bmatrix}$$

$$= \begin{bmatrix} {}^2\dot{P}_{1i} - {}^2\omega_{2,0k}^2\, {}^2P_{1j} + {}^2\omega_{2,0j}^2\, {}^2P_{1k} \\ {}^2\dot{P}_{1j} - {}^2\omega_{2,0i}^2\, {}^2P_{1k} + {}^2\omega_{2,0k}^2\, {}^2P_{1i} \\ {}^2\dot{P}_{1k} - {}^2\omega_{2,0j}^2\, {}^2P_{1i} + {}^2\omega_{2,0i}^2\, {}^2P_{1j} \end{bmatrix}$$

$$+\varepsilon \begin{bmatrix} {}^2\dot{H}_{1i} - {}^2\omega_{2,0k}^2\, {}^2H_{1j} - {}^2V_{2,0k}^2\, {}^2P_{1j} + {}^2\omega_{2,0j}^2\, {}^2H_{1k} + {}^2V_{2,0j}^2\, {}^2P_{1k} \\ {}^2\dot{H}_{1j} - {}^2\omega_{2,0i}^2\, {}^2H_{1k} - {}^2V_{2,0i}^2\, {}^2P_{1k} + {}^2\omega_{2,0k}^2\, {}^2H_{1i} + {}^2V_{2,0k}^2\, {}^2P_{1i} \\ {}^2\dot{H}_{1k} - {}^2\omega_{2,0j}^2\, {}^2H_{1i} - {}^2V_{2,0j}^2\, {}^2P_{1i} + {}^2\omega_{2,0i}^2\, {}^2H_{1j} + {}^2V_{2,0i}^2\, {}^2P_{1j} \end{bmatrix}$$

From dynamic equilibrium:

$${}^BM_A\, {}^A\vec{F}_A - {}^B\vec{F}_B - {}^B\vec{f}_A + \varepsilon\left({}^BM_A\, {}^A\vec{T}_A + {}^BD_A\, {}^A\vec{F}_A - {}^B\vec{T}_B - {}^B\vec{t}_A\right) = 0$$

$${}^BM_A\, {}^A\vec{F}_A - {}^B\vec{F}_B - {}^B\vec{f}_A = 0$$

$${}^BM_A\, {}^A\vec{T}_A + {}^BD_A\, {}^A\vec{F}_A - {}^B\vec{T}_B - {}^B\vec{t}_A = 0$$

$${}^2\vec{F}_2 = \left[{}^2M_1\right]^{-1}\left\{{}^2\vec{f}_1\right\}$$

$${}^1\vec{F}_1 = \left[{}^1M_0\right]^{-1}\left\{{}^2\vec{F}_2 + {}^1\vec{f}_0\right\}$$

$${}^2\vec{T}_2 = \left[{}^2M_1\right]^{-1}\left\{{}^2\vec{t}_1 - {}^2D_1\, {}^2\vec{F}_2\right\}$$

$${}^1\vec{T}_1 = \left[{}^1M_0\right]^{-1}\left\{{}^2\vec{T}_2 + {}^1\vec{t}_0 - {}^1D_0\, {}^1\vec{F}_1\right\}$$

7. Conclusions

The presented method, based on dual-number representation, has demonstrated be a powerful tool for solving a great variety of problems, that imply motions simultaneity off rotation and translation of rigid bodies in the space; the aforementioned, allows establishing dual rotation matrices. Robotics is a field wherein dual numbers have been employed to describe the motion of a rigid body, in particular of serial robotic arms. The methodology proposed is useful for robotic arms with cylindrical, prismatic and rotational joints. Once established the dual angles $\hat{\theta}$ and $\hat{\alpha}$, if the dual part of $\hat{\theta}$ is zero, the mechanism has only revolute joints, otherwise if the primary part of $\hat{\theta}$ is zero, only exist prismatic joints. So the developed methodology can be generalized to different topologies, which is a great advantage that allows that only one program solves a great variety of topologies.

The dynamic model is treated by using the dual momentum, wherein the inertial forces are computed by means of a set of linear equations, thus a $6 \times n$ vector of forces is calculated, and in consequence one obtains a complete description of the robotic manipulator. An appropriate way of dual numbers programming will yield a suitable software alternative to simulate and analyze different serial robotic manipulators topologies.

8. Acknowledgments

The authors gratefully acknowledge the support of CONACYT, IPN and ICyTDF for research projects and scholarships. They also would like to thank the anonymous reviewers for their valuable comments and suggestions.

9. References

Al-Widyan, K.; Qing Ma, Xiao & Angeles, J. (2011). The robust design of parallel spherical robots.

Bandyopadhyay, S. (2004). Analytical determination of principal twists in serial, parallel and hybrid manipulators using dual vectors and matrices. *Journal of Mechanism and Machine Theory*, Vol. 39, (2004), pp. (1289-1305), ISSN: 0094-114X.

Bandyopadhyay, S. (2006). *Analysis and Design of Spatial Manipulators: An Exact Algebraic Approach using Dual Numbers and Symbolic Computation*. Ph. D. Thesis, Department of Mechanica Engineeriring, Indian Institute of Science.

Bayro-Corrochano, E. & Kähler, D. (2000). Motor algebra approach for computing the kinematics of robot manipulators. *Journal of Robotic Systems*, Vol. 17, 9, (September 2000), pp. (495-516), DOI: 10.1002/1097-4563

Bayro-Corrochano, E. & Kähler, D. (2001), Kinematics of Robot Manipulators in the Motor Algebra, In: *Geometric computing with Clifford algebras*, Springer, ISBN: 3-540-41198-4 Institute of Computer Science and Applied Mathematics, University of Kiel.

Brodsky, V. &Shoham, M. (1998). *Derivation of dual forces in robot manipulators.* Journal of Mechanism and Machine Theory, 33: 1241-1248.

Cecchini, E., Pennestri, E., & Vergata, T. (2004). A dual number approach to the Kinematic analysis of spatial linkages with dimensional and geometric tolerances. *Proceedings of Design Engineering Technical Conferences and Computers and Information in Engineering Conference*, Salt Lake City, Utah, USA.

Cheng, H.H. (1994). Programming with dual numbers and its applications in mechanisms design. *Engineering with Computers*, Springer.

Fischer, I. (2003). Velocity analysis of mechanisms with ball joints. *Journal of Mechanics Research Communications*, Vol. 30, 1, January-February 2003, pp. (69-78), doi: 10.1016/S0093-6413(02)00350-6

Fisher, I. S. (1998). *Dual Number Methods in Kinematics, Statics and dynamics.* (1st Edition), CRC Press, ISBN: 9780849391156, U. S. A.

Fisher, I. S. (1998). The dual angle and axis of a screw motion. *Journal of Mechanisms and Machine Theory,* Vol. 33, 3, (April 1998), pp. (331 - 340), DOI: 10.1016/S0094-114X(97)00039-6

Fisher, I. S. (2000). Numerical analysis of displacements in spatial mechanisms with ball joints. *Journal of Mechanisms and Machine Theory,* Vol. 35, 11, (November 2000), pp. (1623 - 1640), doi:10.1016/S0094-114X(99)00058-0

Funda, J. (1988). *A Computational Analysis of Line-Oriented Screw Transformations in Robotics.* Technical Report, University of Pennsylvania, U. S. A.

Gu, Y.L. & Luh, J. Y. S. (1987). Dual-Number Transformation and Its Applications To Robotics.

Keler, M. L. (2000). *On the theory of screws and the dual method.* Proceedings of A Symposium Commemorating the Legacy, Words and Life of Sir Robert Stawell Ball Upon the 100th Anniversary of a Treatise on the Theory of Screws, University of Cambridge, Trinnity College.

Kiat Teu, K.; Kim, W.; Fuss, F. K. & Tan, J.(2006). The analysis of golf swing as a kinematic chain using dual Euler angle algorithm.

Moon, Y-M. & Kota, S.(2002). Automated synthesis of mechanisms using dual-vector algebra. *Mechanisms and Machine Theory,* (February 2002), pp. (143-166), doi: 10.1016/S0094-114X(01)00073-8

Page, A.; Mata, V.; Hoyos, J. V. & Porcar, Rosa. (2007) Experimental depermination of instantaneous screw axis in human motions. Error analysis

Pennestrí, E. &Stefanelli, R. (2007). Linear Algebra and numerical algorithms using dual numbers. *Journal of Multi-body System Dynamics,* Vol. 18, 3, pp. (323-344)

Pennock, G. R. & Mattson, K. G. (1996). Forward position problem of two PUMA-type robots manipulating a planar four-bar linkage payload.

Pennock, G. R. & Meehan P. J. (2000). Geometric insight into dynamics of a rigid body using the theory of screws.

Sai-Kai, C. (2000). Simbolic computation of Jacobian of manipulators using dual number transformations.

Seilig, J.M. (1999). *Geometrical Methods in Robotics.* (1st Edition), Springer, ISBN: 0387947280, New Jersey, U. S. A.

Wang, J.; Liang, H-Z. & Sun Z. (2010). Relative Coupled Dynamics and Control using Dual Number. *Systems and Control in Aeronautics and Astronautics (ISSCAA), 2010 3rd International Symposium on*

Yang, J. & Wang, X. (2010). The application of the dual number methods to scara kinematics.

Ying, N.; Kim, W.; Wong, Y. & Kan, H. K. (2004). Analysis of passive motion characteristics of the ankle joint complex using dual Euler angle parameters. Clinical Biomechanics, Vol. 19, 2, (February 2004), pp. (153-160), doi: 10.1016/j.clinbiomech. 2003.10.005

5

On the Stiffness Analysis and Elastodynamics of Parallel Kinematic Machines

Alessandro Cammarata
University of Catania, Department of Mechanical and Industrial Engineering
Italy

1. Introduction

Accurate models to describe the elasticity of robots are becoming essential for those applications involving high accelerations or high precision to improve quality in positioning and tracking of trajectories. Stiffness analysis not only involves the mechanical structure of a robot but even the control system necessary to drive actuators. Strategies aimed to reduce noise and dangerous bouncing effects could be implemented to make control systems more robust to flexibility disturbances, foreseing mechanical interaction with the control system because of regenerative and modal chattering (1). The most used approaches to study elasticity in the literature encompass: the *Finite Element Analysis* (FEA), the *Matrix Structural Analysis* (MSA), the *Virtual Joint Method* (VJM), the *Floating Frame of Reference Formulation* (FFRF) and the *Absolute Nodal Coordinates Formulation* (ANCF).

FEA is largely used to analyze the structural behavior of a mechanical system. The reliability and precision of the method allow to describe each part of a mechanical system with great detail (2). Applying FEA to a robotic system implies a time-consuming process of re-meshing in the pre-processing phase every time that the robot posture has changed. Optimization all over the workspace of a robot would require very long computational time, thus FEA models are often employed to verify components or subparts of a complex robotic system.

The MSA includes some simplifications to FEA using complex elements like beams, arcs, cables or superelements (3–5). This choice reduces the computational time and makes this method more efficient for optimization tasks. Some authors recurred to the superposition principle along with the virtual work principle to achieve the global stiffness model (6–8). Others considered the minimization of the potential energy of a PKM to find the global stiffness matrix (9), while some approaches used the total potential energy augmented adding the kinematic constraints by means of the Lagrange multipliers (10; 11).

The first papers on VJM are based on pseudo-rigid body models with "virtual joints" (12–14). More recent papers include link flexibility and linear/torsional springs to take into account bending contributes (15–19). These approaches recur to the Jacobian matrix to map the stiffness of the actuators of a PKM inside its workspace; especially for PKMs with reduced mobility, it implies that the stiffness is limited to a subspace defined by the dofs of its end-effector. Pashkevich *et al.* tried to overcome this issue by introducing a multidimensional lumped-parameter model with localized 6-dof virtual springs (20).

Finally, the FFRF and ANCF are powerful and accurate formulations, based on FEM and continuum mechanics, to study any flexible mechanical system (21). The FFRF is suitable

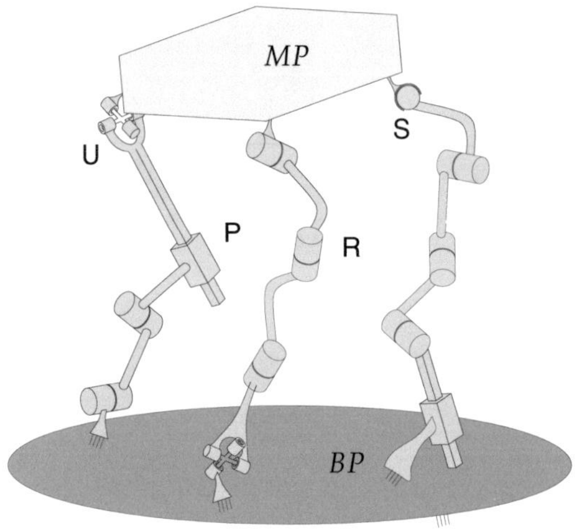

Fig. 1. Schematic drawing of a PKM: P prismatic joint, R revolute joint, S spherical joint, U universal joint

for large rotations and small deformations, while the ANCF is preferred for large rotations and large deformations. Notwithstanding, both the two formulations usually require great computational efforts to be extended to complex robots or to optimization techniques involving the whole robot's workspace.
In this chapter we propose a formulation to study the elastostatics and elastodynamics of PKMs. The method is linear and tries to combine some feature existing in the literature to build a solid framework, the outlines of which are described in Section 2. We start from a MSA approach based on the minimization of the strain energy in which all joints are introduced by means of constraints between nodal displacements. In this way we avoid Lagrange multipliers and the introduction of joints becomes straightforward. Unlike VJM methods based on lumped stiffness, we use 3D Euler beams to simulate links and to distribute stiffness to the flexible structure of a robot, as described in Section 3. The same set of nodal displacement arrays is used to obtain the generalized stiffness and inertia matrix, the latter being lumped or distributed, as discussed in Sections 4 and 5. Besides, the flexibility of the proposed method allows us to provide useful extension to compliant PKMs with joint flexures. The ease in setting up, the direct control of joints and the speed of execution make the procedure adapt for optimization routines, as described in Section 6. Finally, some feasible applications are described in Section 7 studying an articulated PKMs with four dofs.

2. Outlines of the algorithm

Before introducing the reader to the proposed methodology, we have to clarify the reasons of this work. The first question that might arise is: *Why use a new method without recurring to well confirmed formulations existing in the literature?* The right answer is essentially tied to the simplicity of the proposed formulation. The method is addressed to designers that want to implement software to study the elastodynamics of PKMs, as well as to students and researchers that wish to create their own customized algorithm. The author experienced that the elastodynamics study of a complex robotic system is not a trivial issue, mainly when dealing with some features concerning the optimization of performances in terms of elasticity or admissible range of eigenfrequencies. Performing these analyzes often needs for a global optimization all over the workspace of a robot too cumbersome to be faced with conventional formulations. Further, considering that the elastodynamics behavior of a robot changes according to its pose, an accurate analysis should be carried out several times to capture the right response inside the robot's workspace, drastically affecting the computational cost. The focused issue becomes even more complicated when constrained optimization routines, based on indices of elastostatics/dynamics performances, are implemented to work in all the workspace. In the latter case the search for local minimum configurations needs for a simple and robust mathematical framework adapt to iterative procedures. Working with ordinary resources, in terms of CPU speed and memory, can make optimization prohibitive unless the complex flexible multibody formulations would be simplified to meet requirements. Therefore, the second question might be: *Why simplify a complex formulation and do not create a simpler one instead?* The sought formulation is what the author is going to explain in this chapter.

Let us start considering a generic PKM. It is essentially a complex robotic system with parallel kinematics in which one or more limbs connect a base platform to a moving platform, as shown in Fig. 1. The latter contains a tool, often referred to as *end-effector*, necessary to perform a certain task or, sometimes, as in the case of flight simulators or assembly stations, the end effector is the moving platform itself. The limbs connecting the two platforms are composed of links constrained by joints. A limb can be a serial kinematic chain or an articulated linkage with one or more closed kinematic chains or loops.

In performing our analysis we have to choose what is flexible and what is rigid as well. Generally, each body is flexible and the notion of rigid body is an abstraction that becomes a good approximation if strains of the structure are small when compared to displacements. Thus, considering a link flexible or rigid depends on many aspects as: material, geometry, wrenches involved in the process. Besides, some tasks might need for high precision to be accomplished, then an accurate analysis should take care of deformations to fulfill the requirements without gross errors. Here, we model the MP and BP as rigid bodies because, for the most part of industrial PKMs, these are usually one order of magnitude stiffer than the remaining links. The latter will be either flexible or rigid depending on the assumptions made by the designer. As already pointed out in the Introduction, we use 3D Euler beams to represent links, even if the treatment can be extended to superelements, as reported in (22). The formulation is linear and only small deformations are considered. Given a starting pose of the MP, the IKP allows us to find the robot's configuration; then, the elastodynamics—statics—is performed around this undeformed configuration. It might be useful to lock the actuated joints in order to avoid rigid movements and to isolate only the flexible modes.

Below, we summarize all steps necessary to find the elastodynamics equations of a PKM:

1. Solve the inverse kinematic problem (IKP) in order to know the starting pose, i.e. the undeformed configuration, of the PKM. Here, we make the assumption that the configuration is *frozen*, meaning that no coupling of rigid body and elastic motions is considered.
2. Distinguish rigid and flexible links, and discretize the latter into the desired number of flexible elements. The base and moving platforms are modeled as rigid.
3. Introduce nodes and then nodal-arrays for each node. Each flexible part has two end-nodes at its end-sections; the rigid links have a single node at their center of mass.
4. Introduce joint-matrices and arrays for each joint.

5. Individuate the couples of bodies linked by a joint and distinguish among three cases: rigid-flexible, flexible-flexible and flexible-rigid.
6. Find the equations expressing dependent nodal-array in terms of independent nodal-arrays, then find the generalized stiffness and inertia matrices. The latter change whether lumped or distributed method is used.
7. Introduce the global array $\mathbf{q}$ of independent nodal coordinates. This array contains all the independent nodal arrays in the order defined by the reader.
8. Expand all matrices expressing each generalized stiffness and inertia matrix in terms of $\mathbf{q}$ by means of the Boolean matrices $\mathbf{B}_1$ and $\mathbf{B}_2$. Then, sum all contributes to find the generalized stiffness matrix $\mathbf{K}_{PKM}$ and inertia matrix $\mathbf{M}_{PKM}$ of the PKM.
9. Introduce the array $\mathbf{f}$ of generalized nodal wrenches and, finally, write the elastodynamics equations.

3. Mathematical background and key concepts

In a mechanical system flexible bodies storage and exchange energy like a tank is able to storage and supply water. The energy associated to deformation is termed *strain energy* while the aptitude of a body for deformation is tied to the property of *stiffness*. For a continuum body the stiffness is distributed and the strain energy changes according to the variation of the displacement field of its points. In a discrete flexible element inner points' displacements depend on displacements of some points or *nodes*.

3.1 Nodal and joint-array

Robotic links can be well described by means of 3D-beams, that is, flexible elements with two end-nodes, as shown in Fig. 2. The expression of the strain energy depends on the kind of displacements chosen for rotations: slopes, Euler angles, quaternions, and so on, and on the entity of displacement: large or small. Here, we choose a linear formulation based on small displacements and Euler angles to describe rotations. Based on these assumptions, the strain energy is a positive-definite quadratic form in the nodal displacement coordinates of the end-nodes arrays of the beam, where a nodal displacement array $\mathbf{u} = \begin{bmatrix} u_x \; u_y \; u_z \; u_\varphi \; u_\theta \; u_\psi \end{bmatrix}^T$ has six scalar *displacements*, three translational and three rotational. Hereafter, subscripts and superscripts will be, respectively, referred to the beam and to one of the two end-nodes of a beam.

Beams belonging to the same link are contiguous, while joints couple beams belonging to two adjoining links. To express the kinematic bond existing between the two nodes, or sections, coupled by the joint, a constraint equation is introduced in which the nodal displacements of the two nodes are tied through the means of an array of joint displacements. Figure 2 describes two beams linked by a prismatic joint of axis parallel to the unit vector $\mathbf{e}$. The two nodal arrays $\mathbf{u}_1^2$ and $\mathbf{u}_2^1$ are tied together by means of the translational displacement s of the prismatic joint P and by the 6-dimensional joint-array $\mathbf{h}^P = \begin{bmatrix} \mathbf{e}^T \; \mathbf{0}^T \end{bmatrix}^T$, i.e.,

$$\mathbf{u}_1^2 = \mathbf{u}_2^1 + \mathbf{h}^P s \tag{1}$$

We stress that eq.(1) describes a constraint among displacements, then deformations, and not nodal coordinates. In general, $\mathbf{H}^j$ is a $6 \times m(j)$ joint-matrix where $m(j)$ is the dimension of the joint-array $\boldsymbol{\theta}^j$. The joint-matrix $\mathbf{H}^j$ and the joint-array $\boldsymbol{\theta}^j$ depend on the type of joint: the former

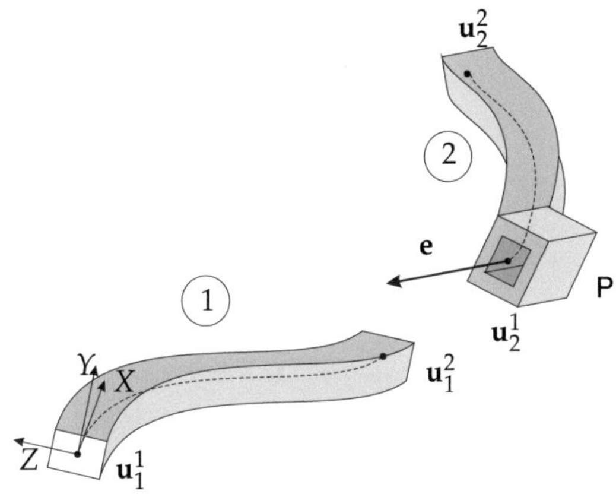

Fig. 2. Notation of two 3D Euler beams coupled by a joint.

containing unit vectors indicating geometric axes, the latter containing joint displacements, either linear s^j, for translations, or angular θ^j, for rotations. Below, two more examples of joints are provided:

Revolute joint:

$$\mathbf{h}^R = \begin{bmatrix} \mathbf{0}^T & \mathbf{e}^T \end{bmatrix}^T, \quad \theta^R = \theta \tag{2}$$

where $\mathbf{e}$ is the unit vector along the axis of the revolute joint R and θ is the angular displacement about the said axis.

Universal joint:

$$\mathbf{H}^U = \begin{bmatrix} \mathbf{0} & \mathbf{0} \\ \mathbf{e}^1 & \mathbf{e}^2 \end{bmatrix}, \quad \boldsymbol{\theta}^U = \begin{bmatrix} \theta^1 & \theta^2 \end{bmatrix}^T \tag{3}$$

where $\mathbf{e}^1$ and $\mathbf{e}^2$ are the unit vectors along the axes of the universal joint U and θ^1 and θ^2 are the angular displacements about the axes of U.

Other joints, i.e. cylindrical, spherical and so on, can be created combining together elementary prismatic and/or revolute joints. The described constraint equations are used to consider joints contribute to elastodynamics in a direct way without recurring to Lagrangian multipliers to introduce joint constraints, (10). In the next section the above equation will be used to obtain joint displacements in terms of nodal displacements.

3.2 Strain energy and stiffness matrix

The strain energy $V_i(\mathbf{u}_i^1, \mathbf{u}_i^2)$ of a flexible body is a nonlinear scalar function of nodal deformations, here expressed via nodal displacements. For the case of a 3D Euler beam, considered in this analysis, the strain energy V_i of the ith-beam turns into a positive-definite quadratic form of the stiffness matrix $\mathbf{K}_i$ in twelve variables, i.e. the nodal displacements of the end-nodes arrays $\mathbf{u}_i^1$ and $\mathbf{u}_i^2$. By introducing the 12-dimensional array $\tilde{\mathbf{u}}_i = \begin{bmatrix} \mathbf{u}_i^{1T} & \mathbf{u}_i^{2T} \end{bmatrix}^T$, the strain energy assumes the following expression

$$V_i = \frac{1}{2}\tilde{\mathbf{u}}_i^T \mathbf{K}_i \tilde{\mathbf{u}}_i \tag{4}$$

The 12×12 stiffness matrix $\mathbf{K}_i$ of a 3D Euler beam with circular cross-section, and for the case of homogeneous and isotropic material, depends on geometrical and stiffness parameters as:

cross section area A, length of the beam L, torsional constant J, mass moment of inertia I, the Young module E and shear module G. For our purposes, it is convenient to divide $\mathbf{K}_i$ into blocks, i.e.

$$\mathbf{K}_i = \begin{bmatrix} \mathbf{K}_i^{1,1} & \mathbf{K}_i^{1,2} \\ \mathbf{K}_i^{2,1} & \mathbf{K}_i^{2,2} \end{bmatrix} \tag{5}$$

in which $\mathbf{K}_i^{2,1} = (\mathbf{K}_i^{1,2})^T$ and the other blocks are defined as

$$\mathbf{K}_i^{1,1} = \frac{E}{L} \begin{bmatrix} A & 0 & 0 & 0 & 0 & 0 \\ 0 & \frac{12I}{L^2} & 0 & 0 & 0 & \frac{6I}{L} \\ 0 & 0 & \frac{12I}{L^2} & 0 & -\frac{6I}{L} & 0 \\ 0 & 0 & 0 & \frac{GJ}{E} & 0 & 0 \\ 0 & 0 & -\frac{6I}{L} & 0 & 4I & 0 \\ 0 & \frac{6I}{L} & 0 & 0 & 0 & 4I \end{bmatrix} \tag{6a}$$

$$\mathbf{K}_i^{1,2} = \frac{E}{L} \begin{bmatrix} -A & 0 & 0 & 0 & 0 & 0 \\ 0 & -\frac{12I}{L^2} & 0 & 0 & 0 & \frac{6I}{L} \\ 0 & 0 & -\frac{12I}{L^2} & 0 & -\frac{6I}{L} & 0 \\ 0 & 0 & 0 & -\frac{GJ}{E} & 0 & 0 \\ 0 & 0 & \frac{6I}{L} & 0 & 4I & 0 \\ 0 & -\frac{6I}{L} & 0 & 0 & 0 & 4I \end{bmatrix} \tag{6b}$$

$$\mathbf{K}_i^{2,2} = \frac{E}{L} \begin{bmatrix} A & 0 & 0 & 0 & 0 & 0 \\ 0 & \frac{12I}{L^2} & 0 & 0 & 0 & -\frac{6I}{L} \\ 0 & 0 & \frac{12I}{L^2} & 0 & \frac{6I}{L} & 0 \\ 0 & 0 & 0 & \frac{GJ}{E} & 0 & 0 \\ 0 & 0 & \frac{6I}{L} & 0 & 4I & 0 \\ 0 & -\frac{6I}{L} & 0 & 0 & 0 & 4I \end{bmatrix} \tag{6c}$$

where the two diagonal block matrices, respectively, refer to the nodal displacements of the two end-nodes while the extra-diagonal blocks refer to the coupling among nodal displacements of different nodes: in fact, each entry of the generic 6×6 block-matrix $\mathbf{K}_i^{l,m}$ can be thought as a force— torque—at the lth-node of the ith-beam when a unit displacement—rotation—is applied to the mth-node.

3.3 Rigid body displacement

Let us consider a rigid body with center of mass at the point G and a generic point P inside its volume, besides let $\mathbf{d}_P$ be the vector pointing from G to the point P. If the body can accomplish only small displacements/rotations, let $\mathbf{p}$ be the displacement of point G and $\mathbf{r}$, be the axial vector of the small rotation matrix $\mathbf{R}$, (9). Upon these assumptions, the displacement array $\mathbf{u}_G$ of G is defined as $\mathbf{u}_G = \begin{bmatrix} \mathbf{p}^T & \mathbf{r}^T \end{bmatrix}^T$.
the displacement array $\mathbf{u}_P$ can be expressed in terms of $\mathbf{u}_G$ by means of the following equation:

$$\mathbf{u}_P = \mathbf{G}_P \mathbf{u}_G, \quad \mathbf{G}_P = \begin{bmatrix} \mathbf{1} & -\mathbf{D}_P \\ \mathbf{O} & \mathbf{1} \end{bmatrix} \tag{7}$$

where $\mathbf{1}$ and $\mathbf{O}$, respectively, are the 3×3 identity- and zero-matrices and $\mathbf{D}_P$ is the Cross-Product Matrix (C.P.M.) of $\mathbf{d}_P$, (23).

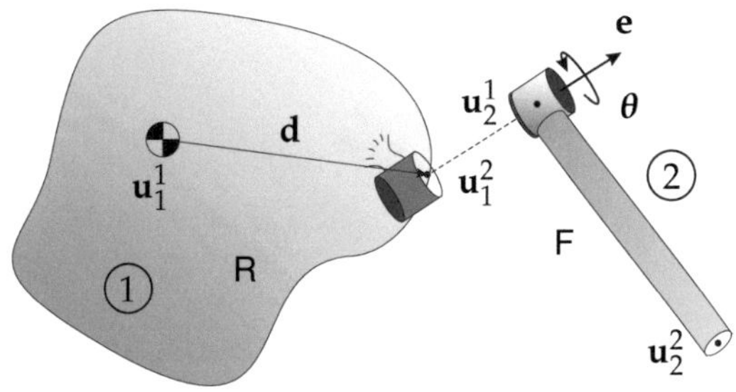

Fig. 3. Case a): Rigid body-flexible beam.

4. Stiffness matrix determination

Let us consider a linkage of flexible beams and rigid bodies connected by means of joints. The strain energy $V(\mathbf{u}_1^1, \mathbf{u}_1^2, \mathbf{u}_2^1, \ldots, \mathbf{u}_{G1}, \mathbf{u}_{G2}, \ldots, \boldsymbol{\theta}^1, \boldsymbol{\theta}^2, \ldots)$ of this system depends on nodal displacement arrays of both rigid and flexible parts and on joint displacement arrays. In the following, we will show how to express V in terms of a reduced set of independent nodal coordinates. In this process, we will start from three elementary blocks composed of rigid and flexible bodies that will be combined to build a generic linkage, for instance, the limb of a PKM. The first and the third case pertain the coupling between a rigid body and a flexible beam by means of a joint; the second case describes the coupling of two beams belonging to two different links. The choice to use two cases to describe the rigid body-flexible body connection is only due to convenience to follow the order of bodies from the base to the moving platform of a PKM. The reader might recur to a unique case to simplify the treatment. The last part of the section is devoted to some insight on joints' stiffness and feasible application to flexures.

4.1 Case a) Rigid body-flexible beam

Figure 3 describes a rigid body R coupled to a flexible beam F by means of a joint. The strain energy V_a of the beam is function of the nodal displacement arrays $\mathbf{u}_2^1$ and $\mathbf{u}_2^2$, i.e.

$$V_a = \frac{1}{2} \begin{bmatrix} \mathbf{u}_2^1 \\ \mathbf{u}_2^2 \end{bmatrix}^T \begin{bmatrix} \mathbf{K}_2^{1,1} & \mathbf{K}_2^{1,2} \\ \mathbf{K}_2^{2,1} & \mathbf{K}_2^{2,2} \end{bmatrix} \begin{bmatrix} \mathbf{u}_2^1 \\ \mathbf{u}_2^2 \end{bmatrix} \tag{8}$$

The array $\mathbf{u}_2^1$ can be expressed in terms of $\mathbf{u}_1^2$ and $\boldsymbol{\theta}$ recalling eq.(1), while $\mathbf{u}_1^2$, in turn, is tied to $\mathbf{u}_1^1$ from eq.(7): upon combining both the equations, we obtain

$$\mathbf{u}_2^1 = \mathbf{G}\mathbf{u}_1^1 + \mathbf{H}\boldsymbol{\theta} \tag{9}$$

where $\mathbf{G}$ depends on $\mathbf{d}$. By substituting the previous equation into eq.(8) we find that $V_a = V(\mathbf{u}_1^1, \mathbf{u}_2^2, \boldsymbol{\theta})$. If the joint is passive, its displacement $\boldsymbol{\theta}$ depends on the elastic properties of the system and, therefore, on the two displacements $\mathbf{u}_1^1$ and $\mathbf{u}_2^2$: thus, it implies that V_a is only function of the two mentioned array, i.e. $V_a = V(\mathbf{u}_1^1, \mathbf{u}_2^2)$. In order to obtain the law for $\boldsymbol{\theta}$ we minimize the strain energy V_a w.r.t. $\boldsymbol{\theta}$:

$$dV_a/d\boldsymbol{\theta} = \mathbf{0}_6^T \tag{10}$$

where $\mathbf{0}_6$ is the six-dimensional zero array. After rearrangements and simplifications, we find

$$\boldsymbol{\theta} = \mathbf{Y}^1\mathbf{u}_1^1 + \mathbf{Y}^2\mathbf{u}_2^2 \tag{11}$$

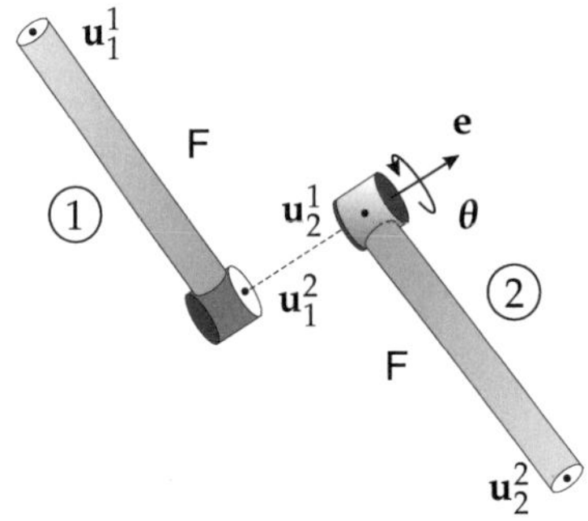

Fig. 4. Case b): Flexible beam-flexible beam.

where

$$\mathbf{Y}^1 = -(\mathbf{H}^T\mathbf{K}_2^{1,1}\mathbf{H})^{-1}\mathbf{H}^T\mathbf{K}_2^{1,1}\mathbf{G} \tag{12a}$$

$$\mathbf{Y}^2 = -(\mathbf{H}^T\mathbf{K}_2^{1,1}\mathbf{H})^{-1}\mathbf{H}^T\mathbf{K}_2^{1,2} \tag{12b}$$

Then, by substituting eq.(11) into eq.(9), we obtain

$$\mathbf{u}_2^1 = \mathbf{X}^1\mathbf{u}_1^1 + \mathbf{X}^2\mathbf{u}_2^2 \tag{13}$$

$$\mathbf{X}^1 = \mathbf{G} + \mathbf{H}\mathbf{Y}^1, \quad \mathbf{X}^2 = \mathbf{H}\mathbf{Y}^2 \tag{14}$$

Let us define the 12-dimensional array $\tilde{\mathbf{u}}_a = \begin{bmatrix} \mathbf{u}_1^{1\,T} & \mathbf{u}_2^{2\,T} \end{bmatrix}^T$ and let us substitute the above expression into V_a, thereby obtaining

$$V_a = \frac{1}{2}\tilde{\mathbf{u}}_a^T\mathbf{K}_a\tilde{\mathbf{u}}_a,\ \mathbf{K}_a = \begin{bmatrix} \mathbf{X}^1 & \mathbf{X}^2 \\ \mathbf{O} & \mathbf{1} \end{bmatrix}^T \begin{bmatrix} \mathbf{K}_2^{1,1} & \mathbf{K}_2^{1,2} \\ \mathbf{K}_2^{2,1} & \mathbf{K}_2^{2,2} \end{bmatrix} \begin{bmatrix} \mathbf{X}^1 & \mathbf{X}^2 \\ \mathbf{O} & \mathbf{1} \end{bmatrix} \tag{15}$$

where $\mathbf{K}_a$ is the 12×12 stiffness matrix sought.

4.2 Case b) Flexible body-flexible body

For the case b) of Fig.4 two beams are coupled by a joint. The strain energy V_b is function of the nodal displacement arrays of the two flexible bodies, i.e.

$$V_b = \frac{1}{2}\begin{bmatrix} \mathbf{u}_1^1 \\ \mathbf{u}_1^2 \end{bmatrix}^T \begin{bmatrix} \mathbf{K}_1^{1,1} & \mathbf{K}_1^{1,2} \\ \mathbf{K}_1^{2,1} & \mathbf{K}_1^{2,2} \end{bmatrix} \begin{bmatrix} \mathbf{u}_1^1 \\ \mathbf{u}_1^2 \end{bmatrix} + \frac{1}{2}\begin{bmatrix} \mathbf{u}_2^1 \\ \mathbf{u}_2^2 \end{bmatrix}^T \begin{bmatrix} \mathbf{K}_2^{1,1} & \mathbf{K}_2^{1,2} \\ \mathbf{K}_2^{2,1} & \mathbf{K}_2^{2,2} \end{bmatrix} \begin{bmatrix} \mathbf{u}_2^1 \\ \mathbf{u}_2^2 \end{bmatrix} \tag{16}$$

The four arrays are not all independent as the following equation stands:

$$\mathbf{u}_1^2 = \mathbf{u}_2^1 + \mathbf{H}\boldsymbol{\theta} \tag{17}$$

The strain energy is, thus, dependent on $\mathbf{u}_1^1, \mathbf{u}_2^1, \mathbf{u}_2^2$ and $\boldsymbol{\theta}$: $V_b = V(\mathbf{u}_1^1, \mathbf{u}_1^2, \mathbf{u}_2^1, \mathbf{u}_2^2) \equiv V(\mathbf{u}_1^1, \mathbf{u}_2^1, \mathbf{u}_2^2, \boldsymbol{\theta})$. Here, we choose to minimize V_b w.r.t. $\boldsymbol{\theta}$, as for the case a), and $\mathbf{u}_2^1$. The reader should notice that our choice is not unique, it is only a particular reduction process necessary for our purposes, it means that the reader might develop a treatment in which $\mathbf{u}_2^1$ is not dependent anymore.

Now, by imposing that the derivative of V_b w.r.t. $\boldsymbol{\theta}$ vanishes, we obtain

$$\boldsymbol{\theta} = \mathbf{F}^1\mathbf{u}_1^1 + \mathbf{F}^2\mathbf{u}_2^1 \tag{18}$$

where

$$\mathbf{F}^1 = -(\mathbf{H}^T\mathbf{K}_1^{2,2}\mathbf{H})^{-1}\mathbf{H}^T\mathbf{K}_1^{2,1} \tag{19a}$$

$$\mathbf{F}^2 = -(\mathbf{H}^T\mathbf{K}_1^{2,2}\mathbf{H})^{-1}\mathbf{H}^T\mathbf{K}_1^{2,2} \tag{19b}$$

Following the previous condition, even the dependent nodal-array $\mathbf{u}_2^1$ must minimize $V_b = V(\mathbf{u}_1^1, \mathbf{u}_1^2(\mathbf{u}_2^1, \boldsymbol{\theta}(\mathbf{u}_1^1, \mathbf{u}_2^1)), \mathbf{u}_2^1, \mathbf{u}_2^2)$; therefore, by applying the chain-rule, we obtain

$$\frac{dV_b}{d\mathbf{u}_2^1} \equiv \frac{\partial V_b}{\partial \mathbf{u}_1^2}\frac{\partial \mathbf{u}_1^2}{\partial \mathbf{u}_2^1} + \frac{\partial V_b}{\partial \mathbf{u}_2^1} \equiv \frac{\partial V_b}{\partial \mathbf{u}_1^2}(\mathbf{1}_6 + \mathbf{H}\mathbf{F}^2) + \frac{\partial V_b}{\partial \mathbf{u}_2^1} = \mathbf{0}_6^T \tag{20}$$

The array $\mathbf{u}_2^1$ is then written in terms of $\mathbf{u}_1^1, \mathbf{u}_2^2$, i.e.

$$\mathbf{u}_2^1 = \mathbf{G}^1\mathbf{u}_1^1 + \mathbf{G}^2\mathbf{u}_2^2 \tag{21}$$

where the 6×6 matrices $\mathbf{G}^1$ and $\mathbf{G}^2$ have the following expressions:

$$\begin{aligned}\mathbf{G}^1 = &-(\mathbf{K}_1^{2,2} + \mathbf{K}_2^{1,1} + \mathbf{F}^{2^T}\mathbf{H}^T\mathbf{K}_1^{2,2} + \mathbf{F}^{2^T}\mathbf{H}^T\mathbf{K}_1^{2,2}\mathbf{H}\mathbf{F}^2)^{-1}\\ &(\mathbf{K}_1^{2,1} + \mathbf{K}_1^{2,2}\mathbf{H}\mathbf{F}^1 + \mathbf{F}^{2^T}\mathbf{H}^T\mathbf{K}_1^{2,1} + \mathbf{F}^{2^T}\mathbf{H}^T\mathbf{K}_1^{2,2}\mathbf{H}\mathbf{F}^1)\end{aligned} \tag{22a}$$

$$\mathbf{G}^2 = -(\mathbf{K}_1^{2,2} + \mathbf{K}_2^{1,1} + \mathbf{F}^{2^T}\mathbf{H}^T\mathbf{K}_1^{2,2} + \mathbf{F}^{2^T}\mathbf{H}^T\mathbf{K}_1^{2,2}\mathbf{H}\mathbf{F}^2)^{-1}\mathbf{K}_1^{1,2} \tag{22b}$$

The joint-arrays $\boldsymbol{\theta}^j$ becomes,

$$\boldsymbol{\theta} = \mathbf{Y}^1\mathbf{u}_1^1 + \mathbf{Y}^2\mathbf{u}_2^2 \tag{23}$$

$$\mathbf{Y}^1 = \mathbf{F}^1 + \mathbf{F}^2\mathbf{G}^1,\ \mathbf{Y}^2 = \mathbf{F}^2\mathbf{G}^2 \tag{24}$$

The dependent nodal-array $\mathbf{u}_1^2$ is obtained by substituting eq.(21) and eq.(23) into eq.(17):

$$\mathbf{u}_1^2 = \mathbf{X}^1\mathbf{u}_1^1 + \mathbf{X}^2\mathbf{u}_2^2 \tag{25}$$

$$\mathbf{X}^1 = \mathbf{G}^1 + \mathbf{H}\mathbf{Y}^1,\ \mathbf{X}^2 = \mathbf{G}^2 + \mathbf{H}\mathbf{Y}^2 \tag{26}$$

Let $\tilde{\mathbf{u}}_b = \left[\mathbf{u}_1^{1^T}\ \mathbf{u}_2^{2^T}\right]^T$ be the 12-dimensional array of independent nodal displacements, then the final expression of V_b in terms $\tilde{\mathbf{u}}_b$ is

$$V_b = \frac{1}{2}\tilde{\mathbf{u}}_b^T\mathbf{K}_b\tilde{\mathbf{u}}_b \tag{27}$$

$$\mathbf{K}_b = \begin{bmatrix}\mathbf{1} & \mathbf{O}\\ \mathbf{X}^1 & \mathbf{X}^2\end{bmatrix}^T \begin{bmatrix}\mathbf{K}_1^{1,1} & \mathbf{K}_1^{1,2}\\ \mathbf{K}_1^{2,1} & \mathbf{K}_1^{2,2}\end{bmatrix} \begin{bmatrix}\mathbf{1} & \mathbf{O}\\ \mathbf{X}^1 & \mathbf{X}^2\end{bmatrix} + \begin{bmatrix}\mathbf{G}^1 & \mathbf{G}^2\\ \mathbf{O} & \mathbf{1}\end{bmatrix}^T \begin{bmatrix}\mathbf{K}_2^{1,1} & \mathbf{K}_2^{1,2}\\ \mathbf{K}_2^{2,1} & \mathbf{K}_2^{2,2}\end{bmatrix} \begin{bmatrix}\mathbf{G}^1 & \mathbf{G}^2\\ \mathbf{O} & \mathbf{1}\end{bmatrix} \tag{28}$$

where $\mathbf{K}_b$ is the 12×12 stiffness matrix.

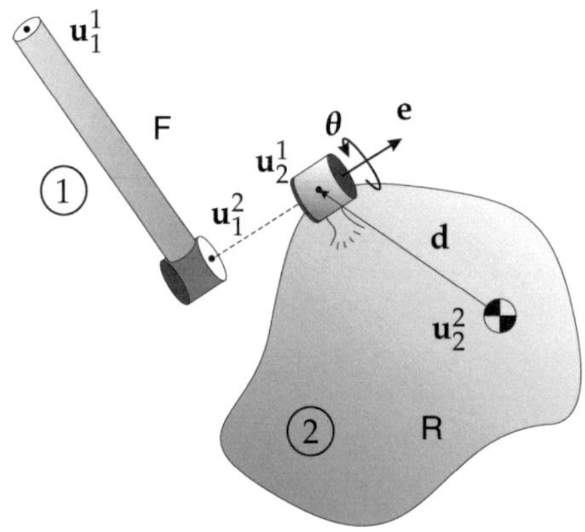

Fig. 5. Case c): Flexible beam-rigid body.

4.3 Case c) Flexible body-rigid body

The case c) describes a beam coupled to a rigid body by means of a joint, as shown in Figure 5. The expressions involving the case c) can be easily obtained by extension of those of the case a), hence, we write only the final results for brevity:

$$\mathbf{Y}^1 = -(\mathbf{H}^T\mathbf{K}_1^{2,2}\mathbf{H})^{-1}\mathbf{H}^T\mathbf{K}_1^{2,1} \tag{29a}$$

$$\mathbf{Y}^2 = -(\mathbf{H}^T\mathbf{K}_1^{2,2}\mathbf{H})^{-1}\mathbf{H}^T\mathbf{K}_1^{2,2}\mathbf{G} \tag{29b}$$

$$\mathbf{X}^1 = \mathbf{H}\mathbf{Y}^1 \tag{30a}$$

$$\mathbf{X}^2 = \mathbf{G} + \mathbf{H}\mathbf{Y}^2 \tag{30b}$$

The strain energy V_c associated to the beam becomes

$$V_c = \frac{1}{2}\tilde{\mathbf{u}}_c^T\mathbf{K}_c\tilde{\mathbf{u}}_c, \quad \mathbf{K}_c = \begin{bmatrix} \mathbf{1} & \mathbf{O} \\ \mathbf{X}^1 & \mathbf{X}^2 \end{bmatrix}^T \begin{bmatrix} \mathbf{K}_1^{1,1} & \mathbf{K}_1^{1,2} \\ \mathbf{K}_1^{2,1} & \mathbf{K}_1^{2,2} \end{bmatrix} \begin{bmatrix} \mathbf{1} & \mathbf{O} \\ \mathbf{X}^1 & \mathbf{X}^2 \end{bmatrix} \tag{31}$$

where $\tilde{\mathbf{u}}_c = \begin{bmatrix} \mathbf{u}_1^{1T} & \mathbf{u}_2^{2T} \end{bmatrix}^T$ is the 12-dimensional array of independent nodal displacements and $\mathbf{K}_c$ is the 12×12 generalized stiffness matrix of the case c).

4.4 Joint's stiffness and flexure joints

The final part of the present section is devoted to show some feasible extension of the formulation to flexure mechanisms. Similar concepts can be applied even to ordinary joints to take into account joint stiffness. In order to reproduce the counterparts of mechanical joints, in a continuous structure it is a common strategy to recur to flexure joints, in fact, zones where the geometry and shape are designed to increase the compliance along specified degrees of freedom (*dofs*). An ideal flexure joint should allow for only motions along its *dofs*, while withstanding to remaining motions along its degrees of constraint (*docs*).

Figure 6 shows the cases of ideal and real flexure revolute joints. While for the ideal case the nodal displacements $\mathbf{u}_1^2$ and $\mathbf{u}_2^1$ of the two flexible beams (1) and (2), coupled by the joint, are tied by the usual constraint equation

$$\mathbf{u}_1^2 = \mathbf{u}_2^1 + \mathbf{H}\delta\boldsymbol{\theta} \tag{32}$$

for the real case $\mathbf{H} \equiv \mathbf{1}_6$. The joint displacement array is now denoted with $\delta\boldsymbol{\theta}$.
Referring to Figure 7, let us consider three different configurations of the flexure joints: an undeformed and unloaded configuration in which the joint-array is $\boldsymbol{\theta}_o$; a preloaded initial configuration with the joint-array $\boldsymbol{\theta}_i$ and a final configuration in which $\boldsymbol{\theta}_f = \boldsymbol{\theta}_i + \delta\boldsymbol{\theta}$, being $\delta\boldsymbol{\theta}$ an array of small displacements around the initial joint-array $\boldsymbol{\theta}_i$. For the following explanation, we refer only to the ideal case of Figure 6. Let $\mathbf{K}_\theta$ be the $m(j) \times m(j)$ joint stiffness matrix and let $\mathbf{w}$ be the generic wrench acting on the flexure joint; then, for the three configurations, we can write

$$\mathbf{w}_o = \mathbf{0}_6 \tag{33a}$$

$$\mathbf{w}_i = \mathbf{K}_\theta(\boldsymbol{\theta}_i - \boldsymbol{\theta}_o) \equiv \mathbf{K}_\theta \Delta\boldsymbol{\theta}_i \tag{33b}$$

$$\mathbf{w}_f = \mathbf{K}_\theta(\boldsymbol{\theta}_f - \boldsymbol{\theta}_o) \equiv \mathbf{K}_\theta \Delta\boldsymbol{\theta}_f \tag{33c}$$

where $\Delta\boldsymbol{\theta}_f = \Delta\boldsymbol{\theta}_i + \delta\boldsymbol{\theta}$. The strain energy V_{θ_f} of the flexure joint in its final configuration simply reduces to

$$V_{\theta_f} = \frac{1}{2}\Delta\boldsymbol{\theta}_f^T \mathbf{K}_\theta \Delta\boldsymbol{\theta}_f \tag{34}$$

The above expressions can be simplified considering $\boldsymbol{\theta}_o = \mathbf{0}_6$ for the unloaded configuration. We do not further discuss on flexure joints, leaving the reader to derive three new cases, similar to those discussed above, taking into account joint stiffness.

5. Mass matrix determination

In this section two ways to include masses/inertias are discussed: the *lumped approach* and the *distributed approach*. The former concentrates masses on nodes of both rigid and flexible parts; the latter considers the real distribution of masses inside beams. As will be explained in the text, the two methods produce good results, particularly when an accurate degree of partitioning is chosen for flexible bodies. Finally, we focus our attention on a way to consider joints with mass and inertia.

5.1 Lumped approach

Reducing mass and inertia of a rigid body to a particular point, the center of mass, without changing dynamic properties of the system, is a common procedure. On the contrary, for flexible bodies every reduction process is an approximation generating mistakes. Let us refer to Fig. 8 in which a link is divided into four beams. In the lumped approach the mass

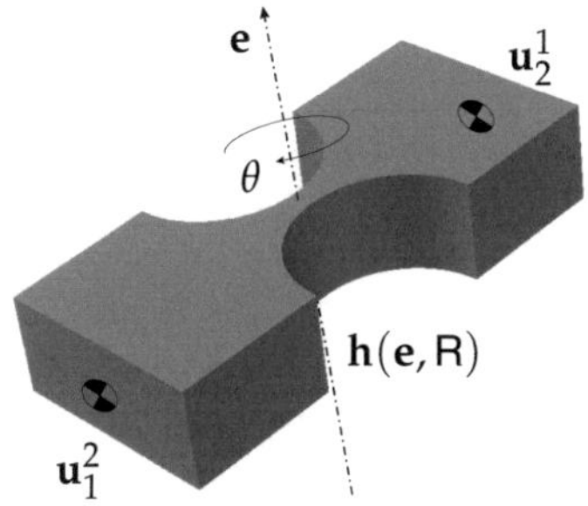

(a) Ideal flexure joint

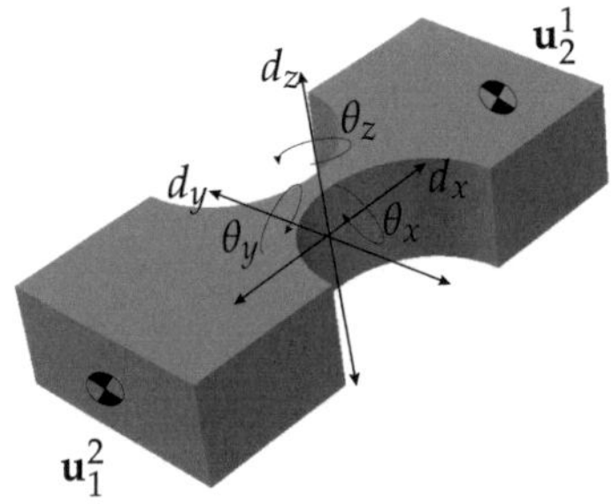

(b) Real flexure joint

Fig. 6. Flexure revolute joint.

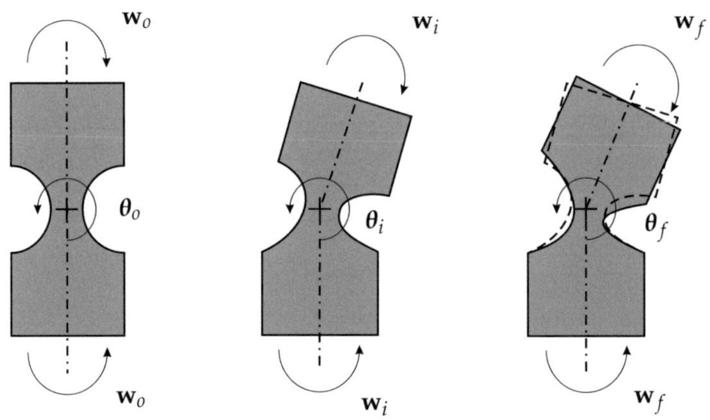

Fig. 7. Flexure joint: a) Undeformed configuration; b) starting preloaded configuration; c) small rotated configuration about the starting preloaded configuration.

and inertia of each beam is concentrated on its end-nodes. Here, we choose a symmetric distribution in which the mass m is divided by two, but the reader can use another distribution according to the case to be examined, as instance beams with varying cross section. The first node has a mass of $m/2$ while any other node, but the fourth, bears a mass m because it receives half a mass from each of the two contiguous beams coupled at its section. The fourth beam of the link is attached to a joint. According to what explained in the previous section, even the mass is concentrated only on the independent joints: it means that the mass of the last beam has to be concentrated on the fourth node, thereby the latter carrying a mass equal to $1/2m + m = 3/2m$. Analogous arguments, not reported here for conciseness, may be used to describe inertias.

The lumped approach concentrates masses and inertias on all the independent nodes, belonging to both rigid and flexible bodies. Mathematically, a 6×6 mass dyad $\widetilde{\mathbf{M}}_i$ is associated at the ith-independent node, defined as

$$\widetilde{\mathbf{M}}_i = \begin{bmatrix} m_i\mathbf{1} & \mathbf{O} \\ \mathbf{O} & \mathbf{J}_i \end{bmatrix} \tag{35}$$

where m_i and $\mathbf{J}_i$ are the mass and the 3×3 inertia matrix, respectively, of either a rigid body, if the independent node is at the center of mass of the said body, or of a beam's end-node. The generalized inertia matrix $\mathbf{M}_{PKM}$ of a PKM is readily derived upon assembling in diagonal blocks the previous inertia dyads, following the order chosen to enumerate all independent nodes inside the global array of independent nodal coordinates, hence

$$\mathbf{M}_{PKM} = diag(\widetilde{\mathbf{M}}_1, \widetilde{\mathbf{M}}_2, \ldots, \widetilde{\mathbf{M}}_n) \tag{36}$$

5.2 Distributed approach

The distributed approach considers the true distribution of mass inside a flexible beam. Particularly, it is possible to find a 12×12 matrix $\mathbf{M}_i$ referred to the twelve nodal coordinates of a beam's end-nodes. This matrix can be divided into blocks, whose entries are reported below, as already done for the stiffness matrix $\mathbf{K}_i$, i.e.

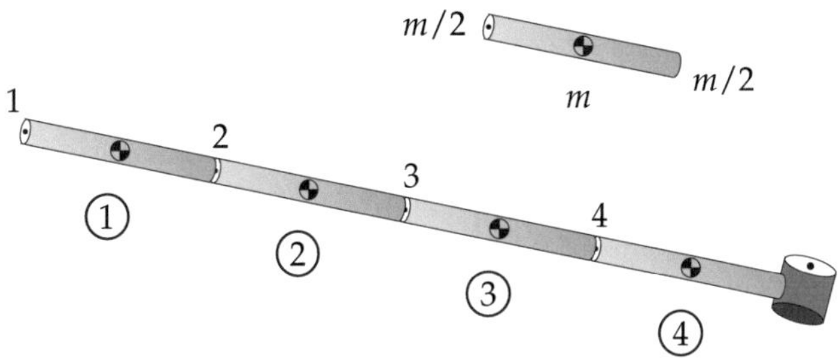

Fig. 8. Lumped distribution of mass.

$$\mathbf{M}_i^{1,1} = \rho A_i L_i \begin{bmatrix} \frac{1}{3} & 0 & 0 & 0 & 0 & 0 \\ 0 & \frac{13}{35} + \frac{6I_z}{5\rho A_i L_i^2} & 0 & 0 & 0 & \frac{11L_i}{210} + \frac{I_z}{10\rho A_i L_i} \\ 0 & 0 & \frac{13}{35} + \frac{6I_z}{5\rho A_i L_i^2} & 0 & \frac{-11L_i}{210} - \frac{I_y}{10\rho A_i L_i} & 0 \\ 0 & 0 & 0 & \frac{I_x}{3\rho A_i} & 0 & 0 \\ 0 & 0 & \frac{-11L_i}{210} - \frac{I_y}{10\rho A_i L_i} & 0 & \frac{L_i^2}{105} + \frac{2I_y}{15\rho A_i} & 0 \\ 0 & \frac{11L_i}{210} + \frac{I_z}{10\rho A_i L_i} & 0 & 0 & 0 & \frac{L_i^2}{105} + \frac{2I_z}{15\rho A_i} \end{bmatrix} \tag{37}$$

$$\mathbf{M}_i^{1,2} = \rho A_i L_i \begin{bmatrix} \frac{1}{6} & 0 & 0 & 0 & 0 & 0 \\ 0 & \frac{9}{70} - \frac{6I_z}{5\rho A_i L_i^2} & 0 & 0 & 0 & -\frac{13L_i}{420} + \frac{I_z}{10\rho A_i L_i} \\ 0 & 0 & \frac{9}{70} - \frac{6I_y}{5\rho A_i L_i^2} & 0 & \frac{13L}{420} - \frac{I_y}{10\rho A_i L_i} & 0 \\ 0 & 0 & 0 & \frac{I_x}{3\rho A_i} & 0 & 0 \\ 0 & 0 & -\frac{13L_i}{420} + \frac{I_z}{10\rho A_i L_i} & 0 & \frac{-L_i^2}{140} - \frac{I_y}{30\rho A_i} & 0 \\ 0 & \frac{13L_i}{420} - \frac{I_z}{10\rho A_i L_i} & 0 & 0 & 0 & \frac{-L_i^2}{140} - \frac{I_z}{30\rho A_i} \end{bmatrix} \tag{38}$$

$$\mathbf{M}_i^{2,2} = \rho A_i L_i \begin{bmatrix} \frac{1}{3} & 0 & 0 & 0 & 0 & 0 \\ 0 & \frac{13}{35} + \frac{6I_z}{5\rho A_i L_i^2} & 0 & 0 & 0 & -\frac{11L_i}{210} - \frac{I_z}{10\rho A_i L_i} \\ 0 & 0 & \frac{13}{35} + \frac{6I_y}{5\rho A_i L_i^2} & 0 & \frac{11L_i}{210} + \frac{I_y}{10\rho A_i L_i} & 0 \\ 0 & 0 & 0 & \frac{I_x}{3\rho A_i} & 0 & 0 \\ 0 & 0 & \frac{11L_i}{210} + \frac{I_y}{10\rho A_i L_i} & 0 & \frac{L_i^2}{105} + \frac{2I_y}{15\rho A_i} & 0 \\ 0 & -\frac{11L_i}{210} - \frac{I_z}{10\rho A_i L_i} & 0 & 0 & 0 & \frac{L_i^2}{105} + \frac{2I_z}{15\rho A_i} \end{bmatrix} \tag{39}$$

where ρ, L_i, A_i, I_x, I_y and I_z, respectively, are the density, the length, the cross section area and the mass moments of inertia for unit of length of the ith-beam. The matrix $\mathbf{M}_i$ is associated to the kinetic energy T_i of a beam, the latter being defined as a quadratic forms into the time-derivatives $\dot{\mathbf{u}}_i^1$, $\dot{\mathbf{u}}_i^2$ of the nodal displacement arrays $\mathbf{u}_i^1$ and $\mathbf{u}_i^2$:

$$T_i = \frac{1}{2} \begin{bmatrix} \dot{\mathbf{u}}_i^1 \\ \dot{\mathbf{u}}_i^2 \end{bmatrix}^T \begin{bmatrix} \mathbf{M}_i^{1,1} & \mathbf{M}_i^{1,2} \\ \mathbf{M}_i^{2,1} & \mathbf{M}_i^{2,2} \end{bmatrix} \begin{bmatrix} \dot{\mathbf{u}}_i^1 \\ \dot{\mathbf{u}}_i^2 \end{bmatrix} \tag{40}$$

In the previous section we have found how dependent nodal displacement arrays are expressed in terms of independent ones. Let us consider the time-derivative of both sides of eq.(13), we write

$$\dot{\mathbf{u}}_2^1 = \mathbf{X}^1\dot{\mathbf{u}}_1^1 + \mathbf{X}^2\dot{\mathbf{u}}_2^2 \tag{41}$$

in which the matrices $\mathbf{X}^1$ and $\mathbf{X}^2$ are not dependent on time. Similar expressions can be obtained for eqs.(21) and (26) for the case b) and for the case c). It means that the same expressions standing for dependent and independent displacements can be extended at velocity and acceleration level. Therefore, the following matrices $\mathbf{M}_a$, $\mathbf{M}_b$ and $\mathbf{M}_c$ can be written with perfect analogy to their counterparts $\mathbf{K}_a$, $\mathbf{K}_b$ and $\mathbf{K}_c$:

$$\mathbf{M}_a = \begin{bmatrix} \mathbf{X}^1 & \mathbf{X}^2 \\ \mathbf{O} & \mathbf{1} \end{bmatrix}^T \begin{bmatrix} \mathbf{M}_2^{1,1} & \mathbf{M}_2^{1,2} \\ \mathbf{M}_2^{2,1} & \mathbf{M}_2^{2,2} \end{bmatrix} \begin{bmatrix} \mathbf{X}^1 & \mathbf{X}^2 \\ \mathbf{O} & \mathbf{1} \end{bmatrix} \tag{42a}$$

$$\mathbf{M}_b = \begin{bmatrix} \mathbf{1} & \mathbf{O} \\ \mathbf{X}^1 & \mathbf{X}^2 \end{bmatrix}^T \begin{bmatrix} \mathbf{M}_1^{1,1} & \mathbf{M}_1^{1,2} \\ \mathbf{M}_1^{2,1} & \mathbf{M}_1^{2,2} \end{bmatrix} \begin{bmatrix} \mathbf{1} & \mathbf{O} \\ \mathbf{X}^1 & \mathbf{X}^2 \end{bmatrix} + \begin{bmatrix} \mathbf{G}^1 & \mathbf{G}^2 \\ \mathbf{O} & \mathbf{1} \end{bmatrix}^T \begin{bmatrix} \mathbf{M}_2^{1,1} & \mathbf{M}_2^{1,2} \\ \mathbf{M}_2^{2,1} & \mathbf{M}_2^{2,2} \end{bmatrix} \begin{bmatrix} \mathbf{G}^1 & \mathbf{G}^2 \\ \mathbf{O} & \mathbf{1} \end{bmatrix} \tag{42b}$$

$$\mathbf{M}_c = \begin{bmatrix} \mathbf{1} & \mathbf{O} \\ \mathbf{X}^1 & \mathbf{X}^2 \end{bmatrix}^T \begin{bmatrix} \mathbf{M}_1^{1,1} & \mathbf{M}_1^{1,2} \\ \mathbf{M}_1^{2,1} & \mathbf{M}_1^{2,2} \end{bmatrix} \begin{bmatrix} \mathbf{1} & \mathbf{O} \\ \mathbf{X}^1 & \mathbf{X}^2 \end{bmatrix} \tag{42c}$$

with obvious meaning of all terms. The three mass matrices, above defined, are referred to the time-derivatives $\dot{\tilde{\mathbf{u}}}_a$, $\dot{\tilde{\mathbf{u}}}_b$ and $\dot{\tilde{\mathbf{u}}}_c$ of the independent nodal displacement arrays $\tilde{\mathbf{u}}_a$, $\tilde{\mathbf{u}}_b$ and $\tilde{\mathbf{u}}_c$. To clarify some doubt that might arise let us refer to Fig. 3. In this case the mass matrix of the rigid body, see eq.(35), is referred to its center of mass with displacement array $\mathbf{u}_1^1$. The distributed approach first allows us to find the 12×12 mass matrix $\mathbf{M}_2$ of the beam, then the latter is expressed in terms of only independent displacements by means of $\mathbf{M}_a$. Obviously, $\mathbf{M}_2$ and $\mathbf{M}_a$ refer to the same object, the beam; but $\mathbf{M}_a$ *distributes* $\mathbf{M}_2$ into the independent nodes with displacement arrays $\mathbf{u}_1^1$ and $\mathbf{u}_2^2$. This implies that the center of mass of the rigid body carries its own mass/inertia and part of the mass/inertia of the beam. Similar conclusions may be sought for the cases b) and c).

5.3 Joint's mass and inertia

In this final subsection we describe a method to consider mass and inertia of joints. For convenience, let us refer to Fig. 4. The joint is split into two parts, one belonging to the first beam, the remaining to the second beam. Let $\widetilde{\mathbf{M}}_L$ and $\widetilde{\mathbf{M}}_R$, where capital letters stand for left and right, be the mass dyads of the two half-parts of the joint, defined as

$$\widetilde{\mathbf{M}}_L = \begin{bmatrix} m_L\mathbf{1} & \mathbf{O} \\ \mathbf{O} & \mathbf{J}_L \end{bmatrix} \quad \widetilde{\mathbf{M}}_R = \begin{bmatrix} m_R\mathbf{1} & \mathbf{O} \\ \mathbf{O} & \mathbf{J}_R \end{bmatrix} \tag{43}$$

The kinetic energy T_J of the joint can be written in terms of the above matrices $\widetilde{\mathbf{M}}_L$ and $\widetilde{\mathbf{M}}_R$ and of the time-derivatives of the nodal arrays $\dot{\mathbf{u}}_1^2$, $\dot{\mathbf{u}}_2^1$, thus

$$T_J = \frac{1}{2}(\dot{\mathbf{u}}_1^2)^T\widetilde{\mathbf{M}}_L\dot{\mathbf{u}}_1^2 + \frac{1}{2}(\dot{\mathbf{u}}_2^1)^T\widetilde{\mathbf{M}}_R\dot{\mathbf{u}}_2^1 \tag{44}$$

Then, upon recalling eqs.(21) and (26), T_J can be expressed in terms of $\tilde{\mathbf{u}} = \begin{bmatrix} \mathbf{u}_1^{1T} & \mathbf{u}_2^{2T} \end{bmatrix}^T$, i.e.

$$T_J = \frac{1}{2}(\tilde{\mathbf{u}})^T \mathbf{M}_J \tilde{\mathbf{u}} \tag{45}$$

where $\mathbf{M}_J$ is the 12×12 generalized inertia matrix of the joint expressed in terms of independent nodal displacements, respectively, defined as

$$\mathbf{M}_a = \begin{bmatrix} \mathbf{X}^{1T}\widetilde{\mathbf{M}}_R\mathbf{X}^1 + \mathbf{G}^T\widetilde{\mathbf{M}}_L\mathbf{G} & \mathbf{X}^{1T}\widetilde{\mathbf{M}}_R\mathbf{X}^2 \\ \mathbf{X}^{2T}\widetilde{\mathbf{M}}_R\mathbf{X}^1 & \mathbf{X}^{2T}\widetilde{\mathbf{M}}_R\mathbf{X}^2 \end{bmatrix} \tag{46a}$$

$$\mathbf{M}_b = \begin{bmatrix} \mathbf{X}^{1T}\widetilde{\mathbf{M}}_L\mathbf{X}^1 + \mathbf{G}^{1T}\widetilde{\mathbf{M}}_R\mathbf{G}^1 & \mathbf{X}^{1T}\widetilde{\mathbf{M}}_L\mathbf{X}^2 + \mathbf{G}^{1T}\widetilde{\mathbf{M}}_R\mathbf{G}^2 \\ \mathbf{X}^{2T}\widetilde{\mathbf{M}}_L\mathbf{X}^1 + \mathbf{G}^{2T}\widetilde{\mathbf{M}}_R\mathbf{G}^1 & \mathbf{X}^{2T}\widetilde{\mathbf{M}}_L\mathbf{X}^2 + \mathbf{G}^{2T}\widetilde{\mathbf{M}}_R\mathbf{G}^2 \end{bmatrix} \tag{46b}$$

$$\mathbf{M}_c = \begin{bmatrix} \mathbf{X}^{1T}\widetilde{\mathbf{M}}_L\mathbf{X}^1 & \mathbf{X}^{1T}\widetilde{\mathbf{M}}_L\mathbf{X}^2 \\ \mathbf{X}^{2T}\widetilde{\mathbf{M}}_L\mathbf{X}^1 & \mathbf{X}^{2T}\widetilde{\mathbf{M}}_L\mathbf{X}^2 + \mathbf{G}^T\widetilde{\mathbf{M}}_R\mathbf{G} \end{bmatrix} \tag{46c}$$

for the three cases in exam.

6. Linearized elastodynamics equations

In this section we will derive the generalized inertia and stiffness matrices necessary to write the linearized elastodynamics equations. As described in the two previous sections stiffness and inertia matrices of rigid bodies and flexible beams are referred to the independent nodal displacements of the system. Now, one might ask how to combine different matrices to build the global stiffness and inertia matrices. In order to solve this issue let us introduce two Boolean matrices $\mathbf{B}_1$ and $\mathbf{B}_2$ able to map a 6-dimensional displacement array $\mathbf{u}_i$ or a 12-dimensional displacement array $\tilde{\mathbf{u}}$ in terms of a $6n$-dimensional global array $\mathbf{q} = \begin{bmatrix} \mathbf{u}_1 \, \mathbf{u}_2 \ldots \mathbf{u}_n \end{bmatrix}$ containing all the independent displacement arrays of the robot. It is important that the reader would define the order in which every single array $\mathbf{u}_i$ appears inside $\mathbf{q}$. The $6 \times 6n$ matrix $\mathbf{B}_1$ and the $12 \times 6n$ matrix $\mathbf{B}_2$ are defined as:

$$\mathbf{u}_i = \mathbf{B}_1(i)\mathbf{q}, \quad \tilde{\mathbf{u}} \equiv \begin{bmatrix} \mathbf{u}_i \\ \mathbf{u}_j \end{bmatrix} = \mathbf{B}_2(i,j)\mathbf{q} \tag{47}$$

$$B_1(i) = \begin{bmatrix} \mathbf{O}_6 \, \mathbf{O}_6 \ldots \mathbf{1}_6(i) \ldots \mathbf{O}_6 \end{bmatrix}, \quad B_2(i,j) = \begin{bmatrix} \mathbf{O}_6 & \mathbf{O}_6 & \ldots \mathbf{1}_6(i) \ldots & \mathbf{O}_6 \\ \mathbf{O}_6 & \mathbf{1}_6(j) \ldots & \mathbf{O}_6 & \ldots \mathbf{O}_6 \end{bmatrix} \tag{48}$$

The above expressions allow us to convert each nodal displacement array in term of $\mathbf{q}$. As instance, let us take into exam the strain energy V_b of eq.(27), it simply turns into $V_b = \frac{1}{2}\mathbf{q}^T\mathbf{B}_2(i,j)^T\mathbf{K}_b\mathbf{B}_2(i,j)\mathbf{q}$, where i and j indicate the position indices of $\mathbf{u}_1^1$ and $\mathbf{u}_2^2$ inside $\mathbf{q}$. From V_b we can extract a new $6n \times 6n$ matrix $\overline{\mathbf{K}}_b$, that is a stiffness matrix expanded to the final dimension of the problem, defined as

$$\overline{\mathbf{K}}_b = \mathbf{B}_2(i,j)^T\mathbf{K}_b\mathbf{B}_2(i,j) \tag{49}$$

Likewise, the generic expanded $6n \times 6n$ mass matrix $\overline{\mathbf{M}}_i$ of $\mathbf{M}_i$, see eq.(35), can be written as $\overline{\mathbf{M}}_i = \mathbf{B}_1(i)^T\mathbf{M}_i\mathbf{B}_1(i)$, where i is the position index of $\mathbf{u}_i$, i.e. the displacement array of the ith-rigid body's center of mass, inside $\mathbf{q}$. By the same strategy, it is possible to expand every stiffness and inertia matrix. This operation is essential as, *only when referred to the same set*

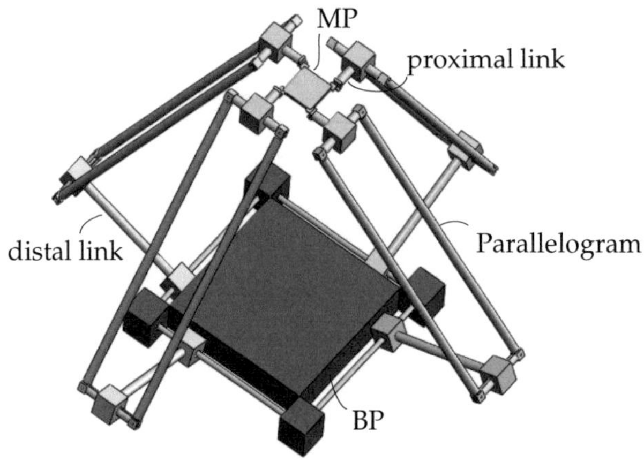

Fig. 9. CAD model of the robot.

of nodal displacement coordinates, these matrices can be summed and combined to obtain the global generalized matrices $\mathbf{K}_{PKM}$ and $\mathbf{M}_{PKM}$ of the robot. The way to use $\mathbf{B}_1$ and $\mathbf{B}_2$ will be shown in detail in the case study of the next section.

Let us introduce the $6n$-dimensional array $\mathbf{f}$ of generalized nodal wrenches, i.e. nodal forces and torques, then, the system of linearized elastodynamics equations becomes

$$\mathbf{M}_{PKM}\ddot{\mathbf{q}} + \mathbf{K}_{PKM}\mathbf{q} = \mathbf{f} \tag{50}$$

The previous system may be used to solve statics around a starting posture of the robot. The homogeneous part of eq.(50), i.e. the left side, may be used to find eigenfrequencies and eigenmodes of the robot, or the zero-input response. As already pointed out, the natural frequencies of the robot change with regard to the pose that the robot is attaining. To determine how stiffness or natural frequencies vary inside the workspace local and global performance indices may be introduced to investigate elastodynamic behavior of PKMs. As instance, let us consider the first natural frequency f_1 mapped inside a robot's workspace. The latter can be analyzed to differentiate areas with high range of frequency from areas in which the elastodynamic performances worsen. The multidimensional integral Ω_1 of f_1, extended to the whole workspace W or part of it, can be a good global index to show how global performances increase or decrease changing some geometrical, structural or inertial parameter, i.e.

$$\Omega_1 = \frac{\int_W f_1 dW}{W} \approx \frac{\sum_{i=1}^{n_w} W_i f_{1i}}{\sum_{i=1}^{n_w} W_i} \tag{51}$$

where, in the approximated discrete formula of the right side, W is divided into n_w hypercubes W_i, while the frequency f_{1i} is calculated at the center point of W_i.

We conclude this section considering an useful application of the method to find singularities. It is well known that as a robot approaches to a singularity configuration it gains mobility. As a consequence, its generalized stiffness matrix becomes singular and its first eigenfrequency goes to zero. Analyzing the variation of f_1 inside the workspace may be useful to avoid zones close to singularity or with low values of frequency. We stress that singularities directly come from kinematics: stiffness and inertial parameters, respectively influencing the elasticity

and the dynamics of a mechanical system, can only amplify or reduce, without creating or nullifying, the effects of the kinematics.
Different considerations can be made for the boundary surface of the workspace. For the latter case, a robot undergoes poses in which one or more legs are completely extended, thus the robot loses dofs associated to those directions normal to the tangent plane at the boundary surface of the workspace. If the displacement of the MP for the corresponding eigenmode, when evaluated at a pose lying on the boundary surface, is normal to the said tangent plane the robot is virtually locked, it means that its stiffness along that direction is high, thus reflecting into an increment of frequency. On the contrary, if the displacement of the MP lies onto the tangent plane its in-plane stiffness, and its natural frequency as well, in theory goes to zero. All remaining cases are included between zero and a maximum value depending on the projection of displacements on the tangent plane. This important conclusion can be summarized by the following statement: ***the value of a given natural frequency of a PKM on the boundary surface of its workspace can be interpreted through the projection of the moving platform's displacements, for the corresponding eigenmode, on the tangent plane to the said surface***. The previous statement is strict only when a three dimensional workspace, e.g. the constant orientation workspace, can be considered. In other cases, one should recur to concepts of projection based on twist theory, beyond the scopes of this chapter.

7. Case study

In this section we apply the method to a complex PKM with 4-dofs. The robot, shown in Fig. 9, is composed of four legs connecting the base frame to a moving platform. Due to the particular kind of constraints generated by the limbs, the moving platform can accomplish three translations and a rotation around the vertical axis. This motion, even referred to as Schönflies motion, is typical of SCARA robots and it is largely used in industry for pick and place applications. Each leg is composed of a distal link connected to the base frame by means of an actuated revolute joint and to a parallelogram linkage, i.e. a Π-joint, by means of a revolute joint. The parallelogram, in turn, is linked to a proximal link by another revolute. Finally, the proximal link is coupled to the MP by a vertical axis revolute joint. All revolute joints, apart from the one fixed to the inertial frame, are passive. We do not further go inside the analysis of the kinematics, citing (24) for more explanations and for any detail pertaining the robot's geometry.

7.1 Application of the method to a generic leg

In order to apply the proposed method each leg is decomposed into three modules. The first module includes the BP and the proximal link, the second the parallelogram linkage, while the last includes the distal link and the MP. We recur to some simplifications that do not change the meaning of the treatment. In general, the two bases of a PKM are one order stiffer than the links composing the structure and can be modeled as rigid without loss of accuracy. Even the short input and output links of a Π-joint can be considered rigid when compared to the slender coupler links. As verified by FEM, the said assumptions are good approximations that simplify the final model introducing rigid-flexible and flexible-rigid connections inside and between each module.
Let us analyze the first module shown in Fig. 10. The distal link is split into three flexible bodies, the choice of discretization being absolutely arbitrary. In this simple case the end-bodies F_1 and F_3 of the link are coupled to two rigid bodies, i.e., the base BP and the input link I of the Π-joint, by means of two revolute joints of axes parallel to the unit vector

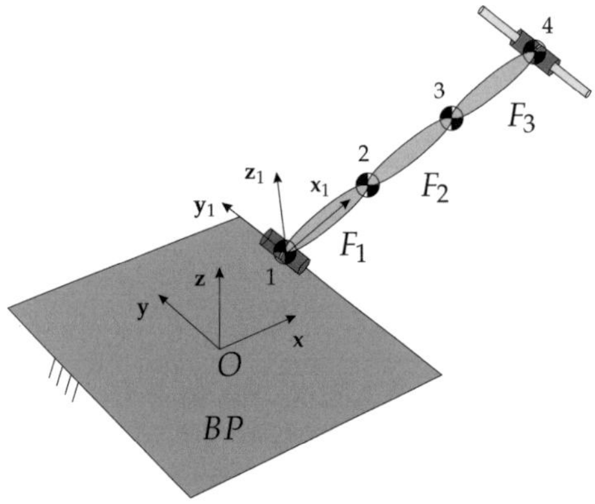

Fig. 10. Drawing of a the first module: Base platform-distal link

e. The remaining flexible body F_2 is internal to the proximal link and coupled to the others bodies by means of fixed connections. Following what explained in the previous sections, the strain energy V_{m1} of the first module is the sum of three components, i.e. the strain energies V_{F_i} of the three beams in which is decomposed, namely

$$V_{m1} = \sum_{i=1}^{3} V_{F_i} = \sum_{i=1}^{3} \frac{1}{2} \tilde{\mathbf{u}}_i^T \mathbf{K}_i \tilde{\mathbf{u}}_i \tag{52}$$

with $\tilde{\mathbf{u}}_1 = \left[\mathbf{u}_1^{1^T} \; \mathbf{u}_1^{2^T} \right]^T$, $\tilde{\mathbf{u}}_2 = \left[\mathbf{u}_2^{2^T} \; \mathbf{u}_2^{3^T} \right]^T$ and $\tilde{\mathbf{u}}_3 = \left[\mathbf{u}_3^{3^T} \; \mathbf{u}_3^{4^T} \right]^T$. The first actuated revolute joint is considered locked to perform the elastodynamics analysis, thereby, $\mathbf{u}_1^1 \equiv \mathbf{u}_{BP}^1 \equiv \overline{\mathbf{u}}^1$. In this way the generalized stiffness matrix of the robot is not singular as rigid body motions of the robot are deleted and the analysis is performed at a frozen configuration. Even for the other three fixed connections at points 2 and 3, similar equations stand: $\mathbf{u}_1^2 \equiv \mathbf{u}_2^2 \equiv \overline{\mathbf{u}}^2$ and $\mathbf{u}_2^3 \equiv \mathbf{u}_3^3 \equiv \overline{\mathbf{u}}^3$. Finally, for the displacement array of the input link R, we can write: $\mathbf{u}_R \equiv \overline{\mathbf{u}}^4$. By substituting into the previous expressions, we derive $\tilde{\mathbf{u}}_1 = \left[\overline{\mathbf{u}}^{1^T} \; \overline{\mathbf{u}}^{2^T} \right]^T$, $\tilde{\mathbf{u}}_2 = \left[\overline{\mathbf{u}}^{2^T} \; \overline{\mathbf{u}}^{3^T} \right]^T$ and $\tilde{\mathbf{u}}_3 = \left[\overline{\mathbf{u}}^{3^T} \; \mathbf{u}_3^{4^T} \right]^T$. The local stiffness matrix $\mathbf{K}_i$ of the ith-body F_i is expressed into the global reference frame. In Figure 10 the first local frame $\{\mathbf{x}_1, \mathbf{y}_1, \mathbf{z}_1\}$, with origin at point 1, and the base global reference frame $\{\mathbf{x}, \mathbf{y}, \mathbf{z}\}$, with origin at point O, are displayed. The set of independent displacements are defined inside the independent displacement array $\mathbf{q}_{M1}$ of the first module: $\mathbf{q}_{M1} = \left[\overline{\mathbf{u}}^1 \; \overline{\mathbf{u}}^2 \; \overline{\mathbf{u}}^3 \; \overline{\mathbf{u}}^4 \right]$, where $\overline{\mathbf{u}}^4$ is the nodal displacement array of the center of mass of the rigid body I. While the first and the second term, i.e. V_{F_1} and V_{F_2}, of the strain energy V_{m1} contain only independent displacements, the last term V_{F_3} is function of the dependent nodal array $\mathbf{u}_3^4$. The flexible body F_3, indeed, is coupled by a revolute joint to the rigid body I, thus, the case c), flexible-rigid, can be applied to express its strain energy only in terms of independent displacements. Following the notation above introduced, we write:

$$V_{F_3} = \frac{1}{2} \tilde{\mathbf{u}}_3^T \mathbf{K}_3 \tilde{\mathbf{u}}_3 \equiv \frac{1}{2} \tilde{\mathbf{u}}_{c3}^T \mathbf{K}_{c3} \tilde{\mathbf{u}}_{c3} \tag{53}$$

where $\tilde{\mathbf{u}}_{c3} \equiv \left[\overline{\mathbf{u}}^{3^T} \; \overline{\mathbf{u}}^{4^T} \right]^T$ and $\mathbf{K}_{c3}$ has been defined in eq.(31). Notice that in order to find $\mathbf{K}_{c3}$ we have to use the 6-dimensional joint array $\mathbf{h}^R(\mathbf{e})$; besides, the position vector $\mathbf{d}$ going

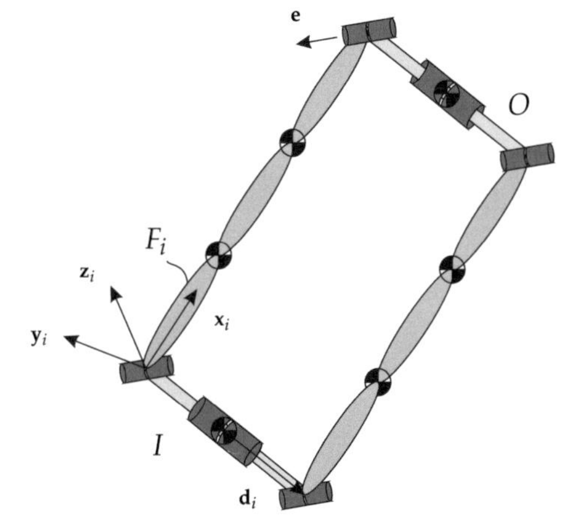

(a) Drawing of a the second module: parallelogram linkage

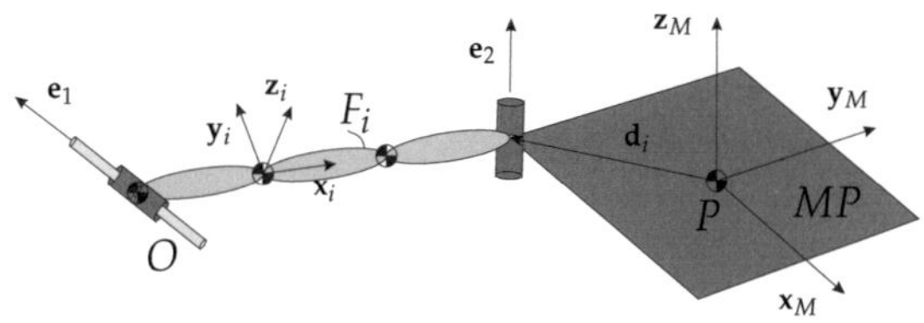

(b) Drawing of a the third module: proximal link-moving platform

from the center of mass of I to the center of the revolute joint, in this case, is the zero vector. Then, by introducing the $12 \times n_{qm1}$ binary-entry matrix $\mathbf{B}_2(\bullet, \bullet)$ mapping the independent nodal-arrays in terms of the array $\mathbf{q}_{M1}$, the expression of the generalized stiffness matrix $\mathbf{K}_{M1}$ can be calculated as

$$\begin{aligned} V_{m1} &= \frac{1}{2}\mathbf{q}_{M1}{}^T\mathbf{K}_{M1}\mathbf{q}_{M1} \\ \mathbf{K}_{M1} &= \mathbf{B}_2(1,2)^T\mathbf{K}_1\mathbf{B}_2(1,2) + \mathbf{B}_2(2,3)^T\mathbf{K}_2\mathbf{B}_2(2,3) + \mathbf{B}_2(3,4)^T\mathbf{K}_{c3}\mathbf{B}_2(3,4) \end{aligned} \tag{54}$$

Here, the matrix $\mathbf{K}_{M1}$ is expressed in terms of $\mathbf{q}_{M1}$. The reader must notice that to obtain $\mathbf{K}_{PKM}$ each matrix has to be expressed in terms of a final n_q-dimensional array $\mathbf{q}$ including *all* the independent nodal displacements. In order to define $\mathbf{q}$, as the modules of a leg are in series, the last node of a module coincides with the first one of the next module and it must be denoted by a unique nodal displacement array. Extension to the final dimension of $\mathbf{q}$ is readily obtained by substituting into eq.(54) a new $12 \times n_q$ binary-entry matrix $\mathbf{B}_2(\bullet, \bullet)$ mapping the independent nodal-arrays in terms of the global array $\mathbf{q}$.
The second module is shown in Fig. 11(a). In this case two rigid-flexible and two flexible-rigid connections must be used to describe the couplings between flexible couplers and input-output rigid bodies I and O. The joint array $\mathbf{h}^R(\mathbf{e})$ remains the same for all the four revolute joints as a matter of fact of the parallelogram architecture. The third module, shown in Fig. 11(b), includes one rigid-flexible and one flexible-rigid connection, respectively, between the distal link and the output link O of the Π-joint and the distal link and the MP. As displayed in the same figure, the two revolute joints to be used to find the joint arrays $\mathbf{h}^R$ have axes of unit vectors $\mathbf{e}_1$ and $\mathbf{e}_2$. We do not describe the calculations to find the generalized

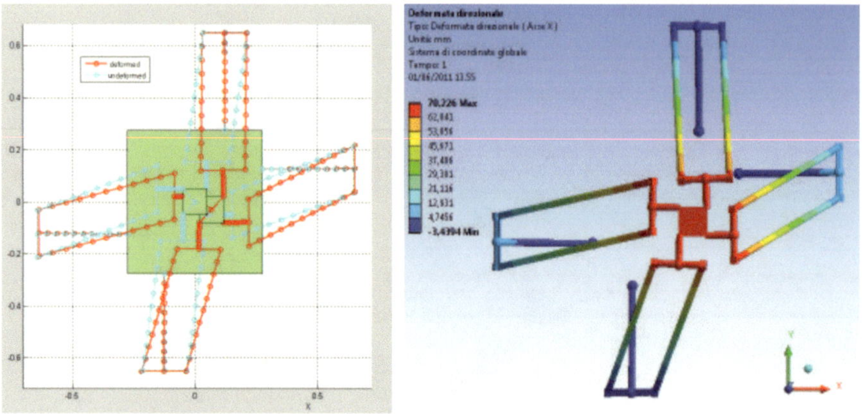

(c) Algorithm model (d) Ansys© model

Fig. 11. Static deformation of the robot.

Disp.	*Algorithm*	*Marc©*	*Ansys©*	*err% Marc©*	*err% Ansys©*
u_x	0.068066	0.068065	0.067436	−0.0008815	−0.933626
u_y	−0.030545	−0.030545	−0.029890	0.003274	−2.191368
u_z	0	0	0	0	0

Table 1. Translational displacements of the end-effector's center node.

stiffness matrices of the two modules as can be readily obtained following procedures similar to the case of the first module.

7.2 Comparison to FEA software and validation

In this subsection the proposed elastodynamics model is compared to FEA results for validation. Two FEA models, with increasing complexity, are implemented in order to establish the nearness of the examined case to the real case. The first model, developed by the commercial software Marc©, considers only 3D-beams and rigid bodies, while joints are modeled by means of relative degrees of freedom between common nodes belonging to two coupled bodies. This model perfectly fits the simplifications of the method in exam. The second model, developed by the commercial software Ansys©, describes a robot with a complex structure closer to reality. Links are solids while joints have finite burdens and provide their function by means of the coupling of surfaces and screws.

7.2.1 Statics

We first compared the static deformation of the robot when an external force of 1000 N, along the x-direction, is applied on the end-effector, when the latter is positioned at its home pose with angle of rotation of MP equal to zero. Figure 11 shows the displacements of our model when compared to Ansys© model, while in Tab. 1 the translational displacements of the end-effector center node are reported.

It can be observed how the first MARC© model perfectly fit to the results of our method. The relative error grows, but still remaining limited, when displacements are compared to Ansys© model. The reason is well understood as it comes from the use of solid bodies and joints to simulate the robot's structure.

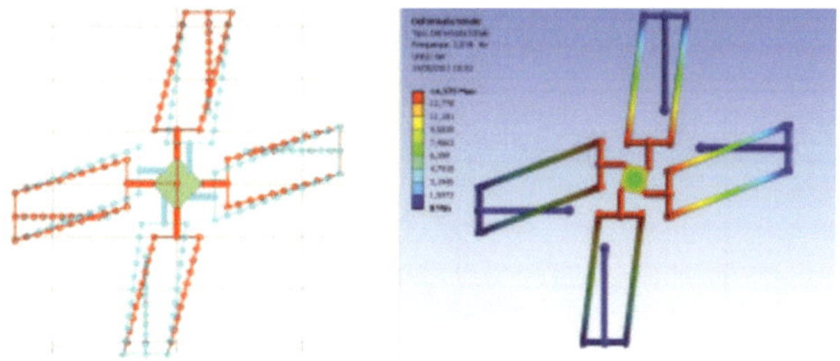

(a) First mode

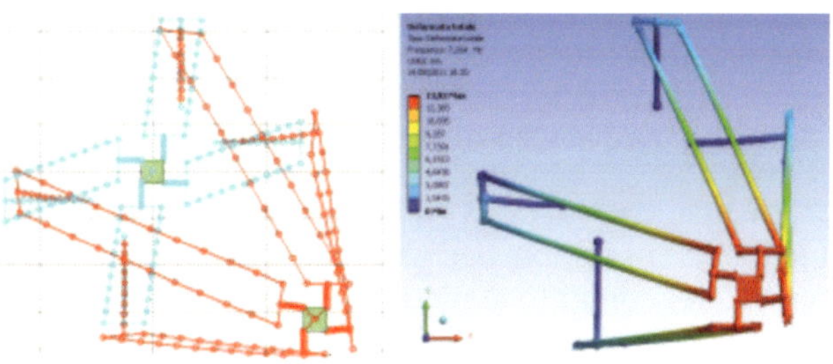

(b) Second mode

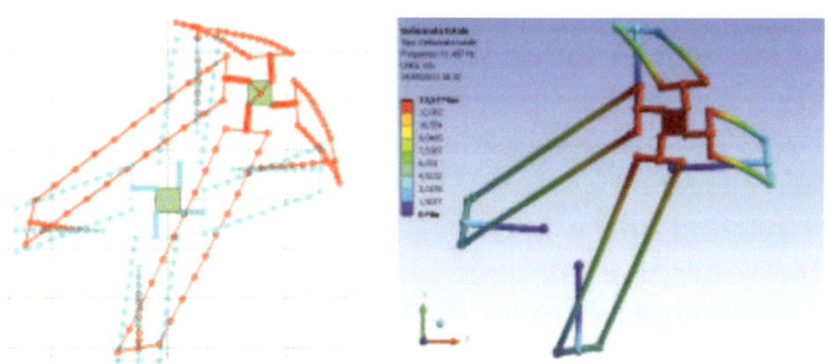

(c) Third mode

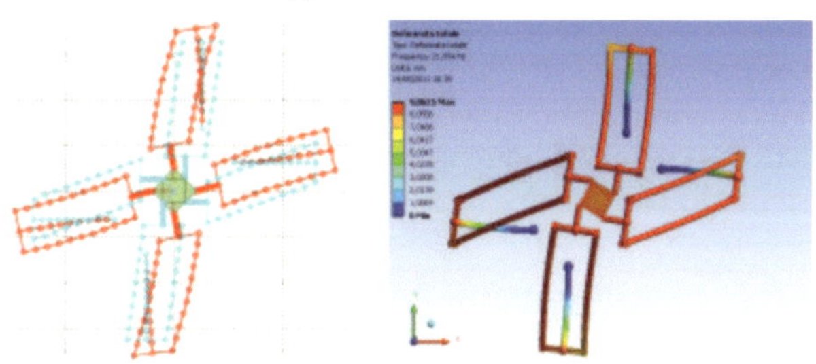

(d) Fourth mode

Fig. 12. Modes comparison: Algorithm *vs*. Ansys©.

7.2.2 Natural modes and frequencies

As in the case of statics, the elastodynamics model of the 3T1R robot is used to compare natural modes and frequencies to FEA software. We report only the comparison to Ansys©, as more indicative of a feasible application of the method to a real case. Figure 12 shows the first four natural modes obtained when the robot is attaining its home pose. In Table 2 the first ten natural frequency of the robot, at the same pose, are reported. Results show good agreement

Freq.	Algorithm [Hz]	Ansys© [Hz]	err%
1	2.920	3.019	3.28%
2	7.062	7.204	1.97%
3	11.275	11.487	1.85%
4	20.834	21.554	3.34%
5	25.480	25.722	0.94%
6	25.545	25.804	1.00%
7	26.028	26.181	0.58%
8	28.306	28.830	1.82%
9	30.368	31.295	2.96%
10	31.060	32.286	3.80%

Table 2. The first ten natural frequencies of the robot at the home pose.

with Ansys© model. Some discrepancies still occur due to the same reasons explained for the static case and to the use of flexible bodies to simulate all links and platforms in Ansys©. This choice has been taken in order to avoid asymmetric contacts between rigid and flexible solids leading to convergence mistakes. In turn, we used a stiffer material to approximate rigid behavior of the MP and rigid links.

7.2.3 Distribution of frequencies inside the workspace

In order to provide a further useful extension of the proposed method, the first natural frequency is calculated and plotted inside the constant orientation workspace of the robot (25). We have chosen elementary cubes of side 5 cm to discretize the workspace of the robot while the angle of rotation of the MP is $\theta_z = 0$. It can be observed that two privileged diagonals divide the workspace into four symmetric areas. These directions coincide with the two diagonals of the squared BP of Fig. 9, meaning that, at the home pose, geometric symmetry reflects itself into the elastic behavior of the robot. The boundary of the constant orientation workspace shows areas with high range of frequency along with other areas in which the first natural frequency reaches values close to zero (Hz). As already outlined in the text, this behavior is due to the MP's displacement (deformation) in correspondence of the first eigenmode: if at a certain pose, in which the analysis is performed, the displacement is along a *doc* of the MP, the ensuing frequency will be high; conversely, if it is along a *dof* of the MP, the frequency will come near zero.

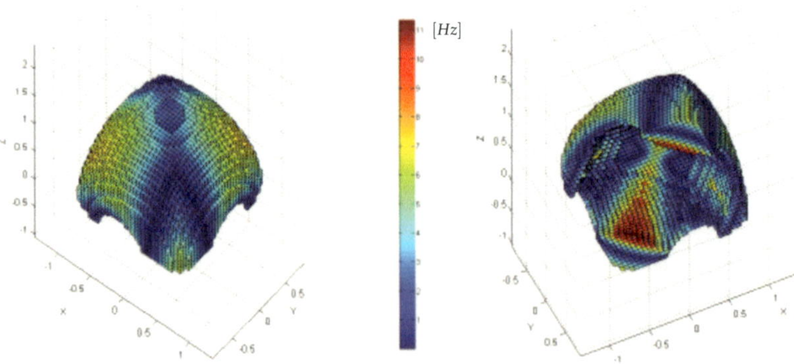

Fig. 13. Distribution of the first natural frequency inside the robot's constant orientation workspace.

8. Conclusions

This chapter has discussed a method, based on the Matrix Structural Analysis, to study the linearized elastodynamics of PKMs. Base and moving platforms are considered rigid, while links can be modeled as rigid or flexible parts, the latter being decomposed into two or more flexible bodies. Here, we used 3D Euler beams but the method can be extended to superelements with two end-nodes. Joints are directly included, without recurring to Lagrange multipliers, by means of kinematic constraints between nodal displacement arrays. Three cases have been taken into account to model the rigid-flexible, flexible-flexible and flexible-rigid coupling of bodies by means joints. Each case yields equations, linking dependent, independent nodal displacement arrays and joint displacements as well, to be used to find generalized stiffness and inertia matrices. The latter are then combined as elementary blocks to find the global matrices of the whole system. Some useful extension to compliant mechanism has been introduced, while two strategy, the lumped and the distributed one, have been explained to include mass/inertia into the model. Feasible applications of the method pertain: the study of natural frequencies inside the robot's workspace by means of local and global indices, the singularity finding, the optimization of elastodynamic performances varying geometric, structural or inertial parameters.
Finally, the method has been applied to an articulated four-dofs PKMs with Schönflies motions. A modular approach is used to split each of the four legs into three modules. Results, compared to commercial software, revealed good accuracy in determining natural frequency range, while drastically reducing the time of computation avoiding the annoying and time-consuming FEM meshing routines.

9. References

[1] Tyapin, I., Hovland, G. & Brogårdh, T. (2008). Kinematic and Elastodynamic Design Optimisation of the 3-DOF Gantry-Tau Parallel Kinematic Manipulator, In: *Proceedings of the Second International Workshop on Fundamental Issues and Future Research Directions for Parallel Mechanisms and Manipulators*, September 21-22, Montpellier, France.

[2] Zienkiewicz, O. C. & Taylor, R. L. (2000). *Solid mechanics - Volume 2*, Butterworth Heinemann, London.

[3] Martin, H. C. (1966). *Introduction to matrix methods of structural analysis*, McGraw-Hill Book Company.

[4] Wang, C.K. (1966). *Matrix methods of structural analysis*, International Textbook Company.

[5] Przemieniecki, J. S. (1985). *Theory of Matrix Structural Analysis*, Dover Publications, Inc, New York.

[6] Huang, T., Zhao, X. & Withehouse, D.J. (2002). Stiffness estimation of a tripod-based parallel kinematic machine, *IEEE Trans. on Robotics and Automation*, Vol. 18(1).

[7] Li, Y.W., Wang, J.S. & Wang, L.P. (2002). Stiffness analysis of a Stewart platform-based parallel kinematic machine, In: *Proceedings of IEEE ICRA: Int. Conf. On Robotics and Automation*, May 11-15, Washington, US.

[8] Clinton, C.M., Zhang, G. & Wavering, A.J. (1997). Stiffness modeling of a Stewart-platform-based milling machine, In: *Trans. of the North America Manufacturing Research Institution of SME*, May 20-23, Vol. XXV, pp 335-340, Lincoln, NB, US.

[9] Al Bassit, L., Angeles, J., Al-Wydyan, K. & Morozov., A. (2002). The elastodynamics of a Schönflies -Motion generator, *Technical Report TR-CIM-02-06*, Centre for Intelligent Machines, McGill University, Montreal, Canada.

[10] Deblaise, D., Hernot, X. & Maurine, P. (2006). A Systematic Analytical Method for PKM Stiffness Matrix Calculation, In: *Proceedings of the 2006 IEEE International Conference on Robotics and Automation*, May, Orlando, Florida.

[11] Gonçalves, R. S. & Carvalho, J. C. M. (2008). Stiffness analysis of parallel manipulator using matrix structural analysis, In: *EUCOMES 2008, 2-nd European Conference on Mechanism Science*, Cassino, Italy.

[12] Wittbrodt, E., Adamiec-Wójcik, I. & Wojciech, S. (2006). *Dynamics of Flexible Multibody Systems*, Springer.

[13] Gosselin, C.M. (1990). Stiffness mapping for parallel manipulator, *IEEE Trans. on Robotics and Automation*, vol. 6, pp 377-382.

[14] Quennouelle, C. & Gosselin, C.M. (2008). Kinemato-Static Modelling of Compliant Parallel Mechanisms: Application to a 3-PRRR Mechanism, the Tripteron, In: *Proceedings of the Second International Workshop on Fundamental Issues and Future Research Directions for Parallel Mechanisms and Manipulators*, September 21-22, Montpellier, France.

[15] Briot, S., Pashkevich, A. & Chablat, D. (2009). On the optimal design of parallel robots taking into account their deformations and natural frequencies, In: *Proceedings of the ASME 2009 International Design Engineering Technical Conferences & Computers and Information in Engineering Conference IDETC/CIE*, August 30 - September 2, San Diego, California, USA.

[16] Yoon, W.K., Suehiro, T., Tsumaki, Y. & Uchiyama, M. (2004). Stiffness analysis and design of a compact modified Delta parallel mechanism, *Robotica*, 22(5), pp. 463-475.

[17] Majou, F., Gosselin, C.M., Wenger, P. & Chablat, D. (2004). Parametric stiffness analysis of the orthoglide, In: *Proceedings of the 35th International Symposium on Robotics*, March, Paris, France.

[18] El-Khasawneh, B.S. & Ferreira, P.M. (1999). Computation of stiffness and stiffness bounds for parallel link manipulator, *Int. J. Machine Tools and manufacture*, vol. 39(2), pp 321-342.

[19] Gosselin, C.M. & Zhang, D. (2002). Stiffness analysis of parallel mechanisms using a lumped model, *Int. J. of Robotics and Automation*, vol. 17, pp 17-27.

[20] Pashkevich, A., Chablat, D. & Wenger, P. (2009). Stiffness analysis of overconstrained parallel manipulators, *Mechanism and Machine Theory*, Vol. 44, pp. 966-982.

[21] Shabana, A.A. (2008). *Computational continuum mechanics*, Cambridge University Press, ISBN 978-0-521-88569-0, USA.

[22] Cammarata, A. & Angeles, J. (2011). The elastodynamics model of the McGill Schönflies Motion Generator, In: *Multibody Dynamics 2011*, 4-7 July, Bruxelles, Belgium.

[23] Angeles, J. (2007). *Fundamentals of Robotic Mechanical Systems: Theory, Methods and Algorithms, Third edition*, Springer, ISBN 0-387-29412-0, New York.

[24] Salgado, O., Altuzarra, O., Petuya, V. & Hernández, A. (2008). Synthesis and design of a novel 3T1R fullyparallel manipulator, *ASME Journal of Mechanical Design*, Vol. 130, Issue 4, pp. 1-8.

[25] Merlet, J.-P. (2006). *Parallel robots, Second Edition*, Kluwer Academic Publisher, ISBN-10 1-4020-4132-2(HB), the Netherlands.

6

Parallel, Serial and Hybrid Machine Tools and Robotics Structures: Comparative Study on Optimum Kinematic Designs

Khalifa H. Harib[1], Kamal A.F. Moustafa[1],
A.M.M. Sharif Ullah[2] and Salah Zenieh[3]
[1]*UAE University*
[2]*Kitami Institute of Technology*
[3]*Tawazun Holding*
[1,3]*United Arab Emirates*
[2]*Japan*

1. Introduction

After their inception in the past two decades as possible alternatives to conventional Computer Numerical Controlled (CNC) machine tools structures that dominantly adapt serial structures, Parallel Kinematic Machines (PKM) were anticipated to form a basis for a new generation of future machining centers. However this hope quickly faded out as most problems associated with this type of structures still persist and could not be completely solved satisfactorily. This especially becomes more apparent in machining applications where accuracy, rigidity, dexterity and large workspace are important requirements. Although the PKMs possess superior mechanical characteristics to serial structures, particularly in terms of high rigidity, accuracy and dynamic response, however the PKMs have their own drawbacks including singularity problems, inconsistent dexterity, irregular workspace, and limited range of motion, particularly rotational motion.

To alleviate the PKMs' limitations, considerable research efforts were directed to solve these problems. Optimum design methods are among the various methods that are attempted to improve the dexterity as well as to maximize the workspace (Stoughton and Arai, 1993, Huang et al., 2000). Various methods to evaluate the workspace were suggested (Gosselin, 1990; Luh et al., 1996; Conti et al., 1998; Tsai et al., 2006). Workspace optimization is also addressed (Wang and Hsieh, 1998). A new shift in tackling the aforementioned problems came when researchers start to look at hybrid structures, consisting of parallel and serial linkages as a compromise to exploit the advantageous characteristics of the serial and parallel structures. This shift creates new research and development needs and founded new ideas.

Among the early hybrid kinematic designs, the Tricept was considered as the first commercially successful hybrid machine tools. This hybrid machine which was developed by Neos Robotics, has a three-degrees-of-freedom parallel kinematic structure and a standard two-degrees-of-freedom wrest end-effector holding joint. The constraining passive leg of the machine has to bear the transmitted torque and moment between the moving platform and the base (Zhang and Gosselin, 2002). Recently the Exechon machine is introduced as an improvement over the Tricept design. The Exechon adopts a unique overconstrained structure, and it has been improved based on the success of the Tricept (Zoppi, et al., 2010, Bi and Jin, 2011). Nonetheless, regardless of the seemingly promising prospect of the hybrid kinematic structures, comprehensive study and understanding of the involved kinematics, dynamics and design of these structures are lacking. This paper is attempting to provide a comparative study and a formulation for the kinematic design of hybrid kinematic machines. The remainder of this paper is as follows: Section 2 provides a discussion on the mobility of serial, parallel and hybrid kinematic structures and the involved effects of overconstrain on the mobility of the mechanism. Section 3 provides a discussion on kinematic design for hybrid machines and the implication of the presented method. Concluding remarks are presented in Section 4.

2. Mobility of robotic structures

Mobility is a significant structural attribute of mechanisms assembled from a number of links and joints. It is also one of the most fundamental concepts in the kinematic and the dynamic modeling of mechanisms and robotic manipulators. IFToMM defines the mobility or the degree of freedom as the number of independent co-ordinates needed to define the configuration of a kinematic chain or mechanism (Gogu, 2005, Ionescu, 2003). Mobility, M, is used to verify the existence of a mechanism (M > 0), to indicate the number of independent parameters in the kinematic and the dynamic models and to determine the number of inputs needed to drive the mechanism.

The various methods proposed in the literature for mobility calculation of the closed loop mechanisms can be grouped in two categories (Ionescu, 2003): (a) approaches for mobility calculation based on setting up the kinematic constraint equations and their rank calculation for a given position of the mechanism with specific joint location, and (b) formulas for a quick calculation of mobility without need to develop the set of constraint equations. The approaches for mobility calculation based on setting up the kinematic constraint equations and their rank calculation are valid without exception. The major drawback of these approaches is that the mobility cannot be determined quickly without setting up the kinematic model of the mechanism. Usually this model is expressed by the closure equations that must be analyzed for dependency. There is no way to derive information about mechanism mobility without performing kinematic analysis by using analytical tools. For this reason, the real and practical value of these approaches is very limited in spite of their valuable theoretical foundations.

Many formulas based on approach (b) above have been proposed in the literature for the calculation of mechanisms' mobility. Many of these methods are reducible to the Cebychev-Grubler-Kutzbach's mobility formula given by Equation 1 below (Gogu, 2005). Using this formula, the mobility M of a linkage composed of L links connected with j joints can be determined from the following equation.

$$M = 6(L-1-j) + \sum_{i=1}^{j} f_i \tag{1}$$

where f_i is the DOF associated with joint i. Equation 1 is used to calculate the mobility of spatial robotic mechanisms as most industrial robots and machine tools structures are serial structures with open kinematics chains.

2.1 Mobility of planner mechanisms

To gain an insight into the effect of mobility on the kinematic analysis and design of serial, parallel and hybrid kinematic structures, we will also look at the mobility of planner mechanisms, which can be obtained from the following planner Kutzbach-Gruebler's equation (Gogu , 2005, Norton, 2004).

$$M = 3(L - 1 - j) + \sum_{i=1}^{j} f_i \quad (2)$$

where M, L, j and f_i are as defined before in Equation 1. As shown in Figure 1, the robotic structures are arranged in serial, parallel and hybrid kinematic chains, and thus have different number of links and joints. Using Equation 2, all the three structures in Figure 1 have three degrees of freedom, or mobility three. This gives the end-effector two translational degrees-of-freedom to position it arbitrarily in the x-y plane, and one rotational degree-of-freedom to orient it about the z-axis. In the serial kinematic structure all three joints are actuated, whereas for the parallel and hybrid structures only the three prismatic joints are actuated whereas the revolute joints are passive. The parallel kinematic part of the hybrid structure in Figure 1.c, has two degrees of freedom, which is achieved by reducing the number of legs to two and eliminating one of the passive revolute joints.
Figure 2 shows an alternative way to reduce the degrees of freedom of the parallel kinematic mechanism, and hence to reduce the number of actuated prismatic joints. In this example this is done by eliminating one of the revolute joints which connect the legs to the platform. The corresponding leg has a passive prismatic joint to constraint one of the degrees-of-freedom. By removing the revolute joint though the leg becomes a three-force member and hence it will be carrying bending moments necessitating considerable design attention to maintain desired stiffness levels and accuracy. This concept of reducing the degrees of freedom is adopted in the spatial Tricept mechanism to reduce the degrees-of-freedom from six to three. Compared to the mechanism in 1.c, this mechanism has more joints and links, which is not desirable from the design point of view.

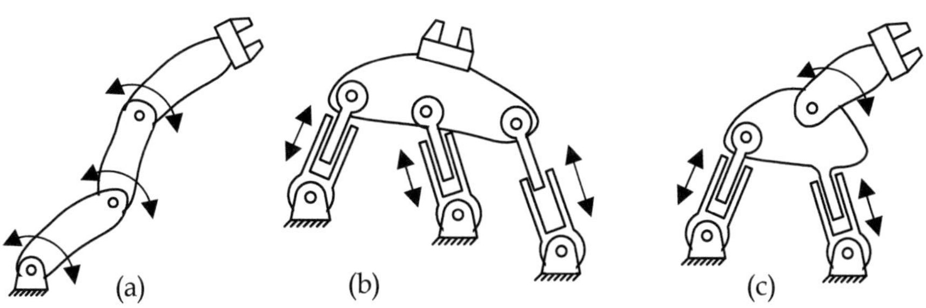

Fig. 1. Schematics of planner 3 degrees-of-freedom robotic structures with a) fully serial (L=4, j=3, $\sum f_i$ =3), b) fully parallel (L=8, j=9, $\sum f_i$ =9), and c) hybrid topologies (L=6, j=6, $\sum f_i$ =6)

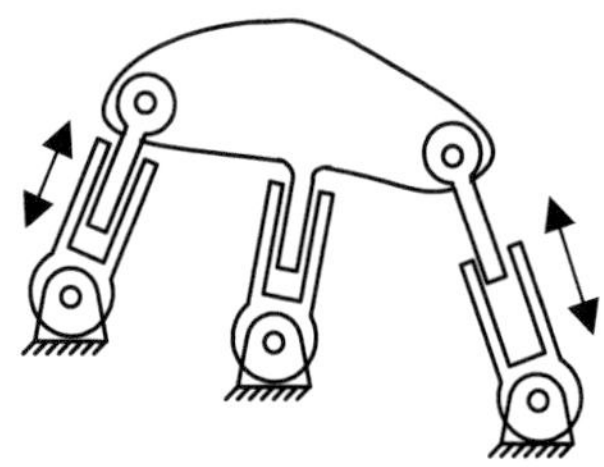

Fig. 2. Schematics of a 2-degrees-of-freedom planner parallel robotic structure, L=7, j=8, $\sum f_i$ =8. The prismatic joint of the middle leg is passive (unactuated)

It should be noted here that the planner mechanisms are realized by necessitating that the involved revolute joints to be perpendicular to the plane and the prismatic joints to be confined to stay in the plane. As such these mechanisms can also be viewed as special cases of spatial mechanisms that are confined to work in a plane through overconstrains and thus Equation 1, with proper modification, rather than Equation 2 could be use, as discussed in the next section,

2.2 Over-constrained mechanisms

Formula for a quick calculation of mobility is an explicit relationship between structural parameters of the mechanism: the number of links and joints, the motion/constraint parameters of the joints and of the mechanism. Usually, these structural parameters are easily determined by inspection without a need to develop a set of kinematic constraint equations. However, not all known formulas for a quick calculation of mobility fit for many classical mechanisms and in particular parallel robotic manipulators (Ionescu, 2003). Special geometric conditions play a significant role in the determination of mobility of such mechanisms, which are called paradoxical mechanisms, or overconstrained, yet mobile linkage (Waldron and Kinzel, 1999). However, as mentioned above, there are overconstrained mechanisms that have full range mobility and therefore they are mechanisms even though they should be considered as rigid structures according to the mobility criterion (i.e. the mobility $M < 1$ as calculated from Equation 1. The mobility of such mechanisms is due to the existence of a particular set of geometric conditions between the mechanism joint axes that are called overconstraint conditions.

Overconstrained mechanisms have many appealing characteristics. Most of them are spatial mechanisms whose spatial kinematic characteristics make them good candidates in modern linkage designs where spatial motion is needed. Another advantage of overconstrained mechanisms is that they are mobile using fewer links and joints than it is expected.

In fact, the planner mechanisms in Figures 1 and 2 can also be viewed as overconstrained spatial mechanisms, and thus the spatial version of Kutzbach-Gruebler's equation (Equation 1), does not work for some of these planner mechanisms. In particular, for the parallel and hybrid kinematic planner mechanisms, Equation 1 will result in negative mobility values suggesting that these mechanisms are rigid structures, although they are not. Since this is not true, it should be concluded that Equation 1 cannot be used for these over-constraint mechanisms (Mavroidis and Roth, 1995). The overconstraint in planner parallel and hybrid kinematic mechanisms is due to the geometrical requirement on the involved joint-axes in relation to each other. To solve the problem when using the spatial version of the Kutzbach-Gruebler's equation for planner mechanisms or for over-constraint mechanisms in general, Equation 1 has to be modified by adding a parameter reflecting the number of overconstaints existing in the mechanism (Cretu, 2007). The resulting equation is called the universal Somo-Malushev's mobility equation. For the case of mechanisms that do not involve any passive degrees of freedom it is written as

$$M = 6(L-1-j) + \sum_{i=1}^{j} f_i + s \tag{3}$$

where s is the number of overconstraint (geometrical) conditions. For example, the parallel kinematic mechanism in Figure 1.b has $L = 8$, $j = 9$, and $\sum f_i = 9$. Using these parameters in Equation 1 gives $M = -3$. However using Equation (3) and observing that there are 6 overconstraints in this mechanism, the mobility will amount to $M = 3$. The overconstraints in this mechanism are due to the necessity for confining the axes of the three prismatic joints to form a plane or parallel planes (two overcosntraints), and for the axes of the three revolute joints of the moving platform (two overconstraints), and the three revolute joints of the base to be perpendicular to the plane formed by the prismatic joints.

3. Kinematic designs of robotic structures

A widely used kinematic design strategy for serial kinematic robotic structures to optimize the workspace is to use the first group of links and joints to position the end-effector and the remaining links and joints to orient the end-effector, and thus breaking the design problem into two main tasks. For the 6-DOF Puma robot schematic shown in Figure 3, the first three links and joint are responsible for positioning the end-effector at the desired position, while the last three joints and links form a 3-DOF concurrent wrest joint that orient the end-effector.

Conventional five axis machining centers achieve similar decoupling by splitting the five axes (three translational axes and two rotational axes) into two groups of axes. One group of serially connected axes is responsible for positioning/orienting the worktable which is holding the workpiece, while the other group of axes moves/orients the spindle (Bohez, 2002).

Unfortunately this strategy cannot be adopted for parallel kinematic structures due to the similarity of the legs and their way of working in parallel. As such decoupling of the two functions (positioning and orienting the end-effector) is not straightforward to do for parallel kinematic structures if not impossible. Partial decoupling has been attempted by Harib and Sharif Ullah (2008) using the axiomatic design approach.

On the other hand, it should be noted here that parallel structures, and to some extent hybrid structures, can be built from identical parts and modules, and thus lend themselves well to adaptation as reconfigurable machines (Zhang, 2006). This attribute is not strongly relevant to serial structures which consist of axes that are stacked on each other making the links and joints differ considerably in terms of size and shape.

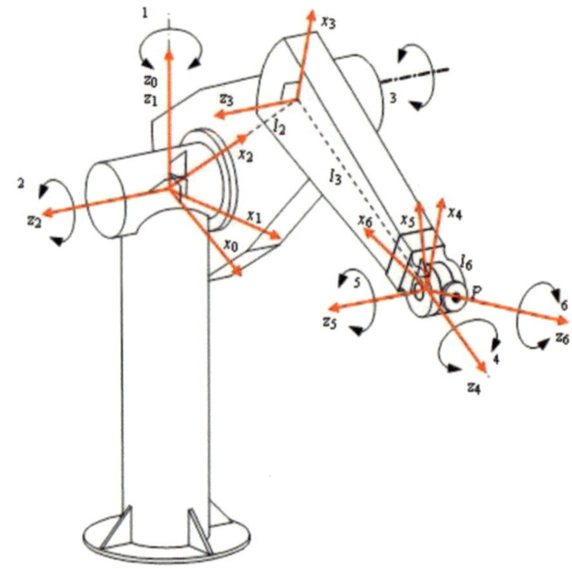

Fig. 3. A schematic of a 6-DOF Puma robot (serial kinematic structure)

3.1 Parallel kinematic designs

A main objective of the optimal design of parallel kinematic machines is to maintain consistent dexterity within the workable space of the machine. Dexterity of the mechanism is a measure of its ability to change its position and orientation arbitrarily, or to apply forces and torques in arbitrary directions. As such the Jacobian matrix of the mechanism is widely used in formulating the dexterity measure. For a six degrees-of-freedom hexapod mechanism (Harib and Srinivasan, 2003), shown in Figure 4, the Jacobian matrix J relates the translational and rotational velocity vectors of the moving platform to the extension rate of the legs as indicated below (Harib and Sharif Ullah, 2008).

$$\left[\dot{l}_1 \cdots \dot{l}_6\right]^T = \mathbf{J}_1 \dot{\mathbf{c}} + \mathbf{J}_2 \boldsymbol{\omega} = \mathbf{J}\left[\dot{\mathbf{c}}^T \quad \boldsymbol{\omega}^T\right]^T \tag{4}$$

where $\mathbf{J} = [\mathbf{J}_1\ \mathbf{J}_2]$ is the Jacobian matrix of the hexapod, which consists of two 6×3 sub-matrices $\mathbf{J}_1$ and $\mathbf{J}_2$ that are given as

$$\mathbf{J}_1 = [\mathbf{u}_1 \cdots \mathbf{u}_6]^T \tag{5}$$

$$\mathbf{J}_2 = [{}^M\mathbf{R}_C\, {}^C\mathbf{a}_1 \times \mathbf{u}_1 \cdots {}^M\mathbf{R}_C\, {}^C\mathbf{a}_6 \times \mathbf{u}_6]^T \tag{6}$$

where $\mathbf{u}_i$ and ${}^C\mathbf{a}_i$ are respectively a unit vector along the ith leg and the position vector of its attachment point to the moving platform in the platform coordinate frame C, and ${}^M\mathbf{R}_C$ is the rotational matrix of the moving platform. The Jacobian matrix $\mathbf{J}$ relates also the external task space forces and torques and the joint space forces as indicated below.

$$[\mathbf{F}\ \ \mathbf{T}]^T = \mathbf{J}^T [f_1 \cdots f_6]^T \tag{7}$$

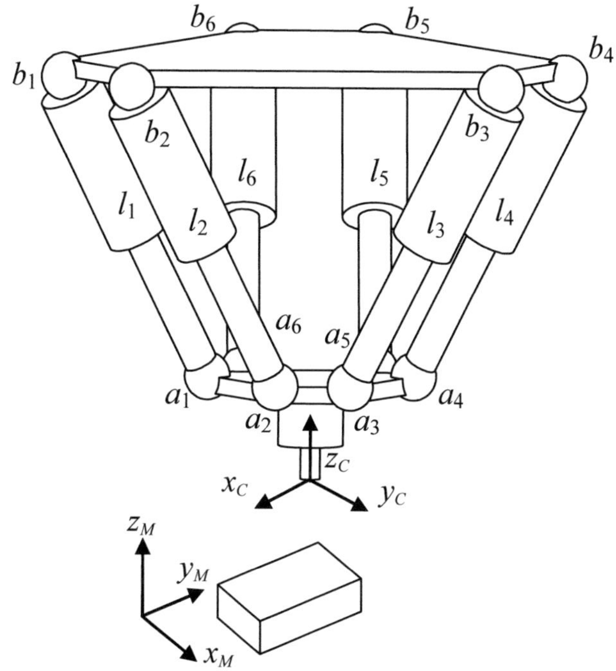

Fig. 4. Typical Construction of a hexapodic machine tools.

where **F** and **T** are respectively the resultants 3-D external force and torque systems applied to the movable platform. This result suggests that to support external force and torque along arbitrary directions, $\mathbf{J}_1$ and $\mathbf{J}_2$ must both have a rank three. Now to support these external force and torque resultants using bounded joint space forces, the condition numbers of $\mathbf{J}_1$ and $\mathbf{J}_2$ must be both as close to unity as possible.
An overall local performance measure *PM* can be obtained from the following relation

$$PM = w\, PM_1 + (1 - w)\, PM_2 \tag{8}$$

where w is a weighing factor in the range $[0 \cdots 1]$ which signify how much emphases is given to translational and rotational dexterities, and PM_1 and PM_2 are respectively performance measures for the translational motion and the rotational motion of the structure, and are defined as (Harib and Sharif Ullah, 2008, Stoughton and Arai, 1993).

$$PM_1 = V' \Big/ \int_{V'} \kappa(\mathbf{J}_1)\, dV \tag{9}$$

$$PM_2 = V' \Big/ \int_{V'} \kappa(\mathbf{J}_2)\, dV \tag{10}$$

In the previous equations, $\kappa(\cdot)$ is the condition number function and V' is the workspace which is a subset of the total reachable space of the mechanism V. PM will then be in the range $[0\cdots1]$, with 1.0 corresponding to the best possible performance, which in turn corresponds to a perfectly conditioned Jacobian matrix.

The workspace of PKMs is another design issue that needs careful attention due to the computational complexity involved. Algorithms proposed in the literature to determine the workspace of PKM structures use the geometric constraints of the structures, including maximum/minimum leg lengths, passive joint limits. The complexity of these computational methods varies depending on the constraints imposed. For example if the cross sectional variation hexapod legs is also considered as a factor to avoid leg collisions considerable computational requirement will be necessary (Conti et. al, 1998). If the considered design would ensure that the operation of the machine is far enough from possibility of leg collisions in the first place considerable design efforts could be saved.

Harib and Sharif Ullah (2008) used the axiomatic design methodology (Suh, 1990) to analyze the kinematic design of PKM structures. In terms of the kinematic functions of PKM structures and based on the aforementioned contemplation, the following basic Functional Requirements (FRs) were identified: (1) The mechanism should be able to support arbitrary 3-D system of forces i.e. PM1 should be as close to unity as possible. (2) The mechanism should be able to support arbitrary 3-D systems of torques i.e. PM2 should be as close to unity as possible. (3) The mechanism should be able to move the cutting tool through a desired workspace. (4) The mechanism should be able to orient the spindle at a desired range within the desired workspace. On the other hand, to achieve the FRs the following two Design Parameters (DPs) are often used: (1) Determine the lengths and strokes of the legs. (2) Determine the orientation of the legs relative to the fixed base and to the moving platform in the home position. From the perspective of AD this implies that the kinematic design of hexapodic machine tools is sort of coupled design. Therefore, gradual decomposition of FRs and DPs are needed to make the system consistent with the AD.

Figure 5 shows a 2-DOF planar parallel kinematics structure. The structure includes two extendable legs with controllable leg lengths l_1 and l_2 and three revolute joints a_1, a_2, and c. The controlled extension of the two legs places the end-effectors point c at an arbitrary position (x, y) in the x-y plane.

The way the function requirements are fulfilled is this design is by assembling the mechanism such that the two legs are orthogonal to each other at the central position of the workspace as shown in Figure 5. This result is coherent with the isotropic configuration that could be obtained for this mechanism (Huang et al., 2004). Away from that position the mechanism is not expected to deviate much from this condition for practical configuration if the limits of the leg lengths are appropriately selected. It is clear that arbitrary strokes and average lengths of the two legs can be selected while maintaining leg orthogonally condition by adjusting the position of b_1 and b_2.

The reachable space of the 2-DOF PKM of Figure 5 is bounded by four circular arc segments with radii $l_{1\text{-}max}$, $l_{1\text{-}min}$, $l_{2\text{-}max}$ and $l_{2\text{-}min}$ and centers b_1 and b_2. With the two legs normal to each other the workspace can be modified along any of the two orthogonal directions independent from the other.

An extension of the previous design method to three DOF planner PKM structures is shown in Figure 6. Selecting the reference point of the mechanism to be the concurrent attachment point of the two orthogonal legs serves the purpose of showing the validity of the previously established result of uncoupled design in terms of the previously defined FRs and DPs. As indicated on Figure 6, with this choice of reference point, the same workspace of the 2-DOF structure is obtained.

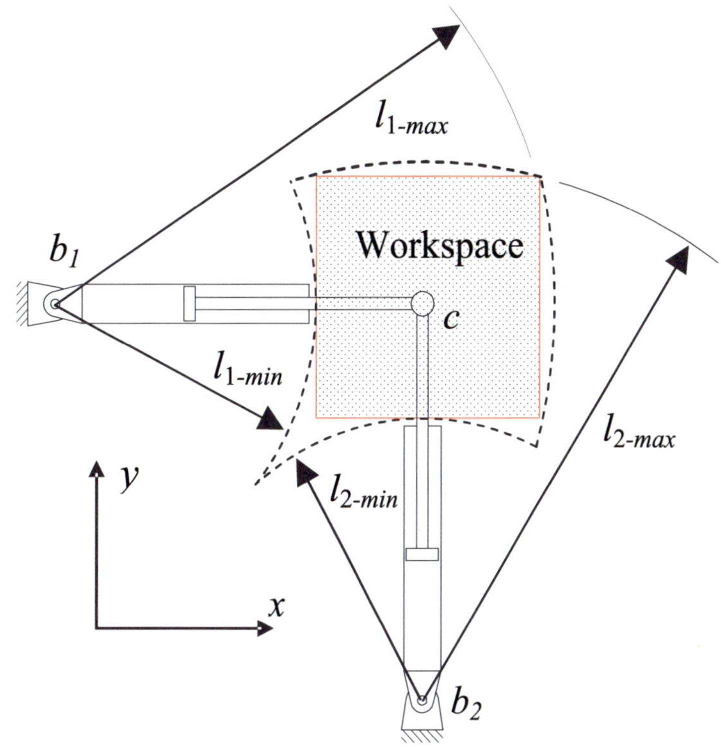

Fig. 5. A 2-DOF Planner PKM System (Harib and Sharif Ullah, 2008)

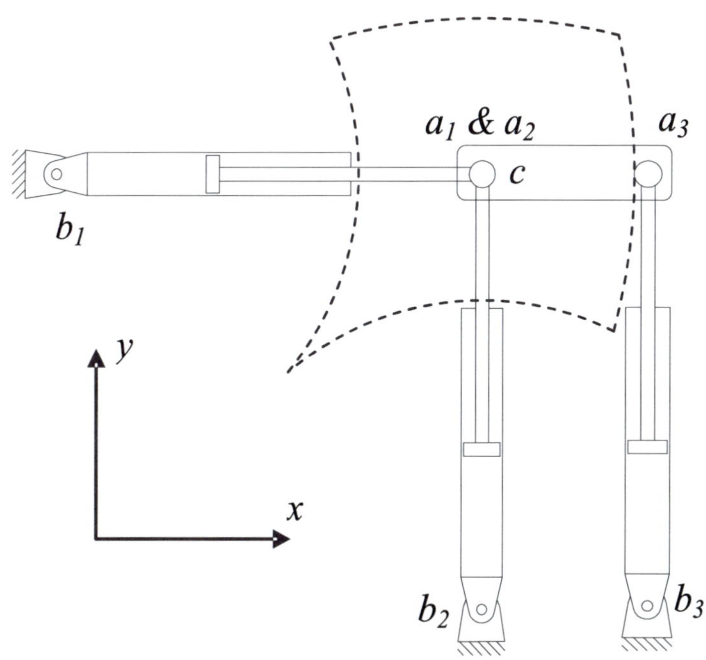

Fig. 6. A 3-DOF Planner PKM System (Harib and Sharif Ullah, 2008)

The previous 3-DOF PKM design of Figure 6 suggests extending the idea to a 6-DOF structure, as shown in Figure 7. The six legs of the suggested structure are arranged such that the idea remains the same (two parallel legs connected by a link and one orthogonal leg) in each of three mutually orthogonal planes. The purpose of the design is to support an arbitrary 6-DOF force and torque system.

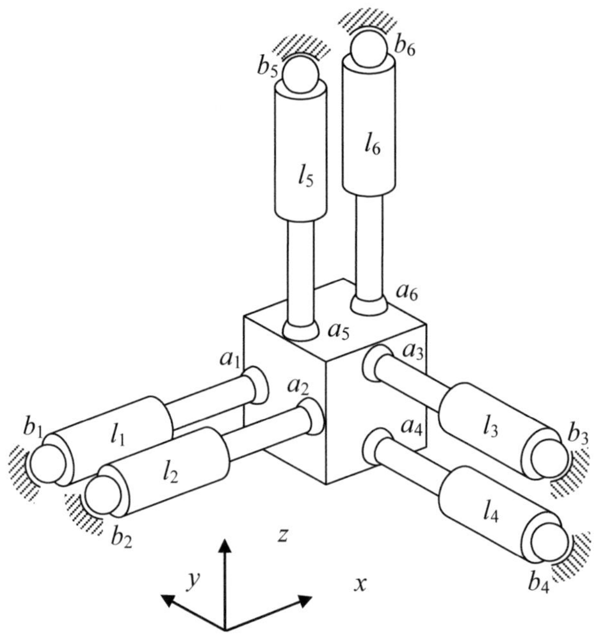

Fig. 7. A schematic of a 6-DOF spatial PKM (Harib and Sharif Ullah, 2008)

While the FRs' and DPs' of the axiomatic design methods are difficult to be decoupled here, this design of the 6 DOF mechanism is shown to be a logical extension from planner mechanisms designed with such design methodology.

3.2 Hybrid kinematic designs

Similar to the serial kinematic robotic design strategy, hybrid kinematic structures could be designed such the first three links and joints, forming the parallel structure, handle the gross positioning of the end-effector. The rest of joints and links could be made to form a concurrent serial kinematic structure that is responsible for orienting the end-effector. Thus this strategy decoupled two main functional requirements (FRs) of the mechanism and their design parameters (DPs). Now, while the serial kinematic part, which is responsible for the orientation of the end-effector, could be a standard wrest joint consisting concurrent revolute joints, the focus could bow be directed on the design of the parallel kinematic part which still requires considerable design attention. The decoupling of the design requirements reduces the design problem to a design of a three-degrees-of-freedom parallel kinematic spatial structure that position the concurrent wrest joint along the x, y and z axes. Although the design requirements on the orientation are not part of the design requirements of the parallel part of the mechanism, ability to support a system of transmitted torque is still part of the design requirements. This is in addition to the requirements of having ability to provide arbitrary motion along three directions and to support associated force system along these directions.

3.2.1 The Exechon mechanism

The Exechon machining center is based on a hybrid five degrees-of-freedom mechanism that consists of parallel and serial kinematic linkages (Zoppi et al., 2010). The parallel kinematic structure of the Exechon is an overconstrained mechanism with eight links and a total of nine joints; three prismatic joints with connectivity one, three revolute joints with connectivity one, and three universal joints with connectivity two. This mechanism is shown schematically in Figure 8.

The number of overconstraint (geometrical) conditions s is 3. These conditions require that the two prismatic joints l_1 and l_2 form a plane, and that the two axes of the joints a_1 and a_2 to be perpendicular to this plane, and the axis of joint a_3 be perpendicular to the axes of joints a_1 and a_2. The parameters of the underlying mechanism can be identified as: $L = 8$, $j = 9$, $\sum f_i$ =12 for all the nine revolute, prismatic and universal joints. The mobility of this mechanism is erroneously calculated by Equation 1 as $M = 0$, which indicates that the mechanism is a structure. Nevertheless, if the geometrical constraints involved in this mechanism are considered and Equation 3 is applied, the mobility is correctly calculated as $M = 3$. These three degrees of freedom obviously correspond to the three actuating linear motors. The overconstraints in this mechanism considerably reduce the required joints, which obviously improves the rigidity of the mechanism. However, the geometric constraints that result in reducing the mobility to three require structural design for the joints to bear the transmitted bending moments and torque components. This requirement is more stringent in the case of the prismatic joints of the three legs. These legs will not be two-force members as in the six DOF hexapodic mechanism and have to be designed to hold bending moments.

The parallel kinematic part can be viewed as a 2-DOF planner mechanism formed by the two struts l_1 and l_2 and the platform, which could be revolved about an axis (the axes of the base joints b_1 and b_2, shown as dashed line in Figure 8) via the actuation of the third strut l_3. To achieve 2-DOF in the planner mechanism, three overconstraints are required. As indicated before these overconstraints come as requirements on the axes of the revolute joints a_1 and a_2 to be normal to the plane formed by l_1 and l_2, and on the third revolute joint a_3 to be normal to the other two joints. Thus the projection of this strut onto the plane is constraining the rotational degree-of-freedom of the moving platform in the plane. This situation resembles the 2-DOF planner mechanism of Figure 2. When this projection onto the plane vanishes (i.e. when the angle between the third strut and the plane made by other two struts is 90 degree), the mechanism becomes singular (attains additional degree-of-freedom).

3.2.2 Alternative hybrid kinematic mechanism

In this section we demonstrate employoing the Axiomatic Design to evaluate a potential design of a 5-axes alternative hybrid kinematic machine tools mechanism consisting of a 3-DOF parallel kinematic structure and a 2-DOF wrest joint. Axiomatic design is a structured design methodology which is developed to improve design activities by establishing criteria on which potential designs may be evaluated and enhanced (Suh, 1990). The general function requirements (FRs) for the proposed hybrid mechanism can be listed as follows. The mechanism should 1) provide required positioning and orientation capabilities, 2) have adequate and consistent dexterity throughout the workspace, 3) have good structural rigidity, and 4) have a large and well shaped workspace. The design parameters (DPs) that could be used to achieve the function requirements concerning the parallel kinematic part of the mechanism include 1) the configuration of the wrest joint, 2) the configuration of the parallel kinematic mechanism, 3) the types of the end joints, and 4) the strokes and average lengths of the legs.

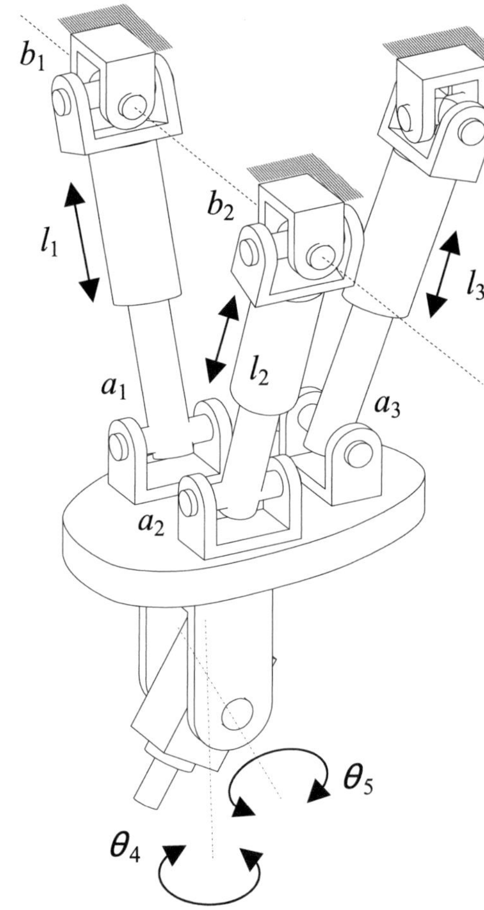

Fig. 8. A schematic of the Exechon hybrid kinematic machine tools mechanism

Based on the discussion in the previous sections and the axiomatic design formulation previously used for planner parallel kinematic structures (Harib and Sharif Ullah, 2008) a kinematic design of an alternative design for a hybrid kinematic machine tools mechanism is proposed. A schematic of the proposed mechanism is depicted in Figure 9 below. The parallel kinematic part has three perpendicular struts when the mechanism is at the center of the workspace, and consists of movable platform and three extendable struts. As shown in Figure 1, the first strut is rigidly connected to the platform, which in turn is connected to other two struts via revolute and universal joints. The struts are connected respectively to the machine frame via universal joints and a spherical joint with connectivity three. The number of overconstraint (geometrical) conditions s is 2. These conditions require that the two prismatic joints l_1 and l_2 form a plane and that the axis of joint a_2 to be perpendicular to this plane. Calculating the mobility using Equation 1 yields $M = 1$. However considering the overconstraints ($s = 2$), the mobility of the mechanism, as calculated by Equation 3, will be $M = 3$.

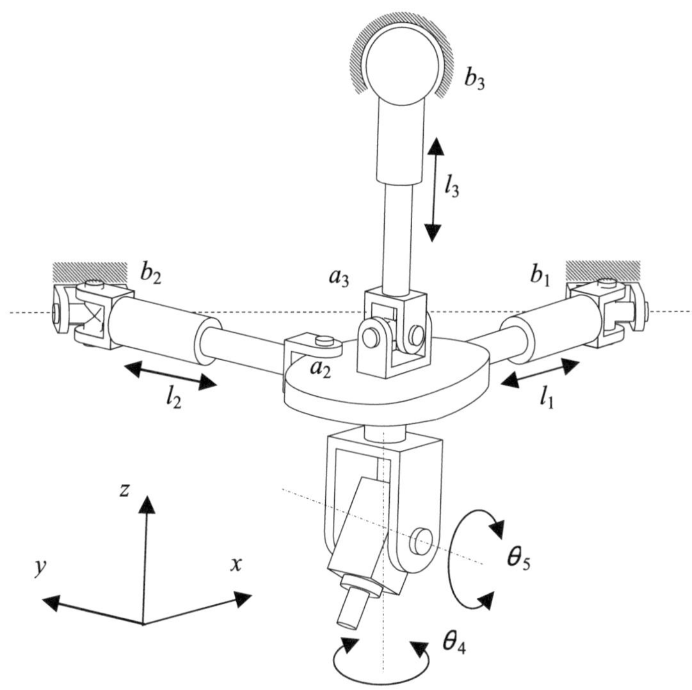

Fig. 9. A schematic of a proposed hybrid machine tools mechanism

In order to reach an optimum design, the Axiomatic Design FRs and DPs are grouped hierarchically. The design problem is also formulated such that the FRs are independent from each other (to fulfill the Independence Axiom), and the DPs are uncoupled at least partially (to fulfill the Information Axiom). Thus, the design strategy is directed to fulfill the FRs using uncoupled DPs first. Figure 10 shows main FRs for a hybrid kinematic mechanism design arranged hierarchically. The fundamental function requirement (FR1 = positioning and orientation capabilities) is split into two independent function requirements (FR11 and FR12) which can be addressed using independent design parameters. FR12 is split into three function requirements (FR121, FR122, FR123). For a given configuration of the parallel kinematic mechanism, the function requirements (FR121, FR122, FR123) can be addressed using the following design parameters:

DP121*i*: the type of the *i*th platform end joint a_i

DP122*i*: the type of the *i*th base end joint b_i

DP123*i*: the stroke of *i*th leg $(l_{i\text{-}max} - l_{i\text{-}min})$

DP124*i*: average lengths of the *i*th leg $(l_{i\text{-}max} + l_{i\text{-}min})/2$

It is worth mentioning here that the joint axes resemble the five axes of the machine tools at the center of the workspace, and could be maintained to be close to this situation by proper design and choice of the leg strokes and mean lengths. Also as an alternative configuration, the 2-DOF wrest joint that hold the spindle could also be replaced by a 2-DOF rotary table, transferring the relative rotational motion to the workpiece. A redundant hybrid structure consisting of a hexapod machine tools and a 2-DOF rotary table is suggested and analyzed by Harib et al. (2007).

4. Conclusions

The considerable interest that is shifted to hybrid kinematic structures to exploit the advantageous features of the serial and parallel kinematic structures and avoiding their drawbacks has brought about some interest in overconstrained hybrid mechanisms. A study on the mobility of the three classes of mechanisms is presented and focuses on the mobility of overconstrained structures in view of their application in parallel and hybrid structures to reduce the number of passive joints. The mobility of the Exechon mechanism is analyzed and discussed as an example of a successful machine tools mechanism. The study of this mechanism reveals that its 3-DOF parallel kinematic part is a revolving 2-DOF planner mechanism. Strategies for kinematic designs of planner parallel mechanisms were developed and discussed based on the axiomatic design methodology. Optimum configurations for planner mechanisms were presented for 2-DOF planner mechanisms and were shown to be extendable to 3-DOF planner and spatial mechanisms by proper choice of joints and constraints. An alternative optimum parallel and hybrid mechanism is discussed and analyzed.

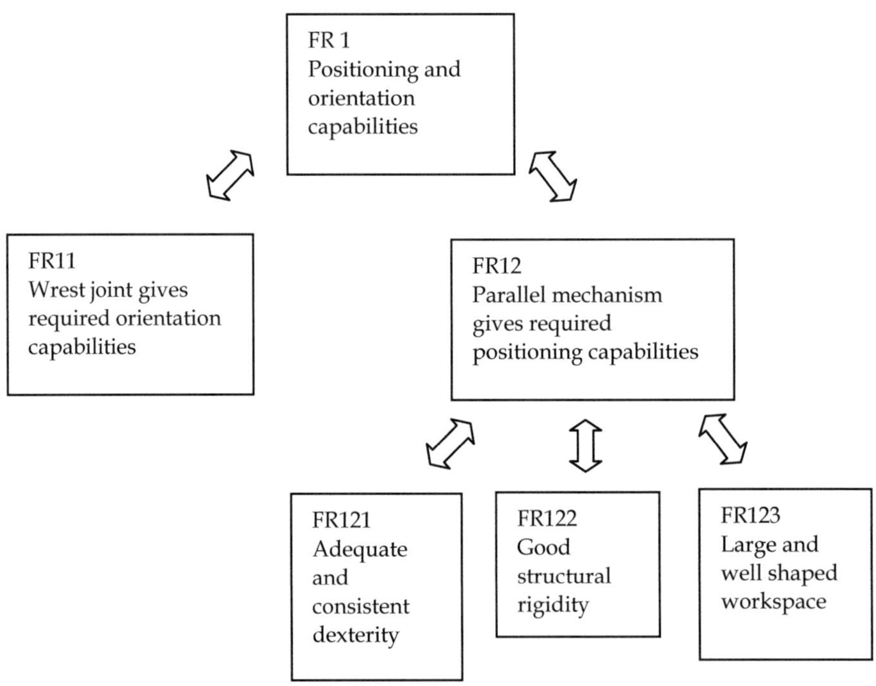

Fig. 10. Main Function Requirements of a hybrid design

5. Acknowledgment

The authors gratefully acknowledge the support of the Emirates Foundation (EF) under Grant No. 2008/052.

6. References

Bi, Z.M., Jin, Y., (2011) Kinematic modeling of Exechon parallel kinematic machine, Journal of Robotics and Computer-Integrated Manufacturing, Vol. 27, Issue 1, February 2011, 186-193

Bohez, E.L.J. (2002) Five-axis milling machine tool kinematic chain design and analysis Int. Journal of Machine Tools & Manufacture 42 Pages 505–520

Cretu, S.M., (2007) TRIZ applied to establish mobility of some mechanisms," Proceedings of the 12th IFToMM World Congress, Besancon, France, 18-21 June

Conti, J.P. Clinton, C.M., Zhang, G. and A. J. Wavering, A.J. (1998). Workspace Variation of a Hexapod Machine Tool, NISTIR 6135, National Institute of Standards and Technology, Gaithersburg, MD, March 1998.

Gogu, G., (2005) Mobility of mechanisms: a critical review," Mechanism and Machine Theory, Vol. 40, p. 1608-1097.

Gosselin, C. (1990). Determination of the Workspace of 6-DOF Parallel Manipulator, Journal of Applied Mechanical Design, 112, 331-336Luh, C., Adkins, F. Haung, E. and Qiu, C. (1996). Working Capapbility Analysis of Stewart Platform Manipulator, ASME Journal of Mechanical Design 118, 220-227.

Harib, K.H., Sharif Ullah, A.M.M. (2008), Axiomatic Design of Hexapod-based Machine Tool Structures, Reliability and Robust Design in Automotive Engineering, SAE/SP-2170: 331-337.

Harib, K.H, Sharif Ullah, A.M.M. and Hammami, H. (2007). A Hexapod-Based Machine Tool with Hybrid Structure: Kinematic Analysis and Trajectory Planning, International Journal of Machine Tools and Manufacture, 47, 1426-1432

Harib, K., Srinivasan, K. (2003) Kinematic and Dynamic Analysis of Stewart Platform-Based Machine Tool Structures, Robotica, 21, (5), 541-554

Huang, T., Li, Li, A., Chetwynd, D.G. and Whitehouse, D.J. (2004). Optimal Kinematic Design of 2-DOF Parallel Manipulators with Well-Shaped Workspace Bounded by a Specified Conditioning Index, IEEE Transactions on Robotics and Automation, 20(3), 538-543

Huang, T., Wang, J., Gosselin, C.M. and Whitehouse, D.J. (2000). Kinematic Synthesis of Hexapods with Specified Orientation Capability and Well-Conditioned Dexterity, Journal of Manufacturing Processes, 2 (1), 36-47.

Ionescu T.G., (2003) Terminology for mechanisms and machine science," Mechanism and Machine Theory, Vol. 38, p. 7-10

Mavroidis C. and Roth B. (1995) Analysis of Overconstrained Mechanisms, Journal of Mechanical Design, Transactions of the ASME, Vol. 117, pp. 69-74.

Norton, R. L., (2004), Design of Machinery, McGraw Hill

Stoughton, R. & Arai, T. (1993). A Modified Stewart Platform Manipulator with Improved Dexterity, IEEE Trans Robotics and Automation, 9 (2), pp. 166-173.

Suh, N.P. (1990). The Principles of Design, New York: Oxford University Press.

Tsai, K.Y. Lee, T.K. and Huang, K.D. (2006). Determining the workspace boundary of 6-DOF parallel manipulators, Robotica, 24(5), 605-611.

Waldron, K.J. and Kinzel, G.L. (1999) Kinematics, Dynamics, and Design of Machinery, John Wiley & Sons

Wang, L.-C.T. and Hsieh, J.-H. (1998). Extreme reaches and reachable workspace analysis of general parallel robotic manipulators, Journal of Robotic Systems 15(3), 145-159.

Zhang, D., Gosselin, C.M.(2002) Kinetostatic Analysis and Design Optimization of the Tricept Machine Tool Family, J. Manufacturing. Science and Engineering., August, Vol. 124, Issue 3, 725-733

Zoppi, M., Zlatanov, D., and Molfino, R. (2010) Kinematics Analysis of the Exechon Tripod, ASME 2010 International Design Engineering Technical Conferences and Computers and Information in Engineering Conference (IDETC/CIE2010), August 15–18, Montreal, Quebec, Canada

7

Design and Postures of a Serial Robot Composed by Closed-Loop Kinematics Chains

David Úbeda, José María Marín, Arturo Gil and Óscar Reinoso
Universidad Miguel Hernández de Elche
Spain

1. Introduction

The robot presented in this chapter is a new binary hybrid (parallel-serial) type climbing system composed by several closed-chains arranged in an open-chain. The originality of the robot resides in the possibility of combining several parallel modules to build a new configuration of the robot according to the intended application. In this chapter, one possible morphology will be covered, destinated to climb metallic cross-linked structures, but we will also study the kinematics and the structure of the simplest modules apart from the final robot.

Hybrid climbing robots are hard to find, but hybrid climbing robots with binary actuators are still less common. In our opinion, binary actuators are interesting, since they allow for an easier control of the robot: only two different positions need to be controlled. This advantage comes at a price, since less points in the workspace can be reached, but hereby, large motion workspace, small volume and multiple degrees of freedom will be some of the new challenges of this kind of robots (Lichter et al., 2002).

In the robot proposed in this chapter, the activation of every lineal actuator of the closed-loop generates a planar and rotational movement of the output link respect to the input one. Several parallel modules can be connected in a serial mode. In this sense, the robot is freely reconfigurable, thus, new modules (translational or rotational) can be added.

A great variety of applications can be reached with the final 2+2 closed-chain disposed in a serial mode proposed system.

As it was mentioned above, it is possible to build complex structures combining parallel modules. Attending some researches, it is not difficult to find many papers of climbing or walking robots (Qi et al., 2009; Nagakubo & Hirose, 1994; Aracil et al., 2006b), but mostly adopt serial mechanism, what makes them less robust and with compromised stability. However, few authors have researched about the use of the hybrid mechanisms to add the desired characteristics with a simple and sensor-less control (Lichter et al., 2002; Chen & Yeo, 2002; Lees & Chirikjian, 1996; Erdmann & Mason, 1988; Goldberg, 1989; Craig, 1989).

The mechanism proposed combines parallel modules to set up a climbing robot, in addition with improve the mentioned characteristics, to outfit the robot with best stability and strength.

Another main feature that contributes originality compared with the related works of similar robots, it is aimed to a discrete workspace. Also we will demonstrate that it is possible to reach enough points to accomplish the required application (climb metallic

structures for inspection and maintenance tasks, construction, petroleum, bridges, etc.), and to achieve similar characteristics according to usual robots destinated to these tasks.
In order to demonstrate that this robot could be used in a continuous workspace, and could be positioned in different planes and surfaces of the metallic structure, we will study the closed chain forward and inverse kinematics, and direct kinematics of the final system consisting of hybrid leg mechanism.
This chapter reviews related works, main important features and applications of some climbing and walking robots. A description of the geometry of a new developed climbing robot with a discrete hybrid (parallel-serial) moving mechanism composed by a closed kinematic chain and binary actuators will be explained. The schematic design of the robot and main postures will be also provided. Moreover, an analysis of the robot's workspace, forward and inverse kinematics of the parallel module, and forward kinematics of the complete serial robot will be also discussed.

2. Related work

Climbing and walking robots are common in industry applications, like as, maintenance activities of nuclear plants, oil refineries, bridges, high voltage towers, medical fields, endoscope devices, and surgical instruments in general. The applications mentioned above are practiced with some problems to access and with hazardous environmental conditions.
To accomplish these tasks, robots need some important features, as reliable or robust, to be able to move over 3D structures, including walls, ceilings, pipes or cylindrical structures (Reinoso et. al, 2001), and they also need to be adaptable into different terrains.
Parallel robots have good performance, and they are perfect to manage manipulation tasks with short manipulation cycles, high speeds and accelerations. These characteristics are very difficult to obtain in serial robots. However, the proposal system combines advantages of serial and parallel robots. For example, thanks to the linear actuators, a parallel robot has a high ratio of payload and deadweight, so using linear actuators is totally justified.
Another desirable characteristics of these robots are that they need powerful torque in the actuators, mainly if they use serial legs for climbing. Although our system uses serial legs for climbing, the combination with parallel modules does that the torque of the actuators is not needed to be very high.
Higher speed is a desirable characteristic, but it is reduced when using legs for climbing, however, in our system, velocity is not a problem because of the parallel modules that are used, similar to Stewart-Gough platforms.
Most common problem in the walking and climbing robots is how to negotiate the boundary of two plain surfaces such as convex or concave corners in 3D. In this paper, we propose a robot model that solves this problem in a right way, using hybrid legs.
The main purpose of this project was to design a very simple robot similar to the Stewart-Gough platform, but combining serial robot abilities that allowed this to do climbing tasks. Probably the most important task to solve in this robot is the control system. To solve this, it is proposed a binary actuation. The binary degrees of freedom in this system are quasi-exponential compared with serial robots, but the approach with a serial robot is increased too. As opposed, our system does not require feedback of any sensor, among other features. Some researchers have studied theses kind of binary actuation robots, but none of them has used hybrid serial-parallel technology.

Similar to parallel robots (Aracil et al., 2006a) this robot can climb the exterior and interior of tubes or metallic structures. According to the kind of structure, the end-effector and the base could carry magnetic foots or suction pads (Kim et al., 2005).
In this chapter, we do not dedicate attention to the fixation system of the end-effector and base of the robot, although a suction pad or magnetic feet are recommended. We are going to concentrate on the kinematics analysis and the postures it can achieve.

3. Schematic design of the robot

As it was introduced above, the main goal of this project was to assemble different parallel modules to set up some new more complex serial ones. All of the linear actuators will be binary, and they will work into ON (stretched)/OFF (shrunken) position, to accomplish a wide workspace.

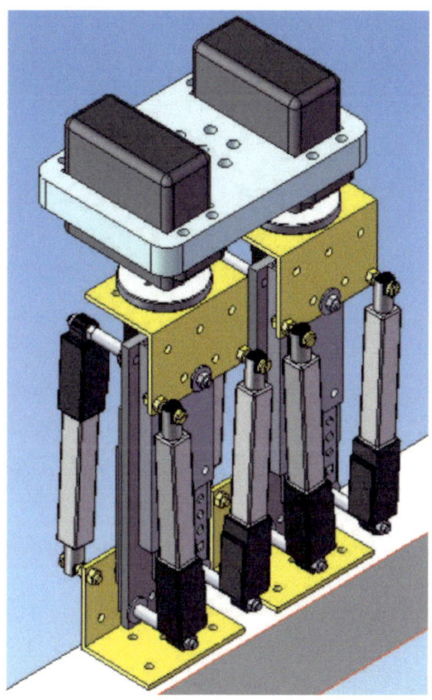

Fig. 1. Hybrid climbing robot

The purpose of this section will be the kinematics study of the closed-chain module, two closed-chain modules to set up a planar serial module, and the 2+2 closed-chain modules to set up a serial open-chain for three-dimensional movements. Another types of structures are possible to run up with the disposal and the number of the closed-chain modules.

3.1 Parallel module

If we focus in the study of a simple closed-chain module, the Figure 2(a) shows such structure, that is composed by two prismatic actuated joints, with two central sliders to limit the lateral movement, and in turn a free rotational joint in the upper side to provide a rotational movement of the end-effector of the module.
As a consequence of the use of a discrete workspace, the actuated joints will be binary, and these modules will have a d_1 translation and a 45 degrees rotation (Figure 2(b)), when their configuration will be P_1 ON, P_2 OFF or vice versa.

The Figure 2(c) refers to both actuators P_1 and P_2 set to ON.

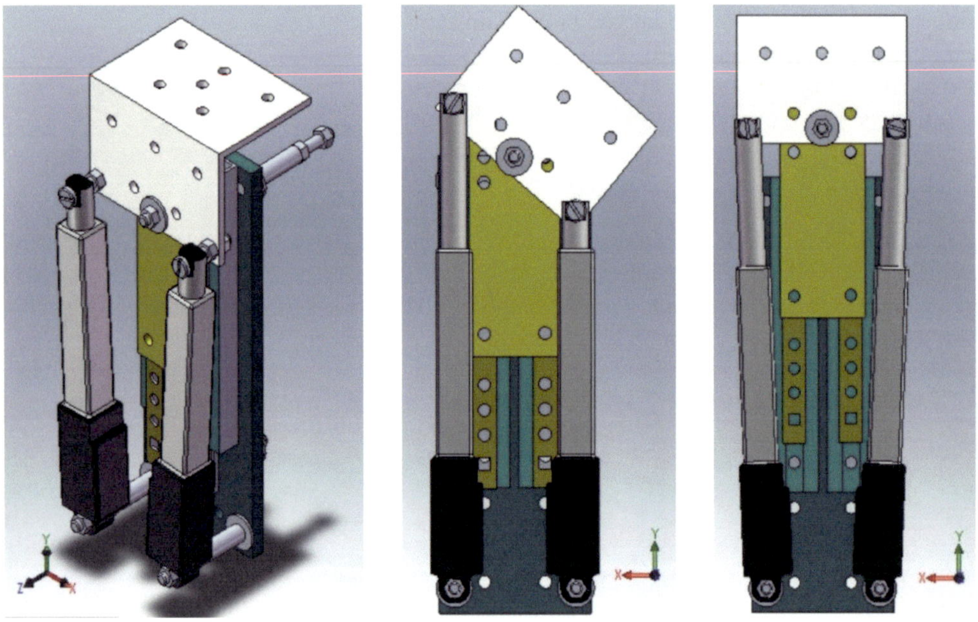

a) Isometric view of the parallel module

b) π/4 rotation: Actuator 2 ON

c) Actuator 1 and 2 ON

Fig. 2. Some views of the closed-chain module

Obviously, the different positions that this module is able to reach are given in Table 1:

Actuator 1	*Actuator 2*	*Translation*	*Rotation*
0	0	0	0°
0	1	d_1	45°
1	0	d_1	-45°
1	1	d_2	0°

Table 1. Positions from one parallel module

3.2 Two parallel modules disposed in a serial mode

In the Figure 3, two parallel modules can be observed. We have disposed them in a serial configuration, leaving one parallel module rotated 180 degrees and disposed in a mirror mode behind the other, to achieve robust and stable postures, and at the same time, it allows to set up 90 degrees rotations (figure 5(b)) of the end-effector around of the free joint axis.

All different positions that these two attached modules are able to reach are summarized in Table 2.

In Figure 4(a), we can observe that the four linear actuators are set to off, and therefore the minimum elongation of the module is obtained.

However, if we need to perform a translation around the axis of the actuators without performing a rotation of the end-effector, we could use the image configuration 4(b) with the 4 actuators set to ON. In that way, there will not be any movement induced by rotational

Actuator P1	*Actuator P2*	*Actuator P3*	*Actuator P4*	*Translation*	*Rotation*
0	0	0	0	0	0°
0	0	0	1	d_1	-45°
0	0	1	0	d_1	45°
0	0	1	1	d_2	0°
0	1	0	0	d_1	-45°
0	1	0	1	$d_1+ d_1$	-90°
0	1	1	0	$d_1+ d_1$	0°
0	1	1	1	$d_1+ d_2$	-45°
1	0	0	0	d_1	45°
1	0	0	1	$d_1+ d_1$	0°
1	0	1	0	$d_1+ d_1$	90°
1	0	1	1	$d_1+ d_2$	45°
1	1	0	0	d_2	0°
1	1	0	1	$d_2+ d_1$	-45°
1	1	1	0	$d_2+ d_1$	45°
1	1	1	1	$d_2+ d_2$	0°

Table 2. Positions from two parallel modules in a serial mode

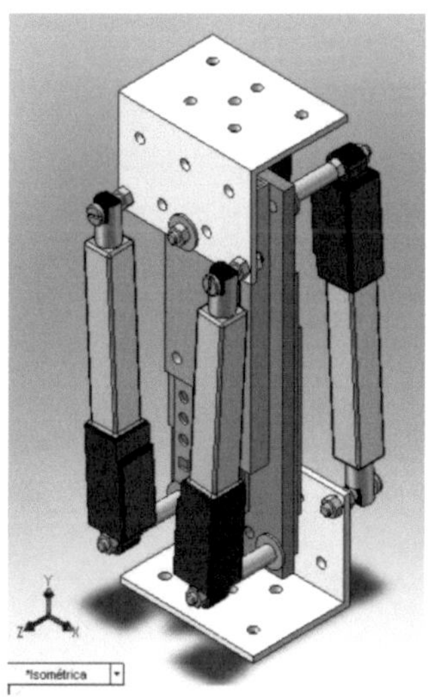

Fig. 3. Two parallel modules to draw up a serial structure

joints. In this pose, it can be observed that the central sliders indicate the distance d_2 between the base and the end-effector, obviously, they will be at its highest point of stretching.
However, it could be needed to reach some points in the workspace that are inclined at 90 degrees according to the base. In order to achieve this, and according to the Table 2, it could be observed in the Figure 5(b), that it can be obtained an inclination of 90 degrees, if the two mirror drives of each parallel module are switched alternately to ON and OFF.
In a similar way, if a 45 degrees inclination according to the base link was needed to reach, we could perform an actuation to ON of one of the linear actuators (figure 5(a)). This could be observed in the Table 2.

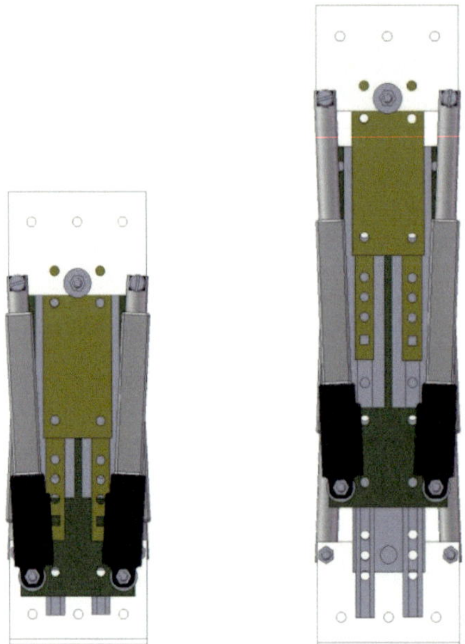

a) Minimum length. Frontal view.

b) Maximum length. Frontal view.

Fig. 4. Minimum and maximum prolongation of the open-chain module

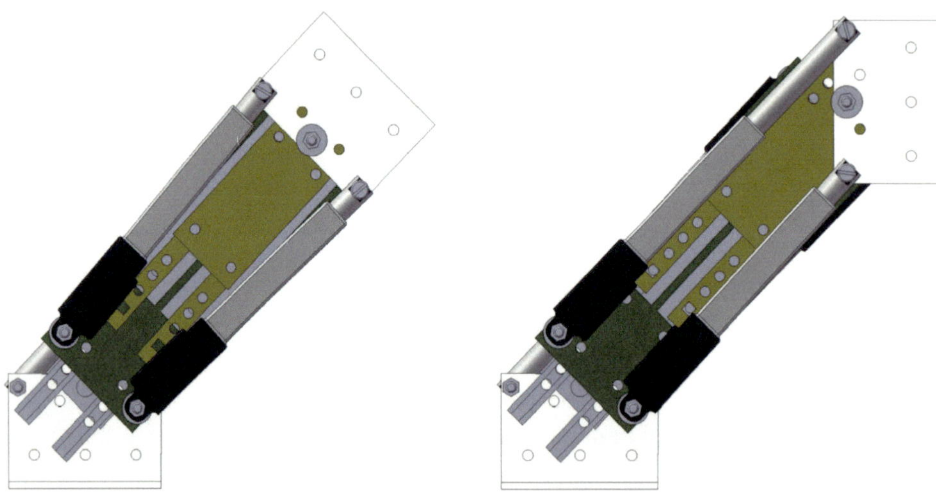

a) 45 degrees inclination

b) 90 degrees inclination

Fig. 5. Different postures of the open-chain module

3.3 2+2 Parallel modules arranged in a serial mode

As was mentioned before, the robot is composed of several parallel modules, and they are able to attach themselves in series to perform more complex structures in order to carry out a particular operation.

The robot in the Figure 1 consists of 2 + 2 parallel modules arranged to each other in a serial configuration and connected by a top link between two actuated rotational joints. According to this configuration, a three-dimensional movement of 90 and 180 degrees is possible to achieve around the rotational axis of the joint, as shown in the Table 3:

Actuator R1	*Actuator R2*	*Translation*	*Rotation*
0	0	0	0°
0	1	d_1	90°
1	0	d_1	-90°
1	1	d_2	180°

Table 3. Positions of the rotational actuator

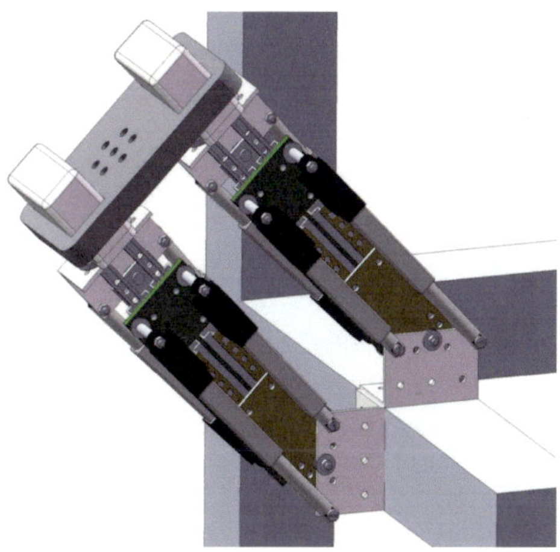

Fig. 6. Posture to a surface change of the structural frame

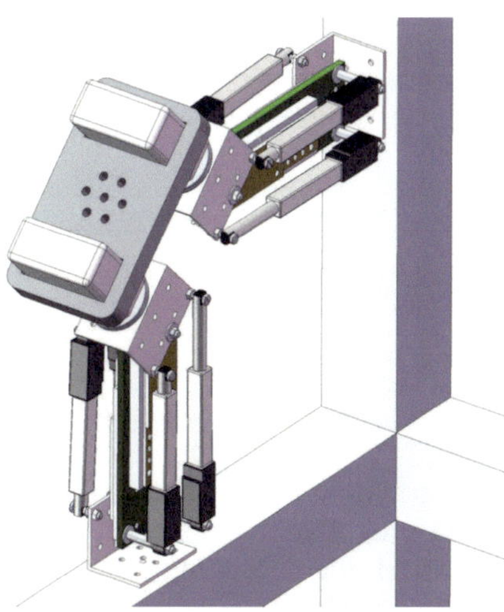

Fig. 7. Posture to evade a structural node: changing the plane

A basic problem that must be solved in the development of this robot, is that it should be able to get around structural nodes. According to the Figure 7, a posture to evade a structural node is shown. Also, the Figure 6 shows a posture to achieve a surface change.
Later in this chapter, we will discuss the kinematics of the modules, so we will not focus on all possible combinations of the actuators of the robot with 2+2 parallel modules arranged in a serial mode.

4. Closed-chain module

4.1 Degrees of freedom of the module

Figure 8(a) shows a CAD model of the closed-chain, and it is composed by two active links with variable length l_1 (link e_2 with e_3) and l_2 (link e_4 with e_5) , and two passive links, e_1 and e_6, with fixed length $2a_1$ and $2a_2$, respectively. A slider keeps the midpoint of the upper passive link e_6 on the line $x=a_1$. There is a fixed link e_1, four revolute joints (1, 3, 5 and 7) and two prismatic joints (2 and 6).
According to the Grübler criterion (Grübler, 1883), the number of active degrees of freedom is given by:

$$F = \lambda(n - j - 1) + \sum_i f_i \tag{1}$$

where:

- n, the number of links in the mechanism, including the fixed link (from e_1 to e_7):

$$n = 7 \tag{2}$$

- λ, degrees of freedom of the space (planar) in which the mechanism is intended to work:

$$\lambda = 3 \tag{3}$$

- j_1, number of prismatic joints

$$j_1 = 3 \tag{4}$$

- j_3, number of revolute joints

$$j_3 = 5 \tag{5}$$

- f_i, DoF permitted by revolute or prismatic joint i

$$f_i = 1 \tag{6}$$

replacing (2), (3), (4), (5), (6 in (1)

$$F = 3(7 - 8 - 1) + 5*1 + 3*1 = 2 \tag{7}$$

These Grübler criterion results could be represented with an equivalent model (figure 8(b)) composed by a prismatic joint plus a solidary revolute joint, that represents reliably the model of figure 8(a). In this model, the P part represents the 3D prismatic joint and the R part represents the 3D revolute joint. The total distance traveled by the slider is equivalent to the prismatic joint distance d of figure 8(a).

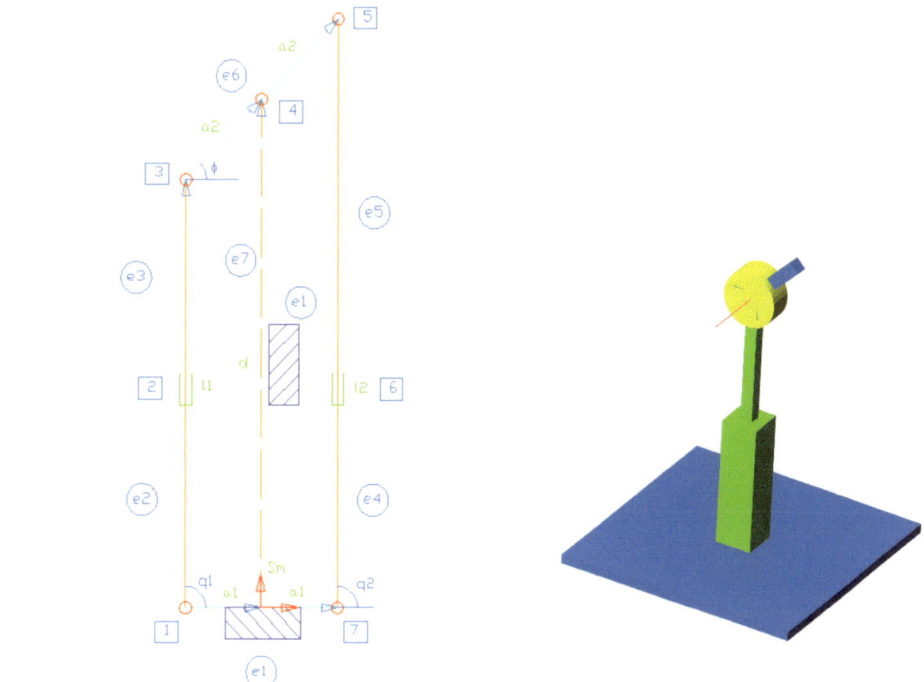

a) DoF: Grübler Criterion b) Equivalent Model

Fig. 8. Closed-chain module

4.2 Inverse kinematics of the parallel module

To study the inverse kinematics of the parallel module of the robot, a series of vectorial equations have been defined to estimate the position and orientation of the base according to the length of the linear actuators and the rotational angles of the rotational joints.

Inverse kinematics pretends to solve the position of the link e_6 of figure 8(a) according to a reference system S_m that is solidary to the ground link. It could be defined as a translation d and a rotation ϕ. In this way, inverse kinematics proposes to solve (l1, l2) as a function of (d, ϕ) parameters.

We could define a movement for the parallel module in different alternative ways. In the next one it is indicated that the mid point of the e_6 link should be at the position (a_1, d) according to the reference system S_m solidary to the ground link.

According to the figure 8(a), two vectorial equations are obtained:

$$\overrightarrow{a_1} + \vec{d} = \overrightarrow{a_2} + \overrightarrow{l_1} \tag{8}$$

$$\overrightarrow{a_1} + \overrightarrow{l_2} = \vec{d} + \overrightarrow{a_2} \tag{9}$$

where, a restriction on e_6 or d link can be observed, because this vector angle will be always 90° according to the ground link a_1. Through a vectorial decomposition of the equations (8), (9), (10) and (11) these new equations are obtained:

$$a_1 = a_2\cos(\phi) + l_1\cos(q_1) \tag{10}$$

$$d = l_1\sin(q_1) + a_2\sin(\phi) \tag{11}$$

$$a_1 + l_2\cos(q_2) = a_2\cos(\phi) \tag{12}$$

$$l_2\sin(q_2) = d + a_2\sin(\phi) \tag{13}$$

and with a new disposition of the equations:

$$a_1 = l_1\cos(q_1) + a_2\cos(\phi) \tag{14}$$

$$d = l_1\sin(q_1) + a_2\sin(\phi) \tag{15}$$

$$-a_1 = l_2\cos(q_2) - a_2\cos(\phi) \tag{16}$$

$$d = l_2\sin(q_2) - a_2\sin(\phi) \tag{17}$$

it could be obtained l_1 link length based on d and ϕ from (14) and (15) equations:

$$\left(a_1 - a_2\cos(\phi)\right)^2 = \left(l_1\cos(q_1)\right)^2 \tag{18}$$

$$\left(d - a_2\sin(\phi)\right)^2 = \left(l_1\sin(q_1)\right)^2 \tag{19}$$

where the addition of both of them:

$$\left(a_1 - a_2\cos(\phi)\right)^2 + \left(d - a_2\sin(\phi)\right)^2 = l_1^2\cos^2(q_1) + l_1^2\sin^2(q_1) \tag{20}$$

and in the next step we will find the value of l_1, in order that q_1 disappears from the equation:

$$l_1 = +\sqrt{\left(a_1 - a_2\cos(\phi)\right)^2 + \left(d - a_2\sin(\phi)\right)^2} \tag{21}$$

Likewise, for l_2:

$$l_2 = +\sqrt{\left(-a_1 + a_2\cos(\phi)\right)^2 + \left(d + a_2\sin(\phi)\right)^2} \tag{22}$$

Only positive solutions are of interest for (l_1, l_2). As well, looking at the equations, with a pair (d, ϕ), a unique pair (l_1, l_2) is obtained and, backwards, with (l_1, l_2) a unique pair (d, ϕ) is obtained too.

4.3 Forward kinematics of the parallel module

Forward kinematics problem has been solved with a numerical method based on least squares method.

The equations (14), (15), (16) and (17) don't allow to find the value of ϕ and d as a length l_1 and l_2 function, because q_1 and q_2 are themselves function of d and ϕ.

We are going to set out the Levenberg-Marquardt numerical method (Levenberg, 1944), (Marquardt, 1963) so the equations (14), (15), (16) and (17) should be redefined as:

$$a_1 = l_1 \cos(q_1) + a_2 \cos(\phi) \tag{23}$$

$$0 = l_1 \sin(q_1) + a_2 \sin(\phi) - d \tag{24}$$

$$-a_1 = l_2 \cos(q_2) - a_2 \cos(\phi) \tag{25}$$

$$0 = l_2 \sin(q_2) - a_2 \sin(\phi) - d \tag{26}$$

An optimization process could be defined with the next functions:

$$f_1(\vec{s}) = l_1 \cos(q_1) + a_2 \cos(\phi) \tag{27}$$

$$f_2(\vec{s}) = l_1 \sin(q_1) + a_2 \sin(\phi) - d \tag{28}$$

$$f_3(\vec{s}) = l_2 \cos(q_2) - a_2 \cos(\phi) \tag{29}$$

$$f_4(\vec{s}) = l_2 \sin(q_2) - a_2 \sin(\phi) - d \tag{30}$$

defining:

$$\vec{f} = \begin{bmatrix} f_1(\vec{s}) \\ f_2(\vec{s}) \\ f_3(\vec{s}) \\ f_4(\vec{s}) \end{bmatrix} \tag{31}$$

where the state vector $\vec{s}$ is defined as:

$$\vec{s} = \begin{bmatrix} d \\ \phi \\ q_1 \\ q_2 \end{bmatrix} \tag{32}$$

and the constraints vector:

$$\vec{y} = \begin{bmatrix} a_1 \\ 0 \\ -a_1 \\ 0 \end{bmatrix} \tag{33}$$

Wherewith, the problem is raised as a minimization of the function:

$$F(\vec{s}) = \sum_{i=1}^{4} \left(f_i(\vec{s}) - y_i \right)^2 \tag{34}$$

For the minimization, we could raise an initial solution $\vec{s}_0$ and update in the direction of the gradient $\frac{\partial J}{\partial s}$

$$\vec{s}_{k+1} = \vec{s}_k + \delta \quad (35)$$

with:

$$\delta = (JJ^T)^{-1} J^T (\vec{y} - \vec{f}) \quad (36)$$

where J is the Jacobian matrix of the robot.

For the algorithm converging, it must indicate an initial solution of the $\vec{s}$. An approximation in order to achieve good results is:

$$d_0 = \frac{l_1 + l_2}{2} \quad (37)$$

$$\phi_0 = \frac{l_2 + l_1}{2a_2} \quad (38)$$

$$q_{10} = \arctan \frac{d_0 - a_2 \sin \phi_0}{a_1 - a_2 \cos \phi_0} \quad (39)$$

$$q_{20} = \arctan \frac{d_0 + a_2 \sin \phi_0}{-a_1 + a_2 \cos \phi_0} \quad (40)$$

The Jacobian matrix is calculated as follows:

$$J = \begin{bmatrix} \frac{\partial f_1}{\partial d} & \frac{\partial f_1}{\partial \phi} & \frac{\partial f_1}{\partial q_1} & \frac{\partial f_1}{\partial q_2} \\ \frac{\partial f_2}{\partial d} & \frac{\partial f_2}{\partial \phi} & \frac{\partial f_2}{\partial q_1} & \frac{\partial f_2}{\partial q_2} \\ \frac{\partial f_3}{\partial d} & \frac{\partial f_3}{\partial \phi} & \frac{\partial f_3}{\partial q_1} & \frac{\partial f_3}{\partial q_2} \\ \frac{\partial f_4}{\partial d} & \frac{\partial f_4}{\partial \phi} & \frac{\partial f_4}{\partial q_1} & \frac{\partial f_4}{\partial q_2} \end{bmatrix} = \begin{bmatrix} 0 & -a_2 \sin \phi & -l_1 \sin q_1 & 0 \\ -1 & a_2 \cos \phi & l_1 \cos q_1 & 0 \\ 0 & a_2 \sin \phi & 0 & -l_2 \sin q_2 \\ -1 & -a_2 \cos \phi & 0 & l_2 \sin q_2 \end{bmatrix} \quad (41)$$

In the performed tests in order to solve forward kinematics, the algorithm converges to the correct solution in only two iterations, with an F<0.0001 error.

Others ways to find the value of δ could be probed, like:

$$\delta = (JJ^T + \lambda I)^{-1} J^T (\vec{y} - \vec{f}) \quad (42)$$

where λ permits to regulate the speed as the function converges. Another way is:

$$\delta = (JJ^T + \lambda diag(J^T J))^{-1} J^T (\vec{y} - \vec{f}) \quad (43)$$

this is known as the Levenberg-Marquardt algorithm.

5. Forward kinematics of the open-chain module

According to the Subsection 3.3 a 2+2 parallel modules disposed in a serial structure could be set up. We are going to start from a complete serial model of the robot. The Figure 1 shows this set up of the robot. An equivalent model is shown in the Figure 9.

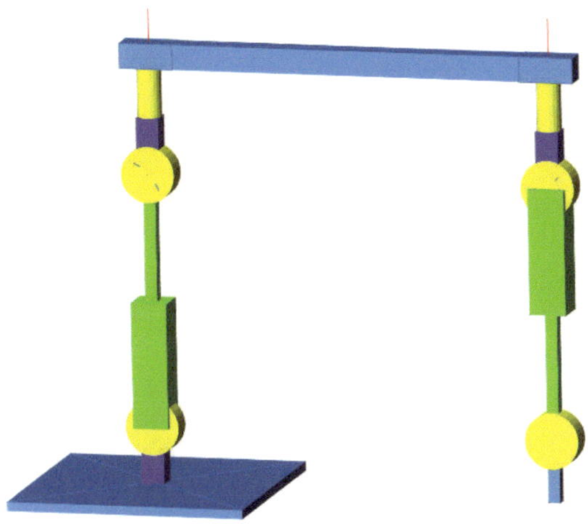

Fig. 9. 3D model of the serial robot

To solve forward kinematics of the open-chain, Denavit-Hartenberg algorithm (Denavit & Hartenberg, 1955; Uicker et al., 1964; Hartenberg & Denavit, 1964) has been used. In order to solve transformation matrices, *The Robotics Toolbox for Matlab* (Corke, 1996) has been used. Firstly, and following D-H convention, we could establish the coordinate axes as follows in the Figure 10. Secondly, the transformation matrix will be solved:

$$^{0}T_1 = \begin{bmatrix} -\sin\phi_1 & 0 & \cos\phi_1 & 0 \\ \cos\phi_1 & 0 & \sin\phi_1 & 0 \\ 0 & 1 & 0 & H_1 \\ 0 & 0 & 0 & 1 \end{bmatrix} \tag{44}$$

$$^{1}T_2 = \begin{bmatrix} 1 & 0 & 0 & 0 \\ 0 & 0 & 1 & 0 \\ 0 & -1 & 0 & L_2 \\ 0 & 0 & 0 & 1 \end{bmatrix} \tag{45}$$

$$^{2}T_3 = \begin{bmatrix} \cos\phi_3 & 0 & \sin\phi_3 & 0 \\ \sin\phi_3 & 0 & -\cos\phi_3 & 0 \\ 0 & 1 & 0 & 0 \\ 0 & 0 & 0 & 1 \end{bmatrix} \tag{46}$$

$$ {}^{3}T_{4} = \begin{bmatrix} \cos\phi_4 & -\sin\phi_4 & 0 & \cos\phi_4 * H_4 \\ \sin\phi_4 & \cos\phi_4 & 0 & \sin\phi_4 * H_4 \\ 0 & 0 & 1 & 0 \\ 0 & 0 & 0 & 1 \end{bmatrix} \tag{47} $$

$$ {}^{4}T_{5} = \begin{bmatrix} \cos\phi_5 & 0 & -\sin\phi_5 & 0 \\ \sin\phi_5 & 0 & \cos\phi_5 & 0 \\ 0 & -1 & 0 & 0 \\ 0 & 0 & 0 & 1 \end{bmatrix} \tag{48} $$

$$ {}^{5}T_{6} = \begin{bmatrix} \cos\phi_6 & 0 & -\sin\phi_6 & 0 \\ \sin\phi_6 & 0 & \cos\phi_6 & 0 \\ 0 & -1 & 0 & 0 \\ 0 & 0 & 0 & 1 \end{bmatrix} \tag{49} $$

$$ {}^{6}T_{7} = \begin{bmatrix} 1 & 0 & 0 & 0 \\ 0 & 0 & -1 & 0 \\ 0 & 1 & 0 & L_6 \\ 0 & 0 & 0 & 1 \end{bmatrix} \tag{50} $$

$$ {}^{7}T_{8} = \begin{bmatrix} \cos\phi_8 & 0 & -\sin\phi_8 & 0 \\ \sin\phi_8 & 0 & \cos\phi_8 & 0 \\ 0 & -1 & 0 & 0 \\ 0 & 0 & 0 & 1 \end{bmatrix} \tag{51} $$

Below, the Table 4 indicates the D-H Parameters of the 8 DoF of the model:

Joint	ϕ	d	a	α
1R	ϕ_1+90°	H_1	0	90°
2R	0	L_2	0	-90°
3R	ϕ_3	0	0	90
4R	ϕ_4	0	H_4	0
5R	ϕ_5	0	0	-90
6R	ϕ_6	0	0	-90
7R	0	L_6	0	90
8R	ϕ_8	0	0	-90

Table 4. D-H Parameters table of the serial model

6. Robot workspace

A preliminary study of the workspace that could reach a set up of 2+2 parallel modules arranged in a serial mode, with actuated rotational joints, have been performed. The goal was to check if it was able to climb a three-dimensional cross-linked structure.

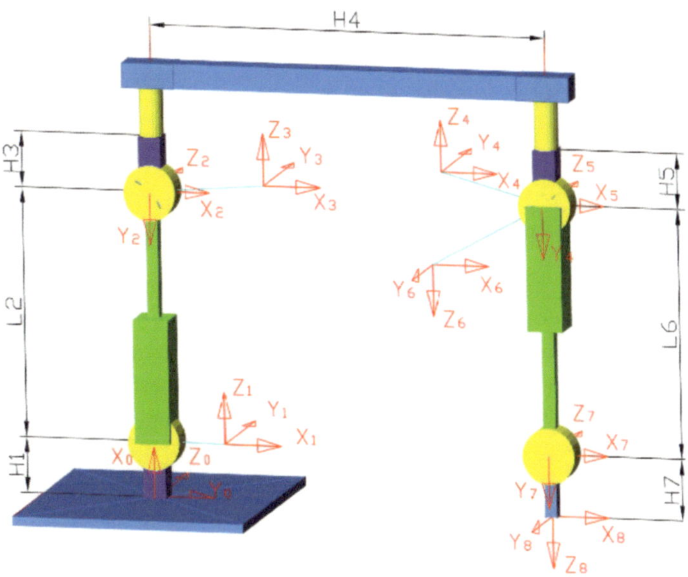

Fig. 10. 3D model of the serial robot with D-H convention axis

For one of the possible workspaces, some of the mathematical combinations of the robot actuators have been obtained, and a vector with all of them has been generated. This vector has been used to obtain different final points of the end-effector. Therefore, every element of the vector will be every final point of the previously described.
We have obtained a 2^{10} elements vector (Figure 11) as a result of the ten joints of the real model. In this vector, the interferences between links were not taken into consideration.
On the other hand, a cross-linked structure and a robot model have been simulated through SolidWorks. The goal was to check if the robot was able to reach enough workspace points and, at the same time, to perform a plane change in the cross-linked structure, and all of this has been shown in the Figures 6 and 7 with the simulated model.

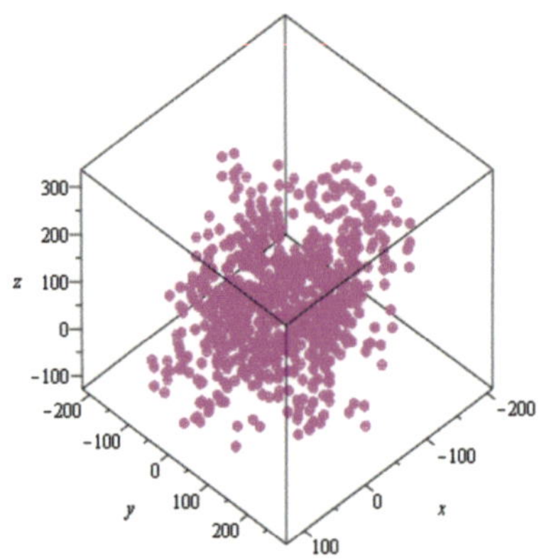

Fig. 11. 1024 points work space

7. Conclusions

Some years ago, new robotic devices with a large number of degrees of freedom and binary actuators were developed to achieve a large motion workspace, to be capable of large fine motion, and have a small-stowed volume. Applications as inspection and maintenance tasks require them to adapt the robot to this kind of hostile environment.

In this way, a new reconfigurable binary climbing robot with closed-chains disposed in an open-chain architecture, has been presented.

Related works has been reviewed at the Section 2, as well as important features and applications of some climbing and walking robots.

Sometimes, the kinematics solution of parallel mechanisms requires using redundant sensors to establish a control loop because it becomes quite complicated. In this chapter, a binary actuators solution is presented, so a sensor-less feature is included.

Linear actuators are directly connected to the base and to the end-effector of the parallel modules, so these actuators are at the same time structural elements of the complete serial robot, and they work in a simultaneous way, which gives them the ability to handle loads much greater than its own weight.

The schematic design of the robot, description of the geometry and main postures have been also provided in the Section 3. In this Section, also has been studied in an independent way the parallel module, the two parallel modules disposed in a serial mode, and the complete robot composed by 2+2 Parallel modules arranged in a serial mode.

Moreover, an analysis of the forward and inverse kinematics of the parallel module, and forward kinematics of the complete serial robot are discussed in the Sections 4 and 5.

Finally the discrete workspace of the robot has been represented in the Section 6.

Future works will consist on determine the inverse kinematics solution of the serial robot, to implement the control system and applying path-planning algorithms to move the robot around of the cross-linked structure.

8. References

Aracil, R.; Saltaren, R. & Reinoso, O. (2006a). A climbing parallel robot. *IEEE Robotics & Automation Magazine,* (March 2006), pp. 16–22, ISSN 1070-9932

Aracil, R.; Saltaren, R.; Sabater, J. & Reinoso, O. (2006b). Robots paralelos: Máquinas con un pasado para una robótica del futuro. *Revista Iberoamericana de automática e informática industrial,* Vol.3, No.1, (January 2006), pp. 16–28, ISSN 1697-7912

Chen, I.M. & Yeo, S. H. (2002). Locomotion and navigation of a planar walker based on binary actuation, *Proceedings of the IEEE International Conference on Robotics and Automation*, pp. 329-334, ISBN 0-7803-7272-7, Washington DC, USA, May, 2002

Corke, P. (1996). A robotics toolbox for MATLAB. *IEEE Robotics and Automation Magazine* Vol.3, No.1, (March 1996), pp: 24–32, ISSN 1070-9932

Craig, J. J. (1989). *Introduction to Robotics : Mechanics and Control* (2nd edition), Prentice-Hall, ISBN 9780131236295

Denavit, J. & Hartenberg, R. S. (1955). A kinematic notation for lower-pair mechanisms based on matrices. *Journal of Applied Mechanics,* Vol.86, pp. 215–221

Erdmann, M. A. & Mason, M. T. (1988). An exploration of sensor-less manipulation. *IEEE Journal of Robotics and Automation,* Vol.4, (August 1988), pp. 369–379

Goldberg, D. (1989). *Genetic algorithms in search, optimization, and Machine learning,* Addison-Wesley, ISBN 0201157675

Grübler, M. (1883). Allgemeine Eigenschaften der ZwanglŁufigen ebenen kinematischen Ketten. *Part I: Zivilingenieur,* Vol.29, pp. 167-200

Hartenberg, R.S. & Denavit, J. (1964). *Kinematic Synthesis of Linkages*, McGraw-Hill, ISBN 978-0070269101, New York

Kim, H.; Kang, T.; Loc, V. G. & Choi, H. R. (2005). Gait planning of quadruped walking and climbing robot for locomotion in 3d environment, *Proceedings of the IEEE International Conference on Robotics and Automation,* pp. 2733–2738, ISBN 0-7803-8914-X, Barcelona, Spain, April, 2005

Lees, D. S. & Chirikjian, G. S. (1996). A combinatorial approach to trajectory planning for binary manipulators, *Proceedings of the IEEE International Conference on Robotics and Automation,* pp. 2749-2754, ISBN: 0-7803-2988-0, Washington DC, USA, April 22-28, 1996

Levenberg, K. (1944). A method for the solution of certain non-linear problems in least squares. *The Quarterly of Applied Mathematics,* Vol.2, (July 1944), pp. 164-168

Lichter, M. D.; Sujan, V. A. & Dubowsky, S. (2002). Computational issues in the planning and kinematics of binary robots, *Proceedings of the IEEE International Conference on Robotics and Automation,* pp. 341–346, ISBN 0-7803-7272-7, Washington DC, USA, May, 2002

Marquardt, D. (1963). An algorithm for least-squares estimation of nonlinear parameters. *SIAM Journal on Applied Mathematics,* Vol.11, No.2, pp: 431-441, ISSN 431-41

Nagakubo, A. & Hirose, S. (1994). Walking and running of the quadruped wall-climbing robot, *Proceedings of the IEEE International Conference on Robotics and Automation,* pp. 1005–1012, ISBN 0-8186-5330-2, Washington DC, USA, May 8-13, 1994

Qi, Z.; Wang, H.; Huang, Z. & Zhang, L. (2009). Kinematics of a quadruped/biped reconfigurable walking robot with parallel leg mechanisms, *ASME/IFToMM International Conference on Reconfigurable Mechanisms and Robots*, pp. 558–564, ISBN 978-88-89007-37-2, London, UK, June 22-24, 2009

Reinoso, O.; Saltaren, R.; Aracil, R.; Almonacid, M. & Perez, C. (2001). Avances en el desarrollo de un robot trepador de estructuras cilíndricas, *XXII Jornadas de Automática*, ISBN 84-699-4593-9, Barcelona, Spain, September, 2001

Uicker, J. J.; Denavit, J. & Hartenberg, R. S. (1964). An interactive method for the displacement analysis of spatial mechanisms. *Journal of Applied Mechanics ASME*, Vol.86, pp: 215–221

8

A Reactive Anticipation for Autonomous Robot Navigation

Emna Ayari, Sameh El Hadouaj and Khaled Ghedira
High Institute of Management, Tunis
Tunisia

1. Introduction

Nowadays, mobile robots are expected to carry out various tasks in all kinds of application fields ranging from manufacturing plants, transportation, nursing service, resource or underwater exploration. In all these applications, robots should navigate autonomously in uncertain and dynamic environments in order to achieve their goals. So, the most current challenge in the development of autonomous robot control systems is making them respond intelligently to changing environments. Navigation in such environments involves many mechanisms such as: object detection, perception, internal building model, decision making, prediction of the future state of the environment and on-line navigation. To attend its goal safely, the robot should minimise interaction with other actors in order to avoid conflict situations. Generally, this problem comes up when many robots and/or actors would have access to the same space at the same time. In this case, the control of autonomous robotic navigation for conflict resolution has been widely studied. Some researchers have been focused on navigation in dynamic environments, where either reactive systems (producing real time behaviour), deliberative systems (introduce reasoning and need much more time to calculate a suitable decision) or hybrid systems (combine deliberative and reactive approaches) have been used in order to attend a known goal.

Typically, reactive systems are used to deal with simple problems (detect an obstacle, go away from an obstacle, follow a wall, etc.). Nevertheless, reactive systems are typically less affected by errors and do not require an explicit model of the environment in order to navigate inside an unknown space. Furthermore, they usually deal only with local information that may be captured at real time. However, in reactive systems, the robot can be derived to a conflict situation with other actors because they ignore prediction and reasoning in the decision process. To face this problem, global planning approaches are used. They consist of elaborating a global plan from beginning state to goal state. These approaches need prior complete information about the state of the environment, so they do not take into account the environment uncertainty. So, in more complex situations, hybrid approaches are used. They combine reactive approaches according to a higher level in order to include anticipation of the state of the environment in the decision process. In these cases, low level control operates in a reactive way (local navigation) whereas high level systems tend to be deliberative. It provides, at each step, a partial moving plan to the robot. But these systems are complex because they need much more time to calculate or to update a suitable trajectory toward a predefined goal. In this situation, it is interesting to introduce prediction

in reactive schemas, without using planning techniques, in order to consider the environment's evolution in the future.
To deal with uncertainty, autonomous navigation involves using systems for navigation control that must be not too computationally expensive, as this would result in a sluggish response. In this case, we choose the fuzzy logic technique because it is faster when the frequency of the environment's changes is high.
In the field of multi-agent systems, several works have encouraged researchers to develop models simulating robot's behaviours in order to achieve a known target (Posadas et al., 2008). They are more flexible and fault tolerant as several simple agents are easier to handle and cheaper to build. Indeed, the term "agent" has been defined as hardware or a software system with certain properties such as autonomy, social ability, reactivity and pro-activity (Ferber, 1995). In fact, there are similarities between robot and agent because they share the same characteristics. So, the mapping from a robot to an agent seems straightforward because each robot represents a physical entity, independent from other robots, with a specific task.
In this paper, we present a reactive anticipation model based on fuzzy logic that takes into account: (1) the reactive navigation in an environment composed of local minimum and moving obstacles, and (2) the anticipation of blocking situations and the prediction of the nature, the velocity and the position of obstacles in the future. This information is used to predict conflict situations without using a motion planning method. In order to validate our work, we evaluate our approach by simulating various scenarios. We also give a comparative study between results obtained by our model and those of some other approaches.
In the remainder of the article, we give, in section 2, an overview of the existing approaches for conflict resolution applied to autonomous robot navigation. In section 3, we present the most used techniques to deal with the uncertainty of perception and we justify our choice of the fuzzy logic method. In section 4, we describe our model that combines reactivity with anticipation in order to deal with the problem of conflict resolution without using a motion planning. In Section 5, we present our experimental results. Finally, we conclude in section 6 and we give perspectives for this work.

2. Existing approaches for conflict resolution

When navigation occurs in an environment that is totally or partially unknown or even dynamically changing, higher degree of autonomy for a mobile robot is required. Thus, a mobile robot should be able to take decisions on-line and to minimise conflict situations in such uncertain and dynamic environments using only sensors' limited information.
In this context, a wide range of approaches have been adopted to suggest solutions to the problem of space conflict when a robot shares the same environment with other actors.

2.1 Reactive approach

Many reactive approaches have been proposed to resolve the problem of autonomous robot navigation. In the following, we mention the most important among them.

- Potential Fields (Huang et al., 2006; Khatib, 1986): this approach relies on creating an artificial repulsion field around obstacles and an attraction field around the goal.
- Vector Field Histogram (Ulrich & Borenstein, 2000): it uses a heading dependent histogram to represent the obstacle's density. So, the robot can move in the direction where there are less obstacles in order to minimise its interaction with them.

- Dynamic Window (Fox et al., 1997) and Curvature Velocity (Simmons, 1996): they search a space of the robot's translational and rotational velocities. Obstacles near the robot are transformed into this space by eliminating all commanded velocities that would cause a collision within a certain time period. Both these methods take into account the kinematics and the dynamics of the robot. Commanded velocities are chosen based on an objective function that considers both progress towards the goal and robot safety.
- Nearness Diagram (Minguez & Montano, 2000): it consists in analysing a situation from two polar diagrams. One diagram is used to extract information of environmental characteristics and identify the immediate goal valley. The second diagram is used to define the safety level between the robot and the obstacles by identifying the closest one.
- Elastic Bands (Quinlan & Khatib, 1993): this method modifies the trajectory of the robot, originally provided by a planner, by using artificial forces which depend on the layout of the obstacles in the way.
- Behaviour-based methods (Jing et al., 2003; Langer et al., 1994): they define fundamental behaviour sets and establish mappings between sensors' information under different situations and reactive behaviours of the mobile robot. The reactive behaviour of the robot can be regarded as a weighted sum of these fundamental behaviours or can be chosen from the behaviour set according to an evaluation function.
- The Velocity Obstacles method (Fiorini & Shiller, 1998): the moving obstacle is transformed into a velocity obstacle. This approach uses the distance between robot and obstacle to minimise conflict at real time. It is considered as a mapping between sensory data and control commands without introducing reasoning in the decision process.

The main drawback of these strategies is that the robot gets into an infinite loop or local minimum when it is moving among multiple obstacles or in conflict situations when it shares the same resource with moving obstacles. To overcome this problem, many methods are proposed. We mention:

- Memory state method that uses a state memory strategy (Zhu & Yang, 2004). The variables from which this method makes ultimate decisions are: "the distance between the robot and the target" and "the distance between the robot and the nearest obstacle".
- Minimum risk approach is based on trial-return behaviour phenomenon (Omid et al., 2009; Wang & Liu, 2005).
- Virtual wall method directs the robot away from the dead-end by placing a virtual wall that bars the limit cycle path (Ordonez et al., 2008). However, these strategies do not take into account the dynamic nature of the environment and the uncertainty of perception. So the robot can be driven into dangerous or conflict situations.

2.2 Global planning approach

Hence, other approaches applied in dynamic environments are proposed with the idea of combining the reactive techniques with global planning methods (Stachniss & Burgard, 2002). At the beginning, a complete plan from present state to goal state is computed. These approaches need prior complete information about the state of the environment, so they do not take into account the uncertainty.

To face this limit, deliberative approaches are appeared. They use a global world model provided by user input or sensory information to generate appropriate actions for the mobile robot to reach the target (Pruski & Rohmer, 1997). This kind of approach enables prediction and reasoning in the decision process by considering the current information and the past information (Nilsson, 1980; Sahota, 1994). The deliberative control architecture comprises three modules: sensing, planning and action modules. First, robot sense it's surrounding and creates a world model of static environment by combining sensory information. Then, it employs planning module to search an optimal path toward the goal and generate a plan for robot to follow. Finally, robot executes the desired actions to reach the target. After a successful action, robot stops and updates information to perform the next motion. Then, it repeats the process until it reaches the goal. It can coordinate multiple goals and constraints within a complex environment (Huq et al., 2008; Yang et al., 2006).

However, in deliberative navigation, accurate model of environment is needed to plan a globally feasible path. The computational complexity of such systems is generally too great to attain the cycle rates needed for the resulting action to keep pace with the changing environments (it is difficult to obtain a completely known map). To perform necessary calculations, enormous processing capabilities and memory is needed.

Therefore, these approaches are not proper in the presence of uncertainty in dynamic or real world.

2.3 Hybrid approach

In more complex situations, other control architectures appeared (Oreback & Christensen, 2003), including the anticipation in the decision process. This combination is known as hybrid architecture (Arkin, 1990) which has two levels: reactive and deliberative. The deliberative level has to determine and offer the reactive level those behavioural patterns that are necessary for the robot to achieve its objectives. The reactive level has to execute these behavioural patterns by guaranteeing real-time restrictions (Fulgenzi et al., 2008; Fulgenzi, 2009).

Practically, these methods are more complex and require more time calculations. They usually use local methods of obstacle avoidance in order to expand the tree and cover the search space. However, local methods are less suited to dynamic environments (Minguez et al., 2002).

In (Schwartz & Sharir, 1983), a general algorithm was developed. It is doubly exponential time, this limit has been lowered by the Canny algorithm described in (Canny et al., 1990) whose running time is exponential in dimension.

The algorithm D* proposed by Stentz (stentz, 1995) is a generalisation of the A* search algorithm in the case of partially known environments. In a finite discretized configuration space, the initial cost of shipping is to move from one configuration to another. A path is first found, and then the robot begins to execute it. If a change in the cost of a path is detected, only the relevant configurations are considered and the optimal path is updated in less time.

Partial motion planning (PMP) (Petti & Fraichard, 2005), the algorithm explicitly takes into account the computation time, constraints and problems safety of navigation in dynamic environment. A tree is grown using a conventional algorithm based on sampling. A node is added to the tree if there is not an inevitable consequence collision. This enables PMP to provide a safe partial path at any time. During the execution of this partial path chosen, another partial path is developed from the end of the previous path developed. This method is applied at real time in dynamic environments, but its major drawback is that it does not consider the uncertainty of the information collected. So it can produce non-executable partial paths.

2.4 Multi-agent systems and robotic simulation

In the field of multi-agent systems, several works have encouraged researchers to develop models simulating robot's behaviours in order to achieve a known target. In fact, there are similarities between robot and agent. So, the mapping from a robot to an agent seems straightforward because each robot represents a physical entity, independent from other robots, with a specific task. Hence, multi-agent simulations models are widely used to solve problems in mobile robotics under dynamic environments. In this way, many approaches are using multi-agent systems to simulate and control autonomous mobile robot in order to resolve the problem of space's conflict by minimising the interaction with agents. For example, (Ros, 2005) proposes a multi-agent system for autonomous robot navigation in unknown environments. In this work, the authors use the case-based reasoning (CBR) techniques in order to solve the problem of local minimum and avoid only static obstacles. In (Ono, 2004), a multi-agent architecture is also proposed to control an intelligent wheelchair. It takes into account only three behaviours: obstacle avoidance (using distance), door passage and wall following. However, it cannot combine behaviours together and it is applied only in static environment. In (Innocenti, 2007), a multi-agent system is proposed as the robot control architecture divided into four sub-systems of agents: perception, behaviour, deliberative and actuator. This architecture is applied in static and dynamic environments and uses the distance between the robot and the moving obstacle in order to predict conflict situations. But this information gives a limited knowledge about the state of the environment and does not allow the robot to take an intelligent decision while navigating in a dynamic and unknown environment. In (Posadas et al., 2008) a multi-agent system is proposed to control the navigation of robot by using a hybrid approach (it uses a motion planning). The architecture is composed of two levels; reactive and deliberative. The communications between these levels are assured by the agents.

2.5 Discussion

Reactive systems are applied in local navigation and used to deal with simple problems. Nevertheless, reactive systems are typically less affected by errors and do not require an explicit models of the environment in order to navigate inside an unknown space. Furthermore, they usually deal only with local information that may be captured at real time. However, reactive systems may fall into local traps or blocking situations because they ignore prediction and reasoning in the decision process. For this reason, the robot can be derived to a conflict situation with other actors sharing the same space. In more complex situations, they are combined according to a higher level in order to include anticipation in the decision process. In these cases, low level control operates in a reactive way (local navigation) whereas high level systems tend to be deliberative and use motion planning method to update the trajectory when there are modifications in the state of the environment. These approaches are called hybrid approaches and are well applied in uncertain and dynamic environments by producing, at each step, a motion planning method that minimise the conflict (Petti & Fraichard, 2005). Nevertheless, building a movement planning requires an important computation time in order to find the most appropriate way. However, if the frequency of environment's changes is high, the use of a planning method becomes not only inefficient, but also useless (if the robot generates plans without using them).

So, in this situation it is interesting to introduce prediction in reactive schemas in order to consider the environment's evolution in the future. Hence, the main concern of this paper is to propose a model that combines reactivity and anticipation in order to resolve the problem of conflict without using a motion planning. Thus, the robot should anticipate the nature and velocity of the obstacles in order to minimise interactions. We use the multi-agent system to simulate the robot's behaviour because there is a mapping between robots, while navigating in dynamic environments, and multi-agent systems.

3. Autonomous navigation in uncertain environment

Autonomous navigation in an uncertain environment involves using systems for navigation control that must not be too computationally expensive, as this would result in a sluggish response. In this case, soft computing methods have played important roles in the design of the robot controllers. The commonly used soft computing methods are: Bayesian Networks and Fuzzy Logic.

3.1 Bayesian networks

Bayesian Networks are models which capture uncertainties in terms of probabilities that can be used to perform reasoning under uncertainty. It epitomises probabilistic dependency models that represent random stochastic uncertainty via its nodes (Darwiche, 2009). The Bayesian inference has been widely used especially in the localisation problem (Thrun, 1998), in the mapping and in the learning mechanisms in mobile robotics. But this technique is very slow and complex (NP-Complex) because it uses a probabilistic reasoning that require much more time to choose a suitable decision. Also, this technique requires a causal model of reality that is not always given. So, its application in autonomous navigation in the case of dynamic environments can be unprofitable.

3.2 Fuzzy logic technique for autonomous navigation

Fuzzy Logic (FL) has been investigated by several researchers to treat the problem of uncertainty in perception. This technique represents uncertainty via fuzzy sets and membership functions. It gives robustness to the system with respect to inaccuracy in data acquisition and uncertainty, and makes definition behaviour and their interactions quite easy by using simple linguistic rules (Klir et al., 1997; Sajotti et al., 1995). It also allows implementing of human knowledge and experience without requiring a precise analytical model of the environment. Probably, the greatest strength of behaviour-based fuzzy approaches is that they operate on/and reason with uncertain perception-based information, which makes them suitable even for difficult environments.

We present in table 1 comparison results between the characteristics of the Bayesian Networks and the Fuzzy Logic. According to this comparison study, we can conclude that the fuzzy logic technique is faster, easier to implement and well applied to autonomous robot navigation.

	Fuzzy Logic	Bayesian Network
Complexity	Simple rules	NP-complex
Reasoning	Fuzzy reasoning	Probabilistic reasoning
Application	Avoidance collision	Localization and mapping
Controller	Fuzzy inference	Bayesian inference
Rapidity	Fast (simple rules)	Slow

Table 1. Comparison between fuzzy logic and Bayesian network.

However, the majority of existing fuzzy logic methods deal only with static environments, and only use the distance between the robot and the obstacle to avoid collision and to minimise conflict with other agents sharing the same space (Bonarini et al, 2003; Selekwa et al., 2008). This kind of information gives a limited knowledge about the state of the environment, so the robot cannot take intelligent decisions. For this reason, in our work, we adopt a fuzzy logic technique to deal with uncertainty. We propose a fuzzy model for autonomous navigation in a dynamic and uncertain environment based on the nature and the velocity of obstacles.

4. Proposed approach

According to Ferber (Ferber, 1995), a multi-agent system is composed of:

1. An environment 'E',
2. A set of objects 'O' in 'E',
3. A set of agents 'A' in 'E',
4. A set of relationships 'R' between agents,
5. A set of operation 'op' enabling agents 'A' to collect, produce, consume and manipulate objects of 'O'.

Basing on this definition, we define our multi-agent system as a set of objects which represent the static objects (have a fixed position) and a set of agents (have a moving position) that represent dynamic objects and the robots. In our model, the principal agent is the "robot". It has its own physical parts including sensors, processors, actuators and communication devices. So, in order to guarantee the safety of the mobile robot, it should be able to navigate by minimising interactions with the other agents navigating in the same space in order to minimise conflict and to achieve a known goal.

This section is organised as follows. We present in subsection 4.1 the perception model of the robot. It allows the robot to perceive its environment in order to take the suitable decision autonomously. In subsection 4.2, we present the kinematic model of the robot. It allows the robot to localise in its environment. In subsection 4.3, we describe the principle of the fuzzy controller technique. In subsection 4.4, we present our fuzzy controllers model. The first controller is described in subsection 4.4.1. It allows the robot to determine its angular velocity. The second controller is presented in subsection 4.4.2. It allows the robot to calculate its linear velocity. We present in subsection 4.4.3 the system rules applied in our fuzzy controllers used to avoid conflict situations.

4.1 The perception model

One of the ultimate goals of robotics is to realise autonomous robots that are able to organise their own internal structure and to achieve their goals through interactions with dynamically changing environments. The robot should take decisions on-line using only sensors providing limited information (without prior information about the position of obstacles and their trajectories) when it navigates autonomously in dynamic spaces.

Our main objective is to make the robot able to predict the nature and the velocity of obstacles (static or moving) in order to minimise conflict situations, to avoid collision and to achieve a specific goal. At this stage, we use a perception model composed of eight ultrasonic sensors. We choose this type of sensors because it has some attractive properties, e.g. cheapness, reliability and soon, which makes it widely used in mobile robots. This type of sensor calculates the distance between the robots.

According to this model of perception, we divide the robot's space into three subspaces controlled by three groups of sensors (see figure 1). The subspaces are: (1) the front area "F" controlled by the first group composed of sensors number 1,2,7,8, (2) the left area "L" controlled by the second group composed of sensors number 3, 4, and (3) the right area "R" controlled by the third group composed of sensors number 5, 6.

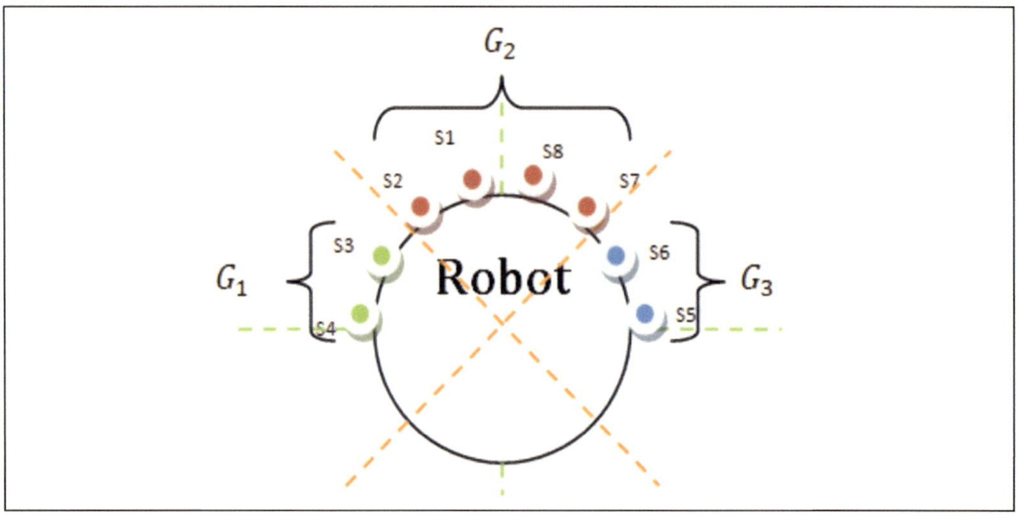

Fig. 1. The Robot's perception areas.

4.2 The kinematic model

In this study, the mobile robot is a system, which is subject to non holonomic constraints. Its position in the environment is represented by P=(x,y,θ), where (x, y) is the position of the robot in the reference coordinate system XOY, and the heading direction θ is taken counter clockwise from the positive direction of X-axis (see figure 2). X'O'Y' is the reference coordinate according to the robot system. It allows the robot to locate the objects in the environment.

The robot is composed of two wheels (left and right). The velocity, acceleration and orientation angle of the robot is assured by the fuzzy controllers.

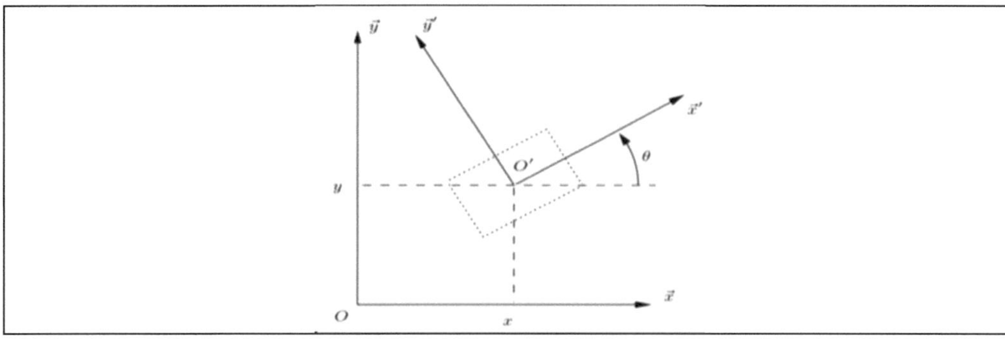

Fig. 2. Robot's kinematic model.

4.3 The fuzzy controller

A Fuzzy Controller (FC) is a control system, whose input is the output of the process to be controlled (sensory data, internal state). Its outputs are commands for the actuators of the process. The ranges of the input and output parameters/variables are represented by membership functions and fuzzy sets. In addition, the interactions between input and output variables/parameters are represented by fuzzy rules. In a nutshell, system input parameters and variables are encoded into fuzzy representations using well defined "If/Then" rules which are converted into their mathematical equivalents. These rules would then determine actions to be taken based on Implication Operators such as Zadeh Min/Max (Zadeh, 1973), or Mamdani Min (Mamdani, 1974). The fuzzified data is then put through a defuzzification process via Center of Gravity, Center of Sum or Mean of Maxima methods to obtain actual commands for the actuators of the process.

In our work, we use the Mamdani fuzzy inference methodology in order to provide the adequate way of modelling the relevance of the controller. For the defuzzification process we choose the Center of Gravity method by applying the formula 1. The crisp value U* is the geometrical center of the output fuzzy value μ(y), where μ(y) is the union of all the contributions of rules whose Degree Of Freedom (DOF) is more than zero, y is the universe of discourse and b is the number of samples.

$$U^* = \frac{\sum_{i=a}^{b} \mu(y) \times y}{\sum_{i=a}^{b} \mu(y)} \qquad (1)$$

4.4 The principle of the behaviour controller based on Fuzzy Logic

The use of fuzzy logic in the design of autonomous navigation behaviours is nowadays quite popular in robotic. The set of behaviours that are being implemented can include, for example, the following of walls, corridors or the avoidance of obstacles. However, usually the existing fuzzy logic methods use only the distance between the robot and the obstacle in order to avoid conflicts and so deal with static environments.

We propose a fuzzy model for the navigation in dynamic and uncertain environments based on"the nature" and "the velocity" of obstacles. For example, if there is an obstacle in front of the robot, it is more logical to reason about its velocity. In fact, the distance between the robot and the obstacle allows it to immediately change the trajectory without taking into account the obstacle nature (mobile or static) and whether the obstacle is going in the same direction of the robot or not. In contrast, the velocity allows the robot to predict if there is conflict in the future. In the reminder of this section, we present robot behaviour modules implemented as fuzzy logic controllers. Each behaviour module receives data input that describes the situation and produces an output to be addressed to the actuators. Our fuzzy architecture is composed of two fuzzy controllers. The first controller is in charge of determining the angular velocity of the two wheels. This controller allows the robot to change its angular orientation based on the prediction of the nature of the obstacle, in order to avoid conflict and to move closer to its target. The second controller uses the velocity of the obstacle. It is in charge of determining whether the robot's speed should be increased (accelerate its speed if there is a free space) or decreased (minimise its speed if there is an obstacle in its trajectory).

4.4.1 Obstacle nature prediction: Time collision concept

Typically ultrasonic sensors calculate the distance between the robot and the obstacle and therefore they do not provide information about the obstacle's nature (mobile or static) and its position in the future state. However, this kind of information is necessary to predict conflict situations in the future. In order to overcome this problem, in our work, the robot uses this distance to calculate new information called "Time Collision" between the robot and the obstacle.

The Time Collision (TC) represents the time left for the robot before a collision occurs with an obstacle. In order to predict the nature and the position of the obstacle in the future, the robot operates as follows. At time Ti, the robot should observe its environment (using the perception model). If it detects an obstacle, it calculates a Time Collision Needed (TCN) representing the time required to collide with this obstacle in the future while keeping the same velocity (see figure 3). At time Ti+1, it repeats the same procedure to recalculate a Time Collision Remaining (TCR) representing the time required to collide the same obstacle in the future while keeping the same velocity (see figure 3). The TC can be obtained by applying the formula 2. Di represents the distance between the robot and the obstacle at time Ti, and VRi represents the velocity of the robot.

$$TC = D_i / VR_i \tag{2}$$

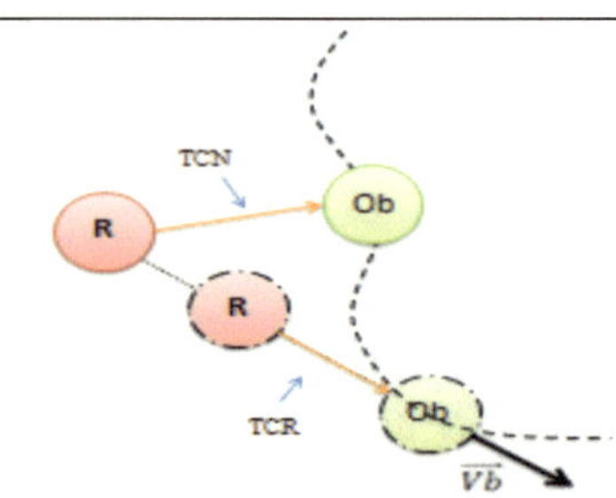

Fig. 3. Illustration of "the Time Collision".

From these two values, the robot can calculate a Difference Time Collision (DTC) with this obstacle by applying formula 3. If the DTC is equal to zero, it means that the obstacle in the trajectory of the robot is static. In this situation, the robot should immediately change its direction in order to avoid local minimum. If the DTC is positive, then the obstacle is considered as a mobile one. In this situation, the robot can expect that the trajectory will be free after a period of time and then it does not need to change its direction. If the DTC is negative, then obstacle is mobile and it is going towards the robot. In this case, the robot should minimise its velocity in order to avoid conflict with this obstacle, and then decide to change the direction completely if it is possible (moves to another subspace, which is safe), or wait until this mobile object moves away (the current subspace will be free), if there is no other free subspace.

$$DTC=TCN-TCR \tag{3}$$

The advantage of this information is that it allows the robot not only to avoid collision and local minimum at real time with obstacles around it, but also to anticipate their natures and their positions in the future so as to predict conflict situations.
We present in figure 4 the FLC of angular velocity. We describe four linguistic variables that are: the DTCL, DTCF, DTCR, and TO. These variables represent respectively: the difference time collision on the left, the difference time collision in the front, the difference time collision on the right and the current target orientation between the robot and the goal. Each

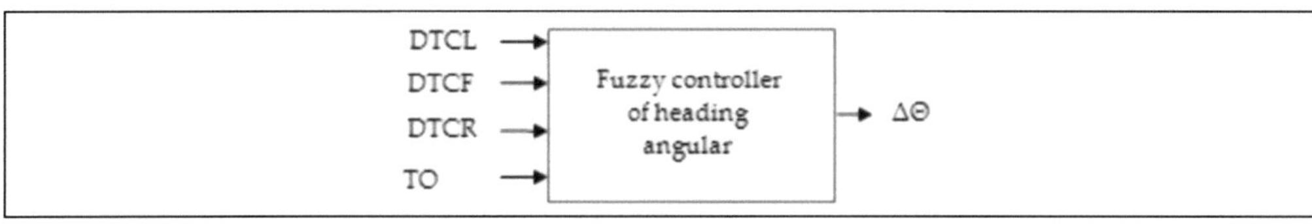

Fig. 4. Fuzzy controller of heading angular

DTC have two membership functions: Fixed Obstacle and Moving Obstacle. The DTCL is used to control the left area. We present in algorithm 1 the reasoning process of the robot that is used to predict the nature of the nearest obstacle in this area. Thus, if the DTCL is

```
if (DTCi) ≤ the time interval Δ then
    The obstacle is static
else
    The obstacle is mobile
     Free space
end if
```

Algorithm 1. The robot's behaviour is based on the prediction of the nature of the obstacles in left and right areas

smaller or equal to Δ (the time interval between two successive perceptions) it means that the obstacle is static; else it is considered as mobile. We can obtain the value of this variable from the formula 4. The same reasoning process is applied to the right area based on the DTCR that can be obtained from the formula 5. The value of DTCF variable can be obtained from the formula 6. Algorithm 2 describes the reasoning mechanism of the robot that is used to predict the nature of the nearest obstacle in the front area. For example, if the DTCF is equal to zero, this means that the obstacle is static. Therefore, the robot should change its trajectory immediately in order to avoid collision. Otherwise, if the DTCF is equal to infinity, this means that the space is free. In order to move toward a specific goal, the robot

```
if (DTCF) =0 then
    The obstacle is static. The robot should change its trajectory
else
    if ((DTCF)>0) and ((DTCF) < + ∞) then
The obstacle is mobile and it is moving away from the robot.
    else
if ((DTCF) <0) and ((DTCF)> −∞) then
The obstacle is mobile and it is going toward the robot.
else
if (DTCF) =- ∞ then
The space is considered as free at ti
else
if (INF (DTCF) =+ ∞ then
No obstacle in front of the robot. Free space
end if
end if
            end if
        end if
end if
```

Algorithm 2. The robot's behaviour is based on the prediction of the nature of the obstacles in front area

should have an idea about the area in which the target exists. For this purpose, the TO which gives an idea about this position is combined with the DTC for each area in order to reach a compromise between "avoid conflict" and "reach goal". The TO has three membership functions that are: L: Left, F: Front, R: Right. The output of this controller is the angular velocity, it has five membership functions: LLT: Large Left Turn, SLT: Small Left Turn, NT: No Turn, SRT: Small Right Turn, LRT: Large Right Turn. Note that figure 5 describes the input of the fuzzy sets involved in the definition of the heading angular. Figure 6 describes the output variable for the angular velocity.

$$DTCL = Sup\,(DTCL_i) \text{ where } i=3, 4 \tag{4}$$

$$DTCR = Sup\,(DTCR_i) \text{ where } i=5, 6 \tag{5}$$

$$DTCF = Inf\,(DTCF_i) \text{ where } i=1, 2, 7, 8 \tag{6}$$

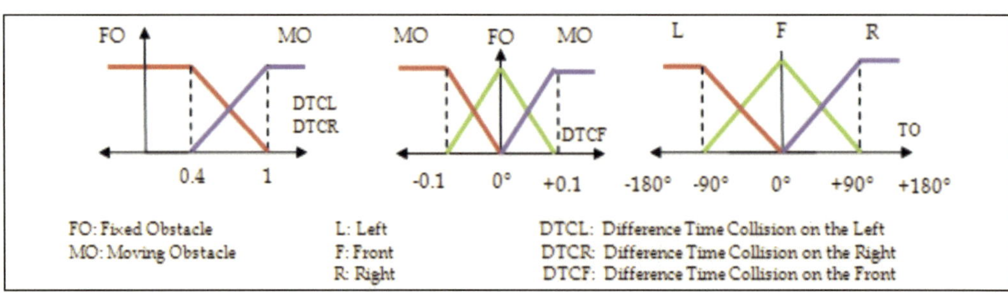

Fig. 5. The definition of angular velocity input membership functions.

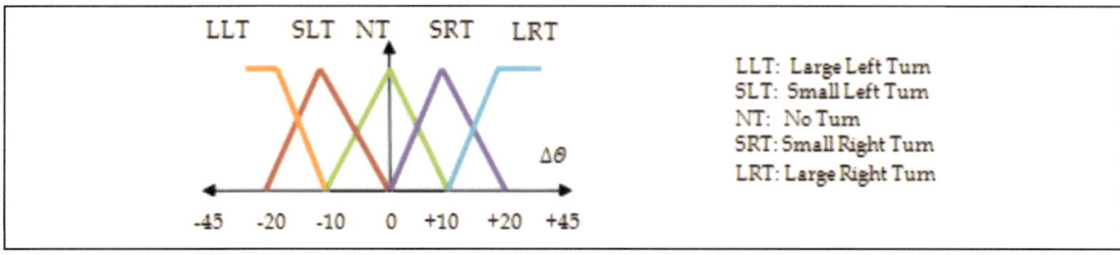

Fig. 6. The definition of angular velocity output membership functions.

4.4.2 Linear velocity prediction: Obstacle velocity concept

The fuzzy controller for angular velocity uses the DTC that gives information about the nature of an obstacle and its trajectory. So, the robot is able to predict the future situation of the environment if it keeps moving in the same direction. While the second fuzzy controller for linear velocity uses the obstacle's velocity in the front area. This information determines whether the robot's speed should be increased or decreased to respond to the nearest situation detected.

Hence, the obstacle's velocity can be calculated according to formula 7 where D represents the distance travelled by the obstacle during the time interval Δ.

$$\vartheta = D/\Delta \tag{7}$$

The distance D is calculated according to formula 8 where X_c and Y_c represent the coordinates of the obstacle at time t_i and X'_c and Y'_c represent the coordinates of the obstacle at $t_i+\Delta$ (see figure 7). The coordinates are obtained according to formula 9.

$$D=\sqrt{(X_c-Y_c)^2+(X'_c-Y'_c)^2} \tag{8}$$

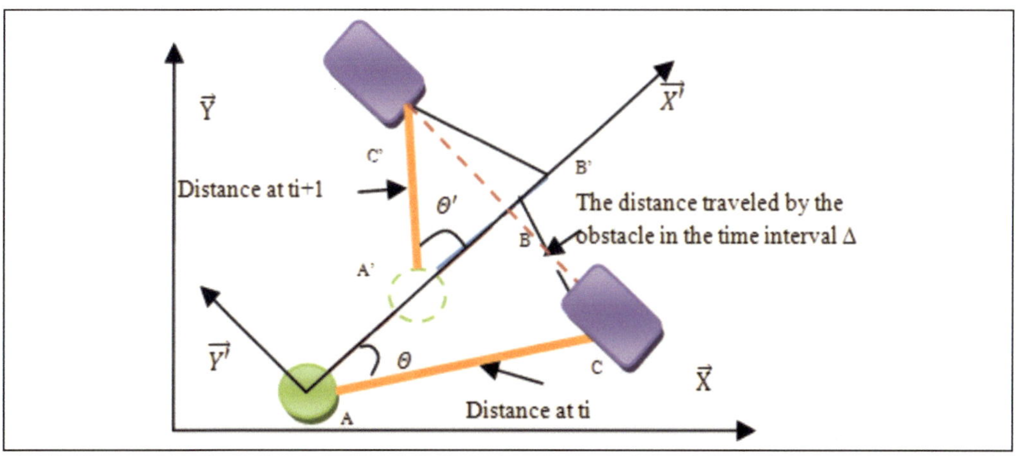

Fig. 7. Illustration of distance traversed by the obstacle.

$$\text{Cord}=\begin{cases} X_c=X_a+(X_b-X_a)\cos\theta-(Y_b-Y_a)\sin\theta \\ Y_c=Y_a+(Y_b-Y_a)\cos\theta+(X_b-X_a)\sin\theta \end{cases} \tag{9}$$

We present in figure 8 the fuzzy logic controller for the linear velocity. This controller determines whether the robot's speed should be increased or decreased. It is used to determine the speed change Δϑ (the linear velocity).

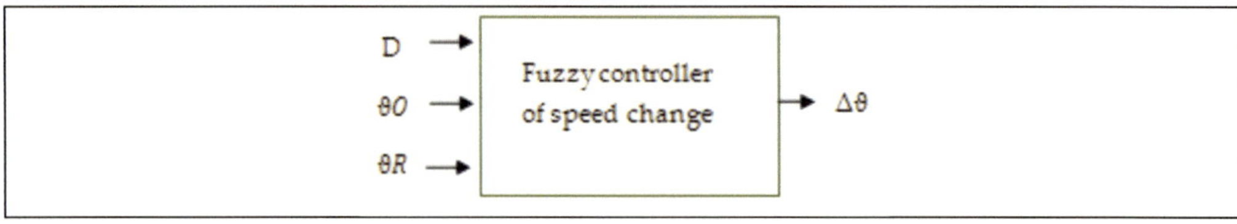

Fig. 8. Fuzzy controller of speed change

The D, ϑO, and the ϑR represent respectively the distance between the robot and the nearest obstacle in the front area, the velocity of the nearest obstacle in the front area and the current velocity of the robot. The input and output membership functions of the fuzzy controller for linear velocity are shown respectively in figure 9 and figure 10.

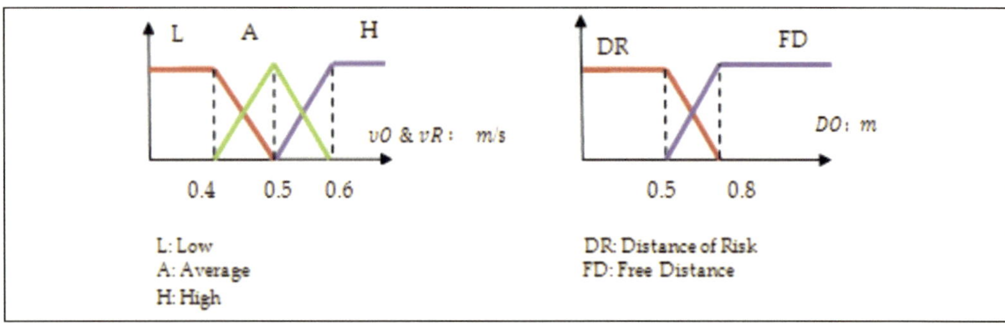

Fig. 9. Input membership functions for the linear velocity

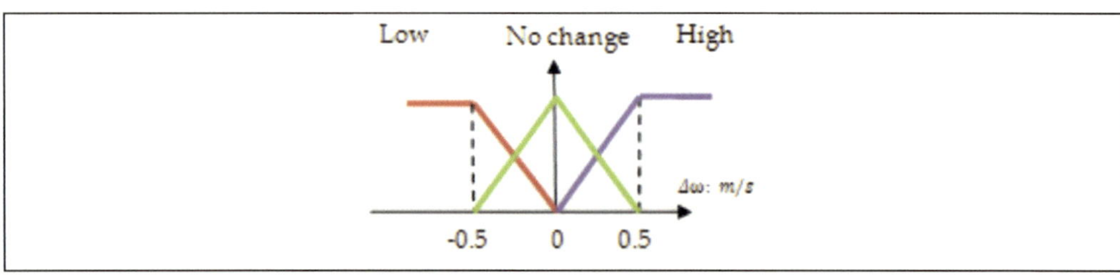

Fig. 10. Output membership functions. Velocity up/down control.

So, the speed of the robot can be influenced by the velocity of the obstacle in the front area. We present in algorithm 3 the reasoning process of the robot used to predict the velocity of the nearest obstacle in this area in order to determine its velocity. For example, if the velocity of the obstacle is smaller than the velocity of the robot, then the robot decreases its speed in order to avoid collision in the near future. If the velocity of the obstacle is larger than the velocity of the robot, the robot keeps the same speed if its velocity and the velocity of the obstacle are close. However, if there is a difference between the speed of the robot and the obstacle, it accelerates.

```
if (VO) =0 then
    The obstacle is static
    The robot must minimise its acceleration.
else
    if (VO < VA) then
        Reduce the velocity of the robot in order to avoid conflict in the near future.
    else
if (VO > VA) then
        Keep the same speed if the velocity of the robot and the velocity of the
obstacle    are close or accelerate if they are different.
else
            Keep the same speed.
        end if
    end if
end if
```

Algorithm 3. The velocity of the robot according to the concept of the velocity of the obstacle

4.4.3 Fuzzy system rules

Robot navigation is actually governed by rules in the fuzzy controller which represent qualitatively the human driving heuristics. The fuzzy logic controllers are applied to coordinate and to combine the various behaviours of the robot in order to choose a suitable decision. The fuzzification converts the input variables into input grades by means of the membership functions shown in figure 5 and figure 9. The inference and aggregation generate a resultant output membership function with respect to fuzzy rules. The defuzzification gives the output membership function shown in figure 6 and in figure 10. Therefore, the total number of rules to determine the angular velocity is N= 24. We can reduce this number into 9 if-else rules by eliminating redundancies (rules that have different values of input variables and the same value of the output variable can be replaced by one rule). We present in table 2 the fuzzy rules for the angular velocity. For example, if DTCF=M (the obstacle in the front area is moving) and TO=F (the target is in front area) then $\Delta\theta$=NT (the robot do not change its trajectory) whatever the value of DTCL and DTCR. Likewise, for the linear velocity there are N=18 rules, but we can reduce them into 9 if-else rules.

The use of a small number of rules is required in dynamic environments, this is especially important when a fast response to the changes is required (short execution and high frequency of sensor readings). We use the method of Center of Gravity Defuzzification to

DTCF		F				M			
DTCL		F		M		F		M	
DTCR		F	M	F	M	F	M	F	M
TO	F	LRT	LRT	SLT	SLT	NT	NT	NT	NT
	L	LRT	LRT	LLT	LLT	NT	NT	LLT	LLT
	R	LRT	LRT	LRT	LRT	NT	LRT	NT	LRT

Table 2. The fuzzy rules for the angular velocity.

calculate the output for the two controllers. The constants of output membership function for the first controller (angular velocity) are shown in figure 6 and the values of the constants of output membership function for the second controller (linear velocity) are shown in figure 10. During simulation work, the robot's normal velocity VN is set to 0.5m/s.

5. Experimentation results

The robot calculates a "TC" with each obstacle around it. The value of "TC" allows it to predict the nature of each obstacle (static or dynamic). Then, the robot can calculate the velocity of each obstacle in order firstly to anticipate the state of the environment in the future and therefore to adjust its speed in order to avoid collisions.
In order to prove the efficiency of the proposed model, we proceed as follows. In a first time, we test our method in static environments (composed of U-shape and T-shape obstacles). Having obtained valid results, we achieve, in a second time, tests in dynamic environments (including moving robots). We have used the Simbad simulation platform.

5.1 The parameters of the robot and the controller in simulation

In simulation, the parameters of the robot are: the maximum linear velocity ϑmax = 1m/s and the maximum angular velocity θmax = 45/s. The height of the mobile robot is 0.78 m, the diameter is 0.4 m, the weight is 50 kg and the radius of the wheel is 0.05m. The Δ time interval between two successive perceptions is 0.4s. This interval time is used to calculate the TC.
In addition, we have defined a variety of basic scenarios for the experimentation stage. In the reminder of this section we detail some of them. For each scenario, the robot is initially positioned at the centre of the environment and starts to work without having any preliminary information. The simulation environment is a square area composed of multiple traps like U-shape and T-shape forming the static obstacle, and moving agents (moving objects and other robots).

5.2 Experimentation results in static environments

Test results in static environments are presented in figure 11. Each scenario shows the robot's environment with the robot's path covered and the detected obstacles.
Scenario 1 The robot is initially positioned in an environment composed of multiple "dead cycle" as shown in figure 11.a. The robot calculates for each trap a DTC in order to predict the nature of the obstacle. The robot's decision depends on this information (e.g. if the DTC is equal to zero then, the obstacle is static and the robot should change its direction). In region 'a' it detects that the DTCF is equal to zero, which means that the robot should change immediately its direction to find a free path towards its target. In region 'b', it changes its behaviour and Turns Right. In region 'c', the robot detects a new local minimum (DTCF=0, DTCR<ΔT and DTCL<ΔT). In this situation, the robot should find a free trajectory in order to move away from this obstacle. When it leaves this local minimum, the robot adjusts its trajectory to minimise the distance between the robot and the target. For each step, the robot reasons about the nature, velocity and the orientation angle in order to choose a direction that will be free in the future (predict the future state using the nature and the velocity of obstacle in order to find a suitable path with fewer constraints). However, in (Wang & Liu, 2005) based on trial-return behaviour phenomenon, the robot searches the nearest exit. Therefore, when the nearest exit is blocked by along wall, the

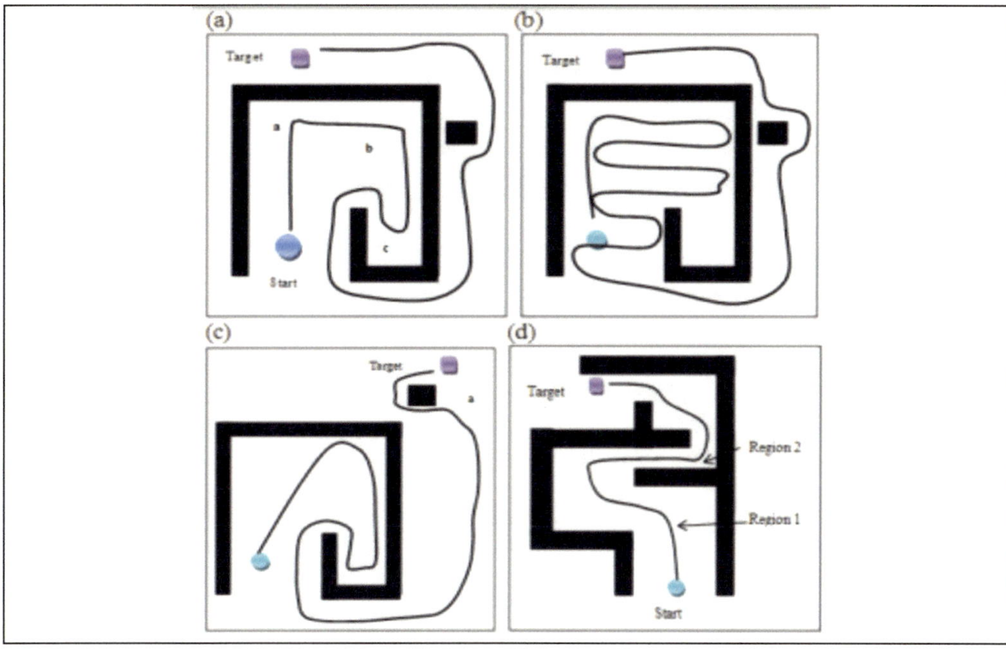

Fig. 11. Experimental results in static environments

nearest exit will be the opening at the right hand side where the wall ends (see figure 11.b). This method takes a large time to find the free end of the wall. However, the problem with trial-return motion is high power consumption and the time spent from start point to target is long when the obstacle is composed of complex traps like U-shape and T-shape. In (Zhu & Yang, 2004), the dead cycle problem is resolved by using a state memory strategy (see figure 11.c). Therefore, there is a situation where the robot cannot go straight toward the target. It has to keep turning around the obstacle (point "a") if the distance between the robot and the obstacle is shorter than the distance between the robot and the target.

Scenario 2 We test our method in an environment composed of corridors (wide and narrow). As shown in figure 11.d the robot moves in a corridor in order to reach its target. The problem is how to ensure the motion's stability without oscillation. In our architecture, there is a compromise between "reach target" and "avoid obstacles". In region 1, the robot crosses a large corridor; it changes its direction when it detects a static obstacle. In region 2, the robot crosses a narrow corridor; in this situation the $DTCR<\Delta T$ and the $DTCL<\Delta T$. Thus, the robot cannot change its trajectory, but it should only adjust its velocity with the velocity of the nearest obstacle in the front area. This reasoning allows the robot to reach its target easily without oscillation.

5.3 Experimentation results in dynamic environments

Scenario 1 Generally it is difficult to deal with narrow passage cases when there are moving actors because there may be oscillation in the trajectory between multiple obstacles. However, we can show, in figure 12, the effectiveness of our method when dealing with this case. The robot navigates in an environment composed of corridors with a moving obstacle. At the first time, the corridor is narrow. In this setting the robot adjusts its velocity to avoid collision with the obstacle without changing the direction because the goal is in the front

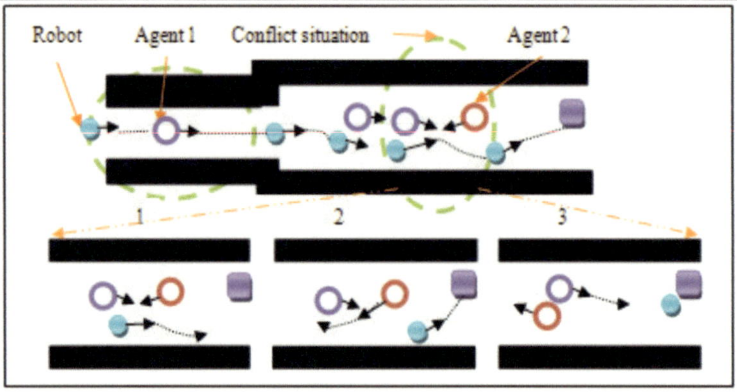

Fig. 12. Experimental results in a dynamic environment: case of conflict situations in narrow and large corridors.

area and there is no free area neither on the left nor on the right (DTC<ΔT on the Left and the Right). When the corridor becomes large, the robot changes its direction because there is a free area on the right. In this trajectory, the robot detects that there is a conflict space (DTCF is negative). With the concept of DTC, the robot can find the trajectory that will be free in the future. Thus, the robot should choose the most adequate direction that minimises states of conflict. So, in our model the robot can go through narrow passages successfully. However, in (Lazkano et al., 2007) a reactive navigation method based on Bayesian Networks is proposed. This method only takes into account the door-crossing behaviour. Its drawback is that it becomes slow when the environment becomes more dynamic because it requires a long computing time.

Scenario 2 We test our method in a dynamic environment composed of multiple traps as shown in figure 13. The robot adjusts its velocity in order to avoid collision with moving

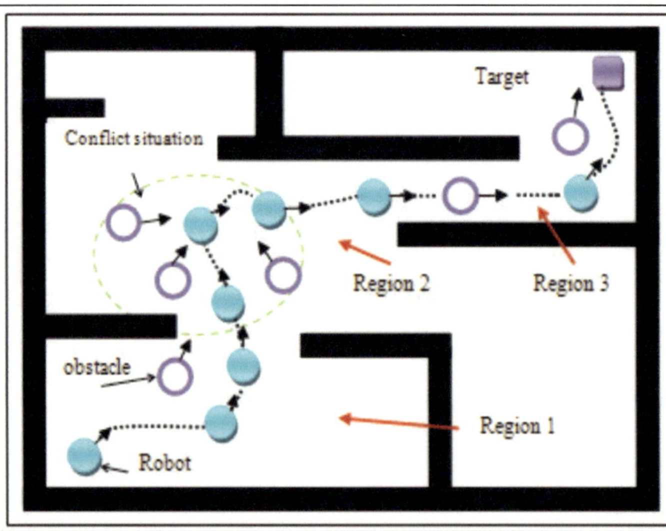

Fig. 13. Experimental results in a dynamic environment: case of conflict situations in a dynamic environment composed of local traps.

obstacles and changes its orientation if it detects a static obstacle. In region 1, it moves away from a U-shape obstacle because it detects that the DTC is equal to zero. In region 2, the robot is in a large corridor with moving obstacles, it calculates the DTC relative to every moving obstacle in order to predict conflict situations. In this setting, the DTC of every obstacle around the robot decreases, which means that the obstacles are going toward the robot. At the first step, the robot calculates the velocity of the nearest moving obstacle in order to adjust its velocity. At the second step, it reasons about the trajectory that it has to choose (minimise interactions with other agents).

According to a large number of simulation experiments, we can conclude that:

1. The robot uses a simple model of perception composed of ultrasonic sensors that provides information at real time.
2. The robot can provide a suitable trajectory in dynamic environments and there are no local minimum encountered.
3. The results provided by our method are satisfactory with the robot's dynamic constraints.
4. The robot can easily predict the nature of obstacles around it, and it uses this kind of information to predict conflict situations with other agents sharing the same resources.
5. The robot can also predict the velocity of each obstacle, using its simple model of perception, to adjust its linear velocity in order to avoid collision with other agents.
6. Our method can be adapted to different cases in dynamic environments.

6. Conclusion and perspectives

In this paper, a new method based on the sensors' information to combine reactivity and anticipation in order to predict conflict situations between robots has been proposed. We have used fuzzy logic to develop a control system that enables the robot to navigate at real time and to minimise its interaction with other agents. Basing on the simulation experiments, we can conclude that our method operates in different cases of dynamic environments. The robot can easily predict the nature of obstacles in order to anticipate conflict situations. It can also predict the velocity of each obstacle and adjust its linear velocity in order to avoid collision. As perspectives for this work, we attend to improve the robot's behaviour by introducing both the ability to learn and the concept of communication between robots in order to explore the environment and to share knowledge.

7. References

Arkin, R. (1990). Integrating behavioural, perceptual and world knowledge in reactive navigation. *Robots and Autonomous Systems*, Vol.6, pp. 105-122

Bonarini, A., Invernizzi, G. & Labella, T. H. (2003). An architecture to coordinate fuzzy behaviours to control an autonomous robot. *Proc. Fuzzy sets Systems*, pp.101-115

Canny, J., Rege, A. & Reif, J. (1990). An exact algorithm for kino dynamic planning in the plane. *In ACM Symp.On Computational Geometry*,pp. 271-280.

Darwiche, A. (2009). Modelling and Reasoning with Bayesian Networks. *New York, NY: Cambridge University Press*

Ferber, J. (1995). Les systèmes multi-agents vers une intelligence collective.*InterEditions*, Paris.

Fiorini, P. & Shiller, Z. (1998). Motion planning in dynamic environments using velocity obstacles. *International.Journal.Robot. Res*, Vol.17 (7), pp. 760-772

Fox, D., Burgard, W. & Thrun, S. (1997). The dynamic window approach to collision avoidance. *IEEE Robotics and Automation Magazine*, pp.23-33

Fulgenzi, C. (2009). Autonomous navigation in dynamic uncertain environment using probabilistic models of perception and collision risk prediction, PhD thesis, INRIA Rhône-Alpes, Grenoble France

Fulgenzi, C., Tay, C., Spalanzani, A. & Laugier, C. (2008). Probabilistic navigation in dynamic environment using Rapidly-exploring Random Trees and Gaussian Processes. *Proc.IEEE/RSJ International Conference on Intelligent Robotsand Systems*, pp.508-513

Huang, W.H., Fajen, R., Fink, J. & Warren, W.H. (2006). Visual navigation and obstacle avoidance using a steering potential function, *Proc. Robotics and Autonomous Systems*, pp. 288-299

Huq, R., Mann, G. K. I. & Gosine, R. G. (2008). Mobile robot navigation usingmotors schema and fuzzy context dependent behaviour modulation. *Appl. Soft. Comput.*, pp. 422-436

Innocenti, B. (2007). A multi-agent architecture with cooperative fuzzy control for a mobile robot. *Proc. Robotics and Autonomous Systems,* Vol. 55, PP. 881-891

Jing, X., Wang, Y. & Tan, D. (2003). Cooperative motion behaviours using biology-modelling behaviour decision-making rules. *Cont. Theory. Appl*, Vol.20 (3), pp. 407-410

Khatib, O. (1986). Real-Time Obstacle Avoidance for Manipulators and Mobile Robots. *In International Journal of Robotics Research*, pp.90-98

Klir, G. J., Yuan, B. & Clair, U. S. (1997). Fuzzy Set Theory: Foundations and Applications. *Prentice-Hall, Upper Saddle River*

Langer, D., Rosenblatt, J. & Hebert, M. (1994). A behaviour-based system for off-road navigation. *Proc.IEEE Transaction. Robot. Automation*, Vol.10, pp. 776-783

Lazkano, E., Sierra, B., Astigarraga, A. & Martnez-Otzeta, J.M. (2007). On the use of Bayesian Networks to develop behaviours for mobile robots. *Robotics and Autonomous Systems*, Vol.55, pp. 253-265

Mamdani, E. H. (1974). Applications of fuzzy algorithms for simple dynamic plants.*Proc.IEEE, 121(12)*, pp. 1585-1588

Minguez, J. & Montano, L. (2000). Nearness diagram navigation: a new real time collision avoidance approach. *Proc. IntelligentRobots and Systems*, pp.2094-2100

Minguez, J., Montano, L., Siméon, N. & Alami, R. (2002). Global nearness diagram navigation. *Proc. IEEE International Conference on Robotics and Automation.*

Nilsson, N. J. (1980). Principles of Artificial Intelligence. *Morgan Kauf-mann Ed, Los Altos, CA*

Omid, R.E.M., Tang, S.H. & Napsiah, I. (2009). Development of a new minimum avoidance system for a behaviour-based mobile robot. Proc.*Fuzzy Sets and Systems*

Ono, Y. (2004). A mobile robot for corridor navigation: A multi-agent approach. *Proc. ACM Southeast Regional Conference, ACM Press*, pp. 379-384

Ordonez, C., Collins, E. G., Selekwa, M.F. & Dunlap, D. D. (2008). The virtual wall approach to limit cycle avoidance for unmanned ground vehicles. *Proc. Robotic and Autonomous System*, vol. 56, pp.645-657

Oreback, A. & Christensen, H. I. (2003). Evaluation of architectures for mobile robotics. *Autonomous Robots*, Vol.14, pp. 33-49

Petti, S. & Fraichard, T. (2005). Safe motion planning in dynamic environments. *IEEE IROS*.

Posadas, J. L., Poza, J.L., Sim, J.E., Benet, G. & Blanes, F. (2008). Agent-based distributed architecture for mobile robot control. *Engineering Applications of Artificial Intelligence*, Vol.21, pp. 805-823

Pruski, A. & Rohmer, S. (1997). Robust path planning for non-holonomic robots.*J. Intell. Robot.Syst: Theory Appl*, 18(4), pp. 329-350

Quinlan, S., Khatib, O. (1993). Elastic bands: Connecting path planning and control. *Proc. IEEE International Conference on Robotics and Automation*, pp. 802-807

Ros, R. (2005). A CBR system for autonomous robot navigation. *Proc. Frontiers in Artificial Intelligence and Applications*, vol.131, pp. 299-306

Sahota, M. K. (1994). Reactive Deliberation: An Architecture for Real Time Intelligent Control in Dynamic Environments. *Proceedings of the AAAI*, pp. 1303–1308.

Sajotti, A., Konolige, K. & Ruspini, E. H. (1995). A multi valued-logic approach to integrating planning and control. *Artificial Intelligence*, pp. 481-526

Schwartz, J. T. & Sharir, M. (1983). General techniques for computing topological properties of algebraic manifolds. *Advances in Applied Mathematics*, 12, 1983.

Selekwa, M. F., Dunlap, D., Shi, D. & Collins, E. (2008). Robot navigation in very cluttered environments by preference-based fuzzy behaviours. *Proc.Robotics and Autonomous Systems*, pp.231-246

Simmons, R. (1996). The curvature-velocity method for local obstacle avoidance. *Proc. International Conference onRobotics and Automation*, pp.2737-2742

Stachniss, C. & Burgard, W. (2002). An integrated approach to goal-directed obstacle avoidance under dynamic constraints for dynamic environments. *Proc. IEEE International Conference on Intelligent Robots and Systems*, pp.508-513

Stentz, A. (1995). The focussed d* algorithm for real-time re-planning. *Proceedings of the International Joint Conference onArtificialIntelligence*.

Thrun, S. (1998). Bayesian landmark learning for mobile robot navigation. *Machine Learning*,Vol.33 (1), pp. 41-76

Ulrich, I. & Borenstein, J. (2000). VFH: Local obstacle avoidance with look-ahead verification. *Proc. IEEE International Conference on Robotics and Automation*, pp.2505-2511

Wang, M. & Liu, J. N. K. (2005). Fuzzy logic based robot path planning in unknown environments. *Proc. Internat. Conf.on Mach. Learn. And Cybernet*, pp.818-818

Yang, X., Moallem, M. & Patel, R. V. (2006). A layered goal-oriented fuzzymotion planning strategy for mobile robot navigation. *IEEE Trans.Syst, Man Cyber Part B: Cybernetics*, 35(6), pp. 1214-1224.

Zadeh, L. A. (1973). Outline of a New Approach to the Analysis of Complex Systems and Decision-Making Approach. *IEEE Trans. on Systems, Man, and Cybernetics SME-3(1)*, pp. 28-45

Zhu, A. & Yang, S. X.(2004). A fuzzy logic approach to reactive navigation of behaviour-based mobile robots. *Proc. IEEE International Conference on Robotics and Automation*, pp.5045-5050

Part 2

Control

9

Singularity-Free Dynamics Modeling and Control of Parallel Manipulators with Actuation Redundancy

Andreas Müller and Timo Hufnagel
University Duisburg-Essen, Chair of Mechanics and Robotics
Heilbronn University
Germany

1. Introduction

The modeling, identification, and control of parallel kinematics machines (PKM) have advanced in the last two decades culminating in successful industrial implementations. Still the acceptance of PKM is far beyond that of the well-established serial manipulators, however. This is mainly due to the limited workspace, the drastically varying static and dynamic properties, leading eventually to singularities, and the seemingly more complex control. Traditionally the number of inputs equals the mechanical degree-of-freedom (DOF) of the manipulator, i.e. the PKM is non-redundantly actuated.

Actuation redundancy is a means to overcome the aforementioned mechanical limitations. It potentially increases the acceleration capability, homogenizes the stiffness and manipulability, and eliminates input singularities, and thus increases the usable workspace as addressed in several publications as for instance Garg et al. (2009); Gogu (2007); Krut et al. (2004); Kurtz & Hayward (1992); Lee et al. (1998); Nahon & Angeles (1989); O'Brien & Wen (1999); Wu et al. (2009).

These advantages are accompanied by several challenges for the dynamics modeling and for the PKM control. A peculiarity of redundantly actuated PKM is that control forces can be applied that have no effect on the PKM motion, leading to mechanical prestress that can be exploited for different second-level control tasks such as backlash avoidance and stiffness modulation Chakarov (2004); Cutkosky & Wright (1986); Kock & Schumacherm (1998); Lee et al. (2005); Müller (2006),Valasek et al. (2005). This also means that the inverse dynamics has no unique solution, which calls for appropriate strategies for redundancy resolution. The implementation of the corresponding model-based control schemes poses several challenges due to model uncertainties, the lack of globally valid parameterizations of the dynamics model, as well to the synchronization errors in decentralized control schemes calling for robust modeling and control concepts Müller (2011c); Müller & Hufnagel (2011).

The basis for model-based control are the motion equations governing the PKM dynamics. Aiming on an efficient formulation applicable in real-time, the motion equations are commonly derived in terms of a minimum number of generalized coordinates that constitute a (local) parameterization of the configuration space Abdellatif et al. (2005); Cheng et al. (2003); Müller (2005); Nakamura & Ghodoussi (1989); Yi et al. (1989). A well-known problem of this formulation is that these minimal coordinates are usually not valid on all of the configuration space, and configurations where the coordinates become invalid are called parameterization singularities. That is, it is not possible to uniquely determine any PKM configuration by one specific set of minimal coordinates. The most natural and practicable choice of minimal coordinates is to use the actuator coordinates. Then, the parameterization singularities are also input singularities. An ad hoc method to cope with this phenomenon is to switch between different minimal coordinates us discussed in Hufnagel & Müller (2011); Müller (2011a). This is a computationally complex approach since it requires monitoring the numerical conditioning of the constraint equations, and the entire set of motion equation must be changed accordingly. Instead of using a minimal number of generalized coordinates together with the switching method, a formulation in terms of the entire set of dependent coordinates of the PKM was proposed in Müller (2011b;c). This gives rise to a large system of redundant equations. Despite the large system of motion equations this formulation is advantageous since it does not exhibit singularities, i.e. it is valid in all feasible configurations of the PKM. Now the peculiarity of RA-PKM is that input singularities can be avoided by means of the actuation redundancy. Consequently, the actuator coordinates represent a valid set of redundant parameters that may give rise to another system of redundant motion equations, but of smaller size, as discussed in the following.

In this chapter the applicability of the standard minimal coordinates formulation is discussed and an alternative formulation in terms of actuator coordinates is presented. The latter formulation is globally valid as long as the PKM does not encounter input singularities, which is the aim of applying redundant actuation. Upon this formulation an amended augmented PD (APD) and computed torque control (CTC) scheme is proposed. These model-based control schemes are shown to achieve exponentially stable trajectory tracking. Experimental results are shown for a prototype implementation of a 2-DOF redundantly actuated PKM.

2. Kinematics of PKM with actuation redundancy

Denoting the joint variables of the PKM with $q^1, \ldots, q^n$, the PKM configuration is represented by the joint coordinate vector $\mathbf{q} \in \mathbb{V}^n$. The kinematic loops of the PKM give rise to a system of r geometric and kinematic constraints

$$\mathbf{0} = \mathbf{h}(\mathbf{q}), \ \mathbf{h}(\mathbf{q}) \in \mathbb{R}^r \tag{1}$$

$$\mathbf{0} = \mathbf{J}(\mathbf{q})\,\dot{\mathbf{q}}, \ \mathbf{J}(\mathbf{q}) \in \mathbb{R}^{r,n}. \tag{2}$$

The configuration space (c-space) of the PKM model is the set of admissible configurations, defined by the geometric constraints (1)

$$V := \{\mathbf{q} \in \mathbb{V}^n | \mathbf{h}(\mathbf{q}) = \mathbf{0}\}. \tag{3}$$

Presumed $\mathbf{J}$ has full rank, the PKM has the DOF $\delta := n - r$. Consequently δ joint variables can be selected as independent coordinates representing a minimal set of generalized coordinates for the PKM and the (2) can be solved in terms of the corresponding independent velocities. Instead of using such independent minimal coordinates a solution can be expressed in terms of actuator coordinates.

To the actuated joints can be associated m joint coordinates summarized in the vector $\mathbf{q}_\mathrm{a}$ so that the vector of joint coordinates can be rearranged as $\mathbf{q} = (\mathbf{q}_\mathrm{p}, \mathbf{q}_\mathrm{a})$, where $\mathbf{q}_\mathrm{p}$ comprises the coordinates of passive coordinates. The constraints (2) can then be rearranged as

$$\mathbf{J}_\mathrm{P}\dot{\mathbf{q}}_\mathrm{P} + \mathbf{J}_\mathrm{a}\dot{\mathbf{q}}_\mathrm{a} = \mathbf{0} \tag{4}$$

with $r \times (n-m)$ matrix $\mathbf{J}_{\mathrm{P}}$.
The form (4) allows to identify two types of singularities. Assume that in regular configurations of the PKM (i.e. no c-space singularities) the constraint Jacobian $\mathbf{J}$ has full rank r. Further assume that the number m of actuators is at least $\delta = n - r$. Then if rank $\mathbf{J}_{\mathrm{P}} = n - m$ and rank $\mathbf{J}_{\mathrm{a}} = \delta$, the PKM motion is always determined by the m actuator coordinates and (4) can be resolved as $\dot{\mathbf{q}}_{\mathrm{P}} = -\mathbf{J}_{\mathrm{P}}^{+}\mathbf{J}_{\mathrm{a}}\dot{\mathbf{q}}_{\mathrm{a}}$ so that

$$\dot{\mathbf{q}} = \widetilde{\mathbf{F}}\dot{\mathbf{q}}_{\mathrm{a}} \tag{5}$$

with

$$\widetilde{\mathbf{F}} = \begin{pmatrix} -\mathbf{J}_{\mathrm{P}}^{+}\mathbf{J}_{\mathrm{a}} \\ \mathbf{I}_{m} \end{pmatrix} \tag{6}$$

that satisfied $\mathbf{J}\widetilde{\mathbf{F}} \equiv \mathbf{0}$, where $\mathbf{J}_{\mathrm{P}}^{+} = \left(\mathbf{J}_{\mathrm{P}}^{T}\mathbf{J}_{\mathrm{P}}\right)^{-1}\mathbf{J}_{\mathrm{P}}^{T}$ is the left-pseudoinverse. In (5) it is assumed that $\dot{\mathbf{q}}_{\mathrm{a}}$ satisfies the constraints. Moreover, δ of them can serve as minimal coordinates.
Since actuation redundancy can eliminate input-singularities it is assumed in the following that the PKM does not encounter input-singularities in the relevant part of the workspace. A configuration $\mathbf{q}$ is called a c-space singularity if rank $\mathbf{J}$ changes in $\mathbf{q}$.

3. Motion equations in actuator coordinates

A PKM is a mechanism with kinematic loops, and the corresponding constraint forces are incorporated via the generalized constraint forces. The Lagrangian motion equations of the PKM can be represented in the standard form

$$\mathbf{G}(\mathbf{q})\,\ddot{\mathbf{q}} + \mathbf{C}(\mathbf{q},\dot{\mathbf{q}})\,\dot{\mathbf{q}} + \mathbf{Q}(\mathbf{q},\dot{\mathbf{q}},t) + \mathbf{J}^{T}(\mathbf{q})\,\boldsymbol{\lambda} = \mathbf{u} \tag{7}$$

where $\boldsymbol{\lambda}$ is the vector of Lagrange multipliers, $\mathbf{G}$ is the generalized mass matrix of the unconstrained system, $\mathbf{C}\dot{\mathbf{q}}$ represents generalized Coriolis and centrifugal forces, $\mathbf{Q}$ represents all remaining forces (possibly including EE loads), and $\mathbf{u}(t)$ are the generalized control forces. In the following a formulation of the equations of motion governing the PKM dynamics are derived in terms of actuator coordinates. Since the columns of $\widetilde{\mathbf{F}}$ constitute a basis for the null-space of $\mathbf{J}$, the generalized constraint reaction forces in (7) can be eliminated by premultiplication with $\widetilde{\mathbf{F}}^{T}$ at the same time reducing the number of equations. On a kinematic level the expression (5) and $\ddot{\mathbf{q}} = \widetilde{\mathbf{F}}\ddot{\mathbf{q}}_{\mathrm{a}} + \dot{\widetilde{\mathbf{F}}}\dot{\mathbf{q}}_{\mathrm{a}}$, where

$$\dot{\widetilde{\mathbf{F}}} = \begin{pmatrix} -\mathbf{J}_{\mathrm{P}}^{+}\dot{\mathbf{J}}\widetilde{\mathbf{F}} \\ \mathbf{0}_{m} \end{pmatrix}, \tag{8}$$

allow substitution of the generalized velocity and acceleration vector $\dot{\mathbf{q}}$ and $\ddot{\mathbf{q}}$, by actuator velocities and accelerations, respectively. This gives rise to the reduced system of motion equations

$$\widetilde{\mathbf{G}}(\mathbf{q})\,\ddot{\mathbf{q}}_{\mathrm{a}} + \widetilde{\mathbf{C}}(\mathbf{q},\dot{\mathbf{q}})\,\dot{\mathbf{q}}_{\mathrm{a}} + \widetilde{\mathbf{Q}}(\mathbf{q},\dot{\mathbf{q}},t) = \mathbf{c} \tag{9}$$

with

$$\widetilde{\mathbf{G}} := \widetilde{\mathbf{F}}^{T}\mathbf{G}\widetilde{\mathbf{F}},\ \widetilde{\mathbf{C}} := \widetilde{\mathbf{F}}^{T}(\mathbf{C}\widetilde{\mathbf{F}} + \mathbf{G}\dot{\widetilde{\mathbf{F}}}),\ \widetilde{\mathbf{Q}} := \widetilde{\mathbf{F}}^{T}\mathbf{Q} \tag{10}$$

and $\mathbf{c}$ represents the actuator forces being part of the overall vector $\mathbf{u}$.
This is a reduced system of m equations. It is crucial to notice that only δ of these m equations are independent. That is, if the PKM is redundantly actuated ($m > \delta$), the projected mass

matrix is $\widetilde{\mathbf{G}}$ is singular. However, the advantage of the formulation (9) is that it already represents a solution for the inverse dynamics problem, in contrast to the minimal coordinate formulations Müller (2005). This will be beneficial for the model-based control.

4. Parameterization singularities of non-redundantly actuated PKM

The selection of actuator coordinates induces a parameterization of the PKM configuration. Commonly a minimal set of δ independent coordinates, denoted $\mathbf{q}_2$, are selected giving rise to δ motion equations. It is well-known, however, that such minimal coordinates are not globally valid in the sense that there are configuration where a particular set of of coordinates does not uniquely determine the PKM motion. Such configurations are called parameterization singularities. For non-redundantly actuated PKM $\delta = m$ actuator coordinates are usually taken as independent coordinates, so that $\mathbf{q}_2 = \mathbf{q}_\mathrm{a}$ and the parameterization singularities are exactly the input singularities. In these cases $\mathbf{J}_\mathrm{a}$ in (4) is rectangular and invertible as long as the non-redundantly actuated PKM does not encounter input singularities.

To explain this phenomenon consider the planar 2$\underline{\text{R}}$RR/$\underline{\text{R}}$R PKM shown in figure 1. This system has a DOF $\delta = 2$, but is actuated by the $m = 3$ actuators at the base joints. Hence it is redundantly actuated with a degree of redundancy of $\rho = m - \delta = 1$. This PKM is naturally parameterized in terms of two of these three actuator coordinates. Now, as outlined above, there are configurations where the PKM motion is cannot be prescribed by $\delta = 2$ coordinates. These parameterization-singularities can be observed if the joint angles of two of these actuators are used as independent coordinates. Figure 2 shows the EE locus corresponding to the input-singularities for three different choices of independent coordinates. The EE traces of the singularities in workspace are the coupler curves of the 4-bar mechanism formed by fixing the middle joint so that the middle links keep aligned.

To cope with the lack of a globally valid parameterization of the PKM configuration a switching method for RA-PKM was proposed in Hufnagel & Müller (2011). The basic idea of this method is to switch to a different set of δ (actuator) coordinates whenever the current set fails. The drawback of this method is that for each set of independent coordinates different set motion equations must be invoked, which increases the implementation effort. Ideally

Fig. 1. Prototype of a planar 2$\underline{\text{R}}$RR/$\underline{\text{R}}$R RA-PKM.

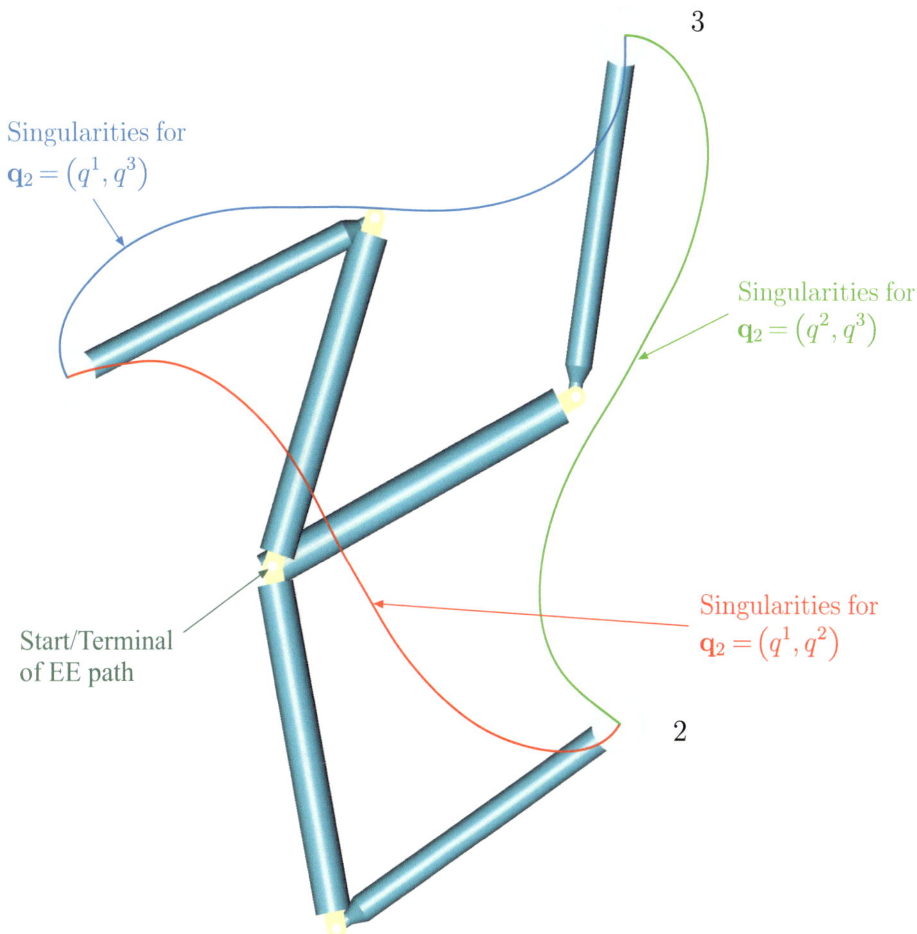

Fig. 2. Different input singularities if the 2 DOF 2$\underline{\text{R}}$R/$\underline{\text{R}}$RR PKM is non-redundantly actuated. The mechanism shown in color is the equivalent non-redundantly actuated mechanisms being instantaneously in an input-singularity.

a formulation should be used that is free from any parameterization singularities within the range of motion of the PKM. It often suggested to use EE coordinates as independent generalized coordinates, so that (9) would govern the PKM dynamics in workspace. It turns out, however, that even this choice suffers from parameter singularities.

Now the main motivation for introduction of redundant actuation is that most, or possibly all, of the input singularities of the non-redundant PKM can be eliminated. Assumption that the RA-PKM does not possess input-singularities, i.e. it can always be controlled by some δ out of the m actuator coordinates, the m input coordinates $\mathbf{q}_a$ constitute feasible coordinates to parameterize the PKM motion. Hence the system (9) is globally valid for the entire motion range. In summary, the redundant formulation (9) is globally valid in the entire motion range of a RA-PKM where it does not exhibit input-singularities. If $m = \delta$, i.e. non-redundant actuation, the formulation (9) reduces to the classical formulation in minimal coordinates Müller (2005).

5. Model-based control schemes in redundant actuator coordinates

While the solution of the inverse dynamics problem of RA-PKM in minimal coordinates involves the pseudoinverse of the $m \times \delta$ control matrix, the formulation (9) in redundant actuator coordinates is already an inverse dynamics solution that can be immediately employed for the feedforward. Therewith an APD control scheme can be introduced as

$$\begin{aligned} \mathbf{c} &= \widetilde{\mathbf{G}}(\mathbf{q})\,\ddot{\mathbf{q}}_{\mathrm{a}}^{\mathrm{d}} + \widetilde{\mathbf{C}}(\dot{\mathbf{q}},\mathbf{q})\,\dot{\mathbf{q}}_{\mathrm{a}}^{\mathrm{d}} + \widetilde{\mathbf{Q}}(\mathbf{q},\dot{\mathbf{q}},t) - \mathbf{K}_{\mathrm{P}}\mathbf{e}_{\mathrm{a}} - \mathbf{K}_{\mathrm{D}}\dot{\mathbf{e}}_{\mathrm{a}} \\ &= \widetilde{\mathbf{F}}^{T}(\mathbf{G}(\mathbf{q})\,\ddot{\mathbf{q}}_{\mathrm{a}}^{\mathrm{d}} + \mathbf{C}(\mathbf{q},\dot{\mathbf{q}})\,\dot{\mathbf{q}}_{\mathrm{a}}^{\mathrm{d}} + \mathbf{Q}(\mathbf{q},\dot{\mathbf{q}},t)) - \mathbf{K}_{\mathrm{P}}\mathbf{e}_{\mathrm{a}} - \mathbf{K}_{\mathrm{D}}\dot{\mathbf{e}}_{\mathrm{a}} \end{aligned} \tag{11}$$

where $\mathbf{q}_{\mathrm{a}}^{\mathrm{d}}(t)$ is the target trajectory and $\mathbf{e}_{\mathrm{a}} := \mathbf{q}_{\mathrm{a}} - \mathbf{q}_{\mathrm{a}}^{\mathrm{d}}$ is the tracking error. The gain matrices $\mathbf{K} = \mathrm{diag}\,(K_1, \ldots, K_m)$ in the linear feed-back measure the errors in the m actuator coordinates.
Further a CTC scheme in terms of actuator coordinates can be introduced as

$$\begin{aligned} \mathbf{c} &= \widetilde{\mathbf{G}}(\mathbf{q})\,\mathbf{v}_{\mathrm{a}} + \widetilde{\mathbf{C}}(\dot{\mathbf{q}},\mathbf{q})\,\dot{\mathbf{q}}_{\mathrm{a}} + \widetilde{\mathbf{Q}}(\mathbf{q},\dot{\mathbf{q}},t) \\ &= \widetilde{\mathbf{F}}^{T}(\mathbf{G}(\mathbf{q})\,\mathbf{v}_{\mathrm{a}} + \mathbf{C}(\mathbf{q},\dot{\mathbf{q}})\,\dot{\mathbf{q}}_{\mathrm{a}} + \mathbf{Q}(\mathbf{q},\dot{\mathbf{q}},t)) \end{aligned} \tag{12}$$

with $\mathbf{v}_{\mathrm{a}} = \ddot{\mathbf{q}}_{\mathrm{a}} - \mathbf{K}_{\mathrm{P}}\mathbf{e}_{\mathrm{a}} - \mathbf{K}_{\mathrm{D}}\dot{\mathbf{e}}_{\mathrm{a}}$.
It is crucial that these control schemes lead to exponentially stable trajectory tracking. This property can be shown as for the minimal coordinates formulation by projection of the error dynamics to a δ subspace of the c-space V. Notice that in $(11)_2$ and $(12)_2$, $\mathbf{q}_{\mathrm{a}}^{\mathrm{d}}(t)$ and $\mathbf{q}_{\mathrm{a}}(t)$ are presumed to satisfy the constraints. If this is not ensured, when using measured values for instance, the formulation $(11)_1$ and $(12)_1$, respectively, is to be used.
At this point it should be remarked that the errors of all $m > \delta$ actuator coordinates must be used in the linear feedback. If only δ independent actuator coordinates are used, the feedback term does not account for the overall error in configurations where the motion is not uniquely determined by these δ actuator motions, i.e. in parameterization-/input-singularities of the non-redundantly actuated PKM. On the other hand the redundant feedback causes counteraction of the m actuators since only δ actuator coordinates are independent but the m feedback commands are not.
While the actuator coordinate formulation offers globally valid motion equations it does not involve the components of the control forces that correspond to the null-space of the control matrix as the inverse dynamics solution in minimal coordinates does.

6. Experimental results

The prototype of the planar 2 DOF 2<u>R</u>RR/<u>R</u>R PKM in figure 1 has been used as testbed for the proposed control schemes in redundant actuator coordinates and the classical formulation in minimal coordinate. The testbed is equipped with a dSPACE DS1103 real-time system operating with a sampling rate of 2.5 kHz. The controller gains were set to $K_{\mathrm{P}} = 500$ and $K_{\mathrm{D}} = 8$, in accordance to the actuator dynamics. The three base joints are actuated by Maxon Re30 DC motors. They are mounted at the vertices of an equilateral triangle with 400 mm

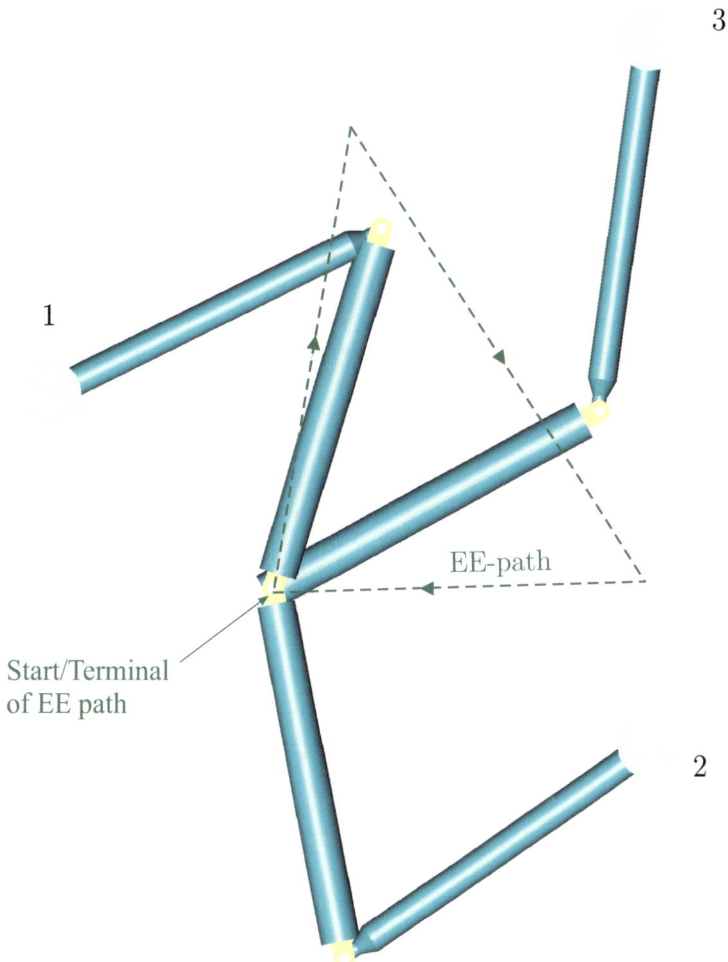

Fig. 3. EE-path and singular curves of the 2DOF RA-PKM.

lateral lengths. Each arm segment has a length of 200 mm, and the total weight of one arm is 134 g. The motion equations (7) are derived in terms of relative coordinates by opening the two kinematic loops. This gives rise to a PKM model (7) comprising $n = 6$ equations in terms of the $n = 6$ joint angles subject to $r = 4$ cut-joint constraints. Hence the DOF of the PKM is $\delta = 2$. the formulation (9) yields $m = 3$ equations in terms of the redundant actuator coordinates (of which $\delta = 2$ are independent). In the experiment the manipulator is controlled along the EE-path in figure 3. Denote with q^1, q^2, q^3 the joint angles of the actuated base joints so that $\mathbf{q}_a = (q^1, q^2, q^3)$. The joint trajectory is determined from the EE-path by solving the inverse kinematics where velocity and acceleration limits are taken into account. The EE path passes all singularity loci shown in 2. That is, a non-redundantly actuated PKM, of which only $\delta = 2$ joints are actuated, exhibits input-singularities for any combination of two actuator coordinates.

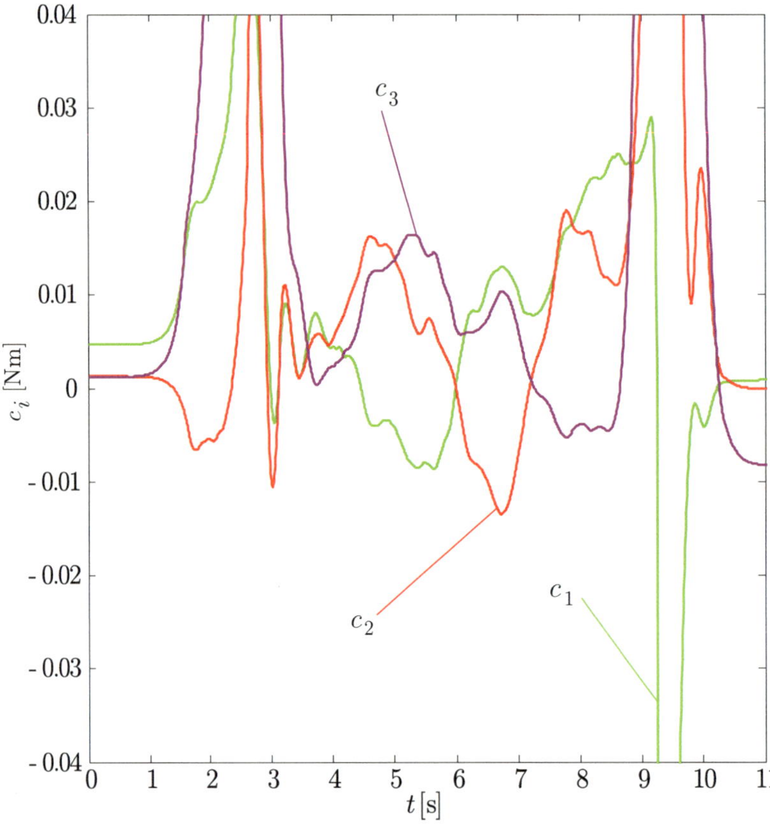

Fig. 4. Actuator torques computed from the CTC in minimal cooridnates if $\mathbf{q}_{\mathrm{a}} = (q^1, q^2)$.

In order to show the effect of parameter singularities of the minimal coordinate formulation figure 4 shows the computed control commands when only the two coordinates $\mathbf{q}_{\mathrm{a}} = (q^1, q^2)$ are used in (9), which corresponds to a non-redundantly actuated PKM. Since for this EE path the PKM has to cross the singularity curve for this combination (red curve in figure 2) once at the start and once just before the end of the EE-trajectory the control torques tend to infinity at these points. Consequently at these points the model does not admit to compute any sensible control torques and leads to instabilities.

In contrast, when controlling the RA-PKM using the CTC (12) in redundant actuator coordinates leads to the drive torques in figure 5. Figure 6 sows the corresponding joint tracking errors. Apparently the redundant coordinate formulation achieves a smooth motion and torque evolution unaffected by any singularities.

In this experiment it is clearly visible that there are non-zero drive torques even if the RA-PKM is not moving. This is a peculiar phenomenon that can only be observed in RA-PKM. It can partially be attributed to the interplay of measurement errors and finite encoder resolutions with actuation redundancy. Due to the actuation redundancy the control forces are not independent so that the RA-PKM attains a configuration that is not determined by the measurement error (as for non-redundant actuation) but by the static equilibrium of the control torques that do not affect the RA-PKM motion, but rather lead to internal prestress. This is a general problem for RA-PKM that was addressed in Müller & Hufnagel (2011).

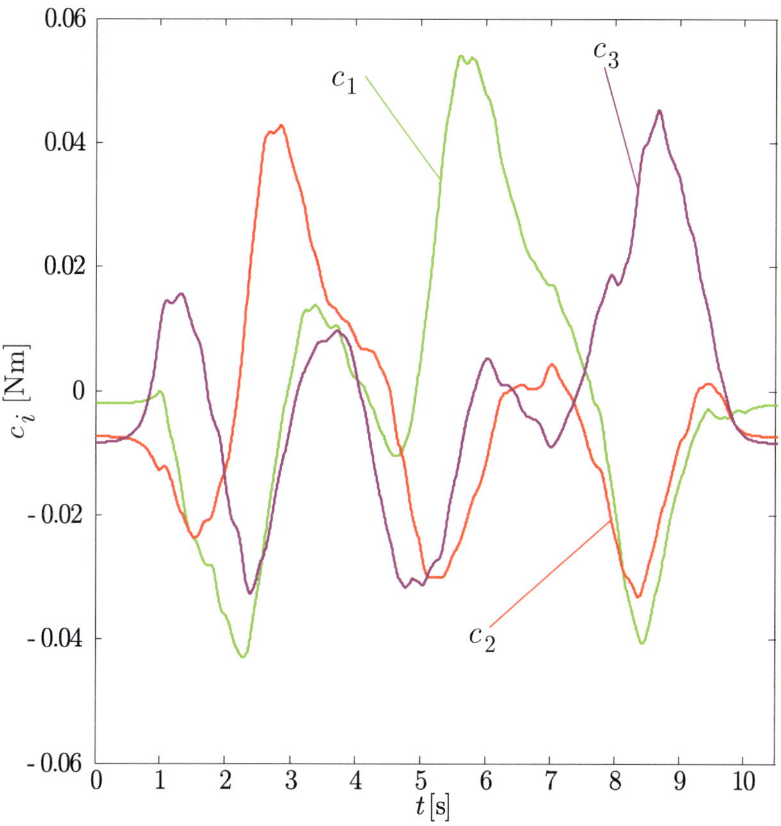

Fig. 5. Actuator torques when the RA-PKM is controlled along the EE-path of figure 3 by the CTC in redundant coordinates.

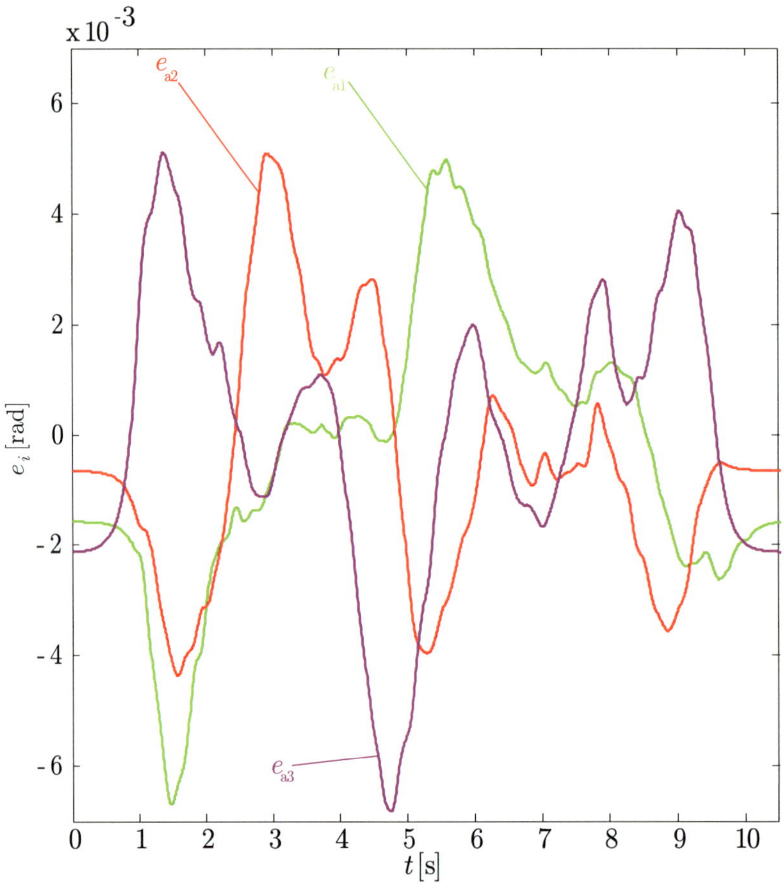

Fig. 6. Joint tracking errors when the RA-PKM is controlled by the CTC in redundant coordinates.

7. Summary

PKM are commonly characterized by inhomogeneous distribution of kinematic and dynamic properties within the work space, and eventually the existence of input-singularities. Actuation redundancy allows to eliminate these singularities, and thus to extend the usable workspace. The PKM motion equations are commonly formulated using a set of minimal coordinates. Moreover, actuator coordinates are usually used as minimal coordinates. Thus input-singularities are also parameterization-singularities of the PKM model, which is critical for any model-based control. In this chapter an alternative formulation of motion equations in terms of redundant actuator coordinates has been proposed, and the corresponding amended form of an augmented PD and computed torque control scheme were presented. The applicability of the proposed methods is confirmed by the experimental results for a planar redundantly actuated PKM.

8. References

H. Abdellatif et al. (2005) High Efficient Dynamics Calculation Approach for Computed-Force Control of Robots with Parallel Structures, IEEE Conference on Decision and Control and European Control Conference (CDC-ECC), 12-15 Dec. 2005, pp. 2024-2029

H. Asada & J.J. E. Slotine (1986) Robot Analysis and Control. New York, Wiley

D. Chakarov (2004) Study of the antagonistic stiffness of parallel manipulators with actuation redundancy, Mech. Mach. Theory, Vol. 39, 2004, pp. 583-601

H. Cheng et al. (2003) Dynamics and Control of Redundantly Actuated Parallel Manipulators, IEEE/ASME Trans. on Mechatronics, Vol. 8, no. 4, 2003, pp. 483-491

M.R. Cutkosky & P.K. Wright (1986) Active Control of a Compliant Wrist in Manufacturing Tasks, ASME J. Eng. for Industry, Vol. 108, No. 1, 1986, pp. 36-43

Garg, V.; Noklely, S.B. & Carretero, J.A. (2009). Wrench capability analysis of redundantly actuated spatial parallel manipulators, *Mech. Mach. Theory*, Vol. 44, No. 5, 2009, pp: 1070-1081

Gogu, G. (2007). Fully-isotropic redundantly-actuated parallel wrists with three degrees of freedom, *Proc. ASME Int. Design Eng. Tech. Conf. (IDETC)*, Las Vegas, NV, 2007, DETC2007-34237

T. Hufnagel & A. Müller (2011) A Realtime Coordinate Switching Method for Model-Based Control of Parallel Manipulators, ECCOMAS Thematic Conference on Multibody Dynamics, Juli 4-7, 2011, Brussels, Belgium

S. Kock & W. Schumacher (1998) A parallel x-y manipulator with actuation redundancy for high-speed and active-stiffness applications, Proc. IEEE Int. Conf. Robot. Autom. (ICRA), Leuven, pp. 2295-2300

Krut, S.; Company, O. & Pierrot, F. (2004) Velocity performance indicies for parallel mechanisms with actuation redundancy, *Robotica*, Vol. 22, 2004, pp. 129-139

Kurtz, R.; Hayward, V. (1992) Multiple-goal kinematic optimization of a parallel spherical mechanism with actuator redundancy, *IEEE Trans. on Robotics Automation*, Vol. 8. no. 5, 1992, pp. 644-651

Lee, J.H.; Li, B.J.; Suh, H. (1998) Optimal design of a five-bar finger with redundant actuation, *Proc. IEEE Int. Conf. Rob. Aut. (ICRA)*, Leuven, 1998, 2068-2074

S.H. Lee et al. (2005) Optimization and experimental verification for the antagonistic stiffness in redundantly actuated mechanisms: a five-bar example, Mechatronics Vol. 15, 2005, pp. 213-238

Müller, A. (2005). Internal Prestress Control of redundantly actuated Parallel Manipulators - Its Application to Backlash avoiding Control, *IEEE Trans. on Rob.*, pp. 668 - 677, Vol. 21, No. 4, 2005

A. Müller (2006). Stiffness Control of redundantly actuated Parallel Manipulators, Proc. IEEE Int. Conf. Rob. Automat. (ICRA), Orlando, May 15-19, 2006, pp. 1153 - 1158

A. Müller (2011). A Robust Inverse Dynamics Formulation for Redundantly Actuated PKM, *Proc. 13th World Congress in Mechanism and Machine Science*, Guanajuato, Mexico, 19-25 June 2011

A. Müller (2011). Motion Equations in Redundant Coordinates with Application to Inverse Dynamics of Constrained Mechanical Systems, *Nonlinear Dynamics*, DOI 10.1007/s11071-011-0165-5

A. Müller (2011) Robust Modeling and Control Issues of Parallel Manipulators with Actuation Redundancy, in A. Müller (editor): Recent Advances in Robust Control - Volume 1: Theory and Applications in Robotics and Electromechanics, InTech, Vienna, Austria, 2011

A. Müller, T. Hufnagel (2011) Adaptive and Singularity-Free Inverse Dynamics Models for Control of Parallel Manipulators with Actuation Redundancy, 8th International Conference on Multibody Systems, Nonlinear Dynamics, and Control, ASME 2011 International Design Engineering Technical Conferences, August 28-31, 2011, Washington, DC

A. Müller, T. Hufnagel (2011) A Projection Method for the Elimination of Contradicting Control Forces in Redundantly Actuated PKM, IEEE Int. Conf. Rob. Automat. (ICRA), May 9-13, 2011, Shanghai, China

Nahon, M.A.; Angeles, J. (1989) Force optimization in redundantly-actuated closed kinematic chains, *Proc. IEEE Int. Conf. Rob. Automat. (ICRA)*, Scottsdale, USA, May 14-19, 1989, pp. 951956

Y. Nakamura & M. Ghodoussi (1989) Dynamics Computation of Closed-Link Robot Mechanisms with Nonredundant and Redundant Actuators, IEEE Tran. Rob. and Aut., Vol. 5, No. 3, 1989, pp. 294-302

O'Brien, J.F.; Wen, J.T. (1999) Redundant actuation for improving kinematic manipulability, *Proc. IEEE Int. Conf. Robotics Automation*, 1999, pp. 1520-1525

Valasek, M. et al. (2005) Design-by-Optimization and Control of Redundantly Actuated Parallel Kinematics Sliding Star, *Multibody System Dynamics*, Vol. 14, no. 3-4, 2005, 251-267

Wu, J. et al. (2009) Dynamics and control of a planar 3-DOF parallel manipulator with actuation redundancy, *Mech. Mach. Theory*, Vol. 44, 2009, pp. 835-849.

B.Y. Yi et al. (1989) Open-loop stiffness control of overconstrained mechanisms/robot linkage systems, Proc. IEEE Int. Conf. Robotics Automation, Scottsdale, 1989, pp. 1340-1345

Position Control and Trajectory Tracking of the Stewart Platform

Selçuk Kizir and Zafer Bingul
Mechatronics Engineering, Kocaeli University
Turkey

1. Introduction

Demand on high precision motion systems has been increasing in recent years. Since performance of today's many mechanical systems requires high stiffness, fast motion and accurate positioning capability, parallel manipulators have gained popularity. Currently, parallel robots have been widely used several areas of industry such as manufacturing, medicine and defense. Some of these areas: precision laser cutting, micro machining, machine tool technology, flight simulators, helicopter runway, throwing platform of missiles, surgical operations. Some examples are shown in Figure 1. Unlike open-chain serial robots, parallel manipulators are composed of closed kinematic chain. There exist several parallel kinematic chains between base platform and end moving platform. Serial robots consist of a number of rigid links connected in serial so every actuator supports the weight of the successor links. This serial structure suffers from several disadvantages such as low precision, poor force exertion capability and low payload-to-weight-ratio. The parallel robot architecture eliminates these disadvantages. In this architecture, the load is shared by several parallel kinematic chains. This superior architecture provides high rigidity, high payload-to-weight-ratio, high positioning accuracy, low inertia of moving parts and a simpler solution of the inverse kinematics equations over the serial ones. Since high accuracy of parallel robots stems from load sharing of each actuator, there are no cumulative joint errors and deflections in the links. Under heavy loads, serial robots cannot perform precision positioning and oscillate at high-speeds. Positioning accuracy of parallel robots is high because the positioning error of the platform cannot exceed the average error of the legs positions. They can provide nanometer-level motion performance. But they have smaller workspace and singularities in their workspace.

The most widely used structure of a parallel robot is the Stewart platform (SP). It is a six degrees of freedom (DOF) positioning system that consists of a top plate (moving platform), a base plate (fixed base), and six extensible legs connecting the top plate to the bottom plate.

SP was invented as a flight simulator by Stewart in 1965 (Stewart, 1965). This platform contained three parallel linear actuators. Gough had previously suggested a tire test machine similar to Stewart's model (Bonev, 2003). In the test machine, six actuators were used as a mechanism driven in parallel. Gough, the first person, developed and utilized this type parallel structure. Therefore, SP is sometimes named as Stewart-Gough platform in the literature. Stewart's and Gough's original designs are shown in Figure 2.

(a) (b) (c)

Fig. 1. Applications of the Stewart Platform: medical, manufacturing and flight simulator (Niesing, 2001; Merlet, 2006; Wikipedia)

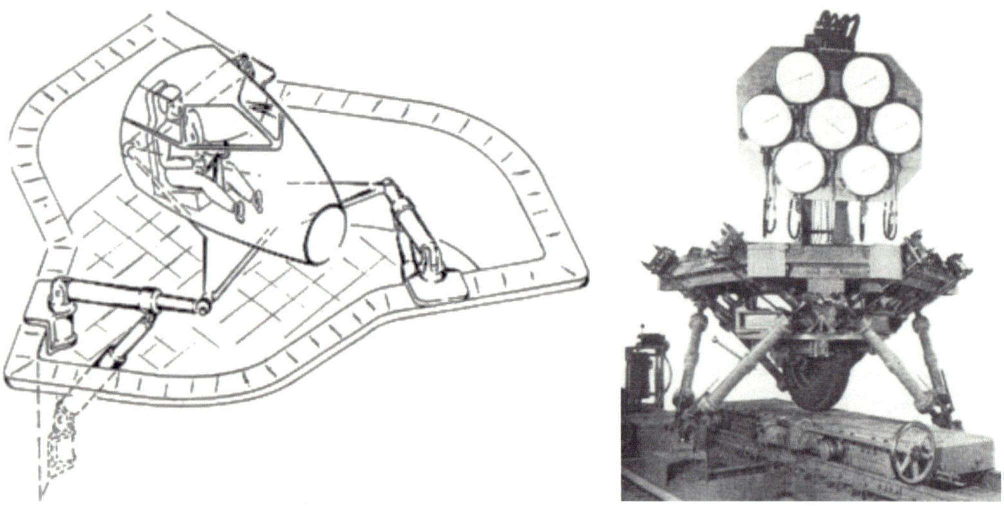

(a) (b)

Fig. 2. Stewart (a) and Gough (b) original design (Bonev, 2003)

SP was not attracted attention during the first 15 years since the first invention. Then, Hunt indicated the advantages of parallel robots. After 1983, researchers realized their high load carrying capacity and high positioning ability of these robots. Researchers were then started to study a detailed analysis of these structures. The widely used structure of SP, where top platform is connected to base platform using 6 linear axis with universal joints, was then developed (Hunt, 1983).

It is a well known fact that the solution of the forward kinematics problem is easier than the inverse kinematics problem for serial robot manipulators. On the other hand, this situation is the just opposite for a parallel robot. Inverse kinematics problem of parallel robot can be expressed as follows: position vector and rotation matrix in Cartesian space is given, and asked to find length of each link in joint space. It is relatively easy to find the link lengths because the position of the connecting points and the position and orientation of the moving platform is known. On the other hand, in the forward kinematics problem, the rotation matrix and position vector of the moving platform is computed with given the link lengths. Forward kinematic of the SP is very difficult problem since it requires the solution of many non-linear equations. In the literature, solutions of the forward (Chen & Song, 1994; Liao et al., 1993; Merlet, 1992; Nauna et al., 1990) and the inverse (Fitcher, 1986; Kim & Chung, 1999; Sefrioui & Gosselin, 1993) kinematics has been given in detail (Kizir et al., 2011).

In this study, design and development stages were given about position control and trajectory tracking of a 6 DOF-Stewart platform using Matlab/Simulink® and DS1103 real time controller. Matlab® (Mathworks Inc.) is a well known and one of the most popular technical computing software package that it is used in a wide area of applications from financial analysis to control designs. Matlab/Simulink® allows easiest way of programming and technical computing to its users. It enables simulations and real time applications of various systems. Third party co-developers improve its abilities allowing using hundreds of hardware. Dspace® company is one of the third party participate of Matlab® that produces rapid control prototyping and hardware-in-the-loop simulation units. DS1103 is a powerful real time controller board for rapid control prototyping (Dspace Inc.).

This chapter is organized in the following manner. System components and real-time controller board are introduced in section 2 and 3, respectively. Position and trajectory tracking control with PID and sliding mode controllers are described in section 4. Finally, experimental results are given in detail.

2. Stewart platform system

The system components are two main bodies (top and base plates), six linear motors, controller, space mouse, accelerometer, gyroscope, laser interferometer, force/torque sensor, power supply, emergency stop circuit and interface board. They are shown in Figure 3.

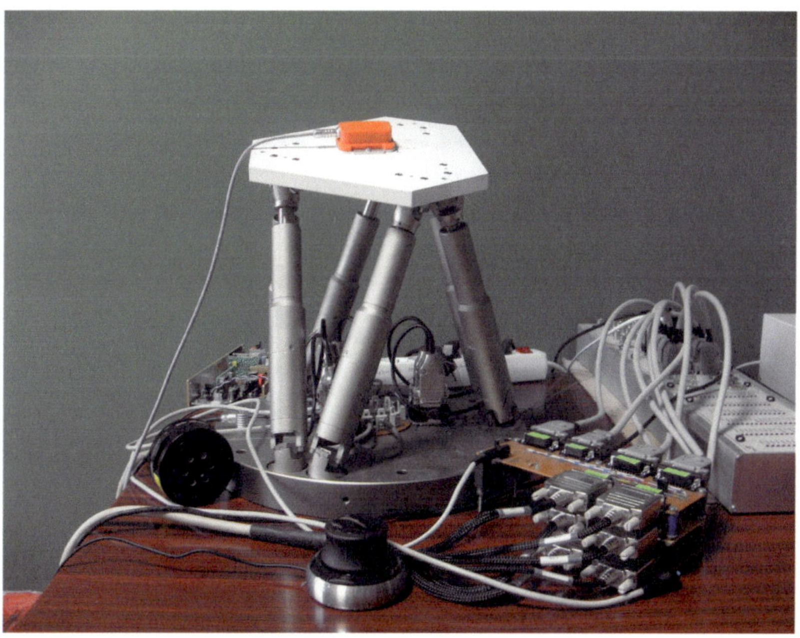

Fig. 3. Stewart platform system

A simple emergency stop circuit was designed to protect the motors, when they move to out of the limits. This circuit controls the power supply which gives the energy to the motors based on the signal of hall-effect sensors on each motor. A switch-mode 150W power supply with inhibit input and EMI filter is used to supply required energy. Also, an interface board was designed between controller and motors.

The Dspace DS1103 real time controller is used to implement control algorithms. DS1103 is a rapid prototyping controller that developed for designing and analyzing complex and difficult control applications. It has various inputs and outputs such as digital, analog digital converter, digital analog converter, serial interface, can-bus, pulse width modulation (PWM) channels and encoders in order to be used lots of peripheral unit like actuators and sensors.

DS1103 has a real time interface (RTI) that allows fully programmable from the Simulink® block diagram environment. A dspace toolbox will be added to Simulink® after installing RTI, so it can be configured all I/O graphically by using RTI. You can implement your control and signal processing algorithms on the board quickly and easily. A general DS1103 controller board system is shown in Figure 4. It consists of a DS1103 controller card in expansion box, CLP1103 input-output connector and led panel, DS817 link card and a computer.

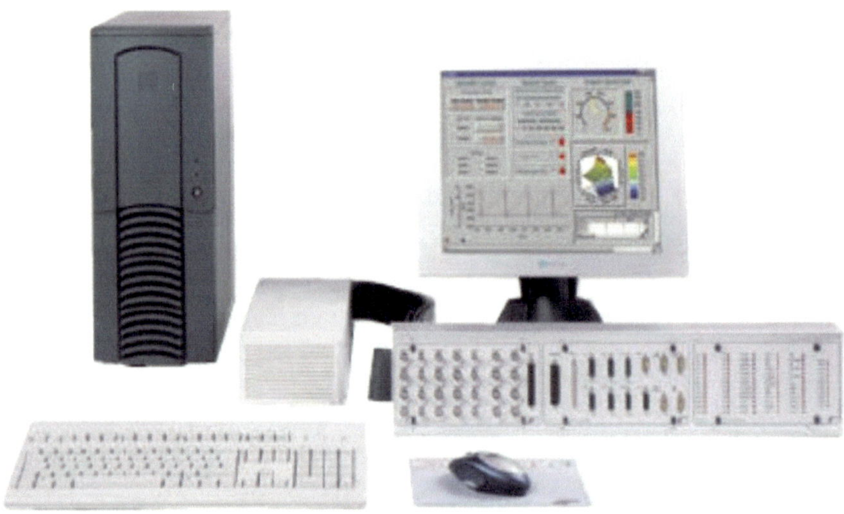

Fig. 4. A general DS1103 set-up

3. DSPACE tool box and design procedures

While Dspace offers various development tools, it is needed at least Control Desk and RTI block set software packages in order to develop projects under Simulink. After installing software, a tool box shown in Figure 5 is added to Simulink®. It can be also opened dspace library shown in Figure 5 typing ‘rti’ in the matlab command window. Block sets in the library are divided into two categories: master processor and slave dsp. While master have blocks such as ADC, serial, encoder, digital I/O, slave has such as PWM, ADC and digital I/O.

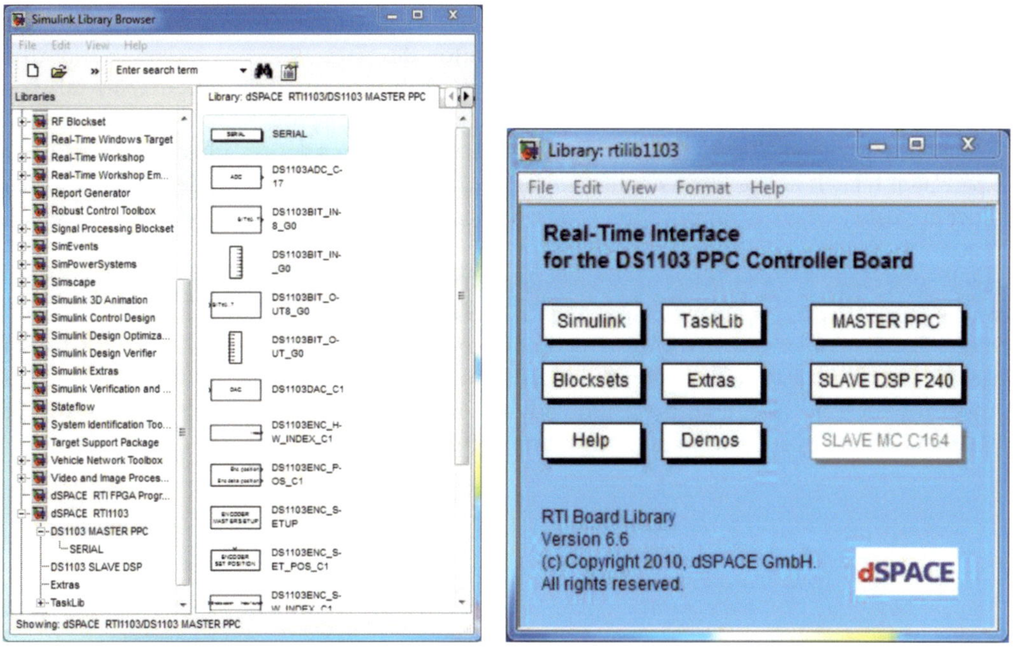

Fig. 5. Dspace toolbox and library

Another software component is the control desk (interface is shown in Figure 6) which allows downloading applications, doing experiments, easily creating graphical user interface and data acquisition.

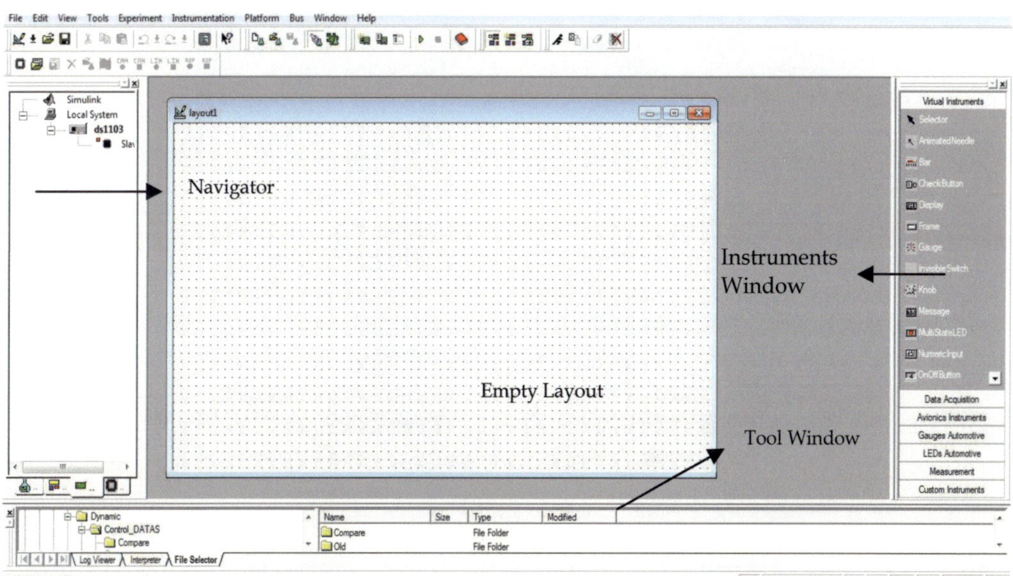

Fig. 6. Control desk interface

As can be seen from Figure 6, panel on the left side is called "Navigator" and it has four tabs: experiment, instrumentation, platform and test automation. All files written for conducting experiment are listed in the experiment tab. Instrumentation tab allows building instrument panels in order to change and monitor the variables of a model. Supported simulations and connected boards are shown in platform tab. Test automation tab has functions about automation tasks, other software solution of Dspace.

Bottom side is called "Tool Window" having log viewer, file selector, interpreter and open experiment tabs. It is seen errors and warnings in the log viewer tab and files under selected folder are listed where an application can be loaded by drag and drop action.

In order to create a GUI for an experiment, it should be opened an empty layout from file-new layout click. A lot of instruments are listed in the instrument selector right side on the control desk. Virtual instruments and data acquisition elements are shown in Figure 7 below. An instrument can be placed on the layout plotting with mouse left clicked after selecting from virtual instruments panel. Its position and size can be changed and its properties such as color, text, precision and etc can be settled according to needs. It can be saved and added to an experiment after completing GUI.

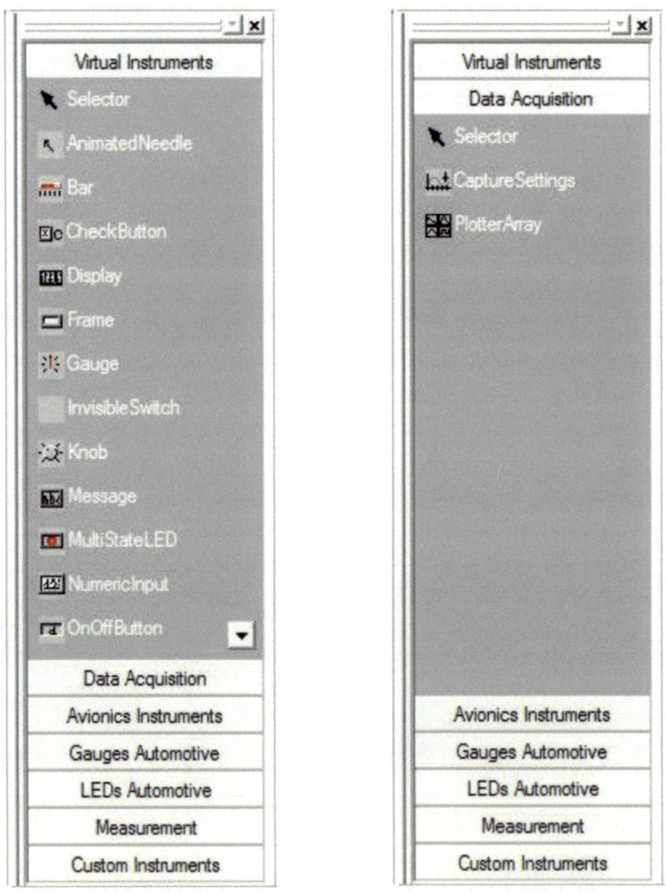

Fig. 7. Virtual instruments and data acquisition in the instruments selector window

All development steps can be illustrated basically in the Figure 8 below. This figure is illustrated for DS1103 in an expansion box. It should be finished all connections before this procedure.

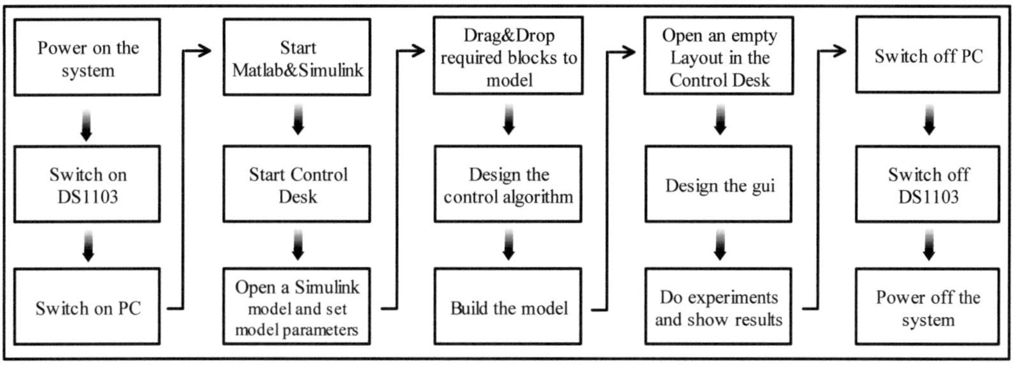

Fig. 8. Basic flow diagram for developing a project

4. Control

A controller is needed to move top platform from initial position to desired position and orientation. It will generate required forces for each motor. Position and trajectory control of the platform can be reduced to leg position control after inverse kinematic and path planning algorithms. A PID (proportional-integrator-derivative) and sliding mode position controllers were developed and implemented. Control algorithms designed in Simulink environment and embedded in the Dspace DS1103 real time controller.

All robots are electro-mechanic devices consisting of actuators, sensors and mechanical structure. In order to control the robots for desired motions kinematic and dynamic equations of the system should be known. Firstly kinematic solution should be computed before controller design. A schematic model of the SP for kinematic solution is illustrated in Figure 9. In the figure, base $B=\{X,Y,Z\}$ and top $T=\{x,y,z\}$ coordinate systems are placed and base and top joint points are labeled as B_i (i=1,2, .. 6) and T_i (i=1,2, .. 6).

It is needed to find leg lengths to reach the moving platform to its desired position and orientation according to fixed platform (inverse kinematics). Required leg vectors (L_i) for given position vector P and orientation matrix R are obtained by using the following equation. Finally, norm of the vectors (L_i) are leg lengths (l_i) (Fitcher, 1986; Kim & Chung, 1999; Sefrioui & Gosselin, 1993).

$$L_i = R_{XYZ} T_i + P - B_i \qquad i:1,2,...,6 \tag{1}$$

In order to have T_i and B_i position vectors based on robot structure, an m-file is written and a Simulink model is designed to obtain inverse kinematic solution by using Equation 1. The model shown in Figure 10 uses the m-file to get required variables and takes the desired position (x, y, z) and orientation (φ, θ, ψ) of the top platform. It outputs the leg lengths. Desired block in this model is shown in Figure 11. The reference inputs can be entered in this block.

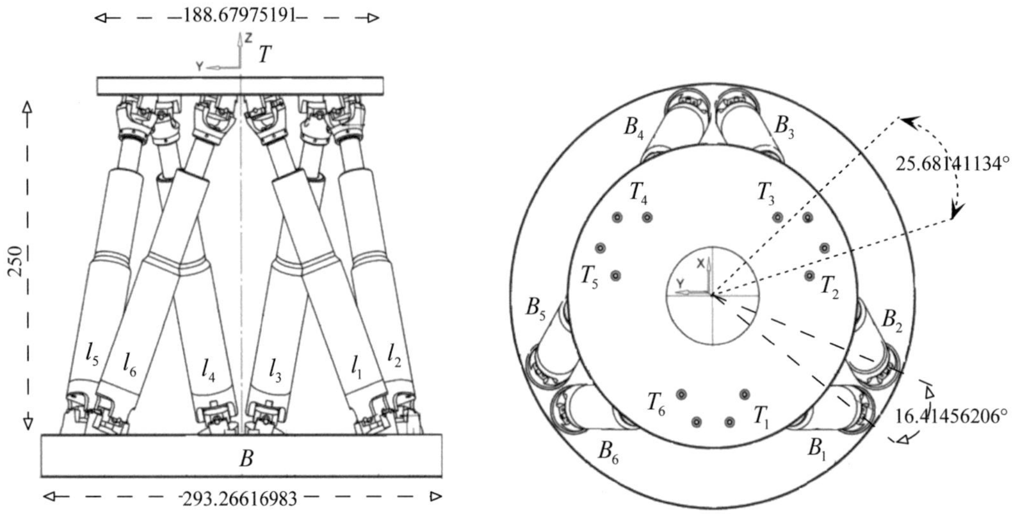

Fig. 9. Schematic diagram of the Stewart platform

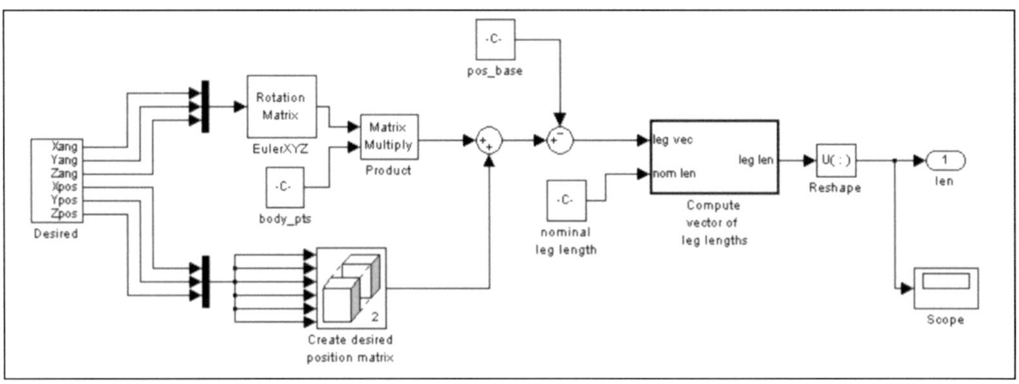

Fig. 10. Simulink model for inverse kinematic solution

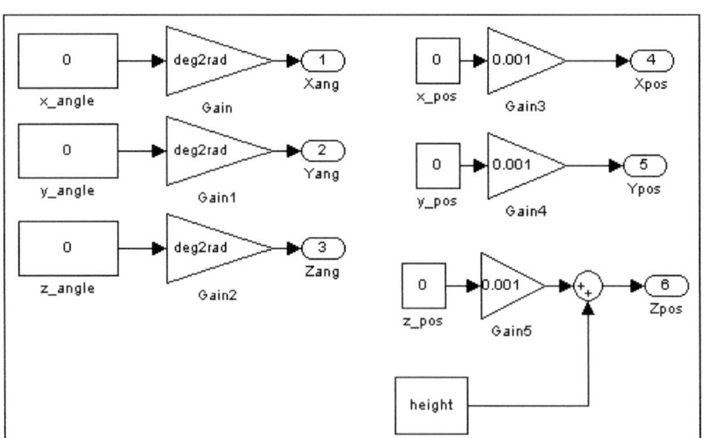

Fig. 11. A subsystem for desired references

4.1 Leg model

The leg system is basically composed of dc motor, precision linear bearing & ball screw and coupling elements. Dc motor model is given below (Küçük & Bingül, 2008).

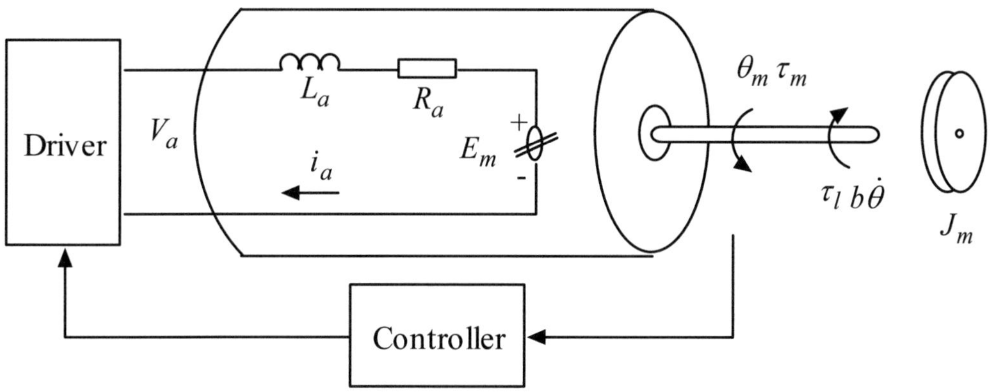

Fig. 12. DC motor model

The symbols represent the following variables here; θ_m is the motor position (*radian*), τ_m is the produced torque by the motor (*Nm*), τ_l is the load torque, V_a is the armature voltage (*V*), L_a is the armature inductance (*H*), R_a is the armature resistance (*Ω*), E_m is the reverse EMF (*V*), i_a is the armature current (*A*), K_b is the reverse EMF constant, K_m is the torque constant.

$$L_a \frac{di_a}{dt} + R_a i_a = V_a - E_m \tag{2}$$

$$E_m = K_b \frac{d\theta_m}{dt} \tag{3}$$

$$\tau_m = K_m i_a \tag{4}$$

$$\tau_m - \tau_l = J_m \frac{d^2\theta_m}{dt^2} \tag{5}$$

4.2 Startup algorithm

Before controller design a startup algorithm is needed to get robot to its home position. The position of each motor is controlled after startup. Motors have incremental encoders therefore firstly they must be brought their zero or home position. When SP system is energized, an index search algorithm looks what the position of the each leg is. The algorithm simply searches index signal of the leg and when it is found encoders are reset by hardware. Designed Simulink model for this purpose is illustrated in Figure 13. Movements to the home position for possible two situations (from upper and lower sides to zero) are shown in Figure 14.

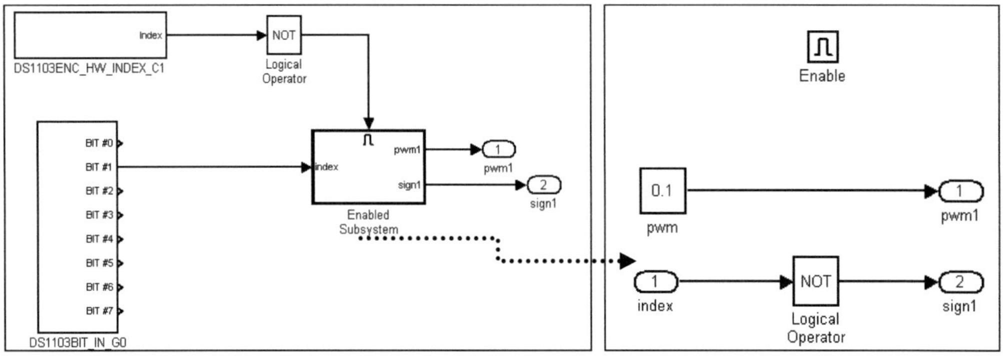

Fig. 13. Simulink model for initialization algorithm

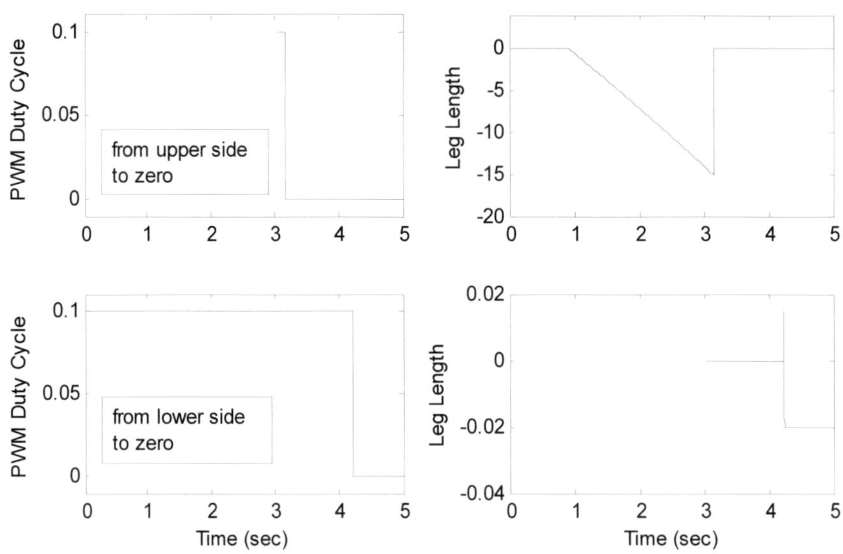

Fig. 14. Initialization routine

4.3 Trajectory generation

For step inputs, the leg lengths obtained from inverse kinematics solution input to independent position control system for each motor. This movement is defined in the joint space. In order to move robot along a straight line, a trajectory planning algorithm is developed. Thus, it can be determined start and stop times of the motion besides desired position and orientation inputs. Also, motors are synchronized each other during the motion. If classical polynomial-based trajectory equations are examined, the following deficiencies are determined: i) there are need many initial and finish values in order to find the polynomial coefficients ii) the acceleration values, especially initially require high levels, iii) the coefficients need to be calculated again each time when the conditions changes. Kane's transition function is used to resolve these shortcomings and it is given the following equation (Reckdahl, 1996).

$$y(t) = y_0 + \left(y_f - y_0\right)\frac{t-t_0}{t_f-t_0} - \frac{y_f - y_0}{2\pi}\sin\left(2\pi\frac{t-t_0}{t_f-t_0}\right) \tag{6}$$

where $y(t)$ is the position function, y_0 is the initial position, y_f is the finish position, t is time, t_0 is initial time and t_f is the finish time. An example of the trajectory generation is given below (Figure 15) using Equation 6. As can be seen from figure, position, velocity and acceleration curves are given for two seconds and velocity and acceleration start and finish with zero.

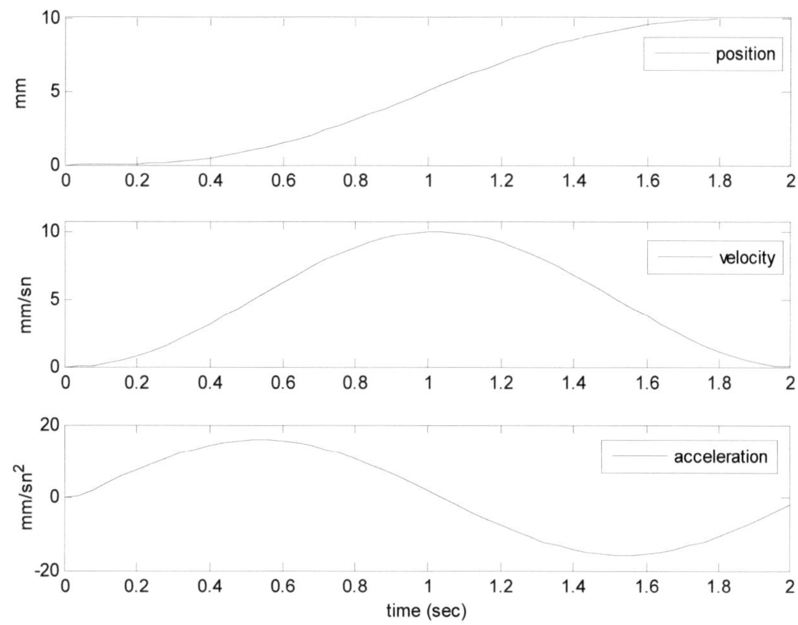

Fig. 15. An example of trajectory generation with Kane function

Equation 6 was embedded in Simulink block. Only end position and path period is given to this structure and other parameters are automatically calculated. This form of motion starts and finishes with zero velocity and zero acceleration. Position, velocity and acceleration values are quite soft changes. This is very important for motors to start and stop more softly. Main model of the trajectory planning with reference inputs is shown in Figure 16 below. Detail of the blocks named 'path' in the Figure 16 is shown in Figure 17 which implements the Equation 6.

4.4 PID controller

PID control is one of the classical control methods and widely used in the industrial applications. The difference between the set point and the actual output is represented by the $e(t)$ error signal. This signal is applied to a PID controller, control signal, $u(t)$ is as follows.

$$u(t) = K_P e(t) + K_I \int e(t)dt + K_D \frac{d}{dt}e(t) \tag{7}$$

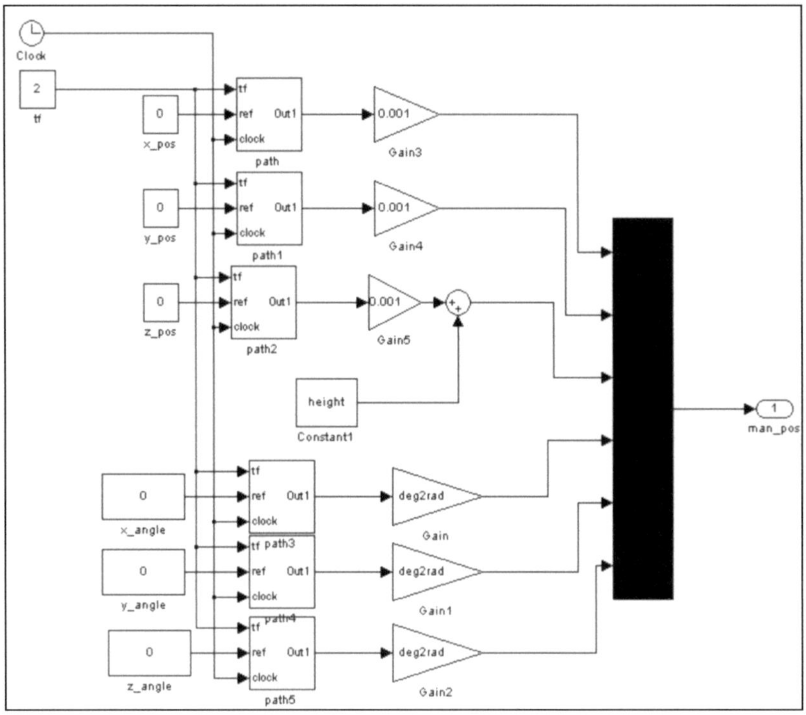

Fig. 16. Reference inputs with trajectory planning

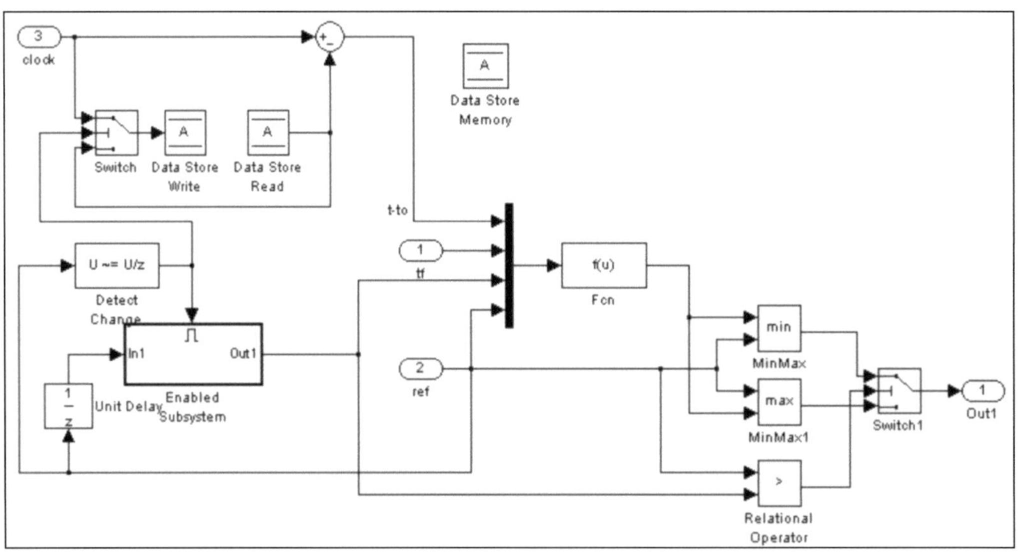

Fig. 17. Implementing Equation 6 in Simulink model

General control schema is summarized as follows: initialization, reference input, inverse kinematic, measurement, closed loop controller, input/outputs and additional blocks for safety reasons. Main PID Simulink model diagram is given Figure 18 below. The model

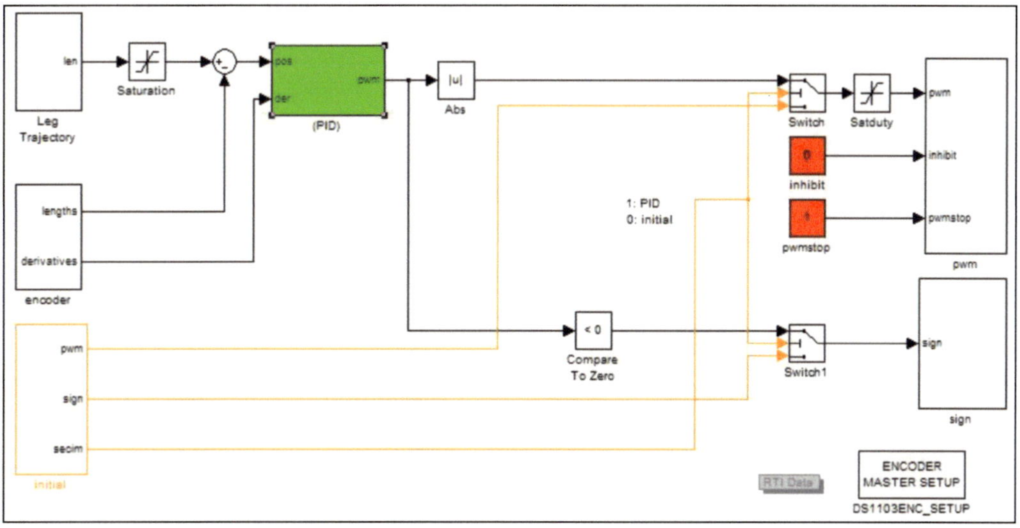

Fig. 18. Main PID controller Simulink model

contains some subsystems such as leg trajectory, encoder, initial, PID, pwm and sign. These subsystems perform the tasks mentioned above.

Project has a Control Desk interface for experiments and it is shown below. All system information can be entered through this interface. It contains variables that can be used in the development phase. Reference input values can be easily entered through the interface.

Leg trajectory subsystem detail was given before, so it will be continued giving other blocks. Firstly, encoder subsystem given in Figure 20 is described. Each encoder is read using an encoder block and then pulses are converted to metric unit (mm) and scaled. Round subsystem shown in Figure 21 is used to eliminate errors less than 500 nanometer.

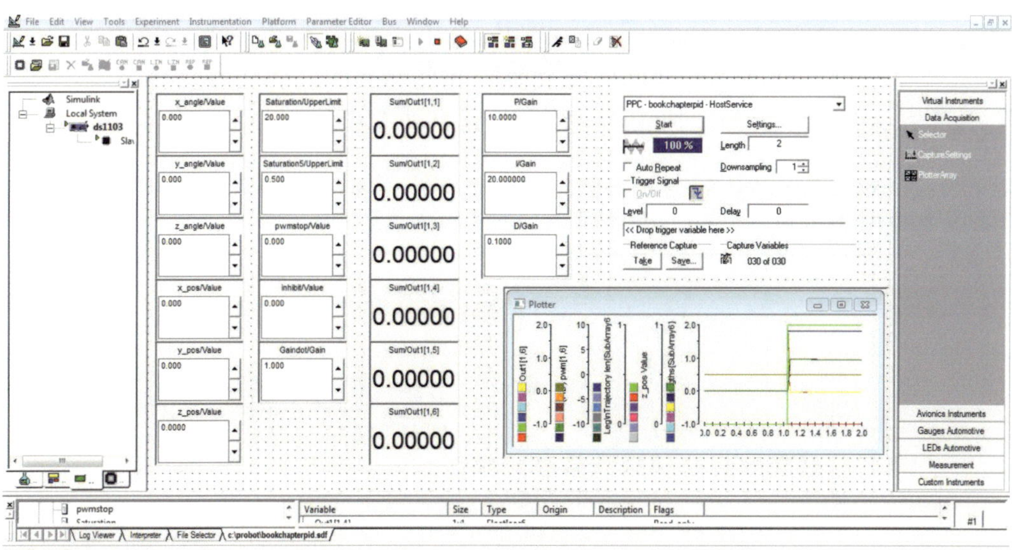

Fig. 19. Control Desk GUI for data acquisition and parameter update

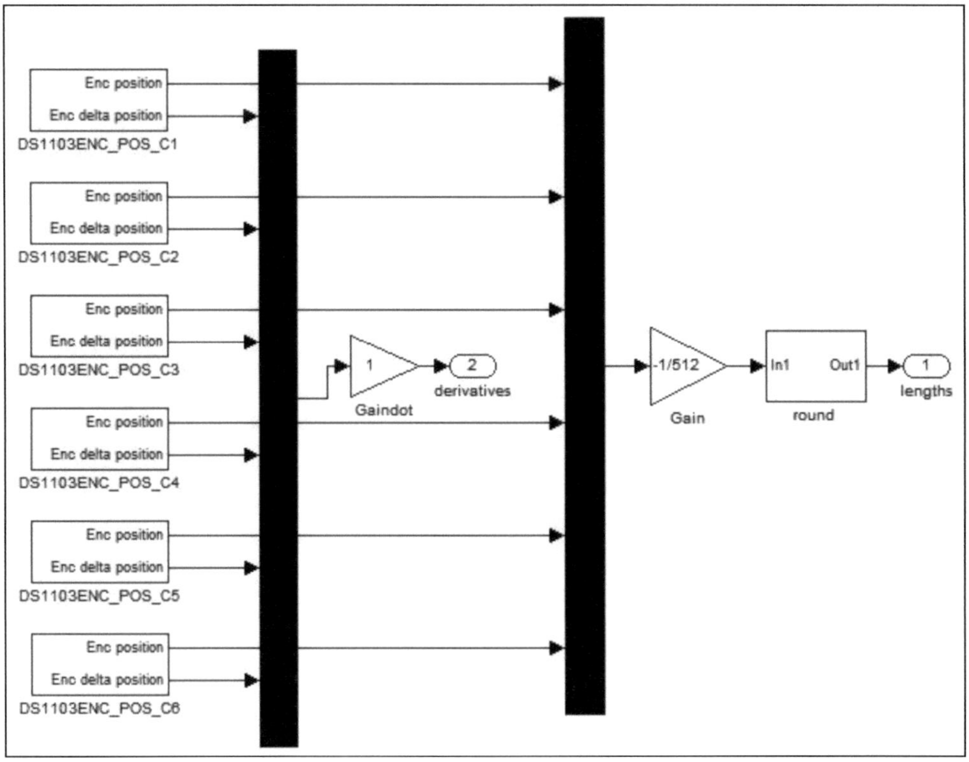

Fig. 20. Encoder subsystem

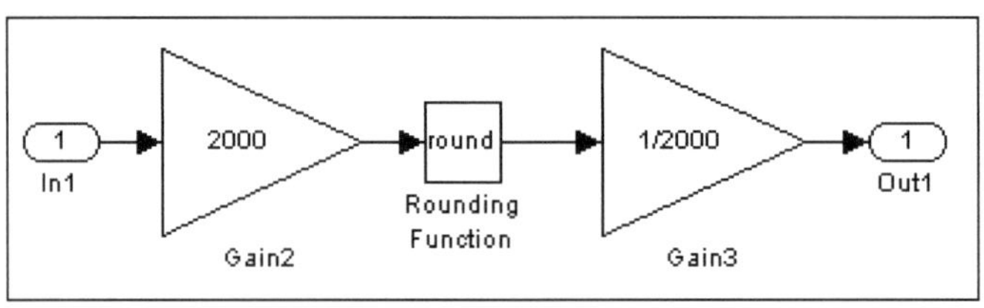

Fig. 21. Round subsystem

A PID controller is added for each leg. These subsystems are shown in figure below. It is a classic way of creating simple and efficient closed control loops.

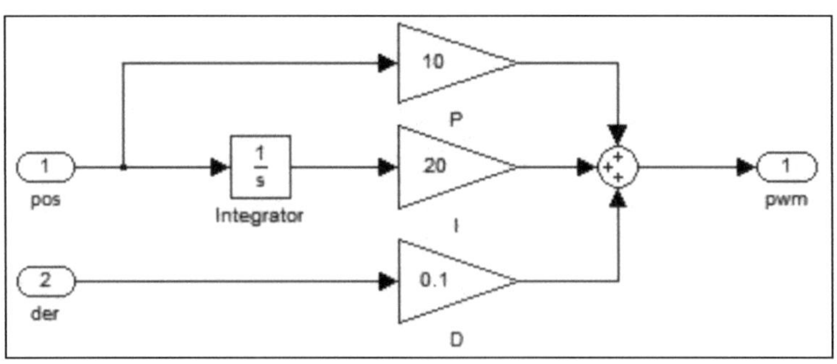

Fig. 22. PID subsystem in main model and simple PID structure

Initial subsystem model is shown in Figure 23 and its details were given before. It takes the index signals of the motors and produces a predefined duty cycle value for PWM generation, motor direction signals and status of the initialization routine.

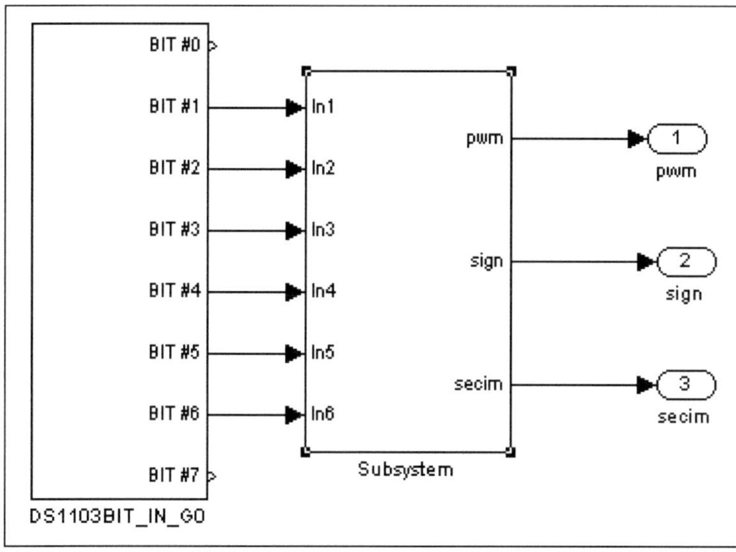

Fig. 23. Initial subsystem

Motors are controlled using 25 KHz PWM signals for amplitude and sign signals for motor directions according to controller outputs. In order to generate PWM signals slave dsp of the DS1103 is used. PWM block in the main model is given below. Saturation blocks are used to determine upper limit of the PWM duty cycles. In Figure 24, PWM and sign subsystems in the main model are shown.

4.4.1 Position control

After creating controller model and user interfaces, experiments can be done and results can be observed. Firstly, PID parameters were determined via trial-error experiments in order to obtain desired responses. A lot of experiments can be done simply and system responses can be taken easily. Output data can be saved '*.mat' extension in order to analyze in detail in Matlab. Some real time responses are given below. For 1 *mm* motion along the *z* direction, responses of the legs with references and control outputs are shown in Figure 25.
An orientation step response in *x* direction and a 500 *nm* step response in *z* direction were given in Figure 26. As can be seen from figures, PID parameters were selected to obtain fast rising time, no steady state error and smaller overshoot. PID controller works in a wide range between 500 *nm* to 100 *mm* with good control behavior.

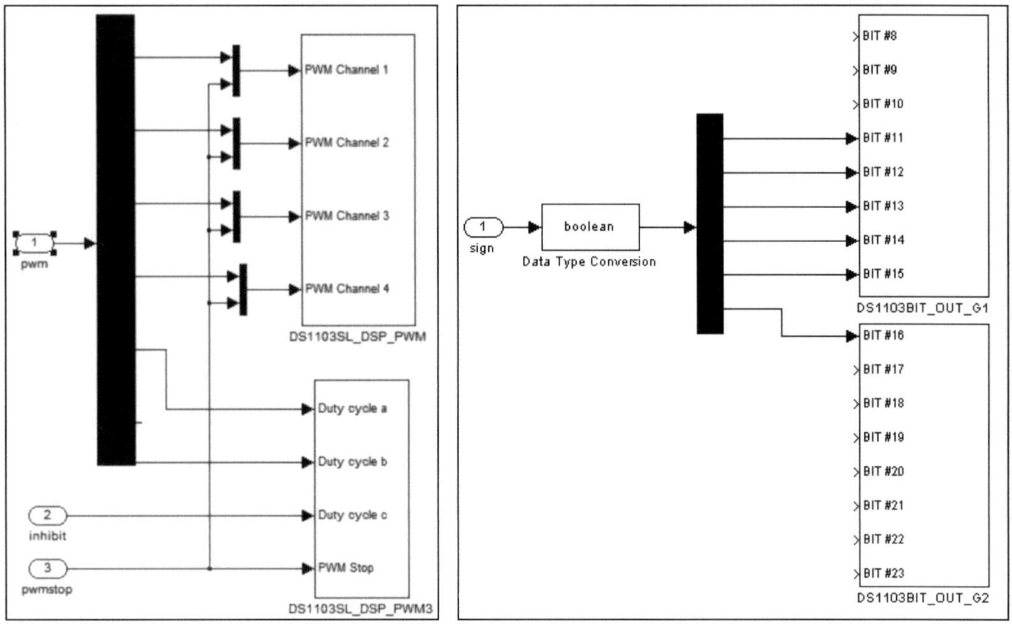

Fig. 24. PWM and Sign subsystems shown in the main model

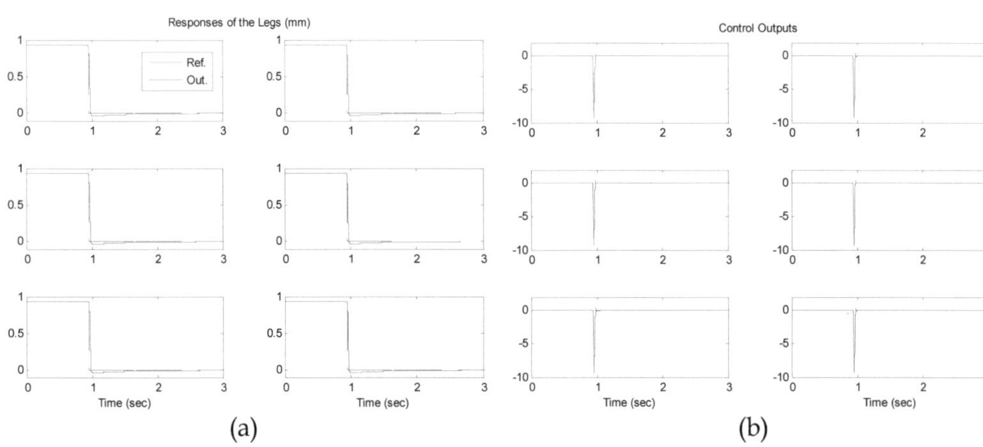

Fig. 25. (a) 1 *mm* step response of the top position in *z* direction (b) PID controller outputs

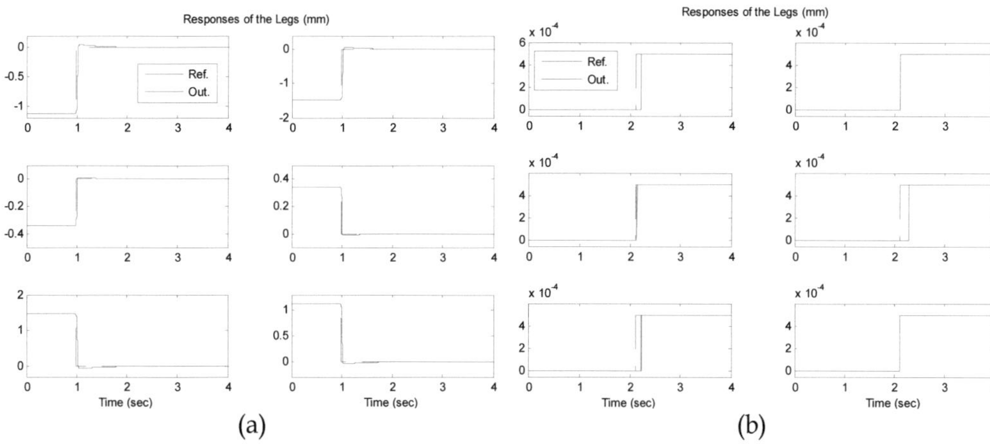

Fig. 26. (a) 1° rotation in x direction (b) 500 nm linear motion in z direction

4.4.2 Trajectory control

Several trajectory experiments were performed using trajectory generation algorithm mentioned in section 4.3. If motion time and end points are entered in to the user interface, the trajectory is created automatically and motion starts. In order to show the performance of trajectory tracking, some examples are given below. For these examples, references, trajectories and leg errors are illustrated in Figure 27-31. Several cases are examined in the results.

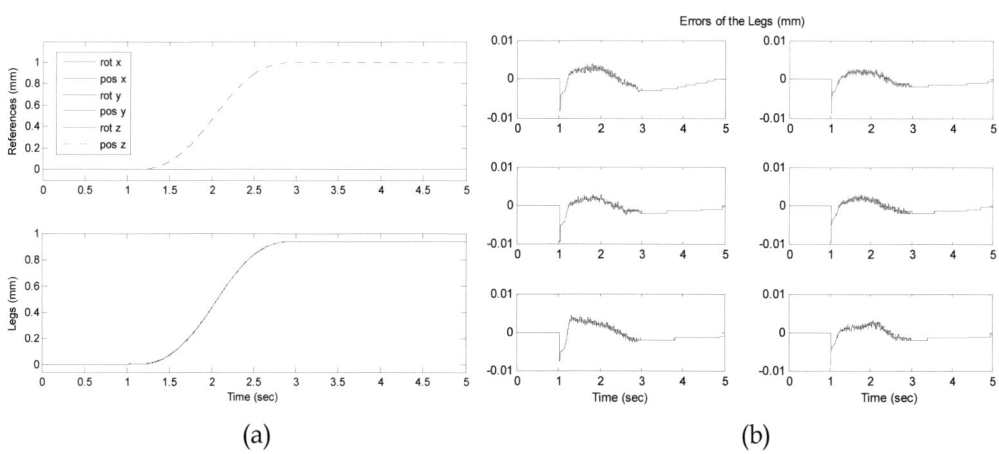

Fig. 27. (a) Trajectory tracking in z direction (b) Errors of the legs

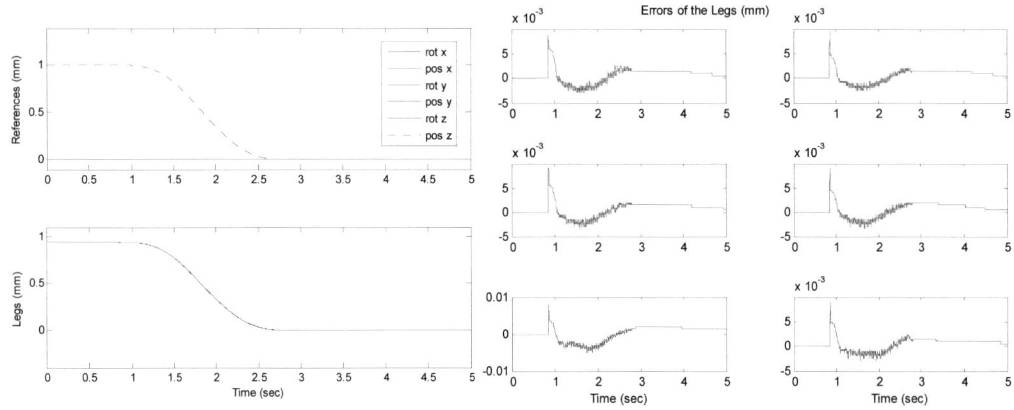

(a) (b)

Fig. 28. (a) Trajectory tracking in z direction (b) Leg errors

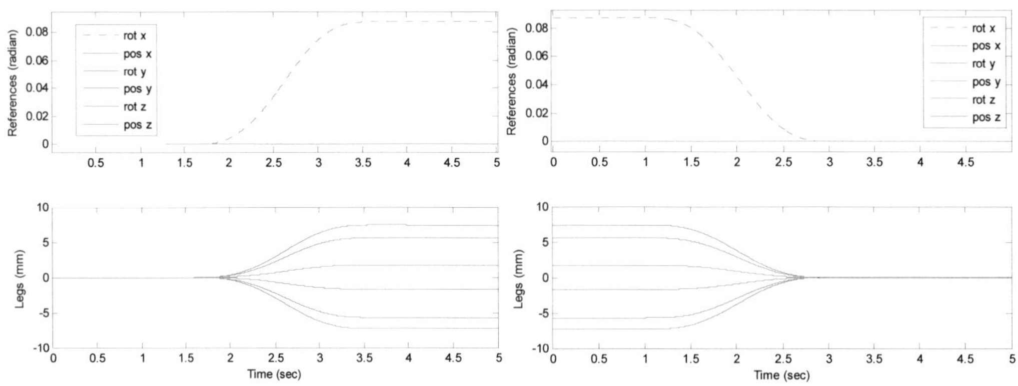

(a) (b)

Fig. 29. (a) Rotation in x direction (b) Rotation in x direction

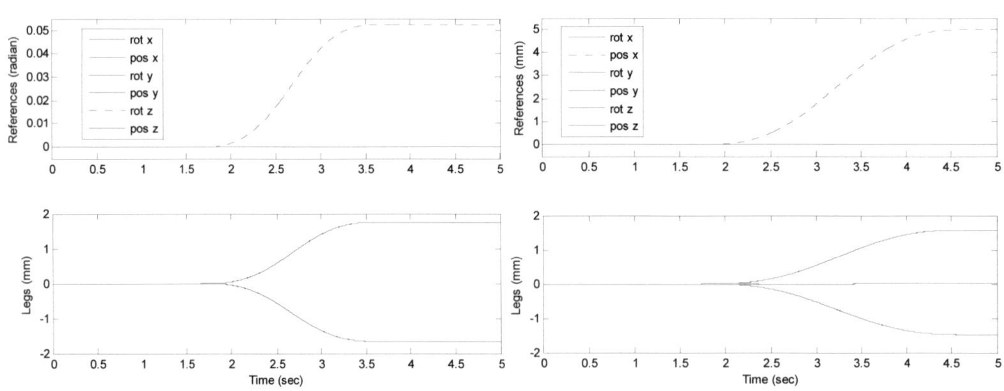

(a) (b)

Fig. 30. (a) Rotation in z direction (b) Linear motion in x direction

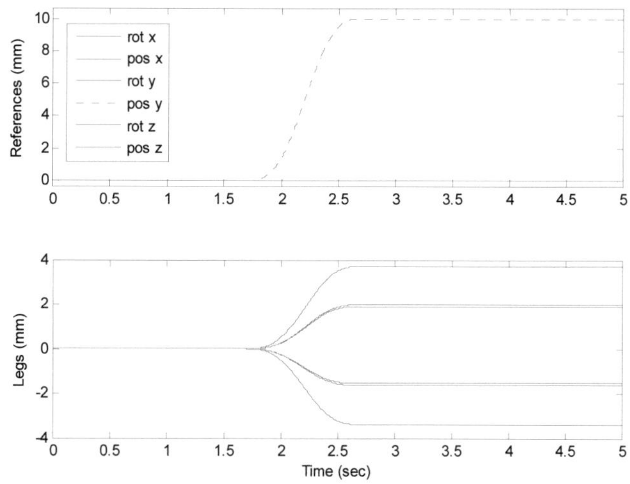

Fig. 31. Linear motion in *y* direction

4.5 Sliding mode controller

Nonlinear control has a very important role in the robot control applications. An important reason for this situation is to create knowledge-based systems which simplify the modeling of complex dynamics in the robot control. SMC is one of the suitable methods used in the knowledge-based systems (Küçük & Bingül, 2008).

SMC is a special case of the variable structure control systems. Variable structure control systems have a structure using feedback control laws and decision making laws together. Decision-making rule called as switching function selects a special feedback control structure according to the behavior of the system. Variable structure control system is designed to force the system states to slide a special surface called the sliding surface in the state space. Once the sliding surface is reached, the SMC tries to keep the states very close to the sliding surface (Küçük & Bingül, 2008).

If it is considered the change in the position error, second order equation of motion given with Equation 2, 3, 4 and 5 can be written as follows according to $x_1 = \dot{\theta}_r - \dot{\theta}_m$ (Utkin, 1993).

$$\begin{aligned} \dot{x}_1 &= x_2 \\ \dot{x}_2 &= -a_1 x_1 - a_2 x_2 + f(t) - bu \end{aligned} \tag{8}$$

a_1, a_2 and b are the positive parameters and $f(t)$ is a function depending on load torque, reference input and their derivatives in Equation 8.

For discontinuous control:

$$u = u_0 sign(s), \qquad s = cx_1 + x_2 \tag{9}$$

and as Equation 10 is linear and doesn't depend on $f(t)$, sliding mode on the s = 0 line allows to decreasing error exponentially.

$$cx_1 + \dot{x}_1 = 0 \tag{10}$$

Derivative of the sliding surface is:

$$\dot{s} = cx_2 - a_1x_1 - a_2x_2 + f(t) - bu_0 sign(s) \tag{11}$$

From equation,

$$bu_0 > \left| cx_2 - a_1x_1 - a_2x_2 + f(t) \right| \tag{12}$$

s and $\dot{s}$ have opposite signs and the state $s = 0$ will approach the sliding line after a while. Inequality given with Equation 12 determines the required voltage to force the system to sliding mode (Utkin, 1993).
A candidate Lyapunov function can be selected as follows for stability analysis (Kassem & Yousef, 2009),

$$v = \frac{1}{2}\sigma^2 \tag{13}$$

The stability condition from Lyapunov's second theorem,

$$\frac{1}{2}\frac{d\sigma^2}{dt} = \sigma\dot{\sigma} \le -K\left|\sigma\right| \tag{14}$$

where K is a positive constant.
After theoretical steps, sliding mode controller was designed in Simulink similar to PID controller. Main model is shown in Figure 32. Details of some subsystems different from using subsystems in PID will be given only.

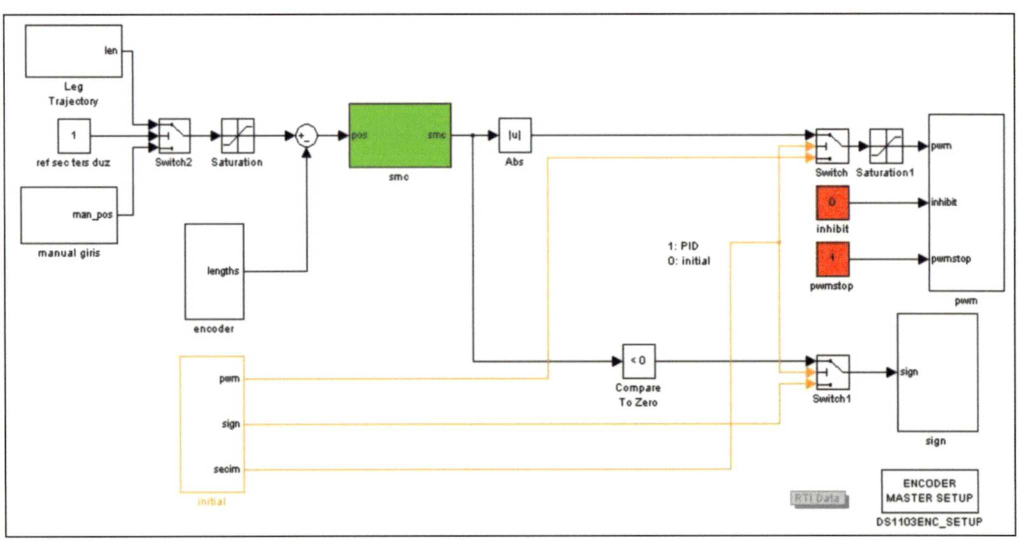

Fig. 32. Main sliding mode controller model

"smc" subsystem is shown in the Figure 33. This model contains sliding mode control and integrator algorithm for one leg. In order to reduce the chattering, a rate limiter block was added to output. In order to eliminate the steady state error, an integrator was added to the

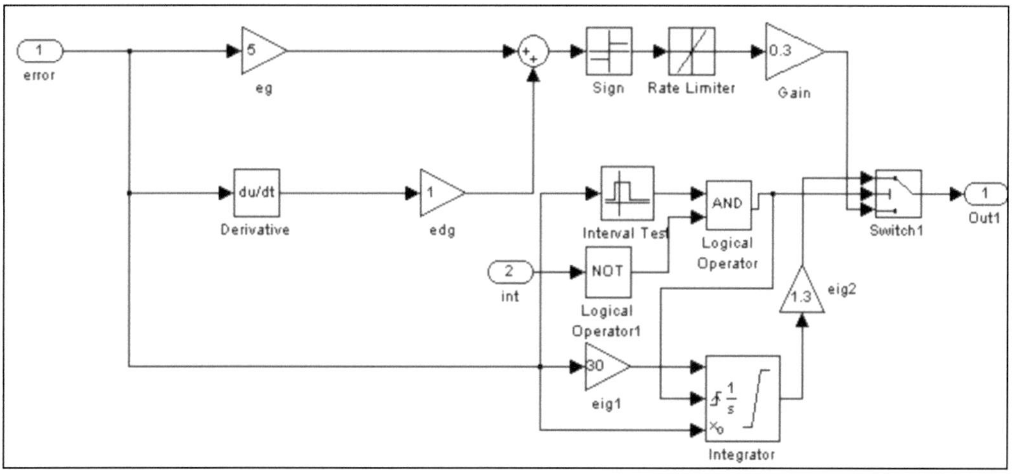

Fig. 33. Simulink model of SMC with integrator for one leg

controller. This integrator is switched on only small limited range between ± 0,008 mm. This integrator does not affect the performance of sliding mode controller. It does not slow down the system response. Also, integrator is disabled during trajectory tracking by switching.

4.5.1 Position control

Some real time responses for position control are given below. In Figure 34, errors of the legs were shown in the motions linear and rotation in the *x* and *z* direction with 15 *mm* and 20° inputs. As can be seen from the figures, overshoot and steady state error are very small. But, system response is slower.

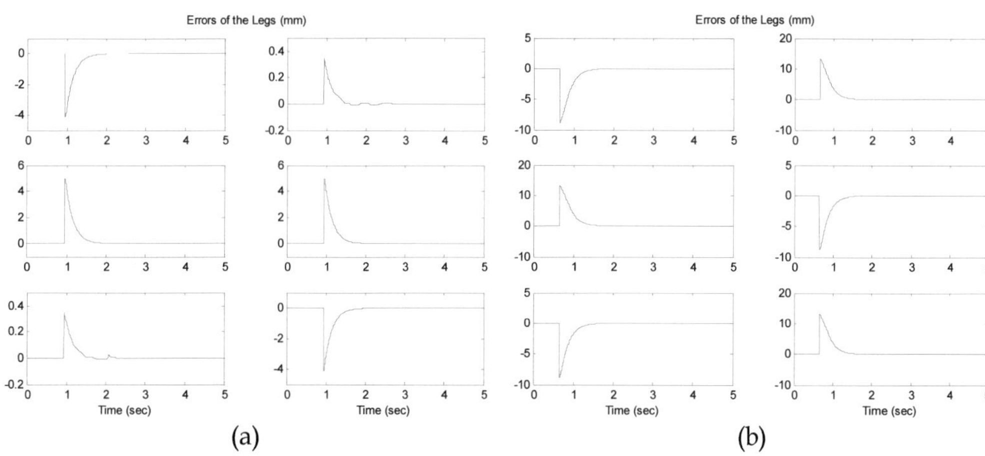

Fig. 34. (a) Linear motion in *x* direction with 15 *mm* reference (b) Rotation in *z* direction with 20° reference

Figure 35 shows a phase diagram of the system with SMC. In the phase diagram, the states of the system are leg position and leg velocity. As can be seen from the figure, SMC pushes states to sliding line and the states went to the desired values along sliding line when 5 *mm* step input along the *z* axis in Cartesian space was applied to the system.

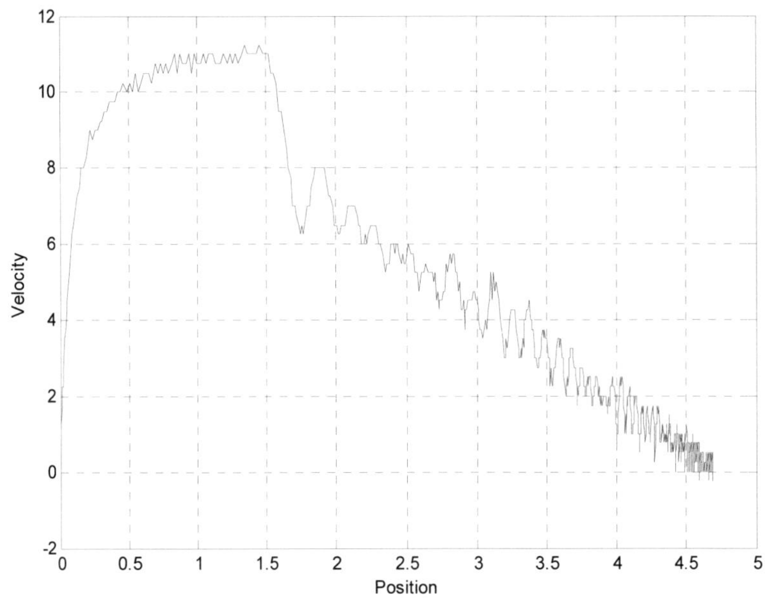

Fig. 35. Phase diagram of the SMC position control

4.5.2 Trajectory control

Different situations in trajectory control are considered in this section. These are shown in Figure 36-38. As can be seen from the figures legs followed the desired trajectories synchronous.

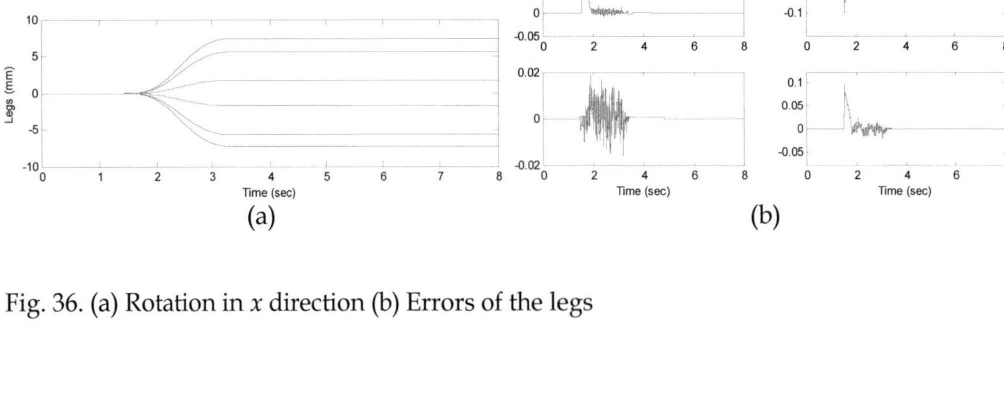

Fig. 36. (a) Rotation in x direction (b) Errors of the legs

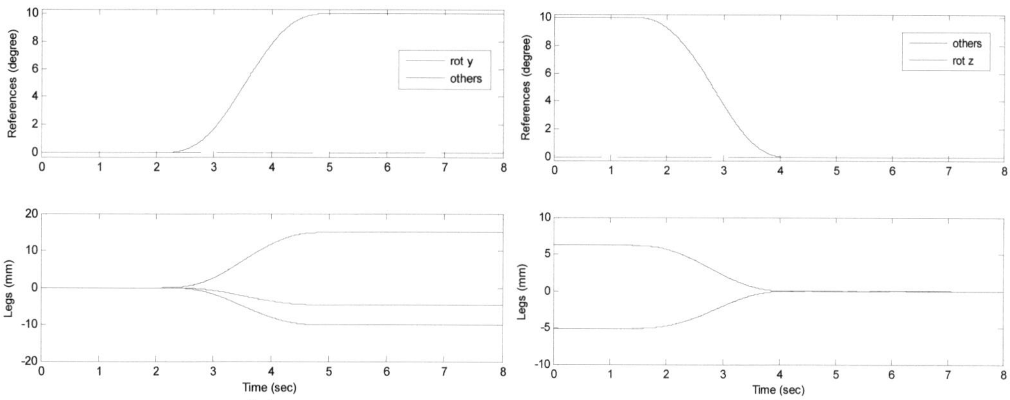

(a) (b)

Fig. 37. (a) Rotation in y and (b) z direction

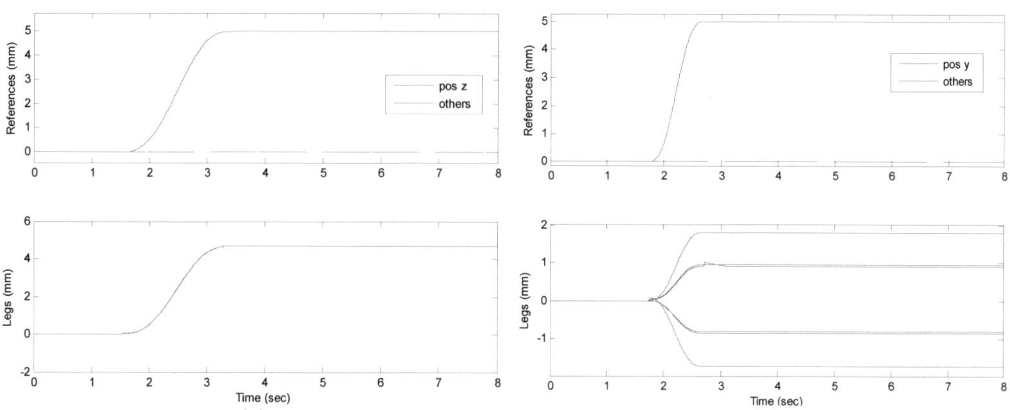

(a) (b)

Fig. 38. (a) Linear motion in z and (b) in y direction

5. Conclusion

In this study, a high precision 6 DOF Stewart platform is controlled by a PID and sliding mode controller. These controllers were embedded in a Dspace DS1103 real time controller which is programmable in the Simulink environment. Design details and development stages of the PID and SMC are given from subsystems to main model in Simulink. This study can be a good example to show how a real time controller can be developed using Matlab/Simulink and Dspace DS1103. In order to test the performance of the controllers, several position and trajectory tracking experiments were conducted. Step inputs are used for position control and Kane transition function is used to generate trajectory. In the position experiments using both controllers, there is no steady state error and moving plate of the SP is positioned to the desired target with an error less than 0.5 μm. Sliding mode controller is better performance in terms of overshoot than PID but PID has faster response due to high gain. In the tracking experiments, PID and SMC have similar responses under no load. If nonlinear external forces are applied to moving platform, control performance of the SMC will be better than PID.

6. Acknowledgment

This work is supported by The Scientific and Technological Research Council of Turkey (TUBITAK) under the Grant No. 107M148.

7. References

Bonev, I. (2003). The True Origins of Parallel Robots, 06.04.2011, Available from: http://www.parallemic.org/Reviews/Review007.html

Chen, N.X.; Song, S.M. (1994). Direct position analysis of the 4-6 Stewart Platform, *ASME J. of Mechanical Design*, Vol. 116, No. 1, (March 1994), pp. (61-66), ISSN 1050-0472

Dspace Inc., 06.04.2011, Available from: http://www.dspaceinc.com/en/inc/home.cfm

Hunt, K.H. (1983). Structural kinematics of in-parallel-actuated robot-arms, *ASME J. Mech., Trans. Automat. Des.*, Vol. 105, No. 4, (December 1983), pp. (705–712), ISSN 0738-0666

Fitcher, E.F. (1986). A Stewart Platform-Based Manipulator: General Theory and Practical Construction, *Int. J. of Robotics Research*, Vol. 5, No. 2, (June 1986), pp. (157-182), ISSN 0278-3649

Kassem, A.M.; Yousef, A. M. (2009). Servo DC Motor Position Control Based on Sliding Mode Approach, *5th Saudi Technical Conference and Exhibition STCEX 2009*, January 2009

Kim, D.; Chung, W. (1999). Analytic Singularity Equation and Analysis of Six-DOF Parallel Manipulators Using Local Structurization Method, *IEEE Transactions on Robotics and Automation*, Vol. 15, No. 4, (August 1999), pp. (612-622), ISSN 1042-296X

Kizir, S. ; Bingül, Z. ; Oysu, C. ; Küçük, S. (2011). Development and Control of a High Precision Stewart Platform, *International Journal of Technological Sciences*, Vol. 3, No. 1, pp. (51-59)

Küçük, S.; Bingül, Z. (2008). *Robot Dinamiği ve Kontrolü*, Birsen press, ISBN 978-975-511-516-0, İstanbul

Liao, Q.; Seneviratne, L.D.; Earles, S.W.E. (1993). Forward kinematic analysis for the general 4-6 Stewart Platform, *IEEE/RSJ International Conference on Intelligent Robots and Systems IROS'93*, ISBN 0-7803-0823-9, Yokohama, Japan, July 1993

Mathworks Inc., 06.04.2011, Available from: http://www.mathworks.com/

Merlet, J.P. (1992). Direct kinematics and assembly modes of parallel manipulators, *Int. J. of Robotics Research*, Vol. 11, No. 2, (April 1992), pp. (150-162), ISSN 0278-3649

Merlet, J.P. (Ed(s).). (2006). *Parallel Robots*, Springer, ISBN-10 1-4020-4133-0, Netherlands

Nauna, P.; Waldron, K.J.; Murthy, V. (1990). Direct kinematic solution of a Stewart Platform, *IEEE Trans. Robotics Automat.*, Vol. 6, No. 4, (August 1990), pp. (438-444), ISSN 1042-296X

Niesing, B. (2001). Medical Engineering, *Fraunhofer Magazine*, Vol. 2

Reckdahl, K.J. (1996). Dynamics and control of mechanical systems containing closed kinematic chains, *Phd Thesis*, Stanford University

Sefrioui, J.; Gosselin., C.M. (1993). Singularity analysis and representation of planar parallel manipulators, *Robot. Autom. Syst.*, Vol. 10, No. 4, pp. (209-224)

Stewart, D. (1965). A Platform with Six Degrees of Freedom, *Proceedings of the Institute of Mechanical Engineering*, Vol. 180, Part 1, No. 5, pp. (371-386)

Utkin, V.I., (1993). Sliding mode control design principles and applications to electric drives, *IEEE Transactions on Industrial Electronics*, Vol. 40, No. 1, pp. (23–36), ISSN 1042-296X

Wikipedia, 06.04.2011, Available from: http://en.wikipedia.org/wiki/Stewart_platform

11

Obstacle Avoidance for Redundant Manipulators as Control Problem

Leon Žlajpah and Tadej Petrič
Jožef Stefan Institute, Ljubljana
Slovenia

1. Introduction

One of the goals of robotics research is to provide control algorithms that allow robotic manipulators to move in an environment with objects. The contacts with these objects may be part of the task, e.g. in the assembly operations, or they may be undesired events. If the task involves some contacts with the environment it is necessary to control the resulting forces. For that purpose, different control approaches have been proposed like hybrid position/force control (Raibert & Craig, 1981) or impedance control (Hogan, 1985), which have also been applied to redundant manipulators (Khatib, 1987; Park et al., 1996; Woernle, 1993; Yoshikawa, 1987). However, in most cases the contact is supposed to occur between the end-effector or the handling object and the object in the workspace. Except in some special cases all other contacts along the body of the robot manipulator are not desired and have to be avoided. In the case when the contacts are not desired, the main issue is how to accomplish the assigned task without any risk of collisions with the workspace objects. A natural strategy to avoid obstacles would be to move the manipulator away from the obstacle into a configuration where the manipulator is not in contact with the obstacle. Without changing the motion of the end-effector, the reconfiguration of the manipulator into a collision-free configuration can be made only if the manipulator has redundant degrees-of-freedom (DOF). The flexibility depends on the degree-of-redundancy, i.e., on the number of redundant DOF. A high degree-of-redundancy is important, especially when the manipulator is working in an environment with many potential collisions with obstacles.

Generally, the obstacle-avoidance (or collision-avoidance) problem can be solved with two classes of strategies: global (planning) and local (control). The global ones, like high-level path planning, guarantee to find a collision-free path from the initial point to the goal point, if such a path exists. They often operate in the configuration space into which the manipulator and all the obstacles are mapped and a collision-free path is found in the unoccupied portion of the configuration space (Lozano-Perez, 1983). However, these algorithms are very computationally demanding and the calculation times are significantly longer than the typical response time of a manipulator. This computational complexity limits their use for practical obstacle avoidance just to simple cases. Furthermore, as global methods do not usually rely on any sensor feedback information, they are only suitable for static and well-defined environments. On the other hand, local strategies treat obstacle avoidance as a control problem. Their aim is not to replace the higher-level, global, collision-free path planning but to make use of the capabilities of low-level control, e.g., they can use the sensor information to change the path if the obstacle appears in the workspace or it moves. Hence, they are suitable when the obstacle position is not known in advance and must be detected in real-time during the task execution. A significant advantage of local methods is that they are less computationally demanding and more flexible. These characteristics make local methods good candidates for on-line collision avoidance, especially in unstructured environments. However, the drawback is that they may cause globally suboptimal behavior or may even get stuck when a collision-free path cannot be found from the current configuration.

With the problem of the collision avoidance of redundant manipulators, there have been different approaches to the local methods proposed by many researchers in the past (Brock et al., 2002; Colbaugh et al., 1989; Glass et al., 1995; Guo & Hsia, 1993; Khatib, 1986; Kim & Khosla, 1992; Maciejewski & Klein, 1985; McLean & Cameron, 1996; Seraji & Bon, 1999; Volpe & Khosla, 1990). The approach proposed by Maciejewski and Klein (Maciejewski & Klein, 1985) is to assign to the critical point an avoiding task space vector, with which the point is directed away from the obstacle. Colbaugh, Glass and Seraji (Colbaugh et al., 1989; Glass et al., 1995) used configuration control and defined the constraints representing the obstacle-avoidance. The next approach is based on potential functions, where a repulsive potential is assigned to the obstacles and an attractive potential to the goal position (Khatib, 1986; Kim & Khosla, 1992; McLean & Cameron, 1996; Volpe & Khosla, 1990). The fourth approach uses the optimization of an objective function maximizing the distance between the manipulator and the obstacles (Guo & Hsia, 1993). Most of the proposed methods solve the obstacle-avoidance problem at the kinematic level. Velocity null-space control is an appropriate way to control the internal motion of a redundant manipulator. Some of the control strategies are acceleration based or torque based, considering also the manipulator dynamics (Brock et al., 2002; Khatib, 1986; Newman, 1989; Xie et al., 1998). However, it is established that certain acceleration-based control schemes exhibit instabilities (O'Neil, 2002). An alternative approach is the augmented Jacobian, as introduced in Egeland (1987), where the secondary task is added to the primary task so as to obtain a square Jacobian matrix that can be inverted. The main drawback of this technique are the so-called algorithmic singularities. They occur when the secondary task causes a conflict with the primary task. Khatib investigated in depth the use of the second-order inverse kinematic, either at the torque or acceleration level, starting from Khatib (1987) to recent task-prioritised humanoid applications (Mansard et al., 2009; Sentis et al., 2010).

Here, we want to present some approaches to on-line obstacle-avoidance for the redundant manipulators at the kinematic level and some approaches, which are considering also the dynamics of the manipulator.

Like in most of the local strategies that solve the obstacle-avoidance problem at the kinematic level (Colbaugh et al., 1989; Glass et al., 1995; Guo & Hsia, 1993; Kim & Khosla, 1992; Maciejewski & Klein, 1985; Seraji & Bon, 1999), the aim of the proposed strategies is to assign each point on the body of the manipulator, which is close to the obstacle, a motion component in a direction away from the obstacle. The emphasis is given to the definition of the avoiding motion. Usually, the avoiding motion is defined in the Cartesian space. As obstacle avoidance is typically a one-dimensional problem, we use a one-dimensional operational space for each critical point. Consequently, some singularity problems can be avoided when not enough "redundancy" is available locally. Additionally, we propose an approximative calculation of the motion that is faster that the exact one. Another important issue addressed in this paper is how the obstacle avoidance is performed when there are more simultaneously active obstacles in the neighborhood of the manipulator. We propose an algorithm that considers all the obstacles in the neighborhood of the robot.

Most tasks performed by a redundant manipulator are broken down into several subtasks with different priorities. Usually, the task with the highest priority, referred to as the main task, is associated with the positioning of the end-effector in the task space, and other subtasks are associated with the obstacle avoidance and other additional tasks (if the degree-of-redundancy is high enough). However, in some cases it is necessary (e.g., for safety reasons) that the end-effector motion is not the primary task. As, in general, task-priority algorithms do not always allow simple transitions or the changing of priority levels between the tasks (Sciavicco & Siciliano, 2005), we propose a novel formulation of the primary and secondary tasks, so that the desired movement of the end-effector is in fact a secondary task. The primary task is now the obstacle avoidance and it is only active if we approach a pre-defined threshold, i.e., the critical distance to one of the obstacles. While far from the threshold, our algorithm allows undisturbed control of the secondary task. If we approach the threshold, the primary task smoothly takes over and only allows joint control in the null-space of the primary task. A similar approach can also be found in Sugiura et al. (2007), where they used a blending coefficient for blending the end-effector motion with the obstacle-avoidance motion, and in Mansard et al. (2009) where they proposed a generic solution to build a smooth control law for any kind of unilateral constraints.

Next, we propose strategies that are also considering the dynamics. In this case, it is reasonable to define the obstacle avoidance at the force level, i.e., the forces are supposed to generate the motion that is necessary to avoid the obstacle. We discuss three approaches regarding the sensors used to detect the obstacles: no sensors, tactile sensors and proximity sensors or vision. First of all, we want to investigate what happens if the manipulator touches an obstacle, especially how to control the contact forces and how to avoid the obstacle after the contact. Therefore, we propose a strategy that utilizes the self-motion caused by the contact forces to avoid an obstacle after the collision. The main advantage of this strategy is that it can be applied to the systems without any contact or force sensors. However, a prerequisite for this strategy to be effective is that the manipulator is backdrivable. As an alternative for stiff systems (having high-ratio gears, high friction, etc.), we propose using tactile sensors. Finally, we deal with proximity sensors and we propose a virtual forces strategy, where a virtual force component in a direction away from the obstacle is assigned to each point on the body of the manipulator, which is close to an obstacle. Like other classical methods for obstacle avoidance this one prevents any part of the manipulator touching an obstacle. Also here we address the problem of multiple obstacles in the workspace, which have to be simultaneously avoided.

The computational efficiency of all the proposed algorithms (at the kinematic level and considering the dynamics) allows the real-time application in an unstructured or time-varying environment. The efficiency of the proposed control algorithms is illustrated by simulations of highly redundant planar manipulator moving in an unstructured and time-varying environment and by experiments on a real robot manipulator.

2. Background

The robotic systems under study are serial manipulators. We consider redundant systems, i.e., the dimension of the joint space n exceeds the dimension of the task space m. The difference between n and m will be denoted as the degree of redundancy r, $r = n - m$. Note that in this definition the redundancy is not only a characteristics of the manipulator itself but also of the task. This means that a nonredundant manipulator may also become a redundant manipulator for a certain task.

2.1 Modelling

Let the configuration of the manipulator be represented by the n-dimensional vector $\boldsymbol{q}$ of joint positions, and the end-effector position (and orientation) by the m-dimensional vector $\boldsymbol{x}$ of the task positions (and orientations). Then, the kinematics can be described by the following equations

$$\boldsymbol{x} = \boldsymbol{f}(\boldsymbol{q}) \qquad \dot{\boldsymbol{q}} = \mathbf{J}^{\#}\dot{\boldsymbol{x}} + \mathbf{N}\dot{\boldsymbol{q}} \qquad \ddot{\boldsymbol{q}} = \mathbf{J}^{\#}(\ddot{\boldsymbol{x}} - \dot{\mathbf{J}}\dot{\boldsymbol{q}}) + \mathbf{N}\ddot{\boldsymbol{q}} \tag{1}$$

where $\boldsymbol{f}$ is an m-dimensional vector function representing the manipulator's forward kinematics, $\mathbf{J}$ is the $m \times n$ manipulator's Jacobian matrix, $\mathbf{J}^{\#}$ is the generalized inverse of the Jacobian matrix $\mathbf{J}$ and $\mathbf{N}$ is a matrix representing the projection into the null space of $\mathbf{J}$, $\mathbf{N} = (\mathbf{I} - \mathbf{J}^{\#}\mathbf{J})$.

For the redundant manipulators the static relationship between the m-dimensional generalized force in the task space $\boldsymbol{F}$, and the corresponding n-dimensional generalized joint space force $\boldsymbol{\tau}$ is

$$\boldsymbol{\tau} = \mathbf{J}^T\boldsymbol{F} + \mathbf{N}^T\boldsymbol{\tau} \tag{2}$$

where $\mathbf{N}^T$ is a matrix representing the projection into the null space of $\mathbf{J}^{T\#}$.

Assuming the manipulator consists of rigid bodies the joint space equations of motion can be written in the form

$$\boldsymbol{\tau} = \mathbf{H}\ddot{\boldsymbol{q}} + \boldsymbol{h} + \boldsymbol{g} - \boldsymbol{\tau}_F \tag{3}$$

where $\boldsymbol{\tau}$ is an n-dimensional vector of control torques, $\mathbf{H}$ is an $n \times n$ inertia matrix, $\boldsymbol{h}$ is an n-dimensional vector of Coriolis and centrifugal forces, $\boldsymbol{g}$ is an n-dimensional vector of gravity forces, and the vector $\boldsymbol{\tau}_F$ represents torques due to external forces acting on the manipulator.

2.2 Kinematic control

For velocity control the following kinematic controller can be used

$$\dot{\boldsymbol{q}} = \mathbf{J}^{\#}\dot{\boldsymbol{x}}_c + \mathbf{N}\dot{\boldsymbol{\varphi}} \tag{4}$$

where $\dot{\boldsymbol{x}}_c$ and $\dot{\boldsymbol{\varphi}}$ represent the task space control law and the arbitrary joint velocities, respectively. The task space control $\dot{\boldsymbol{x}}_c$ can be selected as

$$\dot{\boldsymbol{x}}_c = \dot{\boldsymbol{x}}_e + \mathbf{K}_p\boldsymbol{e} \tag{5}$$

where $\boldsymbol{e}$, $\boldsymbol{e} = \boldsymbol{x}_d - \boldsymbol{x}$, is the tracking error, $\dot{\boldsymbol{x}}_e$ is the desired task space velocity, and $\mathbf{K}_p$ is a constant gain matrix. To perform the additional subtask, the velocity $\dot{\boldsymbol{\varphi}}$ is used. Let p be a function representing the desired performance criterion. Then, to optimize p we can select $\dot{\boldsymbol{\varphi}}$ as

$$\dot{\boldsymbol{\varphi}} = \mathbf{K}_p\nabla p \tag{6}$$

Here, ∇p is the gradient of p and $\mathbf{K}_p$ is a gain.

2.3 Torque control

To decouple the task space and null-space motion we propose using a controller given in the form

$$\boldsymbol{\tau}_c = \mathbf{H}(\mathbf{J}^{\#}(\ddot{\boldsymbol{x}}_c - \dot{\mathbf{J}}\dot{\boldsymbol{q}}) + \mathbf{N}(\boldsymbol{\phi} - \dot{\mathbf{N}}\dot{\boldsymbol{q}})) + \boldsymbol{h} + \boldsymbol{g} \tag{7}$$

where $\ddot{x}_c$ and ϕ represent the task space and the null-space control law, respectively. The task space control $\ddot{x}_c$ can be selected as

$$\ddot{x}_c = \ddot{x}_d + \mathbf{K}_v\dot{e} + \mathbf{K}_p e \tag{8}$$

where e, $e = x_d - x$, is the tracking error, $\ddot{x}_d$ is the desired task space acceleration, and $\mathbf{K}_v$ and $\mathbf{K}_p$ are constant gain matrices. The selection of $\mathbf{K}_v$ and $\mathbf{K}_p$ can be based on the desired task space impedance. To perform the additional subtask, the vector ϕ is given in the form

$$\phi = \mathbf{N}\ddot{\varphi} + \dot{\mathbf{N}}\dot{\varphi} + \mathbf{K}_n\dot{e}_n, \qquad \dot{e}_n = \mathbf{N}(\dot{\varphi} - \dot{q}) \tag{9}$$

where $\dot{\varphi}$ is the desired null space velocity and $\mathbf{K}_n$ is an $n \times n$ diagonal gain matrix. The velocity $\dot{\varphi}$ is defined by the subtask. E.g., let p be a function representing the desired performance criterion. To optimize p we can select $\dot{\varphi}$ as (6).

3. Obstacle-avoidance strategy

The obstacle-avoidance problem is usually defined as how to control the manipulator to track the desired end-effector trajectory while simultaneously ensuring that no part of the manipulator collides with any obstacle in the workspace of the manipulator. To avoid any obstacles the manipulator has to move away from the obstacles into the configuration where the distance to the obstacles is larger (see Fig. 1). Without changing the motion of the end-effector, the reconfiguration of the manipulator into a collision-free configuration can be done only if the manipulator has redundant degrees-of-freedom (DOF). Note that the flexibility or the *degree-of-redundancy* of the manipulator does not depend only on the number of redundant DOF but also on the "location" of the redundant DOF. Namely, it is possible that the redundant manipulator cannot avoid an obstacle, because it is in a configuration where the avoiding motion in the desired direction is not possible. A high degree-of-redundancy is important, especially when the manipulator is working in an environment with many potential collisions with obstacles.

A good strategy for obstacle avoidance is to identify the points on the robotic arm that are near obstacles and then assign to them a motion component that moves those points away from the obstacle, as shown in Fig. 1. The motion of the robot is perturbed only if at least one part of the robot is in the critical neighborhood of an obstacle, i.e., the distance is less than a prescribed minimal distance. We denote the obstacles in the critical neighborhood as the *active obstacles* and the corresponding closest points on the body of a manipulator as the *critical points*. Usually, it is assumed that the motion of the end effector is not disturbed by any obstacle. Otherwise, the task execution has to be interrupted and the higher-level path planning has to recalculate the desired motion of the end-effector. If the path-tracking accuracy is not important control algorithms which move the end-effector around obstacles on-line, can be used.

As the obstacle avoidance is supposed to be done on-line, it is not necessary to know the exact position of the obstacles in advance. Of course, to allow the manipulator to work in an unstructured and/or dynamic environment, some sensors have to be used to determine the position of the obstacles or measure the distance between the obstacles and the body of the manipulator. There are different types of sensor systems that can be used to detect objects in the neighborhood of the manipulator. They can be tactile or proximity sensors. The tactile sensors, like artificial skin, can detect the obstacle only if they touch it. On the other hand, the proximity sensors can sense the presence of an obstacle in the neighborhood. We have

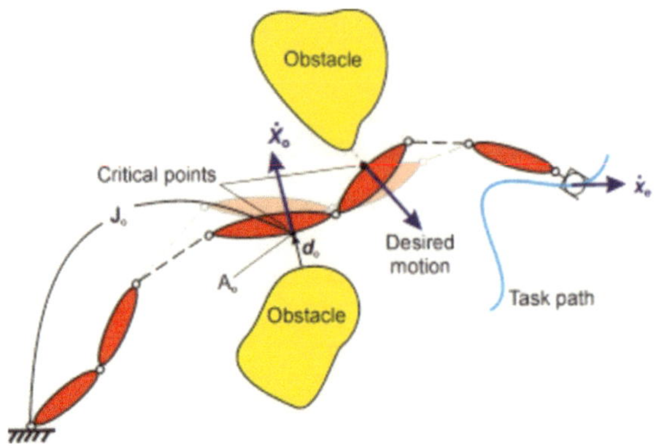

Fig. 1. Manipulator motion in presence of some obstacles

compared the capabilities of a manipulator equipped with both types of sensors. Actually, we have also investigated if and how the manipulator can avoid obstacles without any sensors for the detection of obstacles. As in the case of tactile sensors and when no sensors are used the manipulator has to "touch" the obstacles, we allow a collision with an obstacle. However, after the collision the manipulator should move away from the obstacle and the collision forces should be kept as low as possible.

4. Obstacle avoidance using kinematic control

The proposed velocity strategy considers the obstacle-avoidance problem at the kinematic level. Let $\dot{\boldsymbol{x}}_e$ be the desired velocity of the end-effector, and A_o be the critical point in the neighborhood of an obstacle (see Fig. 1). To avoid a possible collision, one possibility is to assign to A_o such a velocity that it moves away from the obstacle, as proposed in Maciejewski & Klein (1985). Hence, the motion of the end-effector and the critical point can be described by the equations

$$\mathbf{J}\dot{\boldsymbol{q}} = \dot{\boldsymbol{x}}_e \qquad \mathbf{J}_o\dot{\boldsymbol{q}} = \dot{\boldsymbol{x}}_o \tag{10}$$

where $\mathbf{J}_o$ is a Jacobian matrix associated with the point point A_o. There are some possibilities to find a common solution for both equations.

4.1 Exact solution

Let $\dot{\boldsymbol{x}}_c$ in (4) equal $\dot{\boldsymbol{x}}_e$. Then, combining (4) and (10) yields

$$\dot{\boldsymbol{\varphi}} = (\mathbf{J}_o\mathbf{N})^{\#}(\dot{\boldsymbol{x}}_o - \mathbf{J}_o\mathbf{J}^{\#}\dot{\boldsymbol{x}}_e) \tag{11}$$

Now, using this $\dot{\boldsymbol{\varphi}}$ in (4) gives the final solution for $\dot{\boldsymbol{q}}$ in the form

$$\dot{\boldsymbol{q}} = \mathbf{J}^{\#}\dot{\boldsymbol{x}}_c + (\mathbf{J}_o\mathbf{N})^{\#}(\dot{\boldsymbol{x}}_o - \mathbf{J}_o\mathbf{J}^{\#}\dot{\boldsymbol{x}}_e) \tag{12}$$

because $\mathbf{N}$ is both hermitian and idempotent (Maciejewski & Klein, 1985; Nakamura et al., 1987). The meaning of the terms in the above equation can be easily explained. The first term $\mathbf{J}^{\#}\dot{\boldsymbol{x}}_c$ guarantees the joint motion necessary for the desired end-effector velocity. Also, $\dot{\boldsymbol{x}}_c$ is used in (12) instead of $\dot{\boldsymbol{x}}_e$ to indicate that a task space controller can be used to compensate for any task space tracking errors, e.q.

$$\dot{\boldsymbol{x}}_c = \dot{\boldsymbol{x}}_d + \mathbf{K}\boldsymbol{e}. \tag{13}$$

where $\dot{\boldsymbol{x}}_d$ is the desired task space velocity, $\mathbf{K}$ is an m x m positive-definite matrix and $\boldsymbol{e}$ is the task position error, defined as

$$\boldsymbol{e} = \boldsymbol{x}_d - \boldsymbol{x}, \tag{14}$$

where $\boldsymbol{x}_d$ is the desired task space position. The second term in (12), i.e., the homogeneous solution $\dot{\boldsymbol{q}}_h$, represents the part of the joint velocity causing the motion of the point A_o. The term $\mathbf{J}_o\mathbf{J}^{\#}\dot{\boldsymbol{x}}_e$ is the velocity in A_o due to the end-effector motion. The matrix $\mathbf{J}_o\mathbf{N}$ is used to transform the desired critical point velocity from the operational space of the critical point into the joint space. Note that the above solution guarantees that we achieve exactly the desired $\dot{\boldsymbol{x}}_o$ only if the degree of redundancy of the manipulator is sufficient.

4.2 Exact solution using a reduced operational space

The matrix $\mathbf{J}_o\mathbf{N}$ combines the kinematics of the critical point A_o and the null-space matrix of the whole manipulator. Hence, its properties define the flexibility of the system for avoiding the obstacles. We want to point out that the properties of the matrix $\mathbf{J}_o\mathbf{N}$ do not depend only on the position of the point A_o but also on the definition of the operational space associated with the critical point. Usually, it is assumed that all critical points belong to the Cartesian space. Hence, the velocity $\dot{\boldsymbol{x}}_o$ is a 3-dimensional vector and the dimension of the matrix $\mathbf{J}_o\mathbf{N}$ is $3 \times n$. This also implies that 3 degrees-of-redundancy are needed to move one point from an obstacle. Consequently, it seems that a manipulator with 2 degrees-of-redundancy is not capable of avoiding obstacles, and of course, this is not true. For example, consider a planar 3 DOF manipulator that is supposed to move along a line, as shown in Fig. 2. As this is a planar case, the task space is 2-dimensional (e.g. x and y) and the manipulator has 1 degree-of-redundancy. Defining the velocity $\dot{\boldsymbol{x}}_o$ in the same space as the end-effector velocity, i.e., as a 2-dimensional vector, reveals the matrix $\mathbf{J}_o\mathbf{N}$ to have the dimension 2×3. Furthermore, due to 1 degree-of-redundancy the components of the velocity vector $\dot{\boldsymbol{x}}_o$ are not independent. Hence, the rank of $\mathbf{J}_o\mathbf{N}$ is 1, and the pseudoinverse $(\mathbf{J}_o\mathbf{N})^{\#}$ does not exist.

As the obstacle-avoidance strategy only requires motion in the direction of the line connecting the critical point with the closest point on the obstacle, this is a one-dimensional constraint and only one degree-of-redundancy is needed to avoid the obstacle, generally. Therefore, we propose using a reduced operational space for the obstacle avoidance and define the Jacobian $\mathbf{J}_o$ as follows.

Let $\boldsymbol{d}_o$ be the vector connecting the closest points on the obstacle and the manipulator (see Fig. 1) and let the operational space in A_o be defined as one-dimensional space in the direction of $\boldsymbol{d}_o$. Then, the Jacobian, which relates the joint space velocities $\dot{\boldsymbol{q}}$ and the velocity in the direction of $\boldsymbol{d}_o$, can be calculated as

$$\mathbf{J}_{d_o} = \boldsymbol{n}_o^T \mathbf{J}_o \tag{15}$$

where $\mathbf{J}_o$ is the Jacobian defined in the Cartesian space and $\boldsymbol{n}_o$ is the unit vector in the direction of $\boldsymbol{d}_o$, $\boldsymbol{n}_o = \frac{\boldsymbol{d}_o}{\|\boldsymbol{d}_o\|}$. Now, the dimension of the matrix $\mathbf{J}_{d_o}$ is $1 \times n$, and the velocities $\dot{\boldsymbol{x}}_o$ and $\mathbf{J}_{d_o}\mathbf{J}^{\#}\dot{\boldsymbol{x}}_e$ become scalars. Consequently, the computation of $(\mathbf{J}_{d_o}\mathbf{N})^{\#}$ is faster. For example, when calculating the Moore-Penrose pseudoinverse of $(\mathbf{J}_{d_o}\mathbf{N})$ defined as

$$(\mathbf{J}_{d_o}\mathbf{N})^{\#} = (\mathbf{J}_{d_o}\mathbf{N})^T \left(\mathbf{J}_{d_o}\mathbf{N}\,(\mathbf{J}_{d_o}\mathbf{N})^T\right)^{-1} = \mathbf{N}\mathbf{J}_{d_o}^T(\mathbf{J}_{d_o}\mathbf{N}\mathbf{J}_{d_o}^T)^{-1} \tag{16}$$

we do not have to invert any matrix because the term $(\mathbf{J}_{d_o}\mathbf{N}\mathbf{J}_{d_o}^T)$ is a scalar. Going back to our example in Fig. 2, the pseudoinverse $(\mathbf{J}_{d_o}\mathbf{N})^{\#}$ exists and the manipulator can perform the primary task and simultaneously avoid the obstacle, as shown in Fig. 2.

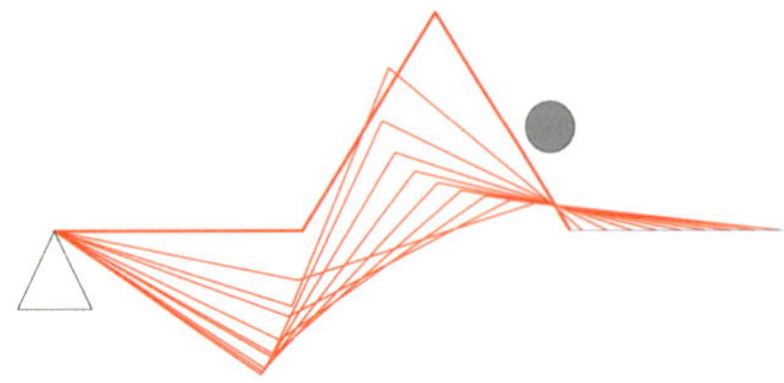

Fig. 2. Planar 3DOF manipulator: tracking of a line and obstacle avoidance using the Jacobian $\mathbf{J}_{d_o}$

4.3 Selection of avoiding velocity

The efficiency of the obstacle-avoidance algorithm also depends on the selection of the desired critical point velocity $\dot{x}_o$. We propose changing $\dot{x}_o$ with respect to the obstacle distance

$$\dot{x}_o = \alpha_v v_o \tag{17}$$

where v_o is the nominal velocity and α_v is the obstacle-avoidance gain defined as

$$\alpha_v = \begin{cases} \left(\frac{d_m}{\|\boldsymbol{d}_o\|}\right)^2 - 1 & \text{for} \quad \|\boldsymbol{d}_o\| < d_m \\ 0 & \text{for} \quad \|\boldsymbol{d}_o\| \geq d_m \end{cases} \tag{18}$$

where d_m is the critical distance to the obstacle (see Fig. 3). If the obstacle is too close ($\|\boldsymbol{d}_o\| \leq d_b$) the main task should be aborted. The distance d_b is subjected to the dynamic properties of the manipulator and can also be a function of the relative velocity $\dot{\boldsymbol{d}}_o$. To assure smooth transitions it is important that the magnitude of $\dot{\boldsymbol{x}}_o$ at d_m is zero. Special attention has to be given to the selection of the nominal velocity v_o. Large values of v_o would cause unnecessarily high velocities and consequently the manipulator would move far from the obstacle. Such motion may cause problems if there are more obstacles in the neighborhood of the manipulator. Namely, the manipulator may bounce between the obstacles. On the other hand, too small value of v_o would not move the critical point of the manipulator away from the obstacle.

For a smoother motion, was is proposed in Maciejewski & Klein (1985) to change the amount of the homogenous solution to be included in the total solution

$$\dot{\boldsymbol{q}}_{EX} = \mathbf{J}^{\#}\dot{\boldsymbol{x}}_c + \alpha_h(\mathbf{J}_{d_o}\mathbf{N})^{\#}(\dot{\boldsymbol{x}}_o - \mathbf{J}_{d_o}\mathbf{J}^{\#}\dot{\boldsymbol{x}}_e) \tag{19}$$

We have selected α_h as

$$\alpha_h = \begin{cases} 1 & \text{for} \quad \|\boldsymbol{d}_o\| \leq d_m \\ \frac{1}{2}\left(1 - \cos\left(\pi\frac{\|\boldsymbol{d}_o\| - d_m}{d_i - d_m}\right)\right) & \text{for} \quad d_m < \|\boldsymbol{d}_o\| < d_i \\ 0 & \text{for} \quad d_i \leq \|\boldsymbol{d}_o\| \end{cases} \tag{20}$$

where d_i is the distance where the obstacle influences the motion. From Fig. 3 it can be seen that in the region between d_b and d_m the complete homogenous solution is included in the motion specification and the avoidance velocity is inversely related to the distance. Between d_m and d_i the avoidance velocity is zero and only a part of the homogenous solution is included. As the homogenous solution compensates for the motion in the critical point due to the end-effector motion, the relative velocity between the obstacle and the critical point

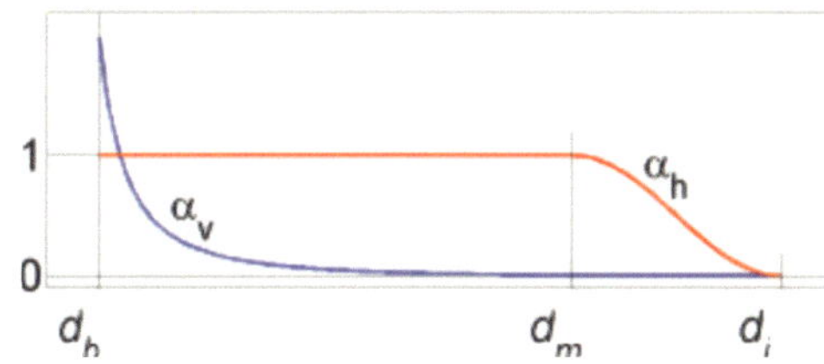

Fig. 3. The obstacle avoidance gain α_v and the homogenous term gain α_h versus the distance to the obstacle

decreases when approaching from d_i to d_m, if the obstacle is not moving, of course. With such a selection of α_v and α_h smooth velocities can be obtained.

The control law (19) can be used for a single obstacle. When more than one obstacle is active at one time then the worst-case obstacle (nearest) has to be used, which results in discontinuous velocities and may cause oscillations in some cases. Namely, when switching between active obstacles the particular homogenous solutions are not equal and a discontinuity in the joint velocities occurs. To improve the behavior we propose to use a weighted sum of the homogenous solution of all the active obstacles

$$\dot{\boldsymbol{q}}_{EX} = \mathbf{J}^{\#}\dot{\boldsymbol{x}}_c + \sum_{i=1}^{n_o} w_i \alpha_{h,i} \dot{\boldsymbol{q}}_{h,i} \tag{21}$$

where n_o is the number of active obstacles, and w_i, $\alpha_{h,i}$ and $\dot{\boldsymbol{q}}_{h,i}$ are the weighting factor, the gain and the homogenous solution for the i-th active obstacle, respectively. The weighting factors w_i are calculated as

$$w_i = \frac{d_i - \|\boldsymbol{d}_{o,i}\|}{\sum_{i=1}^{n_o}(d_i - \|\boldsymbol{d}_{o,i}\|)} \tag{22}$$

Although the actual velocities in the critical points differ from the desired ones, using $\dot{\boldsymbol{q}}_{EX}$ improves the behavior of the system and when one point is much closer to the obstacle than another, then its weight approaches 1 and the velocity in that particular point is close to the desired value.

As an illustration we present a simulation of a planar manipulator with 4 revolute joints. The primary task is to move along a straight line from point P_1 to point P_2, and the motion is obstructed by an obstacle. The task trajectory has a trapezoid velocity profile with an acceleration of $4ms^{-2}$ and a max. velocity of $0.4ms^{-1}$. We chose the the critical distance $d_m = 0.2m$. The simulation results using the exact velocity controller EX (19) are presented in Fig. 4(a).

4.4 Approximate solution

Another possible solution for $\dot{\varphi}$ is to calculate joint velocities that satisfy the secondary goal as

$$\dot{\varphi} = \mathbf{J}_{d_o}^{\#}\dot{x}_o \tag{23}$$

without compensating for the contribution of the end-effector motion and then substitute $\dot{\varphi}$ into (4), which yields

$$\dot{\boldsymbol{q}}_{AP} = \mathbf{J}^{\#}\dot{\boldsymbol{x}}_c + \mathbf{N}\mathbf{J}_{d_o}^{\#}\dot{x}_o \tag{24}$$

This approach avoids the singularity problem of $(\mathbf{J}_{d_o}\mathbf{N})$ (Chiaverini, 1997). The formulation (24) does not guarantee that we will achieve exactly the desired $\dot{x}_o$ even if the degree of redundancy is sufficient because $\mathbf{J}_{d_o}\mathbf{N}\mathbf{J}_{d_o}^{\#}\dot{x}_o$ is not equal to $\dot{x}_o$, in general.

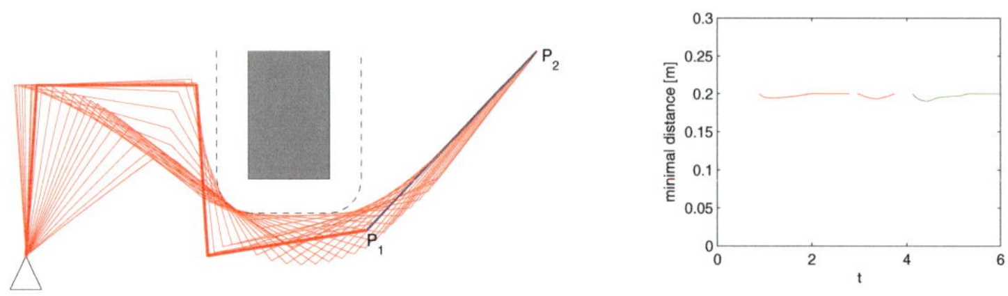

a) EX controller

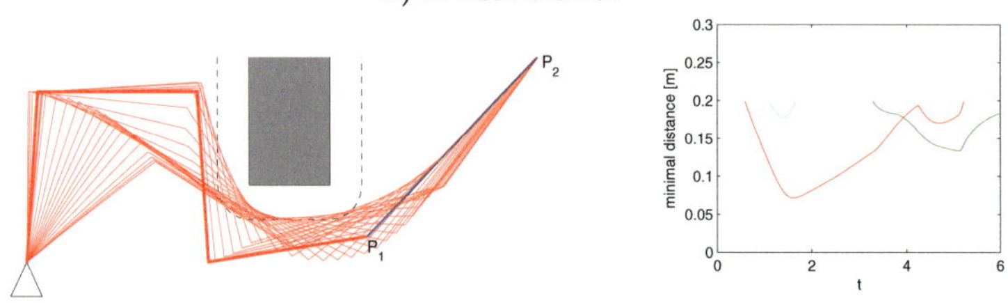

b) AP controller

Fig. 4. Planar 4DOF manipulator tracking a line while avoiding obstacles using velocity control (the dotted line indicates the critical distance)

To avoid the obstacle the goal velocity in A_o is represented by the vector $\dot{\boldsymbol{x}}_o$. Using the original method (12) the velocity in A_o is exactly $\dot{\boldsymbol{x}}_o$. The joint velocities $\dot{\boldsymbol{q}}_{EX}$ assure that the component of the velocity at point A_o (i.e., $\mathbf{J}_o\dot{\boldsymbol{q}}_{EX}$) in the direction of $\dot{\boldsymbol{x}}_o$ is as required. The approximate solution $\dot{\boldsymbol{q}}_{AP}$ gives, in most cases, a smaller magnitude of the velocity in the direction of $\dot{\boldsymbol{x}}_o$ (see $\mathbf{J}_o\dot{\boldsymbol{q}}_{AP}$). Therefore, the manipulator moves closer to the obstacle when $\dot{\boldsymbol{q}}_{AP}$ is used. This is not so critical, because the minimal distance also depends on the nominal velocity v_o, which can be increased to achieve larger minimal distances. Additionally, the approximate solution possesses certain advantages when many active obstacles have to be considered. The joint velocities can be calculated as

$$\dot{\boldsymbol{q}}_{AP} = \mathbf{J}^{\#}\dot{\boldsymbol{x}}_c + \mathbf{N}\sum_{i=1}^{n_o} \mathbf{J}^{\#}_{d_o,i}\dot{x}_{o,i} \qquad (25)$$

where n_o is the number of active obstacles, and therefore, the matrix $\mathbf{N}$ has to be calculated only once. Of course, pseudoinverses $\mathbf{J}^{\#}_{o,i}$ have to be calculated for each active obstacle. For the same system and task as before, the simulation results using the approximate velocity controller AP (24) are presented in Fig. 4(b). We can see that in the case of the AP controller, the links are coming closer to the obstacle as in the case of the EX controller. However, when changing the desired critical point velocity $\dot{x}_o$, i.e., using a higher order in (18), the minimal distance can be increased.

4.5 Obstacle avoidance as a primary task

For a redundant system multiple tasks can be arranged in priority. Let us consider two tasks, T_a and T_b

$$\boldsymbol{x}_a = \boldsymbol{f}_a(\boldsymbol{q}) \qquad \boldsymbol{x}_b = \boldsymbol{f}_b(\boldsymbol{q}) \qquad (26)$$

For each of the tasks, the corresponding Jacobian matrices can be defined as $\mathbf{J}_a$ and $\mathbf{J}_b$, and their corresponding null-space projections as $\mathbf{N}_a$ and $\mathbf{N}_b$. Assuming that task T_a is the primary task, Eq. (4) can be rewritten as

$$\dot{\boldsymbol{q}} = \mathbf{J}_a^{\#}\dot{\boldsymbol{x}}_a + \mathbf{N}_a\mathbf{J}_b^{\#}\dot{\boldsymbol{x}}_b \qquad (27)$$

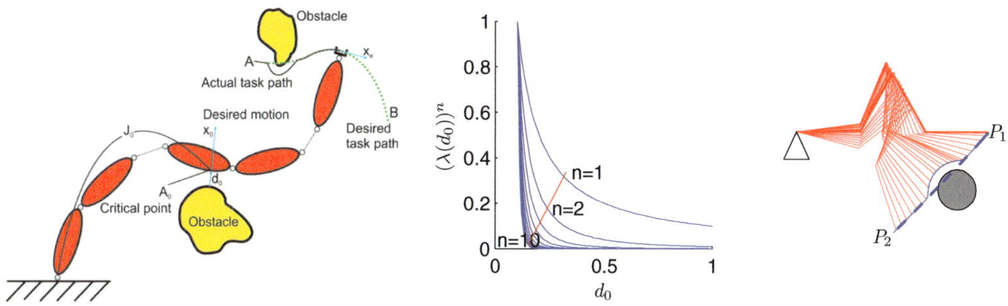

Fig. 5. Robot motion in the presence of some obstacle (left figure). Obstacle-avoidance proximity gain to the power of n (middle figure) and the planar 4DOF manipulator tracking line while avoiding the obstacle (right figure).

In many cases it would be of benefit to have the possibility to change the priority of particular subtasks. Using formulation (27) this cannot be done in a smooth way. Therefore, we propose a new definition of the velocity $\dot{\boldsymbol{q}}$. The velocity $\dot{\boldsymbol{q}}$ is now defined as

$$\dot{\boldsymbol{q}} = \mathbf{J}_a^{\#}\dot{\boldsymbol{x}}_a + \mathbf{N}_a'\mathbf{J}_b^{\#}\dot{\boldsymbol{x}}_b, \tag{28}$$

where the matrix $\mathbf{N}_a'$ is given as

$$\mathbf{N}_a' = \mathbf{I} - \lambda(\boldsymbol{x}_a)\mathbf{J}^{\#}\mathbf{J}, \tag{29}$$

where $\lambda(\boldsymbol{x}_a)$ is a scalar measure of how "active" is the primary task T_a, scaling the vector $\boldsymbol{x}_a$ to the interval $[0,1]$. When the primary task T_a is active the $\lambda(\boldsymbol{x}_a) = 1$ and the value when the task T_a is not active $\lambda(\boldsymbol{x}_a) = 0$.

The proposed algorithm allows a smooth transition in both ways, i.e., between observing the task T_a and the task T_b in null-space of the task T_a or just the unconstrained movement of the task T_b. It can be used for different robotic tasks. When applied to obstacle avoidance, task T_a is the obstacle avoidance and the end-effector motion is the task T_b. Before, we have assumed that the end-effector motion is not disturbed by an obstacle. Now, it is assumed that the motion of the end effector can be disturbed by any obstacle (see Fig. 5). If such a situation occurs, usually the task execution has to be interrupted and higher-level path planning has to be employed to recalculate the desired motion of the end effector. However, if the end-effector path tracking is not essential, we can use the proposed control (28). Consequently, no end-effector path recalculation or higher-level path planning is needed.

Let the primary task T_a be the motion in the direction $\boldsymbol{d}_0$ and the motion of the end-effector be the task T_b. Using the reduced operational space yields

$$\mathbf{J}_a = \mathbf{J}_o, \tag{30}$$

$$\mathbf{J}_b = \mathbf{J}. \tag{31}$$

Next, let the avoiding velocity $\dot{\boldsymbol{x}}_{d_0}$ be defined as

$$\dot{\boldsymbol{x}}_{d_0} = \lambda\left(\boldsymbol{d}_0\right)\boldsymbol{v}_0, \tag{32}$$

where $\boldsymbol{v}_0$ is a nominal velocity and $\lambda\left(\boldsymbol{d}_0\right)$ is defined as

$$\lambda(\boldsymbol{d}_0) = \begin{cases} \left(\dfrac{d_m}{||\boldsymbol{d}_0||}\right)^n, \; n = 1,2,3... & ||\boldsymbol{d}_0|| \geq d_m \\ 1 & ||\boldsymbol{d}_0|| < d_m \end{cases} \tag{33}$$

where $n = 1, 2, 3...$ and d_m is the critical distance to the obstacle. Then eq. (28) can be rewritten in the form

$$\dot{\boldsymbol{q}} = \mathbf{J}_o^{\dagger}\lambda\left(\boldsymbol{d}_0\right)\boldsymbol{v}_0 + \mathbf{N}_0'\mathbf{J}^{\#}\dot{\boldsymbol{x}}_c. \tag{34}$$

Here, $\dot{\boldsymbol{x}}_c$ is the task controller for the end-effector tracking and $\mathbf{N}_0'$ is given by

$$\mathbf{N}_0' = \mathbf{I} - \lambda\left(\boldsymbol{d}_0\right)\mathbf{J}_o^{\dagger}\mathbf{J}_o. \tag{35}$$

Formulation (34) allows unconstrained joint movement, while $\lambda(\boldsymbol{d}_0)$ is close to zero ($\lambda(\boldsymbol{d}_0) \approx 0$). Thus, the robot can track the desired task space path, while it is away from the obstacle. On the other hand, when the robot is close to the obstacle ($\lambda(\boldsymbol{d}_0) \approx 1$), the null space in (35) takes the form $\mathbf{N}_0' = \mathbf{N}_0$, and only allows movement in the null space of the primary task, i.e., the obstacle-avoidance task. In this case, we can still move the end effector, but the tracking error can increase due to the obstacle-avoiding motion.

4.6 Singular configurations

An important issue in the control of redundant manipulators is singular configurations where the associated Jacobian matrices lose the rank. Usually, only the configuration of the whole manipulator is of interest, but in obstacle avoidance we have also to consider the singularities of two manipulator substructures defined by the critical point A_o: (a) the part of the manipulator between the base and the point A_o and (b) the part between A_o and the end-effector. Although it can be assumed that the end-effector Jacobian $\mathbf{J}^{\#}$ is not singular along the desired end-effector path (otherwise the primary task can not be achieved), this is not always true for the matrix $\mathbf{J}_o\mathbf{N}$. Namely, when part (a) is in the singular configuration then $\mathbf{J}_o$ is not of full rank and when part (b) is in the singular configuration then $\mathbf{J}_o$ retains the rank but $\mathbf{J}_{d_o}\mathbf{N}$ becomes singular. Hence, when approaching either singular configuration the values of $\dot{\boldsymbol{q}}_h$ become unacceptably large. As the manipulator is supposed to move in an unstructured environment it is practically impossible to know when $\mathbf{J}_o\mathbf{N}$ will become singular. Therefore, a very important advantage of the proposed Jacobian $\mathbf{J}_{d_o}$ compared to $\mathbf{J}_o$ is that the system has significantly fewer singularities when $\mathbf{J}_{d_o}$ is used.

5. Obstacle avoidance using forces

Impedance control approaches for obstacle-avoidance were first introduced by Hogan (Hogan, 1985). These approaches make use of the additive property of impedances to supplement an impedance controller with additional disturbance forces to avoid the obstacles. The disturbance forces are generated from the artificial potential field. Lee demonstrated this approach with his reference adaptive impedance controller and gave promising results for a simulated 2-DOF robot (Lee et al., 1997).

The advantage of these approaches is that the dynamic behavior of the manipulator as it interacts with obstacles is adjustable through the gains in the obstacle-induced disturbing force. However, this approach is tightly coupled with the control scheme and requires the use of a compliance controller, which may not be desirable, depending on the task.

5.1 Obstacle avoidance without any sensors

First we want to investigate what happens if the manipulator collides with an obstacle. We are especially interested in how to control the manipulator so that it avoids the obstacle after the collision and how to minimize the contact forces. When the task itself includes contacts with the environment (e.g. assembly), the manipulator is equipped with an appropriate sensor to measure the contact forces and the controller includes a force control loop. But when the contacts between the manipulator and an obstacle can take place anywhere on the body of the manipulator, it is questionable whether the forces arising from such contacts can be measured. Assuming that the contact forces are not measurable and no other sensors to detect the obstacles are present, the contact forces have to be considered in the controller as disturbances. Now the problem is, how to generate a motion that would move a part of the manipulator away from the obstacle. To solve this problem we propose to follow a very basic principle: *an action causes a reaction*. In other words, if a manipulator acts with a force on an obstacle then the obstacle acts with a force in the opposite direction on the manipulator and our idea is to take advantage of this reaction force to move the manipulator away from the obstacle. To make such a motion possible, the control must not force the manipulator to oppose the reaction force (e.g. by preserving the configuration). This means that the system should be compliant to these external forces. A prerequisite for such an approach is that the manipulator is *backdrivable*, meaning that any force at the manipulator is immediately felt at the motors, so the manipulator reacts rapidly, drawing back from the source of the force.

To decouple the task space and the null-space motion we propose to use the controller (7). Actually, from the obstacle-avoidance point of view, any controller for the redundant manipulators could be used provided that the controller outputs are the joint torques. However, this is not enough to decouple the task space and null-space motion. Namely, torques applied through the null-space of $\mathbf{J}^{T\#}$, i.e., $\mathbf{N}^T\boldsymbol{\tau}$, can affect the end-effector acceleration, depending on the choice of the generalized inverse. It turns out for redundant systems that only the so-called "dynamically consistent" generalized inverse $\bar{\mathbf{J}}$ defined as

$$\bar{\mathbf{J}} = \mathbf{H}^{-1}\mathbf{J}^T(\mathbf{J}\mathbf{H}^{-1}\mathbf{J}^T)^{-1} \tag{36}$$

is the unique generalized inverse that decouples the task space and the null-space motion, i.e., assures that the task space acceleration is not affected by any torques applied through the null space of $\bar{\mathbf{J}}^T$, and that the end-effector forces do not produce any accelerations in the null-space of $\mathbf{J}$ (Featherstone & Khatib, 1997).

Using the inertia weighted generalized inverse in Eq. (7) yields

$$\boldsymbol{\tau} = \mathbf{H}(\bar{\mathbf{J}}(\ddot{\boldsymbol{x}}_c - \dot{\mathbf{J}}\dot{\boldsymbol{q}}) + \bar{\mathbf{N}}(\boldsymbol{\phi} - \dot{\bar{\mathbf{N}}}\dot{\boldsymbol{q}})) + \boldsymbol{h} + \boldsymbol{g} \tag{37}$$

Combining (3) and (37), and considering Eqs. (8) and (9) yields

$$\mathbf{H}\ddot{\boldsymbol{q}} + \boldsymbol{h} + \boldsymbol{g} - \boldsymbol{\tau}_F = \mathbf{H}(\bar{\mathbf{J}}(\ddot{\boldsymbol{x}}_d + \mathbf{K}_v\dot{\boldsymbol{e}} + \mathbf{K}_p\boldsymbol{e} - \dot{\mathbf{J}}\dot{\boldsymbol{q}}) + \bar{\mathbf{N}}(\ddot{\boldsymbol{\varphi}} + \dot{\bar{\mathbf{N}}}\dot{\boldsymbol{\varphi}} + \mathbf{K}_n\dot{\boldsymbol{e}}_n - \dot{\bar{\mathbf{N}}}\dot{\boldsymbol{q}})) + \boldsymbol{h} + \boldsymbol{g} \tag{38}$$

which simplifies to

$$\bar{\mathbf{J}}(\ddot{\boldsymbol{e}} + \mathbf{K}_v\dot{\boldsymbol{e}} + \mathbf{K}_p\boldsymbol{e}) + \bar{\mathbf{N}}(-\ddot{\boldsymbol{q}} + \ddot{\boldsymbol{\varphi}} + \dot{\bar{\mathbf{N}}}\dot{\boldsymbol{\varphi}} + \mathbf{K}_n\dot{\boldsymbol{e}}_n - \dot{\bar{\mathbf{N}}}\dot{\boldsymbol{q}}) = -\mathbf{H}^{-1}\boldsymbol{\tau}_F \tag{39}$$

where $\boldsymbol{\tau}_F$ represents the influence of all external forces caused by the contacts with obstacles

$$\boldsymbol{\tau}_F = \sum_{i=1}^{a_o} \mathbf{J}_{o,i}^T \boldsymbol{F}_{o,i} \tag{40}$$

Premultiplying (39) with $\mathbf{J}$ yields

$$\ddot{\boldsymbol{e}} + \mathbf{K}_v\dot{\boldsymbol{e}} + \mathbf{K}_p\boldsymbol{e} = -\mathbf{J}\mathbf{H}^{-1}\boldsymbol{\tau}_F \tag{41}$$

Note that the contact forces affect the motion in the task space, which results in the tracking error of the end-effector. Of course, if the obstacle avoidance is successful the contact forces vanish and the task position error converges to zero. The proper choice of $\mathbf{K}_v$ and $\mathbf{K}_p$ assures the asymptotical stability of the homogeneous part of the system, $\ddot{e} + \mathbf{K}_v\dot{e} + \mathbf{K}_p e = 0$. A detailed analysis of the influence of the external forces is given in Žlajpah & Nemec (2003). Next we analyse the behavior in null-space. Premultiplying (39) with $\bar{\mathbf{N}}$ yields

$$-\bar{\mathbf{N}}\mathbf{H}^{-1}\tau_F = \bar{\mathbf{N}}(-\ddot{q} + \ddot{\varphi} + \dot{\bar{\mathbf{N}}}\dot{\varphi} + \mathbf{K}_n\dot{e}_n - \dot{\bar{\mathbf{N}}}\dot{q}) \tag{42}$$

Rearranging Eq. (42) and using the relations $\ddot{e}_n = \bar{\mathbf{N}}(\ddot{\varphi} - \ddot{q}) + \dot{\bar{\mathbf{N}}}(\dot{\varphi} - \dot{q})$ and $\bar{\mathbf{N}}\mathbf{H}^{-1} = \mathbf{H}^{-1}\bar{\mathbf{N}}^T$, we obtain

$$\bar{\mathbf{N}}(\ddot{e}_n + \mathbf{K}_n\dot{e}_n) = -\bar{\mathbf{N}}\mathbf{H}^{-1}\bar{\mathbf{N}}^T\tau_F = -\mathbf{H}_n^{\ddagger}\tau_F \tag{43}$$

where $\mathbf{H}_n$ is the *null-space effective inertia matrix* describing the inertial properties of the system in the null-space

$$\mathbf{H}_n = \bar{\mathbf{N}}^T\mathbf{H}\bar{\mathbf{N}}$$

and $\mathbf{H}_n^{\ddagger}$ is the generalized inverse of $\mathbf{H}_n$, defined as

$$\mathbf{H}_n^{\ddagger} = \bar{\mathbf{N}}\mathbf{H}^{-1}\bar{\mathbf{N}}^T$$

The selection of the null space dynamic properties is subjected to the subtask that the manipulator should perform. Actually, in most cases it is required that the null space velocity tracks a given desired null space velocity $\dot{\varphi}$. For good null space velocity tracking, the gain matrix $\mathbf{K}_n$ should be high, which means that the system is stiff in the null space. On the other hand, when the manipulator collides with an obstacle, the self-motion is initiated externally by the contact force. As we have already mentioned, in this case the system should be compliant in the null-space. Therefore, the gain matrix $\mathbf{K}_n$ should be low. As both requirements for $\mathbf{K}_n$ are in conflict, a compromise has to made when selecting $\mathbf{K}_n$ or the on-line adaptation of $\mathbf{K}_n$ has to be used. The problem with the second possibility is that we have to be able to detect the current state, i.e., if the manipulator is in contact with an object. If this is possible, then it is easy to set low gains when the collision occurs and high gains when the manipulator is "free". If we cannot detect the contact and the probability of collisions is high, then it is rational to select a low $\mathbf{K}_n$, but we must be aware that too low values of $\mathbf{K}_n$ may cause instability in the null-space. The lower bounds for $\mathbf{K}_n$ can be obtained with a Lyapunov analysis (Žlajpah & Nemec, 2003).

As an illustration we use the same example as before, where the manipulator is supposed to have 4 revolute joints. The primary task is to move along a straight line from point P_1 to point P_2, and the motion is obstructed by an obstacle. The task trajectory has a trapezoid velocity profile with an acceleration of $4ms^{-2}$ and a max. velocity of $0.4ms^{-1}$. The control algorithm is given by Eq. (37) (CF). The task space controller parameters (Eq. 8) are $\mathbf{K}_p = 1000\mathbf{I}s^{-2}$ and $\mathbf{K}_v = 80\mathbf{I}s^{-1}$, which are tuned to ensure good tracking of the task trajectory (stiff task space behavior). The null space controller is a modified version of the controller (9)) $\phi = -\mathbf{K}_n\dot{q}$, i.e., the desired null-space velocity is set to zero. We have compared two sets of null-space gains: (i) Low $\mathbf{K}_n$, which ensures compliant null-space behavior, and (ii) Medium $\mathbf{K}_n$, which makes the null-space more stiff. The simulation results are presented in Figs. 6 and 7.

Although the manipulator has finished the desired task in both cases, we can see that making the null-space more compliant results in decreased contact forces. As expected, the impact force does not depend on the stiffness in the null space and cannot be decreased by increasing

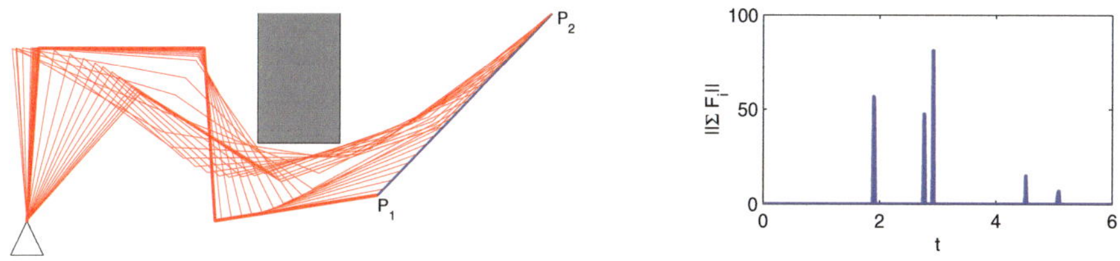

Fig. 6. Planar 4DOF manipulator tracking a line while avoiding obstacles without using any sensors to detect the obstacles (CF); compliant in null space

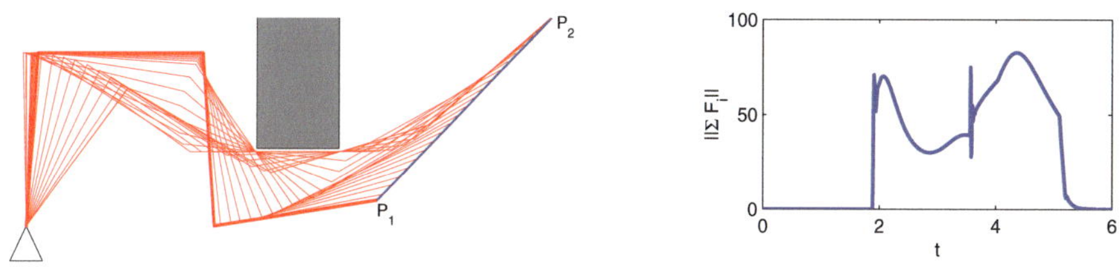

Fig. 7. Planar 4DOF manipulator tracking a line while avoiding obstacles without using any sensors to detect the obstacles (CF); stiff in null space

the compliancy in the null space. Actually, the impact forces are the main problem with this type of control. Namely, the magnitude of the impact forces cannot be controlled with the controller, the controller can decrease the contact forces after the impact. The magnitude of the impact forces depends primarily on the kinetic energy of the bodies that collide and the stiffness of the contact. Therefore, this approach to obstacle avoidance is limited to cases where the manipulator is moving slowly or the manipulator body (or obstacles) is covered with soft material, which reduces the impact forces. Note that the impact forces (the magnitude and the time of occurrence) are not the same in these examples due to the different close-loop dynamics of the system.

5.2 Obstacle avoidance with tactile sensors

As already mentioned, the obstacle-avoidance approach based on contact forces without any contact sensors cannot be applied to manipulators that are not backdrivable, like manipulators with high-ratio gears. The alternative strategy is a sensor based motion control, where a kind of tactile sensors mounted on a manipulator detect the contact with an obstacle. The main advantage of using the tactile sensor information in control is that the obstacle avoidance becomes "active", meaning the avoiding motion is initiated by the controller. So, it can be applied to any manipulator, irrespective of the backdrivability of the manipulator.

With tactile sensors the collisions can be detected. Our approach is to identify the points on the manipulator that are in contact with obstacles and to assign to them additional virtual force components that move the points away from the obstacle (see Fig. 8). We propose that these forces are not included into the close-loop controller, but they are applied as the virtual external forces to the manipulator.

Suppose that $\boldsymbol{F}_o$ is acting at point A_o somewhere on the link i (see Fig. 8).

The static relation between the force $\boldsymbol{F}_o$ and the corresponding joint torques $\boldsymbol{\tau}_o$ is

$$\boldsymbol{\tau}_o = \mathbf{J}_o^T \boldsymbol{F}_o \tag{44}$$

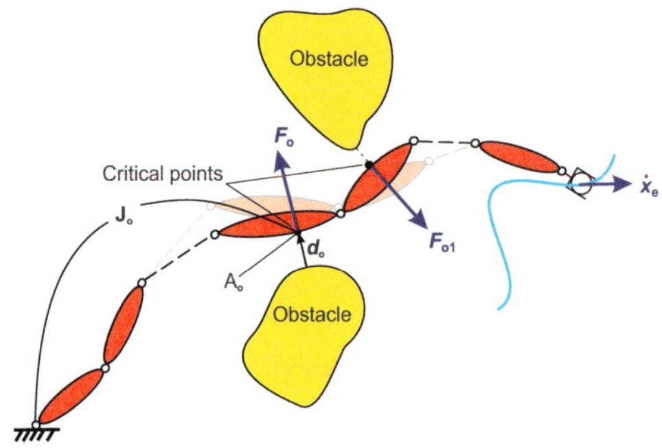

Fig. 8. Manipulator motion in the presence of some obstacles: links in contact are moved away from obstacles by additional virtual forces

where $\mathbf{J}_o$ is a Jacobian matrix associated with the point A_o. Applying $\boldsymbol{\tau}_o$ to the system yields the equation of motion in the form

$$\boldsymbol{\tau} = \mathbf{H}\ddot{\boldsymbol{q}} + \boldsymbol{h} + \boldsymbol{g} - \boldsymbol{\tau}_F - \boldsymbol{\tau}_o \tag{45}$$

which is the same as Eq. (3), except that the torques due to the virtual forces forces $\boldsymbol{\tau}_F$ are added. In general, by applying the torques $\boldsymbol{\tau}_o$ as defined in Eq. (44), the motion of the end-effector and the self-motion of the manipulator are influenced. Note that one of the goals of obstacle avoidance is to disturb the end-effector motion as little as possible. As we are adding virtual forces, it is not necessary that the applied virtual forces correspond to the "real" forces. Therefore, only torques that do not influence the end-effector motion are proposed to be added to generate the obstacle-avoidance motion. In general, the force $\boldsymbol{F}_o$ can be substituted by a force acting in the task space

$$\boldsymbol{F}_{oe} = \mathbf{J}^{T\#}\mathbf{J}_o^T\boldsymbol{F}_o \tag{46}$$

and by joint torques acting in the null-space of $\mathbf{J}^{T\#}$

$$\boldsymbol{\tau}_{oN} = \mathbf{N}^T\mathbf{J}_o^T\boldsymbol{F}_o = \mathbf{N}^T\boldsymbol{\tau}_o \tag{47}$$

Substituting $\boldsymbol{\tau}_{oN}$ for $\boldsymbol{\tau}_o$ in Eq. (45) yields

$$\boldsymbol{\tau} = \mathbf{H}\ddot{\boldsymbol{q}} + \boldsymbol{h} + \boldsymbol{g} - \boldsymbol{\tau}_F - \bar{\mathbf{N}}^T\boldsymbol{\tau}_o \tag{48}$$

The efficiency of the obstacle-avoidance algorithm depends on the selection of the desired force $\boldsymbol{F}_o$. In our approach, the virtual force $\boldsymbol{F}_o$ depends on the location of the critical point A_o, i.e., the locations of the tactile sensors that detect the contact. As the positions of the sensors are known in advance, it is easy to get the corresponding Jacobian matrix $\mathbf{J}_o$ for each sensor. Additionally, each sensor also has a predefined avoiding direction $\boldsymbol{n}_o$. We define the virtual forces $\boldsymbol{F}_o$ as

$$\boldsymbol{F}_o = \alpha_t f_o \boldsymbol{n}_o \tag{49}$$

where α_t is the obstacle-avoidance gain. We propose that α_t depends on the duration of the contact and that the achievedvalue is preserved for some time after the contact between the manipulator and the obstacle is lost (see Fig. 9)

$$\alpha_t = \begin{cases} 0 & \text{for} \quad t < t_s \\ e^{T_i(t-t_s)} & \text{for} \quad t_s \leq t < t_e \\ e^{T_i(t_e-t_s)}e^{-T_d(t-t_e)} & \text{for} \quad t_e \leq t \end{cases} \tag{50}$$

where T_i and T_d are the constants for the increase of the gain value and the delayed action, and t_s and t_e represent the time when the contact occurs and the time when the contact is lost, respectively. With the appropriate selection of T_i and T_d a robust behavior can be obtained.

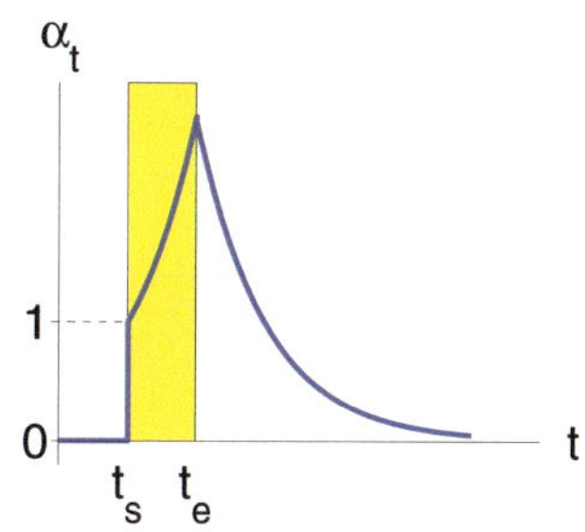

Fig. 9. The obstacle-avoidance gain α_t versus the duration of the contact

The next issue is how the obstacle avoidance is performed when there are more simultaneously active obstacles in the neighborhood of the manipulator. Using the proposed obstacle-avoidance formulation the problem of many simultaneously active obstacles can be solved very efficiently. The additivity of the torques makes it possible to avoid multiple obstacles by using the sum of the torques due to the relevant virtual forces,

$$\boldsymbol{\tau}_o = \sum_{i=1}^{a_o} \mathbf{J}_{o,i}^T \boldsymbol{F}_{o,i} \tag{51}$$

and considering this in Eq. (47) yields

$$\boldsymbol{\tau}_{o,N} = \bar{\mathbf{N}}^T \sum_{i=1}^{a_o} \mathbf{J}_{o,i}^T \boldsymbol{F}_{o,i} \tag{52}$$

where a_o is the number of active obstacles. It is clear that when more than one obstacle is active it is necessary to calculate only the transpose of the Jacobian $\mathbf{J}_{o,i}^T$ for each critical point and not the generalized inverse $\bar{\mathbf{J}}_{o,i}$, as is the case with velocity-based strategies. The redundancy of the manipulator is considered in the term $\bar{\mathbf{N}}^T$, which does not depend on the location of particular critical points $A_{o,i}$. Hence, there is no limitation on a_o regarding the degree-of-redundancy. In the case when a_o is greater than the degree-of-redundancy, the manipulator is pushed into a configuration where the virtual forces compensate each other, i.e., $\boldsymbol{\tau}_o = 0$. Actually, such situations can occur even when a_o is less than the degree-of-redundancy, e.g. when one link is under the influence of more than one obstacle. The force formulation has its advantages computationally, e.g. in Eq. (52) the term $\bar{\mathbf{N}}^T$ is calculated only once.

For the close-loop control the controller (37) is used again. Augmenting (38) with virtual forces the behavior of the system with contact sensors is described by

$$\mathbf{H}\ddot{\boldsymbol{q}} + \boldsymbol{h} + \boldsymbol{g} - \boldsymbol{\tau}_F - \bar{\mathbf{N}}^T\boldsymbol{\tau}_o = \mathbf{H}(\bar{\mathbf{J}}(\ddot{\boldsymbol{x}}_d + \mathbf{K}_v\dot{\boldsymbol{e}} + \mathbf{K}_p\boldsymbol{e} - \dot{\mathbf{J}}\dot{\boldsymbol{q}}) + \bar{\mathbf{N}}(\ddot{\boldsymbol{\varphi}} + \dot{\bar{\mathbf{N}}}\dot{\boldsymbol{\varphi}} + \mathbf{K}_n\dot{\boldsymbol{e}}_n - \dot{\bar{\mathbf{N}}}\dot{\boldsymbol{q}})) + \boldsymbol{h} + \boldsymbol{g} \tag{53}$$

Actually, the term $\bar{\mathbf{N}}^T\boldsymbol{\tau}_o$ is also part of the controller and should be on the right-hand side of Eq. (53), but we put it on the left-hand side to emphasize its role. Eq. (53) simplifies to

$$\bar{\mathbf{J}}(\ddot{\boldsymbol{e}} + \mathbf{K}_v\dot{\boldsymbol{e}} + \mathbf{K}_p\boldsymbol{e}) + \bar{\mathbf{N}}(-\ddot{\boldsymbol{q}} + \ddot{\boldsymbol{\varphi}} + \dot{\bar{\mathbf{N}}}\dot{\boldsymbol{\varphi}} + \mathbf{K}_n\dot{\boldsymbol{e}}_n - \dot{\bar{\mathbf{N}}}\dot{\boldsymbol{q}}) = -\mathbf{H}^{-1}(\bar{\mathbf{N}}^T\boldsymbol{\tau}_o + \boldsymbol{\tau}_F) \tag{54}$$

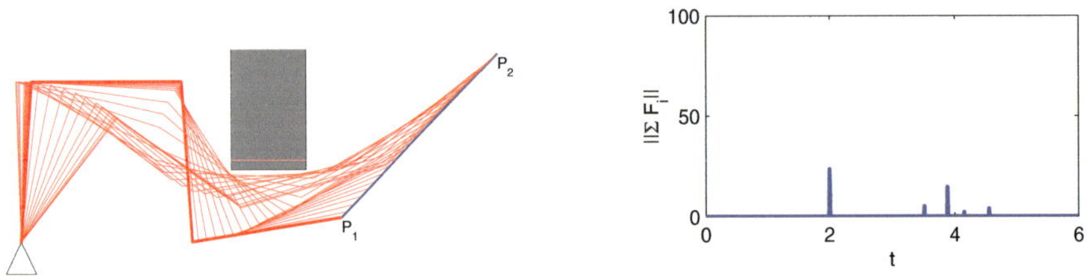

Fig. 10. Planar 4DOF manipulator tracking a line while avoiding obstacles using tactile sensors and virtual forces (TF controller)

Premultiplying (54) with **J** yields

$$\ddot{e} + \mathbf{K}_v \dot{e} + \mathbf{K}_p e = -\mathbf{J}\mathbf{H}^{-1}\boldsymbol{\tau}_F \tag{55}$$

which is the same as Eq. (41), and premultiplying (54) with $\bar{\mathbf{N}}$ yields after simplifications

$$\bar{\mathbf{N}}\ddot{e}_n + \bar{\mathbf{N}}\mathbf{K}_n \dot{e}_n = -\mathbf{H}_n^{\ddagger}(\boldsymbol{\tau}_o + \boldsymbol{\tau}_F) \tag{56}$$

From Eqs. (55) and (56) we can see that the task space and the null-space motion are influenced by the contact forces. However, these forces decrease after the impact because of the avoiding motion.

Next, we present the simulation results of the same task as before for the system where the tactile sensors (TF) were used to detect the obstacle. The close loop controller was the same as for the CF case (ii) approach, which assures stiff null space behavior. The avoidance motion was generated using Eqs. (49) – (50) with the parameters $f_o = 100N$, $T_i = 6s$ and $T_d = 8s$. The results, see Fig. 10, show that with tactile sensors we can decrease the contact forces after the contact, but the impact force cannot be decreased. Unfortunately, the magnitude of the impact forces is not controllable and hence this approach also requires low velocities and a soft contact.

5.3 Obstacle avoidance with proximity sensors

When proximity sensors are used to detect obstacles, the collisions between the manipulator and obstacles can be avoided. Also here, our approach is to identify the points on the manipulator that are near obstacles and to assign to them force components that move the points away from the obstacle (see Fig. 8). The strategy is similar to those given in (Brock et al., 2002), although it was developed independently.

Suppose that $\boldsymbol{F}_o$ is acting at point A_o somewhere on the link i (see Fig. 8). Applying $\boldsymbol{\tau}_o$ (see Eq. 44) to the system yields the equation of motion in the form

$$\boldsymbol{\tau} = \mathbf{H}\ddot{\boldsymbol{q}} + \boldsymbol{h} + \boldsymbol{g} - \boldsymbol{\tau}_o \tag{57}$$

which is the same as Eq. (3), except that the real external forces $\boldsymbol{\tau}_F$ are replaced by the virtual forces $\boldsymbol{\tau}_o$. As we are using virtual forces, only torques that do not influence the end-effector motion are considered

$$\boldsymbol{\tau}_{oN} = \mathbf{N}^T \mathbf{J}_o^T \boldsymbol{F}_o = \mathbf{N}^T \boldsymbol{\tau}_o \tag{58}$$

Substituting $\boldsymbol{\tau}_{oN}$ for $\boldsymbol{\tau}_o$ in Eq. (57) yields

$$\boldsymbol{\tau} = \mathbf{H}\ddot{\boldsymbol{q}} + \boldsymbol{h} + \boldsymbol{g} - \bar{\mathbf{N}}^T \boldsymbol{\tau}_o \tag{59}$$

The main difference compared to the system with tactile sensors is how the virtual forces $\boldsymbol{F}_o$ are generated. Now, the virtual force $\boldsymbol{F}_o$ depends on the location of the critical point and the closest point on the obstacle. Clearly, the location of all the objects in the workspace of the manipulator has to be known. This information can be provided by a higher control level that has access to sensory data. As sensor systems are not our concern, we will assume that the sensor can detect obstacles in the workspace of the manipulator and that it outputs the direction and the distance to the closest point obstacle, and the position of the critical point on the manipulator.
Let A_o be the critical point and $\boldsymbol{d}$ the vector connecting the closest point on the obstacle and A_o (see Fig. 8). To avoid a possible collision a virtual force $\boldsymbol{F}_o$ is assigned to A_o, defined as

$$\boldsymbol{F}_o = \alpha_f f_o \boldsymbol{n}_o \tag{60}$$

where f_o is a scalar gain representing the nominal force, $\boldsymbol{n}_o$ is the unit vector in the direction of $\boldsymbol{d}$, and α_f is the obstacle-avoidance gain. The gain α_f should depend on the distance to the obstacle, as shown in Fig. 11.

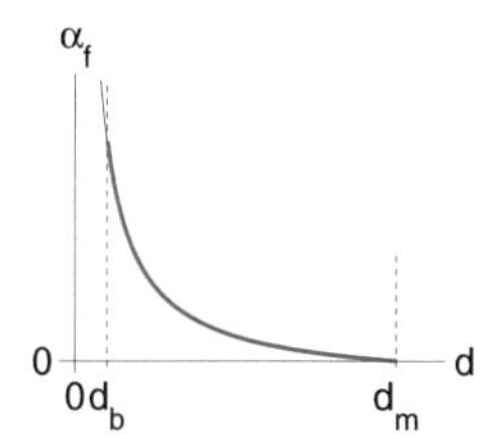

Fig. 11. The obstacle-avoidance gain α_f versus the distance to the obstacle

There are two distances characterizing the changes in the value of the gain: the critical distance d_m and the abort distance d_b. If the distance between the manipulator and the object is greater than d_m then the motion of the manipulator is not perturbed. When the distance is decreasing, the force should increase smoothly (to assure smooth transitions it is important that the magnitude of $\boldsymbol{F}_o$ at d_m is zero). However, if the manipulator is too close to the obstacle (less than d_b) the main task should be, for safety reasons, aborted so that the manipulator can avoid the obstacles (such a situation can occur, especially if moving obstacles are present in the workspace). The distance d_b is subjected to the dynamic properties of the manipulator and can also be a function of the relative velocity between the critical point on the manipulator and the obstacle. The gain α_f can be chosen arbitrarily as long as it has the prescribed form. We propose using the following function

$$\alpha_f = \begin{cases} \left(\frac{d_m}{\|\boldsymbol{d}_o\|}\right)^2 - 1 & \text{for} \quad \|\boldsymbol{d}_o\| < d_m \\ 0 & \text{for} \quad \|\boldsymbol{d}_o\| \geq d_m \end{cases} \tag{61}$$

Special attention has to be given to the selection of the nominal force f_o. Large values of f_o can cause unnecessarily high accelerations and velocities. Consequently, the manipulator could move far from the obstacle. Such a motion may cause problems if there are more obstacles in the neighborhood of the manipulator. Namely, the manipulator may bounce between the obstacles. On the other hand, too small values of f_o would not move the critical point sufficiently away from the obstacle.

When there are more simultaneously active obstacles in the neighborhood of the manipulator, the sum of the torques due to the relevant virtual forces is used,

$$\boldsymbol{\tau}_o = \sum_{i=1}^{a_o} \mathbf{J}_{o,i}^T \boldsymbol{F}_{o,i} \tag{62}$$

and considering this in Eq. (58) yields

$$\boldsymbol{\tau}_{o,N} = \bar{\mathbf{N}}^T \sum_{i=1}^{a_o} \mathbf{J}_{o,i}^T \boldsymbol{F}_{o,i} \tag{63}$$

where a_o is the number of active obstacles.
To decouple the task space and the null-space motion we propose as before the controller (37). Combining (48) and (37), and considering Eqs. (8) and (9) yields

$$\mathbf{H}\ddot{\boldsymbol{q}} + \boldsymbol{h} + \boldsymbol{g} - \bar{\mathbf{N}}^T\boldsymbol{\tau}_o = \mathbf{H}(\bar{\mathbf{J}}(\ddot{\boldsymbol{x}}_d + \mathbf{K}_v\dot{\boldsymbol{e}} + \mathbf{K}_p\boldsymbol{e} - \dot{\mathbf{J}}\dot{\boldsymbol{q}}) + \bar{\mathbf{N}}(\ddot{\boldsymbol{\varphi}} + \dot{\bar{\mathbf{N}}}\dot{\boldsymbol{\varphi}} + \mathbf{K}_n\dot{\boldsymbol{e}}_n - \dot{\bar{\mathbf{N}}}\dot{\boldsymbol{q}})) + \boldsymbol{h} + \boldsymbol{g} \tag{64}$$

As before, the term $\bar{\mathbf{N}}^T\boldsymbol{\tau}_o$ is also part of the controller and should be on the right-hand side of Eq. (64), but we put it on the left-hand side to emphasize its role.
One of the reasons for using the above control law is that the null-space velocity controller (9) can be used for other lower-priority tasks. Hence, to optimize p we can select $\dot{\boldsymbol{\varphi}}$ in (9) as

$$\dot{\boldsymbol{\varphi}} = \mathbf{H}^{-1}k_p\nabla p \tag{65}$$

Note that when the weighted generalized inverse of $\mathbf{J}$ is used, the desired null space velocity has to be multiplied by the inverse of the weighting matrix (in our case $\mathbf{H}^{-1}$) to assure the convergence of the optimization of p (Nemec, 1997).
Next we analyse the behavior of the close-loop system. Premultiplying Eq. (64) by $\mathbf{H}^{-1}$ yields

$$\ddot{\boldsymbol{q}} - \mathbf{H}^{-1}\bar{\mathbf{N}}^T\boldsymbol{\tau}_o = \bar{\mathbf{J}}(\ddot{\boldsymbol{x}}_d + \mathbf{K}_v\dot{\boldsymbol{e}} + \mathbf{K}_p\boldsymbol{e} - \dot{\mathbf{J}}\dot{\boldsymbol{q}}) + \bar{\mathbf{N}}(\ddot{\boldsymbol{\varphi}} + \dot{\bar{\mathbf{N}}}\dot{\boldsymbol{\varphi}} + \mathbf{K}_n\dot{\boldsymbol{e}}_n - \dot{\bar{\mathbf{N}}}\dot{\boldsymbol{q}})$$

and by using (1) the above equation can be rewritten in the form

$$\bar{\mathbf{J}}(\ddot{\boldsymbol{e}} + \mathbf{K}_v\dot{\boldsymbol{e}} + \mathbf{K}_p\boldsymbol{e}) + \bar{\mathbf{N}}(-\ddot{\boldsymbol{q}} + \ddot{\boldsymbol{\varphi}} + \dot{\bar{\mathbf{N}}}\dot{\boldsymbol{\varphi}} + \mathbf{K}_n\dot{\boldsymbol{e}}_n - \dot{\bar{\mathbf{N}}}\dot{\boldsymbol{q}}) = -\mathbf{H}^{-1}\bar{\mathbf{N}}^T\boldsymbol{\tau}_o \tag{66}$$

The dynamics of the system in the task space and in the null-space can be obtained by premultiplying Eq. (66) by $\mathbf{J}$ and $\bar{\mathbf{N}}$, respectively. Premultiplying (66) with $\mathbf{J}$ yields

$$\ddot{\boldsymbol{e}} + \mathbf{K}_v\dot{\boldsymbol{e}} + \mathbf{K}_p\boldsymbol{e} = 0 \tag{67}$$

since $\mathbf{J}\bar{\mathbf{J}} = \mathbf{I}$, $\bar{\mathbf{N}}\mathbf{H}^{-1} = \mathbf{H}^{-1}\bar{\mathbf{N}}^T$, and $\mathbf{J}\bar{\mathbf{N}} = \mathbf{0}$. The proper choice of $\mathbf{K}_v$ and $\mathbf{K}_p$ assures the asymptotical stability of the system. Furthermore, it can be seen that the virtual forces do not affect the motion in the task space. Next, premultiplying (66) by $\bar{\mathbf{N}}$ yields

$$\bar{\mathbf{N}}(-\ddot{\boldsymbol{q}} + \ddot{\boldsymbol{\varphi}} + \dot{\bar{\mathbf{N}}}\dot{\boldsymbol{\varphi}} + \mathbf{K}_n\dot{\boldsymbol{e}}_n - \dot{\bar{\mathbf{N}}}\dot{\boldsymbol{q}}) = -\bar{\mathbf{N}}\mathbf{H}^{-1}\bar{\mathbf{N}}^T\boldsymbol{\tau}_o \tag{68}$$

because $\bar{\mathbf{N}}\bar{\mathbf{J}} = \mathbf{0}$. Rearranging Eq. (68) and using the relation $\ddot{\boldsymbol{e}}_n = \bar{\mathbf{N}}(\ddot{\boldsymbol{\varphi}} - \ddot{\boldsymbol{q}}) + \dot{\bar{\mathbf{N}}}(\dot{\boldsymbol{\varphi}} - \dot{\boldsymbol{q}})$ we obtain

$$\bar{\mathbf{N}}(\ddot{\boldsymbol{\varphi}} - \ddot{\boldsymbol{q}} + \dot{\bar{\mathbf{N}}}(\dot{\boldsymbol{\varphi}} - \dot{\boldsymbol{q}}) + \mathbf{K}_n\dot{\boldsymbol{e}}_n) = -\bar{\mathbf{N}}\mathbf{H}^{-1}\bar{\mathbf{N}}^T\boldsymbol{\tau}_o = -\mathbf{H}_n^{\ddagger}\boldsymbol{\tau}_o \tag{69}$$

From Eq. (69) we can see that the obstacle-avoidance motion is not controlled directly by $\boldsymbol{F}_o$. The force $\boldsymbol{F}_o$ initiates the motion, but the resulting motion depends mainly on the null-space controller (9). Although the null-space controller has in this case the same structure as in the case of the contact forces approach, the gains $\mathbf{K}_n$ can be selected to meet the requirements of the subtask the manipulator should perform, i.e., in most cases to track the desired null space velocity. Hence, the gain matrix $\mathbf{K}_n$ should be high. Consequently, to perform satisfactory obstacle avoidance the nominal force f_o must be higher to predominate over the velocity controller when necessary.
In the following the simulation results for the simple task are shown. The task space controller parameters are the same as in the previous example. To avoid the obstacles the proximity sensor distance was selected as $d_m = 0.2m$. The virtual forces were calculated using Eq. (40) with the parameter $f_o = 800N$. The simulation results, see Fig. 12, clearly show that the obstacle is avoided without a deviation of the end-effector from the assigned task.

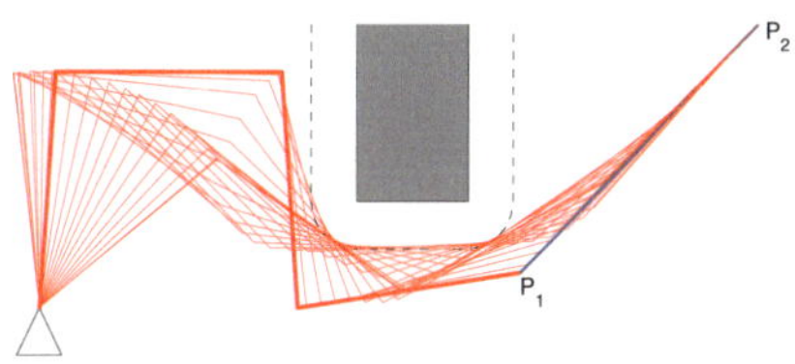

Fig. 12. Planar 4DOF manipulator tracking a line while avoiding obstacles using a virtual forces approach (VF)

6. Experimental results

The proposed algorithms were tested on the laboratory manipulator (see Fig. 13 and two KUKA LWR robots (see Fig. 14). The laboratory manipulator was specially developed for testing the different control algorithms. To be able to test the algorithms for the redundant systems the manipulator has four revolute DOF acting in a plane. The link lengths of the manipulator are $l = (0.184, 0.184, 0.184, 0.203)m$ and the link masses are $m = 0.83, 0.44, 0.18, 0.045)kg$. The manipulator is a part of the integrated environment for the design of the control algorithms and the testing of these algorithms on a real system (Žlajpah, 2001).

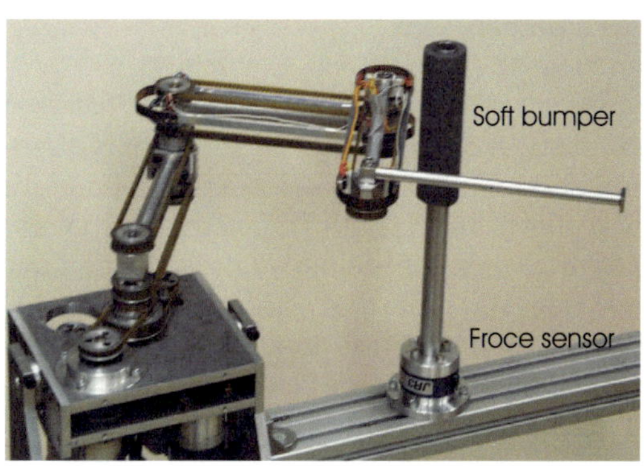

Fig. 13. Experimental manipulator with external force sensor

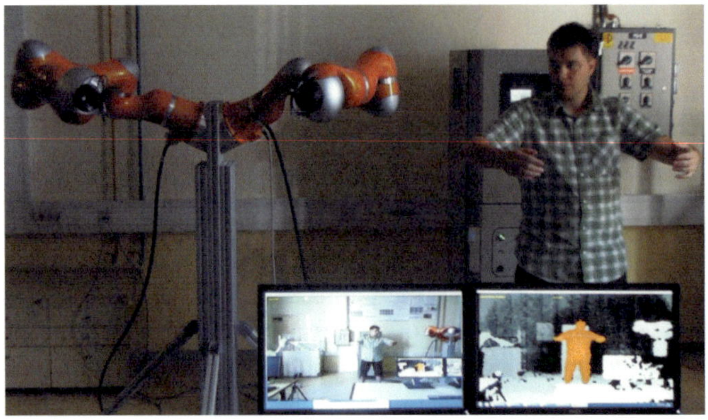

Fig. 14. Experimental setup with two KUKA LWR robots for bimanual movement imitation.

Fig. 15. Planar 4DOF manipulator tracking a path in an unstructured environment with three obstacles using velocity-based control (sampled every 1s)

6.1 Velocity controller

The task in these experiments was tracking the path $\boldsymbol{x}_d = [0.4 - 0.2\sin(2\pi t/8), -0.1 + 0.1\sin(2\pi t/4)]^T$ and the motion of the manipulator was obstructed by three obstacles (see Fig. 15). In the current implementation the vision system is using a simple USB WebCam that can recognize the scene and output the position of all the obstacles in less that 0.04s. To avoid the obstacles the proximity sensor distance was selected as $d_m = 0.08m$. The rate of the velocity controller was 200Hz (the necessary joint velocities for the avoiding motion are calculated in less than 0.5ms). The experimental results are given in Fig. 15. As we can see, the obstacles were successfully avoided.

6.2 Obstacle avoidance as a primary task

We applied our algorithm to two Kuka LWR robots as shown in Fig. 14. Our algorithm is used as a low-level control to prevent self-collision, i.e., a collision between the robots themselves. As mentioned previously, the desired movement of the robot is a secondary task. The task of collision avoidance is only observed if we approach a pre-defined threshold. While far from the threshold the algorithm allows direct control of the separate joints ($\dot{\boldsymbol{q}}_n$). If we approach the threshold, the task of collision avoidance smoothly takes over and only allows joint control in the null space projection of this task. Note that $\dot{\boldsymbol{q}}_n$ is in joint space.
The task for both arms in this experiment was to follow the human demonstrator in real-time. The human motion is captured using the Microsoft Kinect sensor. Microsoft Kinect is based on arange camera developed by PrimeSense, which interprets 3D scene information from a continuously-projected infrared structured light. By processing the depth image, the PrimeSense application programming interface (API) enables tracking of the user's movement in real time. Imitating the motion of the user's arm requires some basic understanding of

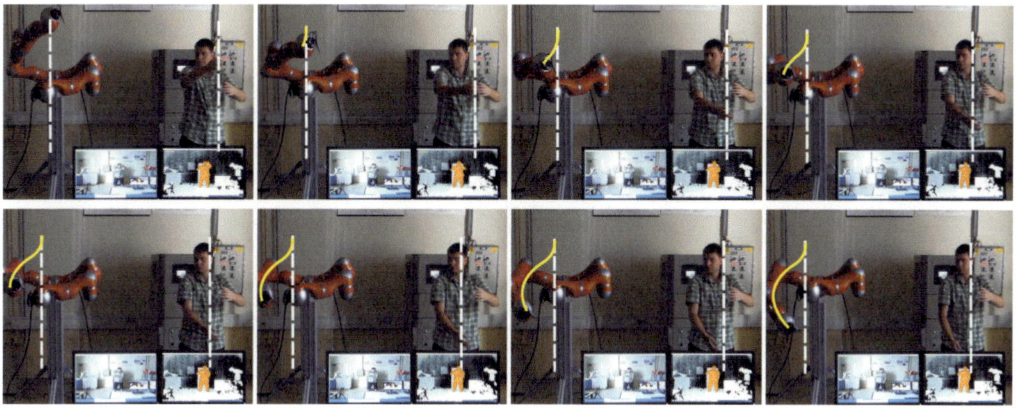

Fig. 16. A sequence of still photographs shows the movement of two Kuka LWR robots, while they successfully avoids each other. The desired movement for the robots is imitated in real time using the Microsoft Kinect sensor for the tracking.

human physiology. The posture of each arm may be described by four angles - three angles in the shoulder joint and one in the elbow. The shoulder joint enables the following motion (Hayes et al., 2001): arm flexion, arm abduction and external rotation. These angles are calculated from the data obtained with Microsoft Kinect.

A sequence for successful self collision-avoidance is shown in Fig. 16. Here, we can see that the robot angles are similar when the humans hands are away from the threshold, i.e., the robots are not close together. On the other hand, when close together, the robots properly adapt their motion to prevent a collision.

6.3 Contact forces

First we tested the behavior of the manipulator when no sensors were used to detect the obstacles. The desired task was to track the circular path and the motion of the manipulator was obstructed by an obstacle (the rod; see Fig. 13). To be able to monitor the contact forces the rod was mounted on a force sensor. Note that the force information measured by this sensor was not used in the close loop controller.

The controller was based on the algorithm (7) with the task controller (8) and null space controller (9) and we compared three sets of null space controller parameters. In the first case (a) the controller assured very stiff null space behavior, in the second (b) the controller assured medium stiffness in null space, and in the last case (c) the manipulator was compliant in the null space. To prevent high impact forces, the bumper was covered with soft material and the manipulator joint velocities were low.

The experimental results are shown in Fig. 17. First we can see that in case (a) the manipulator pushes the bumper more and more and finally, the task has to be aborted due to the very large contact forces. Next, comparing the responses one can see that although the motion is almost equal in both cases, the forces are lower in case (b) (compliant in null-space). Summarizing, the experimental results proved that the contact forces can be decreased by increasing the null space compliance.

6.4 Tactile sensors

Next we tested the efficiency of the tactile sensors. In our experiments we used simple bumpers on each link as tactile sensors. The sensor can detect an object when it touches the

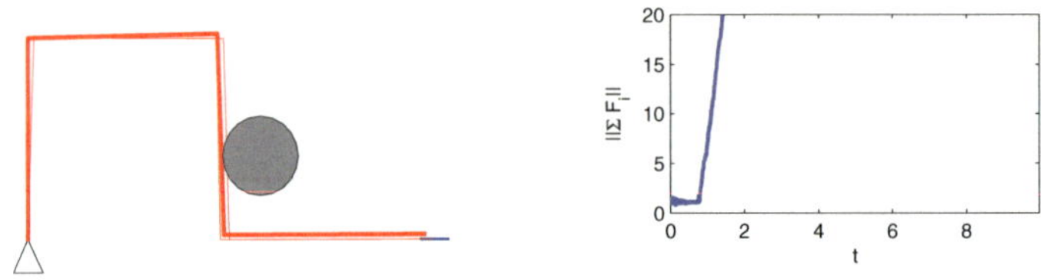

(a) stiff null-space behavior

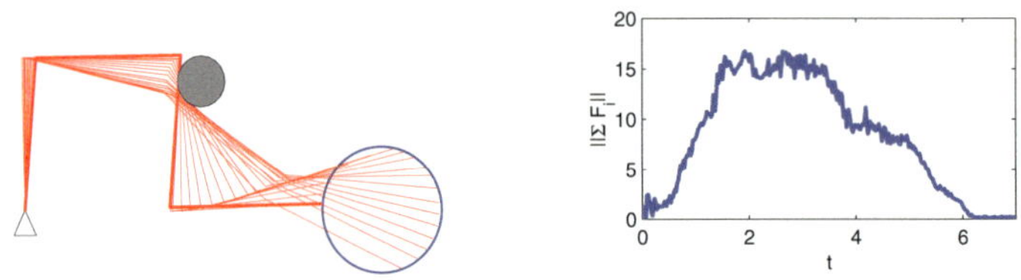

(b) compliant null-space behavior

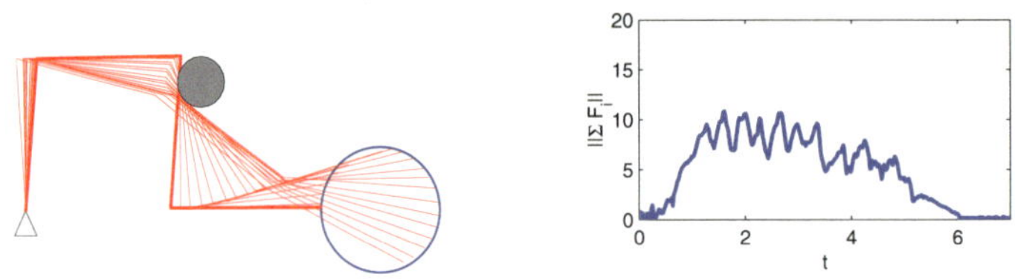

(c) more compliant null-space behavior

Fig. 17. Planar 4DOF manipulator tracking a circle while avoiding obstacles without any sensor for obstacle detection

object. In our case each switch needs a force of $2N$ to trigger it. This means that the sensor can detect an object if the contact force is greater then $\sim 2-4N$, depending on the particular contact position on the bar. The main drawback of this type of sensor is that it can only detect the link and the side of the link where the contact occurs, and not the exact position of the contact.

The desired task in these experiments was tracking the linear path and as before, the motion of the manipulator was obstructed by the rod. The virtual forces were calculated using Eqs. (49) – (50). As our sensor can detect only the side of the link where the contact occurs and not the exact position of the contact, we used the middle of the link as the approximation for the contact point and the avoiding direction was perpendicular to the link.

The experimental results are shown in Fig. 18. The figures show the contact forces norm $\|\boldsymbol{F}_{\text{ext}}\|$ and the configurations of the manipulator. The results clearly show that the manipulator avoids the obstacle after the collision. The behavior of the manipulator after the contact with the obstacle depends mainly on the particular nominal virtual force f_o and the time constants T_i and T_d. Tuning these parameters results in different behaviors of the system. With experiments we have found that it is possible to tune these parameters so that the manipulator slides along the obstacle with minimal impact forces and chattering.

6.5 Virtual forces

Finally, we tested the VF strategy. The desired task was tracking the linear path and the motion of the manipulator was obstructed by a different number of obstacles. To detect the obstacles a vision system was used. In the current implementation the vision system used a simple USB WebCam, which can recognize the scene and output the position of all obstacles in less than

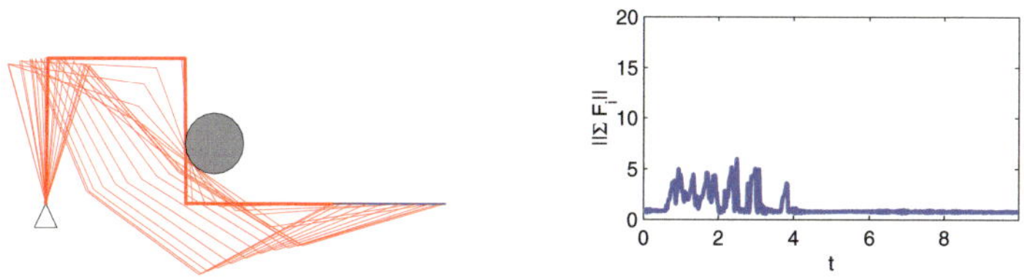

Fig. 18. Planar 4DOF manipulator tracking a circle while and avoiding obstacles using bumper and a virtual forces controller

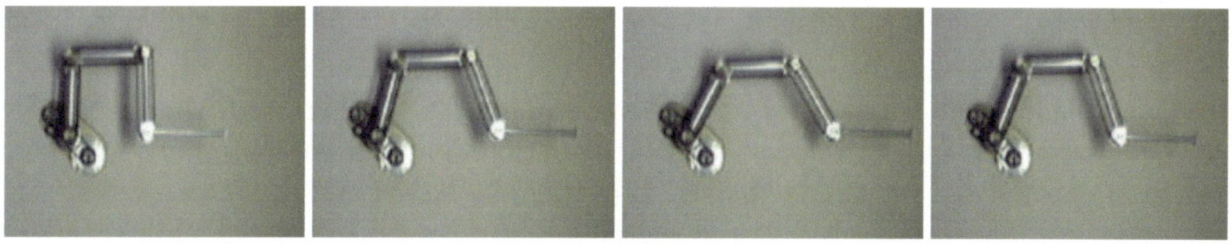

a) no obstacles

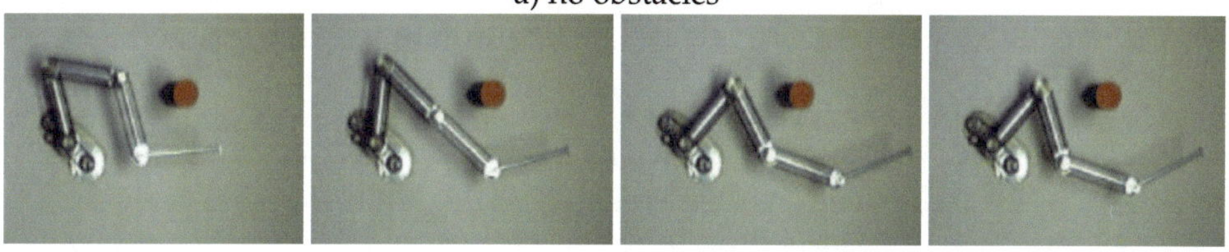

b) one obstacle

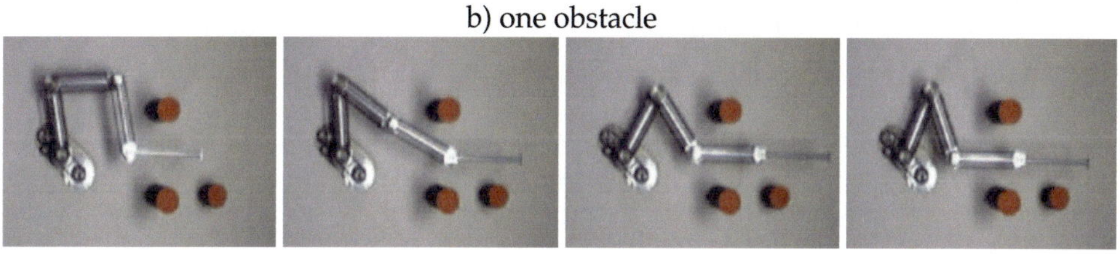

c) three obstacles

Fig. 19. Planar 4DOF manipulator tracking a path in an unstructured environment using a vision system to detect obstacles

0.04s. To avoid the obstacles the proximity sensor distance was selected as $d_m = 0.18m$ and the nominal virtual force as $f_o = 10N$. The rate of the torque controller was 400Hz (the necessary virtual forces for the avoiding motion were calculated in less than 0.5ms). The experimental results are given in Fig. 19. We can clearly see the difference in the motion when no obstacles are present and when one or more obstacles are present.

7. Conclusion

The presented approaches for on-line obstacle avoidance for redundant manipulators are a) based on redundancy resolution at the velocity level or b) considering also the dynamics of the manipulator. The primary task is determined by the end-effector trajectories and for the obstacle avoidance the internal motion of the manipulator is used. The goal is to assign each point on the body of the manipulator, which is close to the obstacle, a motion component in a direction that is away from the obstacle.

In the case of kinematic control (a) this is a velocity component. We have shown that it reasonable to define the avoiding motion in a one-dimensional operational space. In this way some singularity problems can be avoided when not enough "redundancy" is available locally. Additionally, the calculation of the pseudoinverse of the Jacobian matrix $\mathbf{J}_o$ is simpler as it includes scalar division instead of a matrix inversion. Using an approximate calculation of the avoiding velocities has its advantages computationally and it makes it easier to consider more obstacles simultaneously.

The second group of control algorithms (b) used in case b) is based on real or virtual forces. We compare three approaches regarding the sensors used to detect the obstacles: proximity sensors or vision, tactile sensors and no sensors. When proximity sensors are used we propose virtual forces strategy, where a virtual force component in a direction away from the obstacle is assigned to each point on the body of the manipulator, which is close to an obstacle. The algorithm based on the virtual forces avoids the problem of singular configurations and can be also easily applied when many obstacles are present. Additionally, the proposed control scheme enables us to use the null-space velocity controller for additional subtasks like the optimization of a performance criterion. Next, we have shown that under certain conditions obstacle avoidance can also be done without any information about the position and the size of the obstacles. This can be achieved by using a strategy that utilizes the self-motion caused by the contact forces to avoid an obstacle after the collision. Of course, an obstacle can be avoided only after a contact. The necessary prerequisite for this strategy to be effective is that the manipulator is backdrivable. As an alternative for the stiff systems we propose the use of tactile sensors. Here, a tactile sensor detects an obstacle and the controller generates the avoiding motion. The drawback of the last two control approaches is that they do not prevent the collision with the obstacle. Hence, they can only be applied if the collision occurs at a low speed so that the impact forces are not too high.

For the tasks where end-effector tracking is not essential for performing a given task we proposed a modified prioritized task control at the velocity level. The proposed approach enables a soft continuous transition between two different tasks. The obstacle-avoidance task only takes place when the desired movement approaches a given threshold, and then smoothly switches the priority of the tasks. The usefulness of this approach was shown on a two Kuka LWR robot to prevent a collision between them.

The computational efficiency of the proposed algorithms allows real-time application in an unstructured or time-varying environment. The simulations of highly redundant planar manipulators and the experiments on a four-link planar manipulator confirm that the proposed control algorithms assure an effective obstacle avoidance in an unstructured environment.

8. References

Brock, O., Khatib, O. & Viji, S. (2002). Task-Consistent Obstacle Avoidance of Motion Behavior for Mobile Manipulation, *Proc. IEEE Conf. Robotics and Automation*, Washington D.C, pp. 388 – 393.

Chiaverini, S. (1997). Singularity-robust task-priority redundancy resolution for real-time kinematic control of robot manipulators, *IEEE Trans. on Robotics and Automation* 13(3): 398 – 410.

Colbaugh, R., Seraji, H. & Glass, K. (1989). Obstacle Avoidance for Redundant Robots Using Configuration Control, *J. of Robotic Systems* 6(6): 721 – 744.

Egeland, O. (1987). Task-space tracking with redundant manipulators, *Robotics and Automation, IEEE Journal of* 3(5): 471 –475.

Featherstone, R. & Khatib, O. (1997). Load Independance of the Dynamically Consistent Inverse of the Jacobian Matrix, *Int. J. of Robotic Research* 16(2): 168 – 170.

Glass, K., Colbaugh, R., Lim, D. & Seraji, H. (1995). Real-Time Collision Avoidance for Redundant Manipulators, *IEEE Trans. on Robotics and Automation* 11(3): 448 – 457.

Guo, Z. & Hsia, T. (1993). Joint Trajectory Generation for Redundant Robots in an Environment with Obstacles, *J. of Robotic Systems* 10(2): 119 – 215.

Hayes, K., Walton, J. R., Szomor, Z. R. & Murrell, G. A. (2001). Reliability of five methods for assessing shoulder range of motion., *The Australian journal of physiotherapy* 47(4): 289–294.

Hogan, N. (1985). Impedance Control: An Approach to Manipulation: Part 1: Theory, Part 2: Implementation, Part 3: Applications, *Trans. of ASME J. of Dynamic Systems, Measurement, and Control* 107: 1 – 24.

Khatib, O. (1986). Real-Time Obstacle Avoidance for Manipulators and Mobile Robots, *Int. J. of Robotic Research* 5: 90 – 98.

Khatib, O. (1987). A Unified Approach for Motion and Force Control of Robot Manipulators: The Operational Space Formulation, *IEEE Trans. on Robotics and Automation* 3(1): 43 – 53.

Kim, J. & Khosla, P. (1992). Real-Time Obstacle Avoidance Using Harmonic Potential Functions, *IEEE Trans. on Robotics and Automation* 8(3): 338 – 349.

Žlajpah, L. & Nemec, B. (2003). Force strategies for on-line obstacle avoidance for redundant manipulators, *Robotica* 21(6): 633 – 644.

Lee, S., Yi, S.-Y., Park, J.-O. & Lee, C.-W. (1997). Reference adaptive impedance control and its application to obstacle avoidance trajectory planning, *Intelligent Robots and Systems, 1997. IROS '97., Proceedings of the 1997 IEEE/RSJ International Conference on*, Vol. 2, pp. 1158 – 1162 vol.2.

Lozano-Perez, T. (1983). Spatial Planning: A Configuration space approach, *IEEE Trans. on Computers* C-32(2): 102 – 120.

Maciejewski, A. & Klein, C. (1985). Obstacle Avoidance for Kinematically Redundant Manipulators in Dynamically Varying Environments, *Int. J. of Robotic Research* 4(3): 109 – 117.

Mansard, N., Khatib, O. & Kheddar, A. (2009). A unified approach to integrate unilateral constraints in the stack of tasks, *Robotics, IEEE Transactions on* 25(3): 670 –685.

McLean, A. & Cameron, S. (1996). The Virtual Springs Method: Path and Collision Avoidance for Redundant Manipulators, *Int. J. of Robotic Research* 15(4): 300 – 319.

Nakamura, Y., Hanafusa, H. & Yoshikawa, T. (1987). Task-Priority Based Redundancy Control of Robot Manipulators, *Int. J. of Robotic Research* 6(2): 3 – 15.

Nemec, B. (1997). Force Control of Redundant Robots, *in* M. Guglielmi (ed.), *Preprits of* 5th *IFAC Symp. on Robot Control, SYROCO'97*, Nantes, pp. 215 – 220.

Newman, W. S. (1989). Automatic Obstacle Avoidance at High Speeds via Reflex Control, *Proc. IEEE Conf. Robotics and Automation*, Scottsdale, pp. 1104 – 1109.

O'Neil, K. (2002). Divergence of linear acceleration-based redundancy resolution schemes, *Robotics and Automation, IEEE Transactions on* 18(4): 625 – 631.

Park, J., Chung, W. & Youm, Y. (1996). Design of Compliant Motion Controllers for Kinematically Redundant Manipulators, *Proc. IEEE Conf. Robotics and Automation*, pp. 3538 – 3544.

Raibert, M. H. & Craig, J. J. (1981). Hybrid Position/Force Control of Manipulators, *Trans. of ASME J. of Dynamic Systems, Measurement, and Control* 102: 126 – 133.

Sciavicco, L. & Siciliano, B. (2005). *Modelling and Control of Robot Manipulators (Advanced Textbooks in Control and Signal Processing)*, Advanced textbooks in control and signal processing, 2nd edn, Springer.

Sentis, L., Park, J. & Khatib, O. (2010). Compliant control of multicontact and center-of-mass behaviors in humanoid robots, *Robotics, IEEE Transactions on* 26(3): 483 –501.

Seraji, H. & Bon, B. (1999). Real-Time Collision Avoidance for Position-Controlled Manipulators, *IEEE Trans. on Robotics and Automation* 15(4): 670 – 677.

Sugiura, H., Gienger, M., Janssen, H. & Goerick, C. (2007). Real-time collision avoidance with whole body motion control for humanoid robots, *Intelligent Robots and Systems, 2007. IROS 2007. IEEE/RSJ International Conference on*, pp. 2053 –2058.

Volpe, R. & Khosla, P. (1990). Manipulator Control with Superquadratic Artificial Potential FUnctions: Theory and Experiments, *IEEE Trans. on Systems, Man, Cybernetics* 20(6).

Žlajpah, L. (2001). Integrated environment for modelling, simulation and control design for robotic manipulators, *Journal of Intelligent and Robotic Systems* 32(2): 219 – 234.

Woernle, C. (1993). Nonlinear Control of Constrained Redundant Manipulators, *in* J. A. et al. (ed.), *Computational Kinematics*, Kluwer Academic Publishers, pp. 119 – 128.

Xie, H., Patel, R., Kalaycioglu, S. & Asmer, H. (1998). Real-Time Collision Avoidance for a Redundant Manipulator in an Unstructured Environment, *Proc. Intl. Conf. On Intelligent Robots and Systems IROS'98*, Victoria, Canada, pp. 1925 – 1930.

Yoshikawa, T. (1987). Dynamic Hybrid Position / Force Control of Robot Manipulators Description of Hand Constraints and Calculation of Joint Driving, *IEEE Trans. on Robotics and Automation* 3(5): 386 – 392.

12

Nonlinear Dynamic Control and Friction Compensation of Parallel Manipulators

Weiwei Shang and Shuang Cong
University of Science and Technology of China
P.R. China

1. Introduction

Comparing with the serial ones, parallel manipulators have potential advantages in terms of high stiffness, accuracy and speed (Merlet, 2001). Especially the high accuracy and speed performances make the parallel manipulators widely applied to the following fields, like the pick-and-place operation in food, medicine, electronic industry and so on. At present, the key issues are the ways to meet the demand of high accuracy in moving process under the condition of high speed. In order to realize the high speed and accuracy motion, it's very important to design efficient control strategies for parallel manipulators.

In literatures, there are two basic control strategies for parallel manipulators (Zhang et.al., 2007): kinematic control strategies and dynamic control strategies. In the kinematic control strategies, parallel manipulators are decoupled into a group of single axis control systems, so they can be controlled by a group of individual controllers. Proportional-derivative (PD) control(Ghorbel et.al., 2000; Wu et.al., 2002), nonlinear PD (NPD) control (Ouyang et.al., 2002; Su et.al., 2004), and fuzzy control (Su et.al., 2005) all belong to this type of control strategies. These controllers do not always produce high control performance, and there is no guarantee of stability at the high speed. Unlike the kinematic control strategies, full dynamic model of parallel manipulators is taken into account in the dynamic control strategies. So the nonlinear dynamics of parallel manipulators can be compensated and better performance can be achieved with the dynamic strategies.

The traditional dynamic control strategies of parallel manipulators are the augmented PD (APD) control and the computed-torque (CT) control (Li & Wu, 2004; Cheng et.al., 2003; Paccot et.al., 2009). In the APD controller (Cheng et.al., 2003), the control law contains the tracking control term and the feed-forward compensation term. The tracking control term is realized by the PD control algorithm. The feed-forward compensation term contains the dynamic compensation calculated by the desired velocity and desired acceleration on the basis of the dynamic model. Compared with the simple PD controller, the APD controller is a tracking control method. However, the feed-forward compensation can not restrain the trajectory disturbance effectively, thus the tracking accuracy of the APD controller will be decreased. In order to solve this problem, the CT controller including the velocity feed-back is proposed based on the PD controller (Paccot et.al., 2009). The CT control method yields a controller that suppresses disturbance and tracks desired trajectories uniformly in all configurations of the manipulators. Both the APD controller and the CT controller contain two parts including the PD control term and the dynamic compensation term. For the presence of nonlinear factors such as modeling error and nonlinear friction in the dynamic models of the parallel manipulators, those traditional controllers can not achieve good control accuracy.

In order to overcome the uncertain factors in parallel manipulators, nonlinear control methods and friction compensation method are developed in this chapter. Firstly, in order to restrain the modeling error of parallel manipulators, a nonlinear PD (NPD) control algorithm is used to the APD controller, and a so-called augmented NPD (ANPD) controller is designed. Secondly, considering the feed-forward compensation term in the ANPD controller can not restrict the external disturbance, and the tracking accuracy will be affected when the disturbance exists. Thus the NPD controller is combined with the CT controller further, and a new control method named nonlinear CT (NCT) controller is developed. Thirdly, in order to compensate the nonlinear friction of parallel manipulators, a nonlinear model with two-sigmoid-function is introduced to modeling the nonlinear friction. This nonlinear friction model enables reconstruction of viscous, Coulomb, and Stribeck friction effects of parallel manipulators, and the nonlinear optimization tool is used to estimate the parameters in this model. In addition to the theoretical development, all the proposed methods in this chapter are validated on an actual parallel manipulator. The experiment results indicate that, compared with the conventional controllers, the proposed ANPD and NCT controller can get better trajectory tracking accuracy of the end-effector. Moreover, the experiment results also demonstrate that the nonlinear friction model is more accurately to compensate the friction, and is robust against the trajectory and the velocity changes.

2. Dynamic modelling

The experiment platform is a 2-DOF parallel manipulator with redundant actuation. As shown in Fig. 1, a reference frame is established in the workspace of the parallel manipulator. The unit of the frame is meter. The parallel manipulator is actuated by three servo motors located at the base A1, A2, and A3, and the end-effector is mounted at the common joint O, where the three chains meet. Coordinates of the three bases are A1 (0, 0.25), A2 (0.433, 0), and A3 (0.433, 0.5), and all of the links have the same length $l = 0.244$ m. The definitions of the joint angles are shown in the Fig. 1, q_{a1}, q_{a2}, q_{a3} refer to the active joint angles and q_{b1}, q_{b2}, q_{b3} refer to the passive joint angles.

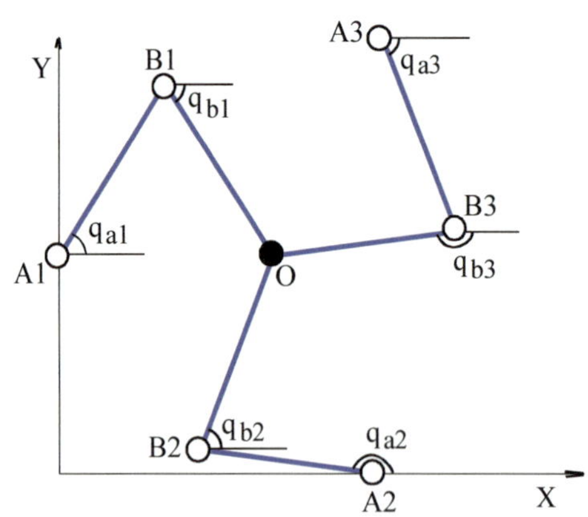

Fig. 1. Coordinates of the 2-DOF parallel manipulator with redundant actuation

Cutting the parallel manipulator at the common point O in Fig. 1, one can have an open-chain system including three independent planar 2-DOF serial manipulators, each of which contains an active joint and a passive joint. The dynamic model of the parallel manipulator equals to the model of the open-chain system plus the closed-loop constraints, thus the dynamic model of the whole parallel manipulator can be formulated by combining the dynamics of the three serial manipulators under the constraints.

As we know, the dynamic model of each planar 2-DOF serial manipulator can be formulated as (Murray et.al., 1994)

$$\mathbf{M}_i\ddot{\mathbf{q}}_i + \mathbf{C}_i\dot{\mathbf{q}}_i + \mathbf{f}_i = \boldsymbol{\tau}_i \tag{1}$$

where $\mathbf{q}_i = \begin{bmatrix} q_{ai} & q_{bi} \end{bmatrix}^T$, q_{ai} and q_{bi} are the active joint and passive joint angle, respectively; $\mathbf{M}_i$ is inertia matrix, and $\mathbf{C}_i$ is Coriolis and centrifugal force matrix, which are defined as

$$\mathbf{M}_i = \begin{bmatrix} \alpha_i & \gamma_i \cos(q_{ai} - q_{bi}) \\ \gamma_i \cos(q_{ai} - q_{bi}) & \beta_i \end{bmatrix}$$

$$\mathbf{C}_i = \begin{bmatrix} 0 & \gamma_i \sin(q_{ai} - q_{bi})\dot{q}_{bi} \\ -\gamma_i \sin(q_{ai} - q_{bi})\dot{q}_{ai} & 0 \end{bmatrix}$$

where α_i, β_i, γ_i, $i = 1,2,3$ are the dynamic parameters which are related with the physical parameters such as mass, center of mass, and inertia. In Eq.(1), $\boldsymbol{\tau}_i = \begin{bmatrix} \tau_{ai} & \tau_{bi} \end{bmatrix}^T$ is joint torque vector, where τ_{ai} is the active joint torque, the passive joint torque $\tau_{bi} = 0$. Vector $\mathbf{f}_i = \begin{bmatrix} f_{ai} & f_{bi} \end{bmatrix}^T$ is the friction torque, where f_{ai} and f_{bi} are the active joint friction and passive joint friction, respectively. The friction parameters of the active joints and the passive joints are identified simultaneously for the parallel manipulator (Shang et.al., 2010). And from the identified results, one can find that the friction parameters of the passive joints are much smaller than those of the active joints. Thus, compared with the active joints friction f_{ai}, the passive joint friction f_{bi} is much smaller and it can be neglected (Shang et.al., 2010). Generally, the active joint friction torque f_{ai} can be formulated by using the Coulomb + viscous friction model as

$$f_{ai} = sign(\dot{q}_{ai}) f_{ci} + f_{vi}\dot{q}_{ai} \tag{2}$$

where f_{ci} represents the Coulomb friction, and f_{vi} represents the coefficient of the viscous friction.

Combining the dynamic models of three 2-DOF serial manipulators, the dynamic model of the open-chain system can be expressed as

$$\mathbf{M}\ddot{\mathbf{q}} + \mathbf{C}\dot{\mathbf{q}} + \mathbf{f} = \boldsymbol{\tau} \tag{3}$$

where the definition of the symbols is similar to those in Eq.(1), only the difference is that the symbols in Eq.(3) represent the whole open-chain system not a 2-DOF serial manipulator. Based on Eq.(3) of the open-chain system and the constraint forces due to the closed-loop constraints, the dynamic model of the parallel manipulator can be written as

$$\mathbf{M}\ddot{\mathbf{q}} + \mathbf{C}\dot{\mathbf{q}} + \mathbf{f} = \boldsymbol{\tau} + \mathbf{A}^T\boldsymbol{\lambda} \tag{4}$$

where $\mathbf{A}^T\boldsymbol{\lambda}$ represents the constraint force vector, here matrix $\mathbf{A}$ is the differential of the closed-loop constrained equation and $\boldsymbol{\lambda}$ is a unknown multiplier representing the magnitude of the constraint forces. Fortunately, $\mathbf{A}^T\boldsymbol{\lambda}$ can be eliminated, by finding the null-space of matrix $\mathbf{A}$ (Muller, 2005). With the Jacobian matrix $\mathbf{W}$, we have

$$\dot{\mathbf{q}} = \mathbf{W}\dot{\mathbf{q}}_e \tag{5}$$

where $\dot{\mathbf{q}} = \begin{bmatrix} \dot{q}_{a1} & \dot{q}_{a2} & \dot{q}_{a3} & \dot{q}_{b1} & \dot{q}_{b2} & \dot{q}_{b3} \end{bmatrix}^T$ represents the velocity vector of all the joints, $\dot{\mathbf{q}}_e = \begin{bmatrix} \dot{q}_x & \dot{q}_y \end{bmatrix}^T$ represents the velocity vector of the end-effector, and the Jacobian matrix $\mathbf{W}$ is defined as

$$\mathbf{W} = \begin{bmatrix} r_1\cos(q_{b1}) & r_1\sin(q_{b1}) \\ r_2\cos(q_{b2}) & r_2\sin(q_{b2}) \\ r_3\cos(q_{b3}) & r_3\sin(q_{b3}) \\ -r_1\cos(q_{a1}) & -r_1\sin(q_{a1}) \\ -r_2\cos(q_{a2}) & -r_2\sin(q_{a2}) \\ -r_3\cos(q_{a3}) & -r_3\sin(q_{a3}) \end{bmatrix}, \text{ where } r_i = \frac{1}{l\sin(q_{bi} - q_{ai})}$$

Considering the constraint equation $\mathbf{A}\dot{\mathbf{q}} = \mathbf{0}$, then one can have $\mathbf{A}\mathbf{W}\dot{\mathbf{q}}_\mathbf{e} = \mathbf{0}$ with the Jacobian relation Eq.(5). The velocity vector $\dot{\mathbf{q}}_e$ of the end-effector contains independent generalized coordinates, so one can get $\mathbf{A}\mathbf{W} = \mathbf{0}$, or equivalently, $\mathbf{W}^T\mathbf{A}^T = \mathbf{0}$. With this result, the term of $\mathbf{A}^T\boldsymbol{\lambda}$ can be eliminated, and the dynamic model Eq. (4) can be written as

$$\mathbf{W}^T\mathbf{M}\ddot{\mathbf{q}} + \mathbf{W}^T\mathbf{C}\dot{\mathbf{q}} + \mathbf{W}^T\mathbf{f} = \mathbf{W}^T\boldsymbol{\tau} + \mathbf{W}^T\mathbf{A}^T\boldsymbol{\lambda} = \mathbf{W}^T\boldsymbol{\tau} \tag{6}$$

In order to study dynamic control and trajectory planning of the parallel manipulator both in the task space, we will further formulate the dynamic model in the task space on the basis of the dynamic model Eq. (6) of the joint space. Differentiating the Jacobian Eq. (5) yields

$$\ddot{\mathbf{q}} = \dot{\mathbf{W}}\dot{\mathbf{q}}_e + \mathbf{W}\ddot{\mathbf{q}}_e \tag{7}$$

and substituting Eqs. (5) and (7) into Eq. (6), the dynamic model in the task space can be written as

$$\mathbf{W}^T\mathbf{M}\mathbf{W}\ddot{\mathbf{q}}_e + \mathbf{W}^T(\mathbf{M}\dot{\mathbf{W}} + \mathbf{C}\mathbf{W})\dot{\mathbf{q}}_e + \mathbf{W}^T\mathbf{f} = \mathbf{W}^T\boldsymbol{\tau} \tag{8}$$

If the friction torques of the passive joints is neglected, then Eq. (8) can be further simplified. Let $\boldsymbol{\tau}_a$ and $\mathbf{f}_a$ be the actuator and friction torque vector of the three active joints respectively, then $\mathbf{W}^T\boldsymbol{\tau} = \mathbf{S}^T\boldsymbol{\tau}_a$, and $\mathbf{W}^T\mathbf{f} = \mathbf{S}^T\mathbf{f}_a$. Here, $\mathbf{S}$ is the Jacobian matrix between the velocity of the end-effector and the velocity of three active joints, and $\mathbf{S}$ is written as

$$\mathbf{S} = \begin{bmatrix} r_1\cos(q_{b1}) & r_1\sin(q_{b1}) \\ r_2\cos(q_{b2}) & r_2\sin(q_{b2}) \\ r_3\cos(q_{b3}) & r_3\sin(q_{b3}) \end{bmatrix}$$

Then, the dynamic model in the task space can be written as

$$\mathbf{W}^T\mathbf{MW}\ddot{\mathbf{q}}_e + \mathbf{W}^T(\mathbf{M}\dot{\mathbf{W}} + \mathbf{CW})\dot{\mathbf{q}}_e + \mathbf{S}^T\mathbf{f}_a = \mathbf{S}^T\boldsymbol{\tau}_a \tag{9}$$

The above Eq.(9) can be briefly expressed as

$$\mathbf{M}_e\ddot{\mathbf{q}}_e + \mathbf{C}_e\dot{\mathbf{q}}_e + \mathbf{S}^T\mathbf{f}_a = \mathbf{S}^T\boldsymbol{\tau}_a \tag{10}$$

where $\mathbf{M}_e = \mathbf{W}^T\mathbf{MW}$ is the inertial matrix in the task space, and $\mathbf{C}_e = \mathbf{W}^T(\mathbf{M}\dot{\mathbf{W}} + \mathbf{CW})$ is the Coriolis and centrifugal force matrix in the task space.
The dynamic model Eq. (10) in the task space also satisfies the similar structural properties to the dynamic model of the open-chain system and the 2-DOF serial manipulator as follows (Cheng et.al., 2003):

a. $\mathbf{M}_e$ is symmetric and positive.
b. $\dot{\mathbf{M}}_e - 2\mathbf{C}_e$ is skew-symmetric matrix.

3. Nonlinear dynamic control by using the NPD

There are two conventional dynamic controllers for parallel manipulators: APD controller and CT controller. The common feature of the two controllers is eliminating the tracking error by linear PD control. However, the linear PD control is not robust against the uncertain factors such as modeling error and external disturbance. To overcome this problem, the NPD control can be combined with the conventional control strategies to improve the control accuracy and disturbance rejection ability.

3.1 NPD controller

As well as we know, the linear PD controller takes the form

$$u_L(t) = k_p e(t) + k_d \dot{e}(t) \tag{11}$$

where k_p and k_d are the proportional and derivative constants respectively, and $e(t)$ is the system error.
The nonlinear PD (NPD) controller has a similar structure as the linear PD controller (11), the NPD controller may be any control structure of the form

$$u_N(t) = k_p(\cdot)e(t) + k_d(\cdot)\dot{e}(t) \tag{12}$$

where $k_p(\cdot)$ and $k_d(\cdot)$ are the time-varying proportional and derivative gains, which may depend on system state, input or other variables.
Currently, several NPD controllers have been proposed for robotic application (Xu et.al., 1995; Kelly & Ricardo, 1996; Seraji et.al., 1998). The NPD controller has superior trajectory tracking and disturbance rejection ability compared with the linear PD controllers for robot control. The NPD controller proposed by Han has a simple structure as (Han, 1994)

$$u_H(t) = k_p fun(e(t), \alpha_1, \delta_1) + k_d fun(\dot{e}(t), \alpha_2, \delta_2) \tag{13}$$

where the function fun can be defined as

$$fun(x,\alpha,\delta)=\begin{cases}|x|^{\alpha}\,sign(x), & |x|>\delta\\ x/\delta^{1-\alpha}, & |x|\le\delta\end{cases} \tag{14}$$

where α refers to the nonlinearity, specially the NPD will degenerate into the linear PD when $\alpha=1$; δ refers to the threshold of the error (or error derivative), and it is at the same magnitude with the error (or error derivative). The NPD controller (13) can be rewritten as the form (12), then $k_p(\cdot)$ can be derived as

$$k_p(e)=\begin{cases}k_p|e|^{\alpha_1-1} & |e|>\delta_1\\ k_p\delta_1^{\alpha_1-1} & |e|\le\delta_1\end{cases} \tag{15}$$

Similarly, $k_d(\cdot)$ can be expressed as

$$k_d(\dot{e})=\begin{cases}k_d|\dot{e}|^{\alpha_2-1} & |\dot{e}|>\delta_2\\ k_d\delta_2^{\alpha_2-1} & |\dot{e}|\le\delta_2\end{cases} \tag{16}$$

In (15) and (16), α_1 and α_2 can be determined in the interval [0.5, 1.0] and [1.0, 1.5], respectively. This choice makes the nonlinear gains with the following characteristics (Han, 1994): on one hand, large gain for small error and small gain for large error; on the other hand, large gain for large error rate and small gain for small error rate. Such variations of the gains result in a rapid transition of the systems with favorable damping. In addition, the NPD controller is robust against the changes of the system parameters and the nonlinear factors. Thus the NPD controller (13) is suitable to the trajectory tracking of the high-speed planar parallel manipulator.

3.2 Augmented NPD controller

The augmented NPD (ANPD) controller developed here is designed by replacing the linear PD in the APD controller with the NPD algorithm. According to the APD controller and the NPD control algorithm (13), based on the dynamic model (10), the control law of the ANPD controller can be written as (Shang et.al., 2009)

$$\tau_A=\mathbf{M}_e\ddot{\mathbf{q}}_e^d+\mathbf{C}_e\dot{\mathbf{q}}_e^d+\mathbf{S}^T\mathbf{f}_a+\mathbf{K}_p(\mathbf{e})\mathbf{e}+\mathbf{K}_d(\dot{\mathbf{e}})\dot{\mathbf{e}} \tag{17}$$

where $\dot{\mathbf{q}}_e^d$ and $\ddot{\mathbf{q}}_e^d$ are the desired velocity and acceleration of the end-effector. The control law (17) can be divided into three terms according to different functions. The first term is the dynamics compensation defined by the desired trajectory, which can be written as

$$\tau_{A1}=\mathbf{M}_e\ddot{\mathbf{q}}_e^d+\mathbf{C}_e\dot{\mathbf{q}}_e^d \tag{18.a}$$

The second term is the friction compensation, which can be written as

$$\tau_{A2}=\mathbf{S}^T\mathbf{f}_a \tag{18.b}$$

The third term is the tracking error elimination, which can be written as

$$\tau_{A3}=\mathbf{K}_p(\mathbf{e})\mathbf{e}+\mathbf{K}_d(\dot{\mathbf{e}})\dot{\mathbf{e}} \tag{18.c}$$

where $\mathbf{e} = \mathbf{q}_e^d - \mathbf{q}_e$ is the position error of the end-effector; $\mathbf{K}_p(\mathbf{e})$ and $\mathbf{K}_d(\dot{\mathbf{e}})$ are symmetric, positive definite matrices of time-varying gains. From (15) and (16), $\mathbf{K}_p(e)$ and $\mathbf{K}_d(\dot{e})$ can be expressed as

$$\mathbf{K}_p(e) = diag\left(k_p|x_1|^{\alpha_1 - 1}, k_p|x_2|^{\alpha_1 - 1}\right) \tag{19}$$

$$\mathbf{K}_d(\dot{e}) = diag\left(k_d|y_1|^{\alpha_2 - 1}, k_d|y_2|^{\alpha_2 - 1}\right) \tag{20}$$

where k_p and k_d are the positive constant gains. The variables x_i, y_i, $i = 1,2$ are determined by the following rules: if $|e_i| > \delta_1$, then $x_i = e_i$, else $x_i = \delta_1$; if $|\dot{e}_i| > \delta_2$, then $y_i = \dot{e}_i$, else $y_i = \delta_2$; $\alpha_1, \alpha_2, \delta_1$, and δ_2 are the designed parameters which should be tuned in practice.

In the following, we will prove the asymptotic stability of the parallel manipulator system controlled by the ANPD controller (17). Firstly, we will introduce two lemmas (Kelly and Ricardo, 1996).

Lemma 1: Let $\alpha(\cdot)$ be a class K function and $f: \Re \to \Re$ a continuous function. If $f(x) \geq \alpha(|x|)$ $\forall x \in \Re$, then $\int_0^x f(\sigma)d\sigma > 0$, $\forall x \neq 0 \in \Re$ and $\int_0^x f(\sigma)d\sigma \to \infty$ as $|x| \to \infty$.

Lemma 2: Consider the continuous diagonal matrix $K_p : \Re^2 \to \Re^{2\times 2}$

$$K_p(e) = \begin{bmatrix} k_{p1}(e_1) & 0 \\ 0 & k_{p2}(e_2) \end{bmatrix}$$

Assume that there exist class K functions $\alpha_i(\cdot)$ such that

$$x k_{pi}(x) \geq \alpha_i(|x|),\ x \in \Re, i = 1,2$$

then $\int_0^{\mathbf{e}} \xi^T \mathbf{K}_p(\xi)d\xi > 0$, $\forall \mathbf{e} \neq 0 \in \Re^2$, and $\int_0^e \xi^T \mathrm{K}_p(\xi)d\xi \to \infty$ as $|e| \to \infty$.

Next, we will give brief proof for Lemma 2 (Kelly and Ricardo, 1996). Define $f(e_i) = k_{pi}(e_i)e_i$, From Lemma 1, one can get

$$\int_0^{e_i} f(\xi_i)d\xi_i > 0, \quad \forall e_i \neq 0 \in \Re \tag{21}$$

which is equivalent to

$$\int_0^{e_i} k_{pi}(\xi_i)\xi_i d\xi_i > 0, \quad \forall e_i \neq 0 \in \Re \tag{22}$$

Therefore, the function $\int_0^e \xi^T \mathbf{K}_p(\xi)d\xi$ is positive definite. Also, Lemma 1 ensures that above integral is radically unbounded with respect to $\mathbf{e}$, and this implies $\int_0^e \xi^T \mathbf{K}_p(\xi)d\xi \to \infty$ as $|\mathbf{e}| \to \infty$.

Theorem 1: If the nonlinear gains $\mathbf{K}_p(\cdot)$ and $\mathbf{K}_d(\cdot)$ are defined by (19) and (20) respectively, the parallel manipulator system controlled by the ANPD control law (17) is asymptotically stable.

Proof: Choose the Lyapunov function candidate as

$$V(\mathbf{e},\dot{\mathbf{e}}) = \frac{1}{2}\dot{\mathbf{e}}^T \mathbf{M}_e \dot{\mathbf{e}} + \int_0^{\mathbf{e}} \xi^T \mathbf{K}_p(\xi) d\xi \tag{23}$$

where

$$\int_0^{\mathbf{e}} \xi^T \mathbf{K}_p(\xi) d\xi = \int_0^{e_1} \xi_1 k_{p1}(\xi_1) d\xi_1 + \int_0^{e_2} \xi_2 k_{p2}(\xi_2) d\xi_2$$

Considering the structural properties (a), the inertial matrix $\mathbf{M}_e$ is symmetric and positive definite matrix, thus the first term in (23) is positive definite. In addition, the integral term can be interpreted as a potential energy induced by the position error-driven part of the controller. Next, we will proof that the second term in (23) is positive definite. Considering $k_{pi}(e_i)$ is defined as

$$k_{pi}(e_i) = \begin{cases} k_{pi}\left|e_i\right|^{\alpha_i - 1}, & \left|e_i\right| > \delta \\ k_{pi}\delta_i^{\alpha_i - 1}, & \left|e_i\right| \le \delta_i \end{cases} \tag{24}$$

Define class K functions $\alpha_i(\cdot)$ as

$$\alpha_i(\left|e_i\right|) = \begin{cases} \varepsilon_i e_i \left|e_i\right|^{\alpha_i - 1}, & \left|e_i\right| > \delta_1 \\ \varepsilon_i e_i \delta_i^{\alpha_i - 1}, & \left|e_i\right| \le \delta_1 \end{cases} \text{, and } k_{pi} > \varepsilon_i > 0 \tag{25}$$

With the Lemma 2, one can get the integral term in (23) is a radically unbounded positive definite function. Thus $V(\mathbf{e},\dot{\mathbf{e}})$ is a positive function. Differentiating $V(t)$ with respect to time yields

$$\dot{V}(\mathbf{e},\dot{\mathbf{e}}) = \dot{\mathbf{e}}^T \mathbf{M}_e \ddot{\mathbf{e}} + \frac{1}{2}\dot{\mathbf{e}}^T \dot{\mathbf{M}}_e \dot{\mathbf{e}} + \mathbf{e}^T \mathbf{K}_p(\mathbf{e})\dot{\mathbf{e}} \tag{26}$$

Combine the control law (17) and the dynamic model (10), the closed-loop system equation can be written as

$$\mathbf{M}_e \ddot{\mathbf{e}} + \mathbf{C}_e \dot{\mathbf{e}} + \mathbf{K}_p(\cdot)\mathbf{e} + \mathbf{K}_d(\cdot)\dot{\mathbf{e}} = 0 \tag{27}$$

Multiplying both sides of the above equation by $\dot{\mathbf{e}}^T$, and then substituting the resulting equation into (26) yields

$$\dot{V} = -\dot{\mathbf{e}}^T \mathbf{K}_d(\cdot)\dot{\mathbf{e}} + \frac{1}{2}\dot{\mathbf{e}}^T (\dot{\mathbf{M}}_e - 2\mathbf{C}_e)\dot{\mathbf{e}} \tag{28}$$

Considering the structural properties (b), then one can have $\dot{\mathbf{e}}^T (\dot{\mathbf{M}}_e - 2\mathbf{C}_e)\dot{\mathbf{e}} = 0$ and

$$\dot{V} = -\dot{\mathbf{e}}^T \mathbf{K}_d(\cdot)\dot{\mathbf{e}} \tag{29}$$

As $\mathbf{K}_d(\cdot)$ is a symmetric, positive definite matrix, then $\dot{V}$ is a semi-negative definite matrix, thus the parallel manipulator system is stable.

Now since $V(t) \geq 0$ and $\dot{V}(t) \leq 0$, $V(t)$ is bounded and decreasing, thus $V(t)$ converges to a limit. From the definition of $V(t)$, it implies that both $\mathbf{e}$ and $\dot{\mathbf{e}}$ are bounded. Since $\mathbf{M}_e$ is uniform positive definite, then $\mathbf{M}_e^{-1}$ exists and bounded, thus the closed-loop system equation (27) can be written as

$$\ddot{\mathbf{e}} = -\mathbf{M}_e^{-1}\left(\mathbf{C}_e\dot{\mathbf{e}} + \mathbf{K}_p(\cdot)\mathbf{e} + \mathbf{K}_d(\cdot)\dot{\mathbf{e}}\right) \tag{30}$$

So $\ddot{\mathbf{e}}$ is also bounded and $\ddot{V}(t)$ is bounded. Thus, $\dot{V}(t)$ is uniformly continuous. With the Barbalat Lemma (Slotine & Li, 1991), one knows $\dot{\mathbf{e}} \to 0$ as $t \to \infty$, and this implies $\mathbf{e} \to 0$ as $t \to \infty$.

One can note that $\boldsymbol{\tau}_A$ in the control law (17) is the actuator torque of the task space, but in fact, we need the actuator torque $\boldsymbol{\tau}_a$ of the active joints. In practice, a solution that has a minimum weighted Euclidian norm is selected as the actual control input. The actual control input vector of the active joints can be written as

$$\boldsymbol{\tau}_a = (\mathbf{S}^T)^+\left(\mathbf{M}_e\ddot{\mathbf{q}}_e^d + \mathbf{C}_e\dot{\mathbf{q}}_e^d + \mathbf{K}_p(\mathbf{e})\mathbf{e} + \mathbf{K}_d(\dot{\mathbf{e}})\dot{\mathbf{e}}\right) + \mathbf{f}_a \tag{31}$$

where $(\mathbf{S}^T)^+ = \mathbf{S}(\mathbf{S}^T\mathbf{S})^{-1}$ is the pseudo-inverse of $\mathbf{S}^T$, satisfying $\mathbf{S}^T(\mathbf{S}^T)^+ = \mathbf{I}$. For the parallel manipulator with redundant actuation, the singularity is eliminated in the effective workspace (Shang et.al., 2010). Thus, the pseudo-inverse matrix $(\mathbf{S}^T)^+$ will not be close to the singularity for this parallel manipulator with redundant actuation.

3.3 Nonlinear computed torque control

An obvious drawback of the traditional CT controllers is the elimination of the tracking error by linear PD algorithm. However, the linear PD algorithm is not robust against the uncertain factors such as modeling error and nonlinear friction. To overcome this problem, the NPD algorithm can be combined with the conventional control strategies to improve the control accuracy. The NCT controller developed in this chapter is designed by replacing the linear PD in the CT controller with the NPD algorithm.

According to the NPD algorithm (13), based on the dynamic model (10), the control law of the NCT controller can be written as (Shang & Cong, 2009)

$$\boldsymbol{\tau}_N = \mathbf{M}_e\ddot{\mathbf{q}}_e^d + \mathbf{C}_e\dot{\mathbf{q}}_e + \mathbf{S}^T\mathbf{f}_a + \mathbf{M}_e\left(\mathbf{K}_p(\mathbf{e})\mathbf{e} + \mathbf{K}_d(\dot{\mathbf{e}})\dot{\mathbf{e}}\right) \tag{32}$$

The control law (32) can be divided into three terms according to the different functions. The first term is the dynamics compensation defined by the desired acceleration and the actual velocity of the end-effector, which can be written as

$$\boldsymbol{\tau}_{N1} = \mathbf{M}_e\ddot{\mathbf{q}}_e^d + \mathbf{C}_e\dot{\mathbf{q}}_e \tag{33.a}$$

The second term is the friction compensation, which can be written as

$$\boldsymbol{\tau}_{N2} = \mathbf{S}^T\mathbf{f}_a \tag{33.b}$$

The third term is the tracking error elimination, which can be written as

$$\boldsymbol{\tau}_{N3} = \mathbf{M}_e\left(\mathbf{K}_p(\mathbf{e})\mathbf{e} + \mathbf{K}_d(\dot{\mathbf{e}})\dot{\mathbf{e}}\right) \tag{33.c}$$

where $\mathbf{K}_p(\mathbf{e})$ and $\mathbf{K}_d(\dot{\mathbf{e}})$ are symmetric, positive definite matrices of time-varying gains. From (15) and (16), $\mathbf{K}_p(\mathbf{e})$ and $\mathbf{K}_d(\dot{\mathbf{e}})$ can be expressed as

$$\mathbf{K}_p(\mathbf{e}) = diag\left(k_{p1}|x_1|^{\alpha_1-1}, k_{p2}|x_2|^{\alpha_1-1}\right) \tag{34}$$

$$\mathbf{K}_d(\dot{\mathbf{e}}) = diag\left(k_{d1}|y_1|^{\alpha_2-1}, k_{d2}|y_2|^{\alpha_2-1}\right) \tag{35}$$

where k_{pi}, k_{di}, $i=1,2$ are positive constant gains. The variables x_i, y_i are determined by the following rules: if $|e_i| > \delta_1$, then $x_i = e_i$, else $x_i = \delta_1$; if $|\dot{e}_i| > \delta_2$, then $y_i = \dot{e}_i$, else $y_i = \delta_2$. α_1, α_2, δ_1, and δ_2 are the designed parameters which should be tuned in practice.
In the following, the asymptotic stability of the parallel manipulator system controlled by the NCT controller (32) will be proven.
Theorem 2: If the nonlinear gains $\mathbf{K}_p(\cdot)$ and $\mathbf{K}_d(\cdot)$ are defined by (34) and (35) respectively, the parallel manipulator system controlled by the NCT controller (32) is asymptotically stable.
Proof: Choose the Lyapunov function candidate as

$$V(\mathbf{e},\dot{\mathbf{e}}) = \frac{1}{2}\dot{\mathbf{e}}^T\dot{\mathbf{e}} + \int_0^{\mathbf{e}} |\xi|^T K_p(\xi) d\xi \tag{36}$$

where $\int_0^{\mathbf{e}} |\xi|^T \mathbf{K}_p(\xi) d\xi = \int_0^{e_1} |\xi_1| k_{p1}(\xi_1) d\xi_1 + \int_0^{e_2} |\xi_2| k_{p2}(\xi_2) d\xi_2$. Obviously, the first term in (36) is positive definite. In addition, the integral term can be interpreted as the potential energy induced by the position error-driven part of the controller. Next, one can prove that the second term in (36) is positive definite. Considering $k_{pi}(e_i)$ is defined as

$$k_{pi}(e_i) = \begin{cases} k_{pi}|e_i|^{\alpha_i-1}, |e_i| > \delta_1 \\ k_{pi}\delta_i^{\alpha_i-1}, |e_i| \le \delta_1 \end{cases} \tag{37}$$

and define class K functions $\alpha_i(\cdot)$ as

$$\alpha_i(|e_i|) = \begin{cases} \varepsilon_i|e_i|^{\alpha_i}, & |e_i| > \delta_1 \\ \varepsilon_i|e_i|\delta_i^{\alpha_i-1}, & |e_i| \le \delta_1 \end{cases}, \text{ and } k_{pi} > \varepsilon_i > 0 \tag{38}$$

From (37) and (38), one knows $|e_i| k_{pi}(e_i) \ge \alpha_i(|e_i|)$. With the Lemma 2, one can get $\int_0^{e_i} |\xi_i|^T k_{p_i}(\xi_i) d\xi_i > 0$, and $\int_0^{\mathbf{e}} |\xi|^T \mathbf{K}_p(\xi) d\xi \to \infty$ as $|\mathbf{e}| \to \infty$. So one can get the integral term in (36) is a radically unbounded positive definite function. Thus $V(\mathbf{e},\dot{\mathbf{e}})$ is a positive definite function. Differentiating $V(\mathbf{e},\dot{\mathbf{e}})$ with respect to time yields

$$\dot{V}(\mathbf{e},\dot{\mathbf{e}}) = \dot{\mathbf{e}}^T\ddot{\mathbf{e}} + \mathbf{e}^T\mathbf{K}_p(\mathbf{e})\dot{\mathbf{e}} \tag{39}$$

Combine the control law (32) and the dynamic model (10) and consider $\mathbf{S}^T\boldsymbol{\tau}_a = \boldsymbol{\tau}_N$, the closed-loop system equation can be written as

$$\mathbf{M}_e\left(\ddot{\mathbf{e}} + \mathbf{K}_p(\cdot)\mathbf{e} + \mathbf{K}_d(\cdot)\dot{\mathbf{e}}\right) = 0 \tag{40}$$

Since $\mathbf{M}_e$ is uniform positive definite, then $\mathbf{M}_e^{-1}$ exists and bounded, thus the closed-loop system equation (40) can be written as

$$\ddot{\mathbf{e}} + \mathbf{K}_p(\cdot)\mathbf{e} + \mathbf{K}_d(\cdot)\dot{\mathbf{e}} = 0 \tag{41}$$

Multiplying both sides of the above equation by $\dot{\mathbf{e}}^T$, and then substituting the resulting equation into (39) yields

$$\dot{V} = -\dot{\mathbf{e}}^T \mathbf{K}_d(\cdot)\dot{\mathbf{e}} \tag{42}$$

As $\mathbf{K}_d(\cdot)$ is a symmetric, positive definite matrix, then $\dot{V}$ is a semi-negative definite matrix, thus the closed-loop system is stable. Considering the closed-loop equation (41) is autonomous system, and defining the region $\mathbf{\Omega}$ as

$$\mathbf{\Omega} = \left\{ \begin{bmatrix} \mathbf{e} \\ \dot{\mathbf{e}} \end{bmatrix} : \dot{V}(\mathbf{e}, \dot{\mathbf{e}}) = 0 \right\} = \left\{ \begin{bmatrix} \mathbf{e} \\ \dot{\mathbf{e}} \end{bmatrix} = \begin{bmatrix} \mathbf{e} \\ 0 \end{bmatrix} \in \Re^4 \right\} \tag{43}$$

Thus $\begin{bmatrix} \mathbf{e} \\ \dot{\mathbf{e}} \end{bmatrix} = \begin{bmatrix} 0 \\ 0 \end{bmatrix}$ is the largest invariant set of $\mathbf{\Omega} = \left\{ \begin{bmatrix} \mathbf{e} \\ \dot{\mathbf{e}} \end{bmatrix} : \dot{V}(\mathbf{e}, \dot{\mathbf{e}}) = 0 \right\}$, and constitutes an asymptotically stable equilibrium point. By using the LaSalle's theorem, one can get that the closed-loop system of the parallel manipulator is asymptotically stable.

4. Nonlinear friction model and identification

In this section, the friction compensation method based on a nonlinear friction model is developed for the parallel manipulator. This nonlinear friction model enables reconstruction of viscous, Coulomb, and Stribeck friction effects of the parallel manipulator. Identification experiments are carried out, and parameters in the nonlinear friction model are estimated by nonlinear optimization.

4.1 Nonlinear friction modeling

In order to reconstruct the nonlinear friction effect, the nonlinear friction model can be formulated as (Hensen et.al., 2000; Kostic et.al., 2004)

$$f(\dot{\theta}) = B_v \dot{\theta} + \sum_{k=1}^{3} f_k \left(1 - \frac{2}{1 + e^{2\omega_k \dot{\theta}}}\right), \quad k = 1,2,3 \tag{44}$$

where the first term represents the viscous friction and B_v is the viscous friction coefficient. The other terms model the Coulomb and Stribeck friction effects. The parameters f_k represent the magnitude of the Coulomb friction and the Stribeck curve. The parameters ω_k determine the slope in the approximation of the sigmoid function in the Coulomb friction and the Stribeck curve.

Obviously, the nonlinear friction model is an odd continuous function. Since $f(\dot{\theta})$ is clearly zero at $\theta = 0$, the model does not capture the static friction. The friction model does not describe stiction, because the system will always slide for an applied force unequal to zero. The stiction regime will be approximated, if the slope of the function near $\dot{\theta} = 0$ is very steep. Then the model can still give acceptable simulation results, i.e., angular displacement during stiction is neglectable. On the other hand, a continuous friction function will facilitate the numerical solution if such a model is used in parameter identification.

In (44), there are three sigmoid functions. If more sigmoid functions are selected, the estimation accuracy with this model will be better, but the friction model will have more parameters and it will be more complicated. So for this nonlinear friction model, a suitable number of the sigmoid function is important. One can also analyze this problem with the neural network. The nonlinear terms in (44) can be constructed with a two layers neural network, i.e., one hidden layer and one output layer. Defining the weight matrices for the first and second layer as $\mathbf{W}_1$ and $\mathbf{W}_2$, the neural network output can be written as (Hensen et.al., 2000)

$$f'(\dot{\theta}) = \mathbf{W}_2^T \sum(\mathbf{W}_1\dot{\theta} + b_1) + b_2 \tag{45}$$

where b_i represents the bias value for the neurons in the i-th layer and $\sum(\cdot)$ is a nonlinear operator with $\sum(x) = [\sigma(x_1) \;\; \sigma(x_2) \;\; \sigma(x_3)]^T$, the activation function $\sigma(x) = 1 - \frac{2}{1+e^{2x}}$. From (44), the parameter b1 and b2 are both zero. The weight matrix for the first layer and the second layer can be written as $\mathbf{W}_1 = [\omega_1 \;\; \omega_2 \;\; \omega_3]^T$ and $\mathbf{W}_2 = [f_1 \;\; f_2 \;\; f_3]^T$ respectively. As we known, increasing the number of the hidden neurons, the approximation performance with the network will be better. However, too many hidden neurons will make the network more complicated and the training time may be longer. In practice, suitable number of the hidden neurons should be selected. In order to model the nonlinear friction of the parallel manipulator, two hidden neurons are enough, that is to say two sigmoid functions will be selected.

If the friction of the passive joints is neglected, according to (44), one can define the nonlinear friction model for the 2-DOF planar parallel manipulator as follows

$$f_{ai} = B_{vi}\dot{q}_{ai} + f_{1i}(1 - \frac{2}{1+e^{2\omega_{1i}\dot{q}_{ai}}}) + f_{2i}(1 - \frac{2}{1+e^{2\omega_{2i}\dot{q}_{ai}}}) + d_i\,,\; i = 1,2,3 \tag{46}$$

where the first term represents the viscous friction and B_{vi} is the viscous friction coefficient of the ith active joint; d_i represents the zero drift of the motion control board; the remaining terms model the Coulomb and Stribeck friction effects of the ith active joint. The parameter f_{1i} and f_{2i} represent the magnitude of the Coulomb friction and the Stribeck curve. The parameters ω_{1i} and ω_{2i} determine the slope in the approximation of the sigmoid function in the Coulomb friction and the Stribeck curve.

4.2 Nonlinear friction identification

In the dynamic model Eq. (10), the dynamic parameters can be calculated directly, and only the parameters in the nonlinear friction model Eq. (46) need to be identified. In Eq. (10), the mass, length and joint angles all united into the standard units. The corresponding torque has the unit N.m. Since the commanded torque for the motion control board of the parallel manipulator is digital value, the proportion should be obtained between the torque of the unit N.m and the commanded digital value of the torque (Shang et.al., 2008). Defining the dynamic torque $(\mathbf{S}^T)^+(\mathbf{M}_e\ddot{\mathbf{q}}_e + \mathbf{C}_e\dot{\mathbf{q}}_e) = \mathbf{D}$ and the proportion is k, the dynamic model Eq. (10) can be rewritten as

$$\mathbf{D}\cdot k+\mathbf{f}_a=\boldsymbol{\tau}_a \tag{47}$$

Substituting the nonlinear friction model (46) into (47), one can define the optimization function J as follows

$$J=\sum_{j=1}^{N}\sum_{i=1}^{3}\left(\tau_{ai}^j-k(D_i^j)-(B_{vi}\dot{q}_{ai}^j+f_{1i}(1-\frac{2}{1+e^{2\omega_{1i}\dot{q}_{ai}^j}})+f_{2i}(1-\frac{2}{1+e^{2\omega_{2i}\dot{q}_{ai}^j}})+d_i)\right)^2 \tag{48}$$

where τ_{ai}^j and D_i^j represent the actuator torque and the dynamic torque of the ith active joint in the jth configuration respectively. And $\dot{q}_{ai}^j$ represents the velocity of the ith active joint in the jth configuration.

The parameters B_{vi}, f_{1i}, f_{2i}, ω_{1i}, ω_{2i}, d_i, and the proportion k, a total of 19 parameters, are selected as the optimization variables. These parameters will be estimated by making the optimization function J minimum. Parameter optimization procedures are programmed with Matlab, and the nonlinear optimization function *fmincon* finding a constrained minimum of a function of several variables is called for in Matlab. In order to use the *fmincon*, the first step is set the initial value, the lower limit value and the upper limit value of the 19 optimization variables. Then (48) is defined as the optimized function of *fmincon*. The third step is getting the variables τ_{ai}^j, D_i^j, and $\dot{q}_{ai}^j$ in (48). Next we will give the procedures about getting the variables τ_{ai}^j, D_i^j, and $\dot{q}_{ai}^j$ in our actual identification experiment.

In actual identification experiment, the end-effector of the parallel manipulator is driven to track a circular trajectory. The center coordinates of the circle are (0.29, 0.25) and radius is 0.07 , the unit is meter, this circle motion is repeated clockwise for 15 times. The parallel manipulator is controlled by the PD controller in the task space, the actuator torque is also the control input, thus τ_{ai}^j is a variable known. The control input is selected in the null-space of the matrix $\mathbf{S}^T$, thus the actuator torque τ_{ai}^j in (48) is also in the null-space of the matrix $\mathbf{S}^T$. And this selection will make the control input used in the identification experiment minimum. For the parallel manipulator, only angles of the active joints can be measured directly by the absolute optical-electrical encoders. The angular velocity of the active joints is obtained by numerical differentiation of the active joint angles, and a low-pass filter is adopted to filter the angular velocity signal, then we will get the variable $\dot{q}_{ai}^j$. The angular acceleration of the joints is obtained by numerical differentiation of the filtered angular velocity. With the velocity and the acceleration of the joints, and considering the kinematics of the parallel manipulator, the actual velocity and acceleration of the end-effector can be obtained. Thus D_i^j can be calculated with these variables. With the actual values of the variable τ_{ai}^j, D_i^j, and $\dot{q}_{ai}^j$, the unknown parameters of the parallel manipulator are identified and results are shown in Table 1.

4.3 Coulomb + viscous friction identification

In order to compare with the nonlinear friction model, a common *Coulomb + viscous* friction model containing the viscous friction and Coulomb friction effect is established for the parallel manipulator. The friction model can be written as

$$f_{ai}=sign(\dot{q}_{ai})f_{ci}+f_{vi}\dot{q}_{ai}+d_i\,,\ i=1,2.3 \tag{49}$$

where f_{ci} represents the Coulomb friction; f_{vi} represents the coefficient of the viscous friction; d_i represents the zero drift of the motion control board.

parameters	values	parameters	values	parameters	values	parameters	values
k	508.7	ω_{21}	-16.4	ω_{12}	-18	f_{23}	500
B_{v1}	892.8	d_1	-2.6	ω_{22}	5.1	ω_{13}	-0.9
f_{11}	1040.1	B_{v2}	1396.4	d_2	-21.9	ω_{23}	10
f_{21}	-268.0	f_{12}	-309.0	B_{v3}	402.6	d_3	30
ω_{11}	0.7	f_{22}	-61.8	f_{13}	-867.7		

Table 1. Identification results of the nonlinear friction model.

With the analysis of the identification of the nonlinear friction model, the corresponding work of the *Coulomb* + *viscous* friction model is much simpler. Substituting the *Coulomb* + *viscous* friction model (49) into (47), one can get a linear equation about the identified parameters as follows

$$[\mathbf{D} \quad \mathbf{K}][k \quad f_{v1} \quad f_{v2} \quad f_{v3} \quad d_1+f_{c1} \quad d_1-f_{c1} \quad d_2+f_{c2} \quad d_2-f_{c2} \quad d_3+f_{c3} \quad d_3-f_{c3}]^T = \boldsymbol{\tau}_a \quad (50)$$

where

$$\mathbf{K} = \begin{bmatrix} \dot{q}_{a1} & 0 & 0 & u_1 & l_1 & 0 & 0 & 0 & 0 \\ 0 & \dot{q}_{a2} & 0 & 0 & 0 & u_2 & l_2 & 0 & 0 \\ 0 & 0 & \dot{q}_{a3} & 0 & 0 & 0 & 0 & u_3 & l_3 \end{bmatrix}$$

For simplicity, parameter combinations $d_i + f_{ci}$ and $d_i - f_{ci}$ are viewed as identified parameters, and the coefficients u_i and l_i of the parameters are determined by the following rules: $u_i = 1, l_i = 0$ when $\dot{q}_{ai} \geq 0$, and $u_i = 0, l_i = 1$ when $\dot{q}_{ai} < 0$.

There are 10 parameters to be identified in Eq. (50), but only three independent equations can be got for each sampling point. So a group of linear equations about the unknown parameters can be got with the sampling data of a continuous trajectory, then the Least Squares method is used to identify the unknown parameters.

The identification experiment designed for the *Coulomb* + *viscous* friction model is the same with the nonlinear friction model discussed in section 4.2. Identification results of the *Coulomb* + *viscous* friction model are shown in Table 2.

parameters	values	parameters	values
k	512.7	$d_1 - f_{c1}$	-261.7
f_{v1}	1534.8	$d_2 + f_{c2}$	212.6
f_{v2}	1415.9	$d_2 - f_{c2}$	-256
f_{v3}	1475.1	$d_3 + f_{c3}$	179.2
$d_1 + f_{c1}$	248.5	$d_3 - f_{c3}$	-129

Table 2. Identification results of the *Coulomb* + *viscous* friction model

5. Experiments

As shown in Fig. 2, the actual experiment platform is a 2-DOF parallel manipulator with redundant actuation designed by Googol Tech. Ltd. in Shenzhen, China. It is equipped with three permanent magnet synchronous servo motors with harmonic gear drives. The active joint angles are measured with absolute optical-electrical encoders. The nonlinear dynamic controllers and the friction compensation method are programmed with the Visual C++, and the algorithms run on a Pentium III CPU at 733MHz. with the sampling period 2ms.

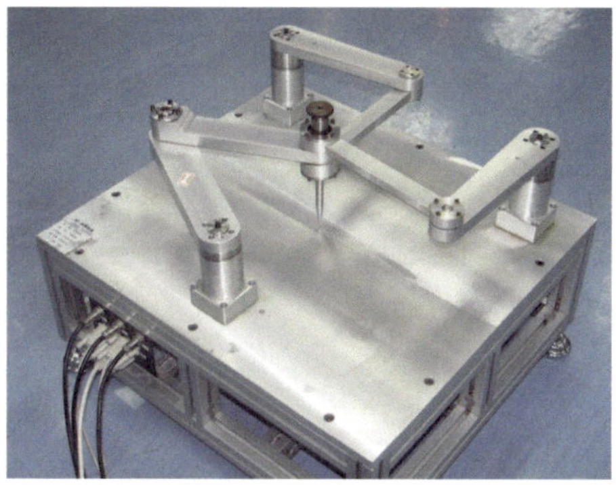

Fig. 2. The prototype of the 2-DOF parallel manipulator with redundant actuation

5.1 Experiments of the ANPD controller

The trajectory tracking control experiment is designed for the parallel manipulator to validate the ANPD controller. The desired trajectory of the end-effector is a straight line, the starting point is (0.22, 0.29) and the ending point is (0.37, 0.21), thus the motion distance is 0.17m. The profile of the desired velocity is an S-type curve (Cheng et.al., 2003). In the experiment, the low-speed and high-speed motions are both tested. For the low-speed motion, the max velocity is 0.2m/s, the max acceleration is 5m/s^2, and the jerk is 200m/s^3. For the high-speed motion, the max velocity is 0.5m/s, the max acceleration is 10m/s^2, and the jerk is 400m/s^3.

In order to implement the ANPD controller (17), the dynamic parameters in (18.a) and the friction parameters in (18.b) must be known. In the experiment, the nominal values of the dynamic parameters are used (Shang et.al., 2008). Then, with the known dynamic parameters, the friction parameters in the *Coulomb + viscous* friction model can be identified by the Least Squares method, as shown in Table 2. In fact, the control parameters in (18.c) are tuned and determined by the actual experiments. The procedures to tune the control parameters in (18.c) can be summarized as follows:

1. Assume $k_{p1} = k_{p2} = k_p$, $k_{d1} = k_{d2} = k_d$. Let $k_d = 0$, $\alpha_1 = 1$, $\alpha_2 = 1$, and increase the value of k_p from zero until the system show a little oscillation to some extent.
2. Keep the value of k_p tuned well in the first stage, and increase the value of k_d to improve the dynamic performance further.
3. Regulate finely the above two values and make tradeoffs between k_p and k_d.
4. Find the maximum error and error rate of the end-effector under the tuned value of k_p and k_d.
5. In the ANPD controller, δ_1 and δ_2 are the threshold of the error and the error rate. If δ_1 is tuned bigger than the maximum error, then the proportional gain $k_p(e_i)$ will always equals to $k_p\delta_1^{\alpha_1 - 1}$; and δ_1 is tuned close to 0, then $k_p(e_i)$ will always equal to $k_p|e_i|^{\alpha_1 - 1}$. So, δ_1 should be made a tradeoff between the maximum error and 0 error. Similar method can be used to tune parameter δ_2. From our actual experiences, the

value of δ_1 is tuned to the half value of the maximum error, and the value of δ_2 is tuned to the half of the maximum error rate. This choice has good control performance and it's easy to implement.

6. For the parameters $\alpha_1 = 1$ and $\alpha_2 = 1$, the proportional gain $k_p(e_i)$ is a constant of k_p, and the derivative gains $k_d(\dot{e}_i)$ is a constant of k_d. Thus the NPD algorithm can be considered as the linear PD algorithm. So decrease the value of α_1 ($0.5 \le \alpha_1 \le 1$), and decrease the value of k_p at the same time to improve the error curve further, and make tradeoffs between the two values. Using this step, one can get the nonlinear proportional gain of the ANPD controller.
7. Increase the value of α_2 ($1 \le \alpha_2 \le 1.5$), and decrease the value of k_d at the same time to improve the error rate curve further, then make tradeoffs between the two values.

Using the above procedures, the ANPD controller parameters are tuned as follow:

$$k_p = 4500\,,\, k_d = 470\,,\ \delta_1 = 3 \times 10^{-4}\,,\ \delta_2 = 3 \times 10^{-3}\,,\ \alpha_1 = 0.7\,,\ \alpha_2 = 1.1$$

In order to make a comparison between the ANPD controller and the APD controller, the same tracking experiments are implemented on the parallel manipulator. We choose the APD controller is because it has nonlinear dynamics compensation and friction compensation. In the APD controller, the control input vector of the three actuated joints can be calculated as (Shang et.al., 2009)

$$\boldsymbol{\tau}_a = (\mathbf{S}^T)^+ \left(\mathbf{M}_e \ddot{\mathbf{q}}_e^d + \mathbf{C}_e \dot{\mathbf{q}}_e^d + \mathbf{K}_{lp}\mathbf{e} + \mathbf{K}_{ld}\dot{\mathbf{e}} \right) + \mathbf{f}_a \tag{51}$$

where $\mathbf{K}_{lp}$ and $\mathbf{K}_{ld}$ are both symmetric, positive definite matrices of constant gains. In the APD controller (51), $\mathbf{M}_e$ and $\mathbf{C}_e$ can be calculated with the nominal dynamic parameters, and $\mathbf{f}_a$ can be calculated with the values of the friction parameters shown in Table 2. The procedures of tuning parameters $\mathbf{K}_{lp}$ and $\mathbf{K}_{ld}$ in APD controller are similar to the procedures of tuning parameters k_p and k_d in ANPD controller. Thus, the tuning procedures (1) to (3) can be used to tune the parameters $\mathbf{K}_{lp}$ and $\mathbf{K}_{ld}$.

The experiment results of the APD and ANPD controller are shown in Fig. 3-4. Fig. 3a and Fig. 3b are the tracking errors of the end-effector at the low-speed on the X-direction and Y-direction respectively. From the experimental curves, one can see that the ANPD controller can decrease the tracking errors during the whole motion process obviously, and the maximum error in the motion is smaller. Fig. 4a and Fig. 4b are the tracking errors of the end-effector at the high-speed on the X-direction and Y-direction respectively. One can find that the tracking errors are much smaller with the ANPD controller than with the APD controller, especially at the acceleration process. And one can conclude that, by the ANPD controller, the performance improvement of trajectory tracking accuracy at the high-speed is more obvious than at the low-speed.

Furthermore, to evaluate the performances of the two controllers, the root-square mean error (RSME) of the end-effector position is selected as the performance index

$$\begin{aligned} RSME &= \sqrt{\frac{1}{N}\sum_{j=1}^{N}\left(e_x^2(j) + e_y^2(j)\right)} \\ &= \sqrt{\frac{1}{N}\sum_{j=1}^{N}\left(\left(x^d(j) - x(j)\right)^2 + \left(y^d(j) - y(j)\right)^2\right)} \end{aligned} \tag{52}$$

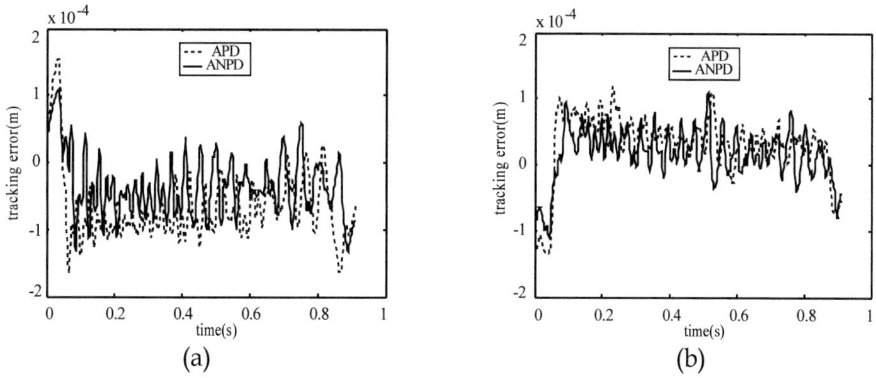

Fig. 3. Tracking errors of the end-effector at the low-speed: (a) X-direction; (b) Y-direction

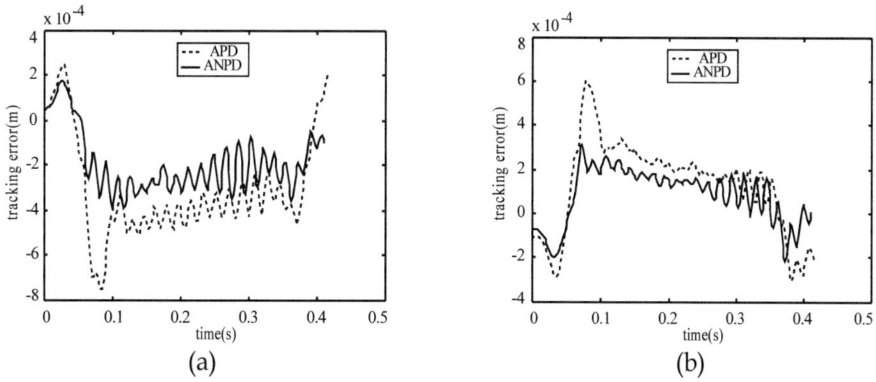

Fig. 4. Tracking errors of the end-effector at the high-speed: (a) X-direction; (b) Y-direction.

where $x^d(j)$ and $y^d(j)$ represent the X-direction and Y-direction position coordinates at the jth sampling point of the desired trajectory respectively; $x(j)$ and $y(j)$ represent the X-direction and Y-direction position coordinates of the jth sampling point of the actual trajectory respectively.

The RSME results of the trajectory tracking experiment of the ANPD and APD controller are shown in Table 3. From the data of the RPE (reduced percentage of error) in Table 3, the ANPD controller can increase the position accuracy of the end-effector above 30%, compared with the conventional APD controller.

	at slow-speed(m)	at high-speed(m)
APD	1.04×10^{-4}	4.55×10^{-4}
ANPD	7.22×10^{-5}	2.78×10^{-4}
RPE	30.6%	38.9%

Table 3. RSME of the APD and ANPD controller

5.2 Experiments of the NCT controller

In order to validate the NCT controller further, the trajectory tracking control experiment is designed for the parallel manipulator. Both the linear and circular trajectories in the workspace are selected as the desired trajectory. For the linear trajectory, the starting point is (0.22, 0.19) and the ending point is (0.35, 0.29), thus the motion distance is 0.164m. The velocity profile of the linear trajectory is an S-type curve (Cheng et.al., 2003), the max velocity is 0.5m/s, the max acceleration is 10m/s^2, and the jerk is 400m/s^3. For the circular trajectory with the constant speed of 0.5m/s, the center is (0.29, 0.25) and the starting point is (0.29, 0.31), thus the radius is 0.06m.

The actual implement of the NCT controller is similar to the ANPD controller, and the dynamic parameters in (33.a) and the friction parameters in (33.b) must be known. In the experiment, the nominal values are selected as the values of the actual dynamic parameters (Shang et.al., 2008). Then, with the known dynamic parameters, the friction parameters can be identified by the Least Squares method (Shang et.al., 2008). And the values of the control parameters in (33.c) are tuned and determined by the actual experiments. The tuning procedures for the ANPD controller can be used to tune the NCT controller. Using those procedures, the NCT controller parameters are tuned as follows: $k_p = 2400$, $k_d = 240$, $\delta_1 = 3\times10^{-4}$, $\delta_2 = 3\times10^{-3}$, $\alpha_1 = 0.7$, $\alpha_2 = 1.1$. Moreover, to demonstrate that the NCT controller can improve the tracking accuracy of the end-effector, experiments using the CT controller are carried out as comparison (Shang & Cong, 2009). The CT controller is chosen because it has friction compensation and feedback dynamics compensation. In the CT controller, the control input vector of the three active joints can be calculated as

$$\boldsymbol{\tau}_a = \left(\mathbf{S}^T\right)^+ \left(\mathbf{M}_e \ddot{\mathbf{q}}_e^d + \mathbf{C}_e \dot{\mathbf{q}}_e + \mathbf{M}_e \left(\mathbf{K}_{lp} e + \mathbf{K}_{ld} \dot{e}\right)\right) + \mathbf{f}_a \tag{53}$$

where $\mathbf{K}_{lp}$ and $\mathbf{K}_{ld}$ are both symmetric, positive definite matrices of constant gains.

In the CT controller (53), the dynamic parameters in $\mathbf{M}_e$ and $\mathbf{C}_e$, and the friction parameters in $\mathbf{f}_a$ are the same with these of the NCT controller. The procedures of tuning parameters of $\mathbf{K}_{lp}$ and $\mathbf{K}_{ld}$ in the CT controller are similar to the procedures of tuning parameters of k_p and k_d in the NCT controller. Thus, the tuning procedures (1), (2), and (3) can be used to tune the parameters of $\mathbf{K}_{lp}$ and $\mathbf{K}_{ld}$. Using the above methods, the CT controller parameters are tuned as follows: $\mathbf{K}_{lp} = diag(20000,\ 20000)$, $\mathbf{K}_{ld} = diag(150,\ 150)$.

The tracking error curves of the end-effector controlled by the CT and NCT controller are shown in Fig. 5-6. Fig. 5 is the linear trajectory tracking errors of the end-effector on the X-direction and Y-direction. From the experiment curves, one can see that the NCT controller can decrease the tracking errors during the whole motion process obviously, and the maximum error in the motion is smaller. Fig. 6 is the circular trajectory tracking errors of the end-effector on the X-direction and Y-direction. From the curves one can see, the tracking accuracy is improved obviously using the NCT controller, compared with the CT controller. The RSME results of the trajectory tracking experiment of the NCT and CT controller are shown in Table 4. From the data of the RPE in Table 4, the NCT controller can increase the position accuracy of the end-effector above 35%, compared with the conventional CT controller.

	Line (m)	Circle (m)
CT	4.77×10^{-4}	4.41×10^{-4}
NCT	3.08×10^{-4}	2.59×10^{-4}
RPE	35.4%	41.3%

Table 4. RSME of the CT and NCT controller

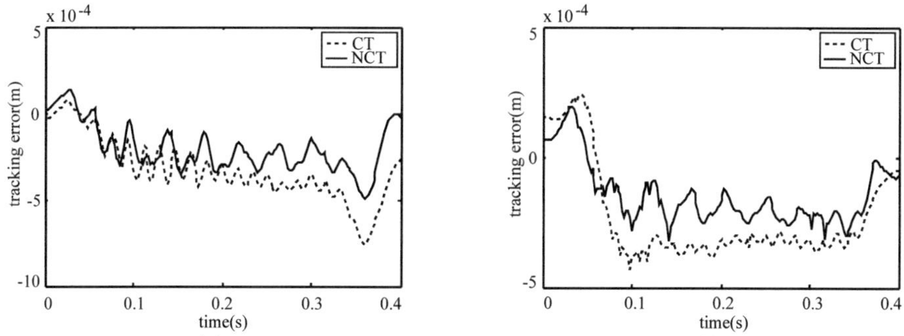

(a) (b)

Fig. 5. Linear trajectory tracking errors of the end-effector: (a) X-direction; (b) Y-direction

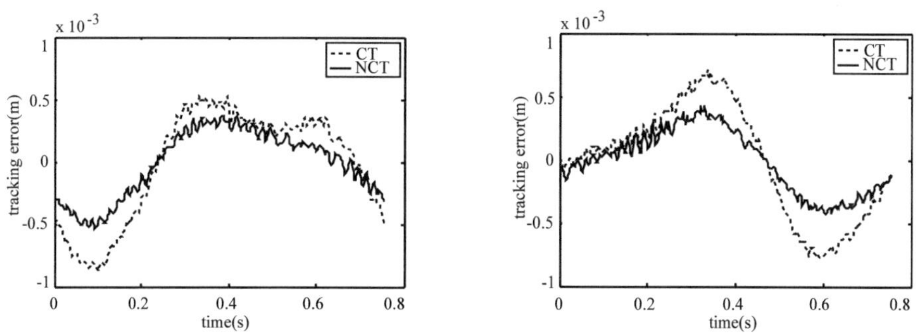

(a) (b)

Fig. 6. Circular trajectory tracking errors of the end-effector: (a) X-direction; (b) Y-direction.

5.3 Experiments of nonlinear friction compensation

In order to compare with the compensation performances of the nonlinear friction model and the Coulomb + viscous friction model, the trajectory tracking experiments are implemented on the parallel manipulator. In the actual experiment, the augmented PD (APD) controller is designed in the task space for the parallel manipulator (Shang et.al., 2009). In the APD controller, the control input vector of the three active joints can be calculated as

$$\boldsymbol{\tau}_a = (\mathbf{S}^T)^+\left(\mathbf{M}_e\ddot{\mathbf{q}}_e^d + \mathbf{C}_e\dot{\mathbf{q}}_e^d + \mathbf{K}_{lp}\mathbf{e} + \mathbf{K}_{ld}\dot{\mathbf{e}}\right) + \mathbf{f}_a \tag{54}$$

where the term $\mathbf{f}_a$ is the friction compensation calculated by the nonlinear friction model (46) with the parameter values in Table 1. Moreover, $\mathbf{f}_a$ can be calculated by the Coulomb + viscous friction model (49) with the parameter values in Table 2. If the term $\mathbf{f}_a$ is neglected in the APD controller (54), it means the friction compensation is not considered in the controller and the friction is ignored in the parallel manipulator.

Both the straight line and the circle in the task space are selected as the desired trajectory to study the friction compensation. For the straight line, the starting point is (0.22, 0.29) and the ending point is (0.37, 0.21), thus the motion distance is 0.17m. The profile of the desired velocity is trapezoidal curve. In the experiment, both the low-speed and high-speed motions are implemented. For the low-speed motion, the maximum velocity is 0.2m/s and the acceleration is 5m/s^2. For the high-speed motion, the maximum velocity is 0.5m/s and the acceleration is 10m/s². In the circle motion with constant speed, the center coordinates of the circle are (0.29，0.25) and radius is 0.04, also both the low-speed motion of 0.2m/s, and the high-speed motion of 0.5m/s are implemented.

Linear trajectory tracking errors of the end-effector at the slow-speed and the high-speed are shown in Fig.7. From the curves one can see, the tracking errors are much smaller with the friction compensation methods based on the *Coulomb* + *viscous* model or the nonlinear model, compared with the without friction compensation method which means the term $\mathbf{f}_a$ is neglected in the APD controller (54). Especially, the maximum error at the acceleration process is decreased greatly with the friction compensation methods. Also one can see that, compared with the friction compensation based on the *Coulomb* + *viscous* model, the tracking accuracy has improved further at the low-speed, and the improvement at the high-speed is even more apparent by using the friction compensation based on the nonlinear model.

Circular trajectory tracking errors of the end-effector at the slow-speed and the high-speed are shown in Fig.8. From the curves one can see, the tracking accuracy is improved obviously using the two friction compensation methods, compared with the without friction compensation method. Also one can see that, with the friction compensation based on the nonlinear model, the tracking error is decreased at the low-speed, and the improvement at the high-speed is more obvious than the friction compensation based on the *Coulomb* + *viscous*.

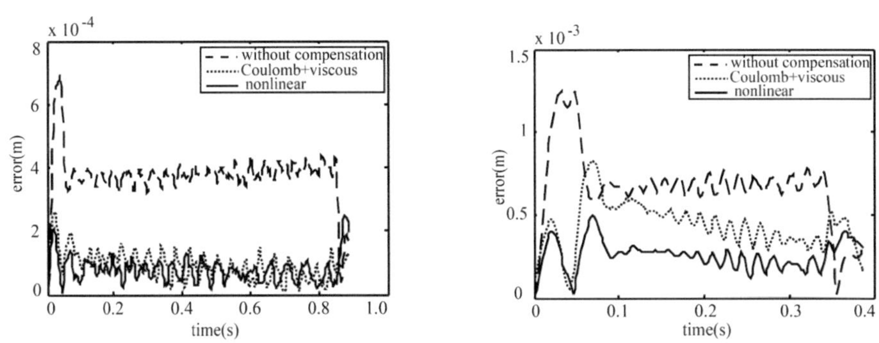

(a) (b)

Fig. 7. Linear trajectory tracking error of the end-effector: (a) at the low-speed; (b) at the high-speed.

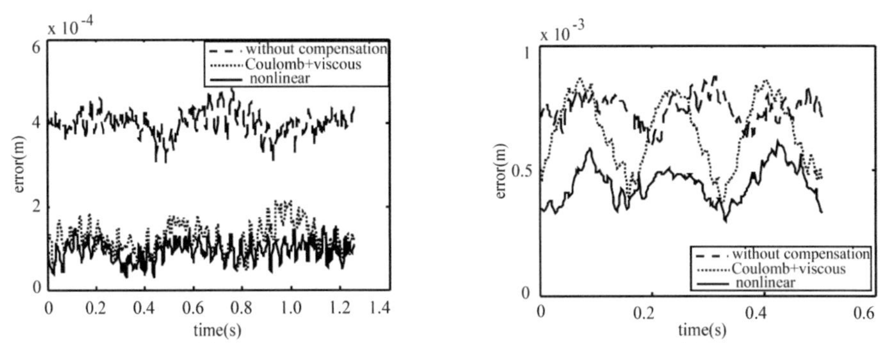

(a) (b)

Fig. 8. Circular trajectory tracking error of the end-effector: (a) at the low-speed; (b) at the high-speed

Furthermore, the RSMEs of the trajectory tracking experiment are shown in Table 5. From the data in the table one can see, by using the two friction compensation methods, the RSMEs are much smaller than the method ignoring friction compensation. And the RSMEs of the friction compensation based on the nonlinear model are smaller than the friction compensation with the *Coulomb + viscous* model, especially when the speed is higher.

Friction compensation method	Straight line motion (m)		Circle motion (m)	
	0.2m/s	0.5m/s	0.2m/s	0.5m/s
Without compensation	3.83×10^{-4}	7.07×10^{-4}	4.00×10^{-4}	7.45×10^{-4}
Coulomb + viscous model	1.03×10^{-4}	4.56×10^{-4}	1.29×10^{-4}	6.68×10^{-4}
Nonlinear model	8.88×10^{-5}	2.71×10^{-4}	9.53×10^{-5}	4.49×10^{-4}

Table 5. RSME of the trajectory tracking experiments

6. Conclusions

In order to realize the high-speed and high-accuracy motion control of parallel manipulator, nonlinear control method is used to improve the traditional dynamic controllers such as the APD controller and the CT controller. The common feature of the two controllers is eliminating tracking error by linear PD control, and the friction compensation is realized by using the Coulomb + viscous friction model. However, the linear PD control is not robust against the uncertain factors such as modeling error and external disturbance. To overcome this problem, the NPD control is combined with the conventional control strategies and two nonlinear dynamic controllers are developed. Moreover, a nonlinear model is used to construct the friction of the parallel manipulator, and the nonlinear friction can be compensated effectively. Our theory analysis implies that, the proposed controllers can guarantee asymptotic convergence to zero of both tracking error and error rate. And for its simple structures and design, the proposed controllers are easy to be realized for the industry applications of parallel manipulators. Our experiment results show that, the position error of the end-effector decrease obviously with the proposed controllers and the nonlinear friction compensation method, especially at the high-speed. So the nonlinear dynamic controller and nonlinear friction compensation can realize high-speed and high-accuracy trajectory tracking of the parallel manipulator in practice. Also these new methods can be used to other manipulators, such as serial ones, or parallel manipulator without redundant actuation to realize high-speed and high accuracy motion.

7. Acknowledgments

This work was supported by the National Natural Science Foundation of China with Grant No. 50905172, the Anhui Provincial Natural Science Foundation with Grant No.090412040, and the Fundamental Research Funds for the Central Universities.

8. References

Cheng H., Yiu Y.K., Li Z.X. (2003) Dynamics and control of redundantly actuated parallel manipulators. *IEEE Trans. Mechatronics*, 8(4): 483-491

Ghorbel F.H., Chetelat O., Gunawardana R., Longchamp R. (2000) Modeling and set point control of closed-chain mechanisms: theory and experiment. *IEEE Trans. Control Syst. Tech.*, 8(5):801-815

Hensen R.H.A., Angelis G.Z., Molengraft M.J.G., Jager A.G., Kok J.J. (2000) Grey-box modeling of friction: An experimental case-study. *European Journal of Control* 6(3):258-267

Han J.Q. (1994) Nonlinear PID controller. *Acta Automatica Sinica*, 20(4): 487-490.

Kelly R., Ricardo C. (1996) A class of nonlinear PD-type controller for robot manipulator. *Journal of Robotic Systems*, 13: 793-802

Kostic D., Jager B., Steinbuch M., Hensen R. (2004) Modeling and identification for high-performance robot control: an RRR-robotic arm case study. *IEEE Trans. Contr. Syst. Techn.* 12(6): 904-919

Li Q., Wu F.X. (2004) Control performance improvement of a parallel robot via the design for control approach. *Mechatronics*, 14(8): 947-964

Merlet J.P. (2000) *Parallel robots*. Norwell, MA: Kluwer

Muller A. (2005) Internal preload control of redundantly actuated parallel manipulators - Its application to backlash avoiding control, *IEEE Trans. Robotics*, 21(4), 668 - 677

Murray R., Li Z. X., Sastry S. (1994) A Mathematical Introduction to Robotic Manipulation. CRC Press

Ouyang P.R., Zhang W.J., Wu F.X. (2002) Nonlinear PD control for trajectory tracking with consideration of the design for control methodology. In: *Proc. of the IEEE Int. Conf. Robot. Autom.*, Washington; May, 2002, pp. 4126-4131

Paccot F., Andreff N., Martinet P. (2009) A review on the dynamic control of parallel kinematic machines: theory and experiments. *International Journal of Robotics Research*, 28(3): 395-416

Seraji H. (1998) A new class of nonlinear PID controllers with robotic applications. *Journal of Robotic Systems*, 15(3): 161-181

Shang W.W., Cong S., Zhang Y.X. (2008) Nonlinear friction compensation of a 2-DOF planar parallel manipulator. *Mechatronics*, 18(7): 340-346

Shang W. W., Cong S. (2009) Nonlinear computed torque control for a high speed planar parallel manipulator, *Mechatronics*, 19(6): 987-992

Shang W. W., Cong S., Li Z. X., Jiang S. L. (2009) Augmented nonlinear PD controller for a redundantly actuated parallel manipulator. *Advanced Robotics*, 23: (12-13), 1725-1742

Shang W. W., Cong S., Kong F. R. (2010) Identification of dynamic and friction parameters of a parallel manipulator with actuation redundancy, *Mechatronics*, 20(2): 192-200.

Shang W. W., Cong S., Jiang S. L. (2010) Dynamic model based nonlinear tracking control of a planar parallel manipulator, *Nonlinear Dynamics*, 60(4): 597-606

Slotine J. -J. E., Li W. P. (1991) *Applied nonlinear control*, Englewood Cliffs, N. J.: Prentice Hall.

Su Y.X., Duan B.Y., Zheng C.H., Zhang Y.F. Chen G.D., Mi J.W. (2004) Disturbance-rejection high-precision motion control of a Stewart platform. *IEEE Trans. Control Syst.* Tech., 12(3): 364-374

Su Y.X., Zheng C.H., Duan B.Y. (2005) Fuzzy learning tracking of a parallel cable manipulator for the square kilometer array. *Mechatronics*, 15(6):731-746

Wu F.X., Zhang W.J., Li Q., Ouyang P.R. (2002) Integrated design and PD control of high-speed closed-loop mechanisms. *J. Dyn. Syst., Meas., Control*, 124(4): 522-528

Xu Y., Hollerbach J.M., Ma D. (1995) A nonlinear PD controller for force and contact transient control. *IEEE Control Systems Magazine*, 15: 15-21.

Zhang Y.X., Cong S., Shang W.W., Li Z.X., and Jiang S.L. (2007) Modeling, identification and control of a redundant planar 2-Dof parallel manipulator. *Int. J. Control, Autom. Syst.*, 5(5):559-569

13

Estimation of Position and Orientation for Non–Rigid Robots Control Using Motion Capture Techniques

Przemysław Mazurek
Department of Signal Processing and Multimedia Engineering
West Pomeranian University of Technology, Szczecin
Poland

1. Introduction

Robots are well established in science and technique. They are used in different environments and they have different structures. Typical robot movements are rapid and steepy when the movement direction changes occurs. It is not necessary to replicate a biological nature based solution for most tasks, so such movements are acceptable and simpler to obtain. Control algorithms are simpler for such cases, development and settings of such controllers are more straightforward.
Robots are also based on a set of joins and serial or parallel configurations. Different configurations are usefully for selected task and may be not based on biological nature references. Replication of biological nature are not necessary, and for example a wheels that are simple to design have not biological references.
Join based approach of robot design is well established and there are many technical advantages of such structure (Fig. 1). Mechanic of the robots is based mostly on a kind of the skeleton. The endoskeletons design uses a mechanical parts located inside light–weight casing. The exoskeletons design uses a mechanical parts that is casing also. Some robots uses mixed design, where the 'bones' are in endosceleton design and only joints uses exosceleton design. Exosceletons design are used in hostile environments typically.

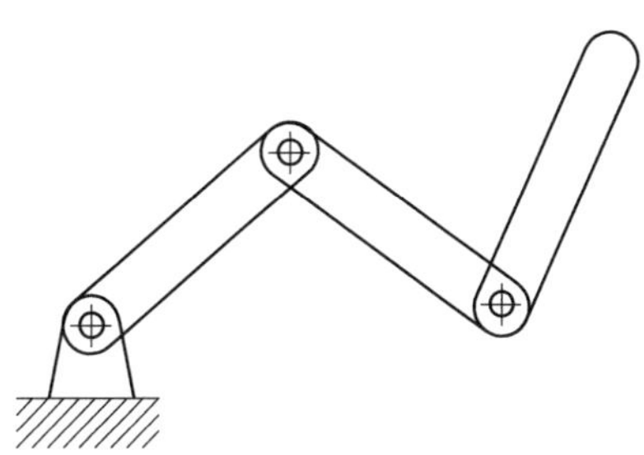

Fig. 1. Rigid actuator

The bones are fixed, so length of the bone or its curvature is not possible to change. Additional actuators for arm extension are used sometimes. Fixed structure of the robot, even if redundant number of degrees of freedom is available, is convenient for analysis and design.

2. Non–rigid robots

Rigid structure is not only–one solution for the robots. The flexible (non–rigid, elastic) robots, complete actuators, and partially flexible actuators are also important for the future robots (Fig. 2). Flexibility of the actuators or overall robot's body is inspired by the biological nature. The giant amount of the species that live in different environments uses flexible bodies or bodies parts with evolutionary success.

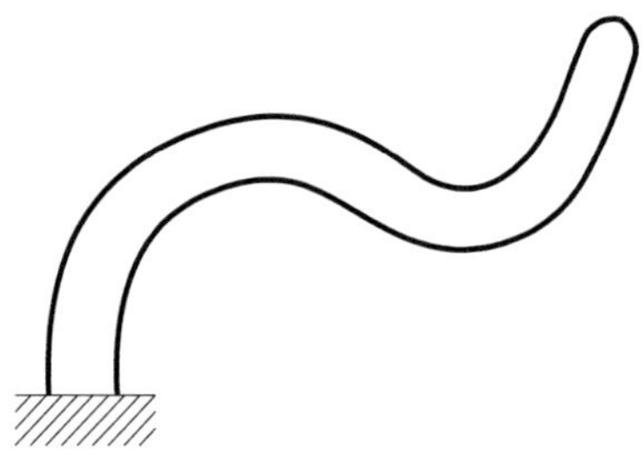

Fig. 2. Non–rigid actuator

Non–rigid robots are active and open research area. Any physical effect related to the flexible movement that is driven by the any factor (continuously or PWM–like) may be applied for intentional movement of robot or actuator. Direct or indirect control of the movement by the electrical signal is desired especially. The Pulse Width Modulation (PWM) control is especially important for simplification of driver.
The pneumatic[Daerden (1999); Daerden & Lefeber (2002); Verrelst (2005)] or hydraulic effects may be used, but the control of them is possible by the electric–to–pneumatic or electric–to–hydraulic conversion devices and is indirect control. The bimetal or memory alloy actuators are controlled by the electricity more directly (exactly there is an electrical energy–to–heat conversion but no additional devices like pumps are necessary).
Progress in the material engineering and market availability of materials, that are sensitive on electricity, gives an ability of application such 'muscles' for skeleton based robots, or even a build an complete body of non–rigid robots.
Non–rigid robots may be characterized by the place of movement. In the rigid robot the movement points are defined by the main gear axis or motor axis. For linear movement the line of the movement is also well defined like for the linear stepping motors for example. Conversion of rotary to linear movement is also used.
The non–rigid robots may be controlled in a hundreds points per muscle. The conventional classification and comparison of actuators, based on the number of degree–of–freedom, is not convenient for such cases. Electrical based control of Electroactive Materials gives building abilities of robots and controlling them in so many of points, giving a new way of robots design. Such robots may change external shape and size (morphing robots).
A few main types of Electroactive Materials are used and developed nowadays.
The simplest are the bimetal strips and coils based on the conversion of electrical energy into heat. The Shape Memory Alloys are also interesting alternatives to bimetal, and the best know is the Nitinol (Nickel titanium). The more advanced actuators like Biometal helix, due significant length changes are also important. The Nitinol was applied in well know Stiquitio hexapod robot legs and derivatives [Conrad & Mills (2004)]. The main drawback of the bimetal and SMA is the speed of the physical changes that is about a few seconds depending on material and design. Heating of such material is controlled by the electricity and could be very rapid, but cooling is depends on the environment of the work.

The Electroactive Polymers (EAPs) are the most promising materials for non–rigid robots design nowadays. The advantages of such materials are applied for rigid robots also, because it is important replacement of the electrical motors. Improved reliability, increased lifetime, reduction of electromagnetic emission are very important for robot design. There are many materials based on the different effects [Bar–Cohen (2004); Besenhard et al. (2001); Capri & Smela (2009); Chanda & Roy (2009); Hu (2007); Kim & Tadokoro (2007); Otake (2010); Wallace et al. (2009)]. The Electronic EAPs uses piezoelectric, electrostatic, electrostrictive and ferroelectric effects nowadays. The Ionic EAPs uses the displacement of ions inside the polymer.
One of the most important task is the measurement of the state of such robot or manipulator. The conventional position and orientation approach is not well fitted, because non–rigid robots are flexible, so huge or infinite number of positions points are possible. Moreover, the estimation of the number of degrees–of–freedom by the simple visual observation of robot movements is not feasible.
The reasonable way is to estimate position and orientation in some points, especially for the end–effector and limited number of selected intermediate points. The overall estimation is possible, using the model based techniques and vision measurements. The vision techniques are well suited for such robots, because they make measurements in hundreds or millions points (pixels in extended cases).
The open–control loop, without knowledge about achieved state, is applicable for very specific cases only, for non–rigid robots. The flexibility of the non–robots have important disadvantage – the forces from manipulated objects and forces from environments influent on the achieved state. Such forces change state and in the worst case all points of the non–rigid robots may differ between the expected position and real one. This is one of the reasons why the closed–control loop for rigid robots and the state estimation are necessary. Vision based technique for rigid robots (visual servoing [Agin (1979); Chaumette (1998); Chaumette & Hutchinson (2008); Corke & Hutchinson (2001); Fung & Chen (2010); Malis at al. (1999); Marchand at al. (2005); Sanderson & Weiss (1983)]) are used from many years, and it is very promising technique for non–rigid robots also.

3. Visual systems for non–rigid robots

Different video tracking schemes for non–rigid robots and actuators are possible, and the selected are presented shortly.

3.1 Conventional motion capture system

Conventional motion capture system (multiple camera vision system [Aghajan & Cavallaro (2009)]) uses a set of cameras located around robot (Fig. 3). Video tracking gives abilities of the robot state estimation what is necessary to control. Such system is very simple for implementation in comparison to other presented tracking schemes. The market availability of such systems for large working area (known as a volumen) like a cubic area with a few meters distance in every direction is important for large scale systems. There are also available systems for small working area about half meter in every direction.
Typical motion capture system uses markers for estimation of the state of human or some objects. The measurements are contact less so significant integration or embedding into robot surface is not necessary. The weight of the robot is preserved. Motion capture system may be used for measurements a very large number of points located on the robot surface. Single or a few cameras are sufficient for estimation of the robot state in most cases.
There are also drawbacks related to the vision techniques. Occlusion reduces a possibility of the state estimation, and the multiple cameras are necessary for reduction of such effects, but

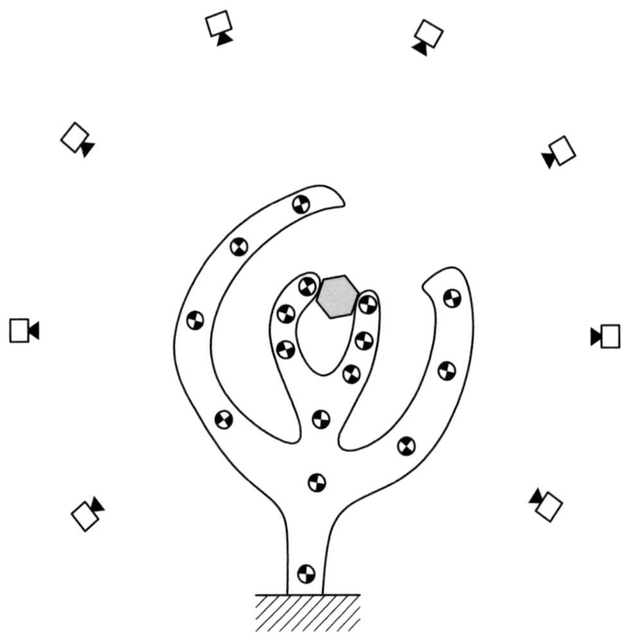

Fig. 3. Motion capture of the non–rigid robot

elimination of the occlusion is not possible for general scenario. Occlusions may occurs due to self occlusions of the robot by the own parts like arms, or may occurs if the environment or operated objects are close to robot.

Internal parts of the robot and related states are hard to estimate, if the cameras are placed around robot. The estimation of the state is based on the outer surfaces, and the estimation of the inner parts of the robot is very difficult task. Such situation occurs for example in estimation task for the propulsion part of the underwater robot that is based on the biological nature species like squids. This is specific design problem, but should be identified on early development stage.

Illumination of the working area influent on the estimation result. The constant environment conditions are recommended. The variable conditions, like bright light sources, may disturb image acquisition by overexposure. Constant light conditions are especially important for the retroreflective markers. Light emitting markers are more robust for variable illumination conditions. Overexposure and underexposure conditions needs expensive HDR (High Dynamic Range) cameras.

High speed cameras are available today (fps $>$ 100 or 1000) but the latency is also very important factor for smooth control of robot, so the image processing part should be integrated into sensors (intelligent cameras are recommended). Most professional motion capture systems uses image processing of acquire image inside camera for bandwidth reduction between camera and computer. Marker detection algorithms are processed in hardware, for reduction processing costs on computer, moreover. High speed cameras reduce distance between position of the marker on two following frames, what gives ability of application simple marker tracking algorithms and assignment algorithms. Gate based approach and nearest neighborhood algorithms for assignment are an example of the simple but an effective algorithms. Assignment is necessary for the tracks of markers maintenance. Assignment is simpler to do if the markers are more unique complex patterns. Position, scale and rotation invariant markers may consist information about unique number of marker. Larger markers

due to additional information about number are less usefully due to size, but the color coded information about number is interesting alternative.
Image processing and state estimation algorithms should be the low–latency and real–time. Fixed processing time or variable with known maximal response time is necessary. Detection, tracking and assignment algorithms should be carefully selected.
The commercial motion systems are mostly closed design, without possibility of the algorithm replacement. There are no available free systems, contemporary.
The conventional systems based on the multiple cameras is not unique, and the similar idea based on the video based estimation is possible for other configurations. Most advantages and disadvantages are preserved in other configurations. Some of them are interesting for new robot design.

3.2 Robot equipped with the vision systems

Some, especially mobile robots, uses own vision system for navigation purposes and objects manipulations. The availability of the own vision systems is important for inspection robots working in an hostile environments, especially for space probes, or planet exploration robot.
Vision systems are used also for remote examination of the current state of the robot in case of the significant motion error. Blocked wheels, failed arms or legs due to unexpected environment case or own failure are possible to detect using vision system used for navigation purposes or objects manipulation. This is typical procedure in space robots nowadays. Vision sensors placed on the flexible arms helps in such situation (Fig. 4), gives ability of failure source inspection, finding solutions and may save (extend live) of a multi million dollar robot.

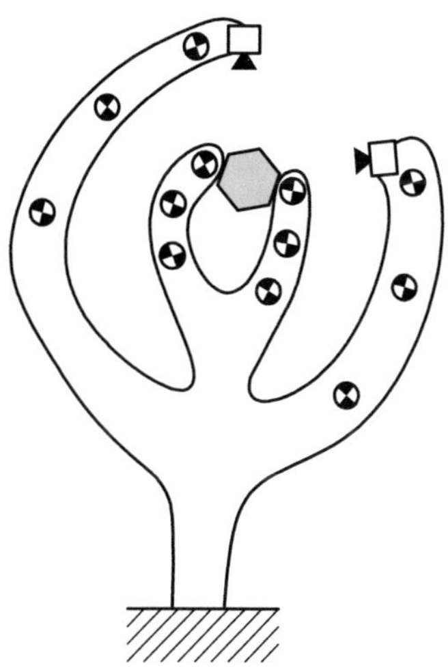

Fig. 4. Non–rigid robot equipped with the vision systems

The conventional sensors may fail and the availability of the vision system gives ability of redundancy also. Proper design uses cameras for the navigation and manipulation task, and many other sensors for movement control. Secondary task of vision system are measurements of state for motion control in case of failure of primary motion control (measurement subsystem).
The non–rigid robots gives interesting ability of application vision system using own multiple cameras. Such robot may change own state and additionally camera position and orientation, creating a different camera configurations on demand. The concept of such robot is similar to amoeba, that have large ability of the shape modification.

The cameras are integrated into robot's flexible body. Range of the work is unlimited and not limited to the unique area (volumen). Different camera configurations may be proposed in real–time and tested for optimal object manipulation or movement. The most challenging task is the multiple or single camera calibration [Daniilidis & Eklundh (2008); Lei et al. (2005); Mazurek (2010; 2009; 2007)]. The estimation of external parameters is especially important for such robots.

3.3 Video sensors on robot's surface

This is specific version of the previous case and inverse motion capture configuration. The cameras are placed on the robot and the fixed set of markers is observed by them. The robot environment is used for the robot's state estimation (Fig.5).

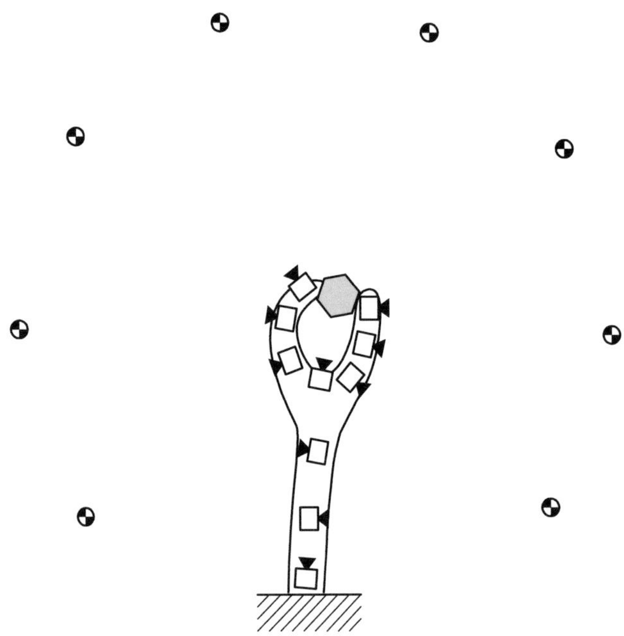

Fig. 5. Cameras placed on the robot surface

It is possible to use cameras for navigation and manipulation purposes and for estimation own state also.
One of the most important factor is the power consumption for such case. The motion capture configuration using passive markers on robot does not need additional power for robot. Inverse motion capture system needs a power supply for camera and acquisition devices. Image processing for inverse case by the external computer is important technique for reduction of the needs of the additional electrical power. The weight of the robot is reduced if the computational part is outside of robot.

3.4 Cooperative robot swarm with multiple cameras

Another possibility when multiple robots (rigid on non–rigid) are equipped with cameras for navigation, manipulation and self measurements. Swarm members are separated robots from the physical point–of–view, but from the logical point–of–view it is a single robot if the cooperation between members of swarm is very close. The self measurement task (Estimation of own parameters) is very interesting, because the state of the particular member of the swarm is obtained from neighborhoods members. Favorable members are inside swarm due to availability of multiple views (multiple independent observations) from neighborhood members. The outer members are partially observed only. The multiple swarm members may cooperate in many ways.

4. Vision based estimation of position and orientation

The images acquired by the camera set, gives information about 3D world using multiple 2D views. Relation between image objects or additional knowledge about object may be used for estimation of position objects and camera. Without additional knowledge a relative, spatial relations are obtained.

4.1 Features and model based approaches

The vision techniques use feature points or model fitting approaches. Both of them are important for establishing relations between real and virtual (computer modeled) world. In the case of motion capture systems the markers (feature points) are placed on robot or deformable model of robot is used (model fitting).
Feature points are existing features of surrounding object in environment (e.g. corners, edges) or intentionally added (e.g. ball shaped markers, or painted chessboard patterns). Estimation of the position (for point like features) and optionally orientation (for edges or patterns) gives ability of estimation of camera position relative to object.
The model fitting approach is based on the 3D model of robot. The camera measurements are related to the estimation of the pixel assignment to the background or robot body. The aim of the fitting is to find the configuration of the model, that gives image for single camera system or images if multiple camera system are used. The corresponding real and virtual (rendered) images are fitted if the configuration of real robot and its model are identical.

4.2 Correspondence by the calibration object

The simplest technique that is used for establishing relations between virtual and real camera is based on the calibration object. This techniques uses physical object with known physical dimension (M) and mathematical model of this object (V). The bridge between the real and virtual world is the calibration object and its model (Fig. 6).
Assuming, that the worlds coordinates (O, X, Y, Z) are defined if fixed relation in virtual and real calibration object, the full correspondence may between objects, projections and cameras is possible (degenerative cases are not considered here). It means, that all particular positions and orientation have exact values. The projections are the images of the markers from the cameras. Acquired image from the real camera is processed for the marker's positions estimation with subpixel accuracy (e.g. center of mass algorithm may be used). The projection of the virtual markers (V) on the virtual camera projection plane is possible using the computer graphics formulas using high, usually floating point accuracy.
During the estimation process of the external parameters the camera, the correspondence is obtained with some error. Markers projections are not identical and cameras parameters are not equal, especially in beginning steps. The error (Fig. 7) between projections (m, v) of markers (M, V) is possible to calculate. Comparison of the 2D positions on projection planes using l_2 value is used typically (Euclidean distance). Iterative calculations with subject of the minimization of this error are used for establish reliable correspondence.
The accumulative l_2 error is computed using the following formula:

$$l_2 = \sqrt{\sum_i d_i^2} = \sqrt{\sum_i (m_i - v_i)^2} \tag{1}$$

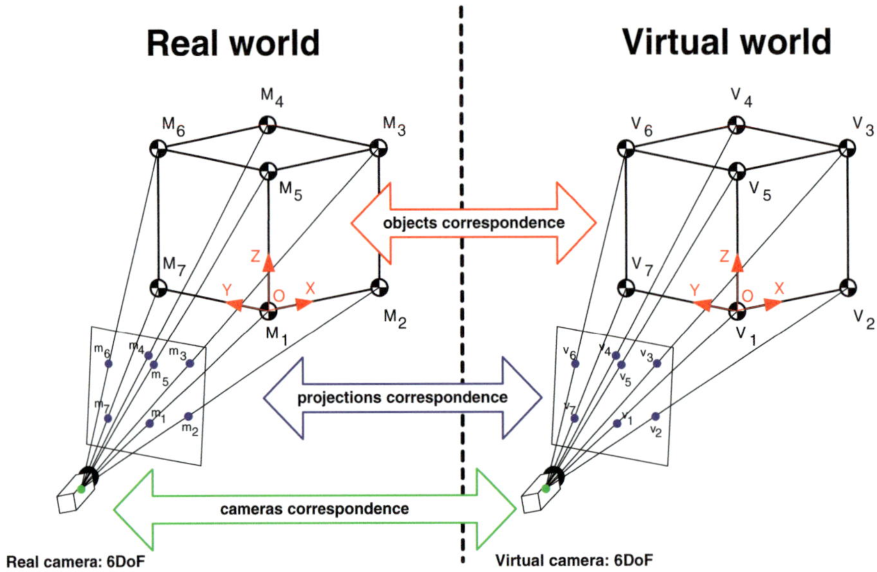

Fig. 6. Correspondences between real and virtual world using 3D calibration object

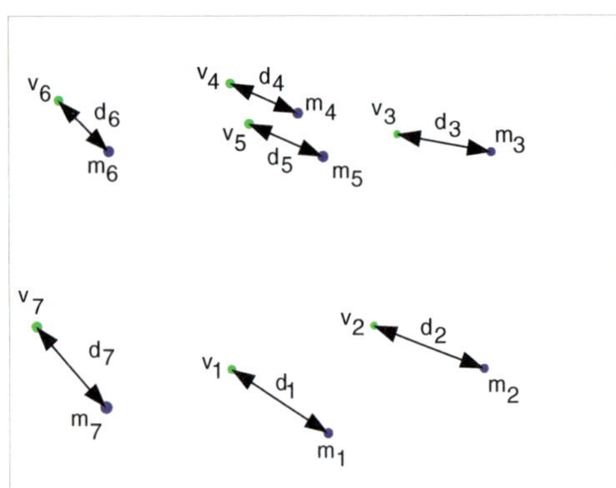

Fig. 7. Comparison of the markers' positions (real and virtual) and local distance errors

.

Minimization process of l_2 value by the movement and rotation of virtual camera is possible using gradient and non–gradient search algorithms. The difference between position of markers' projections d_i are reduced to zero only in ideal case. The estimated position of the real markers is obtained with some accuracy due to acquisition errors (image blur, finite resolution of the imaging senor, camera noises, design of the imaging sensor, and estimation algorithm for the position).

Estimation of the 3D position and orientation using 2D images is possible using the projective geometry, but the application of Euclidean geometry is also possible. Euclidean geometry is a subset of the projective geometry and preserves angles. Using the long focal length camera, for high ratio of the camera distance to the robot work area is possible.

The Euclidean approach is simpler and cheaper for some cases, especially if the robot is very small. Required large distance between camera and object in real scenarios is main drawback (Fig. 8). Estimation of the 3D position is necessary using a few cameras.

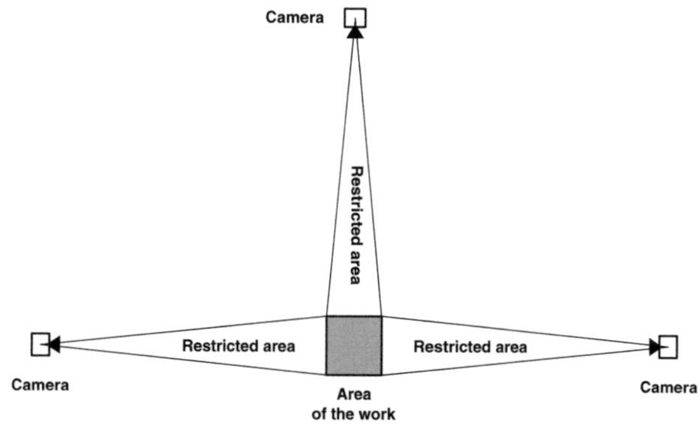

Fig. 8. Example configuration of three cameras for Euclidean geometry based 3D estimation system

The restricted areas and large distance between camera and area of the work requirements are drawback of the Euclidean projections. The perspective projection (Fig. 9) is more applicable for a general case of cameras and different work area configurations.

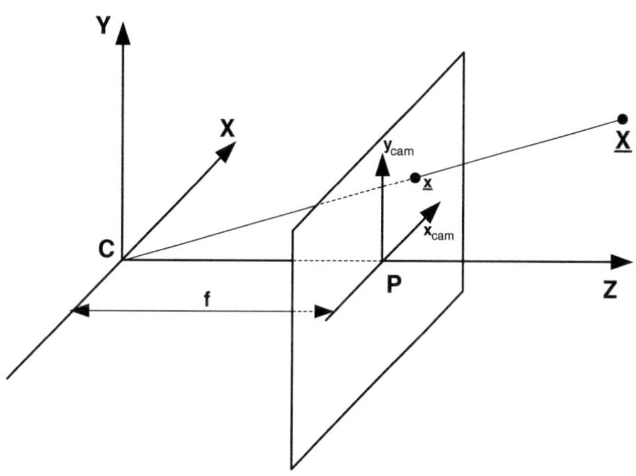

Fig. 9. Perspective projection

Perspective projection uses camera with focal point at position C and projection plane located at distance f, that is focal length. Depending on distance between focal point and point X in the 3D space, the projection x is in different position on projection plane. The projection formulas of point X on projection plane of camera located in arbitrary position in 3D space are available in many computer graphics books [Hartley & Zisserman (2003); Heyden & Pollefeys (2004)].
The perspective projection adds a very important factor – the scale for non–point objects, especially markers. The scale and distance from camera estimation is possible using single camera, depending on the assumed marker estimation technique. Commercial motion capture systems uses very small markers and wide angle cameras (short focal length). The distance is

not well measured, especially for variable light conditions for such configuration. The scale of the larger marker may differ in some direction, so for example the ellipse is observed instead the circle. It gives an ability estimation of full 6 DoF (Degree–of–Freedom) for every large marker.

Correspondence between real and virtual world is used during the calibration of the cameras. Calibrated cameras are used in marker systems or in model fitting approach. The model fitting approach is similar to the calibration process but the instead calibrated object there are two sets of calibrated cameras (real and virtual) and deformable model of the real robot.

5. Markers

Vision tracking techniques for robots are based on the numerous approaches: marker based, object features, or even on complete synthesis of the expected object. All of the them are interesting and the selection is application depended. The most valuable techniques for the controlled environment scenarios are marker based. The uncontrolled environments exist if the unexpected situations may occurs, related to the object occlusions, different lighting conditions, etc.

The marker based techniques are very interesting, because different markers designs are possible. The light emitting markers are especially useful for poor lighting conditions. They need additional power connections (wires) for the bulbs or LEDs. The retroreflective markers reflect surrounding light and no additional power connection are necessary for them. The retroreflective markers are interesting for small size and small power robots, especially.

Controlled environment of the robot's work area gives an ability of the correct light setup for maximization performance of retroreflective markers. Markers may support angular estimation (3DoF) depending on own shape. The simplest matte ball markers are orientation less so only a 3D position (3DoF) is obtained by the triangulation using two or more cameras. The carefully selected set of such markers located at close distance gives ability of estimation of orientation. The larger markers with additional orientation features may support estimation of orientation.

In this paper, the four–sector circle with the boundary ring is used as marker (Fig. 10). Such marker gives an ability of orientation estimation with 180 degree accuracy, position and distance. Complete set of DoF (six of them) is possible to estimate. The estimation of all parameters is limited by the optical visibility of the markers. A low angle case between camera and marker plane are hard to process. This is the reason, why a ball shape markers are preferred, because they have superior visibility. Large markers support estimation of own parameters even for partial occlusions but it is not considered in following tests.

The marker uses boundary ring for improving separation between background and marker, what is important for the scale estimation, because estimation process should be related to the marker, not to the background.

6. Estimation of the position, distance, and rotation of the markers

Estimation of the marker is possible using numerous image processing techniques. The feature based techniques or image synthesis, using the model fitting, are possible also. The feature techniques are based on the corners detection. More advanced techniques uses corners detection for further starting point of the line detection. The estimation quality depends on the marker shape and the number of pixels used for the estimation. The larger number of pixels and larger distant between used pixels are important due to noises and possible occlusions, especially.

Proposed technique use a few techniques for the optimization algorithm. Single technique is not feasible for applications due to computation cost and poor results as it is shown by

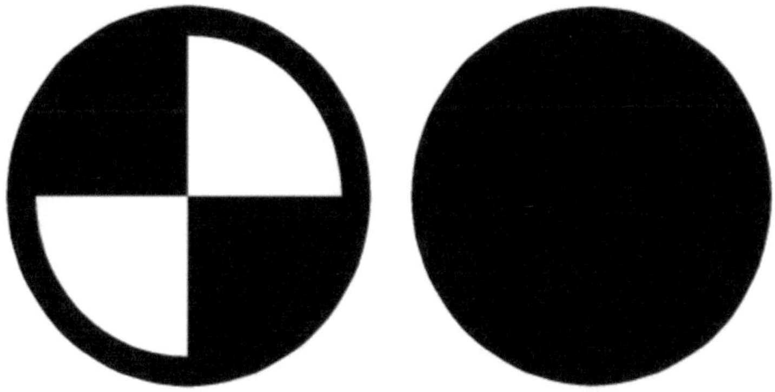

(a) Marker model (b) Mask model

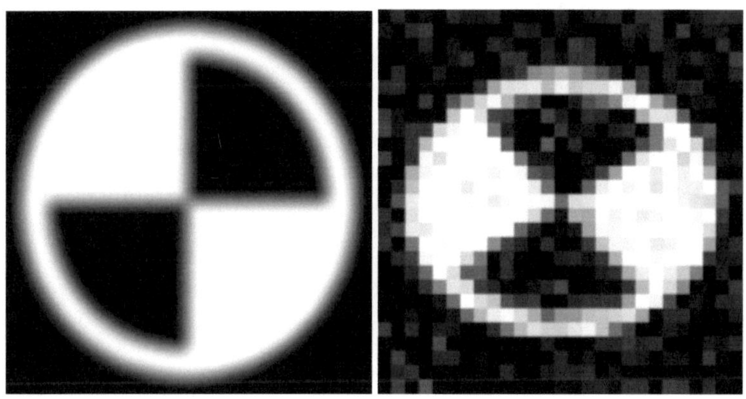

(c) Filtered (blurred) marker before downsampling (d) Example of noised image of marker at low resolution

Fig. 10. Model of marker and noised measurements

the numerical tests. The dedicated renderer of the marker and mask at different positions, scale (distance), 3D rotations, and contrast is used. The contrast fitting is important due to variable light conditions. The white and black points are defined by the two coordinate pairs (Fig. 11). The black (Xb,Yb) and white point (Xw,Yw) define simplest contrast, brightness, and saturation parameters of image transformation.

The first optimization phase is quite simple and the exhaustive search is used for a priori defined spatial and angular resolutions. Positions are tested using subpixel resolutions, 10 times higher resolution in both direction, and rotations using 20 deg. angle resolutions. The scale is not tested, because different scales of markers have common central part. Contrast is also not tested and fixed. The advantages of this phase are the fixed computation cost and possibilities in parallel processing.

The best position obtained from first phase due to obtained l_2 value is tested using optimization in second phase. The selection is driven by the threshold value for l_2 value. Second phase is started in parallel for obtained positions with enough low value of l_2. Second phase is based on the gradient and non–gradient approaches. The constrained optimization is applied in all optimization phases.

During second phase gradient search algorithm is used and after the optimization is stopped (due to achieving error small changes, or after selected number of iterations) the non–gradient

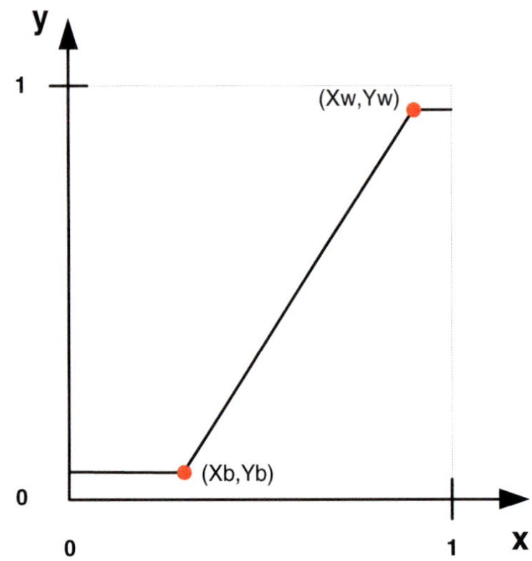

Fig. 11. Contrast curve, with white (w) and black (b) points

algorithm is started. This process is iterated ten times. Such technique gives abilities of exit from local minimal, that is achieved by the gradient search. The non–gradient algorithm when is used alone, supports exit from local minimum (but the convergence is usually very slow).
The gradient algorithm is the minimization procedure from the Matlab Optimization Toolbox (fmincon). The non–gradient algorithm is evolutionary algorithm [Back (T. et al.;T); Michalewicz (1996)], based on mutation. The single parent and child are used at one time evolutionary step. Mutation operator changes relative values of estimated parameters in specific range [Spears (2000)].
The non–gradient phase (Fig.13) uses 1000 iterations and during the single iterations modification of the position (2 DoF), scale (2 DoF), rotation (1 DoF), and contrast (4 DoF) are driven by the uniform random noise generator. The probabilities of mutation of parameter is set to the 0.3. More then one parameter may change during the single iteration. Multiple parameters modified during one iterations reduce influence of local minimum.
The number of iterations and number of repetitions is selected after a lot of tests. The convergence to acceptable level of l_2 is obtained in most cases, but as it is shown later the better results are obtained, if more such optimization processes are started. In parallel processing devices reduce processing time.

7. Performance of proposed estimation technique

Monte Carlo approach Fishman (2000) is used for performance analysis. Application of the Monte Carlo method gives an abilities of testing complex system. The 600 tests are applied using pseudo random number generator for parameters setting. Every test uses 20 iterations (gradient and non–gradient). The Gaussian additive noise is applied to the image (0.2 standard deviation). Values that are not fitted into $(0 - 1)$ range are processed by the contrast curve and saturated according this curve.
The l_2 error is minimized to low values (Fig. 14) what is a numerical, Monte Carlo test based proof of algorithm. Achieving a zero value of l_2 is a very low probable, dependent on the noise level and contrast curve. It means that l_2 error is interesting quality of fitness, that is available during optimization process (due to known model) but not necessary a reliable one.

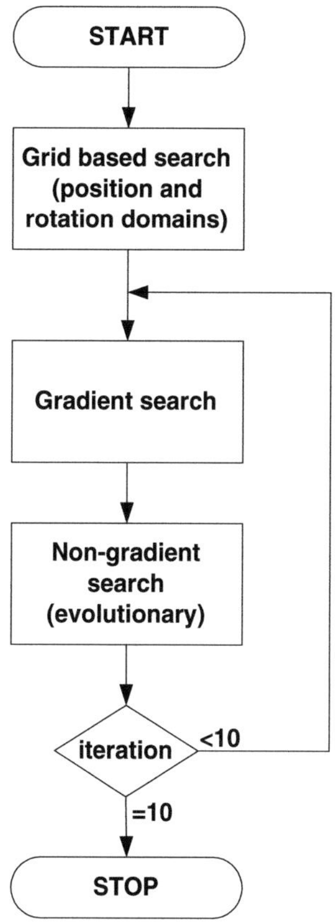

Fig. 12. Optimization scheme

Very interesting are box–plot statistic (Fig. 15), especially the depicted median value of the l_2 error. It is shown, that first step (gradient based) reduces error to low–level, but second step (non–gradient) reduces error to much lower level (more then 2 times). The reduction does not occur significantly by the next repetition of the gradient and non–gradient search. It is very important for practical applications. The gradient algorithm fails in local minima and the solution is possible using the non–gradient algorithm. Applications of the non–gradient algorithm only is not shown in this chapter, and the computation cost is very large (the computation are very slow, and are omitted).

The position error and following errors are calculated using Euclidean distance formula also. All of them are possible to obtain using the synthetic test using Monte Carlo technique and gives an ability of the algorithm test and configuration.

First gradient step does not gives good results (Fig. 16). The mean value of the position error is about half of pixel. The next step (non–gradient based) reduces mean error to values about 0.2. It is important quality improvement. The next steps reduces error, but not significantly. After all 20 steps the mean value is reduced, and histogram is little compressed into left direction, but the computation cost is quite high.

Only z–axis is considered in shown results, that is related to the rotation of the maker around own axis. Rotation errors are reduced significantly (Fig. 17) to the about 0.6 degree (mean value). The reduction occurs after 20 iterations but is not so large.

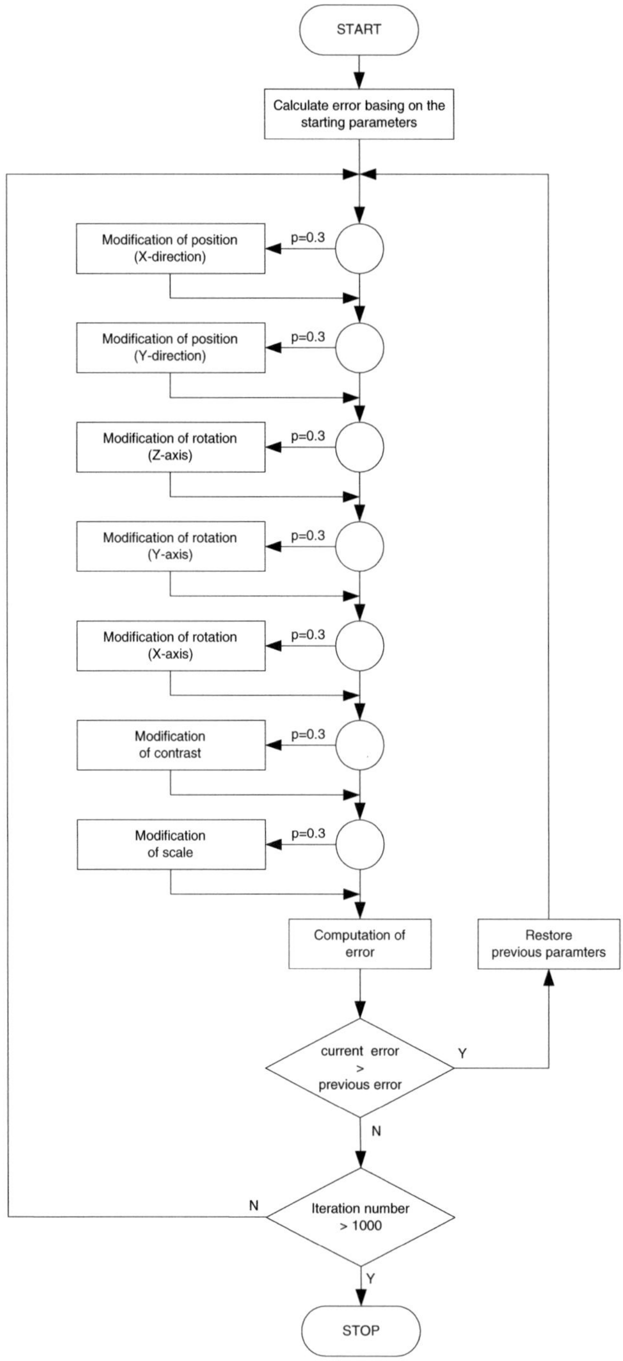

Fig. 13. Evolutionary optimization

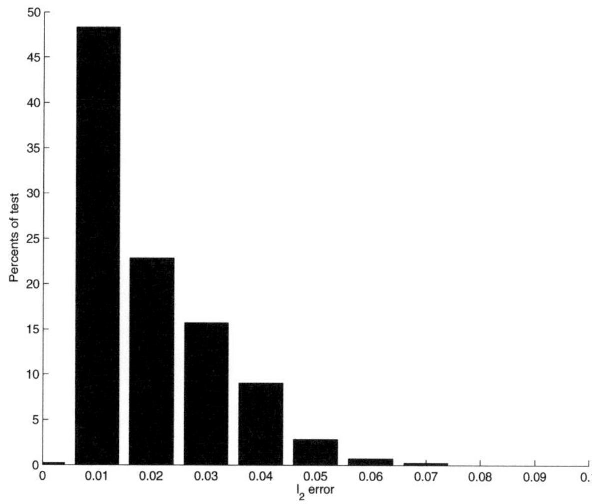

(a)

Fig. 14. l_2 error between image and marker's image model

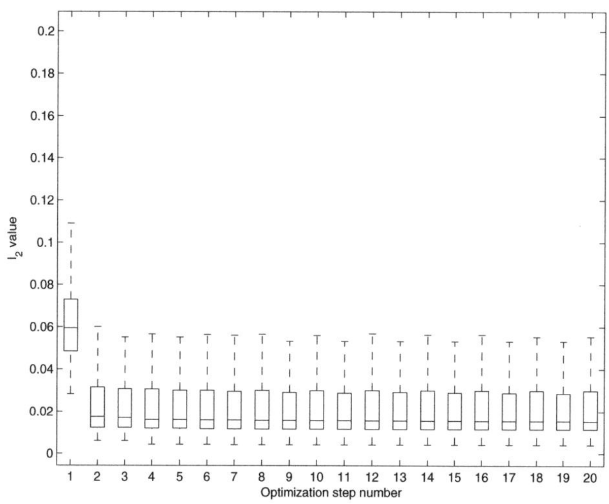

(a)

Fig. 15. Boxplot statistic for optimization step number – gradient based (odd step numbers), non–gradient based (even step numbers)

Known marker size give abilities of distance estimation using single camera. The 24 pixels of diameter correspond to the scale value 0.03. Diameter has variable diameter 24 − 48 pixels in test. The absolute scale error (Fig. 18) is large – 2'nd and 3'rd column preserved about 1/3 cases for errors about 20% of diameter.
Correlation between l_2 value and particular error is very interesting. The following values are obtained: $R = 0.24$ for position, $R = 0.12$ for rotation, and $R = 0.30$ for scale. All tested cases are depicted in Fig. 19 .

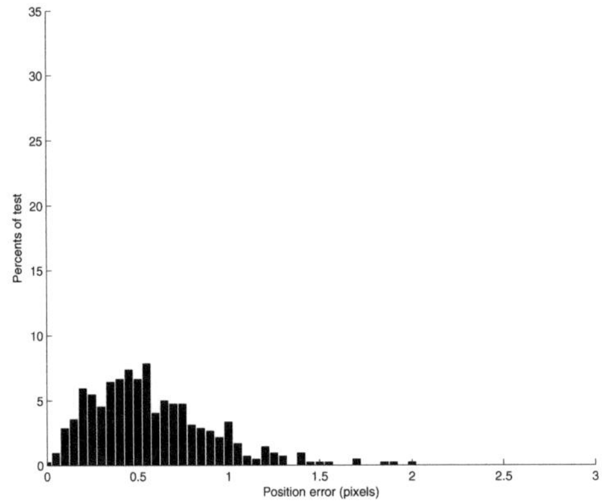

(a) Step=1 gradient based

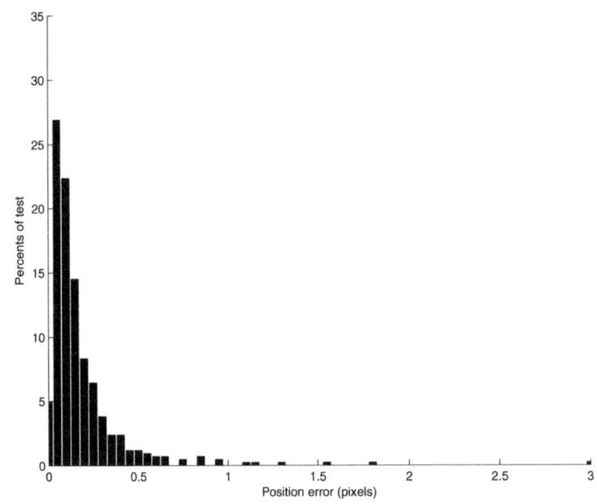

(b) Step=2 non–gradient based

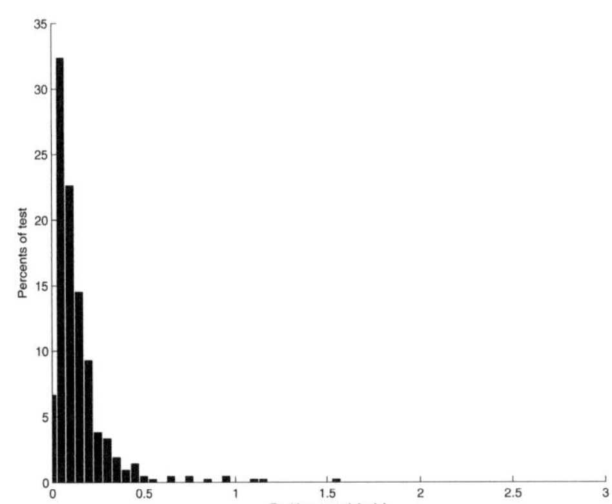

(c) Minimal value after 20 steps (10 iteration of gradient and non–gradient interleaved algorithms)

Fig. 16. Position error

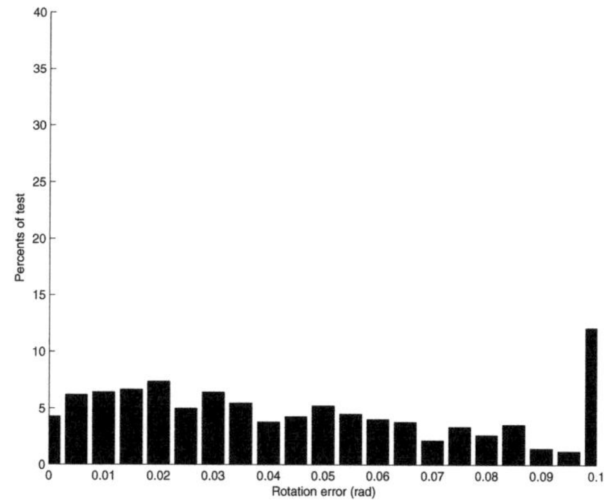

(a) Step=1 gradient based

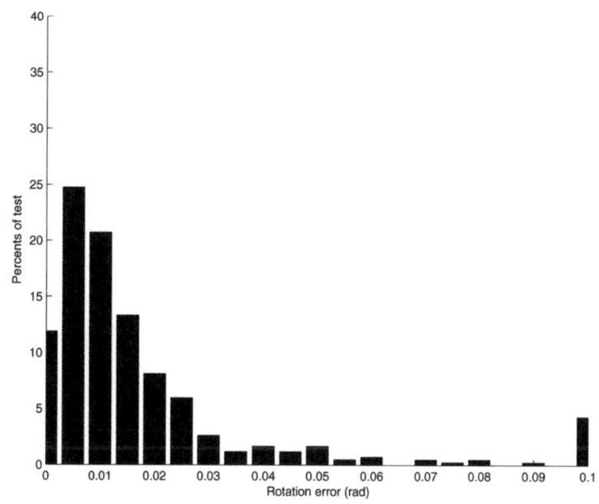

(b) Step=2 non–gradient based

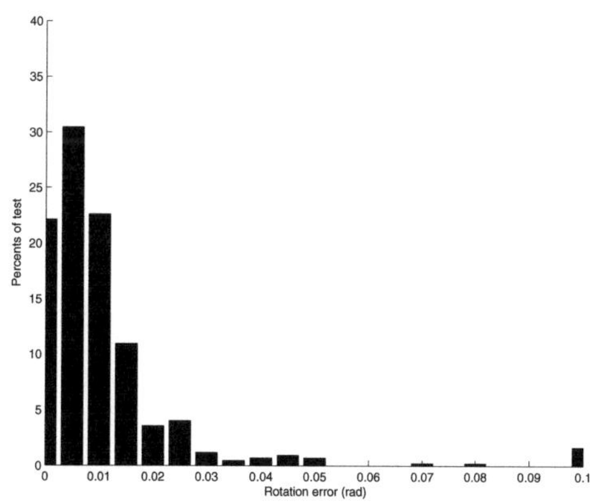

(c) Minimal value after 20 steps (10 iteration of gradient and non–gradient interleaved algorithms)

Fig. 17. Rotation error (z–axis)

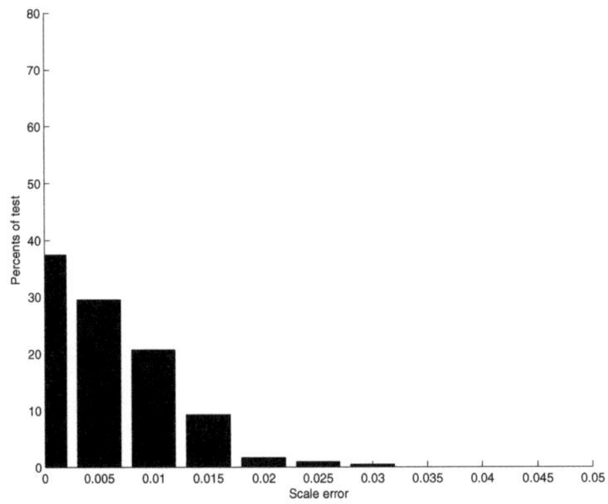

(a) Step=1 gradient based

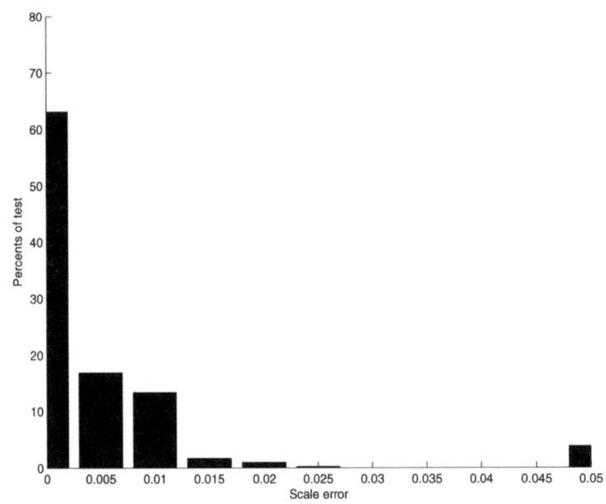

(b) Step=2 non–gradient based

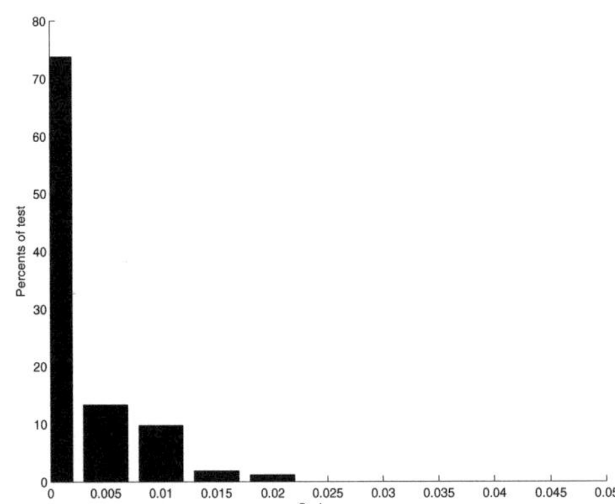

(c) Minimal value after 20 steps (10 iteration of gradient and non–gradient interleaved algorithms)

Fig. 18. Scale (distance) error

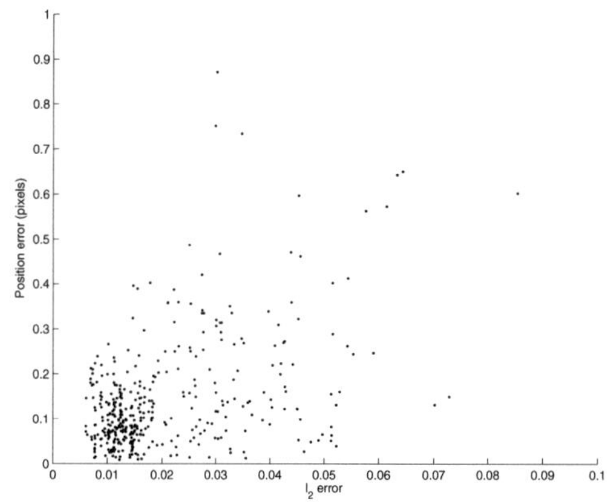

(a) Correlation between image l_2 and position errors

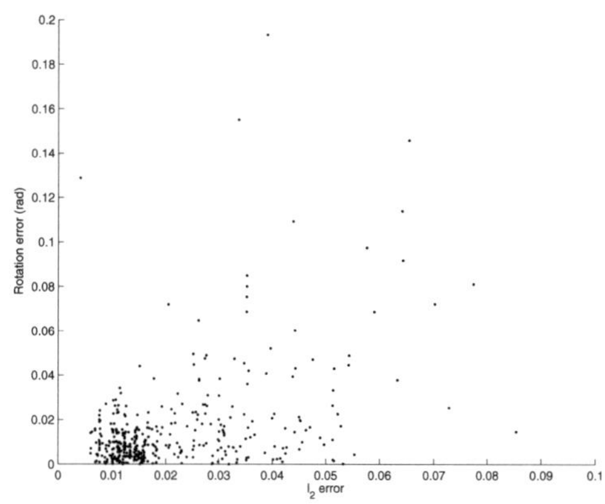

(b) Correlation between image l_2 and rotation errors

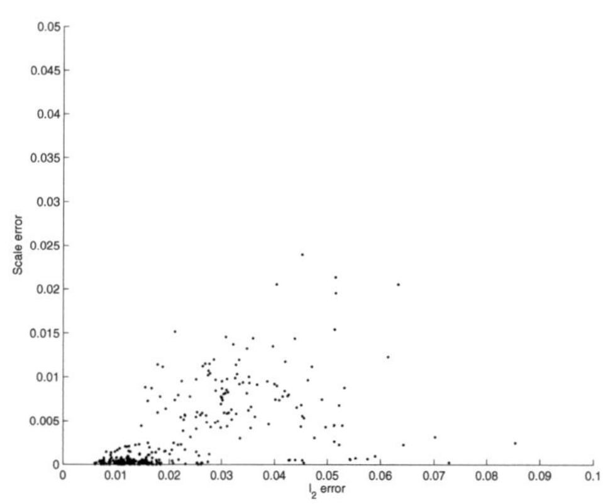

(c) Correlation between image l_2 and scale errors

Fig. 19. Correlation between image l_2 and position, rotation, scale errors

Come discussion is necessary, because correlation coefficients are quite low. there is not direct relation between both errors, like $R = 1/4$, but correlation is high. Most cases create concentration cloud around expected minimal values of both errors. It is well visible for position errors, and if very small l_2 error is measured it is expected that position error is very small also. It looks that position error gives quite large number of pixels used during estimation and the number of pixels influence on the optimization results. The number of pixels for rotation influenced by the rotation probably is lower. This hypothesis should be considered in further works. Improvement of correlation gives abilities of error estimation. This is very important for the tracking algorithms (e.g. Kalman filter) and validation of the measurements. The scale is quite specific, because difference between different scales is defined by the marker's ring. Applications of larger chessboard marker should give better results, but the large markers are not feasible to use.

8. Conclusion

Non–rigid robots are important design for the future robots and different vision based techniques should be applied for the state estimation. Considered technique, based on the larger marker, is promising for state estimation measurements. Estimation of all parameters is possible but the position, rotation, and scale are considered only. The low values of l_2 error corresponds to the low values of the position, rotation and scale errors, and it is a useful estimator of the fitness, but not ideal. The most interesting result is the search scheme, based on the subpixel testing (0.1 pixel accuracy), gradient search and non–gradient search. The next repetition of gradient and non–gradient algorithm does not reduce error so much. Estimation of the parameters (meta level optimization) of non–gradient algorithm is interesting. The 1000 steps are used and reduction of the number of steps is important for the real–time processing. Validation of the proposed algorithm is important for the further optimization and in parallel processing. At this moment, processing time is quite long using Matlab. Optimization of the algorithm and code is necessary together. The visual servoing applications need fast, low latency and computation cost effective solutions. Application of the GPGPU or FPGA are promising computation devices for considered algorithm.

9. Acknowledgments

This work is supported by the UE EFRR ZPORR project Z/2.32/I/1.3.1/267/05 "Szczecin University of Technology – Research and Education Center of Modern Multimedia Technologies" (Poland).

10. References

Aghajan, H. & Cavallaro, A. (2009). *Multi–Camera Networks. Principles and Applications*, Academic Press, ISBN 9780123746337.

Agin, G.J. (1979). *Real Time Control of a Robot with a Mobile Camera* Technical Note 179, SRI International.

Back, T., Fogel D.B., Michalewicz Z. (2000). *Evolutionary Computation 1. Basic Algorithms and Operators*, Institute of Physics Publishing, ISBN 0750306645.

Back, T., Fogel D.B., Michalewicz Z. (2000). *Evolutionary Computation 2. Advanced Algorithms and Operators*, Institute of Physics Publishing, ISBN 0750306653.

Bar–Cohen, Y. (Ed.) (2004). *Electroactive Polymer (EAP) Actuators as Artificial Mulscles. Reality, Potential, and Challenges*, SPIE Press, ISBN 0819452971.

Besenhard, J.O., Gamsjäger, H., Stelzer, F., Sitte, W. (2001). *Electroactive Materials*, Springer–Verlag KG, ISBN 978-3-211-83655-2.

Capri, F., & Smela, E. (Eds.) (2009). *Biomedical Applications of Electroactive Polymer Actuators*, John Wiley & Sons, ISBN 978-0-470-77305-5.

Chaumette, F. (2008). Potential problems of stability and convergence in image–based and position–based visual servoing, In: *The confluence of vision and control, volume 237 of Lecture Notes in Control and Information Sciences*, Kriegman, D., Hager, G., Morse, S., (Eds.), 66–78, Springer–Verlag, ISBN 1852330252, New York.

Chaumette, F. & Hutchinson, S. (2008). Visual Servoing and Visual Tracking, In: *Handbook of Robotics*, Siciliano, B. & Khatib, O., (Eds.), 563–584, Springer, ISBN 978-3-540-23957-4.

Chanda, M. & Roy, S.K. (2009). *Industrial Polymers, Specialty Polymers, and Their Applications*, CRC Press, ISBN 9781420080582.

Conrad, J.M., & Mills, J.W. (1997). *Stiquito(TM): Advanced Experiments with a Simple and Inexpensive Robot*, IEEE Computer Society Press, ISBN 0818674083.

Corke, P. & Hutchinson, S.A. (2001). A new partitioned approach to image–based visual servo control. *IEEE Transactions on Robotics and Automation*, Vol. 17, No. 1, Aug – 2001, 507–515, ISSN 1042-296X.

Daerden, F. (1999). *Conception and realization of pleated pneumatic artificial muscles and their use as compliant actuation elements* PhD Dissertation, Vrije Universiteit Brussel, http://lucy.vub.ac.be/publications/Daerden_PhD.pdf.

Daerden, F. & Lefeber, D. (2002). Pneumatic artificial muscles: actuators for robotics and automation. *European Journal of Mechanical and Environmental Engineering*, Vol. 47, No. 1, 2002, 10–21, ISSN 1371-6980, http://lucy.vub.ac.be/publications/Daerden_Lefeber_EJMEE.pdf.

Daniilidis, K. & Eklundh, J.–O. (2008). 3–D Vision and Recognition, In: *Handbook of Robotics*, Siciliano, B. & Khatib, O., (Eds.), 543–562, Springer, ISBN 978-3-540-23957-4.

Fishman, G.S. (2000). *Monte–Carlo. Concepts, Algorithms, and Applications*, Springer, ISBN 038794527X.

Fung, R.–F. & Chen, K.–Y. (2010). Vision–Based Control of the Mechatronic System, In: *Visual Servoing*, Fung, R.–F., (Ed.), 95–120, Intech, ISBN 978-953-307-095-7.

Hartley, R. & Zisserman, A. (2003). *Multiple View Geometry in Computer Vision*, Cambridge University Press, ISBN 0521540518.

Heyden, A. and & Pollefeys, M. (2004). Multiple View Geometry, In: *Emerging Topics in Computer Vision*, Medioni G., & Kang, S.B, (Eds.), 45–108, Prentice Hall, ISBN 9780131013667.

Hu, J. (2007). *Shape memory polymers and textiles*, CRC Press, ISBN 1845690478.

Kim, K.J. & Tadokoro, S. (Eds.) (2007). *Electroactive Polymers for Robotic Applications. Artificial Muscles and Sensors*, Springer, ISBN 184628371X.

Lei, B.J., Hendriks, E.A., Katsaggelos, A.K. (2005). Camera Calibration for 3D Reconstruction and View Transformation, In: *3D Modeling and Animation: Synthesis and Analysis Techniques for the Human Body*, Sarris, N. & Strintzis, M.G., (Eds.), 70–129, IRM Press, ISBN 1591402999.

Malis, E., Chaumette, F., Boudet, S. (1999). 2.5 D visual servoing. *IEEE Transactions on Robotics and Automation*, Vol. 15, No. 2, 1999, 238–250, ISSN 1042-296X.

Marchand, E., Spindler, F., Chaumette, F. (2005). 3–D Vision and Recognition, In: *Handbook of Robotics*, Siciliano, B. & Khatib, O., (Eds.), 543–562, Springer, ISBN 978-3-540-23957-4.

Mazurek, P. (2010). Mobile system for estimation of the internal parameters of distributed cameras. *Measurement Automation and Monitoring* Vol.56, No.11, 1356–1358, ISSN 0032-4110.

Mazurek, P. (2009). Estimation of state–space spatial component for cuboid Track–Before–Detect motion capture systems. *Lecture Notes in Computer Science*

Vol. 5337 (Computer Vision and Graphics International Conference ICCVG 2008), Springer Verlag, 451–460, ISBN 978-3-642-02344-6.

Mazurek, P. (2007). Estimation Track–Before–Detect motion capture systems state space spatial component. *Lecture Notes in Computer Science* Vol. 4673 (Computer Analysis of Images and Patterns), Springer Verlag, 149-156, ISBN 978-3-540-74271-5.

Michalewicz, A. (2009). *Genetic Algorithms + Data Structures = Evolution Programs*, Springer, ISBN 3540606769.

Otake, M. (2010). *Electroactive Polymer Gel Robots, Modelling and Control of Artificial Muscles*, Springer, ISBN 3540239553.

Sanderson, A.C. & Weiss, L.E. (2008). Adaptive visual servo control of robots, In: *Robot Vision*, Pugh A., (Ed.), 107–116, IFS, ISBN 0903608324.

Spears, W.M. (2000). *Evolutionary Algorithms. The Role of Mutation and Recombination*, Springer, ISBN 3540669507.

Verrelst, B. (2005). *A dynamic walking biped actuated by pleated pneumatic artificial muscles: Basic concepts and control issues* PhD Dissertation, Vrije Universiteit Brussel, http://lucy.vub.ac.be/publications/PhD_Verrelst.pdf.

Wallace, G.G., Spinks, G.M., Kane–Maguire, L.A.P., Teasdale, P.R. (2009). *Conductive Electroactive Polymers. Intelligent Polymer Systems*, CRC Press, ISBN 1420067095.

14

Brushless Permanent Magnet Servomotors

Metin Aydin
Kocaeli University, Department of Mechatronics Engineering, Kocaeli Turkey

1. Introduction

Electrical motors drive a variety of loads in today's world. Almost every industrial process relies on some kind of electrical motors and generators. There exist billions electric motors used in different applications all over the world. Majority of them are small fractional HP motors use in household appliances. However, they used about 5% of the electricity used by the motors. Three phase motors are used in heavier applications and consume substantial amount of electricity. These electric motors operate long hours and consume more than half of the electricity used by motors.

The oldest type of electric motor, wound field DC motor, was the most popular motor for years and easiest for speed control. Although they are replaced by adjustable AC drives in many applications, they are still used in some low power and cost effective applications. The main reason why DC drives faded away over the last decade is that they require converters and maintenance, not to mention their lower torque densities compared to AC motors. Induction motors are also one of the most widely used motors in AC drive applications. They are reliable and don't require maintenance due to the absence of brushes and slip rings. The availability of single phase power is another big plus for these motors. The fact that the rotor windings are present makes the induction motors less efficient and creates cooling problems of the rotor. One crucial drawback of the induction motors is the parameter variation due to the heat caused by the rotor winding.

Variable reluctance motors are also frequently used in the industry and robotics. It's simple and robust stator and rotor structures reduce the cost dramatically compared to other types of motors. The converter requirement is also not very severe. A simple half bridge converter can easily be used to drive the motor. On the other hand, variation of reluctance does also create significant cogging, vibration and audible noise.

As for the synchronous motors, they have benefits and drawbacks of both DC and induction motors. The synchronous motors with field winding can be more efficient than a DC or induction motors and are used in relatively large loads such as generating electricity in power plants. If the rotor winding in synchronous motors is replaced by permanent magnets, another variation of synchronous motors is obtained. These motors are called permanent magnet motors which can be supplied by sinusoidal or trapezoidal currents. These motors have three major types based on their magnet structures as displayed in Fig. 1.

The lack of slip rings and rotor windings as well as high power density, high efficiency and small size make these motors very attractive in the industrial and servo applications. In

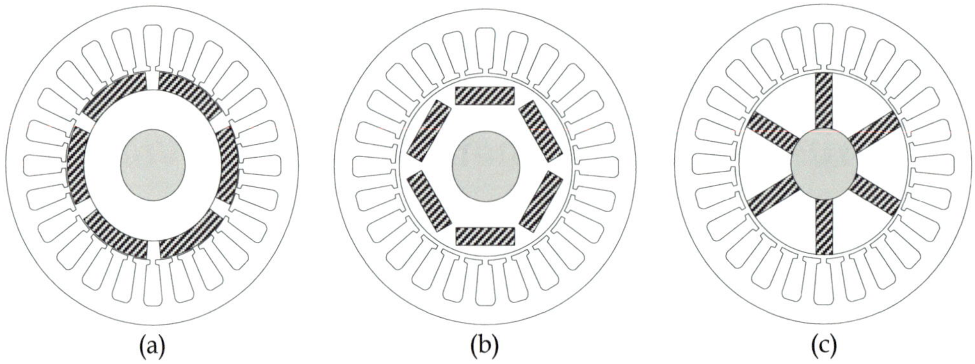

Fig. 1. Surface mounted PM (a), buried PM (b) and spoke type PM (c) motor types

addition, PM servomotors have better torque-speed characteristics and high dynamic response than other motors. Their long operating lives, noise-free operations and high speed ranges are some of the advantages of brushless servomotors.

2. Classification of electric motors

2.1 General motor classification

There are several ways of classifying electric motors by their electrical supply, by rotor structures and stator types. One of the common ways is to categorize them as AC and DC motors as shown in Fig. 2. AC motors use alternating current or voltage as source while DC motors use DC voltage source to supply the windings. DC motors are classified by their field connections such as series, parallel or compound field excitation. AC motors, on the other hand, has two major types: One type is induction motors where rotor magnetic field is generated by electromagnetic induction principles and the other is synchronous motors where the magnetic field is generated by either field winding excitation or permanent magnets. Induction motors could be single or poly-phase and have squirrel-cage or wound rotor. Synchronous motors could have numerous options depending on the rotor type and excitation (Hendershot & Miller, 1995).

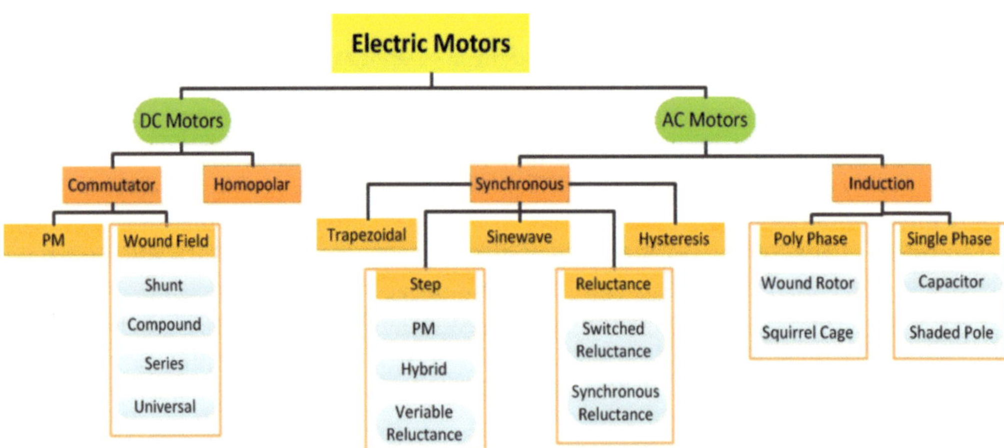

Fig. 2. Fundamental motor classification

Electric motors are also classified by their slots. They are called slotted motors if they do have slots and called non-slotted or slotless motors if they do not have any slot structures. Furthermore, one major classification method is identified by the main flux direction. If the motor has a main flux component which is radial to the shaft, they are called radial flux motors and if the flux component is axial to the motor shaft, then the motors are called axial flux motors where they find various applications because of their structural flexibility.

2.2 Permanent magnet servomotors

There exist various permanent magnet (PM) servomotors in the literature. They can be classified into two main categories, which are surface mounted PM motors where magnets are glued on the rotor surface and buried PM motors where magnets are buried into the rotor.
The use of surface mounted PM motors increases the amount of PM material per pole used in the motor. Using more magnet material usually increases the torque production of the motor while it also increases the motor volume and thus the cost. Buried PM motor and interior PM motor use the flux concentration principles where the magnet flux is concentrated in the rotor core before it gets into the airgap. These motors usually have considerable reluctance torque which arises from the fact that the use of flux concentration in the iron core introduces a position dependent inductance and hence reluctance torque that can be beneficial in certain cases.
PM motors are also classified based on the flux density distribution and the shape of the current excitation. They are listed into two categories, one of which is PM synchronous motors (PMSM) and the other is PM brushless motors (BLDC). PMSM, also called permanent magnet AC (PMAC) motors, has sinusoidal flux density, current and back EMF variation while the BLDC has rectangular shaped flux density, current variation and back EMF. Classification of these two motor types is explained in Table 1.

	PMSM	BLDC
Phase current excitation	Sinusoidal	Trapezoidal
Flux density	Sinusoidal	Square
Phase back EMF	Sinusoidal	Trapezoidal
Power and Torque	Constant	Constant

Table 1. Classification of permanent magnet motors based on their excitation and back EMF waveforms

	Surface PM motor	Buried/Interior PM motor
Convenience	BLDC	PMSM
Flux distribution	Square or Sinusodial	Usually Sinusoidal
Complexity of rotor	Simple	Complex
Speed limit	~1.2 x ω_R	~3 x ω_R or higher
High speed capability	Difficult	Possible
Control	Relatively easy	More complex

Table 2. Basic comparison of surface magnet and buried magnet motors

Fig. 3. Typical servomotor (Courtesy of FEMSAN Motor Co.)

Each PM motor type explained has some advantages over another. For instance, surface magnet motor has very simple rotor structure with fairly small speed limits. Buried or interior PM motors have wide speed ranges but their rotor is more complex than both surface magnet and inset PM rotors. In addition, buried or interior PM motors can go up to very high speeds unlike surface magnet motors although their control is more complex than surface magnet type motors. This comparison is also tabulated in Table 2.

2.3 Permanent magnet servomotor structure

A conventional surface mounted PM servomotor structure is illustrated in Fig. 1 (a). The motor has a stator and a PM rotor. The stator structure is slotted and formed by the laminated magnetic steel. A close picture of a laminated stator is shown in Fig. 4. Polyphase windings are placed into the stator slots although a slotless versions of servomotors are also available. The rotor structure is formed by the permanent magnets mounted on the rotor surface, rotor core and shaft. The rotor core is usually laminated. Fig. 5 shows both the stator and the rotor of a typical permanent magnet servomotor with high energy NdFeB magnets.

Fig. 4. Stator stack showing the servomotor laminations

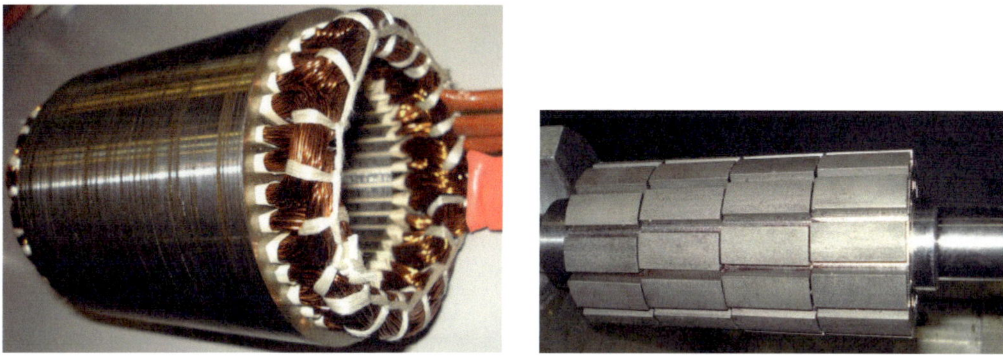

Fig. 5. Stator stack showing the motor laminations

2.4 PM servomotor torque-speed and back-EMF characteristics

Fig. 6 shows typical torque-speed characteristics of a brushless PM servomotor. There are two main torque parameters to describe a PM servomotor: Rated torque (T_R) and maximum torque (T_{max}). In addition, there are two major speed points: Rated speed and maximum speed. The region up to rated speed is called constant torque region and the region between the max speed (ω_{max}) and rated speed (ω_R) is called constant power region. During constant torque region, the motor can be loaded up to rated torque usually without any thermal problem. On the other hand, during constant power region, the motor torque starts to drop but the power stays almost constant. Another important characteristic of a PM motor is maximum load point which shows the overload capability of the motor. During this period, the motor can deliver higher torque for a short time to handle cases such as motor overload, start-up etc.

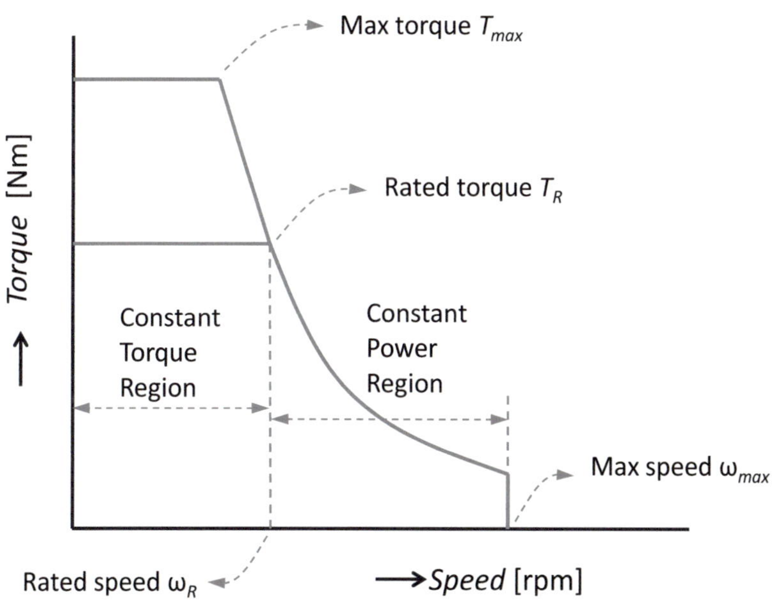

Fig. 6. Torque-speed characteristics of a PM servomotor

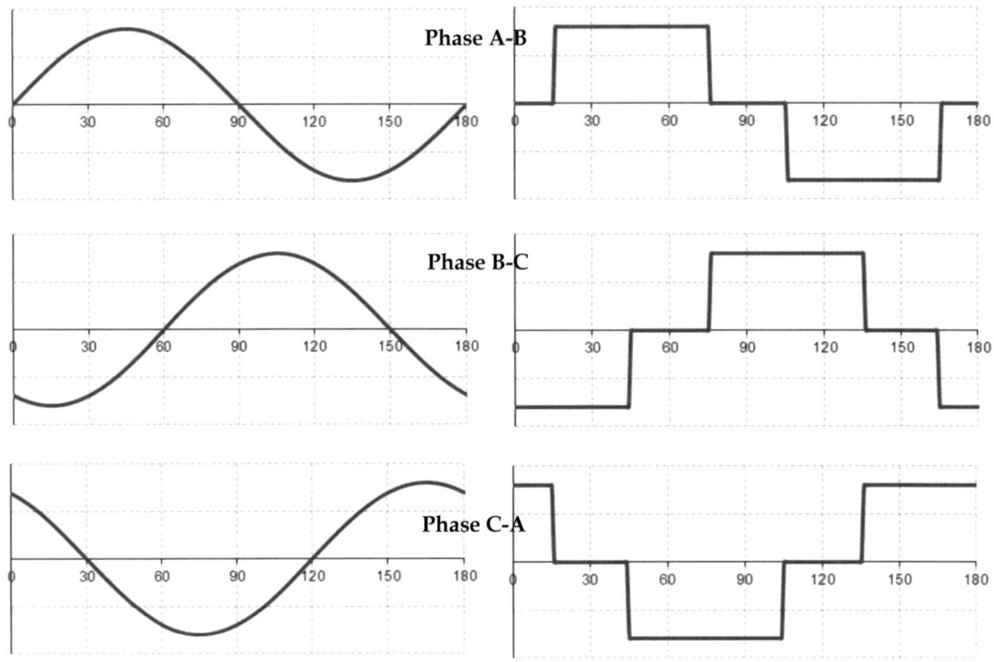

(a) (b)

Fig. 7. Trapeziodal (a) and sinusoidal back-EMF (b) waveforms of a PM servomotor

There are two types of PM servomotor alternatives: Sinusoidal and trapezoidal motors. This is made on the basis of back-EMF waveforms. Trapezoidal servomotors have a back-EMF in trapezoidal manner and sinusoidal servomotors have a sinusoidal back-EMF as illustrated in Fig. 7. In addition to back-EMF, the supply current is trapezoidal and sinusoidal in each individual type of motors.

3. Magnetic materials

3.1 Magnetic steel

There exist various electric steel materials used in servomotors. Material type and grade depends mainly on the application and cost. High quality materials with high saturation and low loss levels are used in high performance and high speed applications while thick and high loss materials are used in low speed and cost effective applications. Non-oriented electrical steels are usually used in electric motor applications. Low magnetic loss and high permeability characteristics are valuable for applications where energy efficient, low loss, low noise and small size are important. One of the most frequently used magnetic steel lamination material is M270-35A (similar to M19 in the US). This material or similar grade is used in most PM servomotor applications. If high saturation levels and low losses at high speeds are required, materials such as Vacoflux50 would be a good option. The BH curve of these materials in addition to materials with high loss and thin high saturation level are all displayed in Fig. 8. Moreover, Table 3 shows the electrical and mechanical properties of various non-oriented electrical steel materials used in different motor applications.

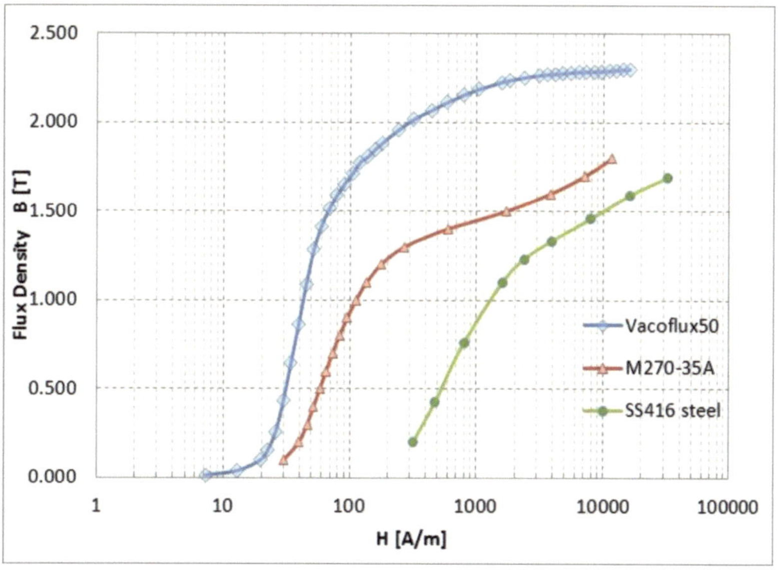

Fig. 8. Examples of steel materials with magnetic and structural properties

Grade EN 10106	Thickness	Maximum specific total loss at 50 Hz		Minimum magnetic polarization at 50 Hz		
		$\hat{J}$ = 1.5 T	1.0 T**	$\hat{H}$ = 2500	5000	10000 A/m
	mm	W/kg	W/kg	T	T	T
M235-35A	0.35	2.35	0.95	1.49	1.60	1.70
M250-35A	0.35	2.50	1.00	1.49	1.60	1.70
M270-35A	0.35	2.70	1.10	1.49	1.60	1.70
M300-35A	0.35	3.00	1.20	1.49	1.60	1.70
M330-35A	0.35	3.30	1.30	1.49	1.60	1.70
M700-35A*	0.35	7.00	3.00	1.60	1.69	1.77
M250-50A	0.50	2.50	1.05	1.49	1.60	1.70
M270-50A	0.50	2.70	1.10	1.49	1.60	1.70
M290-50A	0.50	2.90	1.15	1.49	1.60	1.70
M310-50A	0.50	3.10	1.25	1.49	1.60	1.70
M330-50A	0.50	3.30	1.35	1.49	1.60	1.70
M350-50A	0.50	3.50	1.50	1.50	1.60	1.70
M400-50A	0.50	4.00	1.70	1.53	1.63	1.73
M470-50A	0.50	4.70	2.00	1.54	1.64	1.74
M530-50A	0.50	5.30	2.30	1.56	1.65	1.75
M600-50A	0.50	6.00	2.60	1.57	1.66	1.76
M700-50A	0.50	7.00	3.00	1.60	1.69	1.77
M800-50A	0.50	8.00	3.60	1.60	1.70	1.78
M940-50A	0.50	9.40	4.20	1.62	1.72	1.81
M310-65A	0.65	3.10	1.25	1.49	1.60	1.70
M330-65A	0.65	3.30	1.35	1.49	1.60	1.70
M350-65A	0.65	3.50	1.50	1.49	1.60	1.70
M400-65A	0.65	4.00	1.70	1.52	1.62	1.72
M470-65A	0.65	4.70	2.00	1.53	1.63	1.73
M530-65A	0.65	5.30	2.30	1.54	1.64	1.74
M600-65A	0.65	6.00	2.60	1.56	1.66	1.76
M700-65A	0.65	7.00	3.00	1.57	1.67	1.76
M800-65A	0.65	8.00	3.60	1.60	1.70	1.78
M1000-65A	0.65	10.00	4.40	1.61	1.71	1.80

Grade EN 10106	Conventional density	Resistivity	Yield strength	Tensile strength	Young's Modulus (E) RD	Young's Modulus (E) TD	Hardness HV5 (VPN)
	kg/dm³	μΩcm	N/mm²	N/mm²	N/mm²	N/mm²	-
M235-35A	7.60	59	460	580	185 000	200 000	220
M250-35A	7.60	55	455	575	185 000	200 000	215
M270-35A	7.65	52	450	565	185 000	200 000	215
M300-35A	7.65	50	370	490	185 000	200 000	185
M330-35A	7.65	44	300	430	200 000	220 000	150
M700-35A*	7.80	30	290	405	210 000	220 000	125
M250-50A	7.60	59	475	590	175 000	190 000	220
M270-50A	7.60	55	470	585	175 000	190 000	220
M290-50A	7.60	55	465	580	185 000	200 000	220
M310-50A	7.65	52	385	500	185 000	200 000	190
M330-50A	7.65	50	375	495	185 000	200 000	185
M350-50A	7.65	44	305	450	200 000	210 000	165
M400-50A	7.70	42	305	445	200 000	210 000	160
M470-50A	7.70	39	300	435	200 000	210 000	155
M530-50A	7.70	36	295	430	200 000	210 000	150
M600-50A	7.75	30	285	405	210 000	220 000	125
M700-50A	7.80	25	285	405	210 000	220 000	125
M800-50A	7.80	23	300	415	210 000	220 000	130
M940-50A	7.85	18	300	415	210 000	220 000	130
M310-65A	7.60	59	465	590	175 000	190 000	220
M330-65A	7.60	55	460	585	185 000	205 000	220
M350-65A	7.60	52	375	490	185 000	205 000	185
M400-65A	7.65	44	310	450	185 000	205 000	165
M470-65A	7.65	42	305	445	185 000	205 000	160
M530-65A	7.70	39	300	425	190 000	210 000	145
M600-65A	7.75	36	300	420	190 000	210 000	140
M700-65A	7.75	30	290	395	210 000	220 000	125
M800-65A	7.80	25	300	405	210 000	220 000	130
M1000-65A	7.80	18	295	400	210 000	220 000	125

Table 3. Non-oriented electric steel material properties (Source: Cogent)

3.2 Permanent magnets

Permanent magnet materials have been used in electric motors for decades. One important property of permanent magnets is the maximum energy product (*MEP*) which is the multiplication of residual flux density (B_r) and coercive force (H_r). In other words, *MEP* represents the maximum energy available per unit volume (kJ/m³). *MEP* is also an indication of magnet force. Furthermore, the larger the *MEP*, the smaller the magnet material needed for the same force. Permeability is another important property of the magnets. It is the slope of the demagnetization curve in the linear region. Small permeability means high flux levels before the magnet is irreversibly demagnetized.

Alnico magnets which are Aluminum, nickel, iron and later addition of cobalt based materials was one of the important discoveries in permanent magnet technology and is still widely used today. These magnets can be magnetized in any direction by simply heating the magnet and cooling them in a magnetic field to give a preferred magnetic direction. Traditionally, Alnico magnets were largely used in PM motors. One advantage of Alnico magnets is that they have a high residual flux density (B_r). They have excellent temperature stability and strong corrosion resistance level. Their working temperatures can go up to 500 degrees. However, they can be demagnetized very easily. In addition, the maximum energy product of these magnets is not very high.

Ferrite magnets, also called ceramic magnets, are one of the cheapest magnets manufactured in industry. They have very high intrinsic coercive force (H_{ci}) and therefore, they are very difficult to demagnetize. They can easily be magnetized in a variety of formats. The raw material is so abundant that it is found in numerous applications. This kind of magnet material has a good resistance to corrosion and can operate at high temperatures up to 300 degrees. These materials are used even today for applications where space and cost are not important requirements.

Rare-earth magnets are strong permanent magnets made from the alloys elements such as Neodymium and Samarium. Discovery of these strong magnets have changed the future of permanent magnet motor technology as well as servomotors and the magnetic field can be increased to 1.5T levels. There are two types of rare-earth magnets available: Neodymium magnets and Samarium cobalt magnets.

The first generation rare earth magnets use Samarium and Cobalt (SmCo). One of the biggest advantages of such magnets is that they provide very high MEP compared to Alnicos and Ferrites. This big improvement in high MEP is made possible by the high coercive force. Nonetheless, they are very brittle and both the raw material cost and the production cost are quite high compared to other types of magnets. The revolution of rare earth magnets accelerated with the discovery of Neodymium Iron-Boron (NdFeB) magnets with even higher MEP in 1982. NdFeB magnets are produced by pressing powders in a magnetic field and their energy products can go up to 420 kJ/m^3. This material is much stronger than SmCo and the cost is much lower simply because they are composed of mostly iron which is much cheaper than cobalt. However, they have to be protected against corrosion and their working temperature is also lower compared to SmCo magnets.

A brief comparison of different magnets used in PM motors is illustrated in Table 4. The rare earth magnets are the most common magnet materials used in PM servomotors and the table clearly shows significant benefits of such magnets. NdFeB magnets have higher flux density levels up to 1.5T and higher MEPs but their working temperature is lower (up to 200 °C).

Materials	B_r [T]	Hc [kA/m]	BH_{max} [kJ/m^3]	T_C [°C]	$T_{w\text{-}max}$ [°C]
Alnico	1.2	10	6	500	500
Ferrite	0.43	10	5	300	300
SmCo	Up to 1.1	Up to 820	Up to 240	Up to 820	Up to 350
NdFeB	Up to 1.5	Up to 1033	Up to 422	Up to 380	Up to 200

Table 4. Typical permanent magnet material magnetic properties

NdFeB magnets are more common rare earth magnets than SmCo, cheaper but more brittle. SmCo magnets are widely used in applications in which higher operating temperature and higher corrosion and oxidation resistance are crucial. A basic comparison of the four major types of permanent magnet materials used in motors today is illustrated in Fig. 9.

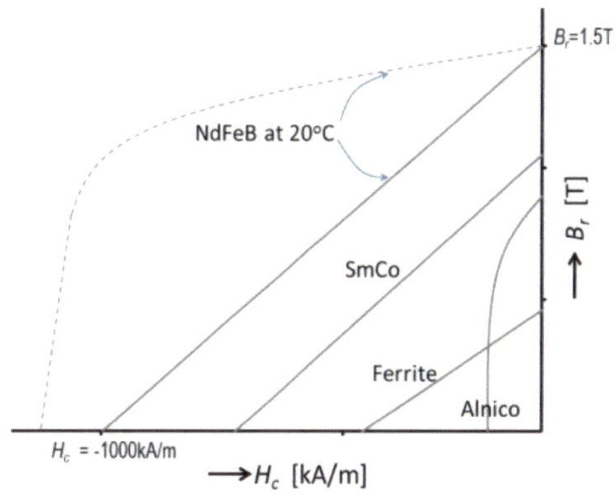

Fig. 9. Flux density versus magnetizing field for the important magnets classes

4. Basic permanent magnet motor design process

Design procedure for any PM servomotor is shown in Fig. 10. This process comprises three main steps: Electromagnetic, structural and thermal designs. Electromagnetic design starts with magnetic circuit modeling and parameter optimization with a given set of design specifications. A series of optimizations such as pole number, loading, current density, dimensional limits etc. have to be performed to find the optimum parameters of the motor before proceeding further. When a design is obtained that meets the technical spec, a quick motor simulation and the influence of parameter variation must be carried out using simulation software such as SPEED (PC-BDC Manual, 2002). A detailed electromagnetic finite element analysis (FEA) either in 2D or 3D is the next step to verify that the design meets the specified torque-speed characteristics and performance. After an electromagnetic design is finalized, structural and thermal analyses (MotorCAD Manual 2004) have to be completed. It should be pointed out that structural analysis is not a necessity at low speed servomotor designs. If the motor does not meet the structural or thermal tests, then the electromagnetic design study should be repeated for a better design. A motor design has to be finalized after a design passes all of the main steps (Aydin et al. 2006).

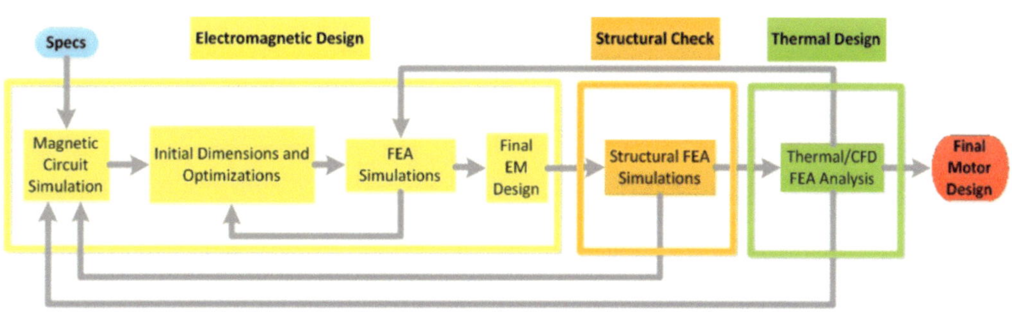

Fig. 10. PM servomotor design process

5. Dynamic model of PM servomotors

Following assumptions are made for the analysis of PM servomotors: The inverter is ideal with no losses; no DC voltage ripple exists in the DC link; the supply current is sinusoidal and no saturation is considered; eddy current and hysteresis loses are negligible; and all motor parameters are constant. Based on these assumptions, permanent magnet servomotor dynamic equations in the synchronous rotating reference frame are written as

$$v_q = r_s i_q + L_q \frac{di_q}{dt} - \omega_e L_d i_d + \omega_e \lambda_f \tag{1}$$

$$v_d = r_s i_d + L_d \frac{di_d}{dt} - \omega_e L_q i_q \tag{2}$$

$$T_m = \frac{3}{2}\frac{P}{2}\left[\lambda_f i_q + \left(L_d - L_q\right) i_d i_q \right] \tag{3}$$

where v_d and v_q are d and q axis voltages, i_d and i_q are d and q-axis currents, r_s is stator resistance, L_d and L_q are d-q axis inductances, ω_e is synchronous speed, λ_f is magnet flux linkage, P is pole number and T_m is the electromagnetic torque of the motor. During constant flux operation, i_d becomes zero and the torque equation becomes

$$T_m = \frac{3}{2}\frac{P}{2}\lambda_f i_q = K_T i_q \tag{4}$$

where K_T is the torque constant of the motor. This equation becomes similar to standard DC motor and therefore provides ease of control. The torque dynamic equation is

$$T_m = T_L + B\omega_m + J\frac{d\omega_m}{dt} \tag{5}$$

equivalent circuit of the steady-state operation of the PM servomotors in d-q reference model is shown in Fig. 11. Independent control of both q-axis and d-axis components of the currents is possible with the vector controlled PM servomotors. Both voltage controlled and current controlled inverters are possible to drive the motor.

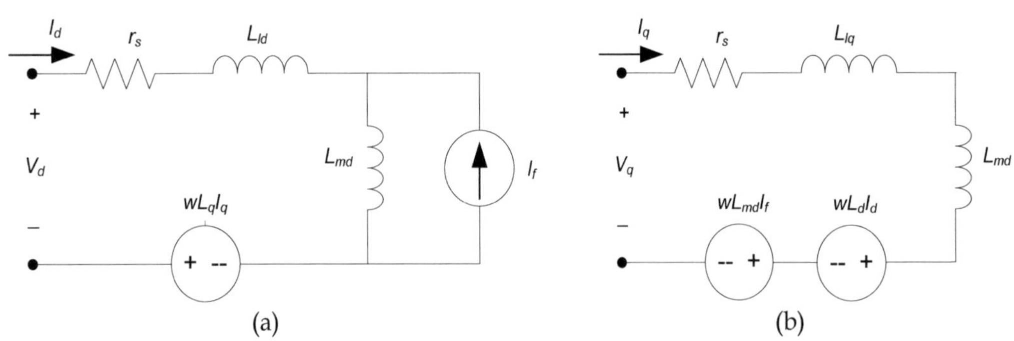

Fig. 11. Equivalent circuit of PM servomotors (a) d-axis equivalent circuit and (b) q-axis equivalent circuit

6. Use of finite element analysis in PM servomotors

The finite element method (FEM) is a numerical method for solving the complex electromagnetic field problems and circuit parameters. It is specifically convenient for problems with non-linear material characteristics where mathematical modeling of the system would be difficult. This method involves dividing the servomotor cross section or volume into smaller areas or volumes. It could be 2D objects in the case of 2D FEM analysis or 3D objects in the case of 3D analysis. The variation of the magnetic potential throughout the motor is expressed by non-linear differential equations in finite element analysis. These differential equations are derived from Maxwell equations and written in terms of vector potential where the important field quantities such as flux, flux direction and flux density can be determined.

The FEM can accurately analyze the magnetic systems which involve permanent magnets of any shape and material. There is no need to calculate the inductances, reluctances and torque values using circuit type analytical methods because these values can simply be extracted from the finite element analysis. Another important advantage of using FEM over analytical approach is the ability to calculate the torque variations or torque components such as cogging torque, ripple torque, pulsating torque and average torque accurately without too much effort.

There are various FEA packages used for motor analysis. FEA packages have 3 main mechanisms which are pre-processor, field solver and post-processor. Model creation, material assignments and boundary condition set-up are all completed in the pre-processor part of the software. Field solver part has 4 main steps to solve the numerical problems. After the pre-process, the software generates the mesh, which is the most important part of getting accurate results. User's experience in generating the mesh has also an important effect on the accuracy of the results. Then, the FEA package computes the magnetic field, performs some analysis such as flux, torque, force and inductance, and checks if the error criteria have been met. If not, it refines the mesh and follows the same steps based on the user's inputs until it reaches the specified error limit. This procedure is shown in Fig. 12. In the post-processor, magnetic field quantities are displayed and some quantities such as force, torque, flux, inductance etc. are all calculated.

7. Torque quality

Permanent magnet servomotors are widely used in many industrial applications for their small size, higher efficiency, noise-free operation, high speed range and better control. This makes quality of their torque an important issue in wide range of applications including servo applications. For example, servomotors used in defense applications, robotics, servo systems, electric vehicles all require smooth torque operation.

One of the most important issues in PM servomotors is the pulsating torque component which is inherent in motor design. If a quality work is not completed during the design stage, this component can lead to mechanical vibrations, acoustic noise, shorter life and drive system problems. In addition, if precautions are not taken, it can lead to serious control issues especially at low speeds. Minimization of the pulsating torque components is of great importance in the design of permanent magnet servomotors.

In general, calculation of torque quality is a demanding task since the torque quality calculation does not only consider the torque density of the motor but also consider the

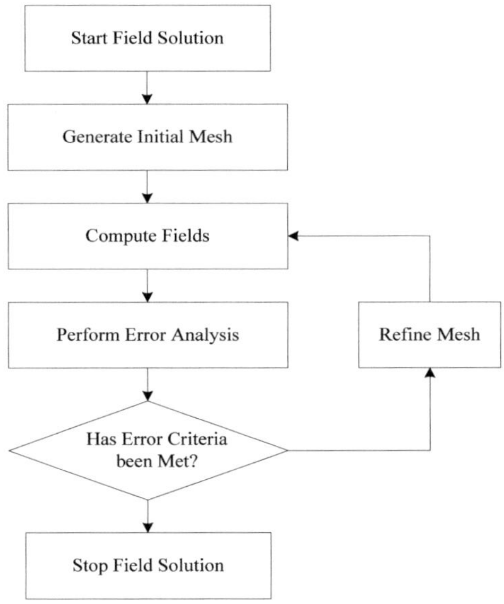

Fig. 12. General procedure for any commercially available FEA software

pulsating torque component. Therefore, a mathematical approach about torque quality should include harmonic analysis of electric drive system rather than a simple sizing of the motor.

Output torque of a PM servomotor has an average torque and pulsating torque components. The pulsating torque consists of cogging torque and ripple torque components. Cogging torque occurs from the magnetic permeance variation of the stator teeth and the slots above the permanent magnets. Presence of cogging torque is a major concern in the design of PM motors simply because it enhance undesirable harmonics to the pulsating torque. Ripple torque, on the other hand, occurs as a result of variations of the field distribution and the stator MMF. At high speed operations, ripple torque is usually filtered out by the inertia of the load or system. However, at low speeds 'torque-ripple' produces noticeable effects on the motor shaft that may not be tolerable in smooth torque and constant speed applications.

Servomotors can also be categorized by the shape of their back EMF waveforms which can take different forms such as sinusoidal and trapezoidal as seen in Fig. 13. Any non-ideal

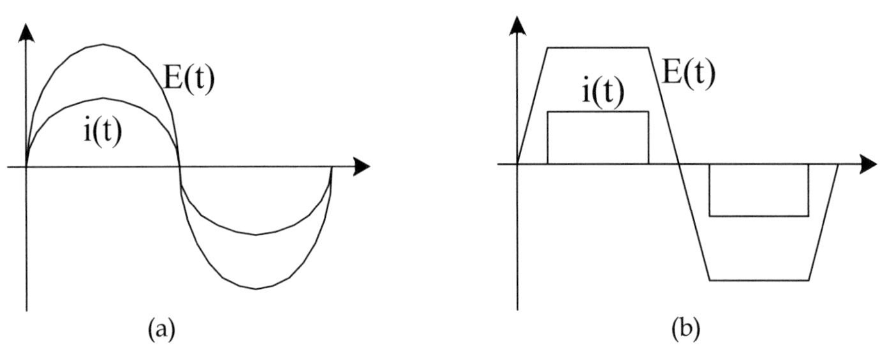

Fig. 13. Current and back EMF waveform options in PM servomotors: (a) sinusoidal back-EMF and current and (b) trapezoidal back-EMF and current

situations such as converter caused disturbed stator current waveform and disturbed back EMF waveform arising from the design cause non-sinusoidal current and airgap flux density waveforms which result in undesired pulsating torque components at the motor output. In other words, if the airgap flux density waveform is disturbed, pulsating torque at the motor shaft becomes inevitable (Jahns & Soong, 1996).

7.1 Electromagnetic torque in PM motors

Definitions of the torque components will be given before getting into the subject any deeper. First, "cogging torque" is defined as the pulsating torque component produced by the variation of the airgap permeance or reluctance of the stator teeth and slots above the magnets as the rotor rotates. In other words, there is no stator excitation involved in cogging torque production of a PM motor. Second, "ripple torque" is the pulsating torque component generated by the stator MMF and rotor MMF. Ripple torque is mainly due to the fluctuations of the field distribution and the stator MMF which depends on the motor structure and the current waveform. This component can take two forms, one of which resulting from the MMF created by the stator windings and the other from MMF created by the rotor magnets. The second form is the torque created by stator MMF and rotor magnetic reluctance variation. In surface mounted PM servomotor, since there exists no rotor reluctance variation, there is no second form of the ripple torque and the ripple torque is mainly created by the first form. The third definition is "pulsating torque" which is defined as the sum of both cogging and ripple torque components (Sebastian et al., 1986 and Ree & Boules, 1989).

In the following analysis, it is assumed that a Y connected three phase unsaturated PM motor used and it has a constant airgap length and symmetrical stator winding. It is also assumed that stator currents contain only odd harmonics and current harmonics of the order of three does not exist. Finally, armature reaction is assumed negligible. For PM motors, at instant t, the instantaneous electromagnetic torque produced by phase A can be written as the interaction of the magnetic field and the phase current circulating in N turns

$$T_a\ (t) = 2pNi_a(t) \int_{-\pi/2mp}^{\pi/2mp} R_g\ L_e\ B(\theta_r,t)\ d\theta_r \tag{6}$$

where R_g is airgap radius of the servomotor, L_e is effective stack length, p is pole pairs and m is the number of phases.

The back-EMF of the motor induced in phase A at the time instant t is given by

$$e_a(t) = 2pN\int_{-\pi/2mp}^{\pi/2mp} R_{mean}\, L_R B(\theta_r,t)\omega_m d\theta_r \tag{7}$$

where ω_m is the rotor angular speed. The back-EMF in phase a can also be written as

$$e_a(t) = \omega_m 2pN\int_{-\pi/2mp}^{\pi/2mp} R_{mean}\, L_R B(\theta_r,t) d\theta_r \tag{8}$$

Substituting (8) into (6), the torque expression becomes

$$T_a(t) = \frac{e_a(t)\cdot i_a(t)}{\omega_m} \tag{9}$$

For the Y-connected three-phase stator winding, the back-EMF in phase A can be written as the summation of odd harmonics including fundamental component:

$$e_a = E_1 \sin \omega t + E_3 \sin 3\omega t + E_5 \sin 5\omega t + E_7 \sin 7\omega t + \ldots \tag{10}$$

and likewise the current in phase A can be written as

$$i_a = I_1 \sin \omega t + I_5 \sin 5\omega t + I_7 \sin 7\omega t + I_{11} \sin 11\omega t + I_{13} \sin 13\omega t + \ldots \tag{11}$$

where E_n is the nth time harmonic peak value of the back EMF, which is produced by n^{th} space harmonic of the airgap magnetic flux density B_{gn} and I_n is the nth time harmonic peak value of current.
The product of back-EMF and current $e_a\, i_a$ is composed of an average component and even-order harmonics for all phases. The total instantaneous torque contributed by each motor phase is proportional to the product of back EMF and phase current. In other words, the total instantaneous torque is the sum of the torques produced by phase a, b, and c and given by,

$$T_m(t) = \frac{1}{\omega_m}\left[e_a(t)\, i_a(t) + e_b(t)\, i_b(t) + e_c(t)\, i_c(t)\right] \tag{12}$$

Since the phase shifts between $e_a\, i_a$ and $e_b\, i_b$ and between $e_a\, i_a$ and $e_c\, i_c$ are $-2\pi/3$ and $2\pi/3$, respectively, the sum ($e_a\, i_a + e_b\, i_c + e_c\, i_c$) will contain an average torque component and harmonics of the order of six. The other harmonics are all eliminated. Thus, the final instantaneous electromagnetic torque equation of a servomotor can be written as

$$T_m(t) = T_0 + \sum_{n=1}^{\infty} T_{6n} \cos n6\omega t \tag{13}$$

where T_0 is the average torque, T_{6n} is harmonic torque components and $n = 1,2,3\ldots.$ In the ideal case, if the back-EMF's and the armature currents are sinusoidal, then the electromagnetic torque is constant and no ripple torque exists as illustrated in Fig. 14. The same quantities are plotted for sinusoidal back EMF and square or trapezoidal stator current waveforms and the presence of the pulsating torque component is observed clearly. The resultant plots including torque pulsations for all cases are shown in Fig. 14.

7.2 Cogging torque

7.2.1 Cogging torque theory

Existence of cogging torque is always a cause of concern in the design of PM servomotors. It in fact demonstrates the quality of a servomotor. This torque component is often desired that the motor produces a smooth torque in a wide speed range. Cogging torque adds unwanted harmonic components to both torque output and the torque-angle curve, which results in torque pulsation. This produces vibration and noise, both of which may be amplified in variable speed drive when the torque frequency coincides with a mechanical resonant frequency of the stator and rotor. In addition, if rotor positioning is required at very low speeds, the elimination of cogging torque component becomes even more crucial and must be eliminated completely during the design stage (Li & Slemon, 1988).

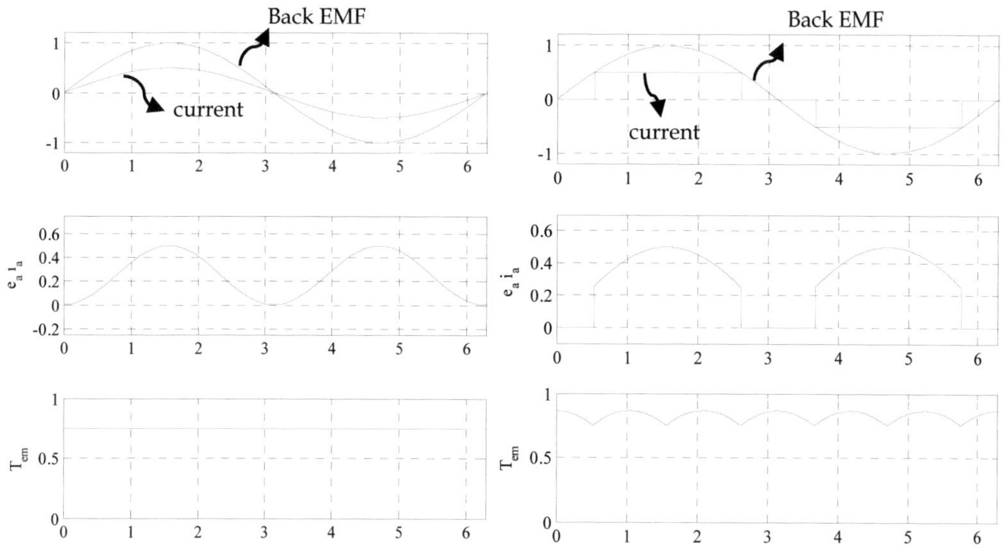

Fig. 14. Torque output for current and back EMF waveforms as a function of electrical cycle

Cogging torque is sensitive to varying rotor position and can be expressed by

$$T_{cog}(\theta_r) = -\frac{1}{2}\phi_g^2 \frac{dR_g}{d\theta_r} \tag{14}$$

where ϕ_g is the airgap flux, R is the reluctance of the airgap and θ_r is the rotor position. Cogging torque increases due to the increased airgap flux as the magnet strength is increased. Nevertheless, the cogging torque results from the non-uniform flux density in the airgap. As the stator teeth become saturated, the flux begins to distribute evenly in the motor airgap and the cogging torque decreases.

In addition, if there is no airgap reluctance variation as in slotless motors, no cogging component occurs. For a slotted stator configuration, the airgap permeance or reluctance is non-uniform because of the shape of the stator, saturation of the lamination material, slot openings and the space between the rotor magnets. This non-uniform reluctance or magnetic flux path causes the airgap flux density to vary with rotor position. This results in cogging torque, and generates vibration.

7.2.2 Minimization of cogging torque component

Cogging torque minimization is a significant concern during the design of brushless PM servomotors, and it is one of the main sources of torque and speed fluctuations especially at low speeds and load with low inertias. A variety of techniques are available for reducing the cogging torque of conventional PM servomotors, such as skewing the slots, shaping or skewing the magnets, displacing or shifting magnets, employing dummy slots or teeth, optimizing the magnet pole-arc, employing a fractional number of slots per pole, and imparting a sinusoidal self-shielding magnetization distribution. A summary of these methods are displayed in Fig. 15 (Bianchi & Bolognani, 2002).

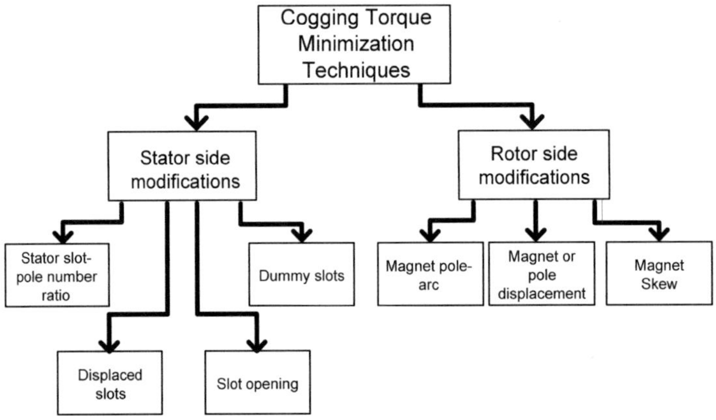

Fig. 15. Summary of cogging torque minimization techniques for PM servomotors

Minimization of cogging torque in PM servomotors can be accomplished by modifications either from stator side or from rotor side. Choosing the appropriate "ratio of stator slot number to rotor pole number" combination is one of the common ways to minimize cogging torque component. This is a design based choice and is the most common method to minimize the unwanted cogging torque components in PM servomotors. Utilizing dummy slots in stator teeth increases the frequency of cogging and reduces its amplitude. Similarly, "displaced slots and slot openings" is a different method to minimize cogging component. In integral slot servomotors (q=1slots/pole/phase), each rotor magnet has the same position relative to the stator slots resulting in cogging torque components which are all in phase, leading to a high resultant cogging torque. Nevertheless, in fractional slot servomotors, where q≠1slots/pole/phase rotor magnets have different positions relative to the stator slots generating cogging torque components which are out of phase with each other. The resultant cogging torque is, thus, reduced since some of the cogging components are partially cancelled out. Even uncommon combinations such as 33, 39 or 45 slots are employed for certain applications to obtain small cogging torque components even though it generates an unbalanced servomotor.

Rotor side cogging torque minimization techniques are more cost effective compared to stator side methods and classified into three different categories: variable or constant magnet pole-arc to pole-pitch ratio, pole displacement and magnet skew. Techniques applied to rotor structure are simpler and less costly than stator side techniques. One of the most effective techniques used in servomotors is to employ an appropriate magnet pole-arc to pole-pitch ratio. Reducing the magnet pole-arc to pole-pitch ratio reduces the magnet leakage flux, but it also reduces the magnet flux, and, consequently, the average torque. Another method of reducing the cogging torque is to employ variable magnet pole-arcs for adjacent magnets such that the phase difference between the associated cogging torques results in a smaller net cogging.

7.2.3 Predicting cogging torque using FEA

Finite element analysis (FEA) can correctly examine the PM servomotors. The motor designers do not need to go through cumbersome circuit type analytical methods because important parameters such as flux, inductance, force and torque can simply and accurately be extracted from the finite element analysis. Even cogging torque component can precisely be calculated using modern FEA software.

Flux 2D software package by Cedrat Co., which is one of the frequently used FEA software in academia and industry, is used in the analyses of the PM servomotor given in Fig. 16 - Fig. 18 (Flux 2D and 3D Tutorial 2002). Cogging torque is obtained using no-load simulations. Rotor structure is rotated for one slot pitch and torque values are calculated using the Flux 2D. Fig. 16 shows both no-load flux density distribution of a 24 slot-8 pole PM servomotor as well as its cogging torque variation over one slot-pitch. Fig. 17 displays the rotor a disc type PM servomotor, its FEA predicted and experimentally verified cogging torque variation. The results show that FEA work well for the cogging torque predictions.

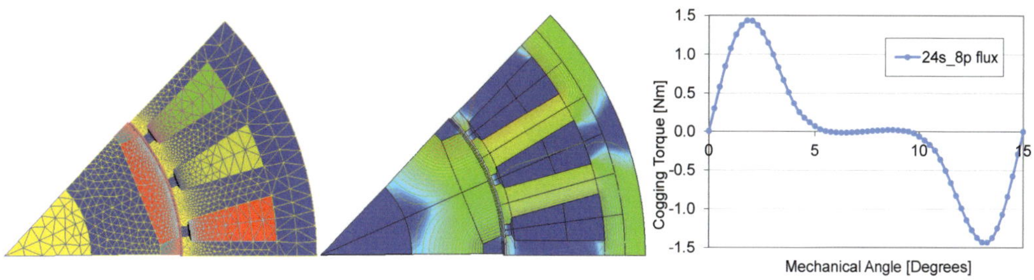

(a) (b) (c)

Fig. 16. 2D-FE Model of 24 slots with 8 poles servomotor (a) mesh structure, (b) flux density distribution and (c) cogging torque variation

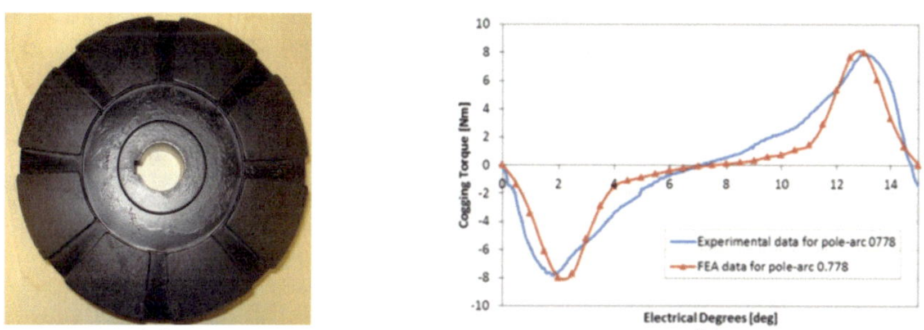

(a) (b)

Fig. 17. Rotor structure of a disc type PM servomotor (a), prediction of cogging torque with FEA and experimental data (b)

7.3 Torque ripple

Torque ripple is another important undesired torque element in PM servomotors. It occurs as a result of fluctuations of the field distribution and the stator MMF. In other words, torque ripple depends on the MMF distribution and its harmonics as well as the magnet flux distribution. At high speeds, torque ripple is usually filtered out by the system inertia. However, at low speeds torque-ripple may produces noticeable effects on motor shaft that may not be tolerable in smooth torque and constant speed servo applications.

Fig. 18 shows an interior permanent magnet (IPM) servomotor geometry, flux lines and flux density distribution at no load operation. If the motor is supplied by a harmonic free excitation, almost no ripple exists at the motor output (Fig. 19). However, if inverter or motor driven harmonics, such as integer slot motors or single segmented rotors with q=1 with no skew, exist in the current excitation, significant torque ripple appears at the motor output and precautions must be taken to lower this component as much as possible. One of common techniques to reduce the torque ripple component and obtain smooth torque output is to use segmented rotor. In order to use this approach, rotor is divided into segments and each piece is rotated with respect to each other to obtain ripple free output. As displayed in Fig. 19, if no segment is used, more than 130% of torque ripple is observed at the motor output. When the rotor is divided into 4 segments, torque ripple is reduced to less than 6% of the average torque which is a reasonable number for most applications.

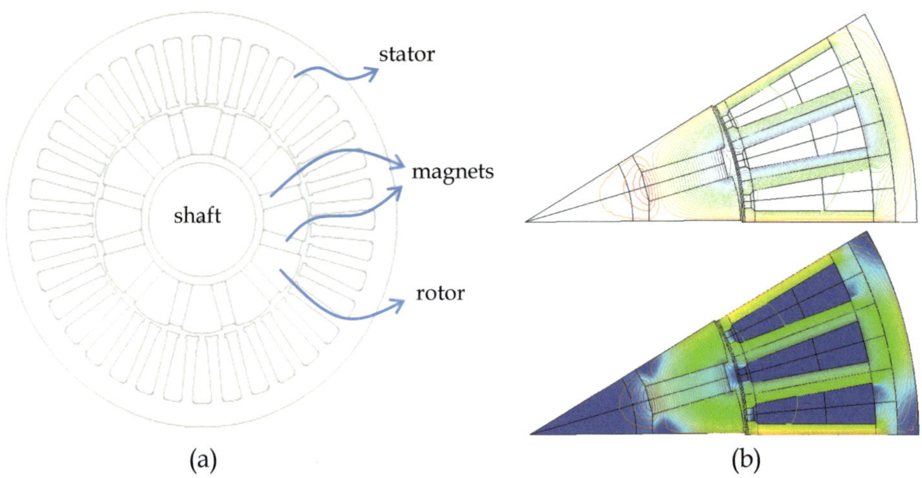

Fig. 18. Spoke type IPM servomotor (a) and flux line and flux distribution (b)

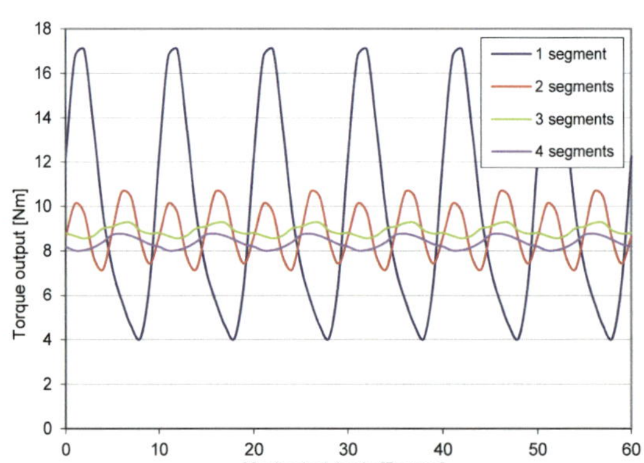

Fig. 19. Torque output variation of the IPM servomotor with low and high torque ripple

8. Control of PM servomotors

Commutation of a brushless pm motor is achieved electronically. Stator winding is energized using an inverter in a sequence. It is crucial to know the position of the rotor so as

to know which winding will be energized. This requires precise information of the rotor position using hall sensors or resolvers. When the rotor magnet poles pass, the position information of the sensor is provided to the controller and inverter drives the motor windings in the correct sequence.
Brushless PM servomotors can have both trapezoidal and sinusoidal back EMF waveforms and are excited with either rectangular or sinusoidal currents. A current regulated voltage source inverter is used to drive the servomotors. Power stage of the converter is combined by a rectifier, DC link and an inverter. Current sensors are used in each phase and fed back to the DSP controller. Position information is frequently obtained either by a resolver or an encoder although hall sensors are preferred for trapezoidal brushless servomotors. The simple system set-up with the main blocks of the system is illustrated in Fig. 20.

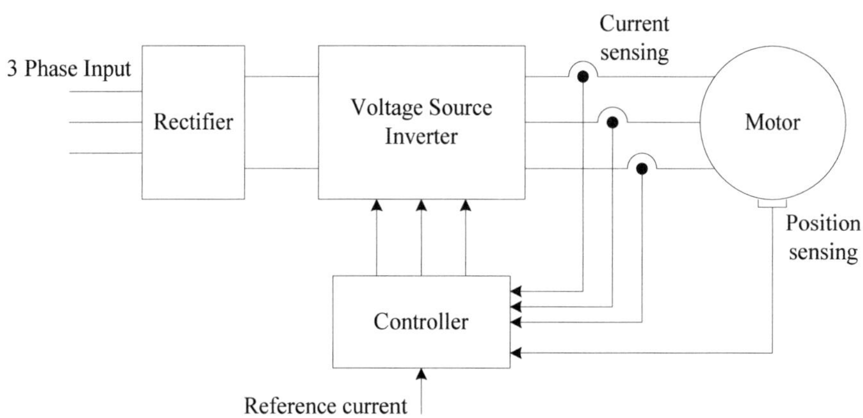

Fig. 20. Permanent magnet servomotor drive

9. Conclusion

Detailed introduction to brushless permanent magnet servomotors used in both industrial and servo applications is provided in this chapter. Motor classification and types, advantages and disadvantages of different PM servomotors and comparison, materials used in motor components are reviewed. Servomotor design process including electromagnetic, structural and thermal steps; softwares used in the analysis, design and optimization of such motors are also enlightened in detail. Torque quality, mathematical output torque equations, cogging and ripple torque components are investigated thoroughly since the torque quality confirms the quality of the servomotor.

10. Acknowledgment

The authors are indebted to CEDRAT Co. for providing the Flux 2D FEA Package and MDS Motor Ltd. for providing some motor pictures and its facilities in preparing this document.

11. References

Flux 2D and 3D Tutorial, Cedrat Co. 2002.

J. D. L. Ree and N. Boules, "Torque production in permanent-magnet synchronous motors," *IEEE Trans. Industry Applications*, vol. 25, no. 1, pp. 107-112, 1989.

J. R. Hendershot and T. J. E. Miller, "Design of Brushless Permanent-Magnet Motors (1995)," Oxford University Press, ISBN 0198593899, UK.

M. Aydin, M. K. Guven, S. Han, T. M. Jahns and W. L. Soong, "Integrated Design Process and Experimental Verification of a 50 kW Interior Permanent Magnet Synchronous Machine", *17th International Conference on Electrical Machines (ICEM 06)*, Crete, Greece, 2006.

Motor-CAD v3.1 software manual, April 2006.

N. Bianchi and S. Bolognani, "Design Techniques for Reducing the Cogging Torque in Surface-Mounted PM Motors", *IEEE Transactions on Industry Applications*, Vol. 38, No. 5, September/October 2002.

SPEED Software, PC-BDC 9.04 User's Manual, February 2010.

T. Sebastian, G. R. Slemon and M. A. Rahman, "Design considerations for variable speed permanent magnet motors", *Proceedings of International Conference on Electrical Machines (ICEM)* 1986, pp.1099-1102.

T.Li, and G. Slemon, "Reduction of cogging torque in PM motors," *IEEE Trans. Magnetics*, vol. 24, no. 6, pp 2901-2903, 1988.

Thomas M. Jahns and Wen L. Soong, "Pulsating Torque Minimization Techniques for Permanent Magnet AC Motor Drives-A Review", *IEEE Transactions on Industry Applications*, pp. Vol. 43, No. 2, April 1996.

15

Fuzzy Modelling Stochastic Processes Describing Brownian Motions

Anna Walaszek-Babiszewska
Opole University of Technology
Poland

1. Introduction

Wiener process, as a special mathematical model of Brownian motions, has been investigated and modelling in many probabilistic examples. In the topic literature it is easy to find many procedures of numeric probabilistic simulations of the Wiener process. Fuzzy modelling does not give us more accurate models than probabilistic modelling. Fuzzy knowledge-based modelling allows to determine linguistic description of non-precise relationships between variables and to derive the reasoning procedure from non-crisp facts. More over, using the notions of probabilities of fuzzy events, it is possible to determine a frequency of a conclusion as well as its expected value.

Wiener process and a random walk are very often used for modelling phenomena in physics, engineering and economy. In the area of robot control theory these processes can represent some time-varying parameters of the environments where the object of control operates. Fuzzy models of these processes can constitute a part of a fuzzy model of a tested complex system.

In paragraph 2. of this chapter, the mathematical descriptions of Brownian motions has been reminded, according to the theory of probability and stochastic processes. Some basics of fuzzy modelling has been presented in paragraph 3., to show the method of creating the knowledge base and rules of reasoning. Attention is focused on identification techniques for building empirical probabilities of fuzzy events from input-output data. Exemplary calculations of knowledge bases for real stochastic processes, as well as, some remarks on future works have been presented in paragraphs 4 and 5.

2. Mathematical models of Brownian motion

The Brownian motion it is well known in physics, a random movement of a particle suspended in a liquid or a gas. The name of the movement is given after the botanist Robert Brown (1827), who was studying the movement of pollen grains suspended in water. There are many similar phenomena, where the time evolutions of the object depend on stochastic, microscopic contacts (collisions) with elements of the surrounded system. In mathematics, many models describing Brownian motion are well known and applied, e.g. the random walk stochastic process, Wiener stochastic process, Langevin stochastic differential equation, general diffusion equations and others.

Observations of the microscopic particle behavior show, that at any time step, the particle is changing its position in the space, according to collisions with liquid particles. Crashes of particles are frequent and irregular. It is usually assumed by mathematicians, that the displacements of the particle $Z_1, Z_2, ..., Z_n, ...$ at particular time steps, are independent, identically distributed random variables. The stochastic process $\{Z_i, i = 1, 2, ..., n., ...\}$ is named *random walk*.

In macroscopic scale, if the time between two observations of the particle, $t - \tau$, is larger than the time between successive crashes, then the increment of the particle positions, $X_t - X_\tau$, is a sum of many small displacements, $X_t - X_\tau = \sum_{i=1,...,k} Z_i$. Since the increments $X_t - X_\tau$ constitute sums of independent, identically distributed random variables, they are normal distributed random variables.

In mathematics, scalar stochastic process $\{X_t, 0 \le t < \infty\}$, is the *Wiener process* if and only if

i. increments $X_t - X_\tau$, $0 \le \tau < t < \infty$ are homogeneous (stationary) and independent for disjoint time intervals,
ii. the initial condition, $P(X_0 = 0) = 1$, is fulfilled,
iii. trajectories of the process $\{X_t, 0 \le t < \infty\}$ are continuous (almost surely),
iv. random variables X_t, are normal distributed, with the probability density function

$$f(t,x) = \frac{1}{\sqrt{2\pi t\sigma^2}} \exp\left(-\frac{x^2}{2t\sigma^2}\right). \tag{1}$$

Wiener process is also known as the *Brownian motion process* (Fisz, 1967; van Kampen, 1990; Kushner, 1983; Sobczyk, 1991).

The increments, $X_t - X_\tau$, $0 \le \tau < t < \infty$, are normal distributed random variables with the expected value and variance as follows:

$$E(X_t - X_\tau) = 0, \; D^2(X_t - X_\tau) = (t - \tau)\sigma^2. \tag{2}$$

Random variables $X_{t_1}, ..., X_{t_n}$, where

$$X_{t_n} = X_{t_1} + (X_{t_2} - X_{t_1}) + ... + (X_{t_n} - X_{t_{n-1}}), \tag{3}$$

are also normal distributed with parameters:

$$E(X_{t_k}) = 0, \; D^2(X_{t_k}) = t_k\sigma^2, \; k=1,2,...,n; \tag{4}$$

and with a non-zero covariance matrix.

If $\sigma^2 = 1$ then $\{X_t, 0 \le t < \infty\}$ is the *standard Wiener process*.

Probability, that a particle occurs in some interval [*a*, *b*], at the moment *t*, is given by the relationship

$$\Pr\{X_t \in [a,b]\} = \int_a^b f(t,x)dx = \frac{1}{\sqrt{2\pi t\sigma^2}} \int_a^b \exp\left(-\frac{x^2}{2t\sigma^2}\right)dx. \tag{5}$$

For any $t_1 \le t_2$ probability density function of the random vector variable (X_{t_1}, X_{t_2}) can be obtained as follows:

$$f(t_1,x_1;t_2,x_2) = f(t_2,x_2 / t_1,X_{t_1} = x_1) f(t_1,x_1) \tag{6}$$

where

$$f(t_2,x_2 / t_1,X_{t_1} = x_1) = \frac{1}{\sqrt{2\pi\sigma(t_2 - t_1)}} \exp\left(-\frac{(x_1 - x_2)^2}{2(t_2 - t_1)\sigma^2} \right) \tag{7}$$

is a conditional probability density function, and $f(t_1,x_1)$ is given by formula (1) with parameters: $E(X_{t_1}) = 0$, $D^2(X_{t_1}) = t_1\sigma^2$.

For any $t_1 \le t_2 \le ... \le t_n$ probability density function of the multidimensional random vector $(X_{t_1},..., X_{t_n})$ can be obtained, taking into account Markov features of the process and using (3), as follows (Sobczyk, 1991):

$$f(t_n,x_n,...,t_1,x_1) = \prod_{i=1,...,n} \frac{1}{\sqrt{2\pi\sigma(t_i - t_{i-1})}} \exp\left(-\sum_{i=1,...,n} \frac{(x_i - x_{i-1})^2}{2(t_i - t_{i-1})\sigma^2} \right). \tag{8}$$

Stochastic vector process $\{[X_1(t),..., X_n(t)],\ 0 \le t < \infty\}$ is called the *nD stochastic Wiener process* if its every component, $\{X_i(t),\ 0 \le t < \infty\}$, $i=1,...,n$, is the scalar stochastic Wiener process and particular scalar stochastic processes are independent.

As an example of the 3*D* stochastic Wiener process we can show three coordinates of the Brownian particle trajectory.

The Wiener process is also the special diffusion stochastic process, fulfilling the Fokker-Planck diffusion equation

$$\frac{\partial f(x,t)}{\partial t} = \gamma \frac{\partial^2 f(x,t)}{\partial x^2}, \quad \lim_{\Delta t \to 0, \Delta x \to 0} \frac{(\Delta x)^2}{\Delta t} = const = 2\gamma \tag{9}$$

where the solution is given by the normal probability density function, and the diffusion coefficient is equal to $\gamma = \sigma^2 / 2$ (van Kampen, 1990).

In macroscopic scale, in physics and in industrial practice, the probability value $f(x)dx$ that scalar variable X assumes its value from the interval $[x, x+dx]$ is equivalent to the quotient n/N (concentration of particles), where n defines the power of subset of particles, whose feature X determines the value over the interval $[x, x+dx]$, and N is the population size. This idea is consistent with Einstein's experiments who considered collective motion of Brownian particles. He assumed that the density (concentration) of Brownian particles $\rho(x,t)$ at point x at time t, met the following diffusion equation:

$$\frac{\partial \rho(x,t)}{\partial t} = \gamma \frac{\partial^2 \rho(x,t)}{\partial x^2} \tag{10}$$

where γ is a diffusion coefficient. The solution has the known exponential form. From the analytical form of the solution the second central moment of the displacement is expressed as

$$E(X_t^{\ 2}) = 2\gamma t \tag{11}$$

Diffusion coefficient, γ, has been expressed by Einstein as a function of macro- and microscopic parameters of the fluid and particles, respectively. Einstein confirmed statistical character of the diffusion law (cited by van Kampen, 1990).

3. Fuzzy knowledge representation of the 'short memory' stochastic process

3.1 Stochastic process with fuzzy states

Let $X(t)$ be a 'short memory' stochastic process, the family of time-dependent random variables, where $X \in \chi \subset R$, $t \in T \subset R$ and B is the Borel σ-field of events. Let p be a probability, the normalized measure over the space (χ, B).

Moreover, assume that according to human experts' suggestions, in the universe of process values, the linguistic random variable has been determined with the set of linguistic values, $L(X)=\{LX_i\}$, $i=1,2,\ldots,I$ e.g. *L(X)={low, middle, high}*, according to Zadeh's definition of the linguistic variable (Zadeh, 1975). The meanings of the linguistic values are represented by fuzzy sets A_i, $i=1,2,\ldots,I$ determined on χ by their membership functions, $\mu_{Ai}(x): \chi \to [0,1]$, which are Borel measurable functions, fulfilling the condition

$$\sum_{i=1}^{I} \mu_{A_i}(x) = 1, \ \forall x \in \chi . \tag{12}$$

According to above assumptions, the probability distribution of linguistic values of the process $X(t)$ can be determined as follows

$$P(X_t) = \{P(A_i\}, i = 1,2,\ldots,I , \tag{13}$$

based on Zadeh's definitions of the probability of fuzzy events (Zadeh, 1968)

$$P(A) = \int_{\chi \subseteq R^n} \mu_A(x) dp . \tag{14}$$

The following conditions must be fulfilled

$$0 \le P(A_i) \le 1 , i=1,2,\ldots,I ; \qquad \sum_{i=1}^{I} P(A_i) = 1 . \tag{15}$$

Let now $t = t_1$, $t = t_2$, $t_2 > t_1$ be fixed, so the stochastic process at that moments is represented by two random variables $(X(t_1), X(t_2))$. Assume, that (χ^2, B, p) is a probability space, where $\chi^2 \subseteq R^2$, B is the Borel σ-field of events and p is a probability, the normalized measure over (χ^2, B). The assumptions mean that the probability distribution $p(x_{t_1}, x_{t_2})$ over the realizations (X_{t_1}, X_{t_2}) exists.

Let also two linguistic random variables (linguistic random vector) (X_{t_1}, X_{t_2}) be generated in χ^2, taking simultaneous linguistic values $LX_i \times LX_j$, $i,j=1,2,\ldots,I$; corresponding collection of fuzzy events $\{A_i \times A_j\}_{i,j=1,\ldots,I}$ is determined on χ^2 by membership functions

$\mu_{A_i \times A_j}(x_{t_1}, x_{t_2})$, *i,j=1,2,…,I*. Membership functions for joint fuzzy events $A_i \times A_j$ should fulfill

$$\sum_i \sum_j \mu_{A_i \times A_j}(x_{t_1}, x_{t_2}) = 1, \ \forall (x_{t_1}, x_{t_2}) \in \chi^2 . \tag{16}$$

The joint 2D probability distribution of linguistic values (fuzzy states) of the stochastic process *X*(*t*) is determined by the joint probability distribution of the linguistic random vector (X_{t_1}, X_{t_2})

$$P(X_{t_1}, X_{t_2}) = \{P(A_i \times A_j)\}_{i,j=1,2,\ldots,I} \tag{17}$$

calculated according to

$$P(A_i \times A_j) = \int_{(x_{t_1}, x_{t_2}) \in \chi^2} \mu_{A_i \times A_j}(x_{t_1}, x_{t_2}) dp \tag{18}$$

and fulfilling

$$0 \le P(A_i \times A_j) \le 1, \ \forall i, j = 1, \ldots, I \ \text{ and } \sum_{i=1}^{I} \sum_{j=1}^{I} P(A_i \times A_j) = 1 \tag{19}$$

(Walaszek-Babiszewska, 2008, 2011). From the joint probability distribution (17), the conditional probability distribution of the fuzzy transition

$$P[(X_{t_2} = A_j) / (X_{t_1} = A_i)] , j=1,2,\ldots,I; \ i=const \tag{20}$$

can be determined according to

$$\begin{aligned} &\{ \ P[(X_{t_2} / (X_{t_1} = A_i)] \ \}_{j=1,\ldots,I} = \\ &= \frac{\{P(X_{t_2} = A_j, X_{t_1} = A_i) \ \}_{j=1,\ldots,I}}{P(X_{t_1} = A_i)} . \end{aligned} \tag{21}$$

The following relationships should be fulfilled for the conditional distributions of fuzzy states (probability of the transitions)

$$\sum_{j=1,\ldots,I} P[(X_{t_2} = A_j / (X_{t_1} = A_i)] = 1; \ i = const. \tag{22}$$

3.2 Rule based fuzzy model

The proposed model of the stochastic process, formulated into fuzzy categories, for two moments t_1, t_2, $t_2 > t_1$, is a collection of file rules, in the following form (Walaszek-Babiszewska, 2008, 2011):

$$\forall A_i \in L(X) , i=1,\ldots,I$$

$$R^{(i)}: w_i[If\,(X_{t_1}\ is A_i)]\,Then(X_{t_2}\ is\ A_1)w_{1/i}$$
$$------------$$
$$Also(X_{t_2}\ is\ A_j)w_{j/i} \tag{23}$$
$$------------$$
$$Also(X_{t_2}\ is\ A_J)w_{J/i}$$

or as a collection of the elementary rules in the form

$$\forall A_i \in L(X)\,,\ \forall A_j \in L(X)\,,\ i,j=1,2,\ldots,I$$

$$R^{(i,j)}: w_{ij}[If\,(X_{t_1}\ is\ A_i)\ Then\ (X_{t_2}\ is\ A_j)] \tag{24}$$

where the weights w_i, $w_{j/i}$, w_{ij} represent probabilities of fuzzy states, determined by (13) – (15), (20) – (22) and (17) - (19), respectively. The weights stand for the frequency of the occurrence of fuzzy events in particular parts of rules and show the probabilistic structure of the linguistic values of the linguistic random vector $\left(X_{t_1}, X_{t_2}\right)$. The weights do not change logic values of the conditional sentences.

3.3 Reasoning procedures

Considering reasoning procedure, we assume that some non-crisp (vague) observed value of the stochastic process at moment t_1 is known and equal to $X_{t_1} = A'$, , or some crisp value $X_{t_1} = x^*_{t_1}$ of the stochastic process at moment t_1 is given. Then, the level of activation of the elementary rule (24) is determined according to one of the following formulas

$$\tau_i = \max_x \min[\mu_{A_i}(x), \mu_{A'}(x)]\,, \tag{25}$$

$$\tau_i = \mu_{A_i}(x^*_{t_1})\,,\ i=1,\ldots,I\,, \tag{26}$$

repectively (Yager & Filev, 1994; Hellendoorn & Driankov, 1997). The conclusion according to the generalized Mamdani-Assilian's type interpretation of fuzzy models has the following form

$$\mu_{A'_{j/i}}(x_{t_2}) = T(\tau_i, \mu_{A_j}(x_{t_2}))\,,\ j=1,\ldots,I;\ i=\text{const}; \tag{27}$$

thus the conclusion derived based on logic type interpretation of fuzzy models is as follows

$$\mu_{A'_{j/i}}(x_{t_2}) = \mathrm{I}(\tau_i, \mu_{A_j}(x_{t_2}))\,,\ j=1,\ldots,I;\ i=const, \tag{28}$$

where T denotes a t-norm and I means the implication operator. Aggregation of the conclusions from particular rules is usually computed by using any s-norm operator (Yager & Filev, 1994; Hellendoorn & Driankov, 1997).

Weights of rules, representing the probability of a fuzzy event in antecedent (w_i), as well as, the conditional probability of a fuzzy event at the consequence part ($w_{j/i}$), can be used to determine probabilistic characteristics of the conclusion. It is worth to note, that fuzzy conclusions (27) and (28) represent some functions, $\varphi[L(X)]$, of linguistic values of the linguistic random variable X_{t_2}. The fuzzy expected value of the following prediction,

$$E\{(X_{t_2}\, is\, \varphi(A_j)) / [X_{t_1}\, is\, A']\} = \bar{A}\,, \tag{29}$$

computed as the aggregated outputs of all active *i-th* file rules, can be determined by the following formula (Walaszek-Babiszewska, 2011)

$$\mu_{\bar{A}}(x_{t_2}) = \sum_i w_i \mu_{A'_i}(x_{t_2}) = \sum_i w_i \sum_j w_{j/i} \mu_{A'_{j/i}}(x_{t_2})\,. \tag{30}$$

where membership functions, $\mu_{A'_{j/i}}$, of the conclusions from elementary rules are given by (27) or (28), depending on the type of input data and the interpretation of a fuzzy model. Also, it is possible to determine probability of the fuzzy conclusion, taking into account a marginal probability distribution $P(X_{t_2})$ of the output linguistic random variable.

4. Creating fuzzy models of stochastic processes - Exemplary calculations

4.1 Fuzzy model of the stochastic time-discrete increments

First example show the fuzzy representation of the simplest form of the considered above stochastic processes, the one-dimensional time-discrete stochastic process of the increments, $\Delta X_t = X_t - X_{t-1}$. The increments, at given *t*, are normal distributed random variables, so it is useful to use the standard normal probability distribution function, over the domain of the process values, $\Delta X \in [-3, 3] = \chi \subset R$ (Table 1). Linguistic random variable, Y_t, with the

$x \in [a,b)$	$p(x)$	Fuzzy sets (events)					Probability of fuzzy events $P(Y)$		
		$\mu_{NH}(x)$	$\mu_{NL}(x)$	$\mu_Z(x)$	$\mu_{PL}(x)$	$\mu_{PH}(x)$			
[-3, -2.5)	0.00486	1	0				P(NH)=		
[-2.5, -2)	0.01654	0.5	0.5				0.014		
[-2, -1.5)	0.044057	0	1					P(NL)=	
[-1.5, -1)	0.091848		1	0				0.220	
[-1, -0.5)	0.149882		0.5	0.5					
[-0.5, 0)	0.191463		0	1					P(Z)=
[0, 0.5)	0.191463			1	0				0.532
[0.5, 1)	0.149882			0.5	0.5				
[1, 1.5)	0.091848			0	1			P(PL)=	
[1.5, 2)	0.044057				1	0		0.220	
[2, 2.5)	0.01654				0.5	0.5	P(PH)=		
[2.5, 3]	0.00486				0	1	0.014		

Table 1. Probability function of random variable X_t, fuzzy sets representing linguistic values *L{Y}* of the linguistic random variable Y_t and probability distribution $P(Y)$

name *'Increment at moment t'* has been assumed, with the set of its linguistic values: *L(Y)={negative high NH, negative low NL, zero Z, positive low PL, positive high PH}*. The linguistic values are represented by respective fuzzy sets. The probability distribution of the linguistic random variable, *P(Y)*, calculated according to (13) - (15), has been presented in Table 1.

Also, the second linguistic random variable, Y_{t-1}, with the name *'Increment at moment t-1'* has been determined with the same set of linguistic values *L(Y)*. Increments of the tested process are independent random variables, so conditional probabilities (probabilities of transitions) fulfill the relationship: $P(Y_t / Y_{t-1}) = P(Y_t)$.

The fuzzy knowledge base for the short memory stochastic process consists of the following, five file rules (25 elementary rules) with respective probabilities (according to Table 1.):

R[1]: 0.014(If Y_{t-1} is NH) Then (Y_t is NH)0.014

Also (Y_t is NL) 0.220

Also (Y_t is Z)) 0.532

Also (Y_t is PL) 0.220

Also (Y_t is PH) 0.014;

R[2]: 0.220 (If Y_{t-1} is NL) Then (Y_t is NH) 0.014

--- (31)

R[5]: 0.014(If Y_{t-1} is PH) Then (Y_t is NH) 0.014

Also (Y_t is PH) 0.014.

In the created rule base of the stochastic process, the same probability distributions for random variables, ΔX_t and ΔX_{t-1}, have been assumed. It is result of the simplification, under the assumption of a constant time interval $\Delta t = 1$.

4.2 Exemplary fuzzy models constructed based on realizations of stochastic processes

4.2.1 Fuzzy model constructed based on data of a floating particle

In the object literature the problem of the fulfilling the Wiener process assumptions by empirical data is often raised, e.g. the expected values of empirical increments are non-zero or increments do not fulfill the criterion of probabilistic independence. These facts have been also observed based on data representing increments of one coordinate, $\Delta x_t = x_t - x_{t-1}$, $\Delta x \in [-3.3, 3.3] = \chi \subset R$, describing the behavior of the particle floating in some liquid. It was assumed, that data stand for the realization of a certain stochastic process *Y(t)*. Also, the linguistic random variable Y_t has been determined, with the name *'Increment at moment t'*.

The set of the linguistic values, *L*(*Y*)={*negative high NH, negative low NL, positive low PL, positive high PH*} has been assumed. In domain χ of the process values, the linguistic values are represented by respective fuzzy sets. Also, second linguistic random variable, Y_{t-1}, with the name *'Increment at moment t-1'* has been determined with the same set of linguistic values *L*(*Y*). For the tested process, the criterion of independent increments is not fulfilled, thus, the conditional probabilities (probabilities of transitions) $P(Y_t / Y_{t-1})$ should be found.

The empirical joint probability of two linguistic random variables, $P(Y_t, Y_{t-1})$, has been calculated according to (16) - (19), based on the joint probability of numeric values of pairs, $p(\Delta x_{t-1}, \Delta x_t)$, as well as, the assumed fuzzy events, representing the linguistic values $L\{Y_t\} = \{NH, NL, PH, PL\}$ (Table 2). Marginal probability $P(Y_{t-1})$ is presented at the last row of the table. It is not a symmetrical distribution, the highest value of the probability, 0.39251, it is a probability that increments take the linguistic value *'Positive Low'*.

Conditional probabilities $P(Y_t / Y_{t-1})$, calculated according to (20) – (22) and presented in Table 3, may be treated as the transitions probabilities from fuzzy states {*NH, NL, PL, PH*} at moment *t*-1 to the particular fuzzy states at moment *t*.

$P(Y_t, Y_{t-1})$				
$L\{Y_t\}$	$L\{Y_{t-1}\}$			
	NH	NL	PL	PH
PH	0.0178	0.05355	0.10702	0.03572
PL	0.0060	0.06555	0.19024	0.09532
NL	0.0953	0.05955	0.02975	0.06555
NH	0.04765	0.03570	0.0655	0.0298
$P(Y_{t-1})$	0.16675	0.21435	0.39251	0.22639

Table 2. Joint probability distribution, $P(Y_t, Y_{t-1})$, of linguistic random variables representing empirical set of increments at moments *t* and *t*-1

$P(Y_t / Y_{t-1})$				
$L\{Y_t\}$	$L\{Y_{t-1}\}$			
	NH	NL	PL	PH
PH	0.10675	0.24983	0.27266	0.15778
PL	0.03600	0.30581	0.48466	0.42104
NL	0.57150	0.27781	0.07580	0.28955
NH	0.28575	0.16655	0.16688	0.13163
$\sum P(Y_t / Y_{t-1})$	1.00000	1.00000	1.00000	1.00000

Table 3. Conditional probability distributions $P(Y_t / Y_{t-1})$ of linguistic random variables

The fuzzy knowledge base of the behavior of some particle, determined by changes of its coordinate Y_t , consists of four file rules (20 elementary rules) with respective probabilities, as follows:

$$
\begin{aligned}
R^1&: 0.16675 \text{ (If } Y_{t-1} \text{ is NH) Then } (Y_t \text{ is NH) } 0.28575\\
&\text{Also } (Y_t \text{ is NL) } 0.57150\\
&\text{Also } (Y_t \text{ is PL) } 0.036\\
&\text{Also } (Y_t \text{ is PH) } 0.10675;\\
R^2&: 0.21435 \text{ (If } Y_{t-1} \text{ is NL) Then } (Y_t \text{ is NH) } 0.16655\\
&\text{---}\\
R^4&: 0.22639\text{(If } Y_{t-1} \text{ is PH) Then } (Y_t \text{ is NH) } 0.13163\\
&\text{-----------------------------}\\
&\text{Also } (Y_t \text{ is PH) } 0.15778.
\end{aligned}
\qquad (32)
$$

Probabilities (weights) at the consequent stand for transitions probabilities.

4.2.2 Fuzzy model of the stochastic increments observed in some technological situation

In a certain technological situation some parameter of a non-homogeneous grain material was measured at discrete moments (Figure 1). It is assumed that observed values $X(n)$, n=1,...,400 represent realization of a certain stochastic process whose variance is high and changes are very quick. For human experts, engineers of the technological process, it is very

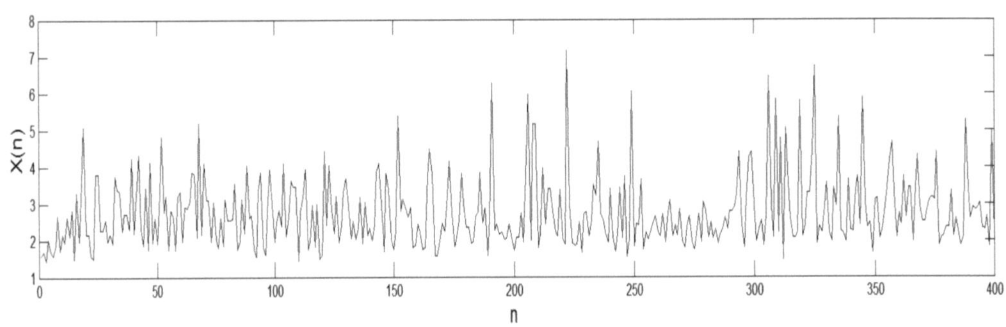

Fig. 1. Realization of the stochastic process $X(n)$

important to recognize a probabilistic character of the changes, especially the changes determined in linguistic categories, like: *Positive Big, Positive Small, Zero, Negative Small, Negative Big*. To determine characteristic of the process with fuzzy states, first, we have calculated the increments

$$DX(n)=X(n)-X(n-1) \tag{33}$$

and a joint probability distribution $p(DX(n),DX(n-1))$ of non-fuzzy values of the process. The range of the increments values, a real number interval [-4.8, 4.8], has been divided into 14 disjoint intervals and the frequency of the occurrence of measurements in particular intervals has been determined. The disjoint intervals have been used for the description of membership functions of particular linguistic values of the set $L\{DX(n)\}=\{NB,NS,Z,PS,PB\}$.

The empirical joint probability distribution of the linguistic random variables, $P(L\{DX(n-1)\}, L\{DX(n)\})$, has been calculated and presented in Table 4. In the last row, the marginal probability values of one linguistic random variable, are presented. It is almost symmetrical distribution, with the highest value of the probability, 0.6114, for the linguistic value of increments equal to '*Zero*'. Conditional probability distributions for particular linguistic values of the variable $DX(n)$ have been also calculated and they represent weights of particular consequent parts of the rule-base fuzzy model (34). The model of the knowledge base consists of the following five file rules with weights:

R1: 0.6114 IF (*DX(n-1)* IS *Z)* THEN (*DX(n)* IS *Z*) 0.6450

ALSO (*DX(n)* IS *NS*) 0.1945

ALSO (*DX(n)* IS *PS*) 0.1462

ALSO (*DX(n)* IS *PB*) 0.0113

ALSO (*DX(n)* IS *NB*) 0.0030

R2: 0.2123 IF (*DX(n-1)* IS *NS*) THEN (*DX(n)* IS *Z*) 0.6739

ALSO (*DX(n)* IS *PS*) 0.2032

ALSO (*DX(n)* IS *NS*) 0.1114

ALSO (*DX(n)* IS *PB*) 0.0111

ALSO (*DX(n)* IS *NB*) 0.0004

R3: 0.1474 IF (*DX(n-1)* IS *PS*) THEN (*DX(n)* IS *NS*) 0.4258 (34)

ALSO (*DX(n)* IS *Z*) 0.4181

ALSO (*DX(n)* IS *NB*) 0.0791

ALSO (*DX(n)* IS *PS*) 0.0714

ALSO (*DX(n)* IS *PB*) 0.0056

R4: 0.0184 IF (*DX(n-1)* IS *NB*) THEN (*DX(n)* IS *Z*) 0.6044

ALSO (*DX(n)* IS *PS*) 0.2363

ALSO (*DX(n)* IS *NS)* 0.1263

ALSO (*DX(n)* IS *PB*) 0.0330

R5: 0.0105 IF (*DX(n-1)* IS *PB*) THEN (*DX(n)* IS *NB*) 0.4762

ALSO (*DX(n)* IS *NS*) 0.4286

ALSO (*DX(n)* IS *Z*) 0.0952.

	P(L{DX(n-1)}, L{DX(n)})				
	L{DX(n-1)}				
L{DX(n)}	NB	NS	Z	PS	PB
PB	0.0051	0.0046	0.0010	0.0	0.0
PS	0.0115	0.0620	0.0609	0.0104	0.0008
Z	0.0017	0.1192	0.3953	0.0895	0.0068
NS	0.0001	0.0235	0.1430	0.0431	0.0023
NB	0	0.0030	0.0112	0.0044	0.0006
$P(L\{DX(n-1)\})$	0.0184	0.2123	0.6114	0.1474	0.0105

Table 4. Joint empirical probability distribution of two linguistic random variables representing increments

To determine the predicted value *DX(n)=b**, for given value (crisp or fuzzy) *DX(n-1)=a**, the reasoning procedure, described in 3.3 is used, e.g. for *DX(n-1)=1.55,* predicted value is approximated as equal to *DX(n)=0.30538.* This value depends on many parameters of the fuzzy model and the reasoning procedure. It is very useful to create the computing system with many options of changing the reasoning parameters. In Fig. 2 the predicted, mean values of the increments has been underlined by thick line.

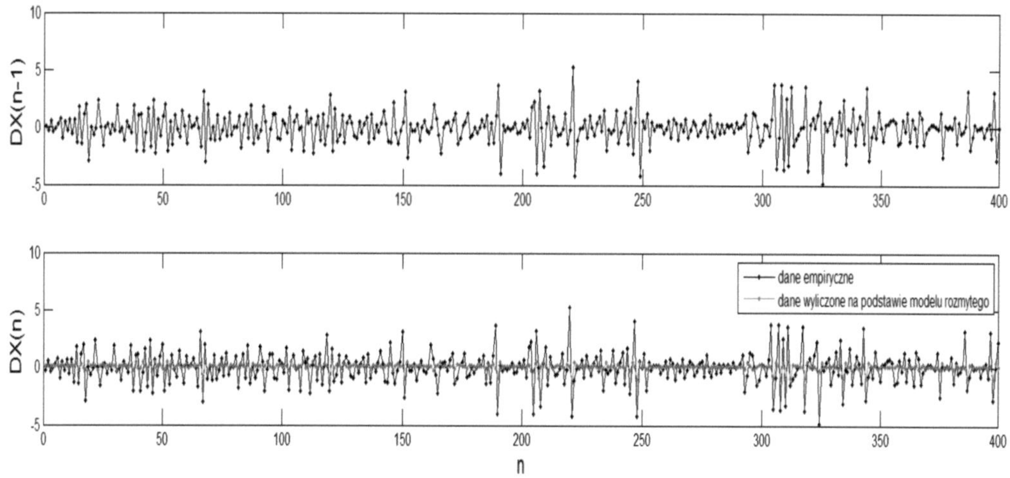

Fig. 2. Realization of the stochastic processes of increments $DX(n)$, $DX(n-1)$ and the predicted mean value

5. Conclusion and future works

In this chapter the new approach to fuzzy modelling has been presented. Knowledge base in the form of weighted fuzzy rules represents in the same time the probability distribution of the fuzzy events occurring in the statements. Considered examples show the creating a few simple models of stochastic increments processes. In the future, in modelling the Wiener process, the time dependent probability of the increments should be taken into account.

6. References

Fisz, M. (1967). *Probability and Statistics Theory* (in Polish), PWN, Warsaw, Poland

Hellendoorn, H. & Driankov, D. (Eds.), (1977). *Fuzzy Model Identification; Selected Approaches*, Springer, ISBN 3-540-62721-9, Berlin, Germany

Kushner, H. (1983). *Introduction to Stochastic Control*, PWN (Polish edition), ISBN 83-01-02212-4, Warsaw, Poland

Sobczyk K. (1996). *Stochastic Differential Equations*, WNT (Polish edition), ISBN 83-204-1971-9, Warsaw, Poland

Van Kampen, N.G. (1990). *Stochastic Processes in Physics and Chemistry*, PWN (Polish edition), ISBN 83-01-09713-2, Warsaw, Poland

Walaszek-Babiszewska, A. (2008). Probability Measures of Fuzzy Events and Linguistic Fuzzy Modelling – Forms Expressing Randomness and Imprecision, In: *Advances on Artificial Intelligence, Knowledge Engineering and Data Bases*, L.A. Zadeh, J. Kacprzyk et al. (Eds.), *Proceedings of the 7th WSEAS International Conference AIKED'08* pp.207-213, ISBN 978-960-6766-41-1, Cambridge, UK, February 20-22, 2008

Walaszek-Babiszewska, A. (2011). *Fuzzy Modelling in Stochastic Environment; Theory, knowledge bases, examples,* LAP Lambert Academic Publishing, ISBN 978-3-8454-1022-7, Saarbrucken, Germany

Yager, R. & Filev, D.P. (1994). *Essentials of Fuzzy Modelling and Control*. John Wiley and Sons, New York, USA

Zadeh, L.A. (1968). Probability Measures of Fuzzy Events. *Journal of Mathematical Analysis and Applications*, Vol.23, No.2, (August 1968), pp. 421-427

Zadeh, L.A. (1975). The Concept of a Linguistic Variable and its Applications to Approximate Reasoning –I. *Information Sciences*, Vol.8, pp. 199-249

Part 3

Optimization

16

Heuristic Optimization Algorithms in Robotics

Pakize Erdogmus[1] and Metin Toz[2]
[1]Duzce University, Engineering Faculty,
Computer Engineering Department
[2]Duzce University, Technical Education Faculty,
Computer Education Department, Duzce
Turkey

1. Introduction

Today, Robotic is an essential technology from the entertainment to the industry. Thousands of articles have been published on Robotic. There are various types of robots such as parallel robots, industrial robots, mobile robots, autonomous mobile robots, health-care robots, military robots, entertainment robots, nano robots and swarm robots. So, this variety brings a lot of problems in Robotic. Inverse kinematic for serial robots, forward kinematic for parallel robots, path planning for mobile robots and trajectory planning for industrial robots are some of the problems in Robotic studied a lot. Some of the problems are solved easily with some mathematical equations such as forward kinematic problem for serial robots and inverse kinematic problem for parallel robots. But the problems consisting of nonlinear equations and higher order terms can't be solved exactly with the classical methods. The forward kinematics problem of the 6 degrees of freedom (DOF) 6x6 type of Stewart Platform can be given as an example to such problems. It has been shown that there are 40 distinct solutions for this problem (Raghavan, 1993). Some of the unsolved problems with classical methods are optimization problems and heuristic optimization techniques are an alternative way for the solution of such problems. The heuristic optimization techniques produce good solutions for the higher order nonlinear problems in an acceptable solution time, when the problems aren't solved with the classical methods (Lee & El-Sharkawi, 2008).
In this chapter, first in Section 2, optimization is shortly described. The introduction and some well-known heuristic algorithms including, Genetic Algorithms(GA), Simulated Annealing(SA), Particle Swarm Optimization(PSO) and Gravitational Search Algorithm(GSA) are reviewed in Section 3. In Section 4, two well-known optimization problems in Robotic are solved with GA and PSO.

2. Optimization

Optimization is of great importance for the engineers, scientists and managers and it is an important part of the design process for all disciplines. The optimal design of a machine, the minimum path for a mobile robot and the optimal placement of a foundation are all optimization problems.
A constrained optimization problem has three main elements; design variables, constraints and objective function/functions. Design variables are independent variables of the

objective function and can take continuous or discrete values. The ranges of these variables are given for the problems. Constraints are the functions of design variables and limit the search space. The objective function is the main function dependent on the design variables. If there is more than one objective function, the problem is called multi-objective optimization problem.
Solving an optimization problem means finding the values of the design variables which minimize the objective function within given constraints. So if the objective function is a maximization problem, it is converted to minimization problem multiplying by -1 as seen in the Figure 1. The mathematical model of an optimization problem is given by equation 1.

$$\text{Minimize } f_{obj}(x_1,x_2,...x_n), \text{ Subject to } \begin{array}{ll} g_i(x_1,x_2,...x_n,a) \le 0, & i=1,2,...,l \\ h_j(x_1,x_2,...x_n,b)=0, & j=1,2,...,m \\ x_k^l \le x_k \le x_k^u, & k=1,2,...n \end{array} \quad (1)$$

Where, $\mathbf{x_1, x_2, ...x_n}$ are design variables, **n** is the number of design variables, **l** is the number of inequality constraints and **m** is the number of equality constraints, **a** and **b** are constant values. $\mathbf{x_k^l}$ and $\mathbf{x_k^u}$ are respectively lower and upper bounds of the design variables.

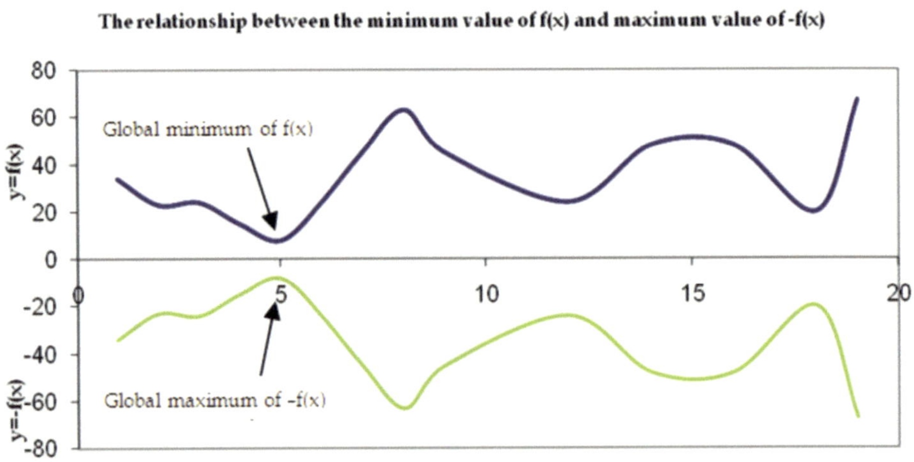

Fig. 1. An objective function conversion to minimization

There are a lot of applications in decision science, engineering, and operations research which can be formulated as constrained continuous optimization problems. These applications include path planning for mobile robots, trajectory planning for robot manipulators, engineering design and computer-aided-design (CAD). Optimal or good solutions to these applications are very important for the system performance, such as low-cost implementation and maintenance, fast execution and robust operation (Wang, 2001).
There are different methods for the solution of the optimization problems. Exact methods and heuristics are two main solution methods. Exact methods find certain solutions to a given problem. But, if the problem size increases, the solution time of the exact methods is unacceptable, because of the fact that solution time increases exponentially when the problem size increases. So, using the heuristics methods for the solution of optimization problems are more practical. (Rashedi et al., 2009). On the other hand, in last decades there

has been a great deal of interest on the applications of heuristic search algorithms to solve the such kind of problems.
The main difficulty encountered in the solution of the optimization problem is the local minimums. If there are a lot of local minimums, then both exact methods and heuristics can be trapped in to the local minimums. Since most of the heuristic algorithms developed a strategy to avoid the local minimums, they have been quite popular recently. The local minimums and global minimum of an objective function with one design variable are seen in the Figure 2.

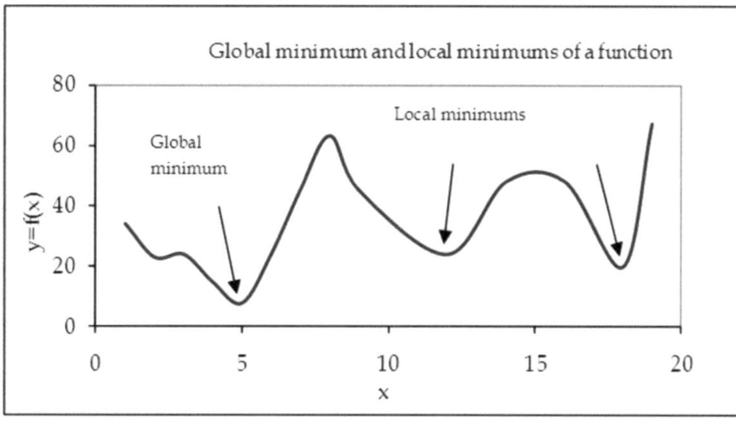

Fig. 2. An objective function with local minimums

3. Heuristic algorithms

Optimization studies drawn attention in 1960's. It was developed a lot of algorithm based on the more sophisticated mathematical background. These algorithms were called exact methods. But, exact methods produced certain solutions only for the limited scope of application. As a result, attention turned to heuristic algorithms. (Fisher et al., 1998). Heuristics algorithms try to find acceptable solutions to the problems using some heuristic knowledge and most of them simulate real life. They use not only pure mathematics, but also algorithms using with basic formulations. While the most important property of heuristic algorithms is that they are designed for the unconstrained optimization problems, they can also be adapted to the constrained optimization problems. The algorithms are designed to find the minimum value of the objective function within the bounds of the constraints . If a solution doesn't satisfy the constraints, this solution is not acceptable, even if the value of the objective function is minimum. So, if there are constraints in a minimization problem, penalty function is added to objective function. The total function is called as fitness function. Namely, if constraints are in feasible region, then there is no penalty and penalty function is equal to zero. If the constraints are not in feasible region, the fitness function is penalized by penalty function.
Heuristic algorithms don't guarantee finding the optimal solutions. They try to find acceptable solutions near to optimum in a reasonable time. These algorithms were studied for both discrete and continuous optimization problems since the 1970's. Researchers have tried to develop adaptive and hybrid heuristics algorithms. By this aim, tens of algorithms were developed in last decade. Heuristic algorithms can be classified as single solution

algorithms and population based algorithms. The first category gathers Local Search (LS), Greedy Heuristic (GH) (Feo et al., 1995), Simulated Annealing (SA) (Kirkpatrick et al., 1983), Tabu Search (TS) (Laguna, 1994) and Iterated Local Search (ILS) (Glover & Garry, 2002). The second category, which is more and more studied, groups evolutionary algorithms such as Genetic Algorithms (GA)(Goldberg, 1989), Ant Colony Optimization (ACO) (Dorigo et al, 1996), Artificial Bee Colony (ABC)(Basturk & Karaboga, 2006), Scatter Search (SS) (Marti et al., 2006), Immune Systems (IS) (Farmer et al., 1986), Differential Evolution Algorithms (DEA) (Storn, 1996), Particle Swarm Optimization (PSO) (Keneddy & Eberhart, 1995), Harmony Search (HS) (Geem & Kim, 2001) and Gravitational Search Algorithm (GSA) (Rashedi et al., 2009). Evolutionary algorithms simulate natural phenomena or social behaviors of animals. So, the algorithms can be subcategorized to these criteria. While SA, GSA, HS simulates natural phenomena, ACO, ABC, PSO simulates the social behaviors of animals. The taxonomy of global optimization algorithms can be found in the related literature (Weise, 2008).

During the last years, hybrid optimization approaches have been popular. Firstly, cooperations have been realized between several heuristic algorithms. Later, cooperations between heuristic algorithms and exact methods have been realized. Since they gather the advantages of both types of algorithm, hybrid algorithms give more satisfied results. (Jourdan et al., 2009).

In single solution heuristic algorithms, the algorithm starts with an initial solution called current solution. This solution can be created randomly and consists of the values of design variables of the optimization problems. The objective function value is calculated with these initial values. If the initial solution satisfies the constraints, fitness function will be the same with the objective function. The second solution, called candidate solution, is created with random values close to the initial solution. Between the two fitness functions, the one which has a minimum value is selected as candidate solution. As long as the iteration proceeds, it is expected that algorithm converges to the global minimum value. But algorithms can be trapped to the local minimums. Heuristic algorithms develop different strategies to avoid to get trapped the local minimums. So, exploration and exploitation are of great importance for finding the global minimum value with the heuristics algorithms. In the first iterations, the algorithm searches the global solution space with big steps in order not to get trapped the local minimums. This is called exploration. In the next iterations, the algorithm searches the solution space with small steps in order to find best minimum. This is called exploitation. It is desired to have a balance between exploration and exploitation in the heuristic algorithms.

3.1 Genetic algorithms

GA was developed in Michigan University by Holland and later it got popularity with the efforts of Goldberg. GA is an adaptive global search method that mimics the metaphor of natural biological evolution. It operates on a population of potential solutions by applying the principle of survival of the fittest to achieve an optimal solution.

In the literature, GA is one of the most applied heuristic optimization algorithms. GA has been applied successfully to a huge variety of optimization problems, nearly in all disciplines, such as materials science, aircraft applications, chemistry, construction, seismology, medicine and web applications. GA has also been applied to the problems in Robotic such as the solution of multimodal inverse kinematics problem of industrial robots

(Kalra et al., 2006), trajectory generation for non-holonomic mobile manipulators (Chen & Zalzala, 1997), generation of walking periodic motions for a biped robot (Selene et al, 2011), the solution of the forward kinematics of 3RPR planar parallel manipulator(Chandra & Rolland, 2011), kinematic design optimization of a parallel ankle rehabilitation robot (Kumar et al., 2011).

GA starts to run with a lot of possible solutions according to the initial population which are randomly prepared. Each individual is encoded as fixed-length binary string, character-based or real-valued encodings. Encoding is an analogy with an actual chromosome (Lee & El-Sharkawi, 2008). A binary chromosome represents the design variables with a string containing 0s and 1s. Design variables are converted to binary arrays with a precision p. The bit number is calculated by equation 2 (Lin & Hajela, 1992).

$$B.N \geq \log_2(((x_k^u - X_k^l)/p)+1) \tag{2}$$

Where, **p** is a precision selected by the program designer. $\mathbf{x_k^u}$ and $\mathbf{x_k^l}$ are respectively upper and lower bounds of the design variables **B.N** is the number of bits representing design variables. If the number of bits is 4, the binary values of the design variables are represented as 0000, 0001, 0010, ..., 1111.

Initial population is generated randomly after coding the variables. Initial population is represented as a matrix. Typical population size varies between 20 and 300. Each row of the population matrix is called as an individual.

Strings are evaluated through iterations, called generations. During each generation, the strings are evaluated using fitness function. Fitness function measures and evaluates the coded variables in order to select the best fitness strings (Saruhan, 2006). Then, it tries to find optimum solutions by using genetic operators. By this way, the best solutions are selected and worsts are eliminated. GA runs according to unconstrained optimization procedure. So, the constrained continuous optimization problems are transformed into unconstrained continuous optimization problem by penalizing the objective function value with the quadratic penalty function. The total function is called fitness function.

Fitness function (FF) values are calculated for each individual as it is seen in equation 3, 4 and 5. In a minimization problem, penalty function is added to objective function. The fitness function (FF), is the sum of objective function (OF) and the penalty function (PF) consisting constraint functions (CF). After elitism, selection, crossover, and mutation are operated, a new population is generated according to the fitness function values. The future of population depends on the evolutionary rules.

$$OF = f_{obj}(x_1, x_2, \dots x_n) \tag{3}$$

$$PF = \sum_{i=1}^{l} R_i(\max[0, g_i(x_1, x_2, \dots x_n, a)])^2 + \sum_{j=1}^{m} Rj(\max[0, \left|h_j(x_1, x_2, \dots x_n, b)\right| - tol])^2 \tag{4}$$

$$FF = OF + PF \tag{5}$$

In the above equations, **a** and **b** are constant values, **l** is the number of inequality constraints, **m** is the number of equality constraints, **n** is the number of variables and **tol** is the tolerance value, for the equality constraints. If $\mathbf{h_j}$'s value is smaller than the tolerance value, it is accepted that equality constraints have been satisfied. If the problem variables satisfy the constraints, g_i and (h_j -tol) values will be negative and PF will be zero. $\mathbf{R}_i$ and $\mathbf{R}_j$ are the penalty coefficients and these values affect the algorithm performance directly.

Selection is to choose the individuals for the generation based on the principle of survival of the best according to the Darwin's theory. The main idea in selection is to create parents from the chromosomes having better fitness function values. Namely the parents are selected from the chromosomes of the first population as directly proportional to their fitness function values. The better fitness function value of a chromosome, the more chance to be a parent. With the selection method, the individuals having worse fitness values disappear in the next generations. The most popular selection methods are roulette wheel and tournament rank. The successful individuals are called parents.

After selection, crossover, which represents mating of two individuals, is applied to the parents. The parents in GA create two children with crossover. There are various kinds of crossover process such as one point crossover, multiple point crossovers and uniform crossover. The crossover operator is applied with a certain probability, usually in the range 0.5-1. This operator allows the algorithm to search the solution space. Namely, exploration is performed in GA with crossover operator. In a basic crossover, the children called offspring are created from mother and father genes with a given crossover probability. Mutation is an another operation in GA and some gens are changed with this operation. But this is not common. Generally mutation rate of binary encoding is specified smaller than 0.1. In contrast to the crossover, mutation is used for the exploitation of the solution space. The last operation is the elitism. It transfers the best individual to the next generation. The evaluation of the previous population with the operators stated above, the new population is generated till the number of generation. Fitness function values are calculated in each new population and the best resulted ones are paid attention among these values. Until the stopping criteria are obtained, this process is repeated iteratively. The stopping criteria may be the running time of the algorithm, the number of generation and for fitness functions giving the same best possible values in a specified time. The pseudo codes of GA are given in Figure 3.

```
init_Popu← Produce initial solution ()
(while stopping criteria not true do)
   for i=1 to generation_number
      calculate fitness function values of init_popu
      choose parents with roulette wheel
      (Parent 1 and Parent 2 are chosen)
      Elitism(Select the best ones in the population)
      Crossover(Create two children for each parent)
      Mutation(Gens are changed with mutation_rate)
      The new ofspring is created
   Next
```

Fig. 3. The pseudo codes of GA

3.2 Simulated annealing

SA uses an analogy of physical annealing process of finding low energy states of solids and uses global optimization method. SA is inspired by Metropolis Algorithm and this approach was firstly submitted to an optimization by Kirkpatrick and his friends in 1983 (Kirkpatrick

et al, 1983). Because of the fact that SA is an effective algorithm and it is easy to implement for the difficult engineering optimization problems, it is also popular for last studies in several different engineering areas. SA is applied to various optimization problem in Robotics such as path planning problem solution(Gao & Tian,2007), the generation of the assembly sequences in robotic assembly(Hong & Cho, 1999), trajectory optimization of advanced launch system (Karsli & Tekinalp, 2005), optimal robot arm PID control, the placement of serial robot manipulator and collision avoidance planning in multi-robot.
SA combines local search and Metropolis Algorithm. Algorithm starts with a current solution at initial temperature. At each temperature, algorithm iterates n times, defined by the program designer. In the iterations for each temperature, a candidate solution that is close to the current solution is produced randomly. If candidate solution is better than the current solution, the candidate solution is replaced with the current solution. Otherwise, the candidate solution is not rejected at once. The random number is produced between 0-1 and compared with the acceptance probability P. P is an exponential function as given by equation 6. If produced random number is smaller than P, the worse solution is accepted as current solution for exploration. Search process progresses until stopping criteria is satisfied. Maximum run time, maximum iteration number, last temperature e.g. may be the stopping criteria.

$$P = e^{-\left(\frac{f(x\_cand)-f(x\_curr)}{T}\right)} \tag{6}$$

For an object function with one design variable, **x_cand** is candidate design variable, **x_curr** is current design variable and **f** is object function, **T** is temperature. At high temperatures, P is close to one. Since the most random number is smaller than one, the possibility of bad solution's acceptance is high for exploration in the first steps of the algorithm. T is decreased along the search process. At low temperatures, P is close to zero. Since the random numbers are bigger than zero, the possibility of bad solution's acceptance approach to zero. When P is equal to zero, the process converges to local search method for exploitation. The pseudo code of SA is given in Figure 4.

```
x_curr← Produce initial solution()
T←T0
while stopping criteria not true  do
    for i=1 to n
        x_cand←Produce a random solution
        if f(x_cand) < f(x_curr) then
            x_ curr ←x_cand
        else
            'Metropolis Algorithm
            x Produce a random number between (0,1)
            if  x < p ( T, x_curr, x_cand) then
                x_curr ← x_cand
            end if
        end if
    end
    update(T)
end while
```

Fig. 4. The pseudo codes of SA Algorithm

Annealing process simulates optimization. Annealing is realized slowly in order to keep the system of the melt in a thermodynamic equilibrium. Convergence to the optimal solution is controlled by the annealing process.
Proper cooling scheme is important for the performance of SA. The proper annealing process is related with the initial temperature, iteration for each temperature, temperature decrement coefficient and stopping criteria. All these criteria can be found in related article (Blum & Roli, 2001). In general, the temperature is updated according to equation 7.

$$T_{k+1} = \alpha T_k \quad (7)$$

Where, $\mathbf{T_{k+1}}$ is the next temperature, $\mathbf{T_k}$ is the current temperature and α is the temperature decrement coefficient, generally selected between 0.80 and 0.99.
Even if SA tries to find global minimum, it can be trapped by local minima. So, in order to overcome this drawback and develop the performance of SA, researchers have developed adaptive or hybridized SA with other heuristics, such as fuzzy logic, genetic algorithms, support vector machines, and distributed/parallel algorithms.

3.3 Particle swarm optimization

PSO was introduced by James Kennedy and Russell Eberhart in 1995 as an evolutionary computation technique (Kennedy & Eberhart, 1995) inspired by the metaphor of social interaction observed among insects or animals. It is simpler than GA because PSO has no evolution operators such as crossover and mutation (Lazinca, 2009).
PSO have many advantages such as simplicity, rapid convergence, a few parameters to be adjusted and no operators (Li & Xiao; 2008). So, PSO is used for solving discrete and continuous problems. It was applied to a wide range of applications such as function optimization, Electrical power system applications, neural network training, task assignment and scheduling problems in operations research, fuzzy system control and pattern identification. PSO was also applied to a lot of different Robotic applications. PSO was applied mobile robot navigation (Gueaieb & Miah, 2008), Robot Path Planning (Zargar & Javadi, 2009) and Swarm Robotic Applications and Robot Manipulators applications.
PSO algorithm is initialized with a group of particles. Each particle is a position vector in the search space and its dimension represents the number of design variables. PSO is started with random initial positions and velocities belong to each particle. For each particle, fitness function's value is computed. Global and local best values are updated. Local best value is the best value of the current particle found so far and the global best value is the best value of all local bests found so far. Velocity and positions are updated according to the global best and local bests. Each particle flies through the search space, according to the local and global best values. Along the iterations, particles converge to the global best. The convergence of the particles to the best solution shows the PSO performance. The rate of position change of the *i*th particle is given by its velocity. In the literature there are different velocity formulas. The first one proposed by Keneddy is given by equation 9. Particles' velocity and positions are updated according to equation 8 and 9.

$$x_i^{k+1} = x_i^k + v_i^{k+1} \quad (8)$$

$$v_i^{k+1} = v_i^k + \varphi_1 \mathrm{rand}()(p_{besti}{}^k - x_i^k) + \varphi_2 \mathrm{rand}()(g_{best} - x_i^k)) \quad (9)$$

Where, **k** is the iteration number, **rand** is a random number, $\mathbf{pbest_i^k}$ is the best value of *i*th particle and **gbest** is the global best value of all particles. $\mathbf{x_i^k}$ and $\mathbf{x_i^{k+1}}$ are respectively the current position and the next position of the *i*th particle. $\mathbf{v_i^k}$ and $\mathbf{v_i^{k+1}}$ are respectively the current velocity and the next velocity of the *i*th particle. The next position of a particle is specified by its current position and its velocity.
PSO simulates social swarm's behaviour. The velocity formula consists of three important components. First part presents the past velocity. The particle generally continues in the same direction. This is called habit. The second part φ_1**rand()(pbest**$_i^k$**-x**$_i^k$**)** presents private thinking. This part is also called self-knowledge and the last part φ_2**rand()(gbest-x**$_i^k$**)** presents the social part of the particle swarm(Kennedy, 1997). When implementing the particle swarm algorithm, some considerations must be paid attention in order to facilitate the convergence and prevent going to infinity of the swarm. These considerations are limiting the maximum velocity, selecting acceleration constants, the constriction factor, or the inertia constant (Valle et al., 2008).
The velocity and position formula with constriction factor (K) has been introduced by Clerc(Clerc, 1999) and Eberhart and Shi (Eberhart & Shi, 2001) as given by equation 10,11 and 12.

$$v_i^{k+1} = K(v_i^k + \varphi_1 \mathrm{rand}()(p_{besti}^k - x_i^k) + \varphi_2 \mathrm{rand}()(g_{best} - x_i^k)) \tag{10}$$

$$x_i^{k+1} = x_i^k + v_i^{k+1} \tag{11}$$

$$K = \frac{2}{\left|2 - \varphi - \sqrt{\varphi^2 - 4\varphi}\right|}, \quad \varphi = \varphi_1 + \varphi_2, \ \varphi > 4 \tag{12}$$

Where, **K** is the constriction factor, φ_1 and φ_2 represent the cognitive and social parameters, respectively. **rand** is uniformly distributed random number. φ is set to 4.1. The constriction factor produces a damping effect on the amplitude of an individual particle's oscillations, and as a result, the particle will converge over time. The pseudo code of PSO is given in Figure 5.

```
Generate initial P particle swarm's random positions and velocities
do
  for i=1:P
    Evaluate fitness function for each particle
    If fitness(Pi) <fitness(Gbest) then Gbest=Pi
    If fitness(Pi) <fitness(Pbest(i)) then Pbest(i)=Pi
    Update velocity of the particle i
    Update position of the particle i
  end
Until stopping criteria is not true
```

Fig. 5. The pseudo codes of PSO

3.4 Gravitational search algorithm

GSA was introduced by Esmat Rashedi and his friends in 2009 as an evolutionary algorithm. It is one of the recent optimization techniques inspired by the law of gravity. GSA was

originally designed for solving continuous problems. Since it is quite newly developed algorithm, it hasn't been applied to a lot of area. GSA was applied to filter modelling (Rashedi et al., 2011), Post-Outage Bus Voltage Magnitude Calculations (Ceylan et al., 2010), clustering (Yin et al., 2011), Scheduling in Grid Computing Systems (Barzegar et al., 2009).
GSA algorithm is based on the Newtonian gravity law: "Every particle in the universe attracts every other particle with a force that is directly proportional to the product of their masses and inversely proportional to the square of the distance between them" (Rashedi et al., 2009).
In GSA, particles are considered as objects and their performances are measured by their masses. GSA is based on the two important formulas about Newton Gravity Laws given by the equation 13 and 14. The first one is as given by the equation 13. This equation is the gravitational force equation between the two particles, which is directly proportional to their masses and inversely proportional to the square of distance between them. But in GSA instead of the square of the distance, only the distance is used. The second one is the equation of accelaration of a particle when a force is applied to it. It is given by equation 14.

$$F = G\frac{M_1 M_2}{R^2} \tag{13}$$

$$a = \frac{F}{M} \tag{14}$$

G is gravitational constant, $\mathbf{M_1}$ and $\mathbf{M_2}$ are masses and **R** is distance, **F** is gravitational force, **a** is acceleration. Based on these formulas, the heavier object with more gravity force attracts the other objects as it is seen in Figure 6.

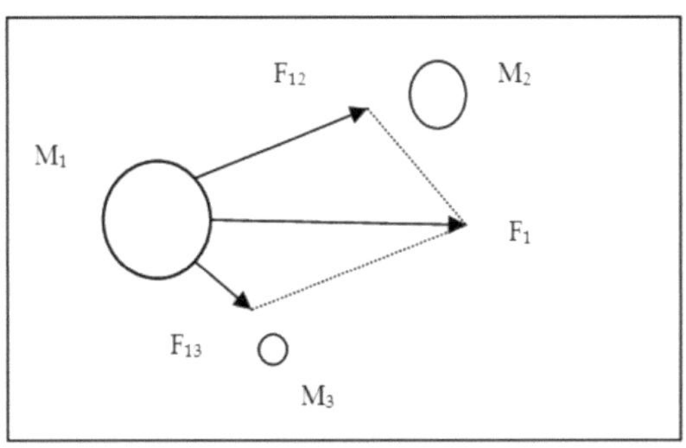

Fig. 6. The Newton Gravitational Force Representation

GSA algorithm initializes the position of the masses(X) given by equation 15.

$$X_i=(x_i^1, x_i^2, \dots , x_i^d, , x_i^n,) \quad i=1,2,3,\dots,N \tag{15}$$

Where, $\mathbf{X_i}$ is the position of *i*th mass. **n** gives the dimension of the masses. N gives the number of particles. $\mathbf{x_i^d}$ represents *i*th particle position in the ***d***th dimension.
The first velocities of the masses are accepted as zero. Until the stopping criterion (maximum iteration), algorithm evaluates the fitness functions of the objects. After the best and worst values are found for the current iteration, the masses of the particles are updated according to the equation 16, 17 and 18.

$$M_{ai} = M_{pi} = M_{ii} = M_i,\ i = 1, 2, \cdots, N \tag{16}$$

$$m_i(t) = \frac{fitness_i(t) - worst(t)}{best(t) - worst(t)} \tag{17}$$

$$M_i(t) = \frac{m_i(t)}{\sum_{j=1}^{N} m_j(t)} \tag{18}$$

In the equation 17, ***fitness$_i$(t)*** represents the fitness value of the ***i***th mass at time t, ***worst(t)*** is the maximum value of all the fitness values and ***best(t)*** is the minimum value of the all fitness values for a minimization problem. For maximization problems, the opposite of this expression is applied. In GSA, active gravitational mass **Ma**, passive gravitational mass **Mp** and inertial mass **Mi** are accepted as they are equal to each other.
Gravitiational constant which is propotional with the time is also updated according to the iteration number given by the equation 19.

$$G(t) = G_0 e^{-\alpha \frac{t}{T}} \tag{19}$$

Where, **α** is a user specified constant, **T** is the total number of iterations, and **t** is the current iteration. This equation is similar to the SA acceptance probability equation given by the equation 6. According to the formula the gravity force is decreasing by the time. The graviational force and total forces are updated as follows.

$$F_{ij}^d(t) = G(t)\frac{M_{pi}(t)M_{aj}(t)}{R_{ij}(t) + \varepsilon}(x_j^d(t) - x_i^d(t)) \tag{20}$$

$$F_i^d(t) = \sum_{j \in Kbest, j \neq i}^{N} rand_j F_{ij}^d(t) \tag{21}$$

F_{ij}^d(t) is the gravity force acting on mass ***i*** from mass ***j*** at time t, **G(t)** is the gravitational constant at time t, **Mpi** is the passive gravitational mass of object i, **Maj** is the active gravitational mass of object j, ε is a small constant, **R_{ij}** is the Euclidean distance between two objects i and j . **F_i^d(t)** is the force that acts on particle ***i*** in dimension ***d***, **rand**$_j$ is a random number between 0 and 1, **Kbest** is the set of first K objects with the best fitness value and biggest mass.The acceleration of an object ***i*** in ***d***th dimension is as follows.

$$a_i^d(t) = \frac{F_i^d(t)}{M_i(t)} \tag{22}$$

The new positions and velocities of the particles are calculated by the equation 23 and 24.

$$v_i^d(t+1) = rand_i \times v_i^d(t) + a_i^d(t) \tag{23}$$

$$x_i^d(t+1) = x_i^d(t) + v_i^d(t) \tag{24}$$

According to the law of motion, particles try to move towards the heavier objects. The heavier masses represent good solutions and they move slowly for the exploitation. The pseudo code of GSA is given in Figure 7.

```
Initialize the gravitational constant(G) and the positions of N masses(Xi)
xi=(xi1, xi2, ... , xid, , xin,) i=1,2,3,...,N
for i=1:max_iteration
   Decrease gravitational constant with the equation 19.
   Evaluate the fitness of each object.
   Calculate the masses with the equation 17, 18.
   Compute the total forces with the equation 21.
   Find the accelerations with the equation 22.
   Compute the velocities with the equation 23.
   Compute the positions with the equation 24.
End
```

Fig. 7. The pseudo codes of GSA

4. PSO and GA applications in robotic

In this section some well-known problems in Robotic were solved with heuristic search algorithms. The first problem is the inverse kinematics problem for a nearly PUMA robot with 6 DOF, and the second problem is the path planning problem for mobile robots.

4.1 The inverse kinematics problem for PUMA robot

Robot kinematics refers to robot motions without consideration of the forces. The forward kinematics is finding the robot's end effector's position and orientation using the given robot parameters and the joint's variables. Also, the inverse kinematics is about finding the robot's joints variables while the robot's parameters and the desired position of the end effector are given (Kucuk & Bingul, 2006). The solution of the robot's forward kinematics is always possible and unique. On the other hand, generally, the inverse kinematics problem has several solutions (Kucuk & Bingul, 2006). The most known and used method for solving robot kinematics problems is Denavit-Hartenberg method. In this method several parameters, namely DH parameters, are defined according to robot's parameters and the replaced coordinate systems as given in Figure 8. These parameters are used to define transformations between the coordinate systems using 4x4 transformation matrices. The multiplication of all the matrices of the robot gives the final robot's end effectors' position and orientation (Kucuk & Bingul, 2006).

The selected robot for this example is a nearly PUMA type robot. Different from the general PUMA robot, the robot used in this example was equipped with an offset wrist. The inverse kinematics of the robot equipped with such a wrist is quite complicated and can be computationally cumbersome (Kucuk & Bingul, 2005). In this example, this problem was solved with GA and PSO. The robot's link parameters and coordinate systems replacements can be seen in Figure 9. Furthermore, according to Figure 9, the DH parameters of the robot can be defined as given in Table 1. Using the DH parameters, the forward kinematics of the robot can be solved easily using robot's transformation matrices. A transformation matrix is a 4x4 matrix and has the form as it is seen in equation 25.

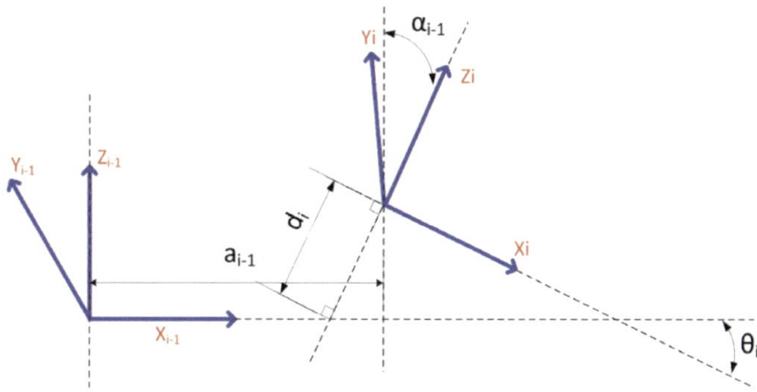

Fig. 8. DH parameters between two coordinate systems

$$T = \begin{bmatrix} & R & & P \\ 0 & 0 & 0 & 1 \end{bmatrix} \tag{25}$$

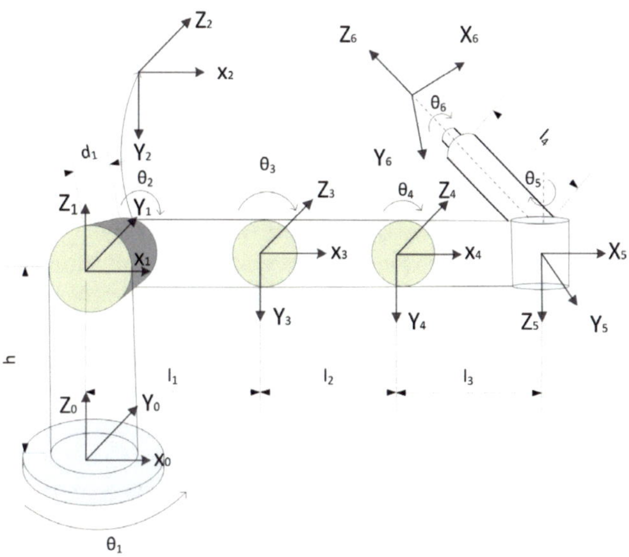

Fig. 9. The nearly Puma robot's link parameters and coordinate systems replacement

I	α_{i-1}	a_{i-1}	d_i	θ_i
1	0	0	h	θ_1
2	$-\pi/2$	0	d_1	θ_2
3	0	l_1	0	θ_3
4	0	l_2	0	θ_4
5	$-\pi/2$	l_3	0	θ_5
6	$\pi/2$	0	l_4	θ_6

Table 1. The DH parameters of the robot

Where, T and R are 4x4 transformation and 3x3 rotation matrices between two consecutive links respectively while P is 3x1 position vector. Detailed information about defining this matrices and vectors can be found in (Kucuk & Bingul, 2006). The transformation matrices of the robot are as follows:

$$
\begin{gathered}
{}_1^0T=\begin{bmatrix} C\theta_1 & -S\theta_1 & 0 & 0 \\ S\theta_1 & C\theta_1 & 0 & 0 \\ 0 & 0 & 1 & h \\ 0 & 0 & 0 & 1 \end{bmatrix}
\quad {}_2^1T=\begin{bmatrix} C\theta_2 & -S\theta_2 & 0 & 0 \\ 0 & 0 & 1 & d_1 \\ -S\theta_2 & -C\theta_2 & 0 & 0 \\ 0 & 0 & 0 & 1 \end{bmatrix}
\quad {}_3^2T=\begin{bmatrix} C\theta_3 & -S\theta_3 & 0 & l_1 \\ S\theta_3 & C\theta_3 & 0 & 0 \\ 0 & 0 & 1 & 0 \\ 0 & 0 & 0 & 1 \end{bmatrix} \\
{}_4^3T=\begin{bmatrix} C\theta_4 & -S\theta_4 & 0 & l_2 \\ S\theta_4 & C\theta_4 & 0 & 0 \\ 0 & 0 & 1 & 0 \\ 0 & 0 & 0 & 1 \end{bmatrix}
\quad {}_5^4T=\begin{bmatrix} C\theta_5 & -S\theta_5 & 0 & l_3 \\ 0 & 0 & 1 & 0 \\ -S\theta_5 & -C\theta_5 & 0 & 0 \\ 0 & 0 & 0 & 1 \end{bmatrix}
\quad {}_6^5T=\begin{bmatrix} C\theta_6 & -S\theta_6 & 0 & 0 \\ 0 & 0 & -1 & -l_4 \\ S\theta_6 & C\theta_6 & 0 & 0 \\ 0 & 0 & 0 & 1 \end{bmatrix}
\end{gathered}
\tag{26}
$$

In the above matrices $C\theta_i$ and $S\theta_i$ (i=1,2,...,6) indicate $\cos\theta_i$ and $\sin\theta_i$ respectively. The forward kinematics of the robot is the forward multiplication of these matrices given by equation 27. The end effector's position in 3D space is defined with the last column of the result matrix.

$$
{}_6^0T={}_1^0T\,{}_2^1T\,{}_3^2T\,{}_4^3T\,{}_5^4T\,{}_6^5T=T=\begin{bmatrix} & R & & P \\ 0 & 0 & 0 & 1 \end{bmatrix}
\tag{27}
$$

In this example, the inverse kinematics of the robot was solved using the most general type of GA and PSO. Before starting to solve the problem with an optimization algorithm, it is needed to define the problem, exactly. The problem presented in this example is finding the robot joint angle values while the robot's parameters and the end effector's position are given. According to problem it can be seen that one individual of the population should have six joint's constraints. They are θ_1, θ_2, θ_3, θ_4, θ_5 and θ_6. So, an individual can be a 1x6 vector. Each component of the individual is for one of the joint's constraints. The range of the each constraint can be defined separately. However, for the sake of simplicity the ranges of the joints were defined between [-pi, pi]. A sample individual can be seen in Figure 10.

π	-π/4	π/2	0	π/5	0

Fig. 10. A sample individual

The most important part of the solution is the object function, since the fitness value of an individual can be defined with the help of this function. In the example, the object function was defined using the desired position values of the end effector of the robot and the obtained position values from individuals using forward kinematic equations of the robot. The Euler distance between the desired position of the end-effector and the results obtained from an individual can be defined as follows.

Let the desired position of the end effector be $P_d=\begin{bmatrix} x_d & y_d & z_d \end{bmatrix}$ and the obtained position knowledge using an individual be $P_i=\begin{bmatrix} x_i & y_i & z_i \end{bmatrix}$. The Euler distance between these two points in 3D space can be obtained as given in equation 28.

$$d_i = \sqrt{\left(x_d - x_i\right)^2 + \left(y_d - y_i\right)^2 + \left(z_d - z_i\right)^2} \tag{28}$$

The individual that offer the smallest distance is the most convenient candidate of the solution. The object function for the problem can be formulated like in equation 29.

$$O_i = p{d_i}^2 \tag{29}$$

$\mathbf{O_i}$ is object function value, **p** is penalty constant and $\mathbf{d_i}$ is the Euler distance calculated by equation 28, for i'th individual.

The problem was solved firstly using GA. The features of the GA was defined as follows: The gene coding type was determined as real-value coding and the selection type was determined as roulette wheel technique while the mutation and the crossover types were determined as one-point crossover and one-point mutation. The GA starts with defining the needed parameters, like crossover and mutation rates, number of individuals, number of iterations (stopping criteria). Then the initial population is defined randomly in the ranges of the constraints and the object and the fitness values of this population are calculated. In each iteration, the elitism, crossover and mutation operations are performed. The new population is generated after these operations and it masked to comply with the range of the constraints. And finally, the new generation's object and fitness values are calculated and the iterations proceeds until to reach the stopping criteria. In the end of the algorithm, the results are presented. The flowchart of the algorithm can be seen in Figure 11.

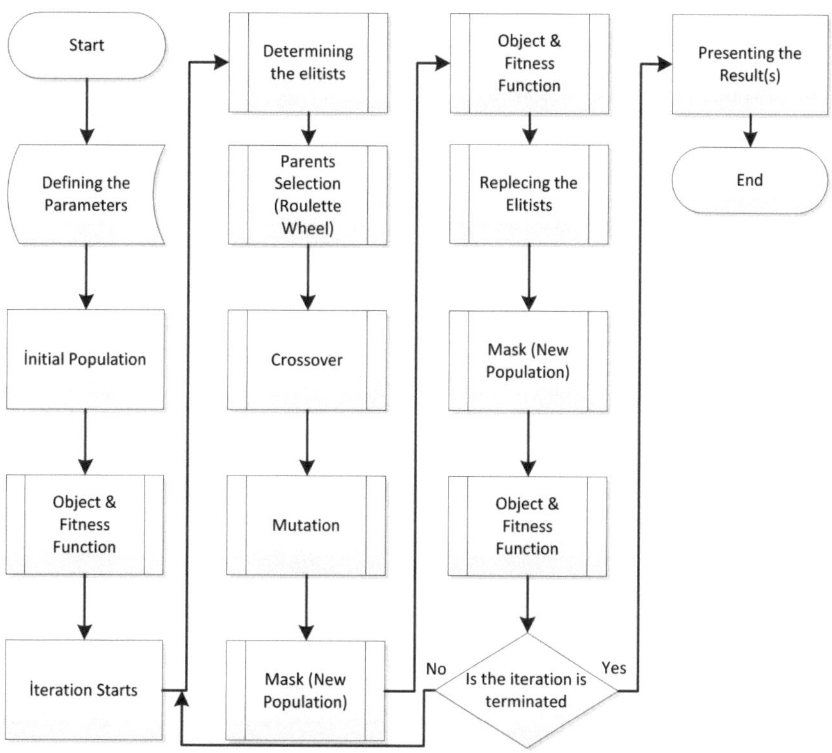

Fig. 11. The flowchart of the GA

The numerical example given below is simply the realization of the algorithm. The robot's first link was replaced in the [0 0 0] coordinates in 3D space and the other link's coordinates were defined according to these coordinates. The aim of the example is to find the robot's joint angles (constraints) that are needed to replace the end-effector of the robot in the goal coordinates. The parameters used in the algorithms were given in Table 2. According to defined parameters, the zero position of the robot's end effector was calculated using zero thetas as [30 15 30]. The solution is the smallest Euler distance between the goal coordinates, [10 5 60], and the each of the individuals. One of the real solutions for this goal coordinates is [0 -pi/2 pi/2 -pi/2 pi/2 0]. The algorithm continues until the stopping criterion is met. In this study, the generation number is the stopping criterion. After running the GA, the constraints' values were found as [-1.0278 -0.5997 -0.6820 -0.8940 0.9335 0] as radian. The coordinates of the end effector can be calculated using these constraints as [9.8143 4.9310 60.0652]. In Figure 12, the two solutions were depicted, the blue one is the sample solution, [0 -pi/2 pi/2 -pi/2 pi/2 0] and the red is the found solution [-1.4238 -1.9043 -0.7396 1.5808 0.9328 0]. The error between the desired and the found end effector's position was [0.1857 0.0690 -0.0652] units.

World Coordinates	Goal Point	Number of Population	Number of Generation	Mutation Rate	Crossover Rate	Penalty	Link Lengths	Zero Position Thetas
[0 0 0]	[10 5 60]	50	2000	0.1	0.9	10	h=30; d1=5; l1=l2=l3=l4=10	[0 0 0 0 0 0]

Table 2. The defined parameters for GA

In this example the most general type of GA was used to solve the problem. It is obvious that more acceptable solutions can be found using different techniques and/or object functions in GA.

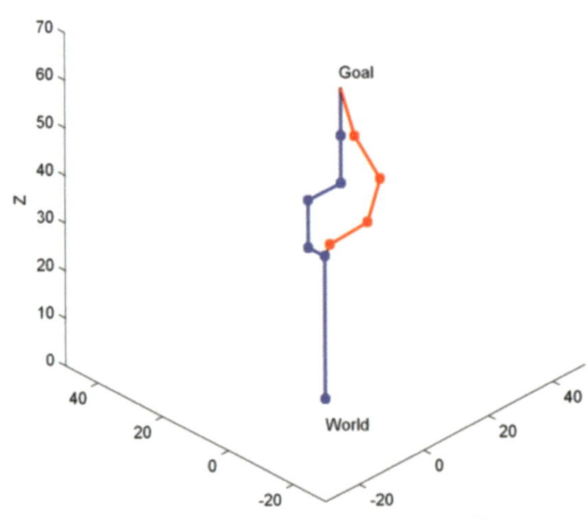

Fig. 12. The sample solution and the solution found with GA

The same problem was solved with PSO algorithm and the solutions were compared with GA. The flowchart of PSO algorithm that was used to solve the problem can be seen in Figure 13 and, the parameters defined for PSO can be seen in Table 3.

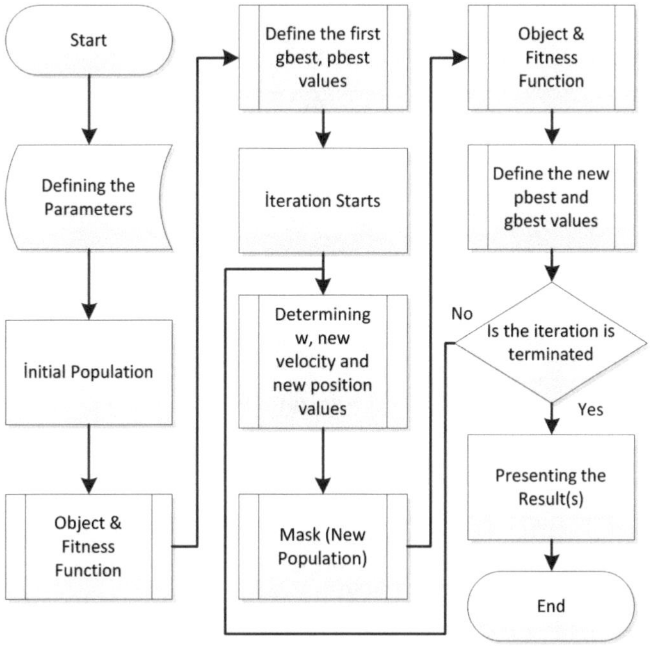

Fig. 13. The flowchart of the PSO algorithm

World Coordinates	Goal Point	Number of Population	Number of Generation	Cognitive Component	Social Component	Penalty	Min. inertia weight	Max. inertia weight	Link Lengths	Zero Position Thetas
[0 0 0]	[10 5 60]	50	2000	2	2	10	0.4	0.4	h=30; d1=5; l1=l2=l3=l4=10	[0 0 0 0 0 0]

Table 3. The defined parameters for PSO

When the algorithm was run, the constraints were found in radian as [-1.3725 -2.5852 1.8546 -0.9442 0.9538 0] and the coordinates of the end effector calculated using these constraints were [9.9979 4.9941 60.0125]. According to these results it can be seen that PSO is found as it serves more convenient solution than GA's solution. In the Figure 14 the two solutions were depicted the blue one is the sample solution, [0 -pi/2 pi/2 –pi/2 pi/2 0] and the red is the found solution [-1.3725 -2.5852 1.8546 -0.9442 0.9538 0].

The convenience of an optimization algorithm to a problem differs from one problem to another and it can only be determined by doing several trials and comparisons. There is no specific algorithm to achieve the best solution for all optimization problems. The comparisons are mainly related to the algorithm's final object function values and the execution time of the algorithm. In the final part of the example a comparison between GA

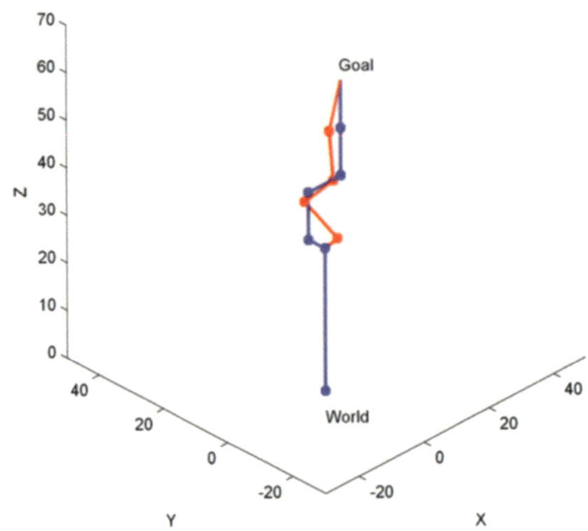

Fig. 14. The sample solution and the found solution using PSO

and PSO for the inverse kinematics problem of the 6 DOF nearly puma robot was presented. For each problem, 100 runs were simulated using the same parameters. The final object function's values and execution times of the two algorithms were presented in a comparative manner using graphs and Tables. The defined parameters for both of the algorithms can be seen in Table 4.

Parameters	GA	PSO
Number of Individuals	100	100
Number of Iterations	1000	1000
Penalty	10	10
World Coordinates	[0 0 0]	[0 0 0]
Goal Coordinates	[10 5 60]	[10 5 60]
Gene Code Type	Real Values	Real Values
Mutation Rate	0.2	***
Crossover Rate	0.9	***
Selection Type	R. Wheel	***
Mutation Type	One Point	***
c1	**	2
c2	**	2
Wmin	**	0.4
Wmax	**	0.9

Table 4. The parameters for GA and PSO for the inverse kinematic problem

Each algorithm was executed under the same condition and on the same computer, and according to the two criterions; the comparison was made between the two algorithms. The first criterion is about the algorithms' final object function values presented in Figure 15. The Figure indicates that both metaheuristic algorithms found the nearly optimum solutions to the problem. On the other hand it can be seen that PSO had more acceptable results than GA. In almost all executions PSO find the exact solutions. However, in 6 executions GA

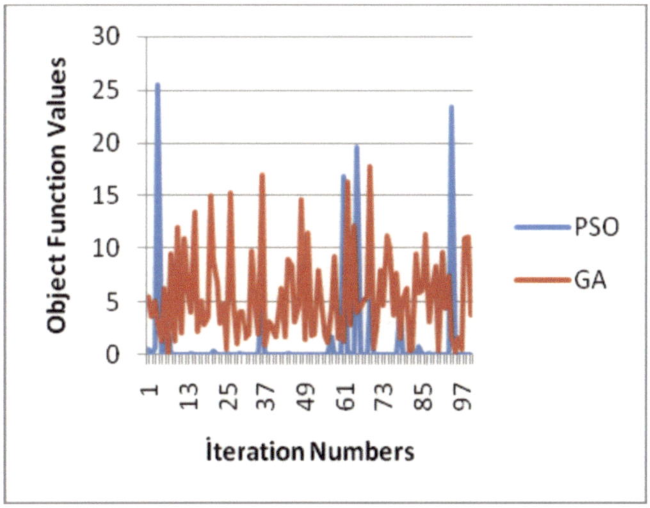

Fig. 15. The object function values of the two algorithms

outperforms PSO. The second criterion is for the execution times of the algorithms. The obtained results, in seconds, were presented in Figure 16. In the Figure, it is obvious that the elapsed time of the PSO is much less than the GA's. As a result, it can be said that PSO produced better results than GA in terms of both final object function's values and the execution times.

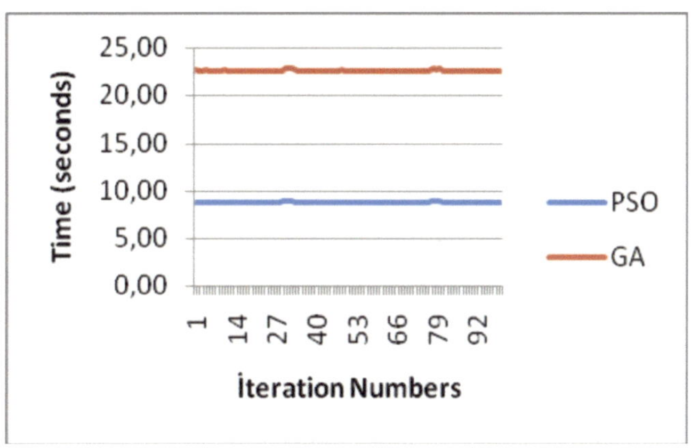

Fig. 16. The execution times of the two algorithms

4.2 Path planning problem for mobile robots

The second example is about path planning for mobile robots. Path planning is one of the most studied topics related to mobile robots. It works for finding the shortest path between the start and goal points while avoiding the collisions with any obstacles. In the example, this problem was solved using GA and PSO.

Path planning can be classified in two categories, global and local path planning. The global type path planning is made for a static and completely known environment while the local path planning is required if the environment is dynamic (Sedighi et al., 2004). In this example, global path planning was performed. The robot's environment was defined as a 10x10 unit size square in 2D coordinate system. In the environment, it was defined several obstacles that have different shapes. The problem is finding the shortest path between pre-defined start and goal points while the coordinates of these points and of the obstacle vertexes are known. A sample environment including obstacles and a sample path can be seen in the Figure 17. In the Figure there are six different shaped obstacles and the path is composed from four points. Two of these points are via points while the others are start and goal points. The mobile robot can reach the goal with tracing the path from the start point. The main object of this problem is to find the shortest path that is not crosses with any obstacles. According to these two constraints, the object function can be defined composing of two parts. The first one is the length of the path and the second one is the penalty function for collisions. The total length of the path can be calculated with the Euler distance between the points on the path if there are two via points that means the path is composed of three parts. The Euler distance between the two points can be simply calculated in 2D environment as in equation 30.

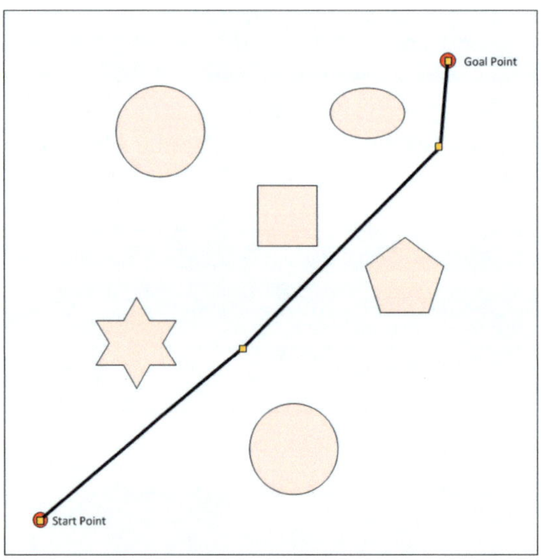

Fig. 17. A sample environment and a path

$$d_i = \sqrt{(x_i - x_{i-1})^2 + (y_i - y_{i-1})^2} \quad i = 1,2,..,n \tag{30}$$

Where, **n** is the number of points on the path. The total length of the path is simply the sum of the distances, equation 31. In the equation, **L** is the total length of the path.

$$L = \sum_{i=1}^{n-1} d_i \quad i = 1,2,..,n \tag{31}$$

The second part of the object function determines the penalty for collision with the obstacles. Determining the collision with an obstacle is quite complicated. The obstacle avoidance technique, used in this study, can be briefly described using Figure 18.

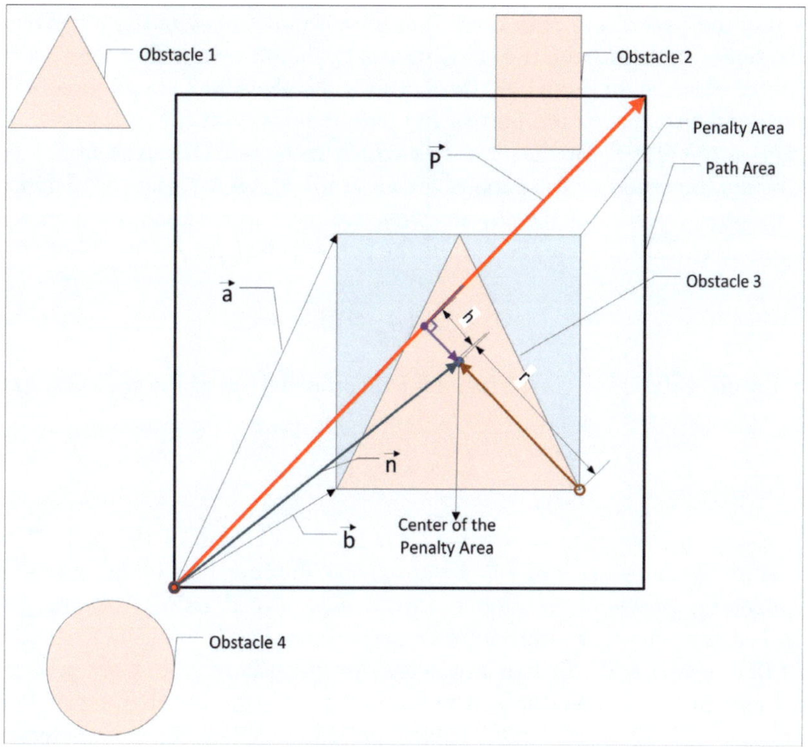

Fig. 18. The penalty calculation for a collision with an obstacle

In the Figure;
Path Area: The rectangular area defined using the maximum and minimum coordinate values of the two points on the path.
Penalty Area: The rectangular area defined using the maximum and minimum coordinate values of the obstacle's vertexes.
$\vec{P}$: The vector between two points of the path, from the first one to the next.
$\vec{a}$ and $\vec{b}$: The vectors from the first point of the $\vec{P}$ to the two vertexes of the penalty area. (There are two additional vectors from the first point of the $\vec{P}$ to the other two vertexes of the penalty area)
$\vec{n}$: The vector from the first point of the $\vec{P}$ to the center of the penalty area.
r : The distance between one vertex and the center of the penalty area.
$h = \frac{|\vec{n} \times \vec{P}|}{|\vec{P}|}$: The distance between the center of the penalty area and the $\vec{P}$ vector.

The collision detection procedure starts with defining the path area, and then the obstacles which are totally or partially located in the path are determined like obstacle 2 and obstacle 3 in the Figure 18. After that, penalty areas for each of the determined obstacle are defined; the penalty area for obstacle 3 is shown in the Figure 18. The following processes are achieved for the determined penalty areas. First, the $\vec{P}$ vector between the two points of the path, and four vectors from the first point of the $\vec{P}$ vector to the vertexes of the penalty area are defined. Afterward, the cross products of the $\vec{P}$ with each of these vectors are achieved and the sign of the each product is determined. If the all cross products have the same sign, this means that the part of the path doesn't cross with obstacle. On the other hand if there are different signs obtained from the cross products, then it means that the part of the path crosses with the obstacle. In Figure 18, the signs for the obstacle 2 are all same while not for the obstacle 3 and that means the part of the path crosses with the obstacle 3. Finally the penalty value is calculated for the obstacles which cross with the part of the path. Euler distance between the center of the penalty area and the $\vec{P}$ vector, and the distance between the center and one vertexes of the penalty area are used to calculate the penalty value as defined in equation 32. In the equation, c_p is the penalty constant for the collisions.

$$P = c_p(1 + r - h)^2 \tag{32}$$

As a result, the object function can be formulated completely as in the equation 33.

$$f = L + \sum_{i=1}^{k} P_i \tag{33}$$

Where, **f** is the final object function value, **L** is the total length of the path, **P** is the total penalty value for the collisions and **k** is the number of the collisions for an individual.
The path planning problem for mobile robots was solved using GA and PSO and a comparison between these two algorithms was presented as it is in the first example. The algorithm's flow charts and other details were not given here since they presented in the chapter and also in the first example. The parameters for the problem were defined as in Table 5, and the problem was firstly solved with GA. The GA's parameters were also defined as in Table 6.

Environment	A 10x10 unit area in 2D space
Obstacles	Seven different shape obstacles
Number of Points of an individual	There are four points. Two of them are via points while the others are start and goal points.
Start Point	[0.2, 0.2]
Goal Point	[8.5, 7.5]

Table 5. The parameters for the path planning problem for mobile robots

Number of Individuals	Number of Iterations	Mutation rate	Crossover Rate	Penalty constant
100	200	0.2	0.9	1000

Table 6. GA parameters

The obtained result can be seen in the Figure 19. It can be seen that GA can find nearly optimum solution to the path planning problem for mobile robots.
The second algorithm is the most general type of the PSO like used in first example. The defined parameters for the algorithm are in the Table 7, and the obtained result from PSO is in the Figure 20, and it is obvious that PSO can find nearly optimum solution to the path planning problem for mobile robots.

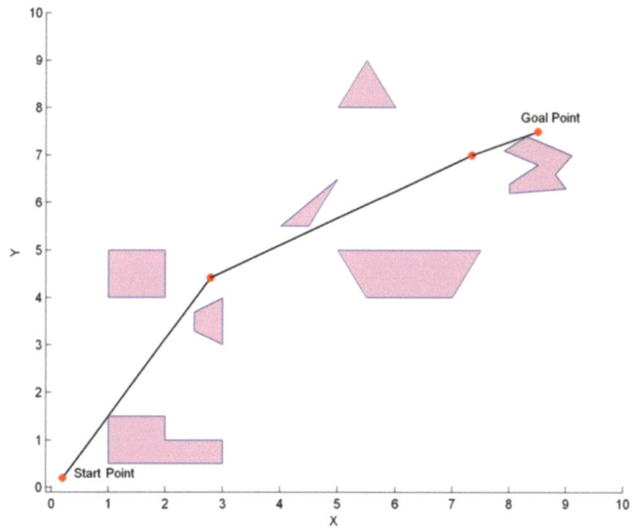

Fig. 19. GA solution

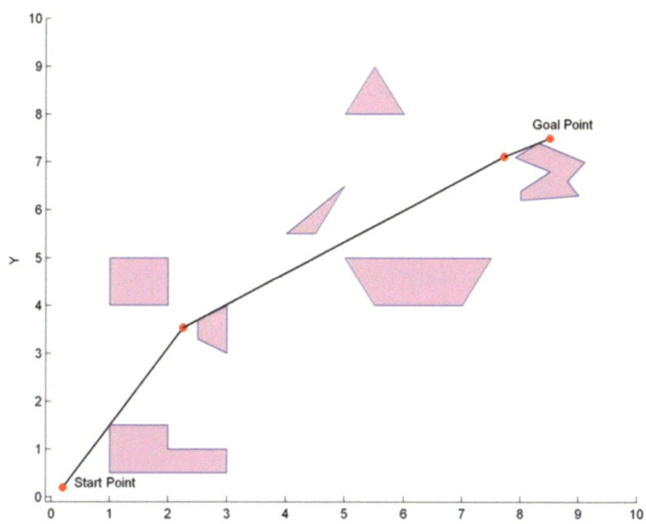

Fig. 20. PSO solution

Number of Individuals	Number of Iterations	Cognitive Component	Social Component	Min. inertia weight	Max. inertia weight	Penalty constant
100	200	2	2	0.4	0.9	1000

Table 7. PSO parameters

For the comparison the same parameters were defined for the two algorithms and each algorithm was run 100 times on the same computer under the same conditions. The parameters were defined as in Table 8.

Parameters	**GA**	**PSO**
Number of Individuals	100	100
Number of Iterations	200	200
Penalty	1000	1000
Start Point	[0.2, 0.2]	[0.2, 0.2]
Goal Point	[8.5, 7.5]	[8.5, 7.5]
Number of Points of an individual	3	3
Gene Code Type	Real Values	Real Values
Mutation Rate	0.2	***
Crossover Rate	0.9	***
Selection Type	R. Wheel	***
Mutation Type	One Point	***
c1	**	2
c2	**	2
Wmin	**	0.4
Wmax	**	0.9

Table 8. The parameters for GA and PSO for the path planning problem

The comparison results for the both algorithms were drawn on the two Figures. In Figure 21, there is a graph for the comparison of the final object function values of the algorithms. Lastly, the graph for the comparison of the algorithms' execution times is in the Figure 22.

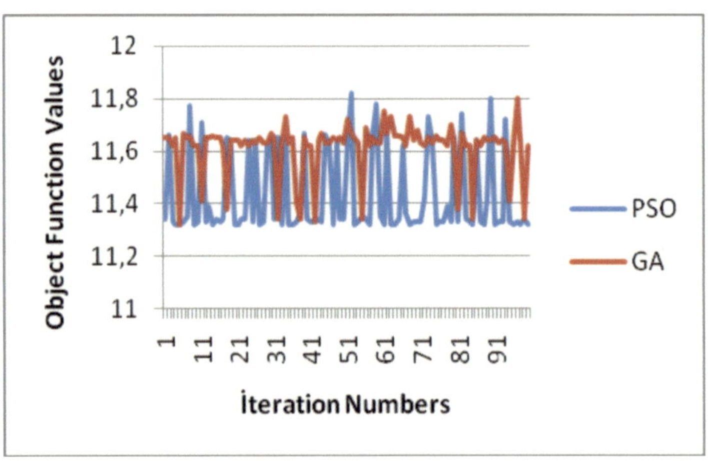

Fig. 21. The object function values of the two algorithms

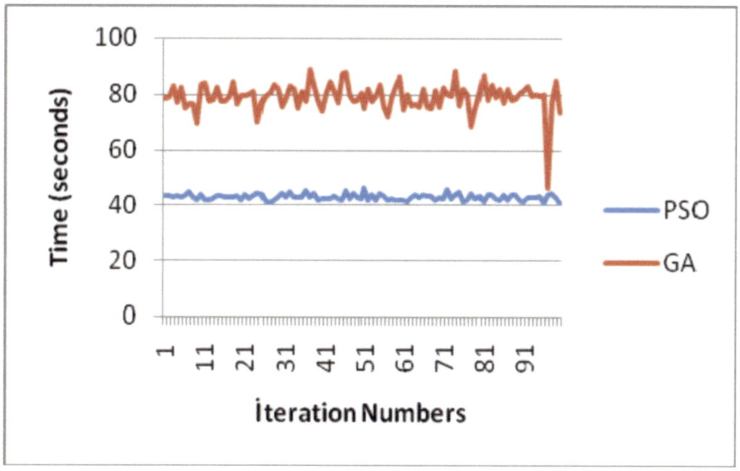

Fig. 22. The execution times of the two algorithms

The perpendicular distance between given start and goal points can be calculated as in equation 34.

$$d = \sqrt{(8.5-0.2)^2 + (7.5-0.2)^2} = 11.0535 \tag{34}$$

The perpendicular distance was calculated directly from start point to goal point and the obstacles were not considered. If the obstacles were considered that means the distance should be longer. The object function values that were calculated from the algorithms are between 11.3 and 11.82, and this means that these results are nearly optimum results. In terms of the comparison, there is no a significant difference about the final object function values. On the other hand, there is a remarkable difference between the two algorithms' execution times. GA's execution time is nearly twice of the PSO's execution times. So, it can be concluded by saying that the both PSO and GA can be used to solve the path planning of the mobile robots, but if the execution time is important, PSO should be preferred.

5. Conclusion

Heuristic algorithms are an alternative way for the solution of optimization problems. Their implementations are easy. Even if they couldn't find the exact optimum point, they find satisfactory results, in a reasonable solution time. In this chapter, two well-known optimization problems in Robotic were solved with PSO and GA. The first problem is the inverse kinematics of the near PUMA robot while the second problem is the path planning problem for mobile robots. These problems were solved with PSO and GA. It has seen that both algorithm give satisfactory results. But PSO outperforms GA in terms of the solution time, because of the fact that it uses little parameters.

6. References

Barzegar, B.; Rahmani, A.M.; Zamanifar, K. & Divsalar, A. (2009). Gravitational emulation local search algorithm for advanced reservation and scheduling in grid computing systems, *Computer Sciences and Convergence Information Technology,. ICCIT '09. Fourth International Conference on*, Vol., No., pp.1240-1245.

Basturk, B. & Karaboga, D. (2006). An Artificial Bee Colony (ABC) Algorithm for Numeric Function Optimization. *IEEE Swarm Intelligence Symposium 2006,* Vol. 8, No. 1, pp. 687-697.

Blum, C. & Roli, A., Metaheuristics in Combinatorial Optimization: Overview and Conceptual Comparasion, Technical Report, *TR/IRIDIA*/2001-13, October 2001.

Ceylan, O.; Ozdemir, A. & Dag, H.(2010). Gravitational search algorithm for post-outage bus voltage magnitude calculations, *Universities Power Engineering Conference (UPEC), 2010 45th International* , Vol., No., pp.1-6.

Chandra, R. & Rolland, L.(2011). On solving the forward kinematics of 3RPR planar parallel manipulator using hybrid metaheuristics, *Applied Mathematics and Computation*, Vol. 217, No. 22, pp. 8997-9008

Chen, M. W. & Zalzala, A. M. S.(1997). Dynamic modelling and genetic-based trajectory generation for non-holonomic mobile manipulators, Original Research Article *Control Engineering Practice*, Vol.5, No.1, pp. 39-48

Clerc, M.(1999). The swarm and the queen: Towards a deterministic and adaptive particle swarm optimization. *Proc. Congress on Evolutionary Computation.*, pp 1951-1957.

Dorigo, M.; Maniezzo, V.; Colorni, A. (1996). Ant system: optimization by a colony of cooperating agents, Systems, *Man, and Cybernetics,* Part B: Cybernetics, IEEE Transactions on , Vol.26, No.1, pp.29-41

Eberhart, R & Shi, Y.(2001). Particle swarm optimization: Developments, applications and resources, *in Proc. IEEE Congr. Evol. Comput.*, Vol. 1,No., pp. 81–86

Farmer, D.; Packard, N. & Perelson, A. (1986). The immune system, adaptation and machine learning, *Physica D,* Vol. 2, pp. 187–204

Feo, T. A. & Resende, M. G.C. (1995). Greedy randomized adaptive search procedures, *Journal of Global Optimization*, Vol. 6, No. 2, pp. 109–133

Fisher, M.L.; Alexander, H. G. & Rinnooy, K. (1998) The Design, analysis and implementation of heuristics, *Management Science*, Vol. 34., No.3, pp 263-265.

Gao,M. & Jingwen, T.(2007), Path planning for mobile robot based on improved simulated annealing artificial neural network, *icnc, Third International Conference on Natural Computation 2007,* Vol. 3, No., pp.8-12.

Geem, Z.W.; Kim, J.H. & Loganathan, G.V. (2001). A new heuristic optimization algorithm: harmony search, *Simulation*, Vol. 76 No. 2 pp. 60–68

Glover, F. & Kochenberger, Gary A. (2002). *Handbook of Metaheuristics,* Kluwer Academic Publishers, Norwell, MA.

Goldberg, D. E. (1989). *Genetic Algorithms in Search Optimization and Machine Learning.* Addison Wesley. pp. 41. ISBN 0201157675.

Gueaieb, W. & Miah, M.S.(2008). Mobile robot navigation using particle swarm optimization and noisy RFID communication, *Computational Intelligence for Measurement Systems and Applications, 2008. CIMSA 2008.* Vol. , No., pp. 111 - 116

Hong, D.S. & Cho, H.S.(1999). Generation of robotic assembly sequences using a simulated annealing, *Intelligent Robots and Systems,* IROS '99 Proceedings. *1999 IEEE/RSJ International Conference on* , Vol.2, No., pp.1247-1252.

Jourdan, L.; Basseur, M. & Talbi, E.-G.(2009). Hybridizing exact methods and metaheuristics: A taxonomy, *European Journal of Operational Research,* Vol. 199, No. 3, pp. 620-629.

Kalra, P.; Mahapatra, P.B. & Aggarwal, D.K. (2006). An evolutionary approach for solving the multimodal inverse kinematics, *Mechanism and Machine Theory,* Vol. 41, No.10, pp. 1213–1229

Karsli, G. & Tekinalp, O. (2005). Trajectory optimization of advanced launch system, *Recent Advances in Space Technologies,* RAST 2005. *Proceedings of 2nd International Conference on* ,Vol., No., pp. 374- 378

Kennedy, J.(1997). The particle swarm: Social adaptation of knowledge, *in Proc. IEEE Int. Conf. Evol. Comput.,* Vol. ,No., pp. 303–308.

Kennedy, J.; Eberhart, R. (1995). Particle Swarm Optimization. *Proceedings of IEEE International Conference on Neural Networks,* Vol.4, No., IV. pp. 1942–1948

Kirkpatrick, S.; Gelatt, D.C & Vechhi, M.P. (1983) Optimization by simulated annealing, *Science* Vol.220, No.4598, pp. 671–680

Kucuk, Serdar, & Bingul, Zafer. (2005). The Inverse Kinematics Solutions of Fundamental Robot Manipulators with Offset Wrist, Proceedings of the 2005 IEEE International Conference on Mechatronics, Taipei, Taiwan, July 2005

Kucuk, Serdar, & Bingul, Zafer. (2006). Robot Kinematics: Forward and Inverse Kinematics, In: Industrial Robotics: Theory, Modelling and Control, Sam Cubero, pp. (117-148), InTech - Open Access, Retrieved from < http://www.intechopen.com/articles/show/title/robot_kinematics__forward_and_inverse_kinematics >

Kumar, J.; Xie, S. & Kean, C. A.(2009). Kinematic design optimization of a parallel ankle rehabilitation robot using modified genetic algorithm, *Robotics and Autonomous Systems,* Vol. 57,No. 10, pp 1018-1027

Laguna, M.(1994). A guide to implementing tabu search. *Investigacion Operative,* Vol.4, No.1, pp 5-25

Lazinca, A. (2009). *Particle Swarm Optimization,* InTech, ISBN 978-953-7619-48-0.

Lee, K. Y. & El-Sharkawi, M. A. (2008). *Modern Heuristic Optimization Techniques Theory and Applications to Power Systems,* IEEE Press, 445 Hoes Lane Piscataway, NJ 08854

Li, J. & Xiao, X.(2008). Multi- Swarm and Multi- Best particle swarm optimization algorithm. *Intelligent Control and Automation, 2008, WCICA 2008, 7th World Congress on* , Vol., No., pp.6281-6286.

Lin, CY & Hajela P.(1992). Genetic algorithms in optimization problems with discrete and integer design variables. *Engineering Optimization* ,Vol. 19, No.4 , pp.309–327.

Martı´, R.; Laguna, M. & Glover F. (2006). Principles of scatter search, *European Journal of Operational Research(EJOR),* Vol. 169, No. 2, pp. 359–372.

Raghavan, M. (1993). The Stewart Platform of General Geometry Has 40 Configurations. *Journal of Mechanical Design,* Vol. 115, pp. 277-282

Rashedi, E.; Nezamabadi-pour, H. & Saryazdi, S.(2009). GSA: a gravitational search algorithm. *Information Science,* Vol. 179, No.13, pp. 2232–2248

Saruhan, H.(2006). Optimum design of rotor-bearing system stability performance comparing an evolutionary algorithm versus a conventional method. *International Journal of Mechanical Sciences,* Vol. 48, No 12. pp 1341-1351

Sedighi , Kamran. H., Ashenayi , Kaveh., Manikas, Theodore. W., Wainwright, Roger L., & Tai, Heng Ming (2004). Autonomous Local Path Planning for a Mobile Robot Using a Genetic Algorithm, The Congress on Evolutionary Computation, Oregon, Portland, June 2004.

Selene, L. C-M.;Castillo, O. & Luis T. A.(2011). Generation of walking periodic motions for a biped robot via genetic algorithms, *Applied Soft Computing*, In Press, Corrected Proof, Available online 20 May 2011.

Storn, R.(1996). On the usage of differential evolution for function optimization, *Fuzzy Information Processing Society*, NAFIPS, Biennial Conference of the North American , vol. , No., pp.519-523

Valle, Y.; Venayagamoorthy, G. K.; Mohagheghi, S.; Hernandez, J.C. & Harley, R. G.(2008). Particle swarm optimization: Basic Concepts,Variants and Applications in Power Systems, *IEEE Transactions On Evolutionary Computation*, Vol. 12, No. 2, pp 171-195.

Wang, T. (2001). *Global Optimization For Constrained Nonlinear Programming*, Doctor of Philosophy in Computer Science in the Graduate College of the University of Illinois at Urbana-Champaign, Urbana, Illinois

Weise, T. (2008). *Global Optimization Algorithms - Theory and Application*, Online as e-book, University of Kassel, Distributed Systems Group, Copyright (c) 2006-2008 Thomas Weise, licensed under GNU, online available http://www.it-weise.de/

Yin, M.; Hu, Y., Yang, F.; Li, X. & Gu, W. (2011). A novel hybrid K-harmonic means and gravitational search algorithm approach for clustering, *Expert Systems with Applications* Vol.38, No. , pp. 9319–9324.

Zargar, A. N. & Javadi, H.(2009). Using particle swarm optimization for robot path planning in dynamic environments with moving obstacles and target, *Third UKSim European Symposium on Computer Modeling and Simulation*, Vol. , No., pp.60-65

17

Multi-Criteria Optimal Path Planning of Flexible Robots

Rogério Rodrigues dos Santos[1], Valder Steffen Jr.[1]
and Sezimária de Fátima Pereira Saramago[2]
[1]*School of Mechanical Engineering, Federal University of Uberlândia, Uberlândia, MG*
[2]*Faculty of Mathematics, Federal University of Uberlândia, Uberlândia, MG*
Brazil

1. Introduction

Determining the trajectory from the initial to the final end-effector positioning represents one of the most common problems in the path-planning design of serial robot manipulators. The movement is established through the specification of a set of intermediate points. In this way, the manipulator is guided along the trajectory without any concern regarding the intermediate configurations along the path. However, there are applications in which the intermediate points have to be taken into account both for path-planning and control purposes. An example of such an application is the case of robot manipulators that are used in welding operations.

In the context of industrial applications, a previous planning is justified, the so-called *off-line programming*, aiming at establishing a precise control for the movement. This planning includes the analysis of the kinematics and dynamics behavior of the system. The reduction of costs and increase of productivity are some of the most important objectives in industrial automation. Therefore, to make possible the use of robotic systems, it is important that one considers the path planning optimization for a specific task.

The improvement of industrial productivity can be achieved by reducing the weight of the robots and/or increasing their speed of operation. The first choice may lead to power consumption reduction while the second results in a faster work cycle. To successfully achieve these purposes it is very desirable to build flexible robotic manipulators. In some situations it is even necessary to consider the flexibility effects due to the joints and gear components of the manipulators for obtaining an accurate and reliable control.

Compared to conventional heavy robots, flexible link manipulators have the potential advantage of lower cost, larger work volume, higher operational speed, greater payload-to-manipulator-weight ratio, smaller actuators and lower energy consumption.

The study of the control of flexible manipulators started in the field of space robots research. Aiming at space applications, the manipulator should be as light as possible in order to reduce the launching costs (Book, 1984). Uchiyama *et al.* (1990), Alberts *et al.* (1992), Dubowsky (1994), to mention only a few, have also studied flexible manipulators for space applications. Shi *et al.* (1998) discussed some key issues in the dynamic control of lightweight robots for several applications.

As a consequence of the interest in using flexible structures in robotics, several papers regarding the design of controllers for the manipulation task of flexible manipulators are found in the literature (Latornell *et al.*, 1998), (Choi and Krishnamurthy, 1994) and (Chang and Chen, 1998).

In Tsujita *et al.* (2004), the trajectory and force controller of a flexible manipulator is proposed. From the point of view of structural dynamics, the trajectory control for a flexible manipulator is dedicated to the control of the global elastic deformation of the system, and the force control is dedicated to the control of the local deformation at the tip of the end-effector. Thus, preferably trajectory and force controls are separated in the control strategy.

Static and dynamic hybrid position/force control algorithms have been developed for flexible-macro/rigid-micro manipulator systems (Yoshikawa *et al.*, 1996). The robust cooperative control scheme of two flexible manipulators in the horizontal workspace is presented in Matsuno and Hatayama (1999). A passive controller has been developed for the payload manipulation with two planar flexible arms (Damaren 2000).

In Miyabe *et al.* (2004), the automated object capture with a two-arm flexible manipulator is addressed, which is a basic technology for a number of services in space. This object capturing strategy includes symmetric cooperative control, visual servoing, the resolution of the inverse kinematics problem, and the optimization of the configuration of a two-arm redundant flexible manipulator.

The effective use of flexible robotic manipulators in industrial environment is still a challenge for modern engineering. Usually there are several possible trajectories to perform a given task. A question that arises when programming robots is which is the best trajectory. There is no definitive solution, since the answer to this question depends on the selected performance index. Focused on industrial applications, the optimal path planning of a flexible manipulator is addressed in the present chapter. The manipulator is requested to perform a task in a vertical plane. Under this condition the gravitational effects are taken into account. Energy consumption is minimized when the movement is conducted through a suitable path. Energy is calculated by means of the evaluation of the joint torque along the path. End-effector accuracy is improved by reducing the vibration effect and increasing manipulability. The determination of the position takes into account the influence of structural flexibility. Weighting parameters are used to set the importance of each objective. The optimization scenario is composed by an optimal control formulation, solved by means of a nonlinear programming algorithm. The improvement obtained through a global optimization procedure is discussed. Numerical results demonstrate the viability of the proposed methodology.

A control formulation to determine the optimal torque profile is proposed. The optimal manipulability is also taken into account. The effect of using end-effector positioning error as performance index is discussed. As a result, the contribution of the present work is the proposition of a methodology to evaluate the influence of different performance indexes in a multi-criteria optimization environment.

The paper is organized as follows. In Section 2, model of deflection, torque and manipulability are presented. Section 3 recalls the general optimal control formulation and the performance indexes are defined. Geometrical insight about the design variables is given. Multi-criteria programming aspects such as Pareto-optimality and objective weighting are presented in section 4. The global optimization strategy is outlined in section

5 while section 6 shows numerical results. The conclusions and perspectives for future work are given in section 7.

2. Manipulator model

2.1 Deflection

Different schemes for modeling of the manipulators have been studied by a number of researchers. The mathematical model of the manipulator is generally derived from energy principles and, for a simple rigid manipulator, the rigid arm stores kinetic energy due to its moving inertia, and stores potential energy due its position in the gravitational field.

A flexible link also stores deformation energy by virtue of its deflection, joint and drive flexibility. Joints have concentrated compliance that may often be modeled as a pure spring storing only strain energy. Drive components such as shafts and belts may appear distributed. They store kinetic energy due to their low inertia, and a lumped parameter spring model often succeeds well to consider such an effect.

The most important modeling techniques for single flexible link manipulators can be grouped under the following categories: assumed modes method, finite element method and lumped parameters technique.

In the assumed modes approach, the link flexibility is usually represented by a truncated finite modal series, in terms of spatial mode eigenfunctions and time-varying mode amplitudes. Although this method has been widely used, there are several ways to choose link boundary conditions and mode eigenfunctions. Some contributions in this field were presented by Cannon and Schmitz (1984), Sakawa *et al.* (1985), Bayo (1986), Tomei and Tornambe (1988), among others. Nagaraj *et al.* (2001), Martins *et al.* (2002) and Tso *et al.* (2003) studied single-link flexible manipulators by using Lagrange's equation and the assumed modes method.

Regarding the finite element formulation, Nagarajan and Turcic (1990) derived elemental and system equations for systems with both elastic and rigid links. Bricout *et al.* (1990) studied elastic manipulators. Moulin and Bayo (1991) also used finite element discretization to study the end-point trajectory tracking for flexible arms and showed that a non-causal solution for the actuating torque enables tracking of an arbitrary tip displacement with any desired accuracy.

By using a lumped parameter model, Zhu *et al.* (1999) simulated the tip position tracking of a single-link flexible manipulator. Khalil and Gautier (2000) used a lumped elasticity model for flexible mechanical systems. Megahed and Hamza (2004) used a variation of the finite segment multi-body dynamics approach to model and simulate planar flexible link manipulator with rigid tip connections to revolute joints.

Santos *et al.* (2007) proposed the computation of flexibility by means of a spring-mass-damper system. According to this analogy, the first spring and damper constants are related to the joint behavior, and the following sets of spring and damper represent link flexibility. The variables and the parameters of the model are interpreted as angular quantities.

In this work the description of the deflection related to a rigid link is proposed. It is achieved by means of an Euler-Bernoulli beam formulation and covers the case for small deflections of a beam subject to lateral loads.

The bending moment M, shear forces Q and deflections w for a cantilever beam subjected to a point load P at the free end are given by

$$M(x) = P(x - L) \tag{1}$$

$$Q(x) = P \tag{2}$$

$$w(x) = \frac{Px^2(3L - x)}{6EI} \tag{3}$$

where L is the length of the link, E is the Young's modulus of the material and I is the moment of inertia. The variable x is the distance between the base of the link and the point where the force is applied. In this work, the error of positioning is measured at the end of each link, which yields

$$w(L) = \frac{PL^3}{3EI}. \tag{4}$$

The linear displacement at the end of each link is then converted into angular displacement through the expression

$$\Delta\theta = \arcsin\left(\frac{w}{L}\right). \tag{5}$$

Considering that the kinematics position of each link is given by a rigid body transformation $T_{i-1}^{i}(\theta)$ the positioning error at the end-effector can be estimated through

$$\delta = \sum_{j=1}^{2} T_j(\theta) - T_j(\theta + \Delta\theta) \tag{6}$$

If there is no load at the end of each link, Eq. (4), it follows that P=0, $\Delta\theta = 0$ and $\delta = 0$, i.e., the link behaves as a rigid body.

2.2 Robot dynamics

Dynamics encompasses relations between kinematics and statics so that the motion of the system is taken into account. To move a robot through a given trajectory, motors provide force or torque to the robotic joints. There are several techniques to model the dynamics of industrial robots. The knowledge about the dynamic behavior of the system is important both to the computational simulation of the movement and to the design of the controller itself (Fu *et al.* 1987).

Characteristics of a two-link planar manipulator follow. The Denavit-Hartenberg parameters are presented in Table 1.

Link	a (m)	α (rad)	d (m)	θ (rad)
1	a_1	0	0	θ_1^*
2	a_2	0	0	θ_2^*

Table 1. Denavit-Hartenberg parameters, (*) joint variable.

The Lagrangian $L = K - P$ is defined by the difference between the kinetic energy K and the potential energy P of the system. The dynamics of the system can be described by the Lagrange's equations as given by:

$$\tau_j = \frac{d}{dt}\left(\frac{\partial L}{\partial \dot{\theta}_j}\right) - \frac{\partial L}{\partial \theta_j} \tag{7}$$

where $\theta_j$are the generalized coordinates (angle of rotational joints in the present case); $\dot{\theta}_j$are the generalized velocities (angular velocity in the present case) and τ_j are the generalized forces (torques in the present case). By developing the Euler-Lagrange formalism, the equations that represent the system dynamics are explicitly obtained (Fu *et al.* 1987), and are expressed through

$$Q(q)\ddot{q} + C(q,\dot{q}) + G(q) = \tau \tag{8}$$

where $q = (\theta_1, \theta_2, \ldots, \theta_n)^T$, $\dot{q} = (\dot{\theta}_1, \dot{\theta}_2, \ldots, \dot{\theta}_n)^T$ and $\ddot{q} = (\ddot{\theta}_1, \ddot{\theta}_2, \ldots, \ddot{\theta}_n)^T$ are joint vectors of dimension $n \times 1$ representing position, velocity and acceleration, respectively. $Q(q)$ is a symmetric $n \times n$ matrix representing inertia, $C(q,\dot{q})$ is a $n \times 1$ vector representing the Coriolis effect, $G(q)$ is a $n \times 1$ vector representing the effects of gravitational acceleration, and $F = (F_1, F_2, \ldots, F_n)^T$ is a $n \times 1$ vector of generalized forces applied at the joints.
The Q, C and G matrices that represent the dynamics of a two-link planar manipulator are described by the Eqs. (9) to (16)

$$Q_{11} = \left(\frac{1}{3}\right) m_1\, a_1^2 + \left(\frac{1}{3}\right) m_2\, a_2^2 + m_2\, a_1^2 + m_2\, a_1\, a_2 \cos(\theta_2) \tag{9}$$

$$Q_{12} = \left(\frac{1}{3}\right) m_2\, a_2^2 + 0.5\, m_2\, a_1\, a_2 \cos(\theta_2) \tag{10}$$

$$Q_{21} = \left(\frac{1}{3}\right) m_2\, a_2^2 + 0.5\, m_2\, a_1\, a_2 \cos(\theta_2) \tag{11}$$

$$Q_{22} = \left(\frac{1}{3}\right) m_2\, a_2^2 \tag{12}$$

$$C_{11} = -m_2\, a_1\, a_2 \sin(\theta_2)\dot{\theta}_1\, \dot{\theta}_2 - 0.5\, m_2\, a_1\, a_2 \sin(\theta_2)\, \dot{\theta}_2^{\,2} \tag{13}$$

$$C_{21} = 0.5\, m_2\, a_1\, a_2 \sin(\theta_2)\, \dot{\theta}_2^{\,2} \tag{14}$$

$$G_{11} = -0.5\, m_1\, g\, a_1 \cos(\theta_1) - 0.5\, m_2\, g\, a_2 \cos(\theta_1 + \theta_2) - m_2\, g\, a_1 \cos(\theta_1) \tag{15}$$

$$G_{21} = -0.5\, m_2\, g\, a_2 \cos(\theta_1 + \theta_2) \tag{16}$$

where $g = 9.81 m/s^2$ is the gravitational constant.
The energy required to move the robot is an important design issue because in real applications energy supply is limited and any energy reduction leads to smaller operational costs. This point could lead to eco-robots design, in which energy supply is one of the key aspects. Due to the close relationship that exists between energy and force, the minimal energy can be estimated from the generalized force $\tau_j(t)$ that is associated to each joint j at time instant t.
Furthermore, it was observed that the resulting trajectory corresponds to robot configurations that are associated with the minimum mechanical energy and small

variations of the torque along the path. This means that an explicit constraint over the maximum torque is not required since it will be implicitly achieved by the present formulation.

2.3 Manipulability

As an approach for evaluating quantitatively the ability of manipulators from the kinematics viewpoint the concepts of manipulability ellipsoid and manipulability measure are used.

The set of all end-effector velocities v which are realizable by joint velocities such that the Euclidean norm satisfies $|\dot{\theta}| \leq 1$ are taken into account. This set is an ellipsoid in the m-dimensional Euclidean space. In the direction of the major axis of the ellipsoid, the end-effector can move at high speed. On the other hand, in the direction of the ellipse minor axis the end-effector can move only at low speed. Also, the larger the ellipsoid the faster the end-effector can move. Since this ellipsoid represents an ability of manipulation it is called as the manipulability ellipsoid.

The principal axes of the manipulability ellipsoid can be found by making use of the singular-value decomposition of the Jacobian matrix $J(\theta)$. The singular values of J, i.e., $\sigma_1, \sigma_2, \ldots, \sigma_m$, are the m larger values taken from the n roots $\left(\sqrt{\lambda_i}, i = 1, \ldots, n\right)$ of the eigenvalues. Then λ_i are the eigenvalues of the matrix $J(\theta)^T J(\theta)$.

One of the representative measures for the ability of manipulation derived from the manipulability ellipsoid is the volume of the ellipsoid. This is given by $c_m w$, where

$$w = \sigma_1 . \sigma_2 \ldots \sigma_m \tag{17}$$

$$c_m = \begin{cases} (2\pi)^{\frac{m}{2}} / [2.4.6 \ldots (m-2).m] & \text{if } m \text{ is even} \\ 2(2\pi)^{\frac{(m-1)}{2}} / [1.3.5 \ldots (m-2).m] & \text{if } m \text{ is odd.} \end{cases} \tag{18}$$

Since the coefficient c_m is a constant value when the dimension m is fixed, the volume is proportional to w. Hence, w can be seen as a representative measure, which is called the manipulability measure, associated to the manipulator joint angle θ.

Due to the direct relation between singular configuration and manipulability (through the Jacobian), the larger the manipulability measure the larger the singular configuration avoidance.

The distance from singular points can be obtained from the solution of an optimization problem in which the following objective function is minimized:

$$f(\theta) = \frac{1}{w} \tag{19}$$

Consequently, the minimization of Equation (19) means to increase the manipulability measure.

3. Optimal control formulation

3.1 Design variables

The design variables are the key parameters that are updated during the workflow, aiming at increasing (or decreasing) the performance index. In this study, the design variables are reference nodes, presented by circles in Figure 1. The abscissa presents the time instants $(t_i = 0, t_f = 1)$ while the ordinate is the joint angle. The value of intermediate joint angles between the references nodes are evaluated by means of a cubic spline interpolation.

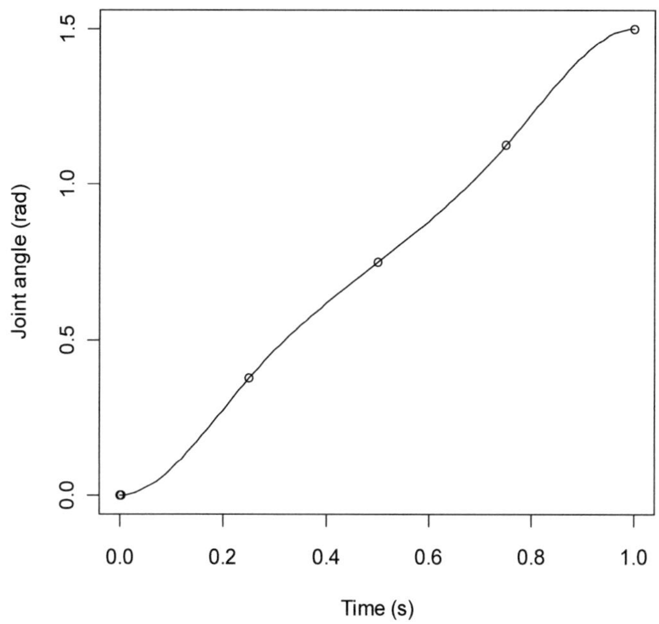

Fig. 1. Reference nodes (o) and joint angle (—).

This approach ensures a smooth transition on the joint angles, velocities and accelerations, which are positive aspects from the mechanical perspective. A smooth movement preserves the mechanism from fatigue effects, for example.

Optimal programming problems for continuous systems are included in the field of the calculus of variations. A continuous-step dynamic system is described by an n-dimensional state vector $\mathbf{x}(t)$ at time t. The choice of an m-dimensional control vector $\mathbf{u}(t)$ determines the time rate of change of the state vector through the dynamics given by the equation below:

$$\dot{\mathbf{x}}(t) = f(\mathbf{x}(t), \mathbf{u}(t), t) \tag{20}$$

A general optimization problem for such a system is to find the time history of the control vector $\mathbf{u}(t)$ for $t_i \leq t \leq t_f$ to minimize a performance index given by

$$J = \varphi[\mathbf{x}(t_f)] + \int_{t_0}^{t_f} L[\mathbf{x}(t), \mathbf{u}(t), t]dt \tag{21}$$

subject to Equation (20) with t_0, t_f, and $\mathbf{x}(t_i)$ specified.

In the present context, the interest is focused on the joint angles and the reference nodes. Performance indexes such as positioning error, manipulability and mechanical power are derived from this information. The variable $x_{i,j} = \theta_j(t_i)$ is an element of the state vector $\mathbf{x}$, which represents the joint angle at each time t_i, related to the joint j. The control vector $u_{k,j}$

represents the position of the reference node k with respect to the joint j. In the present study, the dimension of the state vector is n = 202 (the total traveling time is divided into i=1,...,101 steps for each joint) and the control vector has dimension m = 1,...,10 (five reference nodes for each joint).

3.2 Performance indexes

Initially, the specification of a feasible project is modeled as an optimization problem. To achieve this purpose, let $\mathbf{p}_t=[x_{\text{target}}, y_{\text{target}}]^T$ be the Cartesian target position where the end-effector may intersect when performing a given task. Then, a feasible project is the one whose torque profile is able to conduct each end-effector to a given cartesian position in which the prescribed task will be performed. This profile is obtained by the optimum value of the objective function

$$\varphi[\mathbf{x}(t_f)] = \left[e_1\left(\mathbf{x}(t_f)\right) - p_t\right]^2 \tag{22}$$

where $\mathbf{e}_1(\mathbf{x}(t))$ is the Cartesian position of the robot end-effector, respectively. By using Eq. (22) as the only performance index of the general formulation, Eq. (21), the objective function is

$$J = \left[e_1\left(\mathbf{x}(t_f)\right) - p_t\right]^2 \tag{23}$$

The torque required by the actuators to achieve the final position is approximated by a quadratic expression

$$L_1(\mathbf{x}(t), \mathbf{u}(t), t) = \sum_{j=1}^{2} \tau_{i,j}^2 \tag{24}$$

The manipulability index is evaluated by the expression

$$L_2(\mathbf{x}(t), \mathbf{u}(t), t) = \sum_{j=1}^{2} \left(\frac{1}{w_{i,j}^2}\right) \tag{25}$$

The end-effector positioning error along the path is evaluated by using the equation

$$L_3(\mathbf{x}(t), \mathbf{u}(t), t) = \sum_{j=1}^{2} \delta_{i,j}^2 \tag{26}$$

A number of methods are found in the literature to deal with optimal control (OC) problems (Bryson, 1999), (Bertsekas, 1995). In the present contribution, the results are computed through a classical nonlinear programming (NLP) procedure (Betts, 2001). In this case, there is no need of extra parameter computations and the derivatives are numerically evaluated. This choice characterizes a strong point of the proposed methodology since it provides an efficient formulation to solve the optimal control problem addressed.

Since the NLP procedure requires a finite number of points as design variables, the continuity of the OC variables along the time interval is obtained by interpolating the discrete set along the time. Those objectives can be evaluated individually or combined according to the importance of each objective.

4. Multi-criteria programming problem

In multiple-criteria optimization problems one deals with a design variable vector **u**, which satisfies all constraints and makes as small as possible the scalar performance index that is calculated by taking into account the m components of an objective function vector $J(\mathbf{u})$. This goal can be achieved by the vector optimization problem

$$\min_{\mathbf{u}\in\Omega}\{J(\mathbf{u})|h(\mathbf{u})=0, g(\mathbf{u})\leq 0\} \tag{27}$$

where $\Omega \subset R^n$ is the domain of the objective function (the design space).
An important feature of such multiple-criteria optimization problems is that the optimizer has to deal with objective conflicts (Eschenauer *et al.*, 1990). Other authors discuss the so-called compromise programming, since there is no unique solution to the problem (Vanderplaats, 1999). In this context, the optimality concept used in this work is presented below.

4.1 Pareto-optimality

A vector $\mathbf{u}^* \in \Omega$ is Pareto optimal for the problem (27) if and only if there are no vector $\mathbf{u} \in \Omega$ with the characteristics:

i. $J_k(\mathbf{u}) \leq J_k(\mathbf{u}^*)$ for all $k \in \{1,...,m\}$.
ii. $J_k(\mathbf{u}) < J_k(\mathbf{u}^*)$ for at least one $k \in \{1,...,m\}$.

For all non-Pareto-optimal vectors, the value of at least one objective function J_k can be reduced without increasing the functional values of the other vector components.
Solutions to multi-criteria optimization problems can be found in different ways by defining the so-called substitute problems. Substitute problems represent different form of obtaining the corresponding scalar objective function (Eschenauer *et al.*, 1990).

4.2 Method of objective weighting

Weighting Objectives is one of the most usual (and simple) substitute models for multi-objective optimization problems (Oliveira and Saramago, 2010). It permits a preference formulation that is independent from the individual minimum for positive weights. The preference function or utility function is here determined by the linear combination of the criteria $J_1, \dots, J_m$ together with the corresponding weighting factors $\alpha_1, \dots, \alpha_m$ so that

$$p[J(\mathbf{u})] = \sum_{k=1}^{m} \alpha_k J_k(\mathbf{u}), \mathbf{u} \in \Omega. \tag{28}$$

It is usually assumed that $0 \leq \alpha_k \leq 1$ and $\sum \alpha_k = 1$. It is possible to generate Pareto-optima for the original problem (Equation 27) by varying the weights α_k in the preference function.

4.3 The proposed formulation

Multiple objectives usually have different magnitude values. Numerical comparison among them have no real meaning since they have distinct measurement units and one objective may have a much higher value than another, since they represent different physical quantities. In this context, an initial scaling procedure is justified. In the case of two objective functions considered simultaneously, the following steps are adopted:

1. Select initial parameters $\mathbf{x}_0(t), \mathbf{u}_0(t), t \in [t_0, t_f]$ and $0 \leq \alpha_1 \leq 1$.
2. Set $\alpha_2 = 1 - \alpha_1$.

3. Set $\bar{J}_k = J_k(\mathbf{x}_0, \mathbf{u}_0, t)$.
4. Update $\alpha_k = \frac{\alpha_k}{\bar{J}_k}, k = 1,2$.
5. Set $p[J(\mathbf{u})] = \alpha_1 J_1 + \alpha_2 J_2$.

It follows that $J = 1$ at the beginning of the optimization process. At the end, $0 < J < 1$. By using this scaling procedure, the final objective function value provides a non-dimensional index that describes the percentage of improvement. As an example, the final value J=0.3 means that the overall objective was reduced to 30% of this initial value.

5. Global optimization

Along the investigation of the optimization problem, there are two kinds of solution points (Luenberger, 1984): *local minimum points*, and *global minimum points*. A point $\mathbf{u}^*\in\Omega$ is said to be a *global minimum point* of f over Ω if $f(\mathbf{u}) \geq f(\mathbf{u}^*)$ for all $\mathbf{u}\in\Omega$. If $f(\mathbf{u})> f(\mathbf{u}^*)$ for all $\mathbf{u}\in\Omega$, $\mathbf{u} \neq \mathbf{u}^*$, then $\mathbf{u}^*$ is said to be a *strict global minimum point* of f over Ω.

There are several search methods devoted to find the global minimum of a nonlinear objective function, since it is not an easy task. Well known methods such as genetic algorithms (Vose, 1999), differential evolution algorithm (Price *et al.*, 2005) and simulated annealing (Kirkpatrick, 1983) could be used in this case. The main characteristic of these methods is that the global (or near global) optimum is obtained through a high number of functional evaluations.

As proposed by Santos *et al.* (2005), to use the best feature of local optimization method (low computational cost) and global optimization method (global minimum), it is considered using the so-called tunneling strategy (Levy and Gomez, 1985) (Levy and Montalvo, 1985), a methodology designed to find the global minimum of a function. It is composed of a sequence of cycles, each cycle consisting of two phases: a minimization phase having the purpose of lowering the current function value, and a tunneling phase that is devoted to find a new initial point (other than the last minimum found) for the next minimization phase. This algorithm was first introduced in Levy and Gomez (1985), and the name derives from its graphic interpretation.

The first phase of the tunneling algorithm (minimization phase) is focused on finding a local minimum $\mathbf{u}^*$ of Equation (21), while the second phase (tunneling phase) generates a new initial point $\mathbf{u}^0\neq\mathbf{u}^*$ where $f(\mathbf{u}^0) \leq f(\mathbf{u}^*)$. In summary, the computation evolves through the following phases:

a. Minimization phase: Given an initial point $\mathbf{u}^0$, the optimization procedure computes a local minimum $\mathbf{u}^*$ of $f(\mathbf{u})$. At the end, it is considered that a local minimum is found.
b. Tunneling phase: Given $\mathbf{u}^*$ found above, since it is a local minimum, there exists at least one $\mathbf{u}^0 \in \Omega$, so that $f(\mathbf{u}^0) \leq f(\mathbf{u}^*)$, $\mathbf{u}^0 \neq \mathbf{u}^*$.

In other words, there exists $\mathbf{u}^0 \in Z = \{\mathbf{u} \in \Omega - \{\mathbf{u}^*\} \mid f(\mathbf{u}) \leq f(\mathbf{u}^*)\}$. To move from $\mathbf{u}^*$ to $\mathbf{u}^0$ along the tunneling phase a new initial point $\mathbf{u} = \mathbf{u}^* + \delta$, $\mathbf{u} \in \Omega$ is defined and used in the auxiliary function

$$F(\mathbf{u}) = \frac{f(\mathbf{u}) - f(\mathbf{u}^*)}{[(\mathbf{u} - \mathbf{u}^*)^T(\mathbf{u} - \mathbf{u}^*)]^\gamma} \tag{29}$$

that has a pole in $\mathbf{u}^*$ for a sufficient large value of γ. By computing both phases iteratively, the sequence of local minima leads to the global minimum. Different values for γ are suggested (Levy and Gomez, 1985) (Levy and Montalvo, 1985) for being used in Equation (29) to avoid undesirable points and prevent the search algorithm to fail.

6. Numerical results

Computational evaluation was performed aiming at evaluating the effectiveness of the proposed methodology, as outlined in Figure 2.

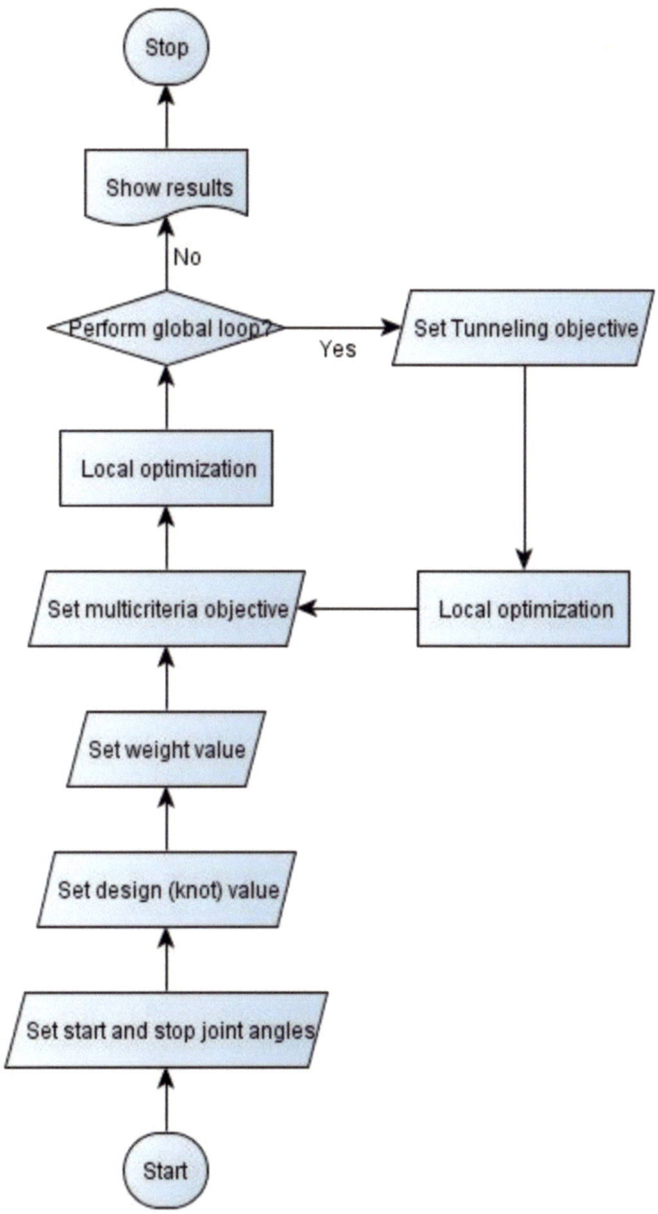

Fig. 2. Computational workflow.

An important point when using multi-objective formulation is the choice of performance indexes. A discussion about the influence of torque, manipulability and end-effector positioning error is presented in the following.

Figure 3 presents the Pareto frontier for the case in which torque and manipulability are considered in the same objective function.

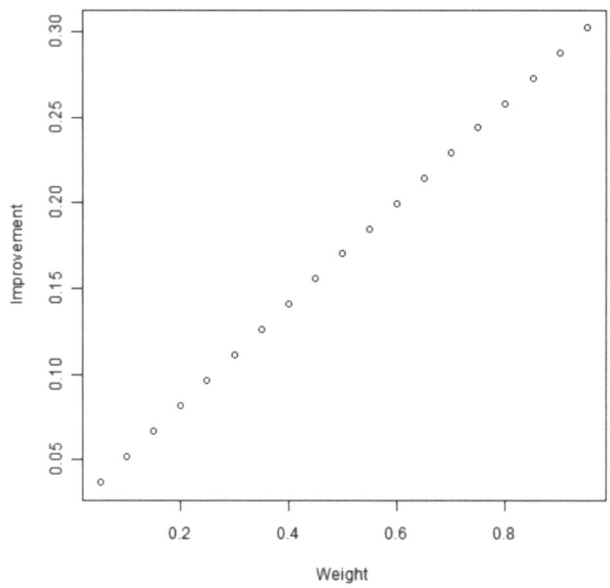

Fig. 3. Minimum value of the performance index.

The abscissa contains several values of the weight factor $\alpha \in (0,1)$. If the factor is zero, only manipulability is taken into account. If the factor is one, only the torque is considered. The factor 0.5 sets the same importance to both objectives. The ordinate is the percentage related to the initial value of the objective function. At the beginning, the objective function value is one. The value 0.10 in the improvement scale means that the final value is 10% of the initial value.

Results presented in the figure confirm that the improvement of manipulability is easier to be achieved by the numerical procedure than the reduction of torque. Those are the final results of the global optimization.

Another important point is the contribution of the global optimization strategy. Figure 4 shows the corresponding improvement achieved.

The abscissa contains several values of the weight factor $\alpha \in (0,1)$. The ordinate represents a range of values where 1.0 means no improvement, that is, no further improvement was obtained with respect to the local minimum. The value 0.75 means that the new (possibly global) minimum has a value corresponding to 75% of the local minimum.

A general view about the contribution of the tunneling strategy to the local minimum is presented in Figure 5. The reduction varies between 0.7 and 1.0, that is, there was a reduction to 70% of the value of the local minimum in the best scenario and no reduction (the corresponding value is 1.0) in the worst case.

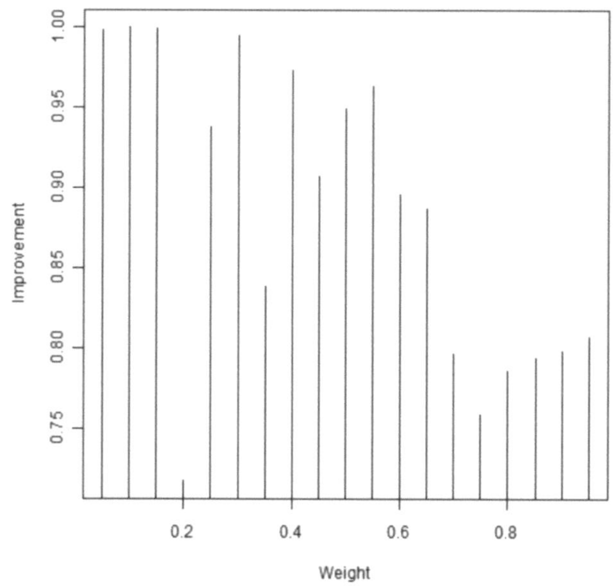

Fig. 4. Contribution of the global strategy.

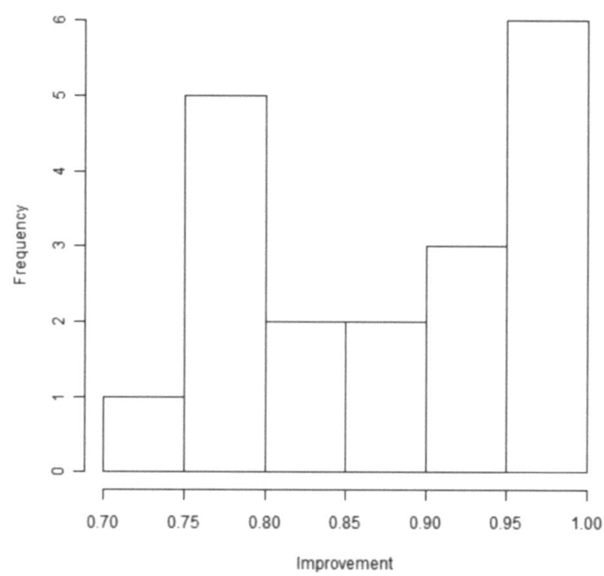

Fig. 5. Range of improvement obtained by the global strategy.

Performance indexes are affected differently by the presence of other objectives and the corresponding priority. The influence of the weight factor on individual objectives is discussed in the following.

The sum of torque is a performance index to be minimized. The higher the importance of the torque in the objective formulation better the improvement achieved by the optimization process. This effect is graphically presented by Figure 6.

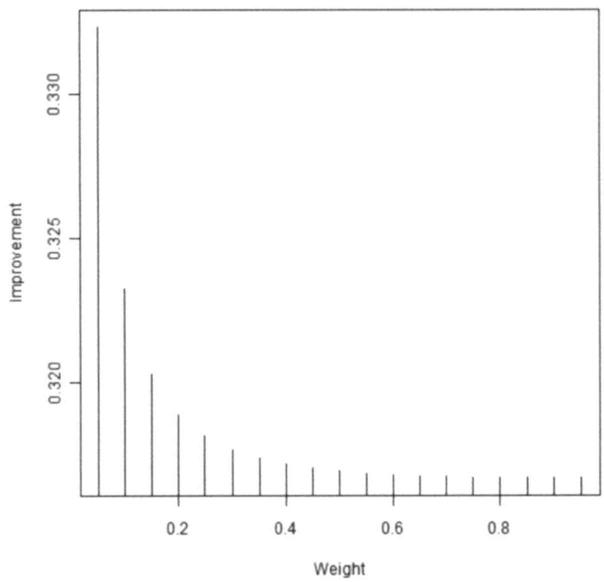

Fig. 6. Influence of weight on the torque.

Manipulability is a performance index to be maximized. It follows that larger the performance index value, better the performance. The influence of the weight coefficient over the manipulability is presented in Figure 7.

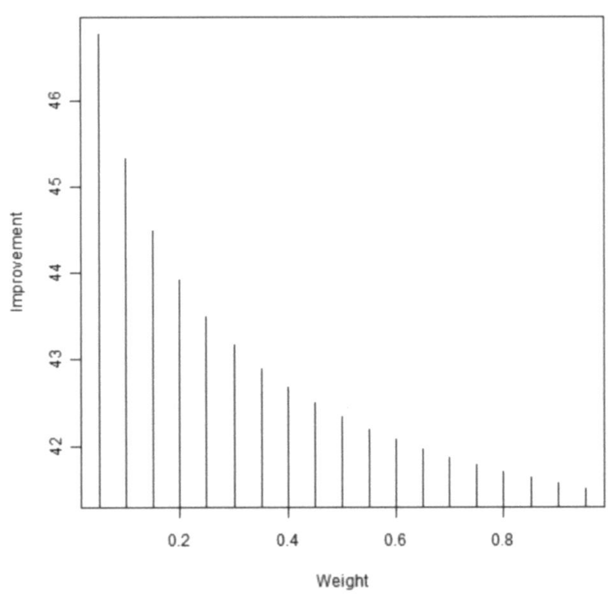

Fig. 7. Influence of weight coefficients on the manipulability.

According to Figure 7, the lower the value of the weight coefficient, better the manipulability. Note that manipulability and torque are conflicting objectives that are addressed by the present formulation.

Results comparing the effects of the end-effector positioning error and torque are presented next.The Pareto frontier for torque and end-effector displacement is shown in Figure 8.

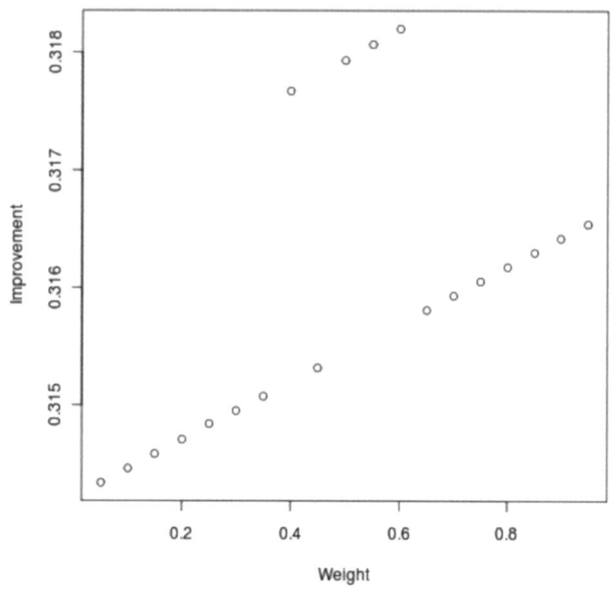

Fig. 8. Minimum value of the performance index.

Despite the small difference in the results, for all cases studied the optimum is between 31% and 32% of the initial value of the objective function. The contribution of the global optimization strategy is also similar for all cases and the global minimum was found between 80.4% and 81.4% of the value of the local minimum.

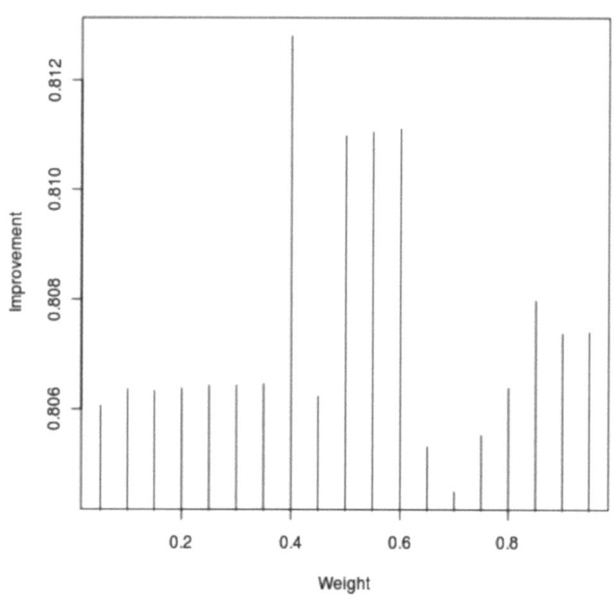

Fig. 9. Contribution of the global strategy.

The average contribution of the tunneling process to the global minimum is shown in Figure 10.

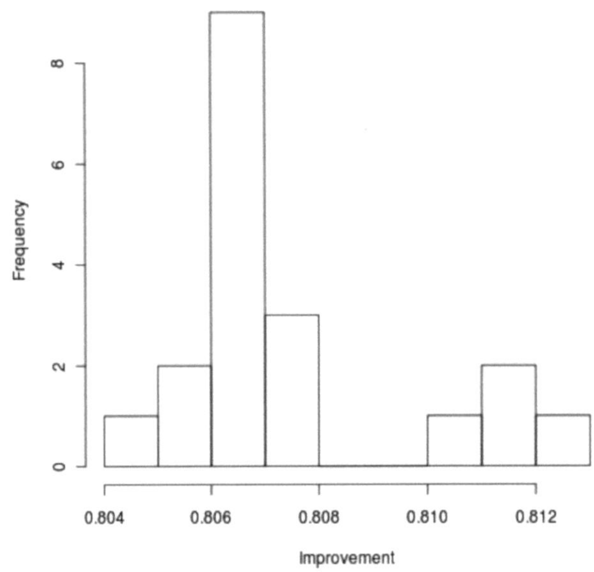

Fig. 10. Range of improvement obtained by the global strategy.

The optimal value of torque index is between 31.6% and 31.9% of the initial value, as presented in Figure 11.

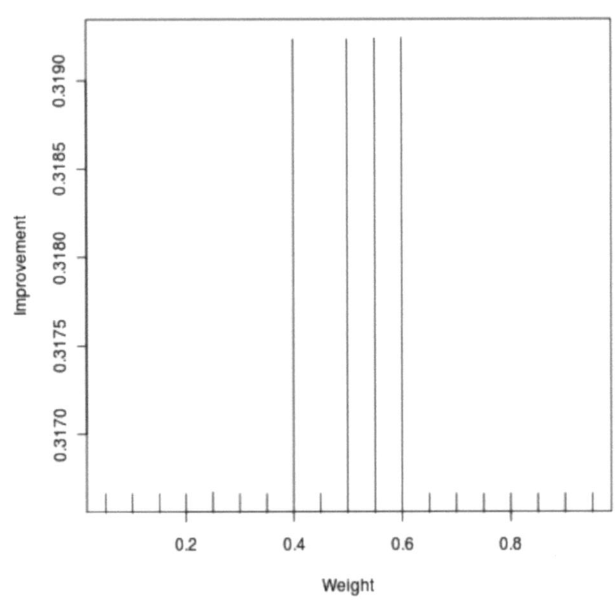

Fig. 11. Influence of weight on the torque.

The end-effector positioning error index was increased about 36 times, as presented in Figure 12.

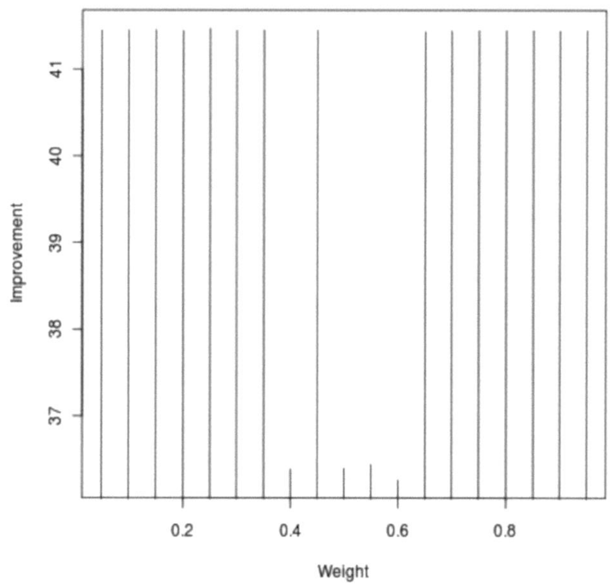

Fig. 12. Influence of weight on the end-effector positioning error.

Results presented in Figures 6 and 7 appear frequently when conflicting objectives are taken into account in the optimization procedure. On the other hand, correlated indexes usually have small deviation in the values obtained, as presented in Figures 11 and 12.

This analysis suggest that torque and manipulability are better choices to compose a multi-criteria analysis as compared with results given by torque and end-effector positioning error. This is justified by the fact that end-effector disturbance is affected by the torque profile. As a result, if the torque is reduced, then the effect of flexibility at the end-effector is also reduced.

7. Conclusion

This work was dedicated to multi-criteria optimization problems applied to flexible robot manipulators. Initially, the model of deflection, torque and manipulability were presented for the system analyzed. Next, optimal control formalism and multi-criteria strategy were outlined. It was concluded that the effectiveness of the numerical procedure depends on the choice of the objective functions and weighting factors.

The first numerical evaluation considered torque and manipulability as performance indexes. The effect of changing the weighting coefficients was presented in Figure 3. This is a typical trend of concurrent objectives, i.e., when one performance index is improved, the other degenerates. In this context it is important to identify the contribution of each index, as shown in Figures 6 and 7.

The effect of the global optimization procedure was also discussed. This point was shown to be effective to obtain the global minimum.

The second numerical evaluation considered the end-effector error positioning and the torque as performance indexes. It was shown that there are no significant changes in the performance index while the weighting factor values are changed. It is explained by the correlation between the objectives, i.e., both indexes are directly affected by the joint torque.

As a result, no further improvement is achieved by changing the relative importance of the objectives.

The numerical experiments conducted during the present research work lead to the following conclusions. The interdependence of the performance indexes is an important aspect that impacts the performance of the numerical method. The evaluation of different objectives that evaluates correlated information increases the computational cost but have no contribution to the optimal design. The use of several weighting factors is recommended. The nonlinear nature of the objective indexes requires a heavy exploration of the design space, aiming at finding a significant improvement for a particular combination of weighing factors. Finally, the use of a global optimization methodology is the most important contribution of this work that will distinguish the proposed methodology as a fast and accurate solver. Few iterations of the tunneling process provided an effective evolution to the global minimum.

From the author's perspective, the effective combination of different techniques is the key to obtain a high performance engineering result. Since this study deals with off-line planning, even a small improvement in the path performed by the robot may lead to expressive economic benefits. This is justified by the fact that the same movement of the robot is repeated several times during the working cycle.

The next step of this research is the evaluation of the effect of uncertainty in the design, through a stochastic approach.

As the proposed methodology is efficient to obtain an improved manipulator trajectory while dealing with the flexibility effect, joint torque and manipulability, the authors believe that the present contribution is a useful tool for robotic path planning design.

8. References

Alberts, T. E., Xia, H. and Chen, Y., 1992, "Dynamic analysis to evaluate viscoelastic passive damping augmentation for the space shuttle remote manipulator system", ASME Journal of Dynamic Systems, Measurement, and Control, Vol. 114, pp. 468–474.

Bayo, E., 1986, "Timoshenko versus Bernoulli beam theories for the control of flexible robots", Proceeding of IASTED International Symposium on Applied Control and Identification, pp. 178–182.

Bertsekas, D. P., 1995, "Dynamic Programming and Optimal Control", Athena Scientific.

Betts, J. T., 2001, "Practical Methods for Optimal Control Using Nonlinear Programming", SIAM 2001, Philadelphia.

Book, W. J., 1984, "Recursive Lagrangian dynamics of flexible manipulator arms", The International Journal of Robotics Research, Vol. 3, No. 3, pp. 87–101.

Bricout, J.N., Debus, J.C. and Micheau, P., 1990, "A finite element model for the dynamics of flexible manipulator", Mechanism and Machine Theory, Vol. 25, No. 1, pp. 119–128.

Bryson, Jr., A. E., 1999, "Dynamic Optimization", Addison Wesley Longman, Inc.

Cannon, R.H. and Schmitz, E., 1984, "Initial experiments on end-point control of a flexible one-link robot", The International Journal of Robotics Research, Vol. 3, No. 3, pp. 62–75.

Chang, Y. C. and Chen, B. S., 1998, "Adaptive tracking control design of constrained robot systems," International Journal of Adaptive Control, Vol. 12, No. 6, pp. 495–526.

Choi, B. O. and Krishnamurthy, K., 1994, "Unconstrained and constrained motion control of a planar 2-link structurally flexible robotic manipulator", Journal of Robotic Systems, Vol. 11, No. 6, pp. 557–571.

Damaren, C. J., 2000, "On the dynamics and control of flexible multibody systems with closed loops", International Journal of Robotics Research, Vol. 19, No. 3, pp. 238–253.

Dubowsky, S., 1994, "Dealing with vibrations in the deployment structures of space robotic systems", in: Fifth International Conference on Adaptive Structures, Sendai International Center, Sendai, Japan, pp. 5–7.

Eschenauer, H. ,Koski, J., Osyczka, A., 1990, "Multicriteria Design Optimization", Berlin, Springer-Verlag.

Fu, K. S., Gonzales, R. C. and Lee, C. S. G., 1987, "Robotics: control, sensing, vision and intelligence", McGraw-Hill.

Khalil, W. and Gautier, M., 2000, "Modeling of mechanical systems with lumped elasticity", Proceedings of the IEEE International Conference on Robotics and Automation, Vol. 4, pp. 3964–3969.

Kirkpatrick, S., Gelatt, C. D. and Vecchi, M. P., 1983, "Optimization by Simulated Annealing", Science, Vol. 220, pp. 671-680.

Latornell, D. J., Cherchas, D. B., and Wong, R., 1998, "Dynamic characteristics of constrained manipulators for contact force control design", International Journal of Robotics Research, Vol. 17, No. 3, pp. 211–231.

Levy, A. V. and Gomez, S., 1985, "The Tunneling Method Ap-plied to Global Optimization. Numerical Optimization," (Ed. P. T. Boggs) R. H. Byrd and R. B. Schnabel, Eds., Society for Industrial and Applied Mathematics, pp. 213-244.

Levy, A. V. and Montalvo, A., 1985, "The Tunneling Algorithm for the Global Minimization of Functions," The SIAM Journal on Scientific and Statistical Computing, Vol. 6, No. 1, 1985, pp. 15-29.

Luenberger, D. G., 1984, "Linear and Nonlinear Programming," 2nd Edition, Addison-Wesley, USA.

Martins, J., Botto, M.A. and Sa da Costa, J., 2002, "Modeling flexible beams for robotic manipulators", Multibody System Dynamics, Vol. 7, No. 1, pp. 79–100.

Matsuno, F. and Hatayama, M., 1999, "Robust cooperative control of two-link flexible manipulators on the basis of quasi-static equations", International Journal of Robotics Research, Vol. 18, No. 4, pp. 414–428.

Megahed, S.M. and Hamza, K.T., 2004, "Modeling and simulation of planar flexible link manipulators with rigid tip connections to revolute joints", Robotica, Vol. 22, pp. 285–300.

Miyabe, T., Konno, A. and Uchiyama, M., 2004, "An Approach Toward an Automated Object Retrieval Operation with a Two-Arm Flexible Manipulator", The International Journal of Robotics Research, Vol. 23, No. 3, March 2004, pp. 275-291.

Moulin, H. and Bayo, E., 1991, "On the accuracy of end-point trajectory tracking for flexible arms by noncausal inverse dynamic solutions", ASME Journal of Dynamic Systems, Measurement, and Control, Vol. 113, pp. 320–324.

Nagaraj, B.P., Nataraju, B.S. and Chandrasekhar, D.N., 2001, "Nondimensional parameters for the dynamics of a single flexible link", in: International Conference on Theoretical, Applied, Computational and Experimental Mechanics (ICTACEM) 2001, Kharagpur, India.

Nagarajan, S. and Turcic, D.A., 1990, "Lagrangian formulation of the equations of motion for the elastic mechanisms with mutual dependence between rigid body and elastic motions, Part 1: Element level equations, and Part II: System equations", ASME Journal of Dynamic Systems, Measurement, and Control, Vol. 112, No. 2, pp. 203–214, and pp. 215–224.

Oliveira, L.S. and Saramago, S.F.P., 2010, "Multiobjective Optimization Techniques Applied to Engineering Problems", Journal of the Brazilian Society of Mechanical Sciences and Engineering, Vol. XXXII, p.94 - 104.

Price, K., Storn, R. and Lampinen, J., 2005, "Differential Evolution - A Practical Approach to Global Optimization", Springer.

Sakawa, Y., Matsuno, F. and Fukushima, F., 1985, "Modelling and feedback control of a flexible arm", Journal of Robotic Systems, Vol. 2, No. 4, pp. 453–472.

Santos, R. R., Steffen Jr., V. and Saramago, S.F.P., 2005, "Solving the inverse kinematics problem through performance index optimization".XXVI Iberian Latin American Congress on Computational Methods in Engineering, Guarapari-ES.CILAMCE.

Santos, R. R., Steffen Jr., V. and Saramago, S.F.P., 2007, "Optimal path planning and task adjustment for cooperative flexible manipulators". 19th International Congress of Mechanical Engineering.

Shi, J.X., Albu-Schaffer, A. and Hirzinger, G., 1998, "Key issues in the dynamic control of lightweight robots for space and terrestrial applications", Proceedings of the IEEE International Conference on Robotics and Automation, Vol. 1, pp. 490–497.

Tomei, P. and Tornambe, A., "Approximate modeling of robots having elastic links", IEEE Transactions on Systems, Man and Cybernetics, Vol. 18, No. 5, pp. 831–840.

Tso, S.K., Yang, T.W., Xu, W.L. and Sun, Z.Q., 2003, "Vibration control for a flexible link robot arm with deflection feedback", International Journal of Non-Linear Mechanics, Vol. 38, pp. 51–62.

Tsujita, K., Tsuchiya, K., Urakubo, T., Sugawara, Z., 2004, "Trajectory and Force Control of a Manipulator With Elastic Links", Journal of Vibration and Control, Vol. 10, pp. 1271–1289.

Uchiyama, M., Konno, A., Uchiyama, T. and Kanda, S., 1990, "Development of flexible dual-arm manipulator tested for space robotics", Proceedings of IEEE International Workshop on Intelligent Robots and System, pp. 375–381.

Vanderplaats, G. N, 1999, "Numerical Optimization Techniques for Engineering Design",3rd edition, VR&D Inc.

Vose, M. D., 1999, "The Simple Genetic Algorithm: Foundations and Theory", MIT Press, Cambridge, MA.

Yoshikawa, T., Harada, K., and Matsumoto, A., 1996, "Hybrid position/force control of flexible-macro/rigid-micro manipulator system", IEEE Transactions on Robotics and Automation, Vol. 12, No. 4, pp. 633–640.

Zhu, G., Ge, S.S. and Lee, T.H., 1999, "Simulation studies of tip tracking control of a single-link flexible robot based on a lumped model", Robotica, Vol. 17, pp. 71–78.

18

Singularity Analysis, Constraint Wrenches and Optimal Design of Parallel Manipulators

Nguyen Minh Thanh[1], Le Hoai Quoc[2] and Victor Glazunov[3]
[1]*Department of Automation, Hochiminh City University of Transport,*
[2] *Department of Science and Technology, People's Committee of Hochiminh City,*
[3]*Mechanical Engineering Research Institute, Russian Academy of Sciences,*
[1,2]*Vietnam*
[3]*Russia*

1. Introduction

In recent years, numerous researchers have investigated parallel manipulators and many studies have been done on the kinematics or dynamics analysis. Parallel manipulators has been only mentioned in several books, as in (Merlet, 2006; Ceccarelli, 2004; Kong, & Gosselin, 2007; Glazunov, et al., 1991). Reference (Gosselin, & Angeles, 1990) has established singularity criteria based on Jacobian matrices when describing the various types of singularity. Then, in (Glazunov, et al. 1990) proposed other singularity criteria for consideration of these problems the screw theory based on the approach of the screw calculus, as in (Dimentberg, 1965). Those criteria are determined by the constraints imposed by the kinematic chains, as in (Angeles, 2004; Kraynev, & Glazunov, 1991), taking into account some problems the Plücker coordinates of constraint wrenches can be applied in (Glazunov, 2006; Glazunov, et al. 1999, 2007, 2009; Thanh, et al. 2009, 2010a).
Dynamical decoupling allows increasing the accuracy for the parallel manipulators presented as in (Glazunov, & Kraynev, 2006; Glazunov, & Thanh, 2008). It is necessary to develop optimal structure have combined (Thanh, et al. 2008), as well as algorithms and multi-criteria optimization (Statnikov, 1999; Thanh, et al. 2010b) obtaining the Pareto set. It is very important to taking into account possible singularity configurations, to find out how they influence the characteristics of constraints restricting working space (Bonev, et al. 2003; Huang, 2004; Arakelian, et al. 2007).
The trend towards highly rapid manipulators due to the demand for greater working volume, dexterity, and stiffness has motivated research and development of new types of parallel manipulator (Merlet, 1991). This paper is focused the constraints and criteria existing in known parallel manipulators in form of a parallel manipulator with linear actuators located on the base.

2. Kinematic of parallel manipulator

In this section, let us consider a 6-DOF parallel manipulator with actuators situated on the base. The mechanical architecture of the considered robot is illustrated in Fig. 1.

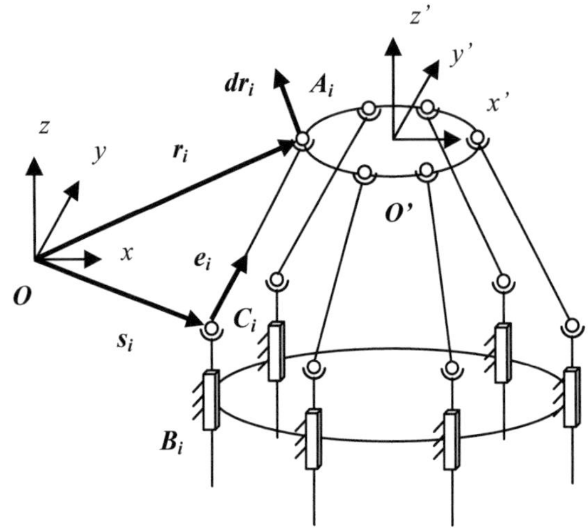

Fig. 1. Parallel manipulator with linear actuators located on the base

The parallel manipulator as seen in Fig. 1 is composed of a mobile platform connected to a fixed base via six kinematic sub-chains (legs) comprising of one prismatic, one universal and one spherical pair (PUS pairs). Parameters of design of the platform and the base form an irregular hexagon positioned in the *(x-y)* plane. A_i, B_i $(i=1,\ldots,6)$ are coordinates of the points of the mobile platform (the output link) and of the base respectively. The points $A_1A_3A_5$ and $A_2A_4A_6$ make form equilateral triangles, the angle ψ_p determines their location and R_p is the radius of the circumscribed circle (Fig. 2, a). Similarly, the angle ψ_b and the radius R_b determines the location of the equilateral triangles $B_1B_3B_5$ and $B_2B_4B_6$ located on the base. Let the distance between the centers of the universal and spherical pairs A_i and C_i of the *i-th* leg be l_i. In addition, the generalized coordinates, which are equal to the distance between the points B_i and C_i are designated θ_i. The radius-vectors of the points A_i and C_i are $r_i(x_{Ai}, y_{Ai}, z_{Ai})$ and $s_i(x_{Ci}, y_{Ci}, z_{Ci})$ respectively $(i=1,\ldots,6)$. We could note that the coordinates of the points B_i and C_i are $x_{Ci}=x_{Bi}$, $y_{Ci}=y_{Bi}$, $z_{Ci}=\theta_i$.

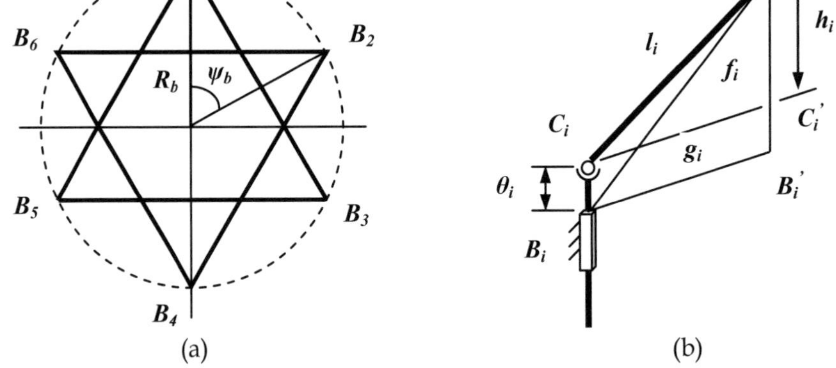

Fig. 2. Parametrical and geometrical design of parallel manipulator

With this approach, the linear actuators can be firmly fixed on the base to reduce high acceleration movements because the power is not used to move heavy actuators but lightweight links. However, the obstacle is a smaller working space in comparison with a Stewart platform, due to the movement of the linear actuators. Moreover, forces acting on the actuator have a perpendicular component, whereas forces exerted upon Stewart actuators have a longitudinal component.

Let us consider an inverse kinematic problem of position of parallel manipulators, which has characteristic relation between the numbers of chains. The manipulator with six kinematic chains offers convenience in optimization of working space in terms of decreased rigidity and load-bearing capacity.

Likewise, the generalized coordinates of the *i-th* segment (the length) which are equal to the distance between the points A_i and B_i, can be expressed as:

$$f_i = \sqrt{(x_{Ai} - x_{Bi})^2 + (y_{Ai} - y_{Bi})^2 + (z_{Ai} - z_{Bi})^2}\ , i = 1,...,6 \tag{1}$$

By geometrical method, the distance between the points C_i and C'_i (Fig. 2, b):

$$g_i = \sqrt{(f_i)^2 - (z_{Ai})^2}\, , i = 1,...,6 \tag{2}$$

when the length of the link l_i is known, the distance between the points A_i and C'_i (Fig. 2, b):

$$h_i = \sqrt{(l_i)^2 - (g_i)^2} \tag{3}$$

We could obtain the generalized coordinate θ_i (Fig. 2, c) as follows:

$$\theta_i = z_{Ai} - h_i \tag{4}$$

It is the solution of the inverse kinematic problem. The inverse kinematics for parallel manipulator can be formulated to determine the required actuator heights for a given pose of the mobile platform with respect to the base. The pose consists of both position and orientation in the Cartesian system. Actuators are considered to act linearly in the vertical direction, parallel to the *z*-axis, in order to simplify the mathematics, although that needs not be the case.

3. Multi-criteria optimization

Influence of singularities on parameters of the working space of the parallel manipulator is a significant factor worth investigating. In these singularity configurations, the system is out of control and that greatly affects its functionality. It is necessary to determine the extent of the lack of control to see how that affects the parameters of the working space. These singularity configurations also affect the optimization results.

The constraint wrenches of zero pitch acting to the output link from the legs are located along the unit screws: $E_i = e_i + \chi e^o_i$, $(i=1,\dots,6)$ where e_i is the unit vector directed along the axis of the line C_iA_i of the corresponding leg, χ is the Clifford factor, $\chi^2=0$ (for a vector, $e_i\, e^o_i=0$). E_i consists of the unit vector e_i and its moment $e^o_i = s_i \times e_i$ corresponding with $e^o_{xi} = s_{Cyi}e_{Czi} - s_{Czi}e_{Cyi}$; $e^o_{yi} = s_{Czi}e_{Cxi} - s_{Cxi}e_{Czi}$; $e^o_{zi} = s_{Cxi}e_{Cyi} - s_{Cyi}e_{Cxi}$ and can be expressed by Plücker coordinates $E_i = (x_i, y_i, z_i, x^o_i, y^o_i, z^o_i)$. These coordinates make form the 6×6 matrix (E):

$$(E) = \begin{pmatrix} x_1 & y_1 & z_1 & x_1^o & y_1^o & z_1^o \\ x_2 & y_2 & z_2 & x_2^o & y_2^o & z_2^o \\ . & . & . & . & . & . \\ . & . & . & . & . & . \\ . & . & . & . & . & . \\ x_6 & y_6 & z_6 & x_6^o & y_6^o & z_6^o \end{pmatrix} \quad (5)$$

Optimization of parameters of the parallel manipulator with linear actuators located on the base is considered. Let us take in account three criteria: working volume, dexterity and stiffness of parallel manipulator. The first criterion N_p is the quantity of the reachable points of the centre of the mobile platform. The second criterion N_c is the average quantity of orientations of the mobile platform in each reachable point. The third criterion D_e is the average module of the determinant $|\det(E)|$ in each configuration. Determinant $|\det(E)|$ constructed from coordinate axes of the drive kinematic couples is used as a third criterion of optimization. Since the value of this criterion is related to one of the important characteristics of the manipulator - its stiffness or load capacity. If determinant are more qualifiers, then the manipulator away from the singularity configuration and the stiffness of the above.

Let us consider optimization of the parameters of the manipulator for different values of the criterion of proximity to singular configurations, as well as the influence of this criterion in the optimization results. We set up four coefficients *H1, H2, H3* and *H4* expressed four parameters of optimization. The coefficient *H1* characterizes the length $l = l_i$ of the links A_iC_i *(i=1,…,6)* (in Fig. 2, b). The coefficient *H2* characterizes the angle ψ_p (Fig. 2, a) determining the location of the triangles $A_1A_3A_5$ and $A_2A_4A_6$ of the mobile platform. The coefficient *H3* characterizes the angle ψ_b determining the location of the triangles $B_1B_3B_5$ and $B_2B_4B_6$ on the base. Moreover, the coefficient *H4* characterizes the relation between the radius R_p and the radius R_b of the circumscribe circles of the platform and of the base respectively.

The algorithm of determination of the Pareto-optimal solutions can be presented as follows:

Step 1. Establish the limits of the parameters of optimization.

$H_{1min} \le H_1 \le H_{1max}$, $H_{2min} \le H_2 \le H_{2max}$, $H_{3min} \le H_3 \le H_{3max}$, $H_{4min} \le H_4 \le H_{4max}$. The number of steps of scanning in the space of parameters is n_p. The limits of the scanned Cartesian coordinates of the centre of the moving platform and the limits of the scanned orientation angles of this platform in interval are $x_{min} \le x \le x_{max}$, $y_{min} \le y \le y_{max}$, $z_{min} \le z \le z_{max}$, $\alpha_{min} \le \alpha \le \alpha_{max}$, $\beta_{min} \le \beta \le \beta_{max}$, $\gamma_{min} \le \gamma \le \gamma_{max}$. As well as the number n_c of steps of scanning in the space of these coordinates and the limitation of changing of the generalized coordinates $\theta_{imin} \le \theta_i \le \theta_{i\,max}$ *(i=1,…,6)*. The limit of the determinant $|\det(E)| \ge \varepsilon$. At this step assume *i=0*, by this the parameters are $H_{10} = H_{1min}$, $H_{20} = H_{2min}$, $H_{30} = H_{3min}$, $H_{40} = H_{4min}$, $N_p = N_c = D_e = 0$.

Step 2. Determine the values of the criteria for all the values of the parameters.

2.1. Determine the parameters $H_{1i}, \ldots, H_{40}$, assume j=0, by this $x_0 = x_{min}$, $y_0 = y_{min}$, $z_0 = z_{min}$, $\alpha_0 = \alpha_{min}$, $\beta_0 = \beta_{min}$, $\gamma_0 = \gamma_{min}$.

2.2. Determine θ_i (i=1,…,6) and $|\det(E)|$; if all the $\theta_{i\,min} \le \theta_i \le \theta_{i\,max}$ (i=1,…,6) and $|\det(E)| \ge \varepsilon$ then $N_c = N_c + 1$, $D_e = D_e + |\det(E)|$; if $x_j \ne x_{j-1}$ or $y_j \ne y_{j-1}$ or $z_j \ne z_{j-1}$ then $N_p = N_p + 1$.

2.3. $j = j+1$, if $j \le n_c$ then go back to 2.2.
2.4. Determine the criteria $N_{pi}= N_p$, $D_{ei}= D_e / N_c$, $N_{ci}= N_c / N_p$; assume $N_p = N_c = D_e= 0$.
2.5. $i = i+1$, if $i \le n_p$ then go back to 2.1.

Step 3. Determine the Pareto-optimal solutions (matrix *(Par)*).

3.1. Assume i= 1, (by this $N_{pi}= N_{p1}$, $D_{ei}= D_{e1}$, $N_{ci}= N_{c1}$), k= 0.
3.2. Determine N_{pi}, D_{ei}, N_{ci}; assume $j= 1$, the criteria of optimal solution $K1=1$, $K2=0$.
3.3. Determine N_{pj}, D_{ej}, N_{cj}; if $N_{pi} > N_{pj}$ or $D_{ei}> D_{ej}$ or $N_{ci}> N_{cj}$ then K2=1; if $N_{pi}= N_{pj}$ and $D_{ei}= D_{ej}$ and $N_{ci}= N_{cj}$ then K2=1.
3.4. If $K2\neq1$ then $K1=0$; $K2=0$; $j=j+1$; if $j \le n_p$ then go back to 3.3.
3.5. If $K1 = 1$ then $k = k + 1$, $Par_{1k}= H_{1i}, \ldots, Par_{7k}= N_{ci}$, $i=i+1$; if $i \le n_p$ then go back to 3.2.

Singularity of the manipulator is determined by closeness to zero of determinant of matrix *(E)* of Plücker coordinates of unit wrenches. Let us fix certain value $\varepsilon>0$ as a criterion of singularity (the manipulator is in singular position if $|\det(E)|\le\varepsilon$). If $\varepsilon=0$ then the construction of the working space of the manipulator shows that the same results we can get without singularity constraint. Giving various values of the criterion of the singularity, we can get interval of the determinant of matrix (*E*).
Further, analysis influences of the criterion of singularity ε, $|\det(E)|\le\varepsilon$ on the value of the working volume. With the value of the criterion of singularity is equal to $\varepsilon=0.01$ there exist *81* available solutions, but only *8* of them are Pareto-optimal. By the condition of the criterion of singularity is equal to $\varepsilon=0.01$ and the condition $\varepsilon=0$, there Pareto-optimal set consists of *6* and *29* solutions correspondingly. Therefore, the value of ε influences on the results of optimization.
Value of the criterion that determines the proximity to singular configurations is equal to zero, we can assume that the constraints associated with the singularity in general, are not imposed in the analysis of each specific configuration. However, the criterion for determining the load capacity occurs. As a result, the number of Pareto-optimal variants varies very much. Here, *29* variants satisfy the conditions of Pareto set.
Limiting possible module of a determinant of matrix (*E*) to singularity configurations changes the Plücker coordinates of the wrenches transmitted on the output link. Methodology for analyzing the singularities on optimization appearing in the parallel manipulator and their impact in the working space is proposed. The practical significance from the fact is the results obtained in this work increase the effectiveness of design automation.

4. Twist inside singularity

The approach based on matrix *(E)* consisting of the Plücker coordinates of the constraint wrenches allows determining the twists of the platform inside singularity (Glazunov, 2006). Let us consider the increases of the Plücker coordinates of the unit screws E_i after an infinitesimal displacement $\$ = (d\varphi, dr) = (dr_x, dr_x, dr_x, d\varphi_x, d\varphi_y, d\varphi_z)^T$ of the platform corresponding to displacement $dr_i = (dx_{Ai}, dy_{Ai}, dz_{Ai})^T$ of the point A_i of the manipulator presented on the Fig. 1.

$$\begin{aligned} dx_{Ai} &= dr_x + d\varphi_y z_{Ai} - d\varphi_z y_{Ai}, \\ dy_{Ai} &= dr_y + d\varphi_z x_{Ai} - d\varphi_x z_{Ai}, \\ dz_{Ai} &= dr_z + d\varphi_x y_{Ai} - d\varphi_y x_{Ai} \end{aligned} \tag{6}$$

The generalized coordinate after mentioned infinitesimal displacement *(dx_i, dy_i, dz_i)* is:

$$\theta_i + d\theta_i = z_{Ai} + dz_{Ai} - \sqrt{l_i^2 - (x_{Ai} + dx_{Ai} - x_{Ci})^2 - (y_{Ai} + dy_{Ai} - y_{Ci})^2} \tag{7}$$

After transformations the increase of the generalized coordinate is:

$$d\theta_i = \frac{\left[(x_{Ai} - x_{Ci})dx_{Ai} + (y_{Ai} - y_{Ci})dy_{Ai} + (z_{Ai} - z_{Ci})dz_{Ai}\right]}{(z_{Ai} - z_{Ci})} \tag{8}$$

The unit screw E_i can be rewritten as E_i+dE_i or as e_i+de_i and $e^o_i + de^o_i$.
Using (6), (7), and (8) the coordinates of the de_i and de^o_i can be expressed as:

$$\begin{gathered} dx_i = \frac{\partial x_i}{\partial \varphi_x}d\varphi_x + \frac{\partial x_i}{\partial \varphi_y}d\varphi_y + \frac{\partial x_i}{\partial \varphi_z}d\varphi_z + \frac{\partial x_i}{\partial r_x}dr_x + \frac{\partial x_i}{\partial r_y}dr_y + \frac{\partial x_i}{\partial r_z}dr_z \\ \cdots\cdots\cdots\cdots\cdots\cdots\cdots\cdots\cdots\cdots \\ dz_i^o = \frac{\partial z_i^o}{\partial \varphi_x}d\varphi_x + \frac{\partial z_i^o}{\partial \varphi_y}d\varphi_y + \frac{\partial z_i^o}{\partial \varphi_z}d\varphi_z + \frac{\partial z_i^o}{\partial r_x}dr_x + \frac{\partial z_i^o}{\partial r_y}dr_y + \frac{\partial z_i^o}{\partial r_z}dr_z \end{gathered} \tag{9}$$

where

$$\frac{\partial x_i}{\partial \varphi_x} = 0,\ \frac{\partial x_i}{\partial \varphi_y} = \frac{z_{Ai}}{l_i},\ \frac{\partial x_i}{\partial \varphi_z} = -\frac{y_{Ai}}{l_i},\ \frac{\partial x_i}{\partial r_x} = \frac{1}{l_i},\ \frac{\partial x_i}{\partial r_y} = 0,\ \frac{\partial x_i}{\partial r_z} = 0,$$

$$\frac{\partial x_i^o}{\partial \varphi_x} = \frac{\left\{(y_{Ai} - y_{Ci})\left[\frac{(y_{Ai} - 2y_{Ci})z_{Ai}}{(z_{Ai} - z_{Ci})} - y_{Ai}\right] + z_{Ci}z_{Ai}\right\}}{l_i},$$

$$\frac{\partial x_i^o}{\partial \varphi_y} = \frac{\left[\frac{(x_{Ai} - x_{Ci})(2y_{Ci} - y_{Ai})z_{Ai}}{(z_{Ai} - z_{Ci})} - x_{Ai}(y_{Ai} - y_{Ci})\right]}{l_i},$$

$$\frac{\partial x_i^o}{\partial \varphi_z} = \frac{\left\{\frac{\left[(y_{Ai} - y_{Ci})x_{Ai} - (x_{Ai} - x_{Ci})y_{Ai}\right](2y_{Ci} - y_{Ai})}{(z_{Ai} - z_{Ci})} - x_{Ai}z_{Ci}\right\}}{l_i},$$

$$\frac{\partial x_i^o}{\partial r_x} = \frac{(x_{Ai} - x_{Ci})(2y_{Ci} - y_{Ai})}{(z_{Ai} - z_{Ci})l_i},\ \frac{\partial x_i^o}{\partial r_y} = \frac{\frac{(y_{Ai} - y_{Ci})(2y_{Ci} - y_{Ai})}{(z_{Ai} - z_{Ci})} - z_{Ci}}{l_i},$$

$$\frac{\partial x_i^o}{\partial r_z} = \frac{(y_{Ci} - y_{Ai})}{l_i},\ i = 1,\ldots,6$$

Other partial derivatives also can be obtained from Eqs. (6), (7), and (8).
By means of the properties of linear decomposition of determinants d[det*(E)*] can be obtained as the sum of *36* determinants (Glazunov, 2006). From this, d[det*(E)*] can be presented as:

$$d[\det(E)] = \frac{\partial[\det(E)]}{\partial\varphi_x d\varphi_x} + \frac{\partial[\det(E)]}{\partial\varphi_y d\varphi_y} + \frac{\partial[\det(E)]}{\partial\varphi_z d\varphi_z} + \frac{\partial[\det(E)]}{\partial r_x dr_x} + \frac{\partial[\det(E)]}{\partial r_y dr_y} + \frac{\partial[\det(E)]}{\partial r_z dr_z} \tag{10}$$

Using (10) the criterion of the singularity locus can be presented as d[det(E)]=0. This condition imposes only one constraint. Therefore, there exist five twists of motions of the platform inside singularity.
For example, let us obtain five inside singularity of manipulator. Set up the coordinates of the vectors be r_i are $r_1(-1, 0, 4)$, $r_2(-0.5, 1, 4)$, $r_3(0.5, 1, 4)$, $r_4(1, 0, 4)$, $r_5(0.5, -1, 4)$, $r_6(-0.5, -1, 4)$; s_i are $s_1(-1.5, 0, 0.866)$, $s_2(-1, 1.5, 0.707)$, $s_3(1, 1.5, 0.707)$, $s_4(1.5, 0, 0.866)$, $s_5(1, -1.5, 0.707)$, $s_6(-1, -1.5, 0.707)$. From here, we can see the generalized coordinates as (0.136, 0.305, 0.305, 0.136, 0.305, 0.305). Matrix (E) is determined as:

$$\begin{pmatrix} 0.158 & 0 & 0.988 & 0 & 1.618 & 0 \\ 0.148 & -0.148 & 0.978 & 1.572 & 1.083 & -0.074 \\ -0.148 & -0.148 & 0.978 & 1.572 & -1.083 & 0.074 \\ -0.158 & 0 & 0.988 & 0 & -1.618 & 0 \\ -0.148 & 0.148 & 0.978 & -1.572 & -1.083 & -0.074 \\ 0.148 & 0.148 & 0.978 & -1.572 & 1.083 & 0.074 \end{pmatrix}$$

The determinant consisting of the Plücker coordinates of the unit screws is det(E) = 0. Their partial derivatives are:

$$\frac{\partial[\det(E)]}{\partial r_x} = -0.02, \quad \frac{\partial[\det(E)]}{\partial r_y} = 0, \quad \frac{\partial[\det(E)]}{\partial r_z} = 0,$$

$$\frac{\partial[\det(E)]}{\partial \varphi_x} = 0, \quad \frac{\partial[\det(E)]}{\partial \varphi_y} = 0.002, \quad \frac{\partial[\det(E)]}{\partial \varphi_z} = 0$$

Using the approach presented above, we find five independent twists inside singularity: $\$_1(1, 0, 0, 0, 0, 0)$, $\$_2(0, 0, 1, 0, 0, 0)$, $\$_3(0, 0, 0, 0, 1, 0)$, $\$_4(0, 0, 0, 0, 0, 1)$, $\$_5(0, 4.433, 0, 1, 0, 0)$. The twist-gradient is calculated to be $\$^*(-0.02, 0, 0, 0, 0.002, 0)$. This twist-gradient is practically important as it offers the highest speed.

5. Dynamical decoupling

In this section, let we consider the reduction of the dynamical coupling of the motors of the parallel manipulator with linear actuators located on the base. The basic idea is to represent the kinetic energy as the quadratic polynomial including only the squares of the generalized velocities (Glazunov, & Kraynev, 2006). The kinetic energy can be expressed by means of the matrix *(E)*.
Let m be the mass and J_x, J_y, J_z be the inertia moments of the platform. Assuming that the mass of the platform is much more than the masses of the legs and using the Eqs. (6)-(8), the kinetic energy T can be expressed as follows (Dimentberg, 1965; Kraynev, & Glazunov, 1991):

$$T = \frac{m}{2}\left[\left(\sum_{i=1}^{6} p_i^o \dot{\theta}_i G_{ii}\right)^2 + \left(\sum_{i=1}^{6} q_i^o \dot{\theta}_i G_{ii}\right)^2 + \left(\sum_{i=1}^{6} r_i^o \dot{\theta}_i G_{ii}\right)^2\right] + \\ + \frac{J_x}{2}\left(\sum_{i=1}^{6} p_i \dot{\theta}_i G_{ii}\right)^2 + \frac{J_y}{2}\left(\sum_{i=1}^{6} q_i \dot{\theta}_i G_{ii}\right)^2 + \frac{J_z}{2}\left(\sum_{i=1}^{6} r_i \dot{\theta}_i G_{ii}\right)^2 \tag{11}$$

where $\dot{\theta}_i$ are the generalized velocities, p_i, q_i, r_i, p^o_i, q^o_i, r^o_i are the components of the matrix $(E)^{-1}$, G_{ii} are the components of the diagonal matrix (G) $(i=1,\ldots,6)$.
The Lagrange equation of motion for a parallel manipulator can be written as:

$$\frac{d}{dt}\left(\frac{\partial T}{\partial \dot{\theta}_i}\right) - \frac{\partial T}{\partial \theta_i} = Q_i \tag{12}$$

where Q_i are the generalized forces $(i=1,\ldots,6)$.
The dynamical coupling can be determined using the Eq. (11). The expression of each generalized force comprises all other generalized velocities and accelerations. In order to reduce the dynamical coupling we represent the kinetic energy as follows:

$$T = \frac{m}{2}\begin{bmatrix} \sum\limits_{i=1}^{6}\left(p_i^o \dot{\theta}_i G_{ii}\right)^2 + 2\sum\limits_{i=1, j=1, i\neq j}^{6} p_i^o p_j^o \dot{\theta}_i G_{ii} \dot{\theta}_j G_{jj} + \\ + \ldots + \sum\limits_{i=1}^{6}\left(r_i^o \dot{\theta}_i G_{ii}\right)^2 + 2\sum\limits_{i=1, j=1, i\neq j}^{6} r_i^o r_j^o \dot{\theta}_i G_{ii} \dot{\theta}_j G_{jj} \end{bmatrix} + \\ + \frac{J_x}{2}\left[\sum_{i=1}^{6}\left(p_i \dot{\theta}_i G_{ii}\right)^2 + 2\sum_{i=1, j=1, i\neq j}^{6} p_i p_j \dot{\theta}_i G_{ii} \dot{\theta}_j G_{jj}\right] + \\ + \ldots + \frac{J_z}{2}\left[\sum_{i=1}^{6}\left(r_i \dot{\theta}_i G_{ii}\right)^2 + 2\sum_{i=1, j=1, i\neq j}^{6} r_i r_j \dot{\theta}_i G_{ii} \dot{\theta}_j G_{jj}\right] \tag{13}$$

According to the Eq. (13) dynamical decoupling can be satisfied if the columns of the following matrix (D) are orthogonal:

$$(D) = \begin{pmatrix} p_1^o G_{11}\sqrt{m} & \ldots & p_6^o G_{66}\sqrt{m} \\ q_1^o G_{11}\sqrt{m} & \ldots & q_6^o G_{66}\sqrt{m} \\ r_1^o G_{11}\sqrt{m} & \ldots & r_6^o G_{66}\sqrt{m} \\ p_1 G_{11}\sqrt{J_x} & \ldots & p_6 G_{66}\sqrt{J_x} \\ q_1 G_{11}\sqrt{J_y} & \ldots & q_6 G_{66}\sqrt{J_y} \\ r_1 G_{11}\sqrt{J_z} & \ldots & r_6 G_{66}\sqrt{J_z} \end{pmatrix}$$

$$(D)=\begin{pmatrix} \sqrt{m} & 0 & 0 & 0 & 0 & 0 \\ 0 & \sqrt{m} & 0 & 0 & 0 & 0 \\ 0 & 0 & \sqrt{m} & 0 & 0 & 0 \\ 0 & 0 & 0 & \sqrt{J_x} & 0 & 0 \\ 0 & 0 & 0 & 0 & \sqrt{J_y} & 0 \\ 0 & 0 & 0 & 0 & 0 & \sqrt{J_z} \end{pmatrix}(E)^{-1}(G)$$

$$(D)=(M)(E)^{-1}(G) \tag{14}$$

Let the axes of the links A_iC_i be parallel to the axes of the links B_iC_i and the matrix *(G)* is unit matrix. Then in order to satisfy the condition of orthogonal columns of the matrix *(D)* the rows of the inverse matrix $(D)^{-1} = (E)(M)^{-1}$ are to be orthogonal. From this, the following matrix *(E)* is proposed:

$$(E)=\begin{pmatrix} 0 & 0 & 1 & 0 & -\sqrt{J_y/m} & 0 \\ 0 & 0 & -1 & 0 & -\sqrt{J_y/m} & 0 \\ 1 & 0 & 0 & 0 & 0 & -\sqrt{J_z/m} \\ -1 & 0 & 0 & 0 & 0 & -\sqrt{J_z/m} \\ 0 & 1 & 0 & -\sqrt{J_x/m} & 0 & 0 \\ 0 & -1 & 0 & -\sqrt{J_x/m} & 0 & 0 \end{pmatrix} \tag{15}$$

The determinant of the matrix *(E)* (15) can be written as:

$$\det(E)=8\sqrt{J_xJ_yJ_z/m^3} \tag{16}$$

The matrix (15) corresponds to the Fig. 3. Here the center of the mass of the platform coincides with the center of the coordinate system xyz and the axes of the links of the legs

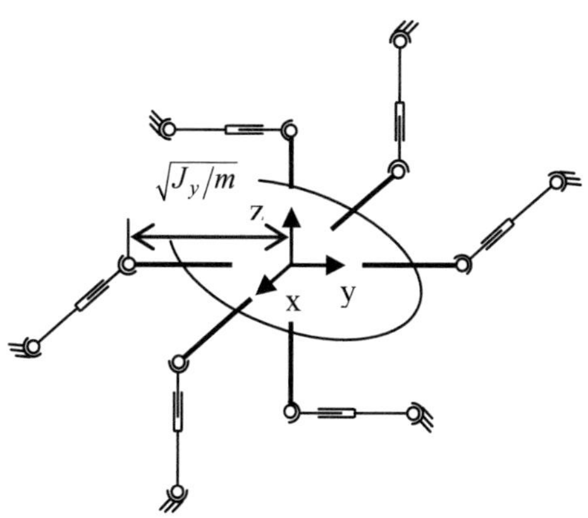

Fig. 3. Parallel manipulator with dynamical decoupling

are parallel to the main central inertia axes of the platform. The proposed approach can be applicable for manipulators characterized by small displacements and high speeds. Moreover, this architecture causes partial kinematic decoupling because if the generalized coordinates corresponding to the opposite legs are equivalent then the moving platform keeps constant orientation.

6. Pressure angles

The parallel manipulators have singularity configurations in which there is an uncontrolled mobility because some of the wrenches acting on the output link are linearly dependent. The local criterion of singular configurations is the singular matrix of the screw coordinates of the wrenches, such as:

$$\det(E) = \varepsilon^* \tag{17}$$

where ε^* is the preassigned minimal determinant value. The pressure angle of the linear dependent sub-chain is equal to $\pi/2$, as a reciprocal twist to five-member group of screws has a perpendicular moment at about any points of the axis. All stalled actuators but one the manipulator has $DOF=1$ and its output link can move along some twist $\Omega = \omega + \chi\omega^0$ ($\chi^2 = 0$) reciprocal to five-member group of the wrenches corresponding to stalled actuators. We can find this twist from the reciprocity condition:

$$mom(\Omega, R_i) = 0,\ i = 1,\ldots,5 \tag{18}$$

In general the six-member group of the unit wrenches of zero parameter $R_i(r_i, r_i^o)$ $(i=1,\ldots,6)$ is acting on the output link of the such manipulators, determinant composed of the screw coordinates of these wrenches as given in (5).
The velocity of any point A_i $(i=1,\ldots,6)$ of the mobile platform can be found as a twist moment relative to this point:

$$V_{A_i} = \omega^0 + \omega \times r_{A_i},\ i = 1,\ldots,6 \tag{19}$$

where r_{Ai} is radius-vectors of the points A_i.
The pressure angle α_i for the stalled actuator *i-th* of the parallel manipulators (Fig.1) can be determined as:

$$\alpha_i = \arccos\left(\frac{V_{A_i} . F_i}{\left|V_{A_i}\right| . \left|F_i\right|}\right),\ i = 1,\ldots,6 \tag{20}$$

where F_i is the force vector on the actuator axis. For normal functions of the manipulator it is necessary that working space be limited by positions:

$$\alpha_i \le \alpha_{KP},\ i = 1,\ldots,6 \tag{21}$$

where α_{KP} is maximum pressure angle is defined by friction coefficient.
The manipulator control system must be provided by algorithm testing the nearness to singular configurations based on the analysis of singular matrix (5) or on the pressure angle determination.

7. Manipulator for external conditions

In Fig. 4, (a, b) the six-DOFs parallel mechanisms and their sub-chain has a parallel connection of links and actuators are shown in (Glazunov, et al. 1999) which were invented by (Kraynev, & Glazunov, 1991). Such mechanisms may be utilized to manipulate the corrosive medium at all actuators that are located out of the working space. Existence of several sub-chains and many closed loops determine the essential complication of the mathematical description of these mechanisms. Screw calculus using screw groups is universal and effective for parallel mechanisms analysis. Here, *1* describes the fixed base, *2* describes the output link and *3* describes the actuators. Addition, A_i expresses the spherical joint center situated on the fixed base; B_j expresses the center of the spherical joints combined with translational; C_j expresses the output link spherical joint centers; l_i, d_j expresses the generalized coordinates and s_j, f_j expresses the link lengths $(i=1,\ldots,6;\ j=1,\ldots,3)$.

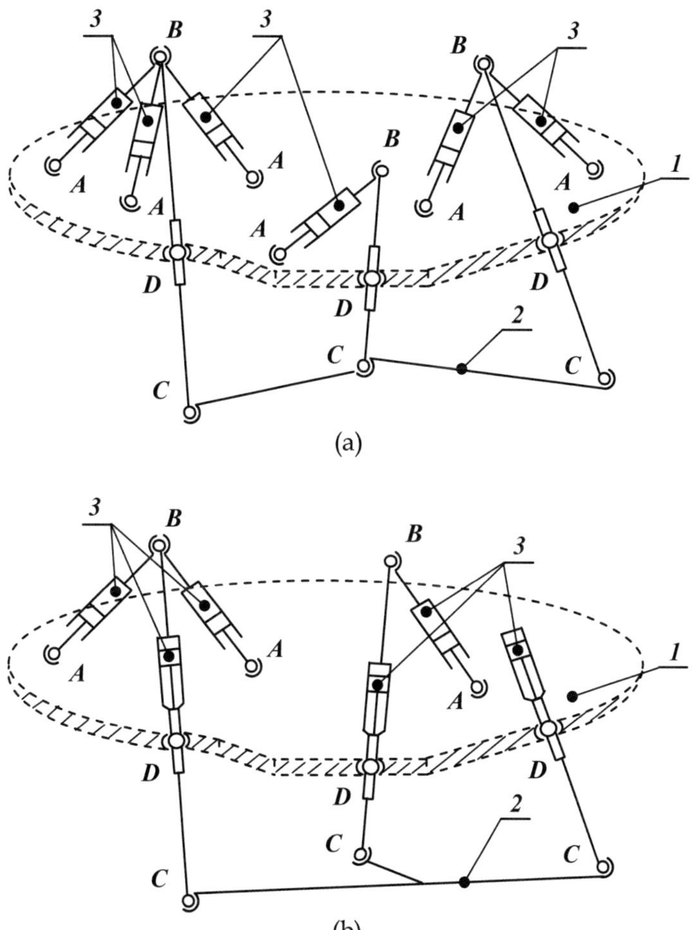

Fig. 4. The six-DOFs parallel mechanisms

In general, the wrench axis corresponding to *i-th* stalled actuator is located in the plane $(A_iB_jC_j)$, passes through center joint C_j and is directed perpendicular to its possible displacement. With the mechanisms as in (Fig. 3, a) the components of the wrench R_i can be find as:

$$r_i = \frac{1}{p_i\left\{a_i + \left[\frac{s_j}{f_j} - \left(\frac{1}{f_j} + \frac{1}{s_j}\right)\frac{(a_i.b_j)}{d_j}\right]b_j\right\}}, ; r_i^0 = \rho_{C_j} \times r_i \tag{22}$$

where p_i - vector defining the wrench axis, a_i - vector from point A_i to point C_j, b_i - vector from point D_j to point C_j and ρ_{C_j} - radius vector point C_j.

Besides, with the mechanism as in (Fig. 4, b) the wrench axis *(j=1, …,3)* coincides with actuator axis. The wrench of the *i-th* stalled actuator *(i=, …,3)* is given as

$$r_i = \frac{1}{l_i}\left\{a_i - \frac{(a_i.b_j)b_j}{d_j^2}\right\}, ; r_i^0 = \rho_{C_j} \times r_i \tag{23}$$

The present approach may be applied for different types of mechanisms such as sub-chains with varied actuator connection using spherical pairs.

8. Conclusion

Thus in this paper various criteria of design and singularity analysis of parallel manipulators are presented. The constraint wrenches imposed to the platform by kinematic chains is proposed to rely on the screw theory by determinants of matrix consisting of the Plücker coordinates of the unit screws. Criteria for design and singularity analysis of parallel manipulators with linear actuators located on the base are presented. The kinematic criterion of singularity corresponds to linear dependence of wrenches supporting the mobile platform; the static criterion corresponds to the limitation of pressure angles. The dynamical decoupling allows increasing the accuracy, parametrical optimization allows designing the mechanisms with optimal working volume, dexterity and stiffness, determination of the twists inside singularity allows finding the differential conditions of singular loci. Furthermore, the use of screw groups in order to determination of the singular zones of the multi-DOFs parallel mechanisms that make form of continuous areas and manipulators for external conditions are expressed.

9. References

Angeles, J. (2004). The Qualitative Synthesis of Parallel Mechanisms, *In Journal of Mechanical Design*, 126: 617-624.

Arakelian, V.; Briot, S. & Glazunov, V. (2007). Improvement of functional performance of spatial parallel mechanisms using mechanisms of variable structure, *In Proceedings of the 12th World Congress in Mechanism and Machine Science*, Besancon, France, 1: 159-164.

Bonev, I.; Zlatanov, D. & Gosselin, C. (2003). Singularity analysis of 3-DOF planar parallel mechanisms via screw theory, *In Transactions of the ASME, Journal of Mechanical Design*, 125: 573-581.

Ceccarelli, M. (2004). Fundamentals of Mechanics of Robotic Manipulations, *Kluwer Academic Publishers.*

Dimentberg, F. (1965). The Screw calculus and its Applications in Mechanics, *Nauka,* (English translation: AD680993, Clearinghouse for Federal Technical and Scientific Information, Virginia).

Glazunov, V. & Kraynev, A. (2006). Design and Singularity Criteria of Parallel mechanisms, *In ROMANSY 16, Robot Design, Dynamics, and Control, Proceedings of 16 CISM-IFToMM Symposium,* Springer Wien New York, 15-22.

Glazunov, V. & Thanh, N.M. (2008). Determination of the parameters and the Twists inside Singularity of the parallel Manipulators with Actuators Situated on the Base, *ROMANSY 17, Robot Design, Dynamics, and Control. In Proceedings of the Seventeenth CISM-IFToMM Symposium,* Tokyo, Japan, 467-474.

Glazunov, V. (2006). Twists of Movements of Parallel Mechanisms inside Their Singularities, *In Mechanism and Machine Theory,* 41: 1185-1195.

Glazunov, V.; Gruntovich, R.; Lastochkin, A. & Thanh, N.M. (2007). Representations of constraints imposed by kinematic chains of parallel mechanisms, *In Proceedings of 12th World Congress in Mechanism and Machine Science,* Besancon, France, 1: 380-385.

Glazunov, V.; Hue, N.N. & Thanh, N.M. (2009). Singular configuration analysis of the parallel mechanisms, *In Journal of Machinery and engineering education,* ISSN 1815-1051, No. 4, 11-16.

Glazunov, V.; Koliskor, A. & Kraynev, A. (1991). Spatial Parallel Structure Mechanisms, *Nauka.*

Glazunov, V.; Koliskor, A.; Kraynev, A. & B. Model, (1990). Classification Principles and Analysis Methods for Parallel-Structure Spatial Mechanisms, *In Journal of Machinery Manufacture and Reliability,* Allerton Press Inc., 1: 30-37.

Glazunov, V.; Kraynev, A.; Rashoyan, G. & Trifonova, A. (1999). Singular Zones of Parallel Structure Mechanisms, *In X World Congress on TMM,* Oulu, Finland, 2710-2715.

Gosselin, C. & Angeles, J. (1990). Singularity Analysis of Closed Loop Kinematic Chains, *In IEEE Trans. on Robotics and Automation,* 6(3): 281-290.

Huang, Z. (2004). The kinematics and type synthesis of lower-mobility parallel robot manipulators, *Proceedings of the XI World Congress in Mechanism and Machine Science,* Tianjin, China, 65–76.

Kong, X. & Gosselin, C. (2007). Type Synthesis of Parallel Mechanisms, *Springer-Verlag Berlin Heidelberg,* 272p.

Kraynev, A. & Glazunov, V. (1991). Parallel Structure Mechanisms in Robotics, *In MERO'91, Sympos. Nation. de Robotic Industr.,* Bucuresti, Romania, 1: 104-111.

Merlet, J.-P. (1991). Articulated device, for use in particular in robotics, *United States Patent 5,053,687.*

Merlet, J.-P. (2006). Parallel Robots, *Kluwer Academic Publishers,* 394p.

Statnikov, R.B. (1999). Multicriteria Design. Optimization and Identification, Dordrecht, Boston, London: *Kluwer Academic Publishers,* 206p.

Thanh, N.M.; Glazunov, V. & Vinh, L.N. (2010). Determination of Constraint Wrenches and Design of Parallel Mechanisms, *In CCE 2010 Proceedings, Tuxtla Gutiérrez, Mexico, 2010, International Conference on Electrical Engineering, Computing Science and Automatic Control, IEEE 2010,* 46-53.

Thanh, N.M.; Glazunov, V.; Tuan, T.C. & Vinh, N.X. (2010). Multi-criteria optimization of the parallel mechanism with actuators located outside working space, *In ICARCV 2010 Proceedings, Singapore, International Conference on Control, Automation, Robotics and Vision, IEEE 2010*, 1772-1778.

Thanh, N.M.; Glazunov, V.; Vinh, L.N. & Mau, N.C. (2008). Parametrical optimization of the parallel mechanisms while taking into account singularities, *In ICARCV 2008 Proceedings, Hanoi, Vietnam, International Conference on Control, Automation, Robotics and Vision, IEEE 2008*, 1872-1877.

Thanh, N.M.; Quoc, L.H. & Glazunov, V. (2009). Constraints analysis, determination twists inside singularity and parametrical optimization of the parallel mechanisms by means the theory of screws, *In CCE 2009 Proceedings, Toluca, Mexico, International Conference on Electrical Engineering, Computing Science and Automatic Control, IEEE 2009*, 89-95.

19

Data Sensor Fusion for Autonomous Robotics

Özer Çiftçioğlu and Sevil Sariyildiz
Delft University of Technology,
Faculty of Architecture, Delft
The Netherlands

1. Introduction

Multi-sensory information is a generic concept since such information is of concern in all robotic systems where information processing is central. In such systems for the enhancement of the accurate action information redundant sensors are necessary where not only the number of the sensors but also the resolutional information of the sensors can vary due to information with different sampling time from the sensors. The sampling can be regular with a constant sampling rate as well as irregular. Different sensors can have different merits depending on their individual operating conditions and such diverse information can be a valuable gain for accurate as well as reliable autonomous robot manipulation via its dynamics and kinematics. The challenge in this case is the unification of the common information from various sensors in such a way that the resultant information presents enhanced information for desired action. One might note that, such information unification is a challenge in the sense that the common information is in general in different format and different size with different merits. The different qualities may involve different accuracy of sensors due to various random measurement errors. Autonomous robotics constitutes an important branch of robotics and the autonomous robotics research is widely reported in literature, e.g. (Oriolio, Ulivi et al. 1998; Beetz, Arbuckle et al. 2001; Wang and Liu 2004). In this branch of robotics continuous information from the environment is obtained by sensors and real-time processed. The accurate and reliable information driving the robot is essential for a safe navigation the trajectory of which is in general not prescribed in advance. The reliability of this information is to achieve by means of both physical and analytical redundancy of the sensors. The accuracy is obtained by coordinating the sensory information from the redundant sensors in a multi-sensor system. This coordination is carried out by combining information from different sensors for an ultimate measurement outcome and this is generally termed as sensor fusion. Since data is the basic elements of the information, sometimes to emphasize this point the fusion process is articulated with data as *data fusion* where the *sensor fusion* is thought to be as a synonym. Some examples are as follows.

> "Data fusion is the process by which data from a multitude of sensors is used to yield an optimal estimate of a specified state vector pertaining to the observed system." (Richardson and Marsh 1988)
>
> "Data fusion deals with the synergistic combination of information made available by various knowledge sources such as sensors, in order to provide a better understanding of a given scene." (Abidi and Gonzales 1992)

> "The problem of sensor fusion is the problem of combining multiple measurements from sensors into a single measurement of the sensed object or attribute, called the *parameter*." (McKendall and Mintz 1992; Hsin and Li 2006)

The ultimate aim of information processing as fusion is to enable the system to estimate the state of the environment and in particular we can refer to the state of a robot's environment in the present case. A similar research dealing with this challenge, namely a multiresolutional filter application for spatial information fusion in robot navigation has been reported earlier (Ciftcioglu 2008) where data fusion is carried out using several data sets obtained from wavelet decomposition and not from individual sensors. In contrast with the earlier work, in the present work, in a multi-sensor environment, fusion of sensory information from different sensors is considered. Sensors generally have different characteristics with different merits. For instance a sensor can have a wide frequency range with relatively poor signal to noise ratio or vice versa; the response time of the sensor determines the frequency range. On the other hand sensors can operate synchronized or non-synchronized manner with respect to their sampling intervals to deliver the measurement outcomes. Such concerns can be categorized as matters of *sensor management* although sensor management is more related to the positioning of the sensors in a measurement system. In the present work data fusion sensor fusion and sensor management issues are commonly are referred to as sensor fusion. The novelty of the research is the enhanced estimation of the spatial sensory information in autonomous robotics by means of multiresolutional levels of information with respect to sampling time intervals of different sensors. Coordination outcome of such redundant information reflects the various merits of these sensors yielding enhanced positioning estimation or estimate the state of the environment. To consider a general case the sensors are operated independently without a common synchronizing sampling command, for instance. The multiresolutional information is obtained from sensors having different resolutions and this multiple information is synergistically combined by means of inverse wavelet transformation developed for this purpose in this work. Although wavelet-based information fusion is used in different applications (Hong 1993; Hsin and Li 2006), its application in robotics is not common in literature. One of the peculiarities of the research is essentially the application of wavelet-based dynamic filtering with the concept of multiresolution as the multiresolution concept is closely tied to the discrete wavelet transform. The multiresolutional dynamic filtering is central to the study together with the Kalman filtering which has desirable features of fusion. Therefore the vector wavelet decomposition is explained in some detail. For the information fusion process extended Kalman filtering is used and it is also explained in some detail emphasizing its central role in the fusion process. In an autonomous robot trajectory the estimation of angular velocity is not a measurable quantity and it has to be estimated from the measurable state variables so that obstacle avoidance problem is taken care of. The angular velocity estimation in real-time is a critical task in autonomous robotics and from this viewpoint, the multiresolutional sensor-based spatial information fusion process by Kalman filtering is particularly desirable for enhanced robot navigation performance. In particular, the multiresolutional sensors provide diversity in the information subject to fusion process. In this way different quality of information with respective merits are synergistically combined.

The motivation of this research is the use of a vision robot for an architectural design and the architectural artifacts therein from the viewpoint of human perception, namely to investigate the perceptual variations in human observation without bias. The similar perception centered research by a human can have an inherent bias due to the interests and background of that human. In this respect, a robot can be viewed as an impartial observer with emulated human perception. Therefore, in this research, the sensory information is treated as robot's visual perception as an emulation of that of a human. A theory for the human perception from a viewpoint of perception quantification and computation is presented earlier (Ciftcioglu, Bittermann et al. 2007; Ciftcioglu 2008). The robot can be a physical real artifact autonomously wandering in an architectural environment. Or alternatively, it can be a virtual robot, wandering in a virtual reality environment. Both cases are equally valid utilization options in the realm of perceptual robotics in architecture. Apart from our interest on human perception of architectural artifacts as motivation, the present research is equally of interest to other adjacent robotics research areas like social robots which are closely related to perception robots. Namely, thanks to the advancements in robotics, today the social robots are more and more penetrating in social life as an aid to many human endeavors. With the advent of rapid progresses in robotics and evolutions on hardware and software systems, many advanced social, service and surveillance mobile robots have been coming into realization in the recent decades; see for instance, *http:/spectrum.ieee.org/robotics*. One of the essential merits of such robots is the ability to detect and track people in the view in real time, for example in a care center. A social robot should be able to keep eye on the persons in the view and keep tracking the persons of concern for probable interaction (Bellotto and Hu 2009). A service robot should be aware of people around and track a person of concern to provide useful services. A surveillance robot can monitor persons in the scene for the identification of probable misbehavior. For such tasks, detecting and tracking multiple persons in often crowded and cluttered scenes in public domain or in a working environment is needed. In all these challenging scenarios perceptual mobile robotics can give substantial contribution for the functionality of such special variety of robots in view of two main aspects. One aspect is vision, which is not the subject-matter of this work. The other aspect is the sensor-data fusion for effective information processing, which is the subject matter of this research where Kalman filtering is the main machinery, as it is a common approach in mobile robotics for optimal information processing.

The further organization of the present work is as follows. After the description of Kalman filtering and wavelet transform in some detail, detailed description of optimal fusion process of information from different multiresolutional levels is presented. The optimality is based on minimum fusion estimation error variance. Finally, autonomous robot implementation is described with the computer experiments the results of which are illustrated by means of both true and estimated trajectories demonstrating the effective multisensor-based, multiresolutional fusion. The work is concluded with a brief discussion and conclusions.

2. Kalman filter

2.1 Description of the system dynamics

Kalman filtering theory and its applications are well treated in literature (Jazwinski 1970; Gelb 1974; Kailath 1981; Maybeck 1982; Brown 1983; Sorenson 1985; Mendel 1987; Grewal and Andrews 2001; Simon 2006). In order to apply Kalman filtering to a robot movement the system dynamics must be described by a set of differential equations which are in state-space form, in general

$$\frac{dx}{dt} = Fx + Gu + w \tag{1}$$

where x is a column vector with the states of the system, F the system dynamics matrix, u is the control vector , and w is a white noise process vector. The process noise matrix Q is related to the process-noise vector according to

$$Q = \mathrm{E}[ww^{\mathrm{T}}] \tag{2}$$

The measurements are linearly related to the states according to

$$z = Hx + v \tag{3}$$

where z is the measurement vector, H is the measurement matrix, and v is measurement noise vector which is element-wise white. The measurement noise matrix R is related to the measurement noise vector v according to

$$R = \mathrm{E}[vv^{\mathrm{T}}] \tag{4}$$

In discrete form, the Kalman filtering equations become

$$\begin{aligned} x_k &= \Phi_k x_{k-1} + \mathrm{K}_\mathrm{k}(\mathrm{z}_\mathrm{k} - \mathrm{H}\Phi_k x_{k-1} - \mathrm{HG}_\mathrm{k} u_{\mathrm{k-1}}) + \mathrm{G}_\mathrm{k} u_{\mathrm{k-1}} \\ \mathrm{z}_\mathrm{k} &= Hx_k + v_k \end{aligned} \tag{5}$$

where Φ_k system transition matrix, K_k represents he Kalman gain matrix and G_k is obtained from

$$G_k = \int_0^T \Phi(\tau)\mathrm{G}(\tau)\mathrm{d}\tau \tag{6}$$

where T is the sampling time interval and the computation of Φ(t) is given shortly afterwards in (13). In this research information processing from the sensors for estimation is concerned. The control signal (***u***) is not involved in the filtering operation. Hence the Kalman filtering equation for this case becomes

$$x_k = \Phi_k x_{k-1} + \mathrm{K}_\mathrm{k}(\mathrm{z}_\mathrm{k} - \mathrm{H}\Phi_k x_{\mathrm{k-1}}) \tag{7}$$

While the filter is operating, the Kalman gains are computed from the matrix Riccati equations:

$$\begin{aligned} M_k &= \Phi_k P_{k-1} \Phi_k^T + Q_k \\ K_k &= M_k H^T (H M_k H^T + R_k)^{-1} \\ P_k &= (I - K_k H) M_k \end{aligned} \tag{8}$$

where P_k is a covariance matrix representing errors in the state estimates after an update and M_k is the covariance matrix representing errors in the state estimates before an update. The discrete process noise matrix Q_k can be found from the continuous process-noise matrix Q according to

$$Q_k = \int_0^T \Phi(\tau) Q \Phi^T(\tau) d\tau \tag{9}$$

where Φ(t) is given in (13). When robot movement is along a straight line with a constant speed v_x, the x component of the system dynamic model is given by

$$x = a_o + v_x t \tag{10}$$

It is to note that the angular speed $\omega=0$. The system dynamics in state-space form is given by

$$\begin{bmatrix} \dot{x} \\ \ddot{x} \end{bmatrix} = \begin{bmatrix} 0 & 1 \\ 0 & 0 \end{bmatrix} \begin{bmatrix} x \\ \dot{x} \end{bmatrix} \tag{11}$$

Where the system dynamics matrix F is given by

$$F = \begin{bmatrix} 0 & 1 \\ 0 & 0 \end{bmatrix} \tag{12}$$

The system transition matrix Φ is computed from inverse Laplace transform of the form

$$\begin{aligned} \Phi(t) &= L^{-1}\left\{(sI - F)^{-1}\right\} = e^{Ft} \\ \Phi_k &= \Phi(t) = \begin{bmatrix} 1 & t \\ 0 & 1 \end{bmatrix} \end{aligned} \tag{13}$$

The discrete fundamental matrix, i.e., system transition matrix can be found from preceding expression by simply replacing time with the sampling time interval of the perception measurements T or

$$\Phi_k = \Phi(T) = \begin{bmatrix} 1 & T \\ 0 & 1 \end{bmatrix} \tag{14}$$

In two dimensional navigation space, i.e., xy plane, the system transition matrix becomes

$$\Phi_k = \begin{bmatrix} 0 & T & 0 & 0 \\ 0 & 1 & 0 & 0 \\ 0 & 0 & 1 & T \\ 0 & 0 & 0 & 1 \end{bmatrix} \tag{15}$$

and the corresponding state vector X is given by

$$X = [x \quad v_x \quad y \quad v_y] \tag{16}$$

In the case of $\omega \neq 0$, i.e., circular movement with an angular velocity, we consider the geometry shown in Figure 1.

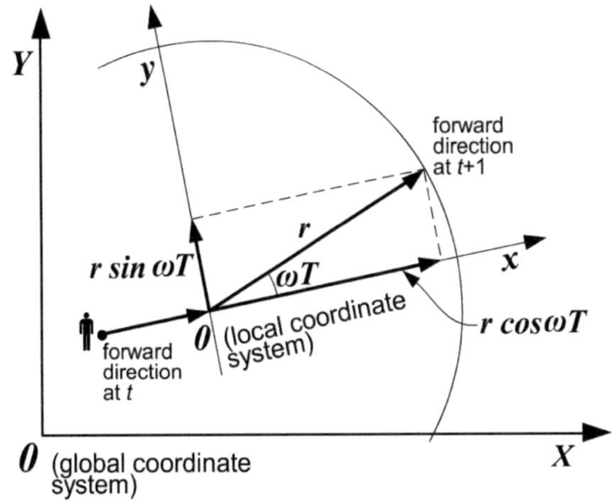

Fig. 1. Geometry with respect to angular deviation during robot navigation

At the local coordinate system, the state variables are

$$\begin{aligned} x_1 &= r\cos(\omega t) \\ \dot{x}_1 &= -r\omega\sin(\omega t) \\ x_2 &= r\sin(\omega t) \\ \dot{x}_2 &= r\omega\cos(\omega t) \end{aligned} \tag{17}$$

So that the system dynamics in state-space form in continuous time is given by

$$\begin{bmatrix} \dot{x}_1 \\ \ddot{x}_1 \\ \dot{x}_2 \\ \ddot{x}_2 \end{bmatrix} = \begin{bmatrix} 0 & 1 & 0 & 0 \\ 0 & 0 & 0 & -\omega \\ 0 & 0 & 0 & 1 \\ 0 & \omega & 0 & 0 \end{bmatrix} \begin{bmatrix} x_1 \\ \dot{x}_1 \\ x_2 \\ \dot{x}_2 \end{bmatrix} \tag{18}$$

The system transition matrix Φ^{ω}_{k} is computed from inverse Laplace transform of the form

$$\Phi_k^{\omega}(t) = L^{-1}\left\{(sI - F_{\omega})^{-1}\right\} = e^{F_{\omega} t} \tag{19}$$

where $(sI\text{-}F_{\omega})$ is given by

$$sI - F_{\omega} = \begin{bmatrix} s & -1 & 0 & 0 \\ 0 & s & 0 & \omega \\ 0 & 0 & s & -1 \\ 0 & -\omega & 0 & s \end{bmatrix} \tag{20}$$

The inverse of (20) yields

$$\begin{bmatrix} \frac{1}{s} & \frac{1}{s^2+\omega^2} & 0 & -\frac{\omega}{s(s^2+\omega^2)} \\ 0 & \frac{1}{s(s^2+\omega^2)} & 0 & -\frac{\omega}{s^2+\omega^2} \\ 0 & \frac{\omega}{s(s^2+\omega^2)} & \frac{1}{s} & \frac{1}{s^2+\omega^2} \\ 0 & \frac{\omega}{s^2+\omega^2} & 0 & \frac{1}{s(s^2+\omega^2)} \end{bmatrix} \quad (21)$$

and the inverse Laplace transform of (21) gives the system transition matrix, for $t=T$, as

$$\Phi_k^{\omega} = \begin{bmatrix} 1 & \frac{\sin(\omega T)}{\omega} & 0 & \frac{\cos(\omega T)-1}{\omega} \\ 0 & \cos(\omega T) & 0 & -\sin(\omega T) \\ 0 & -\frac{\cos(\omega T)-1}{\omega} & 1 & \frac{\sin(\omega T)}{\omega} \\ 0 & \sin(\omega T) & 0 & \cos(\omega T) \end{bmatrix} \quad (22)$$

During the robot navigation we have obtained two system dynamics models; namely rectilinear straight-ahead and angular rotation cases. To endow the robot to be autonomous the angular velocity should be computed during the navigation. If the perception measurements yield a significant angular velocity, the system dynamics model should switch from linear to non-linear. It is interesting to note that if in (22) $\omega=0$, then it reduces to (15) which is the transition matrix for linear case. In other words, (22) represents inherently the linear case, as well as the rotational robot navigation. If the angular velocity is computed at each step of navigation and if it is non-zero, the robot moves along a non-linear trajectory with each time a deviation θ from linear trajectory. The linear and non-linear cases are illustrated in figure 2 and figure 3 where the measurements are from sensory visual perception (Ciftcioglu, Bittermann et al. 2007; Ciftcioglu 2008).

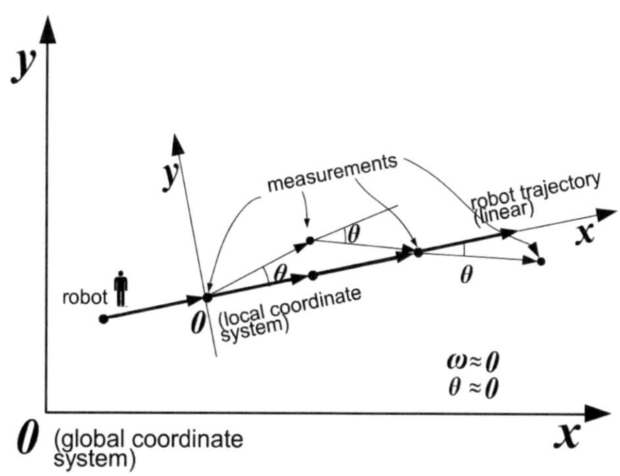

Fig. 2. Measurements along a linear move

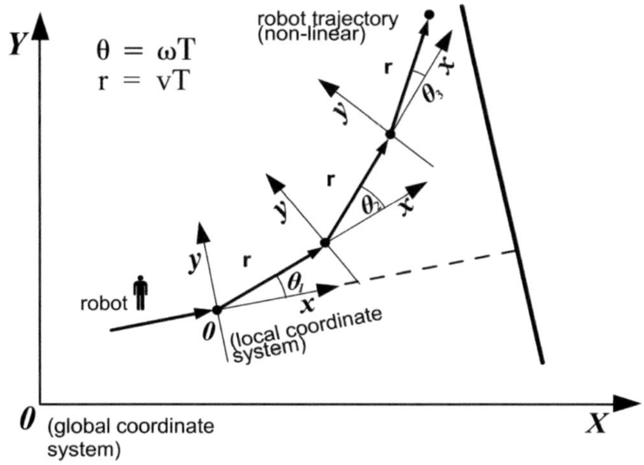

Fig. 3. Robot navigation deviating from a linear move

To compute the angular velocity ω at each step, it is also selected as a state variable, so that the state variables vector given by (16) is modified to

$$X^{\omega} = [x \quad v_x \quad y \quad v_y \quad \omega] \tag{23}$$

However, in this case the system transition matrix in (22) becomes non-linear with respect to ω. In this case Kalman filtering equations should be linearized. This is a form known as extended Kalman filtering.

2.2 Extended Kalman filtering (EKF)

The non-linear state-space form as a set of first-order non-linear differential equations is given by

$$\dot{x} = f(x) + w \tag{24}$$

where x is a vector of the system states, $f(x)$ is a non-linear function of those states, and w is a random zero-mean process. The measurement equation is considered to be a non-linear function of the states according to

$$z = h(x) + v \tag{25}$$

where $h(x)$ is a non-linear measurement matrix, v is a zero-mean random process.
We assume that an *approximate* trajectory x_o is available. This is referred to as the reference trajectory. The actual trajectory x may then be written as

$$x = x_o + \Delta x \tag{26}$$

Hence, (24) and (25) become

$$\begin{aligned} \dot{x}_o + \Delta\dot{x} &= f(x_o + \Delta x) + w \\ z &= h(x_o + \Delta x) + v \end{aligned} \tag{27}$$

The Taylors series expansion yields the linearized model

$$\begin{aligned} \dot{x}_o + \dot{\Delta x} &\approx f(x_o) + \left[\frac{\partial f}{\partial x}\right]_{x=x_o} \Delta x + w \\ z &= h(x_o) + \left[\frac{\partial h}{\partial x}\right]_{x=x_o} \Delta x + v \end{aligned} \tag{28}$$

where

$$\frac{\partial f}{\partial x}\Big|_{x=x_o} = \mathbf{F} = \begin{bmatrix} \frac{\partial f_1}{\partial x_1} \frac{\partial f_1}{\partial x_2} \ldots\ldots \\ \frac{\partial f_2}{\partial x_1} \frac{\partial f_1}{\partial x_2} \ldots\ldots \\ . \\ . \end{bmatrix} \quad \frac{\partial h}{\partial x}\Big|_{x=x_o} = \mathbf{H} = \begin{bmatrix} \frac{\partial h_1}{\partial x_1} \frac{\partial h_1}{\partial x_2} \ldots\ldots \\ \frac{\partial h_2}{\partial x_1} \frac{\partial h_1}{\partial x_2} \ldots\ldots \\ . \\ . \end{bmatrix} \tag{29}$$

If the reference trajectory x_o is chosen to satisfy the differential equation

$$\Delta \dot{x} = f(x_o) \tag{30}$$

In view of (29) and (30), the system dynamics matrix Φ in discrete form for extended Kalman filtering becomes

$$\Phi_k^{\omega} = \begin{bmatrix} 1 & \frac{\sin(\omega T)}{\omega} & 0 & \frac{\cos(\omega T)-1}{\omega} & \omega_x \\ 0 & \cos(\omega T) & 0 & -\sin(\omega T) & \omega_{\dot{x}} \\ 0 & -\frac{\cos(\omega T)-1}{\omega} & 1 & \frac{\sin(\omega T)}{\omega} & \omega_y \\ 0 & \sin(\omega T) & 0 & \cos(\omega T) & \omega_{\dot{y}} \\ 0 & 0 & 0 & 0 & 1 \end{bmatrix} \tag{31}$$

Above, ω_x , ω_y , .. are given by

$$\omega_x = \frac{1}{\omega}\left[(T\cos\omega T - \frac{\sin\omega T}{\omega})\dot{x} + (-T\sin\omega T - \frac{\cos\omega T - 1}{\omega})\dot{y}\right] \tag{32}$$

$$\omega_{\dot{x}} = \left[-\sin\omega T)\dot{x} - \cos\omega T\,\dot{y}\right]T \tag{33}$$

$$\omega_y = \frac{1}{\omega}\left[(T\sin\omega T - \frac{1-\cos\omega T}{\omega})\dot{x} + (-T\cos\omega T - \frac{\sin\omega T}{\omega})\dot{y}\right] \tag{34}$$

$$\omega_{\dot{y}} = \left[\cos\omega T \dot{x} - \sin\omega T \dot{y} \right] T \tag{35}$$

In the extended Kalman filter operation, three measurements are considered. Referring to Figure 3 these are

$$\begin{aligned} \theta &= arctg(y / x) = arctg(x_3 / x_1) && \text{angle} \\ r &= \sqrt{x^2 + y^2} = \sqrt{x_1^2 + x_3^2} && \text{distance} \\ v &= \sqrt{v_x^2 + v_y^2} = \sqrt{x_2^2 + x_4^2} && \text{velocity} \end{aligned} \tag{36}$$

From (36), the linearized measurement matrix in terms of state variables becomes

$$\mathbf{H} = \begin{bmatrix} \frac{-1}{x_1^2 + x_3^2} & 0 & \frac{x_1}{x_1^2 + x_3^2} & 0 & 0 \\ \frac{x_1}{\sqrt{x_1^2 + x_3^2}} & 0 & \frac{x_3}{\sqrt{x_1^2 + x_3^2}} & 0 & 0 \\ 0 & \frac{x_2}{\sqrt{x_2^2 + x_4^2}} & 0 & \frac{x_4}{\sqrt{x_2^2 + x_4^2}} & 0 \end{bmatrix} \tag{37}$$

Above x_1, x_2, x_3, x_4 are the state variables which are defined as $x_1=x$, $x_2=y$, $x_3=v_x$, and $x_4=v_y$, respectively.

2.3 Estimation

In this work, the Kalman filter is an estimator of states of a dynamic system with a minimal error (innovation) variance and in this sense it is optimal. In order to explain the estimation in detail, the filter equations taking the discrete time point *k* as reference are briefly given below. A general dynamic system given in a form

$$x(k+1) = A(k)x(k) + B(k)w(k) \tag{38}$$

$$z(k) = C(k)x(k) + v(k) \tag{39}$$

is terminologically referred to as *state-space*. Above A is the system matrix; B process noise matrix; C is the measurement matrix. Further, *w(k)* and *v(k)* are Gaussian process noise and measurement noise respectively with the properties

$$\begin{aligned} &E\{w(k)\} = 0 \\ &E\{w(k)w(l)^T\} = Q(k) \, for \;\; k = l \\ &\qquad\qquad\qquad\;\; = 0 \; otherwise \end{aligned} \tag{40}$$

$$\begin{aligned} &E\{v(k)\} = 0 \\ &E\{v(k)v(l)^T\} = R(k) \, for \;\; k = l \\ &\qquad\qquad\qquad\;\; = 0 \; otherwise \end{aligned} \tag{41}$$

The estimation in Kalman filter is accomplished recursively which with the notations in the literature became standard matrix equations formulation and it reads

$$x(k+1|k) = A(k)x(k|k) \tag{42}$$

$$P(k+1|k) = A(k)P(k|k)A(k)^T + B(k)Q(k)B(k)^T \tag{43}$$

$$K(k+1) = \frac{P(k+1|k)C(k+1)^T}{C(k+1)P(k+1|k)C(k+1)^T + R(k+1)} \tag{44}$$

So that the updated as the measurements z are available the updated state variables and covariance matrix are

$$\begin{aligned} &x(k+1|k+1) = x(k+1|k) + K(k+1)[z(k+1) - C(k+1)x(k+1|k)] \\ &z(k+1) - C(k+1)x(k+1|k) = innovation \end{aligned} \tag{45}$$

$$P(k+1|k+1) = [I - K(k+1)C(k+1)]P(k+1|k) \tag{46}$$

N-level multiresolutional dynamic system in a vector form can be described by

$$\begin{aligned} &x^{[N]}(k_N+1) = A^{[N]}(k_N)x^{[N]}(k_N), \\ &z^{[i]}(k_i) = C^{[i]}(k_i)x^{[i]}(k_i) + v^{[i]}(k_i) \\ &i = 1,...,N \end{aligned} \tag{47}$$

where i=N is the highest resolution level, so that

$$\begin{aligned} &E\left[w^{[N]}(k_N)\right] = 0, \\ &E\left[w^{[N]}(k_N)w^{[N]}(l_N)^T\right] = Q^{[N]}(k_N), \quad k = l \\ &\qquad = 0 \quad k \neq l \end{aligned} \tag{48}$$

Referring to the measurements $z^{[i]}(k_i)$ at different resolution levels, we write

$$\begin{aligned} &E\left[w^{[i]}(k_i)\right] = 0, \\ &E\left[w^{[i]}(k_i)w^{[i]}(l_i)^T\right] = Q^{[i]}(k_i), \quad k = l \\ &\qquad = 0 \quad k \neq l \end{aligned} \tag{49}$$

and

$$\begin{aligned} &E\left[v^{[i]}(k_i)\right] = 0, \\ &E\left[v^{[i]}(k_i)v^{[i]}(l_i)^T\right] = R^{[i]}(k_i), \quad k = l \\ &\qquad = 0 \quad k \neq l \end{aligned} \tag{50}$$

Kalman filter is used to combine the information from the measurements at different resolutional levels and enhance the state estimation rather than to employ single measurement at each time-step.

3. Wavelets

3.1 Multiresolutional decomposition

Wavelet analysis is basically the projection of data onto a set of basis functions in order to separate different scale information. In particular, in the discrete wavelet transform (DWT) data are separated into wavelet detail coefficients (detail-scale information) and approximation coefficients (approximation-scale information) by the projection of the data onto an orthogonal dyadic basis system (Mallat 1989). In the DWT framework, a signal f(x) is decomposed into approximation and detail components to form a multiresolution analysis of the signal as

$$f(x)=\sum_k a_{jo,k}\phi_{jo,k}(x)+\sum_{j=jo}^{jo+J}\sum_k d_{j,k}\psi_{j,k}(x) \quad j_o,j,k\in\mathbb{Z} \tag{51}$$

where $a_{jo,k}$ denote the approximation coefficient at resolution j_o; $d_{j,k}$ denotes the wavelet coefficient at resolution j; $\phi_{jo,k}(x)$ is a scaling function; $\psi_{j,k}(x)$ is a wavelet function at resolution j, and J is the number of decomposition levels. The coefficients are given by

$$\begin{aligned} a_{jo,k} &= \langle f(x),\phi_{jo,k}\rangle \\ d_{j,k} &= \langle f(x),\psi_{j,k}\rangle \quad j_o,j,k\in\mathbb{Z} \end{aligned} \tag{52}$$

Above $\langle . \rangle$ denotes the inner product in the space of square integrable functions $L^2(\measuredangle)$. Specifically, the dyadic DWT assumes the scaling functions have the property of

$$\phi_{jo,k}(x)=2^{jo/2}\phi(2^{jo}x-k) \tag{53}$$

and the wavelet functions

$$\psi_{j,k}(x)=2^{j/2}\psi(2^{j}x-k) \tag{54}$$

The novel feature of wavelets is that they are localized in time and frequency as to signals. This behaviour makes them convenient for the analysis of non-stationary signals. It is an elementary introduction of wavelets by introducing a scaling function, such that

$$\phi(t)=\sqrt{2}\sum_k g_k\phi(2t-k) \tag{55}$$

A counterpart of this function is called mother wavelet function obtained from

$$\psi(t)=\sqrt{2}\sum_k h_k\phi(2t-k) \tag{56}$$

where l_k and h_k are related via the equation

$$h_k = (-1)^k g_{1-k} \tag{57}$$

The coefficients g_k and h_k appear in the quadrature mirror filters used to compute the wavelet transform. $\phi(t)$ and $\psi(t)$ form orthogonal functions which constitute low-pass and high-pass filters respectively which are spaces in $L_2(\Re)$ where inner product of functions is defined with finite energy. The orthogonal spaces satisfy the property

$$\phi_{m,k}(t) \cup \psi(t)_{m,k} = \phi_{m+1,k}(t) \tag{58}$$

where

$$\phi_{m,k}(t) = 2^{m/2}\phi(2^m t - k) \tag{59}$$

$$\psi_{m,k}(t) = 2^{m/2}\psi(2^m t - k) \tag{60}$$

$m=0$ constitutes the coarsest scale. The simplest filter coefficients are known as Haar filter and given by

$$\begin{aligned} h_h &= [h_1 \;\; h_2] \\ &= \frac{1}{\sqrt{2}}[1 \quad 1] \end{aligned} \tag{61}$$

$$\begin{aligned} g_h &= [g_1 \;\; g_2] \\ &= \frac{1}{\sqrt{2}}[1 \;\; -1] \end{aligned} \tag{62}$$

If one sensor is used at the highest resolutional level i.e., i=3 the measurements at different resolution levels can be obtained by the decomposition scheme shown in figure 4.

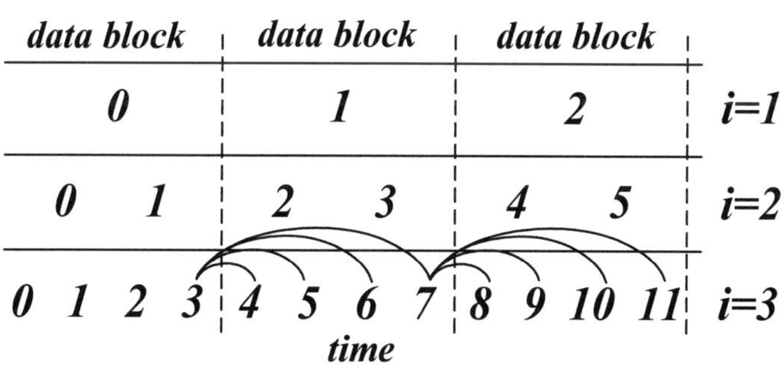

Fig. 4. Measurements at different resolution levels

In this scheme each data block at the highest resolution level (i=3) contains 4 samples. Wavelet decomposition of this block of samples is shown in figure 5.
In figure 5, the measurements are uniform. This means measurement time points in a lower resolution are exactly at the mid of the two points of measurement times at the higher resolutional level, as indicated in figure 4. Within a data block, the state variables at resolution level i are designated as

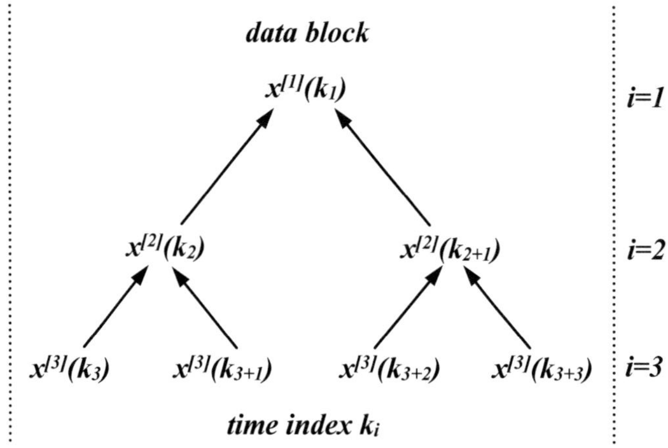

Fig. 5. Wavelet decomposition of state variables in a data block

$$X_m^{[i]} = \begin{bmatrix} x^{[i]}k(i) \\ x^{[i]}k(i+1) \\ \ldots\ldots. \\ x^{[i]}k(i+2^{i-1}) \end{bmatrix} \tag{63}$$

$$x^{[i]}{}_{k(i)} = \begin{bmatrix} x_{k,1}^{[i]} \\ x_{k,2}^{[i]} \\ \ldots. \\ x_{k,p}^{[i]} \end{bmatrix} \tag{64}$$

where m is data block index and p is the number of state variables. In a data block, there are 2^{i-1} state variables. Each state variable has p state components. A lower resolution state variable is computed from

$$x^{[i]}(k_i) = h_1 x^{[i+1]}(k_{i+1}) + h_2 x^{[i+1]}(k_{i+1}+1) \tag{65}$$

where h_1 and h_2 are the Haar low-pass filter coefficients. The details component i.e., high frequency part after the decomposition is computed via

$$y^{[i]}(k_i) = g_1 x^{[i+1]}(k_{i+1}) + g_2 x^{[i+1]}(k_{i+1}+1) \tag{66}$$

where g_1 and g_2 are the Haar high-pass filter coefficients. The reconstruction of the states is carried out by combining (65) and (66) in a matrix equation form as given below.

$$\begin{bmatrix} x^{[i+1]}(k_{i+1}) \\ x^{[i+1]}(k_{i+1}+1) \end{bmatrix} = \boldsymbol{h}^{*T} \boldsymbol{x}^{[i]}(k_i) + \boldsymbol{g}^{*T} \boldsymbol{y}^{[i]}(k_i) \tag{67}$$

where h^* and g^* are mirror filters of h and g counterparts; wavelet decomposition and reconstruction is carried out according to the scheme shown in figures 6 and 7.

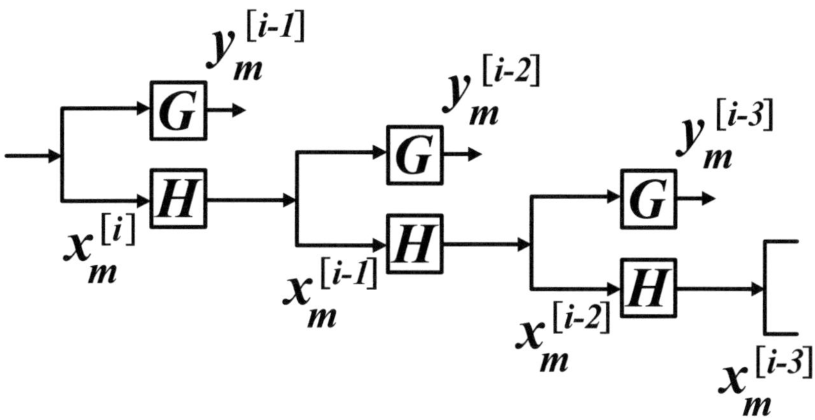

Fig. 6. Wavelet decomposition of state variables in a data block

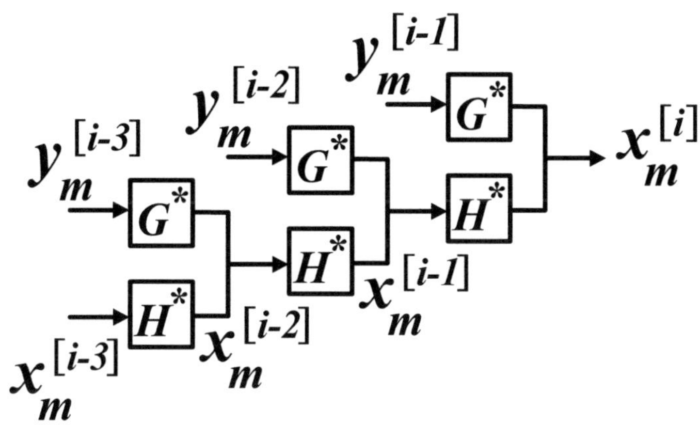

Fig. 7. Wavelet reconstruction of state variables in a data block

The wavelet matrix operator G and the scaling matrix operator H in the decomposition and their counterparts G^* and H^* in the reconstruction contain two-tap Haar filters and they related by

$$G^* = G^T \qquad H^* = H^T \tag{68}$$

The operators G and H are called Quadrature Mirror Filters (QMF) for wavelet decomposition and G^* and H^* QMF for reconstruction. A QMF has the following properties.

$$\begin{aligned} &H^*H + G^*G = 1 \\ &\begin{bmatrix} H^*H & HG^* \\ GH^* & GG^* \end{bmatrix} = \begin{bmatrix} I & 0 \\ 0 & I \end{bmatrix} \end{aligned} \tag{69}$$

where I is the identity matrix and (68) implies that filter impulse responses form an orthonormal set. It is to note that the state variable estimations are carried out at the respective resolution levels, as follows.

$$H^{i+1\to i} = diag\{(1/\sqrt{2})h_h^{(1)},(1/\sqrt{2})h_h^{(2)},....,(1/\sqrt{2})h_h^{(K)}\} \quad (70)$$

where $h_h^{[i]}$ is scaled two-tap Haar lowpass filters on the diagonal; K is the number of filters involved in a decomposition from the resolution level $i+1$ to i. For instance from 2 to 1, then i=1, and K is given by

$$K = 2^{[i-1]} = 1 \quad (71)$$

as this is seen in figure 5 where $2^{[i-1]}$ pairs of state variables in X_m^{i+1} are transformed to $2^{[i-1]}$ lower resolution variables in X_m^i . For the p number of components in a state variable as seen in (64), the H the scaling matrix operator is composed of p number of $H^{i+1\to i}$ matrices at the diagonal as

$$H = diag\{H_{[1]}^{i+1\to i}, H_{[2]}^{i+1\to i},......., H_{[p]}^{i+1\to i}\} \quad (72)$$

where each $H_{[i]}^{i+1\to 1}$ is given by (70). Similarly, for the reconstruction filter, we write

$$G^{i+1\to i} = diag\{(\sqrt{2})g_h^{(1)},(\sqrt{2})g_h^{(2)},....,(\sqrt{2})g_h^{(K)}\} \quad (73)$$

The wavelet matrix operator for G for the wavelet coefficients at resolution level i from the resolution level $i+1$

$$G = diag\{G_{[1]}^{i+1\to i}, G_{[2]}^{i+1\to i},......., G_{[p]}^{i+1\to i}\} \quad (74)$$

where K is given by (71). For the inverse transform scheme given by figure 7, we write

$$H^* = diag\{H_{[1]}^{i\to i+1}, H_{[2]}^{i\to i+1},......., H_{[p]}^{i\to i+1}\} \quad (75)$$

and

$$G^* = diag\{G_{[1]}^{i\to i+1}, G_{[2]}^{i\to i+1},......., G_{[p]}^{i\to i+1}\} \quad (76)$$

Where each $H_{[i]}^{i\to i+1}$ and $G_{[i]}^{i\to i+1}$is given by

$$H^{i\to i+1} = diag\{(\sqrt{2})h_h^{T(1)},(\sqrt{2})h_h^{T(2)},....,(\sqrt{2})h_h^{T(K)}\} \quad (77)$$

$$G^{i\to i+1} = diag\{(1/\sqrt{2})g_h^{T(1)},(1/\sqrt{2})g_h^{T(2)},....,(1/\sqrt{2})g_h^{T(K)}\} \quad (78)$$

Above T indicates transpose.

3.2 Multiresolution by sensory measurements

In subsection A wavelet decomposition is presented where N-level wavelet decomposition scheme lower level measurements are obtained basically by means of wavelet decomposition. This implies that for a state variable all measurements are obtained by a single sensor associated with that state variable. However in the present case we consider multiple sensors for the same state variable while the sensors are operated in different resolutions. Referring to figure 4, 3 sensors of different resolutions are considered. Since sensors are operated independently the measurements are non-uniform, in general. This means measurements in the lower resolution are not necessarily at the mid of the two points of the measurement times at the higher resolutional level. This is depicted in figure 8. Uniform sampling is seen in figure 4.

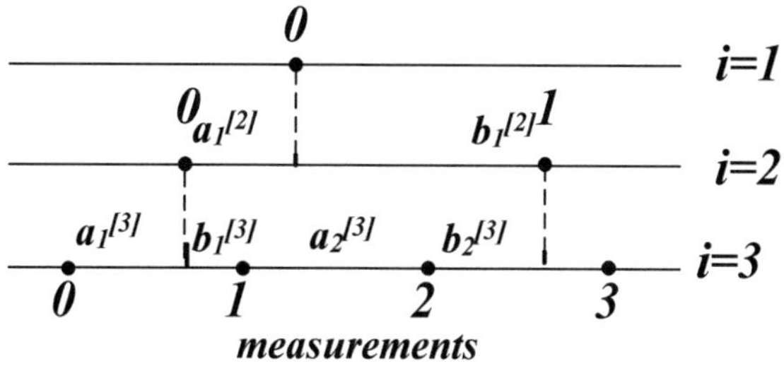

Fig. 8. Non-uniform sampling in a data block of three resolutions

Before explaining the fusion process, the wavelet decomposition for the non-uniform case will be explained in detail since this is central to this study. Decomposing the state variables at time indices *0* and *1* at resolution level *i*=*3* into a single state variable at time index *0* at resolution level *i*=*2* can be achieved by lowpass filter $h^{[2]}(1)$ as follows.

$$h^{[2]}(1) = \begin{bmatrix} \dfrac{b_1^{[3]}}{a_1^{[3]} + b_1^{[3]}} & \dfrac{a_1^{[3]}}{a_1^{[3]} + b_1^{[3]}} \end{bmatrix} \tag{79}$$

which can be written in general form

$$h^{[i]}(1) = \begin{bmatrix} \dfrac{b_{k_i}^{[i+1]}}{a_{k_i}^{[i+1]} + b_{k_i}^{[i+1]}} & \dfrac{a_1^{[i+1]}}{a_{k_i}^{[i+1]} + b_{k_i}^{[i+1]}} \end{bmatrix} \tag{80}$$

where index *i* denotes the resolution level; k_i is the time index at the resolution level *i*; $a_{ki}^{[i+1]}$ and $b_{ki}^{[i+1]}$ are the relative time intervals. The lowpass filter $h^{[i]}(k_i)$ for deriving a coarsened estimate state variable at time index k_i and at resolution level *i* is based on the appropriate pair of estimated state variables at resolution level *i+1*. As the lowpass filter is determined, the highpass filter and the inverse filters can be determined by the filterbank implementation of the Quadrature Mirror Filter (QMF) shown in figures 6 and 7. Hence from lowpass filter $h^{[i]}(k_i)$ the highpass filter $g^{[i]}k(i)$ and the inverse filters $h_{inv}^{[i]}(k_i)$ and $g_{inv}^{[i]}(k_i)$ are determined as given below that they satisfy the constraints given by (69).

$$g^{[i]}(k_i) = \begin{bmatrix} \dfrac{2b_{k_i}^{[i+1]}}{a_{k_i}^{[i+1]} + b_{k_i}^{[i+1]}} & \dfrac{-2a_1^{[i+1]}}{a_{k_i}^{[i+1]} + b_{k_i}^{[i+1]}} \end{bmatrix} \tag{81}$$

$$h_{inv}^{[i]}(k_i) = \begin{bmatrix} \dfrac{0.5(a_{k_i}{}^{[i+1]} + b_{k_i}^{[i+1]})}{b_{k_i}^{[i+1]}} & \dfrac{0.5(a_{k_i}{}^{[i+1]} + b_{k_i}^{[i+1]})}{a_{k_i}^{[i+1]}} \end{bmatrix} \tag{82}$$

and

$$g_{inv}^{[i]}(k_i) = \left[\frac{0.5(a_{k_i}^{[i+1]} + b_{k_i}^{[i+1]})}{2b_{k_i}^{[i+1]}} \quad \frac{-0.5(a_{k_i}^{[i+1]} + b_{k_i}^{[i+1]})}{2a_{k_i}^{[i+1]}} \right] \tag{83}$$

For $a_{ki}^{[i+1]}=b_{ki}^{[i+1]}$, the filters reduce to Haar filters given (61) and (62) and shown in figures 6 and 7.

In this implementation the scaling and wavelet operators H and G for decomposition i+1→i are given by

$$\begin{aligned} H^{i+1\to i} &= diag\left\{h^{[i]}(k_i), h^{[i]}(k_i+1), \ldots, h^{[i]}(k_i+2^{i-1}-1)\right\} \\ G^{i+1\to i} &= diag\left\{g^{[i]}(k_i), g^{[i]}(k_i+1), \ldots, g^{[i]}(k_i+2^{i-1}-1)\right\} \end{aligned} \tag{84}$$

For $a_{ki}^{[i+1]}= b_{ki}^{[i+1]}$ (84) reduces to (70) and (73).

The inverse scaling and wavelet operators H and G for construction i→i+1 are given by

$$\begin{aligned} H^{i\to i+1} &= diag\left\{h_{inv}^{[i]}(k_i)^T, h_{inv}^{[i]}(k_i+1)^T, \ldots, h_{inv}^{[i]}(k_i+2^{i-1}-1)^T\right\} \\ G^{i\to i+1} &= diag\left\{g_{inv}^{[i]}(k_i)^T, g_{inv}^{[i]}(k_i+1)^T, \ldots, g_{inv}^{[i]}(k_i+2^{i-1}-1)^T\right\} \end{aligned} \tag{85}$$

For $a_{ki}^{[i+1]}= b_{ki}^{[i+1]}$ (84) and (85) reduces to (77) and (78).

4. Fusion process as multiresolutinal dynamic filtering (MDF)

The fusion of information is central to this research. Therefore, in the preceding section wavelet decomposition and reconstruction is presented in vector form for the sake of explaining the fusion process in detail. However the wavelet decomposition in this work is not used. This is simply because lower resolution level sensory measurements are obtained from associated sensors and not from wavelet decomposition of the highest resolution level sensory measurements. Therefore only the wavelet reconstruction is relevant. The lower resolution level measurements are used to update the estimated information at this very level. Afterwards, this information is transformed to higher resolution level information by inverse wavelet transform where the inverse transformation wavelet coefficients, that is the detail coefficients, are not involved in this process as they are all zero. Because of this reason the transformed information at a higher resolution level is the same as the information lying in the preceding lower level. But this very information at the higher resolution level timely coincides with the sensory information of this level. This is achieved by non-uniform formulation of wavelet transform. By doing so, the independent operation of multiresolutional sensors is aimed to make the information fusion effective. The actual implementation in this work is explicitly as follows. Referring to figure 8, a data block has four sensory measurement samples at the highest resolution *(i=3)* and one sensory sample in the lowest resolution *(i=1)*. The resolution level between the highest and lowest contains two sensory measurements. By means of inverse wavelet transform the updated estimations at levels *i=1* and *i=2* are transformed to highest level separately providing the estimate of the signal of the resolution index *i=1* and *i=2* and the highest level *(i=3)*. In the level one, a single estimation, in the level two, two updated estimations are projected to highest level. In the level three the estimations are updated for four samples. At all levels the estimations are updated by Kalman filtering for *i=1,2,* and *3*. Signals from different resolutional levels are projected to the highest resolution level so that they all have four samples in a data block. The basic update scheme for dynamic multiresolutional filtering is shown in Fig. 9 where at each resolutional level, when the measurement Z is available, the state variables are updated and when the block *m* is complete the inverse wavelet transform and fusion is performed. During the inverse transformation the wavelet coefficients are all zero due to non-performed wavelet decomposition.

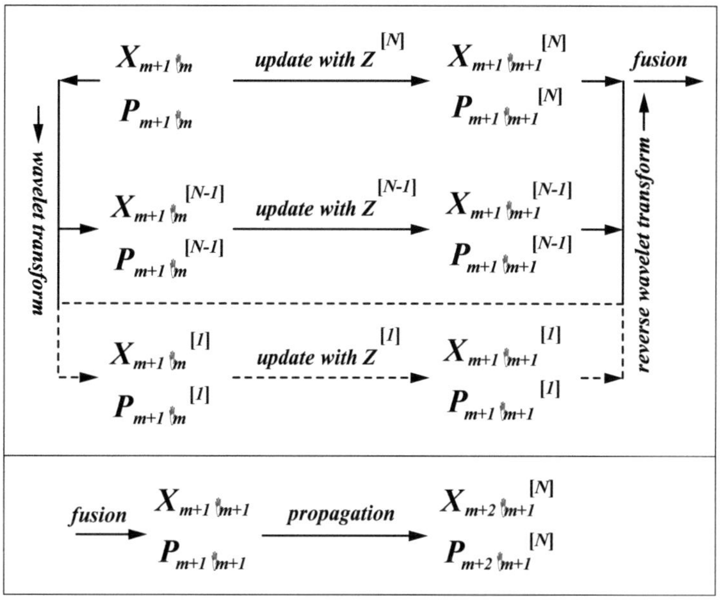

Fig. 9. Wavelet decomposition of state variables in a data block *m*

Explicitly, the basic update scheme is as follows.

$$X_{m+1|m+1}{}^{[i]} = X_{m+1|m}{}^{[i]} + K_{m+1}{}^{[i]}(Z_{m+1}{}^{[i]} - C_{m+1}{}^{[i]}X_{m+1|m}{}^{[i]}) \tag{86}$$

and

$$P_{XX_{m+1|m+1}}{}^{[i]} = (I - K_{m+1}{}^{[i]}C_{m+1}{}^{[i]})P_{XX_{m+1|m}}{}^{[i]} \tag{87}$$

The minimum variance Kalman gain matrix $K_{m+1}{}^{[i]}$ at each level, is determined by

$$K_{m+1}{}^{[i]} = P_{XX_{m+1|m}}{}^{[i]}C_{m+1}{}^{[i]T}\left(C_{m+1}{}^{[i]}P_{XX_{m+1|m}}{}^{[i]}C_{m+1}{}^{[i]T} + R_{m+1}{}^{[i]}\right)^{-1} \tag{88}$$

where the measurent matrix $C_{m=1}{}^{[i]}$ and $R_{m+1}{}^{[i]}$ are given by

$$C_{m+1}^{[i]} = diag\begin{bmatrix} C^{[i]}[(m+1)2^{i-1}], C^{[i]}[(m+1)2^{i-1} - 2^{i-1} + 1], \dots, \\ \dots\dots \qquad , C^{[i]}[(m+1) + 2^{i-1} + 1] \end{bmatrix} \tag{89}$$

$$R_{m+1}^{[i]} = diag\begin{bmatrix} R^{[i]}[(m+1)2^{i-1}], R^{[i]}[(m+1)2^{i-1} - 2^{i-1} + 1], ..., \\ ..... \qquad\qquad ,R^{[i]}[(m+1) + 2^{i-1} + 1] \end{bmatrix} \tag{90}$$

Once, the sequences of updated state variables and error covariances $X_{m+1|m+1}{}^{[N,i]}$ and $P_{m+1|m+1}{}^{[N,i]}$ for *i=1,2,..,N,* are determined, they must be fused to generate an optimal $X_{m+1|m+1}{}^{[NF]}$ and $P_{m+1|m+1}{}^{[NF]}$. For the minimum fusion error covariance $P_{m+1|m+1}{}^{[NF]}$ as derived in (Hong 1991; Hong 1992), the fused estimate $X_{m+1|m+1}{}^{[NF]}$ is calculated as

$$X_{m+1|m+1}{}^{[NF]} = P_{m+1|m+1}{}^{[NF]}\left[\sum_{i=1}^{N}\left(P_{m+1|m+1}{}^{[N,i]}\right)^{-1} X_{m+1|m+1}{}^{[N,i]} - (N-1)\left(P_{m+1|m}{}^{[N]}\right)^{-1} X_{m+1|m}{}^{[N]}\right] \tag{91}$$

where the minimum fusion error covariance $P_{m+1|m+1}{}^{[NF]}$ is given by

$$\left(P_{m+1|m+1}{}^{[NF]}\right)^{-1} = \sum_{i=1}^{N}\left(P_{m+1|m+1}{}^{[N,i]}\right)^{-1} - (N-1)\left(P_{m+1|m}{}^{[N]}\right)^{-1}. \tag{92}$$

The fused estimate $X_{m+1|m+1}{}^{[NF]}$ is a weighted summation of both predicted $X_{m+1|m}{}^{[N]}$ and updated $X_{m+1|m+1}{}^{[N,i]}$, for *i=1,2,..,N*. The sum of the weight factors equal to the identity *I*. This can be seen by substitution of $P_{m+1|m+1}{}^{[NF]}$ given above into the expression of $X_{m+1|m+1}{}^{[NF]}$ in (91). With the estimations in different level of resolutions and finally fusion of the level-wise estimations for unified estimations form a multiresolutional distributed filtering (MDR).

5. Experiments with the autonomous robot

The computer experiments have been carried out with the simulated robot navigation. The state variables vector is given by (93) where *N=i* to represent a general resolutional level.

$$x^{[N]}{}_k(N) = \begin{bmatrix} x_{k,1}^{[N]} \\ x_{k,2}^{[N]} \\ .... \\ x_{k,p}^{[N]} \end{bmatrix} \tag{93}$$

Explicitly,

$$x^{[N]}k(N) = [x, \dot{x}, y, \dot{y}, \omega]$$

where ω is the angular rate and it is estimated during the move. When the robot moves in a straight line, the angular rate becomes zero and the other state variables namely, x and y coordinates and the respective velocities remain subject to estimation. The overall robot trajectory is shown in figure 10 where there are four lines plotted but they are all close to each other due to the scale involved. Broadly one can see approximately a linear trajectory followed by a curve trajectory and approximately another linear trajectory afterwards. The line marked by * sign represents the measurement of the data at the highest resolution level for *i=3*. The line marked by • is the estimation by sensor fusion. The line marked by + sign is the estimation by extended Kalman filtering for the data obtained from the sensor of the highest resolution level *(i=3)*. The line indicated by **o** sign is the reference trajectory. These lines are not explicitly seen in this figure. For explicit illustration of the experimental outcomes the same figure with different zooming ranges and the zooming powers are given in figures 11-18.

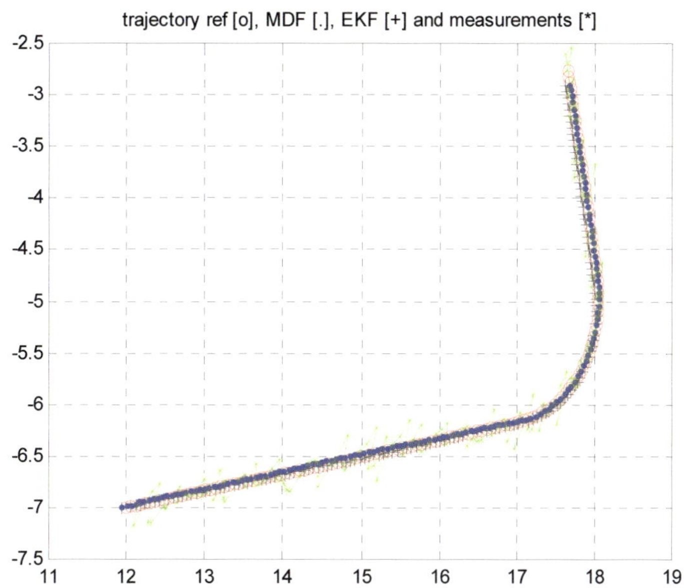

Fig. 10. The overall *measurement, reference, extended Kalman filtering(EKF)* and *multiresolutional distributed filtering* (*MDF)* estimation of robot trajectory. The * sign is for measurement; + for EKF; **o** for reference; • for *MDF* estimated trajectory.

Figure 11 and 12 shows the estimations in a linear mode. Figure 12 is the enlarged form of figure 11. From these figures it is seen that, the Kalman filtering is effective at the first linear part of the trajectory; namely relative to Kalman filtering estimation, the estimation by sensor fusion by MDF is inferior. In this mode the angular velocity is zero, the system matrix is linear and the linear Kalman filter is accurate enough to describe the dynamic system. During this period, the Kalman filter estimations are carried in smallest sampling time intervals. At the same period MDF estimations made in lower resolution levels are extended to the highest resolution level. However during this extension the x and y coordinates do not match exactly the estimates in the highest resolutional level because of time difference between the estimations. Explicitly, in figure 8 the estimation in the level *i=0* is extended to estimation number 3 in the resolutional level *i=3* where there is time difference of more than one sampling time interval. The result is higher estimation error in the MDF and this error appears to be as systematic error in estimation in the form of hangoff error, i.e., error does

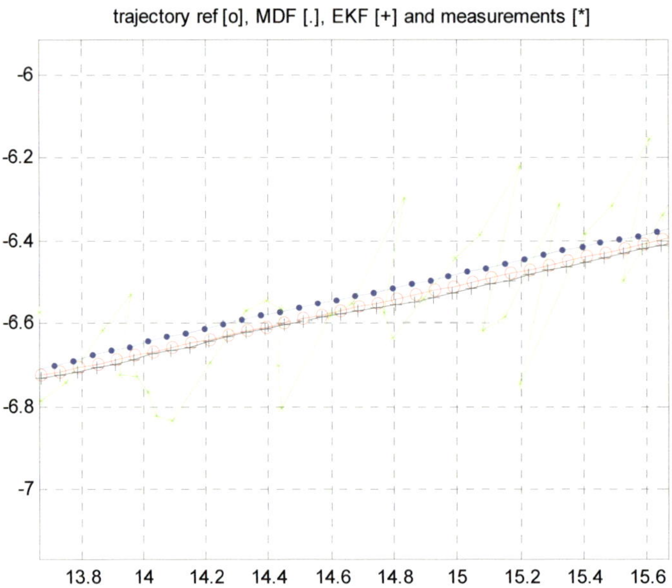

Fig. 11. Enlarged *measurement, reference, extended Kalman filtering(EKF)* and *multiresolutional distributed filtering (MDF)* estimation of robot trajectory in first linear period. The * sign is for measurement; + for EKF; **o** for reference; • for *MDF* estimated trajectory.

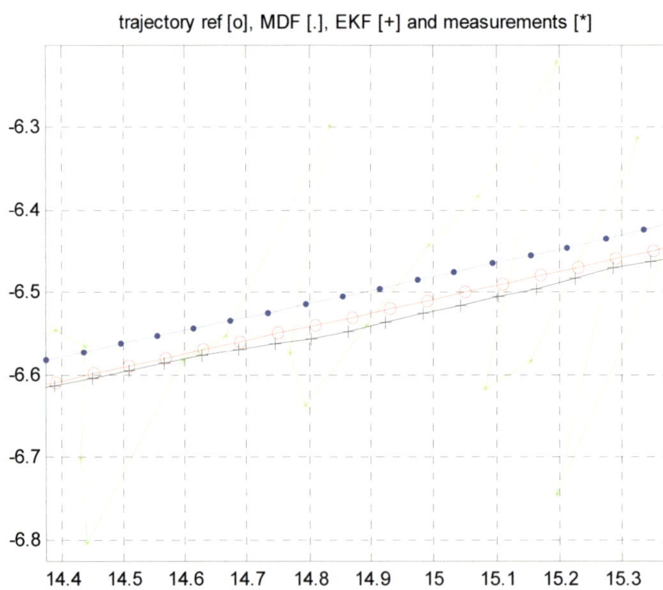

Fig. 12. Enlarged *measurement, reference, extended Kalman filtering(EKF)* and *multiresolutional distributed filtering (MDF)* estimation of robot trajectory in first linear period. The * sign is for measurement; + for EKF; **o** for reference; • for *MDF* estimated trajectory.

not go to zero. In a sensor fusion process such sensor delays are inevitable and thus delay-related effects are inevitable. This research clearly illustrates the extent of such effects which are to be categorized eventually as errors. Consequently one can conclude that the fusion of sensors from different resolutional levels has an inherent peculiarity of latency that turns out to be undesirable outcome in some cases, as it is the case in the present situation, although this is not general as the following figures (13-18) indicate.
Figure 13 and 14 shows the estimations in a bending mode. Figure 14 is the enlarged form of figure 13. In this case estimations by sensor fusion are superior to the estimations by extended Kalman filtering. This can be explained seeing that system matrix involves the angular velocity which makes the system dynamics matrix non-linear. This results in marked separation between the reference trajectory and the estimated trajectory due to the approximation error caused by the Taylor's series expansion and ensuing linearization in the extended Kalman filtering (EKF) in the highest resolution level. One should note that the effect of this approximation error propagated four times in a data block to the time point where fusion and predictions are made for the following data block as seen in figure 4. In this nonlinear period, sensor fusion is very effective and the difference between the estimated outcomes and the reference trajectory is apparently negligibly small. However, this is not exactly so. Because of the delay of the data from the lower resolutional levels to the highest resolutional level as described in the preceding paragraph, there is some difference between the true position and the estimated position. Nevertheless, the true trajectory is almost perfectly identified. The reason for the effectiveness in the lower resolution levels is due to more effective linearization and therefore better state estimations. Although in the lower resolutions levels error in the linearization process for EKF is greater relative to that occurred in the higher resolutional level, such modeling errors are accounted

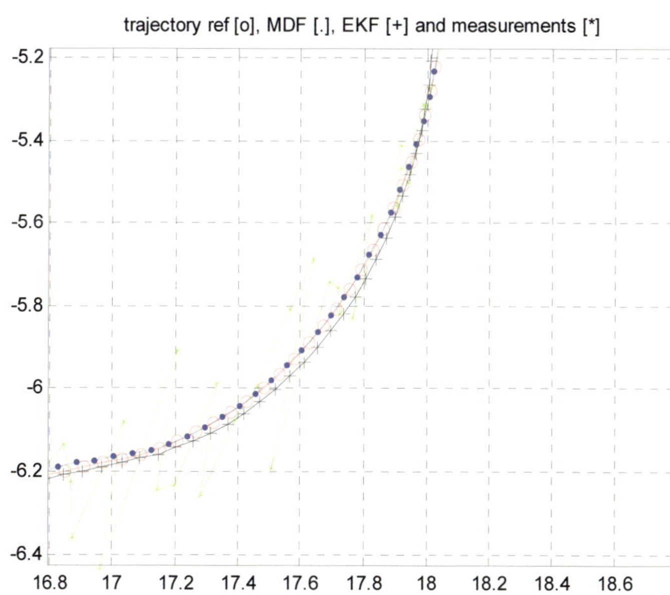

Fig. 13. Enlarged *measurement*, *reference*, *extended Kalman filtering(EKF)* and *multiresolutional distributed filtering* (*MDF*) estimation of robot trajectory in the bending period. The * sign is for measurement; + for EKF; **o** for reference; • for *MDF* estimated trajectory.

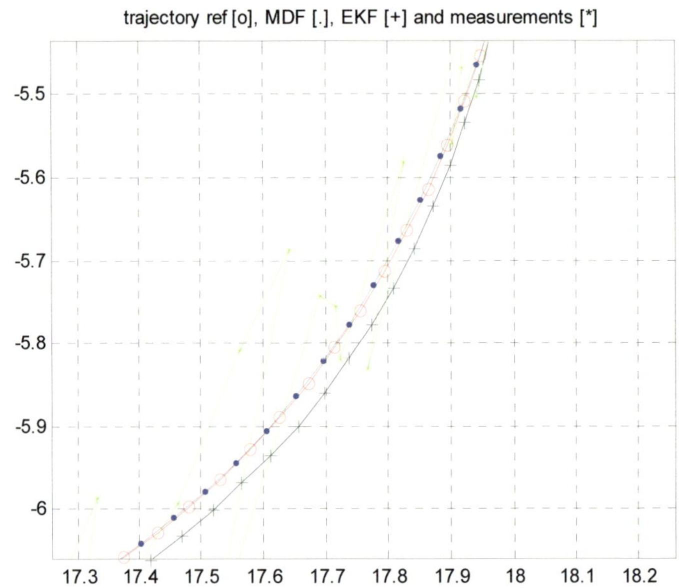

Fig. 14. Enlarged *measurement*, *reference*, *extended Kalman filtering(EKF)* and *multiresolutional distributed filtering* (*MDF)* estimation of robot trajectory in the bending period. The * sign is for measurement; + for EKF; **o** for reference; • for *MDF* estimated trajectory.

for in the process noise and therefore effect of errors due to linearization becomes less important. However, it should be pointed out that, in all resolutional levels, the sensor quality plays essential role on the estimation errors.

Figure 15 shows the trajectory where EKF estimation crosses the reference trajectory. This can be explained as follows. EKF estimations in the highest resolutional level without multiresolutional information, start to deviate from the reference trajectory in the bending mode as seen in figures 13 and 14. In this case Kalman filter tend to make estimations to compensate this deviation error and therefore the deviation start to become smaller. At the same time the bending information namely the angular frequency (ω) becomes effective and these two corrective joint actions in this turbulent transition period make the estimation error minimal and finally the estimated trajectory cross the reference trajectory. It is to note that in this resolutional level the Kalman filter bandwidth is relatively wide justifying the sampling rate which is the highest. As seen in (31), the system matrix is highly involved with the angular frequency and even small estimation error on ω might cause relatively high effects in this non-linear environment. After crossing, the deviations start to increase and after the bending is over it remains constant in the second linear mode in the trajectory, as seen in figures 16 and 17. On the other hand, during this period, the multiresolutional distributed filtering (MDF) estimations improve due to due to incoming bending information, the deviations become smaller and finally it crosses the reference trajectory. This crossing is shown in figure 16. The estimations at the lower resolution level are much accurate than those at the highest resolution level and by means of the sensor fusion process, the fused estimations are quite accurate at the bending mode and afterwards. This is seen in figures 13 through18. Also the effect of the information latency on the position estimation is clearly observed in these figures.

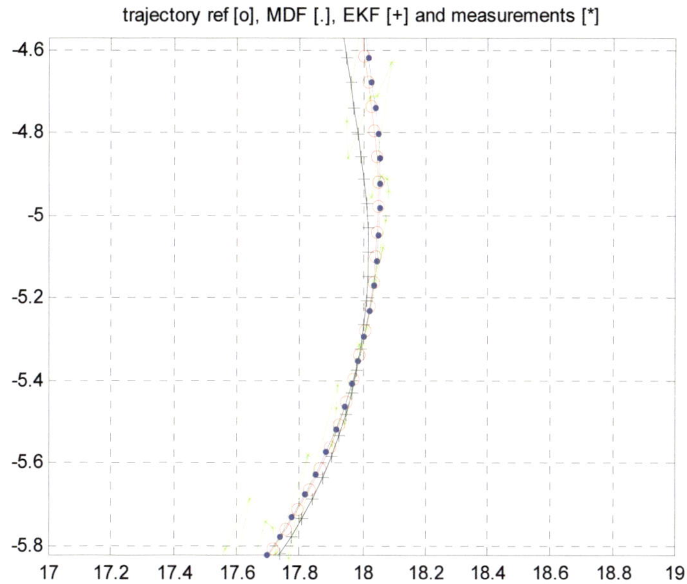

Fig. 15. Enlarged *measurement, reference, extended Kalman filtering(EKF)* and *multiresolutional distributed filtering* (*MDF*) estimation of robot trajectory in the bending period. The * sign is for measurement; + for EKF; **o** for reference; • for *MDF* estimated trajectory.

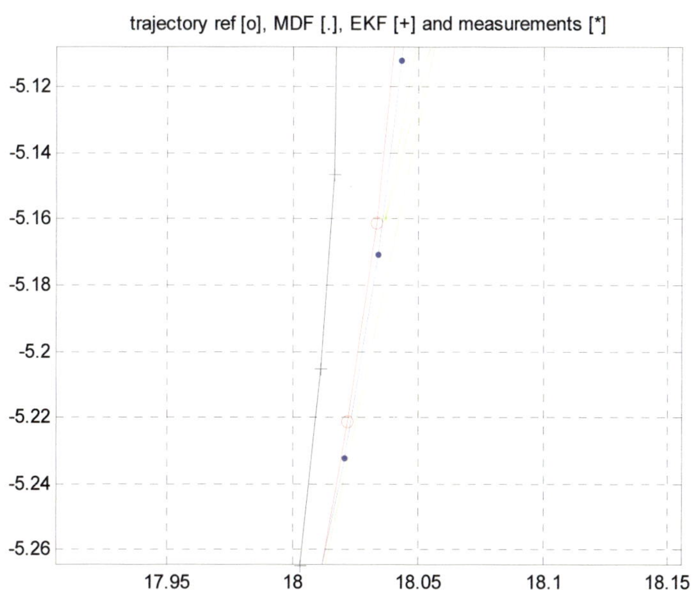

Fig. 16. Enlarged *measurement, reference, extended Kalman filtering(EKF)* and *multiresolutional distributed filtering* (*MDF*) estimation of robot trajectory in the transition between bending and second linear periods. The * sign is for measurement; + for EKF; **o** for reference; • for *MDF* estimated trajectory.

Figure 17 and 18 shows the estimations in the second linear trajectory. They are the enlarged form of figure 10 at this very period. Next to satisfactory MDF estimations, the figures show the

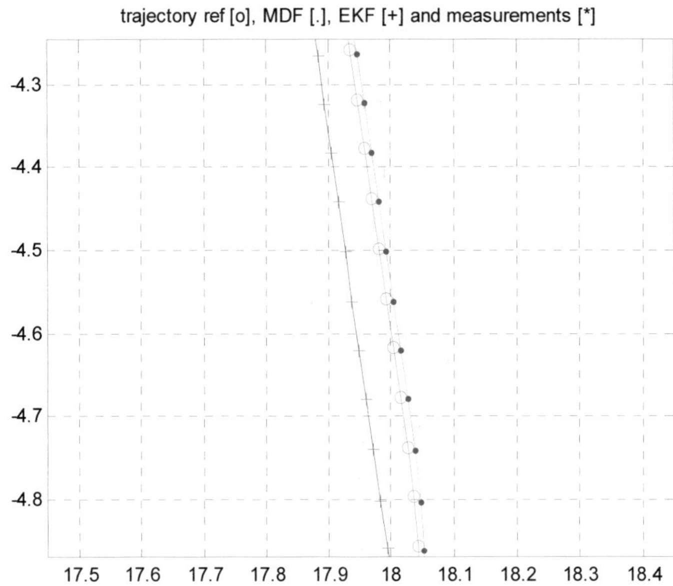

Fig. 17. Enlarged *measurement, reference, extended Kalman filtering(EKF)* and *multiresolutional distributed filtering (MDF)* estimation of robot trajectory in the second linear period. The * sign is for measurement; + for EKF; **o** for reference; • for *MDF* estimated trajectory.

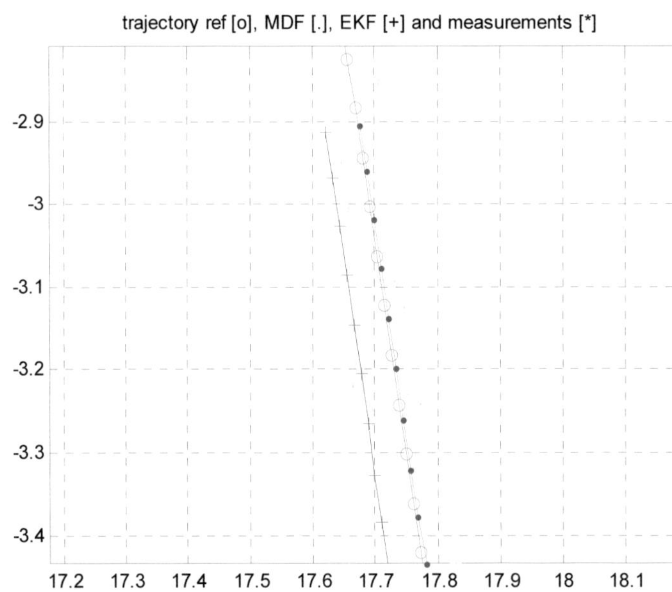

Fig. 18. Enlarged *measurement, reference, extended Kalman filtering(EKF)* and *multiresolutional distributed filtering (MDF)* estimation of robot trajectory in the second linear period. The * sign is for measurement; + for EKF; **o** for reference; • for *MDF* estimated trajectory.

estimations of the Extended Kalman filtering in the highest resolutional level. These estimations have relatively large errors which are due to the system dynamics matrix given by (31) where ω is expected to be zero in this linear period; however it is approximately zero ($\omega \approx 0$) as calculated by Kalman filtering. The small nonzero terms in the matrix cause error in estimations which are interpreted as model errors in the Kalman filtering operation. Further such errors also cause round off errors in the covariance matrix in (43) and finally poor estimation. When the same operation is repeated by switching the matrix forcefully from bending mode to linear mode by putting $\omega=0$ in (31), the Kalman filtering estimation in the last linear period becomes comparable as illustrated in figure 11 and 12. Since the highest resolution level estimations have large errors, they have small contributions to the sensor-data fusion process and therefore the fusion results remain accurate. Figures 13 through 18 represent a firm indication of the effectiveness and robustness of the sensor fusion, in this research.

6. Discussion

In this work the effectiveness of multisensor-based multiresolutional fusion is investigated by means of estimation errors of mobile robot position determination. The comparison is made offline but not real-time. By doing so, a clear view presented about at what conditions the multiresolutional multi-sensor fusion process is effective and also in which circumstances the fusion process may have shortcomings and why. However, the implementation can be carried on in real-time in the form of one block ahead prediction forming the data-sensor fusion, and one step-ahead prediction at the highest resolutional level i.e., for $i=3$ without fusion process. These are illustrated in figure 4. In both cases, i.e., real-time and off-line operations, the merits of the multiresolutional multisensor fusion remains robust although some unfavorable deviation from the existing results in real-time may occur due to a block prediction compared to 1-step-ahead prediction, obviously. Investigations on real-time operation for the assessment of the robustness are interesting since the mobile robot is especially meant for this type of operation.

7. Conclusions

Autonomous mobile robot navigation is a challenging issue where robot should be provided with accurate and reliable position information. Although reliable information can be provided by adding redundant sensors, the enhanced accuracy and precision information can be provided by synergistically coordinating the information from these sensors. In this respect, the present research introduced a novel information fusion concept by inverse wavelet transform using independent multiresolutional sensors. In the linear system description, the highest resolutional sensor provides enough information for optimum information processing by Kalman filtering where residual variance is minimum so that the information delivered by multiresolutional sensors can be redundant depending on the sensors's qualities and associated noises. In situations where system dynamics is non-linear, Kalman filter is still optimal in its extended formulation. However, the estimation errors in this case are dependent on the degree of the non-linearity of the system dynamics. The multiresolutional sensor fusion becomes quite effective in the non-linear case since the partial nonlinearity information of the system in different resolutional scales is available. Sensor quality is always an important factor playing role on the estimation. These features are demonstrated and the fusion process presented can easily be extended to consider real-time operation as well as some cases of probabilistic nature such as missing measurements, sensor failures and other probabilistic occurrences.

8. References

Abidi, M. A. and R. C. Gonzales (1992). Multi-sensor Image Fusion. *Data Fusion in Robotics and Machine Intelligence*. R. S. Blum and Z. Liu, Academic Press.

Beetz, M., T. Arbuckle, et al. (2001). Integrated, Plan-based Control of Autonomous Robots in Human Environments. *IEEE Intelligent Systems* 16(5): 56-65.

Bellotto, N. and H. Hu (2009). Multisensor-based Human Detection and Tracking for Mobile Service Robots. *IEEE Trans. System, Man, and Cybernetics-B* 39(1): 167-181.

Brown, R. G. (1983). *Introduction to Random Signal Analysis and Kalman Filtering*. New York, John Wiley & Sons.

Ciftcioglu, Ö. (2008). Multiresolutional Filter Application for Spatial Information Fusion in Robot Navigation. In: *Advances in Robotics, Automation and Control*, 355-372, J. Aramburo and A. R. Trevino (Eds.), ISBN 78-953-7619-16-9, I-Tech Publishing, Vienna, Austria.

Ciftcioglu, Ö. (2008). Shaping the Perceptual Robot Vision and Multiresolutional Kalman Filtering Implementation. *Int. Journal Factory Automation, Robotics and Soft Computing(3)*: 62-75, ISSN 1828-6984, International Spociety for Advanced Research, *www.internationalsar.org*.

Ciftcioglu, Ö., M. S. Bittermann, et al. (2007). Visual Perception Theory Underlying Perceptual Navigation. *Emerging Technologies, Robotics and Control Systems* International Society for Advanced Research: 139-153.

Gelb, A. (1974). *Applied Optrimal Estimation*. Cambridge, MA, MIT Press.

Grewal, M. S. and A. P. Andrews (2001). *Kalman Filtering Theory and Practice Using MATLAB*. New York, Wiley.

Hong, L. (1991). Adaptive Distributed Filtering in Multi-coordinated Systems. *IEEE Trans. on Aerospace and Electronic Systems* 27(4): 10.

Hong, L. (1992). Distributed Filtering Using Set Models. *IEEE Trans. on Aerospace and Electronic Systems* 28(4): 10.

Hong, L. (1993). Multiresolutional Filtering using Wavelet Transform. *IEEE Trans. on Aerospace and Electronic Systems* 29(4): 1244-1251.

Hsin, H. C. and A. C. Li (2006). Wavelet-based Kalman Filtering in Scale Space for Image Fusion. *Pattern Recognition and Computer Vision*. C. H. C. a. P. S. P. Wang. Singapore, World Scientific.

Jazwinski, A. H. (1970). *Stochastic Processes and Filtering Theory*. New York Academic Press.

Kailath, T. (1981). *Lectures on Wiener and Kalman Filtering*. New York, Springer Verlag.

Mallat, S. G. (1989). A theory for multiresolution signal decomposition:the wavelet representation. *IEEE Trans. on Pattern Analysis and Machine Intelligence*. 11(7): 674-693.

Maybeck, P. S. (1982). *Stochastic Models, Estimation and Control*, Vol II. New York, Academic Press.

McKendall, R. and M. Mintz (1992). Data Fusion Techniques using Robust Statistics. *Data Fusion in Robotics and Machine Intelligence* Academic Press: 211-244.

Mendel, J. M. (1987). *Kalman Filtering and Digital Estimation Techniques*. New York, IEEE.

Oriolio, G., G. Ulivi, et al. (1998). Real-time Map Building and Navigation for autonomous robots in unknown environments. *IEEE Trans. on Systems, Man and Cybernetics - Part B*: Cybernetics 28(3): 316-333.

Richardson, J. M. and K. A. Marsh (1988). Fusion of Multi-Sensor Data. *Int. J. Robotics Research* 7(6): 78-96.

Simon, D. (2006). Optimal State Estimation. New Jersey, Wiley Interscience.

Sorenson, H. W. (1985). *Kalman Filtering: Theory and Application*. New York, IEEE Press.

Wang, M. and J. N. K. Liu (2004). Online Path Searching for Autonomous Robot Navigation. *IEEE Conf. on Robotics, Automation and Mechatronics*, 1-3 December, Singapore: 746-751, vol.2, ISBN 0-7803-8645-0

20

Optimization of H4 Parallel Manipulator Using Genetic Algorithm

M. Falahian, H.M. Daniali* and S.M. Varedi
Babol University of Technology
Iran

1. Introduction

Parallel manipulators have the advantages of high stiffness and low inertia compared to serial ones (Merlet, 2006). Most pick-and-place operations, including picking, packing and palletizing tasks; require four-degree-of-freedom (DOF), i.e. three translations and one rotation around a vertical axis (Company et al, 2003). A new family of 4-DOF parallel manipulator being called H4 that could be useful for high-speed, pick-and-place applications is proposed by Pierrot and Company (Pierrot & Company, 1999). This manipulator offers 3-DOF in translation and 1-DOF in rotation about a given axis. The H4 manipulator is useful for high-speed handling in robotics and milling in machine tool industry since it is a fully-parallel mechanism with no passive chain which can provide high performance in terms of speed and acceleration (Wu et al, 2006). Its prototype, built in the Robotics Department of LIRMM, can reach 10g accelerations and velocities higher than 5 m/s (Robotics Department of LIRMM). Pierrot et al. proved the efficiency of H4 serving as a high-speed pick-and-place robot (Pierrot et al, 2006). Corradini et al. evaluated the 4-DOFs parallel manipulator stiffness by two methods and compared the results (Coradini & Fauroux, 2003). Renaud et al. presented the kinematic calibration of a H4 robot using a vision-based measuring device (Renaud et al, 2003). Tantawiroon et al. designed and analyzed a new family of H4 parallel robots (Tantawiroon & Sangveraphunsiri, 2003). Poignet et al. estimated dynamic parameters of H4 with interval analysis (Poignet et al, 2003).

Parallel manipulators suffer from smaller workspaces relative to their serial counterparts; therefore, many researchers addressed the optimization of their workspaces (Boudreau & Gosselin, 1999; Laribi et al, 2007). But optimization for such a purpose might lead to a manipulator with poor dexterity. To alleviate this drawback some others considered both performance indices and volume of workspace, simultaneously (Li & Xu, 2006; Xu & Li, 2006; Lara et al, 2010).

This chapter deals with an optimal design of H4 parallel manipulator aimed at milling and Rapid-Prototyping applications with three degrees of freedom in translation and one in rotation. The forward and inverse kinematics of the manipulator are solved. The forward kinematics analysis of H4 leads to a univariate polynomial of degree eight. The workspace of the manipulator is parameterized using several design parameters. Some geometric constraints are considered in the problem, as well. Because of nonlinear discontinuous behaviour of the

---

* Corresponding Author

problem, Genetic Algorithm (GA) Method is used here to optimize the workspace. Finally, using GA, the manipulator is optimized based on a mixed performance index that is a weighted sum of global conditioning index and its workspace. It is shown that by introducing this measure, the parallel manipulator is improved at the cost of workspace reduction.

2. Description and mobility analysis of a H4 parallel manipulator

The basic concept of H4 is described by a simple architectural scheme as illustrated in Fig. 1, where joints are represented by lines (Pierrot et al, 2001). The manipulator is based on four independent chains between the base and the End-Effector (EE); each chain is driven by an actuator which is fixed on the base. Let P, R, U and S represent prismatic, revolute, universal, and spherical joints, respectively. Each of the *P-U-U* and *R-U-U* chains must satisfy some geometrical conditions to guarantee that the manipulator offers three translations and one rotation about a given axis (see (Pierrot & Company, 1999) for details). The *U-U* and $(S\text{-}S)_2$ (or $(U\text{-}S)_2$) chains can be considered as "equivalent" in terms of number and type of degrees of motion, so the *P-U-U* (or *R-U-U*) chains can be replaced by $P\text{-}(U\text{-}S)_2$ or $P\text{-}(S\text{-}S)_2$ chains (respectively by $R\text{-}(U\text{-}S)_2$ or $R\text{-}(S\text{-}S)_2$). In this chapter, $P\text{-}(S\text{-}S)_2$ chain is chosen for the mechanism architecture of H4. Fig. 2 shows the architecture of H4 (chain #1 is not plotted for sake of simplicity) (Poignet et al, 2010).

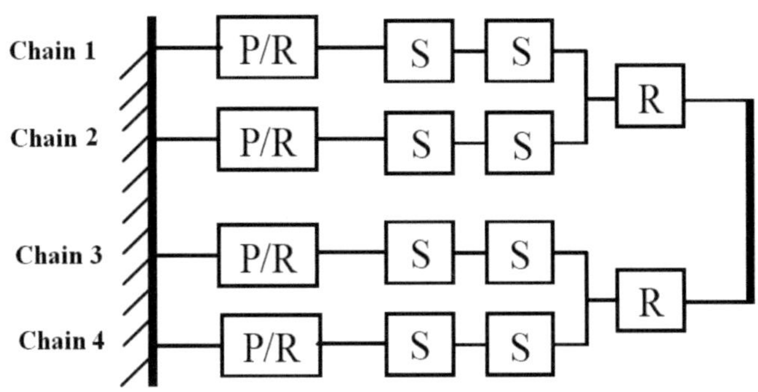

Fig. 1. Architectural scheme of H4

It is noteworthy that the four independent chains are not directly connected to the EE. It is possible to add another revolute joint on this end part and to couple it (with gears, timing belt, etc (Robotics Department of LIRMM)) so that the range of motion obtained on this latter joint can be larger than the end part ones. It is even possible to equip this passive revolute joint with a sensor to improve the robot accuracy. Moreover, the manipulator is a high-speed mechanism and can be easily controlled. So the H4 manipulator has the ability of serving as an efficient pick-and-place robot.
Considering the H4 robotic structure as given in Fig. 2, its geometrical parameters of are defined as follows:

- Two frames are defined, namely {A}: a reference frame fixed on the base; {B}: a coordinate frame fixed on the EE (C_1-C_1).
- The actuators slide along guide-ways oriented along a unitary vector, $\overrightarrow{k_z}$ ($\overrightarrow{k_z}$ is the unity vector parallel to the z axis in the reference frame {A}), and the origin is point $\mathbf{P}_i$, so the position of each point $\mathbf{A}_i$ is given by: $\vec{\mathbf{A}}_i = \vec{\mathbf{P}}_i + \mathbf{q}_i \vec{\mathbf{z}}_i$; for i=1,...4, in which $\mathbf{q}_i$ is the actuator coordinates.

- The parameters $\mathbf{M}_i$, d and h are the length of the rods, the offset of the revolute-joint from the ball-joint, and the offset of each ball-joint from the center of the traveling plate, respectively.
- The pose of the EE is defined by a position vector $\vec{\mathbf{B}} = \begin{bmatrix} x & y & z \end{bmatrix}^T$ and an angle θ, representing its orientation.

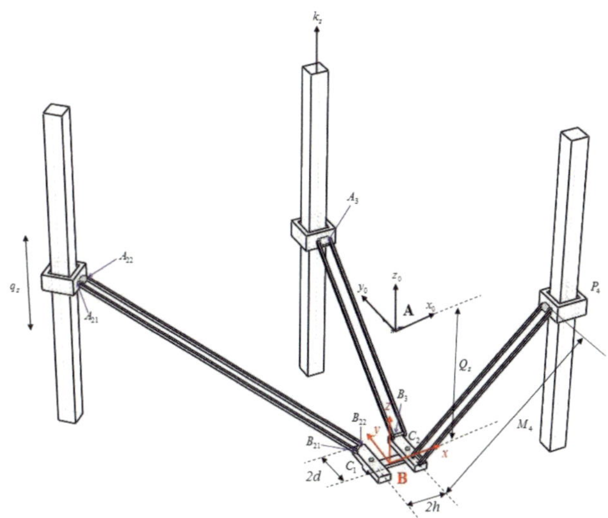

a) Robot with four lines drives and $(S-S)_2$ chains

b) Robot CAD model

Fig. 2. H4 parallel manipulator

Without losing generality, in this chapter we consider $\vec{\mathbf{P}}_i = \begin{bmatrix} a_i & b_i & 0 \end{bmatrix}^T$ for simplicity, Q_z is the offset of {B} from {A} along the direction of $\overrightarrow{k_z}$.
One can effectively analyze the mobility of a H4 parallel manipulator by resorting to screw theory, which is a convenient tool to study instantaneous motion systems that include both rotation and translation in three dimensional spaces (Zhao et al, 2004).
A screw is called a twist when it is used to describe the motion state of a rigid body and a wrench when it is used to represent the force and moment of a rigid body. If a wrench acts on a rigid body in such a way that it produces no work, while the body is undergoing an infinitesimal twist, the two screws are said to be reciprocal (Li & Xu, 2007). In a parallel

manipulator, the reciprocal screws associated with a serial limb represent the wrench constraints imposed on the moving platform by the serial limb. The motions of the moving platform are determined by the combined effect of all the wrench constraints imposed by each limb. Therefore, we can get the following equation:

$$\$_r^T \circ \$ = 0 \tag{1}$$

where $\$_r$ is the reciprocal screw and "$\circ$" represents the reciprocal production of two screws (Dai & Jones, 2007). According to the physical interpretations of reciprocal screws, one can obtain the constraints spaces that should be spanned by all of the reciprocal screws. As far as a H4 parallel manipulator is concerned, each S joint is equivalent to three intersecting non-coplanar R joints, and then the joint twists associated with the ith *P-(S-S)*$_2$*-R* (or *P-U-U-R*) chain form a 6-system, which can be identified in the fixed frame as follows:

$$\begin{aligned} &\$_1^i = \begin{bmatrix} 0 \\ \vec{s}_1^i \end{bmatrix}, \quad \$_2^i = \begin{bmatrix} {}_1\vec{s}_{A_i}^i \\ A_i \times {}_1\vec{s}_{A_i}^i \end{bmatrix}, \quad \$_3^i = \begin{bmatrix} {}_2\vec{s}_{A_i}^i \\ A_i \times {}_2\vec{s}_{A_i}^i \end{bmatrix} \\ &\$_4^i = \begin{bmatrix} {}_1\vec{s}_{B_i}^i \\ B_i \times {}_1\vec{s}_{B_i}^i \end{bmatrix}, \quad \$_5^i = \begin{bmatrix} {}_2\vec{s}_{B_i}^i \\ B_i \times {}_2\vec{s}_{B_i}^i \end{bmatrix}, \quad \$_6^i = \begin{bmatrix} \vec{s}_{C_i}^i \\ C_i \times \vec{s}_{C_i}^i \end{bmatrix} \end{aligned} \tag{2}$$

where $\vec{s}_j^i$ denotes a unit vector along the jth joint axis of the ith chain, for $i = 1,\ldots,4$. Therefore, the kinematic screws of each kinematic chain can be expressed as:

$$[\$^i]^T = \begin{bmatrix} \$_1^i & \$_2^i & \$_3^i & \$_4^i & \$_5^i & \$_6^i \end{bmatrix} \tag{3}$$

Therefore, the reciprocal screws of kinematic chains can be derived as:

$$[\$_{platform}^r]^T = \begin{bmatrix} \$_r^1 & \$_r^2 & \$_r^3 & \$_r^4 \end{bmatrix} \tag{4}$$

Finally one can compute null spaces of the foregoing reciprocal screws which leads to the DOF of the manipulator; namely,

$$\begin{aligned} DoF_1 &= [0 \ \ 0 \ \ 0 \ \ 1 \ \ 0 \ \ 0]^T \\ DoF_2 &= [0 \ \ 0 \ \ 0 \ \ 0 \ \ 1 \ \ 0]^T \\ DoF_3 &= [0 \ \ 0 \ \ 0 \ \ 0 \ \ 0 \ \ 1]^T \\ DoF_4 &= [0 \ \ 0 \ \ 1 \ \ 0 \ \ 0 \ \ 0]^T \end{aligned} \tag{5}$$

These imply that H4 robot has three translational and one rotational DOF. Figure 3 shows the rotation of C_1C_2 link about z-axis as rotational DOF.

3. Kinematic analysis

3.1 Inverse kinematics

The inverse position kinematics problem solves the actuated variables from a given pose of EE. Let $\mathbf{q} = [q_1 \ \ q_2 \ \ q_3 \ \ q_4]^T$ be the array of the four actuator joint variables and

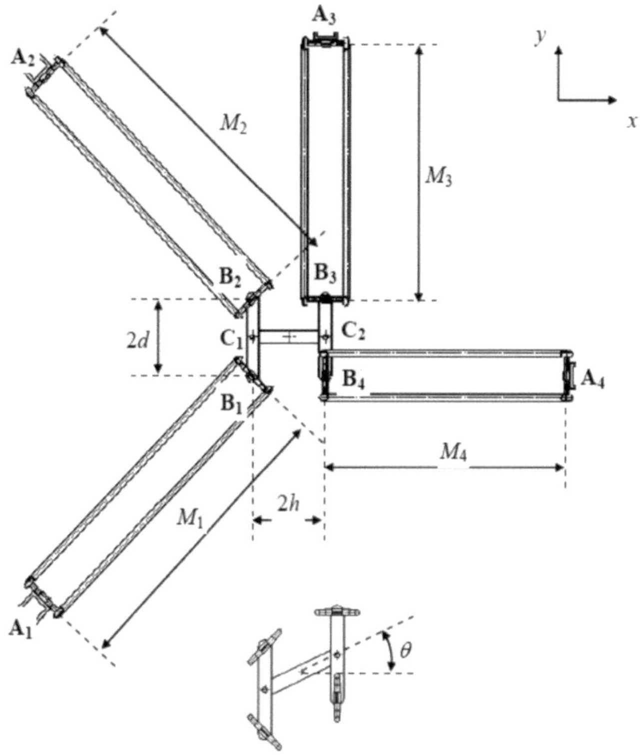

Fig. 3. Design parameters of H4

$\vec{\mathbf{x}} = \begin{bmatrix} x & y & z & \theta \end{bmatrix}^T$ be the array of the pose of the EE. The position of points C_1 and C_2 are given by [4]:

$$\vec{\mathbf{C}}_1 = \vec{\mathbf{B}} + \mathbf{Rot}(\theta)\overrightarrow{\mathbf{BC_1}} \qquad \vec{\mathbf{C}}_2 = \vec{\mathbf{B}} + \mathbf{Rot}(\theta)\overrightarrow{\mathbf{BC}_2} \tag{6}$$

where $\mathbf{Rot}(\theta)$ denotes the rotation matrix of the EE with respect to reference frame and is defined as:

$$\begin{aligned}\mathbf{Rot}(\theta) &= {}^{A}\mathbf{R}_B = \mathbf{R}_z(\theta) \\ &= \begin{bmatrix} cos(\theta) & -sin(\theta) & 0 \\ sin(\theta) & cos(\theta) & 0 \\ 0 & 0 & 1 \end{bmatrix}\end{aligned} \tag{7}$$

Moreover, the position of each point $\mathbf{B_i}$ is given by:

$$\begin{aligned} \vec{\mathbf{B}}_1 &= \vec{\mathbf{C}}_1 + \overrightarrow{\mathbf{C}_1\mathbf{B}_1} \qquad & \vec{\mathbf{B}}_2 &= \vec{\mathbf{C}}_1 + \overrightarrow{\mathbf{C}_1\mathbf{B}_2} \\ \vec{\mathbf{B}}_3 &= \vec{\mathbf{C}}_2 + \overrightarrow{\mathbf{C}_2\mathbf{B}_3} \qquad & \vec{\mathbf{B}}_4 &= \vec{\mathbf{C}}_2 + \overrightarrow{\mathbf{C}_2\mathbf{B}_4} \end{aligned} \tag{8}$$

Therefore, the following can then be written:

$$||A_iB_i||^2 = M_i^{\,2} \tag{9}$$

Then, for the first chain:

$$\overrightarrow{\mathbf{A}_1\mathbf{B}_1} = (\vec{\mathbf{B}} + \mathbf{Rot}(\theta)\overrightarrow{\mathbf{BC}}_1 + \overrightarrow{\mathbf{C}_1\mathbf{B}_1} - \vec{\mathbf{P}}_1) - q_1\vec{\mathbf{z}}_1$$
$$(A_1B_1)^2 = q_1{}^2 - 2q_1d_1.z_1 + \|d_1\|^2 \tag{10}$$

where $\vec{\mathbf{d}}_1 = \vec{\mathbf{B}} + \mathbf{Rot}(\theta)\overrightarrow{\mathbf{BC}}_1 + \overrightarrow{\mathbf{C}_1\mathbf{B}_1} - \vec{\mathbf{P}}_1$. Finally, the two solutions of Eq. 10 are given by:

$$q_1 = \vec{\mathbf{d}}_1.\vec{\mathbf{z}}_1 \pm \sqrt{(\vec{\mathbf{d}}_1.\vec{\mathbf{z}}_1)^2 + M_1{}^2 - \|\mathbf{d}_1\|^2} \tag{11}$$

Similarly, q_1, q_2 and q_4 can be derived as:

$$\begin{aligned}
q_2 &= \vec{\mathbf{d}}_2.\vec{\mathbf{z}}_2 \pm \sqrt{(\vec{\mathbf{d}}_2.\vec{\mathbf{z}}_2)^2 + M_2{}^2 - \|\mathbf{d}_2\|^2} & \vec{\mathbf{d}}_2 &= \vec{\mathbf{B}} + \mathbf{Rot}(\theta)\overrightarrow{\mathbf{BC}}_1 + \overrightarrow{\mathbf{C}_1\mathbf{B}_2} - \vec{\mathbf{P}}_2 \\
q_3 &= \vec{\mathbf{d}}_3.\vec{\mathbf{z}}_3 \pm \sqrt{(\vec{\mathbf{d}}_3.\vec{\mathbf{z}}_3)^2 + M_3{}^2 - \|\mathbf{d}_3\|^2} & \vec{\mathbf{d}}_3 &= \vec{\mathbf{B}} + \mathbf{Rot}(\theta)\overrightarrow{\mathbf{BC}}_2 + \overrightarrow{\mathbf{C}_2\mathbf{B}_3} - \vec{\mathbf{P}}_3 \\
q_4 &= \vec{\mathbf{d}}_4.\vec{\mathbf{z}}_4 \pm \sqrt{(\vec{\mathbf{d}}_4.\vec{\mathbf{z}}_4)^2 + M_4{}^2 - \|\mathbf{d}_4\|^2} & \vec{\mathbf{d}}_4 &= \vec{\mathbf{B}} + \mathbf{Rot}(\theta)\overrightarrow{\mathbf{BC}}_2 + \overrightarrow{\mathbf{C}_2\mathbf{B}_4} - \vec{\mathbf{P}}_4
\end{aligned} \tag{12}$$

3.2 Forward kinematics

Forward kinematic problem solves the pose of the EE from a given actuators variables. It is well-known that forward kinematic problem of parallel manipulators is challenging (Dasgupta & Mruthyunjaya, 2000) and involves the solution of a system of nonlinear coupled algebraic equations in the variables describing the platform posture. This system of nonlinear equations might lead to solutions. Except in a limited number of the problems, one has difficulty in finding exact analytical solutions for the problem. So these nonlinear simultaneous equations should be solved using other methods, namely, numerical or semi-exact analytical methods. Some others believe that the combination of numerical and semi-exact analytical methods can also produce useful results (Hashemi et al, 2007; Varedi et al, 2009). Choi et al. solved forward kinematic problem of H4 and showed that the problem lead to a 16th degree polynomial in a single variable (Choi et al, 2003).

The EE is composed of three parts (two lateral bars and one central bar). Moreover, points $\mathbf{B}_1$, $\mathbf{B}_2$, $\mathbf{B}_3$ and $\mathbf{B}_4$ form a parallelogram. Let ${}^A\mathbf{A}_i$ and ${}^A\mathbf{B}_i$ represent the homogeneous coordinates of the points $\mathbf{A}_i$ in {A} and $\mathbf{B}_i$ in {A}, respectively. Then, one can write (Wu et al, 2006):

$$ {}^A\vec{\mathbf{B}}_i = \begin{bmatrix} x + hE_{1i}c\theta \\ y + hE_{1i}s\theta + dE_{2i} \\ z \\ 1 \end{bmatrix} = \begin{bmatrix} P_i c\theta + x \\ P_i s\theta + y + Q_i \\ z \\ 1 \end{bmatrix}$$
$${}^A\vec{\mathbf{A}}_i = \begin{bmatrix} a_i & b_i & q_i & 1 \end{bmatrix}^T \tag{13}$$

where

$$P_i = hE_{1i},\ Q_i = dE_{2i},\ E_{11} = E_{12} = -1,\ E_{13} = E_{14} = -1,$$
$$E_{21} = E_{24} = 1,\ E_{22} = E_{23} = 1,\ c\theta = cos(\theta),\ s\theta = sin(\theta) \tag{14}$$

Substituting these values in Eq.(9), upon simplifications, yields:

$$(P_i c\theta + x - a_i)^2 + (P_i s\theta + y + Q_i - b_i)^2 + (z - q_i)^2 = M_i^2 \quad i = 1,...,4 \tag{15}$$

Expanding and rearranging Eq.(15) leads to:

$$\begin{aligned}
&\tilde{A}_i x + \tilde{B}_i y + \tilde{C}_i z + \tilde{D}_i + \tilde{E}_i = 0 \quad for \;\; i = 1,...,4 \\
&\tilde{A}_i = 2(P_i c\theta - a_i), \quad \tilde{B}_i = 2(P_i s\theta + Q_i - b_i) \quad \tilde{C}_i = -2q_i \\
&\tilde{D}_i = a_i^2 + b_i^2 + q_i^2 - 2P_i(a_i c\theta + b_i s\theta - Q_i s\theta) - 2Q_i b_i + P_i^2 + Q_i^2 - M_i^2 \\
&\tilde{E}_i = x^2 + y^2 + z^2
\end{aligned} \tag{16}$$

Subtracting Eq.(16) for i=3, 4 from the same equation for i=2, yields to:

$$\Delta A_{23} x + \Delta B_{23} y + \Delta C_{23} z + \Delta D_{23} = 0 \tag{17}$$

$$\Delta A_{24} x + \Delta B_{24} y + \Delta C_{24} z + \Delta D_{24} = 0 \tag{18}$$

where

$$\Delta A_{23} = (\tilde{A}_2 - \tilde{A}_3), \Delta B_{23} = (\tilde{B}_2 - \tilde{B}_3), \Delta C_{23} = (\tilde{C}_2 - \tilde{C}_3), \Delta D_{23} = (\tilde{D}_2 - \tilde{D}_3),$$
$$\Delta A_{24} = (\tilde{A}_2 - \tilde{A}_4), \Delta B_{24} = (\tilde{B}_2 - \tilde{B}_4), \Delta C_{24} = (\tilde{C}_2 - \tilde{C}_4), \Delta D_{24} = (\tilde{D}_2 - \tilde{D}_4),$$

Eqs. (17) and (18) now can be solved for x and y, namely:

$$x = \frac{\Delta_{11} z + \Delta_{12}}{\Delta_0} = e_1 z + e_2 \tag{19}$$

$$y = \frac{\Delta_{21} z + \Delta_{22}}{\Delta_0} = e_3 z + e_4 \tag{20}$$

where

$$e_1 = \frac{\Delta_{11}}{\Delta_0}, e_2 = \frac{\Delta_{12}}{\Delta_0}, e_3 = \frac{\Delta_{21}}{\Delta_0}, e_4 = \frac{\Delta_{22}}{\Delta_0}, \;\; \Delta_0 = \Delta A_{23}\Delta B_{24} - \Delta A_{24}\Delta B_{23},$$
$$\Delta_{11} = \Delta B_{23}\Delta C_{24} - \Delta B_{24}\Delta C_{23}, \;\; \Delta_{12} = \Delta B_{23}\Delta D_{24} - \Delta B_{24}\Delta D_{23},$$
$$\Delta_{21} = \Delta A_{24}\Delta C_{23} - \Delta A_{23}\Delta C_{24}, \;\; \Delta_{22} = \Delta A_{24}\Delta D_{23} - \Delta A_{23}\Delta D_{24},$$

Substituting Eqs.(19) and (20) into Eq.(16) for i=2, yields to the following quadratic equation.

$$\lambda_0 z^2 + \lambda_1 z + \lambda_2 = 0 \tag{21}$$

where

$$\lambda_0 = e_1^2 + e_3^2 + 1, \quad \lambda_1 = 2e_1e_2 + 2e_3e_4 + \tilde{A}_2 e_1 + \tilde{B}_2 e_3 + \tilde{C}_2,$$
$$\lambda_2 = e_2^2 + e_4^2 + \tilde{A}_2 e_2 + \tilde{B}_2 e_4 + \tilde{D}_2$$

Eq.(21) can be solved for z. Substituting this value into Eq.(16) for i=1, upon simplifications leads:

$$\begin{aligned}
&f((c\theta)^4, (c\theta)^3(s\theta)^1, (c\theta)^2(s\theta)^2, (c\theta)^1(s\theta)^3, (c\theta)^0(s\theta)^4, (c\theta)^3(s\theta)^0, \\
&(c\theta)^2(s\theta)^1, (c\theta)^1(s\theta)^2, (c\theta)^0(s\theta)^3, (c\theta)^2(s\theta)^0, (c\theta)^1(s\theta)^1, (c\theta)^0(s\theta)^2, \\
&(c\theta)^1(s\theta)^0, (c\theta)^0(s\theta)^1, (c\theta)^0(s\theta)^0) = 0
\end{aligned} \tag{22}$$

where $f(x_1, x_2, ..., x_n)$ represents a linear combination of $x_1, x_2, ..., x_n$. The coefficients of Eq.(22) are the data depend on the design parameters of the H4 robot. In Eq.(22), we substitute now the equivalent expressions for $c\theta$ and $s\theta$ given as:

$$c\theta = \frac{1-T^2}{1+T^2} \quad , \quad s\theta = \frac{2T}{1+T^2} \quad , \quad T = tan(\theta / 2) \tag{23}$$

Upon simplifications, Eq.(22) leads to a univariate polynomial of degree eight, namely;

$$aT^8 + bT^7 + cT^6 + dT^5 + eT^4 + fT^3 + gT^2 + hT^1 + i = 0 \tag{24}$$

where a, b, c, d, e, f, g, h and i depend on kinematic parameters. The detailed expressions for them are not given here because these expansions would be too large to serve any useful purpose. What is important to point out here is that the above equation admits eight solutions, whether real or complex, among which we only interested in the real ones. Substituting the values of T from Eq.(23) into Eq.(19), Eq.(20) and Eq.(21), complete the solutions.

3.2.1 Numerical example of kinematic analysis

Here, we include a numerical example as shown in Fig.4. The design parameters of H4 are given as:

$$h = d = 6(\text{cm}),\ Q_z = 42(\text{cm}),\ M_1 = M_2 = \sqrt{3}Q_z,\ M_3 = M_4 = \sqrt{2}Q_z \tag{25}$$

Substituting these values in Eq.(13), yields:

$$\begin{aligned}
&\vec{\mathbf{A}}_1 = [-48 \quad -48 \quad 0]^T,\ \vec{\mathbf{B}}_1 = [-6 \quad -6 \quad -42]^T, \\
&\vec{\mathbf{A}}_2 = [-48 \quad 48 \quad 0]^T,\ \ \vec{\mathbf{B}}_2 = [-6 \quad 6 \quad -42]^T, \\
&\vec{\mathbf{A}}_3 = [6 \quad 48 \quad 0]^T,\ \ \ \ \vec{\mathbf{B}}_3 = [6 \quad 6 \quad -42]^T, \\
&\vec{\mathbf{A}}_4 = [48 \quad -6 \quad 0]^T,\ \ \vec{\mathbf{B}}_4 = [6 \quad -6 \quad -42]^T.
\end{aligned}$$

Given, the position and orientation of the EE as $\vec{\mathbf{x}} = \left[5 \quad -5 \quad -30 \quad \pi / 6\right]^T$, inverse kinematics are given by:

$$\vec{\mathbf{q}} = [13.021 \quad -7.488 \quad 9.679 \quad 15.77]^T \tag{26}$$

Next, the forward kinematic problem, for the actuators coordinate as given in Eq.(26), is solved. The polynomial equation in Eq.(24) can be solved for T, namely;

$$\begin{aligned}
&T_{12} = -0.61309 \pm 0.56609i \\
&T_{34} = 0.073172 \pm 0.84245i \\
&T_{56} = 0.028294 \pm 0.88575i \\
&T_7 = 0.267957 \\
&T_8 = -2.8822
\end{aligned} \tag{27}$$

There are only two real solutions, for which $T_7 = 0.2680$ leads to $\vec{\mathbf{x}} = \left[5(cm) \quad -5(cm) \quad -30(cm) \quad 0.524(rad)\right]^T$ and $T_8 = -2.8822$, yields:

$\vec{\mathbf{x}} = \left[3(cm) \quad -7.95(cm) \quad -14.58(cm) \quad -2.47(rad)\right]^T$. However, the latter configuration cannot be realized in practice because of the mutual interference of the parallelograms as shown in Fig.4.

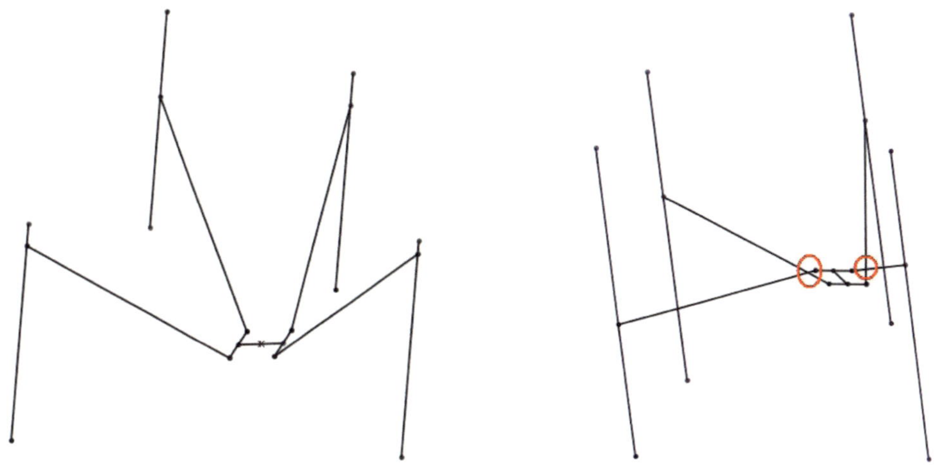

T_7 = 0.2680 T_8= - 2.8822

Fig. 4. The solutions for forward kinematic problem

3.3 Jacobian matrix

Jacobian matrix relates the actuated joint velocities to the EE Cartesian velocities, and is essential for the velocity and trajectory control of parallel robots. The velocity of the EE of H4 can be defined by resorting to a velocity for the translation, $\vec{\mathbf{v}}_B = \left[\dot{x} \quad \dot{y} \quad \dot{z}\right]^T$ and a scalar for the rotation about $\vec{\mathbf{z}}$; namely, $\dot{\theta}$. Thus, the velocity of points $C_1$and C_2 can be written as follows (Wu et al, 2006):

$$\vec{\mathbf{v}}_{c_1} = \vec{\mathbf{v}}_B + \dot{\theta}(\vec{\mathbf{k}}) \times \overrightarrow{\mathbf{BC}_1} \qquad \vec{\mathbf{v}}_{c_2} = \vec{\mathbf{v}}_B + \dot{\theta}(\vec{\mathbf{k}}) \times \overrightarrow{\mathbf{BC}_2} \tag{28}$$

Moreover, since the links $\mathbf{B}_1\mathbf{B}_2$ and $\mathbf{B}_3\mathbf{B}_4$ only have translational motion, the following relations hold:

$$\vec{\mathbf{v}}_{B_1} = \vec{\mathbf{v}}_{B_2} = \vec{\mathbf{v}}_{C_1} \qquad \vec{\mathbf{v}}_{B_3} = \vec{\mathbf{v}}_{B_4} = \vec{\mathbf{v}}_{C_2} \tag{29}$$

On the other hand, velocity of points A_i is given by:

$$\vec{\mathbf{v}}_{A_i} = \dot{q}\overrightarrow{k_z} \tag{30}$$

The velocity relationship can then be written thanks to the classical property; namely,

$$\vec{\mathbf{v}}_{A_i} . \overrightarrow{\mathbf{A}_i\mathbf{B}_i} = \vec{\mathbf{v}}_{B_i} . \overrightarrow{\mathbf{A}_i\mathbf{B}_i} \tag{31}$$

Eq.(31) can be written for i=1,…,4 and the results grouped in a matrix form as:

$$\mathbf{J}_q\dot{\mathbf{q}} = \mathbf{J}_x\dot{\vec{\mathbf{x}}} \tag{32}$$

Where $\dot{\mathbf{x}}$ and $\dot{\mathbf{q}}$ denote the vectors of the EE velocity and input actuated joint rates, respectively ; $\mathbf{J}_q$ and $\mathbf{J}_x$ are the Jacobian matrices, all are defined as:

$$\dot{\mathbf{q}} = \begin{bmatrix} \dot{q}_1 & \dot{q}_2 & \dot{q}_3 & \dot{q}_4 \end{bmatrix}^T$$

$$\mathbf{J}_q = \begin{bmatrix} \overrightarrow{A_1B_1} \cdot \overrightarrow{\mathbf{z}_1} & 0 & 0 & 0 \\ 0 & \overrightarrow{A_2B_2} \cdot \overrightarrow{\mathbf{z}_2} & 0 & 0 \\ 0 & 0 & \overrightarrow{A_3B_3} \cdot \overrightarrow{\mathbf{z}_3} & 0 \\ 0 & 0 & 0 & \overrightarrow{A_4B_4} \cdot \overrightarrow{\mathbf{z}_4} \end{bmatrix}$$

$$\dot{\mathbf{x}} = [\dot{x} \quad \dot{y} \quad \dot{z} \quad \dot{\theta}]^T \tag{33}$$

$$\mathbf{J}_x = \begin{bmatrix} (\overrightarrow{A_1B_1})_x & (\overrightarrow{A_1B_1})_y & (\overrightarrow{A_1B_1})_z & (\overrightarrow{A_1B_1} \times \overrightarrow{BC_1}).\vec{\mathbf{k}} \\ (\overrightarrow{A_2B_2})_x & (\overrightarrow{A_2B_2})_y & (\overrightarrow{A_2B_2})_z & (\overrightarrow{A_2B_2} \times \overrightarrow{BC_1}).\vec{\mathbf{k}} \\ (\overrightarrow{A_3B_3})_x & (\overrightarrow{A_3B_3})_y & (\overrightarrow{A_3B_3})_z & (\overrightarrow{A_3B_3} \times \overrightarrow{BC_2}).\vec{\mathbf{k}} \\ (\overrightarrow{A_4B_4})_x & (\overrightarrow{A_4B_4})_y & (\overrightarrow{A_4B_4})_z & (\overrightarrow{A_4B_4} \times \overrightarrow{BC_2}).\vec{\mathbf{k}} \end{bmatrix}$$

If the mechanism is not in a singular configuration, the Jacobian and its inverse are described as:

$$\mathbf{J} = \mathbf{J}_x^{-1}\mathbf{J}_q \qquad \text{and} \qquad \mathbf{J}^{-1} = \mathbf{J}_q^{-1}\mathbf{J}_x \tag{34}$$

4. Optimization of H4

4.1 Workspace evaluation

For a robot in the context of industrial application and given parameters, it is very important to analyze the volume and the shape of its workspace (Dombre & Khalil, 2007). Calculation of the workspace and its boundaries with perfect precision is crucial, because they influence the dimensional design, the manipulator's positioning in the work environment, and its dexterity to execute tasks (Li & Xu, 2006). The workspace is limited by several conditions. The prime limitation is the boundary obtained through solving the inverse kinematic problem. Further, the workspace is limited by the reachable extent of drives and joints, then by the occurrence of singularities, and finally by the links and platform collisions (Stan et al, 2008). Various approaches may be used to calculate the workspace of a parallel robot. In the present work the boundary of workspace of H4 is determined geometrically (Merlet, 2006).

4.2 Condition number

In order to guarantee the regular workspace to be effective, constraints on the dexterity index are introduced into the design problem. A frequently used measure for dexterity of a manipulator is the inverse of the condition number of the kinematics Jacobian matrix (Hosseini et al, 2011). Indeed, in order to determine the condition number of the Jacobian matrices, their singular values must be ordered from largest to smallest. However, in the presence of positioning and orienting tasks the singular values associated with positioning, are dimensionless, while those associated with orientation have units of length, thereby making impossible such an ordering. This dimensional in-homogeneity can be resolved by introducing a weighting factor/length, which is here equal to the length of the first link (Hosseini et al, 2011). Then, the condition number of homogeneous Jacobian is defined as the ratio of its largest singular value σ_l to its smallest one, σ_s (Gosselin & Angeles, 1991), i.e.

$$\kappa(\mathbf{J}) \equiv \frac{\sigma_l}{\sigma_s} \tag{35}$$

Note that $\kappa(\mathbf{J})$ can attain any value from 1 to infinity, in which they correspond to isotropy and singularity, respectively.

4.3 Performance index

The objective function for maximization is defined here as a mixed performance index which is a weighted sum of global dexterity index (GDI), η_d and space utility ratio index (SURI), η_s (Dasgupta & Mruthyunjaya, 2000) , i.e.,

$$\begin{aligned} \eta &= w_d \eta_d + (1-w_d)\eta_s \\ &= w_d \left[\frac{1}{V} \int_V \frac{1}{\kappa} dV \right] + (1-w_d)\frac{V}{V^*} \end{aligned} \tag{36}$$

where the weight parameter $w_d\,(0 \le w_d \le 1)$ describes the proportion of GDI in the mixed index, and V^* represents the robot size which is evaluated by the product of area of the fixed platform and the maximum reach of the EE in the z direction.

4.4 Design variables

The architectural parameters of a H4 involve the offset of {B} from {A} along the direction of $\vec{k}_z(Q_z)$, length of the offset of the revolute-joint from the ball-joint (d) and the offset of each ball-joint from the center of the traveling plate (h). In order to perform the optimization independent of the dimension of each design candidate, the design variables are scaled by Δq, i.e., the motion range of the actuators. Thus, the design variables become $\vec{\mathbf{\Gamma}} = \left[\frac{d}{\Delta q}, \frac{h}{\Delta q}, \frac{Q_z}{\Delta q} \right]$. However, we have the following limitations for the design variables:

$$1/\kappa(\mathbf{J}) > 0.01,$$

$$0.01 < \frac{d}{\Delta q} < 0.15 \quad , \quad 0.01 < \frac{h}{\Delta q} < 0.15 \quad , \quad 0.35 < \frac{Q_z}{\Delta q} < 0.55$$

4.5 Optimization result of H4

In order to perform an optimal design of H4 parallel robots, an objective function was developed first, then GA is applied in order to optimize the objective function (Xu & Li, 2006). For optimization settings, regarding to the GA approach, normalized geometric selection is adopted (Merlet, 2006), and the genetic operators are chosen to be non-uniform mutation with the ratio of 0.08 and arithmetic crossover with the ratio of 0.8. Moreover, the population size is 30 and the generations' number is set to 150.

4.5.1 Optimization based on maximum workspace volume

First we consider the volume of workspace as the objective function; namely,

$V^*=max(V)$

Subject to

1. $1/\kappa(\mathbf{J}) > 0.01$

$$0.01 < \frac{d}{\Delta q} < 0.15 \quad , \quad 0.01 < \frac{h}{\Delta q} < 0.15 \quad , \quad 0.35 < \frac{Q_z}{\Delta q} < 0.55$$

The solution of this problem is given in Table 1. Moreover, the workspace for $\theta = 0$ and the conditioning index for $\theta = 0$ and z=0 are shown in Fig.5 and Fig.6, respectively. While the workspace size is acceptable, the manipulator suffers from a poor dexterity throughout its workspace.

Volume of workspace *(rad)(cm³)*	Average of conditioning index	Robot's parameters		
		d(cm)	*h(cm)*	Q_z *(cm)*
12582.0	0.042	13.52484	13.88781	35.18892

Table 1. Optimization result for H4

As it is observed the GA reaches a convergence after 30 iterations as depicted in Fig. 7.

4.5.2 Optimization based on GDI

In this section we optimize the average of conditioning index in the workspace. Therefore, the problem is stated as:

$GDI = \max(average\,(1/\kappa(\mathbf{J})))$

Subject to

1. $1/\kappa(\mathbf{J}) > 0.01$
2. $0.01 < \frac{d}{\Delta q} < 0.15 \quad , \quad 0.01 < \frac{h}{\Delta q} < 0.15 \quad , \quad 0.35 < \frac{Q_z}{\Delta q} < 0.55$

As it is expected, the volume of the workspace is very small and only includes a small neighbourhood of a point of the best conditioning index. This optimal design is given in Table 2.

Volume of workspace *(rad)(cm³)*	Average of conditioning index	Robot's parameters		
		d(cm)	*h(cm)*	Q_z *(cm)*
4.1887	0.0705	1.00008	1.09692	35.48742

Table 2. Optimization result for H4

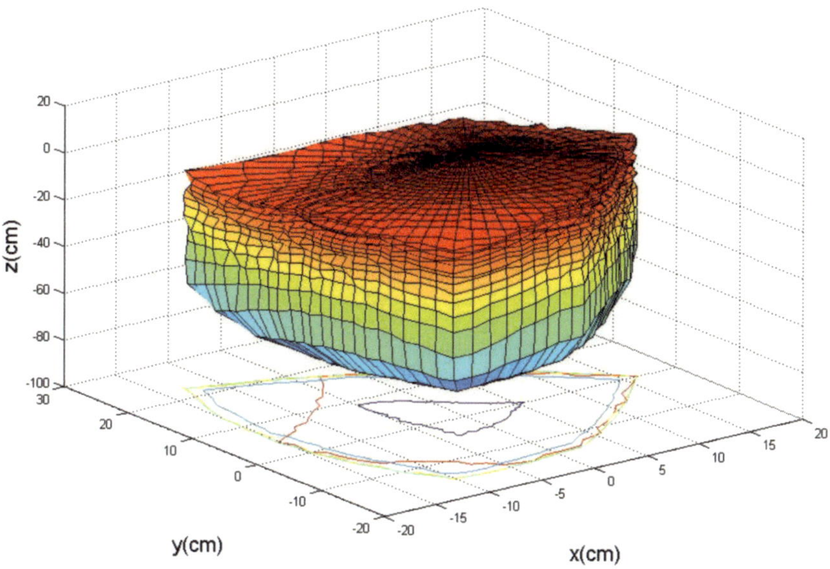

Fig. 5. Workspace of H4 for $\theta = 0$

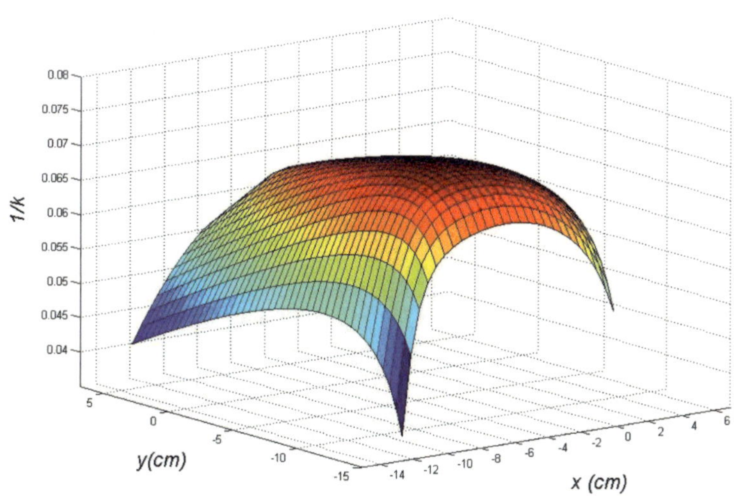

Fig. 6. Conditioning index for z=0 and $\theta = 0$

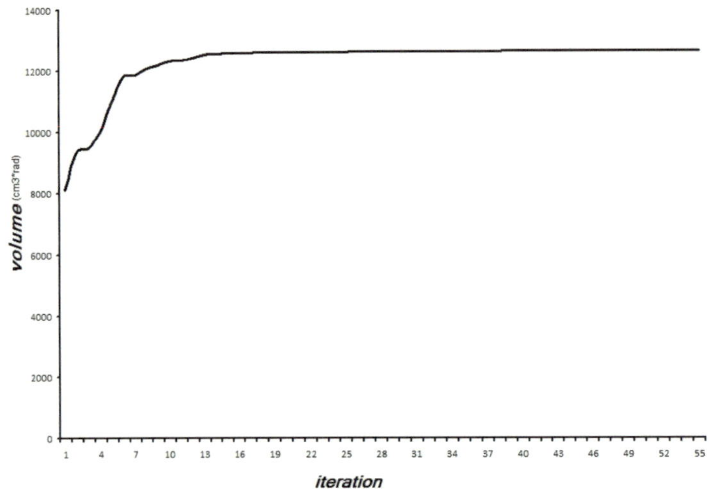

Fig. 7. Convergence of GA

4.5.3 Optimization based on the mixed performance index

For the problem at hand one needs a good fitness function, because the optimization based on maximal workspace volume, decreases the performance indices and the optimization based on GDI decreases the workspace volume. Therefore, one can optimize the manipulator based on performance index that described in subsection 5.3. The optimization results for w_d=0.25, 0.5, 0.75 are given in Table 3.
Moreover, for different values of w_d, the problem is solved and the GDI, SURI and the mixed performance index are calculated and plotted in Fig. 8. As the result, any value of w_d greater than 0.74 leads to a limited workspace and for any values smaller than that has no substantial effects on GDI and the workspace. Therefore, it clearly shows that by introducing this measure, the performance of the manipulator can be improved at a minor cost its workspace volume.

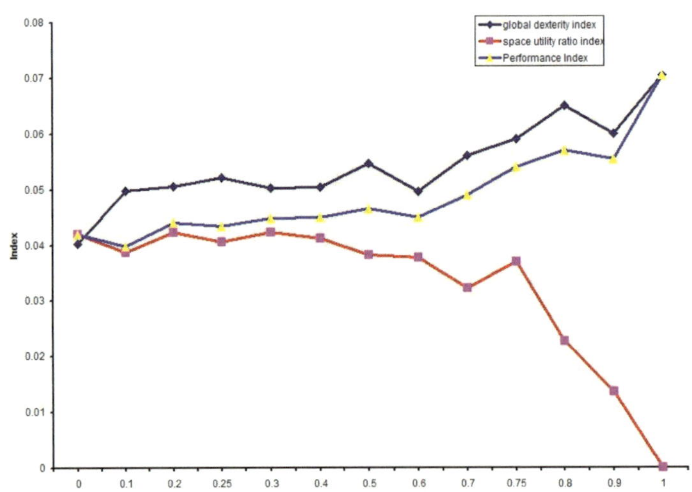

Fig. 8. GDI and SURI and Performance Index versus weight parameter

	$w_d = 0.25$	$w_d = 0.5$	$w_d = 0.75$
Volume of workspace *(rad)(cm³)*	11983	11304	11008
d(cm)	12.14243	12.60003	10.36257
h(cm)	10.38564	9.06147	5.56941
Q_z *(cm)*	37.25841	39.61105	40.69626
GDI	0.0521	0.0547	0.059

Table 3. Optimization results for H4

5. Conclusions

First, the forward and inverse kinematics of H4 parallel manipulator has been studied here, in which the former problem has leaded to a univariate polynomial of degree eight. Then, the optimal design of the manipulator has been addressed. Using genetic algorithm the manipulator has been optimized based on a mixed performance index that is a weighted sum of global conditioning index and its workspace volume. It has been shown that by introducing this measure, the parallel manipulator has been improved at minor cost of its workspace volume.

6. References

Boudreau, R.; Gosselin, C.M. (1999). The synthesis of planar parallel manipulators with a genetic algorithm, , *Journal of Mechanical Design*, 121(4), 1999, pp. 533–537.

Choi, H.B.; Konno, A. & Uchiyama, M. (2003). Closed-form solutions for the forward kinematics of a 4-DOFs parallel robot H4, *Proceedings of IEEE/RSJ International Conference on Intelligent Robots and Systems*, Las Vegas, USA, October, 2003, pp. 3312-3317.

Company, O.; Marquet, F. & Pierrot, F. (2003). A new high-speed 4DoF parallel robot synthesis and modeling issues. *IEEE, Transactions on Robotics and Automation*, Vol.19, No.3, 2003, pp. 411-420.

Coradini, C.; Fauroux, J. (2003). Evaluation of a 4-DOF parallel manipulator stiffness, *Mechanism and Machine Science*, Aug, 2003.

Dai, J.S.; Jones, J.R. (2007). A Linear Algebraic Procedure in Obtaining Reciprocal Screw Systems, *J. Robotic Systems*, 2007, 20(7), pp. 401–412.

Dasgupta, B.; Mruthyunjaya, T.S. (2000). The Stewart platform manipulator: A review, *Mechanism and Machine Theory*, 35, 2000, pp. 15–40.

Dombre, E.; Khalil, W. (2007). Modeling, Performance Analysis and Control of Robot Manipulators, *ISTE*, 2007.

Gosselin, C.; Angeles, J. (1991). A global performance index for the kinematic optimization of robotic manipulators. *ASME J Mech*, December, 1991, 113(3), pp. 220–226.

Hashemi, S.H.; Daniali, H.M. & Ganji, D.D. (2007). Numerical simulation of the generalized Huxley equation by He's homotopy perturbation method, *Applied Mathematics and Computation*, 2007, pp. 157–161.

Hosseini, M.A; Daniali, H.M. & Taghirad, H.D. (2011). "Dexterous Workspace Optimization of a Tricept Parallel Manipulator", *Advanced Robotics*, Vol. 25, 2011, pp. 1697-1712.

Lara-Molina, F.A.; Rosário, J.M. & Dumur, D. (2010). Multi-Objective Design of Parallel Manipulator Using Global Indices, *The Open Mechanical Engineering Journal*, 2010, 4, pp. 37-47.

Laribi, M.A.; Romdhane, L. & Zeghloul, S. (2007). Analysis and dimensional synthesis of the DELTA robot for a prescribed workspace, *Mechanism and Machine Theory*, 42, (2007), pp. 859-870.

Li, Yangmin.; Xu, Qingsong. (2006). A new approach to the architecture optimization of a general 3-PUU translational parallel manipulator. *J Int Robot System*, 2006, 46, pp. 59–72.

Li, Yangmin.; Xu, Qingsong. (2007). Kinematic analysis of a 3-PRS parallel manipulator, *Robotics and Computer-Integrated Manufacturing*, 2007, 23, pp. 395–408.

Merlet, J.P.; (2006). *Parallel robots* (second edition), springer.

Pierrot, F.; Company, O. (1999). H4: a new family of 4-DoF parallel robots, *Int Conf on Advanced Intelligent Mechatronics*, Proceedings of the 1999 IEEE/ASME, pp. 508-513.

Pierrot, F.; Marquet, F. & Company, O. & Gil, T. (2001). H4 parallel robot: modeling, design and preliminary experiments, *Int Conf on Robotics and Automation*, May, 2001.

Poignet, Ph.; Ramdani, N. & Vivas, O.A. (2003). Robust estimation of parallel robot dynamic parameters with interval analysis, *Proceedings of the 42nd IEEE*, Conference on Decision and Control, Maui, Hawaii USA, December, 2003.

Renaud, P.; Andreff, N. & Marquet, F. & Martinet, P. (2003). Vision-based kinematic calibration of a H4 parallel mechanism, *Int Conf on Robotics and Automation*, Proceediogr of the 2003 IEEE, Taipei, Taiwan, September 14-19.

Robotics Department of LIRMM. (n.d.). H4 with rotary drives: a member of H4 family, dedicated to high speed applications, http://www.lirmm.fr/w3rob.

Stan, S.D.; Manic, M. & Mătieş, M. & Bălan, R. (2008). Evolutionary approach to optimal design of 3 DOF Translation exoskeleton and medical parallel robots, *HSI 2008, IEEE Conference on Human System Interaction*, Krakow, Poland, May 25-27, 2008, pp. 720-725.

Tantawiroon, N.; Sangveraphunsiri, V. (2005). Design and analysis of a new H4 family parallel manipulator, *Thammasat Int J. Science Tech, July-September*, Vol. 10, No. 3, 2005.

Varedi, S.M.; Daniali, H.M. & Ganji, D.D. (2009). Kinematics of an offset 3-UPU translational parallel manipulator by the homotopy continuation method, *Nonlinear Analysis: Real World Applications 10*, 2009, pp. 1767–1774.

Wu, Jinbo.; Yin, Zhouping. & Xiong, Youlun. (2006). Singularity analysis of a novel 4-DoF parallel manipulator H4, *Int J Advanced Manuf Tech*, 29, pp. 794–802.

Xu, Qingsong.; Li, Yangmin. (2006). Kinematic analysis and optimization of a New compliant parallel micromanipulator, *Int J of Advanced Robotic Systems*, 2006, Vol. 3, No. 4.

Zhao, J.S.; Zhou, K. & Feng, Z.J. (2004). A theory of degrees of freedom for mechanisms. *Mechanism and Machine Theory*, 39, 2004, pp. 621–643.

21

Spatial Path Planning of Static Robots Using Configuration Space Metrics

Debanik Roy
Board of Research in Nuclear Sciences, Department of Atomic Energy, Government of India, Mumbai India

1. Introduction

Obstacle avoidance and robot path planning problems have gained sufficient research attention due to its indispensable application demand in manufacturing vis-à-vis material handling sector, such as picking-and- placing an object, loading / unloading a component to /from a machine or storage bins. Visibility map in the configuration space (*c-space*) has become reasonably instrumental towards solving robot path planning problems and it certainly edges out other techniques widely used in the field of motion planning of robots (e.g. Voronoi Diagram, Potential Field, Cellular Automata) for *unstructured environment*. The c-space mapping algorithms, referred in the paper, are discussed with logic behind their formulation and their effectiveness in solving path planning problems under various conditions imposed a-priori. The visibility graph (*v-graph*) based path planning algorithm generates the equations to obtain the desired joint parameter values of the robot corresponding to the ith intermediate location of the end - effector in the collision - free path. The developed c-space models have been verified by considering first a congested workspace in 2D and subsequently with the real spatial manifolds, cluttered with different objects. New lemma has been proposed for generating c-space maps for higher dimensional robots, e.g. having degrees-of-freedom more than three. A test case has been analyzed wherein a seven degrees-of-freedom revolute robot is used for articulation, followed by a case-study with a five degrees-of-freedom articulated manipulator (RHINO XR-3) amidst an in-door environment. Both the studies essentially involve new c-space mapping thematic in higher dimensions.

Tomas Lozano Perez' postulated the fundamentals of Configuration Space approach and proved those successfully in spatial path planning of robotic manipulators in an environment congested with polyhedral obstacles using an explicit representation of the manipulator configurations that would bring about a collision eventually [Perez', 1983]. However, his method suffers problem when applied to manipulators with revolute joints. In contrast to rectilinear objects, as tried by Perez', collision-avoidance algorithm in 2D for an articulated two-link planar manipulator with circular obstacles have been reported also [Keerthi & Selvaraj, 1989]. The paradigm of *automatic transformation* of obstacles in the c-space and thereby path planning is examined with finer details [De Pedro & Rosa, 1992], such as *friction* between the obstacles [Erdmann, 1994]. Novel c-space computation algorithm for convex planar algebraic objects has been reported [Kohler & Spreng, 1995], while *slicing* approach for the same is tried for curvilinear objects [Sacks & Bajaj, 1998] & [Sacks, 1999]. Nonetheless, various intricacies of the global c-space mapping techniques for a robot under static environment have been surveyed to a good extent [Wise & Bowyer, 2000]. Although the theoretical paradigms of c-space technique for solving *find-path* problem have been largely addressed in the above literature vis-à-vis a few more [Brooks, 1983], [Red & Truong-Cao, 1985], [Perez', 1987], [Hasegawa & Terasaki, 1988], [Curto & Monero, 1997], the bulging question of tackling collision detection under a typical manufacturing scenario, cluttered with real-life multi-featured obstacles remains largely unattended.

Survey reports on motion planning of robots in general, have been presented, with special reference to path planning problems of lower dimensionality [Schwartz & Sharir, 1988] & [Hwang & Ahuja, 1992]. The find-path problem under sufficiently cluttered environment has been studied with several customized models, such as using distance function [Gilbert & Johnson, 1985], probabilistic function [Jun & Shin, 1988], time-optimized function [Slotine & Yang, 1989], shape alteration paradigms [Lumelsky & Sun, 1990a] and sensorized stochastic method [Acar et al, 2003]. Even, novel *path transform function* for guiding the search for find-path in 2D is reported [Zelinsky, 1994], while the same for manipulators with higher degrees-of-freedom is also described [Ralli & Hirzinger, 1996]. All these treatises are appreciated from the context of theoretical estimation, but lacks in simulating all kinds of polyhedral obstacles.

Based on the c-space mapping, algorithmic path planning in 2D using *visibility* principle is studied [Fu & Liu, 1990], followed by exhaustive theoretical analysis on visibility maps [Campbell & Higgins, 1991]. However, issues regarding computational complexity involved in developing a typical visibility graph, which is O (n^2), 'n' being the total number of vertices in the map, is analyzed earlier [Welzl, 1985]. The concept of *M-line*[1] and its uniqueness in generating near-optimal solutions against heuristic-based search algorithms has also been examined [Lumelsky & Sun, 1990b].

Several researchers have reviewed the facets of path planning problem in a typical spatial manifold. A majority of these models are nothing but extrapolation of proven 2D techniques in 3D space [Khouri & Stelson, 1989], [Yu & Gupta, 2004] & [Sachs et al, 2004]. However, new methods for the generation of c-space in such cases (i.e. spatial) have been exploited too [Brost, 1989], [Bajaj & Kim, 1990] & [Verwer, 1990]. Customized solution for rapid computation of c-space obstacles has been addressed [Branicky & Newman, 1990], using geometric properties of collision detection between *known* static obstacles and the manipulator body, while sub-space method is being utilized in this regard [Red et al, 1987]. The usefulness of several new algorithms using v-graph technique has been demonstrated in spatial robotic workspace [Roy, 2005].

It may be mentioned at this juncture with reference to the citations above, that, although celebrated, a distinct methodology of using c-space mapping for higher dimensional robots as well as in spatial workspace is yet to be tuned. Our approach essentially calls on this lacuna of the earlier researches. We proclaim our novelty in adding new facets to the problem in a generic way, like: a] *rationalizing* configuration space mapping for *higher dimensional* (e.g. 7 or 8 degrees-of-freedom) *robots*; b] *preferential selection* of joint-variables for configuration space plots in 2D; c] extension of 2D path planning algorithm in 3D through *slicing technique* (creation, validation & assimilation of c-space slices) and d] *searching* collision-free path in 3D, using novel *visibility map-based algorithm*.

---

[1] Mean Line, as referred in the literature concerning the visibility graph-based path planning of robots.

The paper has been organized in six sections. The facets of our proposition towards configuration space maps in 3D are discussed in the next section. Section 3 delineates the c-space mapping algorithms, with the logistics and analytical models. The features of the path planning metrics and the algorithm in particular, using the concept of visibility graph, have been reported in section 4. Both 2D and spatial workspaces have been postulated, with an insight towards the analytical modeling, in respective cases alongwith test results. Section 5 presents the case study of robot path planning. Finally section 6 concludes the paper.

2. Configuration space map in 3D space: Our proposition

2.1 Modeling of robot workspace

The robotic environment is modeled through *discretization* of the 3D space into a number of 2D planes (Cartesian workspace), corresponding to a finite range of *waist* /base rotation of the robot[2]. Thus, modeling has been attempted with the sectional view of the obstacles in 2D plane.

The obstacles are considered to be *regular*, i.e. having finite shape and size with standard geometrical features with known vertices in Cartesian co-ordinates. For example, obstacles with shapes such as cube, rectangular paralleopiped, trapezoid, sphere, right circular cylinder, right pyramid etc. have been selected (as primitives) for modeling the environment. A complex obstacle has been modeled as a Boolean combination of these primitives, to have polygonal convex shape preferably. However, concave obstacles can also be used in the algorithms by approximating those to the nearest convex shapes, after considering their 'convex hulls' (polytones). Irregular-shaped obstacles have also been modeled by considering their envelopes to be of convex shapes. Circular obstacles have been approximated to the nearest squares circumscribing the original circles, thereby possessing *pseudo-vertices*.

Features of the developed technique, namely, "Slicing Method", are: i] alongwith shoulder, elbow and wrist (pitch only) rotations, waist rotation of the robot is considered, which is guided by a finite range vis-à-vis a finite resolution; ii] the entire 3D workspace is divided into a number of 2D planes, according to the number of 'segments' of the waist rotation; iii] for every fixed angle of rotation of the waist, a 2D plane is to be constructed, where all other variables like shoulder, elbow and wrist pitch movements are possible; iv] corresponding to each of the 2D slices of the workspace, either one obstacle entirely or a part of it will be generated, depending on the value of the resolution chosen for waist rotation.

Corresponding to each slice, one c-space map (considering only two joint variables at a time) is to be developed and likewise, several maps will be obtained for all the remaining slices. The final combination of the colliding joint variable values will be the union of all those sets of the values for each slice. Nevertheless, the process of computation can be simplified by taking some finite number of slices, e.g. four to five planes. Figure 1 pictorially illustrates the above-mentioned postulation, wherein the robotic workspace consists of various categories of obstacles, like regular geometry (e.g. obstacle 'A', 'B' & 'C') and integrated geometry[3] (e.g. obstacle 'D' & 'E').

---

[2] Base rotation is earmarked for articulated robots, whereas suitable angular divisions of the entire planar area, i.e. 360^0 are considered for robots with non-revolute joints (e.g. prismatic).

[3] Boolean combination of regular geometries is considered.

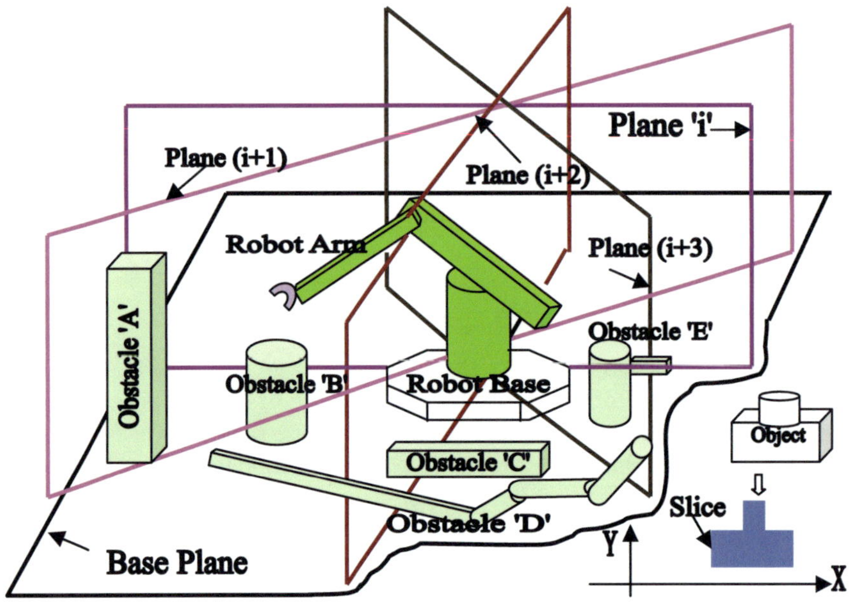

Fig. 1. Schematic view of 'Slicing Model' for a congested spatial robotic environment

By knowing the intercept co-ordinates for each slice, an equivalent 2D *slice workspace* is developed; simply by projecting those intercept lines. Obviously the height of the obstacle will now play a vital role and the projecting length will be equal to the height of the obstacle. In a similar manner, obstacles with varying height (say, slant-top type) can also be considered, with differential length of projection. As before, irregular-shaped obstacles can be approximated by means of some standard regular shape, either uniform or varying height, using the same model.
The total number of configuration space plots for the entire cluttered environment will depend on the number of slices each obstacle has and also thereby the average number of slices obtained. Since each of those sliced c-space will represent obstacle geometries, fully or partially, it is important to label the nodes of the obstacle-slices so produced. In general, if a particular obstacle has got 'k' slices, having 'n' nodes each, then a generalized node of that obstacle will be labeled as, 'n_k'. However, to avoid ambiguity, 'k' is considered alphabetic only. Figure 2 shows a representative obstacle with slices, where node '3_b' signifies the third node of the $b^{th.}$ slice, which is incidentally the second slice of the obstacle.

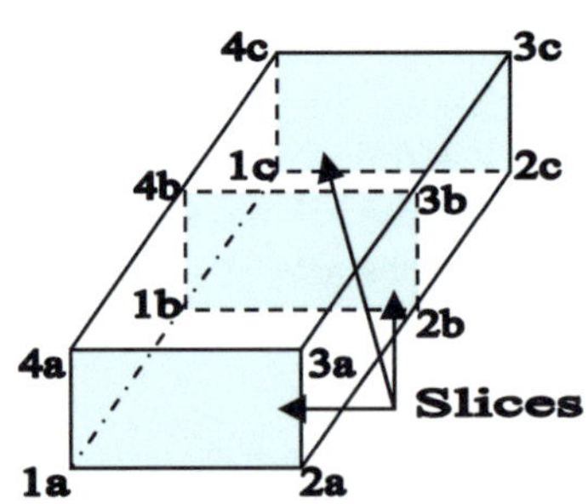

Fig. 2. Node numbering thematic for sliced obstacles

2.2 Paradigms of the C-space mapping algorithms in 2D *sliced* workspace

In the present work, *sliced* c-space maps have been generated considering a two degrees-of-freedom revolute type manipulator having finite dimensions (refer fig. 3) and an environment cluttered with polygonal obstacles. Both manipulator links and obstacles are represented as convex or concave polygons[4].

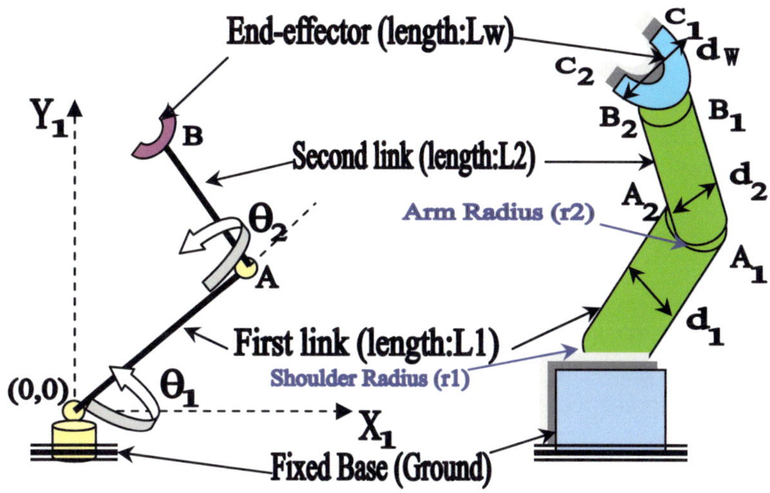

Fig. 3. Representative schematics of a two-link manipulator with revolute joints

The obstacles are considered to be *regular* in shape with fixed dimensions, having a well-defined shape (sectional view) in 2D, preferably convex, for easier calculations. This has been made purposefully as in most of the manufacturing and/or shop-floor activities *geometric* objects are being handled by the robot, for example, loading and unloading of components to/from the machine, handling of semi-finished components between machines, storage and retrieval of finished components into bins etc. The philosophy behind these mapping algorithms is to consider each complex obstacle as a boolean combination of various primitives, viz,. *'Point', 'Line'* and *'Circle'*. That is to say, if the obstacle is theoretically considered as a 'point', 'line' or 'circle' in shape in 2D, then colliding angle of the robot link(s) with those will be obtained and C-space maps can be drawn there from. These algorithms can also be applied for concave objects by considering the 'convex hull' of those and proceeding in the same manner taking that as the *new* obstacle. Similarly, irregular shaped objects can also be tackled with these models, in which *envelope* of the object is to be considered to get the nearest convex shape. Obviously accuracy of the results will suffer to some extent by this approximation, but it would be a reasonable solution for practical situations.

3. Details of the C-space mapping algorithms developed

3.1 Overview of the mapping algorithms

3.1.1 C-space transformation of "POINT"

This algorithm gives the C-space data for an obstacle, considered theoretically as a *point* in Cartesian space. The robot with line representation is being considered here. (refer fig.3).

[4] Concave obstacles are modeled as a combination of several convex polygons.

Algorithm:

1. Input robot base co-ordinates, link lengths, the specified *point*, range of joint-angles & angular resolution.
2. Calculate the distance of the *point* from robot base.
3. Initialize the loop with iteration i=1.
4. Check whether the first link is colliding.
5. Calculate the positional details of the first link (i.e. under colliding conditions), if step 4 is true.
6. Check the collision with the second link, if step 4 is false.
7. Calculate the colliding details of the second link, if step 6 is true.
8. Output the colliding angles for suitable cases.
9. i=i +1.
10. Continue till all combinations of joint - angles are checked.

3.1.2 C-space transformation of "LINE"

Here the obstacle has been considered as a regular polygon, bounded by several straight line-segments, as 'edges'. The algorithm is valid for obstacles having rectangle, square, triangle, trapezium etc. shaped cross-section in the vertical plane.

3.1.3 C-space transformation of "CIRCLE"

This algorithm for collision detection tackles the spherical obstacles with circular cross-section in the vertical plane. Various possible colliding conditions of the circular obstacle with the robot link(s) are depicted in fig. 4. It depends entirely on the location of the obstacle(s) with respect to the location of the robot in the workspace.

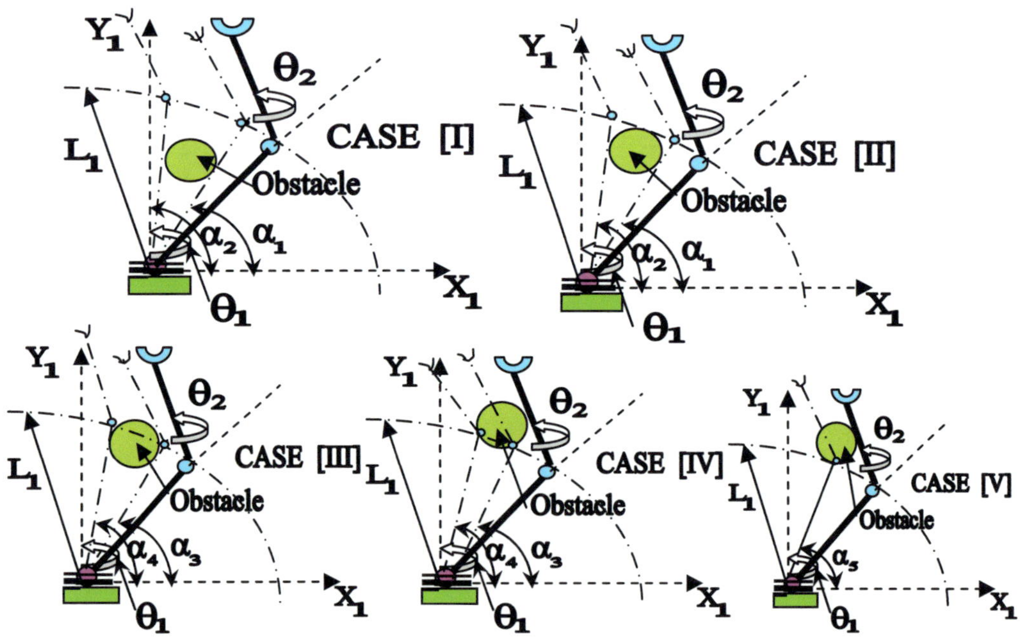

Fig. 4. Various possible colliding combinations of a two-link robot with circular obstacle

Figure 4 shows five different cases of collision, considering only the first link. However, the paradigm is valid for subsequent links also. These cases are:
Case I: Obstacle is fully within the range of the first link.
Case II: Obstacle is within the first link's range, touching the *range circle* internally.
Case III: Obstacle is collidable by the first link, with its centre inside the range of the first link.
Case IV: Same as before, but centre is outside the range of the first link.
Case V: Obstacle is touching the range circle of the first link externally.

3.1.4 C-space transformation with finite dimensions of the robot

Modifications of the previous algorithms for *POINT*, *LINE* and *CIRCLE* obstacles have been considered with finite dimensions of the robot arms (refer fig. 3). Also, planar 3-link manipulator is considered now, where the third link is nothing but the end-effector. Since planar movements are taken into account, only pitch motion of the wrist is considered along with shoulder and elbow rotations. The exhaustive list of input parameters for these cases will be as follows, viz. (i) Robot base co-ordinates (x_b, y_b); (ii) Length of the upper arm or shoulder (l_1); (iii) Length of the fore arm or elbow (l_2); (iv) Length of the end-effector or *wrist* (l_w); (v) Width of the upper arm (d_1); (vi) Width of the fore arm (d_2); (vii) Width of the end-effector (d_w); (viii) Radii of curvature for upper and fore arm (r_1 & r_2 respectively); (ix) The co-ordinates of the *Point*: (x_1, y_1) or *Line*: [(x_1, y_1) & (x_2, y_2) as end - points] or *Circle*: [centre at (x_c, y_c) & radius : 'r'].

3.2 Analytical model of the mapping algorithms

The analytical models of various C-space mapping algorithms, described earlier, have been grouped into two categories, viz. (a) Model for *LINE* obstacles and (b) Model for *CIRCLE* obstacles. These are being described below.

3.2.1 Model for LINE obstacles

The ideation of collision detection phenomena for *Line* obstacle is based on the intersection of the line- segments in 2D considering only the kinematic chain of the manipulator. The positional information, i.e. co -ordinates (x_k, y_k) of the manipulator joints can be generalized as,

$$[x_k, y_k]^T = [x_b, y_b]^T + [\sum_{k=1}^{k=n} l_k \, Cos(\sum_{j=1}^{j=k} \theta_j), \sum_{k=1}^{k=n} l_k \, Sin(\sum_{j=1}^{j=k} \theta_j)]^T$$

$$\forall\, k = 1,2,3,\ldots\ldots,n \;\&\; \forall\, j = 1,2,\ldots\ldots, k \qquad (1)$$

where,
$[x_b, y_b]^T$: Robot base co - ordinate vector in Newtonian frame of reference;
l_k : k th. link - length of the manipulator;
θ_j : j th. joint - angle of the manipulator.
The slope of the *line* (i.e. the edge of the obstacle) with (x_1, y_1) & (x_2, y_2) as end-points is given by,

$$m_0 = |(y_2 - y_1)| / |(x_2 - x_1)| = |\Delta y / \Delta x| \qquad (2)$$

Hence, the co - ordinates of the intersection point between the obstacle edge(s) and the robot link(s) are,

$$x_{int\_k} = (y_k - y_1 - m_k x_k + m_0 x_1) / (m_0 - m_k) \tag{3a}$$

$$y_{int\_k} = [m_0 m_k (x_k - x_1) - m_0 y_k + m_k y_1] / (m_k - m_0) \tag{3b}$$

where,
$[x_{int\_k} , y_{int\_k}]^T$: The intersection point vector for the k $^{th.}$ robot link with the *Line* and
m_k : The slope of the k $^{th.}$ robot link.
For a 3-link planar revolute manipulator, we have, therefore,

$$m_1 = \tan \theta_{1i} ,\text{where } \theta_{1i} \in [\theta_{1\_min} , \theta 1_{\_max}]$$

and

$$m_2 = \tan (\theta_{1i} + \theta_{2j}), \text{ where } \theta_{2j} \in [\theta_{2\_min} , \theta_{2\_max}]$$

with θ_{1i} as defined earlier.
The above model can be extended likewise, considering finite dimension of the manipulator, i.e. having widths of the arms, viz. $\{ d_k \}$.
Nonetheless, considering finite dimensions, the generalized co-ordinates of the manipulator joints can be evaluated from,

$$[x_{Ak}, y_{Ak}]^T = [x_b, y_b]^T + [\sum_{k=1}^{k=n} l_k \text{Cos} (\sum_{j=1}^{j=k} \theta_j) , \sum_{k=1}^{k=n} l_k \text{Sin} (\sum_{j=1}^{j=k} \theta_j)]^T$$
$$+ [d_k/2 \text{ Sin} (\sum_{j=1}^{j=k} \theta_j) , - d_k/2 \text{ Cos} (\sum_{j=1}^{j=k} \theta_j)]^T$$

$$\forall k = 1,2,3,..............,n \;\&\; \forall j= 1,2,..........,k \tag{4}$$

and,

$$[x_{Bk}, y_{Bk}]^T = [x_b, y_b]^T + [\sum_{k=1}^{k=n} l_k \text{Cos} (\sum_{j=1}^{j=k} \theta_j) , \sum_{k=1}^{k=n} l_k \text{Sin} (\sum_{j=1}^{j=k} \theta_j)]^T$$
$$+[- d_k/2 \text{ Sin} (\sum_{j=1}^{j=k} \theta_j) , d_k/2 \text{ Cos} (\sum_{j=1}^{j=k} \theta_j)]^T$$

$$\forall k = 1,2,3,..............,n \;\&\; \forall j= 1,2,..........,k \tag{5}$$

Hence, the co-ordinates of the intersecting point(s) between the robot arm(s) and the *edges* of the obstacle(s) become,

$$x_{intA\_k} = (y_{Ak} - y_1 - m_k x_{Ak} + m_0 x_1) / (m_0 - m_k); \tag{6a}$$

$$y_{intA\_k} = [m_0 m_k (x_{Ak} - x_1) - m_0 y_{Ak} + m_k y_1] / (m_k - m_0); \tag{6b}$$

$$x_{intB\_k} = (y_{Bk} - y_1 - m_k x_{Bk} + m_0 x_1) / (m_0 - m_k); \tag{6c}$$

$$y_{intB\_k} = [\, m_0\, m_k\, (\, x_{Bk} - x_1\,) - m_0\, y_{Bk} + m_k\, y_1\,] \,/\, (\, m_k - m_0\,); \tag{6d}$$

considering two possible collisions per arm at the most.

3.2.2 Model for CIRCLE obstacles

With reference to fig. 4, let the following nomenclatures be defined,

(x_b, y_b): Robot base co-ordinates in Newtonian frame;
l_1 & l_2: Lengths of the first and second link of the robot respectively;
(x_c, y_c): Co-ordinates of the centre of the 'circle' obstacle and
r : Radius of the 'circle'.

Let,

$$d = [\, (\, x_c - x_b\,)^2 + (\, y_c - y_b\,)^2\,]^{1/2} \tag{7}$$

If collision is detected with the first link of the robot, then the range of colliding angles for case I & II (i.e. α_1 & α_2) and for case III & IV (i.e. α_3 & α_4) will be evaluated as shown below,

$$\alpha_{2,1} = \tan^{-1} [(\, y_c - y_b\,) \,/\, (\, x_c - x_b\,)\,] \pm \tan^{-1} [\, r \,/\, (\, d^2 - r^2\,)^{1/2}\,] \tag{8}$$

$$\alpha_{4,3} = \tan^{-1} [(\, y_c - y_b\,) \,/\, (\, x_c - x_b\,)\,] \pm 2 \tan^{-1} [\, (\, s - l_1\,)\, (\, s - d\,) \,/\, s\, (\, s - r\,)\,]^{1/2} \tag{9}$$

where,

$$2\, s = (\, l_1 + d + r\,) \tag{10}$$

Obviously, only one colliding angle, viz. α_5 will be obtained with case V, i.e.

$$\alpha_5 = \tan^{-1} [(\, y_c - y_b\,) \,/\, (\, x_c - x_b\,)\,] \tag{11}$$

When the collision occurs with the second link, i.e. all the values of the first joint-angle are collidable, the ranges for collision will be obtained as given below.
The co-ordinates of the start point of the second link, which serves as the *instantaneous base* of the robot, are given by,

$$[\, x_b', y_b'\,]^T = [\, x_b, y_b\,]^T + [\, l_1 \cos\theta_1, l_1 \sin\theta_1\,]^T \tag{12}$$

The colliding range for the second link is between θ_{2S} and θ_{2f} against case I & II, where,

$$\theta_{2S} = \beta_1 - \theta_{1i} \text{ and } \theta_{2f} = \beta_2 - \theta_{1i},\ \forall\, \theta_{1i}, \text{ where } \theta_{1\_min} \le \theta_{1i} \le \theta_{1\_max} \tag{13}$$

and,

$$\beta_{2.1} = \tan^{-1} [(\, y_c - y_b\,) \,/\, (\, x_c - x_b\,)\,] \pm \tan^{-1} (\, r \,/\, p\,) \tag{14}$$

where,

$$p = (\, h^2 - r^2\,)^{1/2} \tag{15}$$

and,

$$h = [\, (x_c - x_b'\,)^2 + (\, y_c - y_b'\,)^2\,]^{1/2} \tag{16}$$

For case III & IV, the colliding range will be θ_{3S} to θ_{3f}, which can be evaluated as,

$$\theta_{3S} = \beta_3 - \theta_{1i} \text{ and } \theta_{3f} = \beta_4 - \theta_{1i}, \forall \theta_{1i}, \text{ where } \theta_{1i} \in [\theta_{1\_min}, \theta_{1\_max}] \quad (17)$$

and,

$$\beta_{4,3} = \tan^{-1}[(y_c - y_b') / (x_c - x_b')] \pm 2\tan^{-1}[(s' - l_2)(s' - h) / s'(s' - r)]^{1/2} \quad (18)$$

where,

$$2s' = (l_2 + h + r) \quad (19)$$

For case V, the particular formidable value of the joint-angle is,

$$\theta_4 = \tan^{-1}[(y_c - y_b') / (x_c - x_b') - \theta_{1i} \quad (20)$$

The above equations need to be altered for collision checking with finite link dimensions of the manipulator, considering r1 and r_2 as the radii of curvature of the upper arm and fore arm respectively (refer fig. 3). The modifications required are: i] 'l_1' is to be replaced by l_u (= $l_1 + r_1$); ii] 'l_2' is to be replaced by l_f (= $l_2 + r_2$) and iii] 'r' is to be replaced by $r_{nj} = r + d_j/2$, $\forall$ j = 1,2, 3 corresponding to collision with upper arm, fore arm and the end-effector.

3.3 Illustrations using the developed algorithms

The c-space mapping algorithms have been tested with two different robot workspaces in 2D, as detailed below. Technical details of the robot under consideration for these workspaces are highlighted in Table 1.

Type of Robot Considered	Revolute
No. of Links	2
No. of Degrees -of- Freedom	2
Length of the Links	First Link: 5 units; Second Link: 4 units
Co-ordinates of the Robot Base	$x_b = 5$; $y_b = 5$
Ranges of Rotation of the Joints (Anticlockwise)	Case I: For Non-circular Polyhedral Obstacles Joint-angle 1: 0 to 360 deg. Joint-angle 2: 0 to 260 deg. Case II: For Circular Obstacles Joint-angle 1: -40 to 240 deg. Joint-angle 2: -180 to 180 deg.
Resolution of Joint Rotation	5 deg. (for both joints)

Table 1. Technical Features of the Robot Under Consideration

Figure 5 presents a 2D environment with non-circular polygonal obstacles with a revolute type robot located in-between.

After obtaining the relevant c-space data, various plots of joint-angle 1 vs. joint-angle 2 are made. It is to be noted that the final data-points are those, which are common values of formidable angles for the entire obstacle. Obviously, the points, which are inside or on the closed boundary of the curves, are 'collidable' combinations, and, hence, those should not be attempted for robot path planning.

Another case is studied, as shown in fig. 6, with circular obstacles only. There is a distinct difference in the appearance in the C-space maps between obstacles when collision occurs with the first as constrained with the same for the second link.

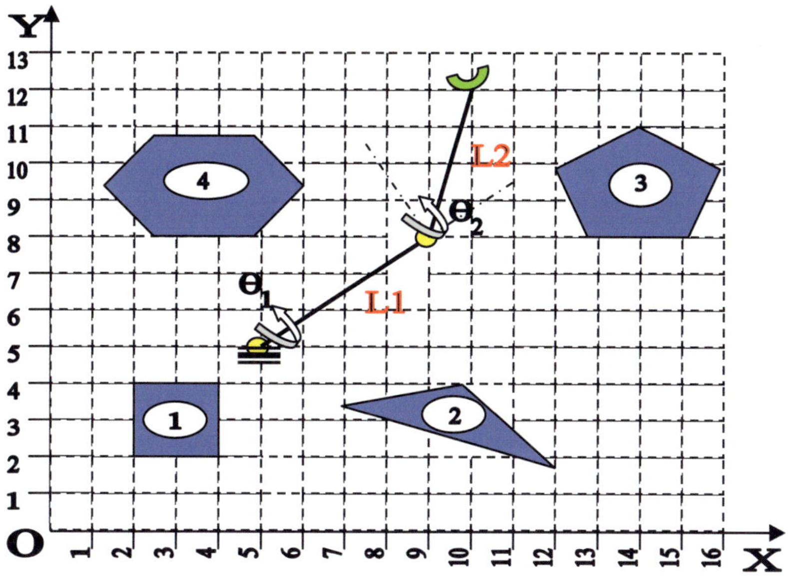

Fig. 5. A representative 2D environment congested with non-circular polygonal obstacles

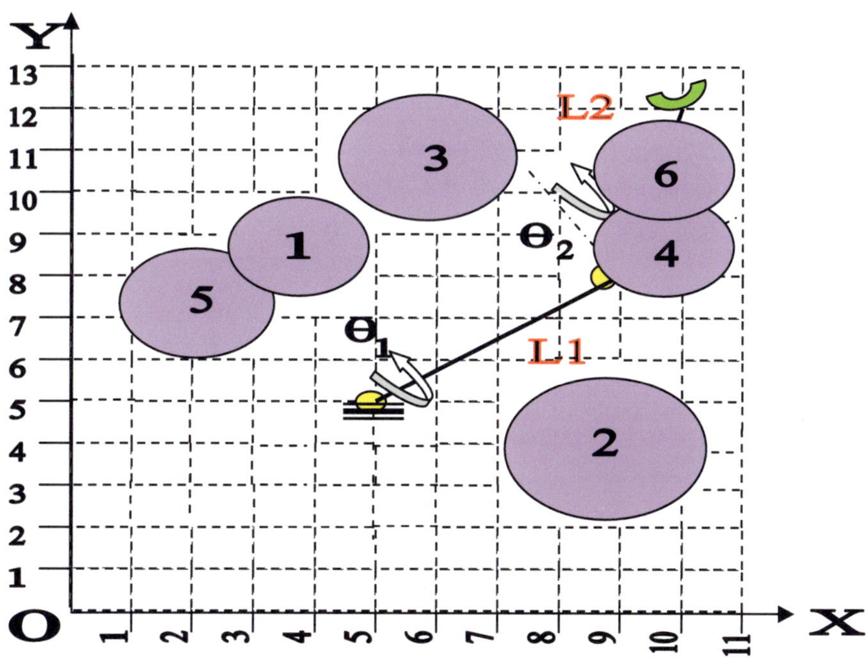

Fig. 6. A representative 2-D environment filled with circular obstacles

Figures 7 and 8 show the final c-space for the above two environments.

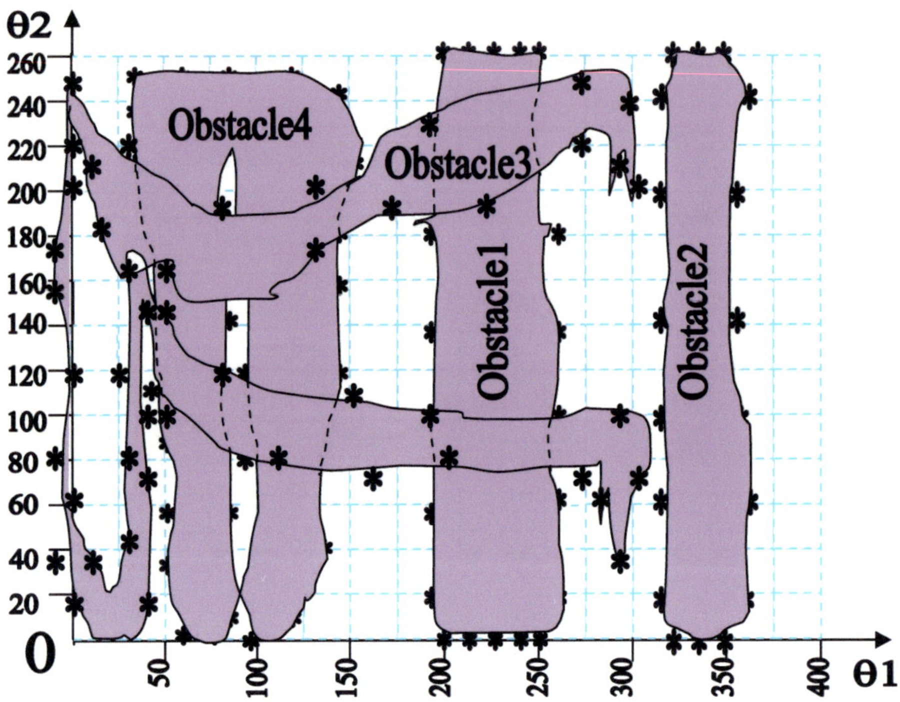

Fig. 7. Final c-space mapping for the environment filled with non-circular polygonal obstacles

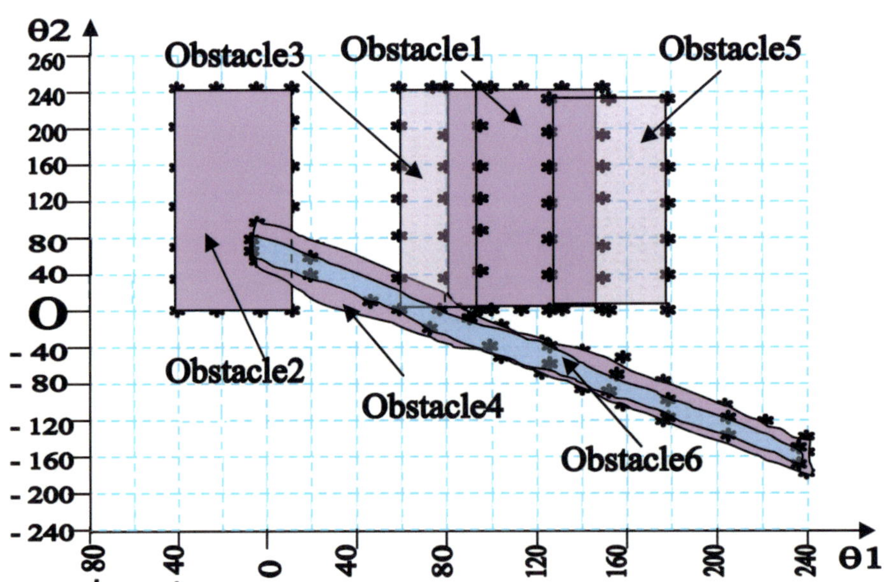

Fig. 8. Final c-space mapping for the environment congested with circular obstacles

3.4 C-space maps for higher dimensionality

The development of c-space is relatively simpler while we have two degrees-of-freedom robotic manipulators. As described in earlier sections, irrespective of the nature of the environment, we can generate simple planar maps, corresponding to the variations in the joint-angles (in case of revolute robots). Thus the mapping between task space and c-space is truly mathematical and involves computationable solutions for inverse kinematics routines. The procedure of generating c-space can be extrapolated to three degrees-of-freedom robots at most, wherein we get 3D plot, i.e. mathematically speaking, *c-space surface*. However, this procedure can't be applied to higher dimensional robots, having degrees-of-freedom more than three. In fact, c-space surface of dimensions greater than three is unrealizable, although it is quite common to have such robots in practice amidst cluttered environment. For example, let us take the case of a workspace for a seven degrees-of-freedom articulated robot, as depicted in fig. 9. Here we need to consider variations in each of the seven joint-angles, viz. θ_1, θ_2,……, θ_7 (the last two degrees-of-freedoms are attributed to the wrist rotations) towards avoiding collision with the obstacles.

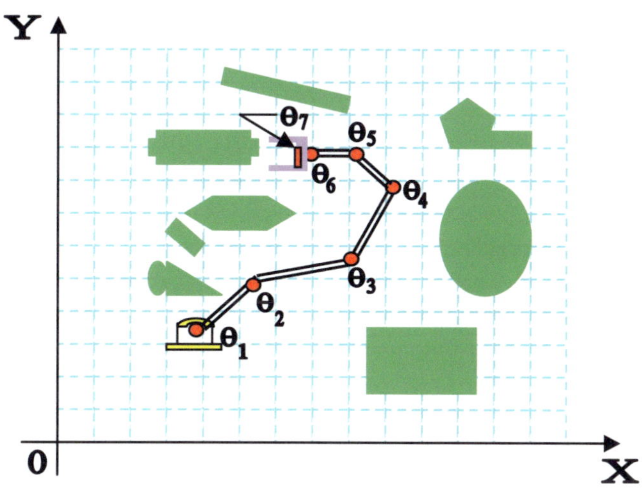

Fig. 9. A representative cluttered environment with seven degrees-of-freedom revolute robot

So, the question arises as how can we tackle this problem of realizing higher dimensionality of c-space mapping. Hence it is a clear case of building *composite c-space map*, with proper characterization of null space. We propose a model for this mapping in higher dimensionality as detailed below.

3.4.1 Lemma

1. Identify the degrees-of-freedom of the robot ['n'] and notify those.
2. The robot is conceptualized as a serial chain of micro-robots of two degrees-of-freedom each.
3. We will consider a total of 'k' planar c-space plots, where k = n/2 if 'n' is even and k = (n+1)/2 if 'n' is odd.
4. If 'n' is even, then the pairs for the planar c-space plots will be: [q_1 - q_2], [q_3 - q_4],……[q_{n-1} - q_n], where 'q' denotes the generalized joint-variable of the manipulator.

5. If 'n' is odd, then the pairs for the planar c-space plots will be: $[q_1 - q_2]$, $[q_3 - q_4]$,......$[q_{n-2} - q_{n-1}]$, $[q_{n-1} - q_n]$.
6. In a way, we are considering several *virtual 2-link mini manipulators,* located at the respective joints of the original manipulator.
7. Out of the plots so generated, select the *most significant* c-space map.
8. One way of accessing the most significant c-space map is to consider finite measurement of the planar area of the c-space. A larger area automatically indicates more complex dynamics of the joint-variables so far as the collision avoidance is concerned.
9. Alternatively, significant c-space plots will be those having multiple disjointed loops, i.e. regions of formidable area. Individually the regions may be of smaller area, but the multiplicity of their occurrence adds complexity to the scenario.
10. Once the most significant c-space map is selected, the locations corresponding to 'S' and 'G' are to be affixed in that plot. This will be achieved using inverse kinematics routine from 'S'(x,y) and 'G' (x,y).
11. For the most significant plot so obtained, all joint-variables, except the two used in the plot will be *constant*. For example, if $[q_3 - q_4]$ plot is the most significant one, then q_1, q_2,......q_{n-1}, q_n are constant except q_3 and q_4.
12. In general, if $[q_i - q_j]$ plot be the most significant, then the set $\{q_1, q_2, \ldots\ldots q_{n-1}, q_n\}$, except $[q_i - q_j]$, will be constant. And, the value of the set $\{q_1, q_2, \ldots\ldots, q_{i-1}\}$ will be ascertained by the inverse kinematic solution of 'S' while the other set, $\{q_{j+1}, q_{j+2}, \ldots\ldots, q_n\}$ will be determined by the inverse kinematic solution of 'G'.

3.4.2 Schematic of the model

Let us take an example of a seven degrees-of-freedom articulated robot, similar to one illustrated in fig. 9. According to the lemma proposed in 3.4.1, there will be four planar c-space plots, namely, $[\theta_1 -- \theta_2]$, $[\theta_3 -- \theta_4]$, $[\theta_5 -- \theta_6]$ and $[\theta_6 -- \theta_7]$. Figure 10 shows a sample view of these segmental c-space maps.

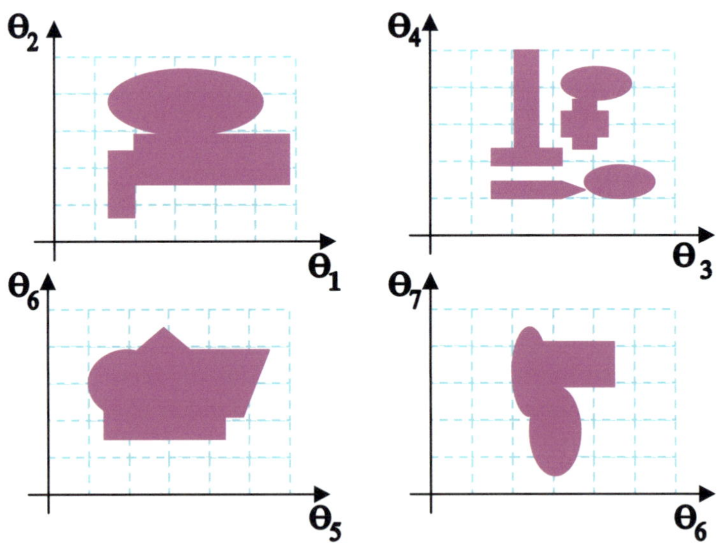

Fig. 10. Sample view of the composite C-space map for a seven degrees-of-freedom robot

As it may be apparent from fig. 10, either [θ_1 -- θ_2] or [θ_3 -- θ_4] plot can be significant, considering *larger area* or *presence of multiple loops* criterion (refer serial no. 8 & 9 of 3.4.1).

3.4.3 Generation of C-space plots: Concept of equivalent circle

In order to compute c-space data points for any particular combination of consecutive joint-variable pair for the higher dimensional robot, we would use a new concept, viz. the formulation of *Equivalent Circle* at the end of amidst the pair of links. Since we are considering *virtual two-link mini-manipulators* for the generation of c-space maps in pair, we would theoretically divide the links in two groups. The links, directly related to the generation of the specific c-space map, are termed as *active links*, while the others are known as *dummy links*. The philosophy of this equivalent circle is to re-represent the higher dimensional manipulator with only the active links and the joints therein, interfaced with circular zone(s) either at the bottom of the first active link or at the tip of the second active link. In general, the equivalent circles are constructed considering full rotational freedom of all the dummy links, located before / after the active links.

For example, if we wish to generate [θ_1 -- θ_2] plot for the seven d.o.f. manipulator, then the *equivalent circle* alias *equivalent formidable zone* is to be constructed adjacent to the end the second link and circumscribing the remaining links. Figure 11 schematically presents the concept of *equivalent formidable zone*, with first two links as active links for a seven d.o.f. manipulator.

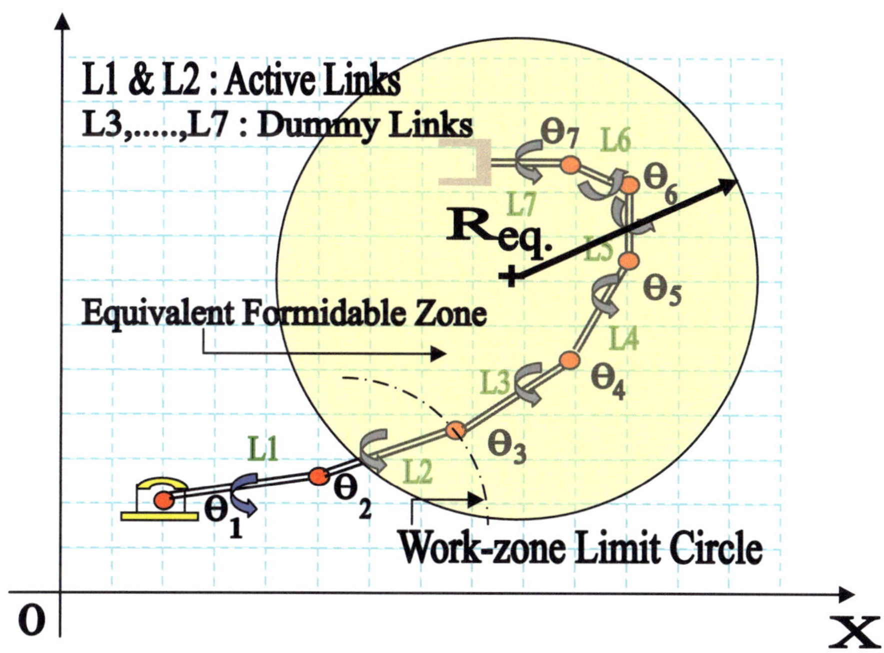

Fig. 11. Schematic view of equivalent formidable zone for a seven d.o.f. manipulator

However it is possible to have two *equivalent formidable zones* in cases where some intermediate links are considered for c-space plots. For example, if the third & fourth links of the manipulator become active links, then there will be two formidable zones, as illustrated in fig. 12. Of course, as per this proposition, there can't be more than two formidable zones for any higher dimensional manipulator.

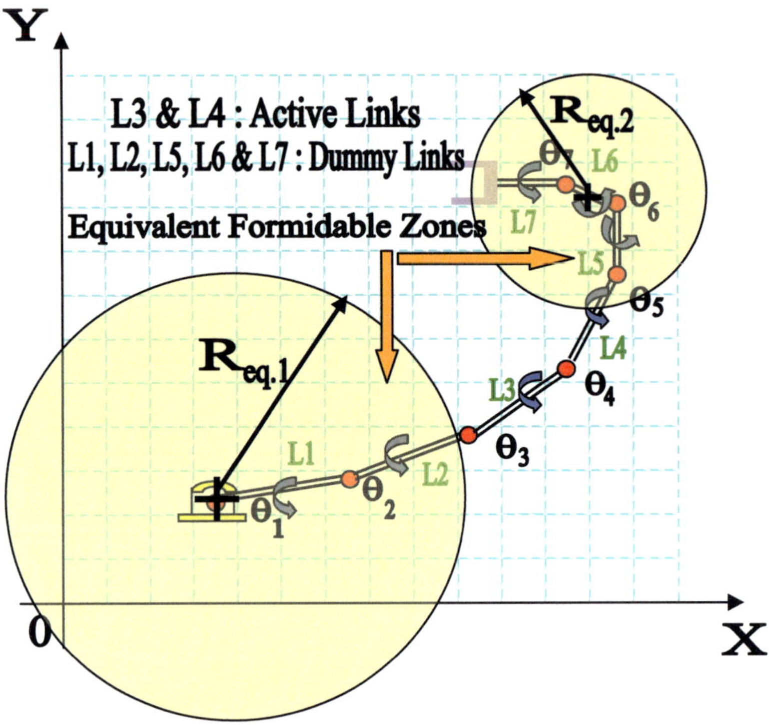

Fig. 12. Occurrence of two equivalent formidable zones for a seven d.o.f. manipulator

It is essential to locate the center of the *equivalent circle* vis-à-vis its radius (equivalent radius, $R_{eq.}$), in order to start computing for colliding combinations. However, the formulations for equivalent radii are not same in the two cases, as cited in figs. 11 & 12. In fact, the center of the equivalent circle, for cases wherein active links are followed by dummy links, will be at the base of the manipulator and its radius will be the summation of the lengths of the dummy links till we reach the first active link. For example, $R_{eq.\ 1}$ in fig. 12 will be the added sum of L1 & L2. Figure 13 shows the computational backup for the evaluation of the *radius* of the equivalent formidable zone / circle in this case, nomenclated as *equivalent radius [type I]*.

Although finding center and calculating equivalent radius [type I] is straight -forward, evaluation of the new *base* for the *virtual two-link robot* is critical. For example, as shown in fig. 12, we need to find out the possible location of the base for the virtual robot, comprising of L3 & L4. This has been explained in fig. 14, wherein we adopt a methodology, called *Least Path*. The least path(s) is/are the straight line-segment(s) joining the centers of equivalent circle [type I] and the obstacles in the vicinity of the virtual robot. The respective locations for the base of the virtual robot will be the point of intersection of the least path and the equivalent circle. Thus, as per fig. 14, there will be three base-points, viz. 'C_p', 'C_q' & 'C_r' corresponding to three obstacles, vide 'p', 'q' & 'r', which are situated within the limit-zone of the virtual robot with links L_k & L_{k+1}. However, this location of the base can range between two extreme points, as detailed in the inset of fig. 14. Two cases may appear here,

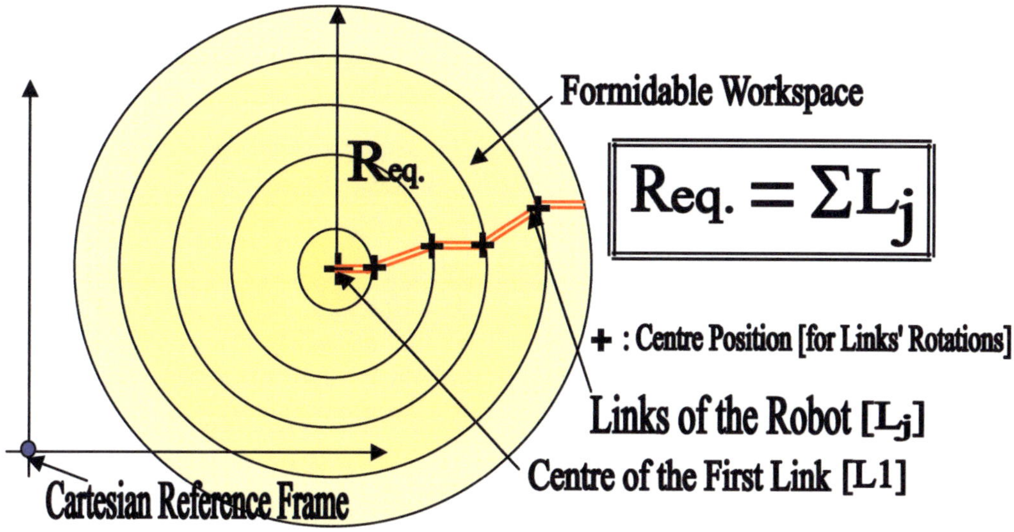

Fig. 13. Schematic showing the analytical layout for the evaluation of equivalent radius [type I]

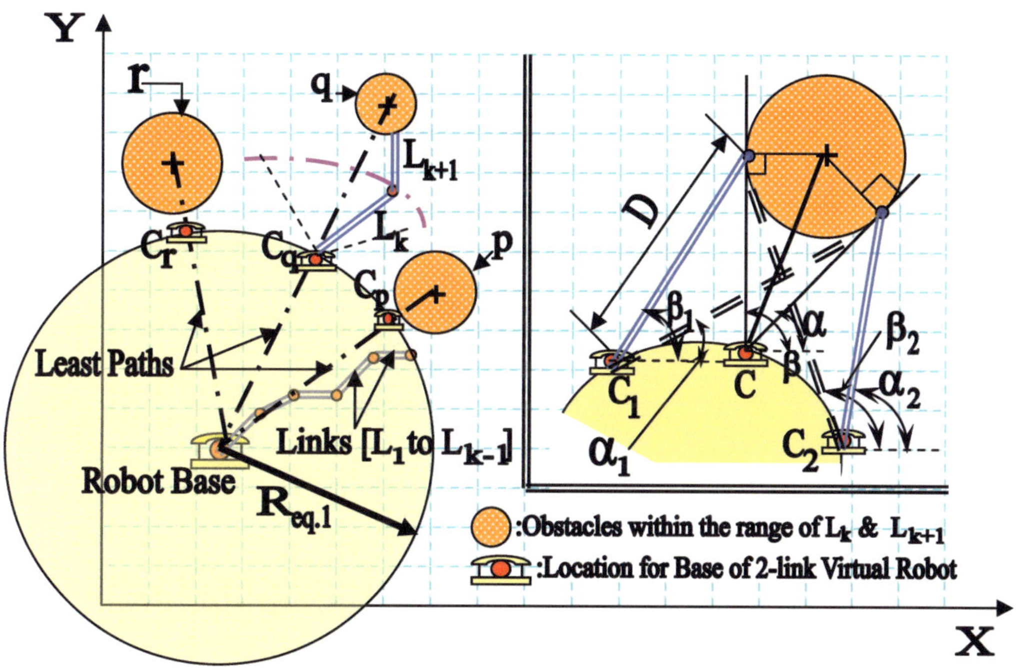

Fig. 14. Locations of the base for the two link virtual robot with respect to equivalent circle [type I]

viz. when the obstacle is a] within the range of both L_k & L_{k+1} and b] outside the range of L_k. Now, considering the first link of the virtual robot is just able to touch the obstacle we can get two extreme positions for the base, e.g. 'C_1' & 'C_2'. As explained earlier, the point 'C' is the other location for the base, situated on the least path. From geometry, we can assign 'D',

which is numerically equal to either L_k or L_{k+1}, depending upon which link is colliding with that obstacle. The collidable range of joint-angles, corresponding to 'C', 'C_1' & 'C_2' will be (β-α), (β_1-α_1) & (β_2-α_2) respectively. Thus, in general a formidable range from α_2 to β_1 should be selected for c-space mapping in (θ_k --θ_{k+1}) plot.
In contrary to this situation, the other one, namely where dummy links are followed by active links, is more intricate so far the thematic is concerned. Figure 15 explains this case of evaluating *equivalent radius [type II]*, the corresponding circular zone being *optimized* between two extremes, viz. maximum and minimum formidable zones. The minimum formidable zone is a circular space, tangent to the work-zone limit circle at 'A' while the maximum formidable zone is a semi-circular area, with two opposite extremities as 'Z_1' & 'Z_2'. Several feasible formidable zones are theoretically possible in-between, with pair of *chordal end-points* as [B_1 - B_1^*] or [B_2 - B_2^*] etc. It may be noted that all the three formidable zones, namely the minimum, maximum & optimum, share the common vertex 'V'.

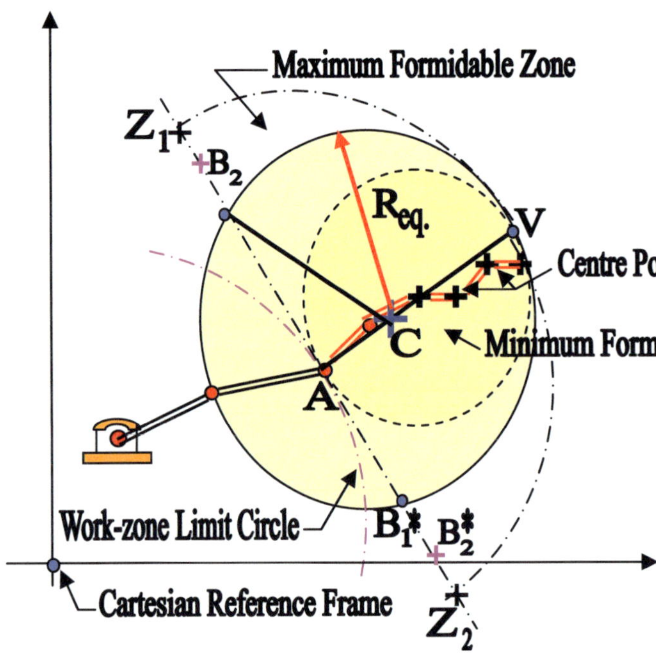

Fig. 15. Schematic showing the disposition of the equivalent formidable circle [type II]

The *equivalent radius [type II]* is evaluated using geometrical attributes, as detailed in fig. 16. Here, the points 'A', 'C' & 'C_m' represent the locations of the centers of the maximum, equivalent & minimum formidable zones respectively. As evident from the figure, the ratio between the two line-segments, viz. the semi-chordal length of the equivalent circle and the radius of the maximum formidable zone is 'k', where $0<k<1$. In-line with the numerical evaluation of '$R_{eq.}$', the location of the center, 'C' can be determined also.[5]

[5] The location of the center is determined by evaluating the length of the line-segment, AC, which is numerically equal to $[(1-k^2)/2]\Sigma L_j$ and it is also at a distance of $(k^2/2)\Sigma L_j$ from the center of the minimum formidable zone, i.e. 'C_m'.

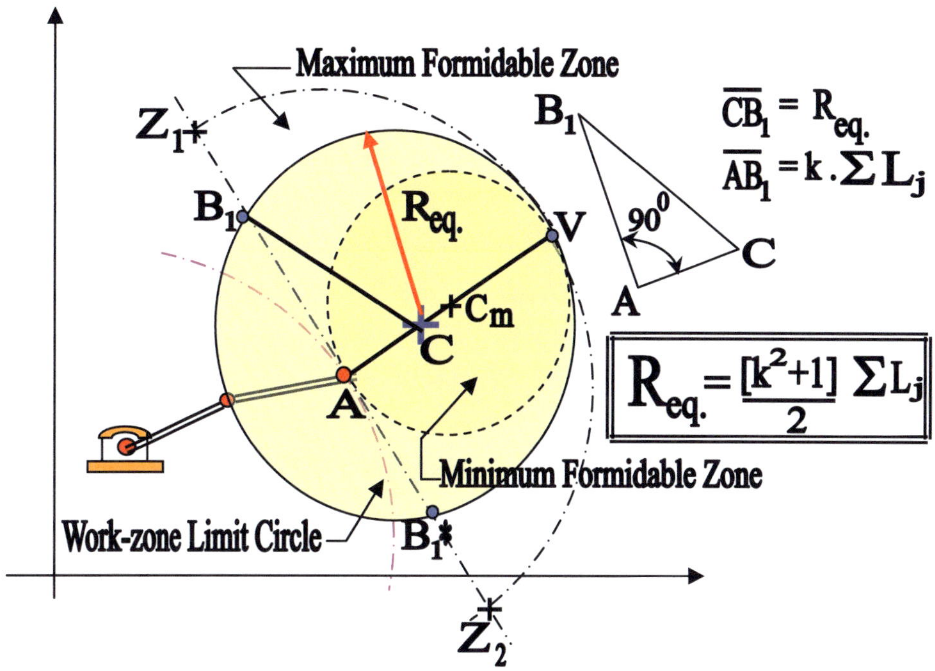

Fig. 16. Schematic showing the analytical layout for the evaluation of equivalent radius [type II]

3.5 Evaluation of C-space plots for higher dimensional robot: Example

Here we will study a specific case for a seven degrees-of-freedom robot, amidst a 2D cluttered environment as shown in fig. 17. The technical parameters of the robot, comprising link-lengths, $\{l_i, \forall i = 1,2,\ldots 7\}$and joint limits $\{\theta_i, \forall i = 1,2,\ldots 7)$, are highlighted in Table 2. Circular obstacles are considered for simplicity in computations. The locations of the respective centers and diameters of the obstacles (expressed in suitable units) are presented in Table 3.

Type of Robot Considered	Revolute
No. of Links	7
No. of Degrees -of- Freedom	7
Length of the Links [in suitable units]	l_1=15.52; l_2=14.87; l_3=13.04; l_4=12.54; l_5=9.0; l_6=5.22 & l_7=8.0
Co-ordinates of the Robot Base	$x_b = 10$; $y_b = 10$
Ranges of Rotation of the Joints (Anticlockwise)	θ_1: -20^0 to 140^0; θ_2: 0^0 to 120^0; θ_3: 0^0 to 80^0; θ_4: -5^0 to 90^0; θ_5: 10^0 to 50^0; θ_6: -5^0 to 55^0; θ_7: 5^0 to 35^0
Resolution of Joint Rotation	3 deg. (for all joints)

Table 2. Technical Facets of the Higher Dimensional Robot Under Consideration

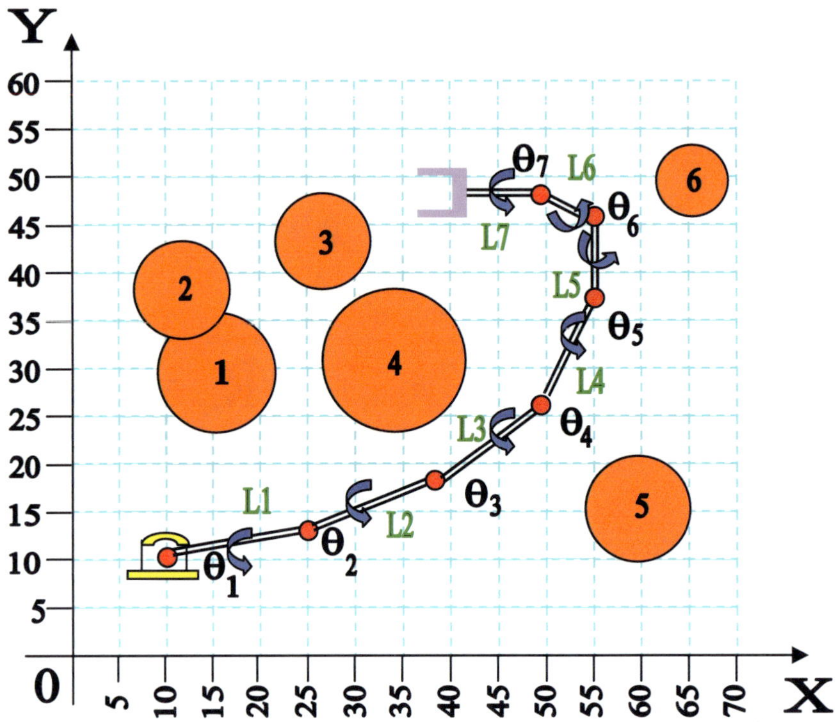

Fig. 17. Workspace layout of the seven degrees-of-freedom articulated robot

Obstacle No.	Diameter	Location of Centre
1	15.88	(x =15, y = 30)
2	13	(x = 12.5, y = 37.5)
3	12.7	(x = 27.5, y = 42.5)
4	19	(x = 35, y = 30)
5	14	(x = 60, y = 15)
6	9.53	(x = 65, y = 50)

Table 3. Obstacle Signature, as per Workspace Layout of Figure 16

Now, in this case of seven degrees-of-freedom revolute robot, we will have four different c-space plots, namely, [θ_1 -- θ_2], [θ_3 -- θ_4], [θ_5 -- θ_6] & [θ_6 -- θ_7]. All of these plots use collision-detection algorithms, described earlier, for each of the obstacles separately, taking into account the concepts of *equivalent circles*. These c-space plots are illustrated in figure 18. A gross estimate reveal that [θ_1 -- θ_2], [θ_3 -- θ_4], [θ_5 -- θ_6] & [θ_6 -- θ_7] plots occupy a planar area measuring (160x120), (80x95), (40,60) & (60x30) sq. units respectively. It is evident from fig. 18 that although complexity-wise both [θ_1 -- θ_2] and [θ_3 -- θ_4] plots are roughly at par, but the former is to be selected as the most significant c-space plot as it is also the largest in size.

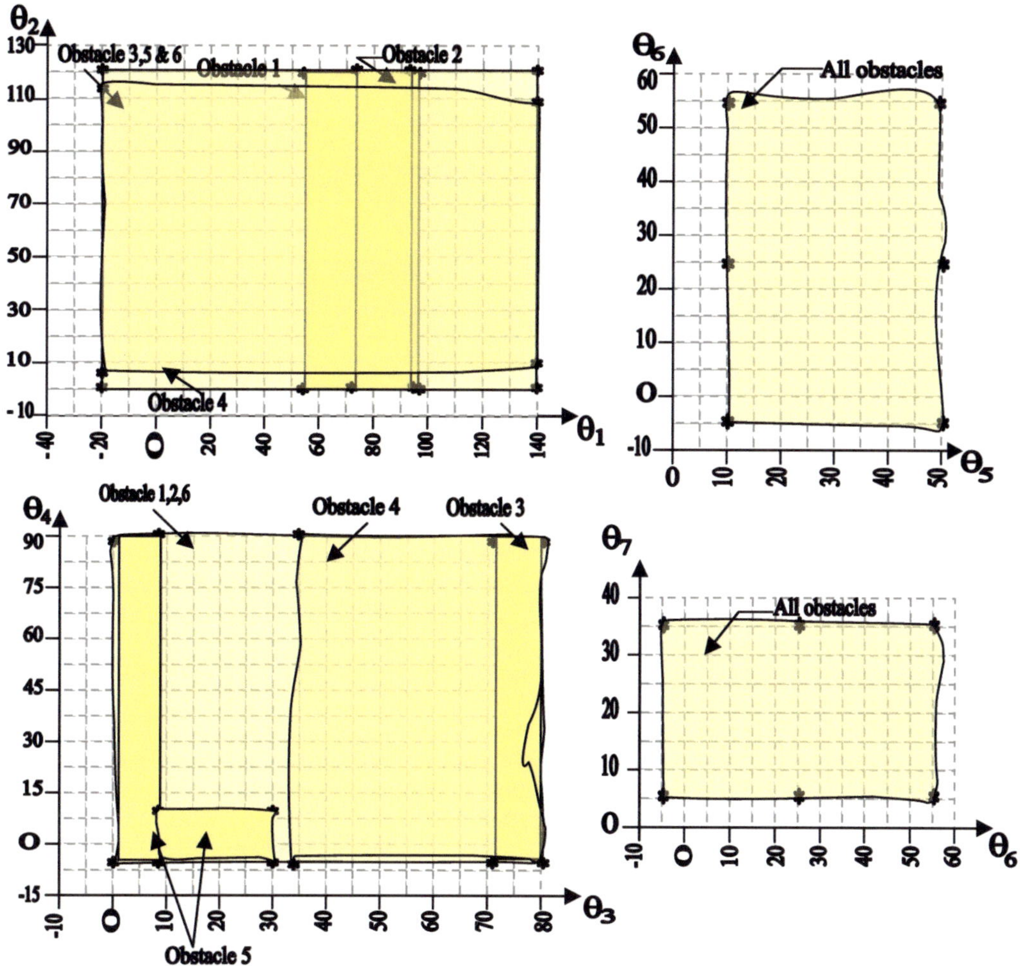

Fig. 18. Four c-space plots for the seven joint revolute robot amidst cluttered workspace of fig. 17

It may be noted that while c-space plot for a 2 d.o.f. robot (working in 2D or 3D task-space) can be composed of irregular non-geometric shapes (refer fig. 7), the same for higher d.o.f. robots are perfectly geometric (refer fig. 18). This is happening because of the incorporation of the concept of 'formidable zones' for higher dimensional robots, wherein we are deliberately allowing the collidable zone to engulf more regions in the c-space. In fact, in most of cases for higher d.o.f. robots, the c-space zones are perfect rectangular in shapes, between the minimum & maximum limits of the participating joint-angles. For example, in fig. 18, (θ_1 vs. θ_2) c-space slice plot the final rectangle is constituted between 4 vertices, viz. θ_{1_min}, θ_{1_max}, θ_{2_min} & θ_{2_max}.

4. Safe path in configuration space: Logistics & algorithm

4.1 Perspective

Based on the formation of c-space maps, collision-free paths are to be ascertained in 2D as well as in 3D. We will analyze the gamut in four functional *quadrants*, which have been conceptualized from the point of view of a] disposition of the obstacles (i.e. planar or spatial) and b] kinematics of the manipulator (i.e. its degrees-of-freedom). Following checker-box illustrates the situation pictorially (refer fig. 19).

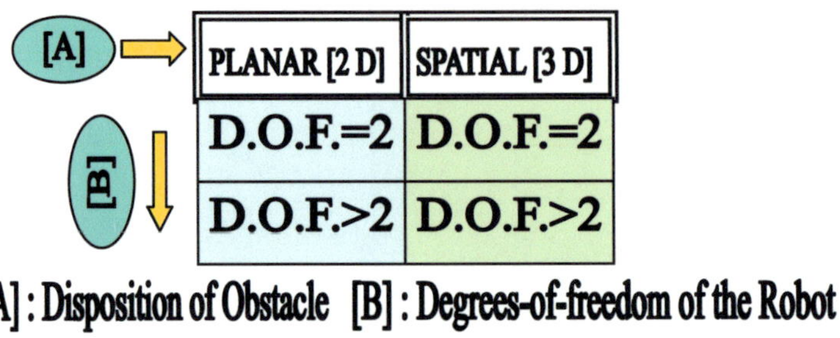

Fig. 19. Schematic of the robotic path planning scenario using Configuration Space approach

In fact, the methodologies to be adopted for different situations of robot path planning vary significantly and those depend on the task-space nature (i.e. planar or spatial) and the robot kinematics (i.e degrees-of-freedom). Besides, the 3D path planning is also dependent upon the nature of the slices produced from the task-space. Those can be identical in nature or non-identical. Table 4 presents the scenario, highlighting the methods used for the collision-free path planning,

Parameter	**COLLISION-FREE PATH PLANNING**					
Task-space	2 D [Planar]		3 D [Spatial]			
Robot Type	D.O.F. = 2	D.O.F. > 2	D.O.F. = 2		D.O.F. > 2	
Method Used for Path Planning	a] C-space Map & b] V-graph	a] (Multiple) C-space Maps ⇒ b] Most Significant C-space Map & c] V-graph	**Identical Slice**	**Non-identical Slice**	**Identical Slice**	**Non-identical Slice**
			a] Sliced C-space Maps ⇒ b] V-graph based Paths & c] Final Path	a] Sliced C-space Maps ⇒ b] V-graph based Paths &c] *Intersection* of the Feasible Paths	a] (Multiple) C-space Maps ⇒b] Most Significant C-space Map & c] V-graph for each slice & d] Final Path	a] (Multiple) C-space Maps ⇒b] Most Significant C-space Map & c] V-graph for each slice & d] *Union* of the Feasible Paths

Table 4. Illustrative Summary of the Methods Used for Collision-free Path Planning of Robots

4.2 Logistics of visibility graph formulation: Our model

The workspace of the robot has been modeled by formulating the *Visibility Matrix* of the *visibility graph*[6] of the cluttered environment. This matrix has been conceived as a kind of 'adjacency' relationship and framed by knowing the necessary visibility information about the nodes of the graph. Figure 21 illustrates the visibility matrix, [Vij], as developed from the environment shown in fig. 20, which depicts a typical sub-visibility graph, generated out of several polygonal obstacles known a-priori (i.e. with pre-fixed locations).

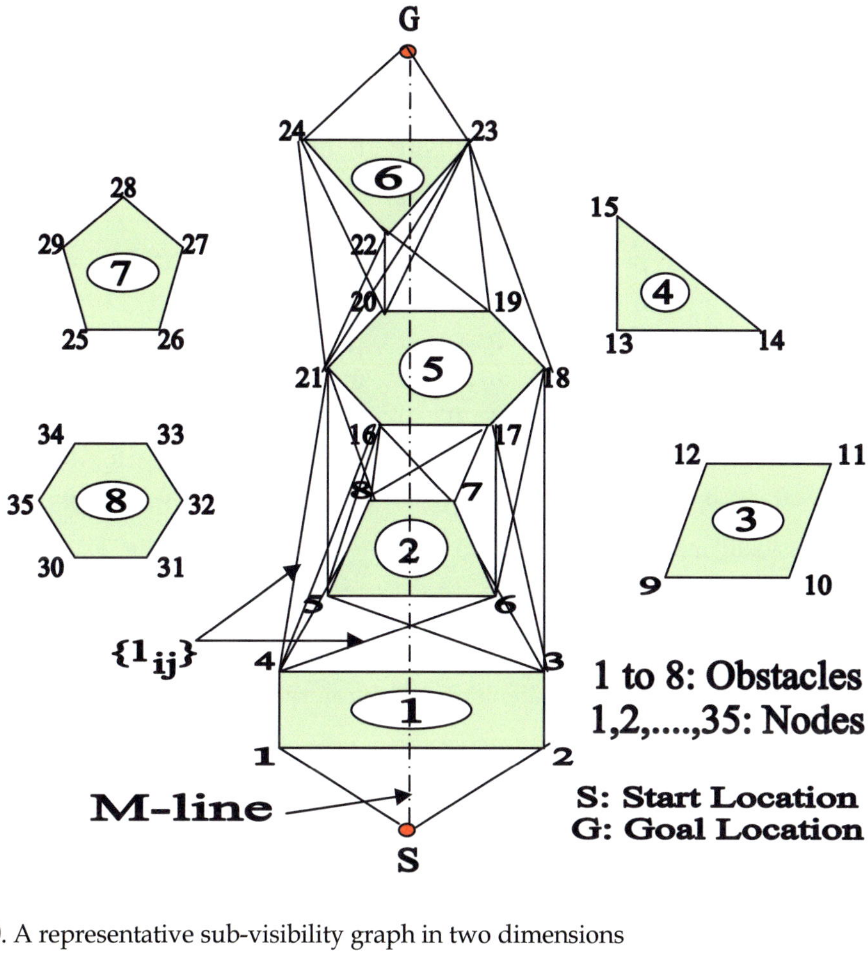

Fig. 20. A representative sub-visibility graph in two dimensions

The matrix is of the order (N + 2) x (N + 2), 'N' being the total number of intermediate nodes of the graph. The full matrix is formed by adding the 'start' (S) and 'goal' (G) nodes, making [V ij] a square matrix. Each row of [Vij] gives the visibility information of that very node. For example, the fifth row of the matrix signifies that the node no. 4 (considering 'S' as the first node) can 'see' nodes 5, 6, 8, 16 & 21 only.

[6] In order to reduce computational burden, 'Sub-visibility Graph' technique has been adopted in the present study. It considers only those obstacles in the robot workspace, which collide directly with the M-line.

	S	1	2	3	4	5	6	7	8	16	17	18	19	20	21	22	23	24	*G*
S –	0	1	2	0	0	0	0	0	0	0	0	0	0	0	0	0	0	0	0
1 –	0	0	2	0	4	0	0	0	0	0	0	0	0	0	0	0	0	0	0
2 –	0	0	0	3	0	0	0	0	0	0	0	18	0	0	0	0	0	0	0
3 –	0	0	0	0	4	0	6	7	0	0	17	18	0	0	0	0	0	0	0
4 –	0	0	0	0	0	5	6	0	8	16	0	0	0	0	21	0	0	0	0
5 –	0	0	0	0	0	0	6	0	8	16	0	0	0	0	21	0	0	0	0
6 –	0	0	0	0	0	0	0	7	0	0	17	18	0	0	0	0	0	0	0
7 –	0	0	0	0	0	0	0	0	8	16	17	18	0	0	0	0	0	0	0
8 –	0	0	0	0	0	0	0	0	0	16	17	0	0	0	21	0	0	0	0
16 –	0	0	0	0	0	0	0	0	0	0	17	0	0	0	21	0	0	0	0
17 –	0	0	0	0	0	0	0	0	0	0	0	18	0	0	0	0	0	0	0
18 –	0	0	0	0	0	0	0	0	0	0	0	0	19	0	0	0	23	0	0
19 –	0	0	0	0	0	0	0	0	0	0	0	0	0	20	0	22	23	0	0
20 –	0	0	0	0	0	0	0	0	0	0	0	0	0	0	21	22	23	24	0
21 –	0	0	0	0	0	0	0	0	0	0	0	0	0	0	0	22	23	24	0
22 –	0	0	0	0	0	0	0	0	0	0	0	0	0	0	0	0	23	24	0
23 –	0	0	0	0	0	0	0	0	0	0	0	0	0	0	0	0	0	24	*G*
24 –	0	0	0	0	0	0	0	0	0	0	0	0	0	0	0	0	0	0	*G*
G –	0	0	0	0	0	0	0	0	0	0	0	0	0	0	0	0	0	0	0

Fig. 21. The visibility matrix developed from the environment shown in fig. 20

Features of the visibility matrix are listed below:

i. Nodes are numbered in ascending order from 'S' to 'G' maintaining counter-clockwise sense for each obstacle. Backtracking of the nodes is not allowed. Symbolically, if 'n_r' is the particular node under consideration which can see nodes $n_{j1}, n_{j2}, \ldots, n_{jp}, \ldots, n_{jk}$ then:

$$n_{j1} > n_r$$

and

$$n_{r-1} \leq n_{jp} \leq N \tag{21}$$

where 'n_{jp}' is any general node of the graph, *visible* by the node 'n_r' and 'N' is the goal node of the nodal series, namely 1,2,3,........,N.

ii. Numbering of nodes is exhaustive and independent of the obstacle nomenclature. In other words, 'n_{jp}' is invariant to obstacle number and also does not have any correlation with any specific obstacle geometry in any form.

iii. The entire matrix has got two parts symmetrically disposed off by the diagonal. Because of the reason stated earlier, the generalized element, 'a_{ij}' of [Vij], which signifies the visibility information of the $j^{th.}$ node as *viewable* with the $i^{th.}$ node as *viewer*, and can be expressed mathematically as:

$$a_{ij} = 0 \text{ or } j \text{ , } \forall\, j \geq i$$

$$a_{ij} = 0 \ \forall \ j \leq i$$

$$a_{i1} = 0 \ \forall \ i$$

$$a_{Nj} = 0 \ \forall \ j \tag{22}$$

iv. For simplicity in computation, the original square matrix [Vij] of order (N+2) has been truncated to a square matrix of order (N+1), by deleting the first column and the last row. Since all the elements of these row and column are zero as per proposition, this modification will not alter the final result. Obviously, structure of this reduced matrix depends on the modeling of the robot environment and the total number of nodes present.

v. It has been found from the composite evaluations that the total number of computations required for the path planning algorithms is slightly less than O (N^2), 'N' being the total number of nodes in the visibility graph, corresponding to the workspace under investigation.

vi. Essentially the visibility matrix reduces to the following structure in its most practical form, viz.:

$$[Vij] = \begin{bmatrix} 0 & 0 & d & d & d & 0 \\ 0 & 0 & 0 & 0 & d & d \\ 0 & 0 & 0 & 0 & d & 0 \\ 0 & 0 & 0 & 0 & 0 & d \\ 0 & 0 & 0 & 0 & 0 & d \\ 0 & 0 & 0 & 0 & 0 & 0 \end{bmatrix}$$

where, 'd' signifies the locations for non-zero entry. The left triangular matrix will be zero in a majority of cases, alongwith the diagonal elements. However, the visibility matrix may include some non-zero entries too corresponding to 'sculptured obstacles' with multiple vertices. With this structure of [Vij], which is time-optimized, the nodal lines can be computed as:

$$\{Lij\} = \sum_{i=1}^{i=N} C_i\,(a_{ij}\,^*) \tag{23}$$

where, {Lij} is the nodal line vector, (a_{ij} *) is the non-zero [a_{ij}] and C_i (a_{ij} *) is the cardinality of a_{ij} *. For example, C_i (a_{ij} *) for the 'S' node (i.e. the first row of [Vij] with i = 1) becomes 2.

In addition, the total number of imaginary lines in the visibility graph can be computed as:

$$\{Lij^*\} = \{Lij\} - \sum_{k=1}^{k=N} d_k \tag{24}$$

where, 'd_k' is the number of edges of the $k^{th.}$ obstacle.

vii. A quick estimation of the computational time for the algorithmic path planning using a finalized visibility graph of the robot workspace reveals the following:

$$\tau \propto \{Lij\} \text{ or } \{Lij^*\} \tag{25}$$

where, 'τ' is a factor representing the computational time and the memory requirement factor, say ξ, will be as follows:

$$\xi \propto \{Lij^*\} \tag{26}$$

Also the range of 'τ' may be estimated for all practical computational situations as,

$$O(N) < \tau \leq O(N^{3/2}) \tag{27}$$

It is to be noted that the lower bound of 'τ' is certainly beyond O (N), while the upper bound can marginally reach $O(N^{3/2})$, as 'N' tends to some larger value.
Regarding circular obstacles in 2D plane, a trade-off has been attained between the approximation to the nearest polygonal shape and the computational burden. For example, a perfectly circular-shaped object can be approximated with a circumscribing square-shaped object, but it will be about 80 % less efficient in comparison to an approximation with an octagonal shape. Hence, the decision for the optimal selection for approximation for a circular obstacle remains with the overall complexity of the visibility graph, i.e. essentially the value of 'N' generated thereby.

4.3 Development of the path planning algorithm in 2D plane

The new heuristic algorithm, namely, Angular Deviation Algorithm, has been developed to obtain near-optimal path for the manipulator amidst obstacles in a planar workspace. The formulation of the heuristics and subsequently the solution phase are based on A* search technique, in general. Following legends have been used in formulating the algorithm.
S: The 'start' location of the robot end-effector (in Cartesian or C-Space);
G: The 'goal' location of the robot end-effector (in Cartesian or C-Space);
SG : The imaginary line joining 'S' and 'G';
$L_{M\text{-}Line}$: The geometric length of the imaginary line joining 'S' & 'G', i.e. the 'M-Line';
x : An intermediate level in the graph search process;
V_{x_j} : $j^{th.}$ visible node from $x^{th.}$ node in the visibility graph;
$x\ V_{x\_j}$: The nodal line, joining the $x^{th.}$ node and the $j^{th.}$ visible node (from $x^{th.}$ node);
i : Iteration number of the graph search process.
This algorithm relies on *angular deviation* as the necessary computing heuristic, which is in-built in nature. It considers each line-segment, $\{ l_{ij} \}$, where, $l_{ij} \in \{ l \}$, joining the nodes, say, n_i and n_j, where $(n_i, n_j) \in \{ n \}, \forall\, i, j \in I$, of the sub-visibility graph and computes the angular deviation of that $\{ l_{ij} \}$ with respect to the M-line. The logic of this algorithm is to minimize the Angular Heuristic Function, as generated from the angular deviations, at each level of searching. Hence, in a cluttered environment the near-optimal path can be chosen by considering only those line-segments, which are comparatively closer to the M-line.
Steps:

1. Initialize the search with i=1.
2. For i=1, loop starts with 'S': note V_{S_1}, V_{S_2}, ..., V_{S_p}.
3. Compute: α_{S_1} = Ang (SG, SV_{S_1}); α_{S_2} = Ang (SG, SV_{S_2}),.......... α_{S_p} = Ang (SG, SV_{S_p}.).
4. Check: min. (α_{S_1} , α_{S_2} ,............, α_{S_p}).
5. If V_{S_p}. = 'G', then stop.

Else,

6. i = i + 1.
7. Begin the next level of search from the $x^{th.}$ node with min.(α_{S_x}).
8. Compute: { α_{x_j} } = { Ang (SG, XV_{x_j}) }, where $x < j \leq N$, 'N' being the total number of nodes in the graph.
9. Go on searching likewise till 'G' occurs and finally note the nodes of the optimal path, so achieved.

4.4 Paradigms of path planning in 3D space for two degrees-of-freedom robots

4.4.1 Model for C-space slices and path generation

The concept of discretization of robot workspace in preferential 2D slices has been applied for generating safe path in a spatial manifold. As a result, multiple c-space slices are generated depending upon the features of the individual slices. Safe paths are then determined, using the *Angular deviation algorithm*, separately for each such c-space slice produced. Thus, if a spatial workspace is segregated in 'k' slices, then there will be 'k' c-space slices also. Figure 22 schematically presents the view of the *sliced c-space maps* for a known environment.

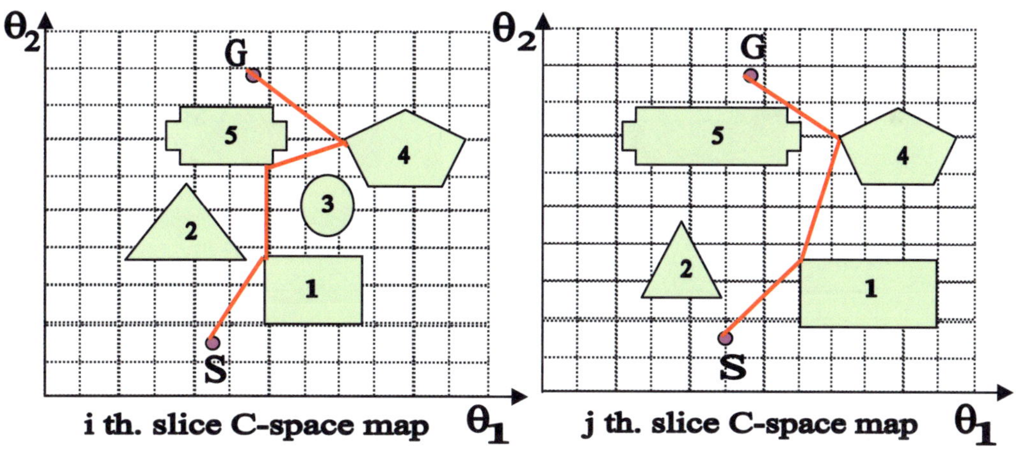

Fig. 22. Schematic view of the sliced c-space maps for a two degrees-of-freedom robot workspace

It may be noted that we need to generate *c-space slices*, as shown in fig. 22, for all the slices equally since our c-space mapping algorithms are in 2D and those are based on planar collision avoidance principles concerning *Point*, *Line* & *Circle* obstacles. Since the total number of slices for a specific environment is fixed a-priori, it may so happen that a particular slice of an object is not falling under the obstruction zone of the robot. In that case, that particular slice of that object will not appear in the corresponding c-space slice (e.g. refer $j^{th.}$ slice c-space map of fig. 22, wherein the slice for obstacle 3 is absent). Nonetheless, the axiom followed is *if the last slice of any obstacle is collidable, then all its previous slices ought to be. But the vice-versa is not true.*

Once the requisite c-space slice maps are generated, we need to evaluate the *safe* paths in each of these sliced c-space maps using the visibility-based Angular deviation algorithm. Thus a set of paths will be obtained and the cardinality of the set will be equal to the number of slices. Finally we will take the *intersection* of the possible paths, as only intersection set will represent the optimal path in true sense. However, intersection won't be the solution for situations where slice(s) for obstacle(s) is/are absent in a particular c-space slice. For example, with reference to fig. 22, considering two c-space slices in total, we have to follow the path shown in the first map, i.e. the $i^{th.}$ slice map.

On the other hand, in situations where all the object-slices are present in all the c-space slices, then intersection can be advantageous, as we can omit longer routes via nodes in certain instances. A typical case is exemplified in fig. 23. Here a particular object is shown to have slightly different geometries and the path between 'S' & 'G' also varies accordingly as shown. In case (a), we are unable to consider 2' as 'node', because of the proposition of visibility graph and the path (viz. S⇒ ……1⇒2⇒3⇒G) is bound to pass through the stipulated node 2 only. However, node 2' lies very much inside the boundary of the c-space obstacle and in fact, it is closer to 'G' as compared to node 2. Thus the path shown in case (b) is the optimal solution (viz. S⇒ ……..1⇒2'⇒G) and in fact, it is also the intersection of the two alternatives.

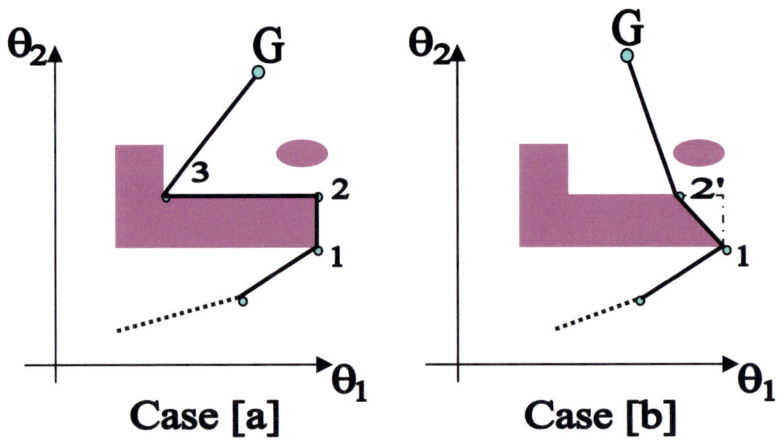

Fig. 23. Selection of path using intersection of alternatives (paths)

4.4.2 Quantitative evaluation of C-space slice points

In order to evaluate the c-space points mathematically, the relevant algorithm generates the intercept co-ordinates (X & Y) corresponding to each 'slice', which are governed by the rotational range of the robot waist and the finite resolution of the waist rotation. The program is applicable only to rectangular 3D solid obstacles, e.g. cube, rectangular parallelopiped, pyramid etc., either directly or after duly transformed from spherical or semi-spherical obstacles. The model is being illustrated schematically through fig. 24.

The relevant formulation vis-à-vis algorithm of the concerned model is described in detail below. Consider figure 24, let:

w : Width of the obstacle;

d : Distance between the robot and the obstacle ;

(x_b, y_b) : Co-ordinates of the robot base;

(x_1, y_1) & (x_2, y_2) : Co-ordinates of the edge of the obstacle in consideration in 2D elevation;

$\theta_{b\_max.}$ & $\theta_{b\_min.}$: Maximum and minimum values of the base rotational edge ;

θ_S: Slicing value of the base rotational angle.

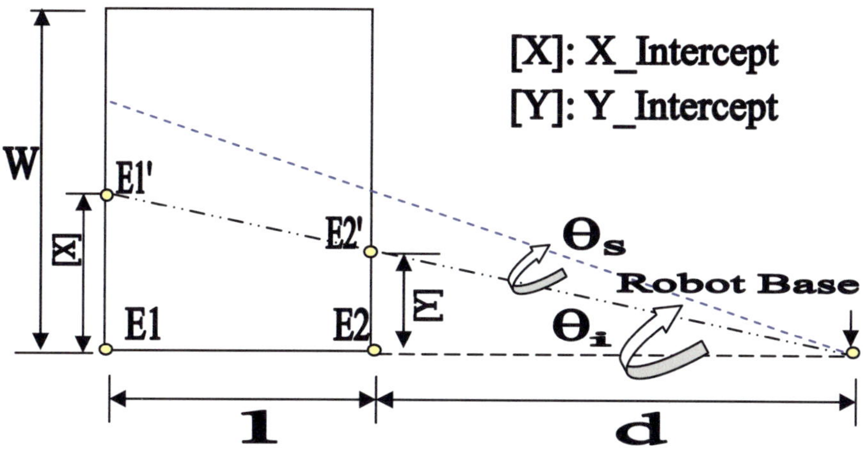

Fig. 24. Schematic representation of the dimensional metrics of a 2D 'Slice'

The range of base rotation is computed as,

$$r_{base} = (\theta_{b\_max.} - \theta_{b\_min.}) \tag{28}$$

Length of the 'edge' of the obstacle is,

$$l = [(x_2 - x_1)^2 + (y_2 - y_1)^2]^{1/2} \tag{29}$$

Now, only one slice is possible, if,

$$d (\pi \theta_S / 180) > w \tag{30}$$

In situations where more than one slice is possible for a particular obstacle, two cases can appear.

Case I: Robot base is in-line with the obstacle

In this case, let $S = d (\pi \theta_i / 180)$, where $\theta_S \le \theta_i \le r_{base}$.
If $S \le w$, then 'slice' is possible and co-ordinates of the intercept of the slices are given by,

$$x_{int\_1} = x_1 + [l \tan \theta_i / (l/d)] [1 + (l/d)] \tag{31}$$

$$y_{int\_1} = y_1 + [l \tan \theta_i / (l/d)] [1 + (l/d)] \tag{32}$$

$$x_{int\_2} = x_2 + [l \tan \theta_i / (l/d)] \tag{33}$$

$$y_{int\_2} = y_2 + [l \tan \theta_i / (l/d)] \tag{34}$$

where, (x_{int_1}, y_{int_1}) and (x_{int_2} , y_{int_2}) are one set of co-ordinates corresponding to one slice. With θ_i varying within its range with an increment of θ_S, the other set of slice co-ordinates will be obtained.

Case II: Robot base is not in-line with the obstacle

In this case,

$$\theta_{in} = \tan^{-1} [\mid (y_2 - y_b) / (x_2 - x_b) \mid] \tag{35}$$

Also,

$$S' = d\,[\,\pi(\theta_j - \theta_{in}) / 180\,],\ \forall\, j,\ \text{where}\ \theta_{in} \le \theta_j \le r_{base}. \quad (36)$$

If $S' \neq 0$ and $S' \leq w$, then slice is possible and co-ordinates of the intercept of the slices are given by,

$$x_{int\_1n} = x_1 + [\,l \tan(\theta_j - \theta_{in}) / (l/d)\,]\,[\,1 + (l/d)\,] \quad (37)$$

$$y_{int\_1n} = y_1 + [\,l \tan(\theta_j - \theta_{in}) / (l/d)\,]\,[\,1 + (l/d)\,] \quad (38)$$

$$x_{int\_2n} = x_2 + [\,l \tan(\theta_j - \theta_{in}) / (l/d)\,] \quad (39)$$

$$y_{int\_2n} = y_2 + [\,l \tan(\theta_j - \theta_{in}) / (l/d)\,] \quad (40)$$

As before, (x_{int_1n} , y_{int_1n}) and (x_{int_2n} , y_{int_2n}) are one set of co-ordinates corresponding to one slice. With θ_j varying within its range with an increment of θ_S, the other set of slice co-ordinates will be obtained. Selection of 'safe' nodes of the robot end-effector in the 3D space depends on the elemental results, as obtained from the corresponding planar analysis. Symbolically, if the collision-free path for one particular 'slice' is represented as,

$$\{ P_{S\_k} \} = \{ S, X_1, X_2, \ldots\ldots\ldots\ldots\ldots, G \}_{S\_k} \quad (41)$$

where, X_1, X_2, ..., represent the serial number of the 'safe' nodes (may not be in the same order as the node nos., viz, 1,2,3,........) and 's_k' is the $k^{th.}$ slice, then the final path will be the union of all such feasible combinations, viz.,

$$\{ P \} = \bigcup_{k=1}^{k=n} \{ P_{S\_k} \} \quad (42)$$

where, 'n' is the total number of slices generated.

4.5 Evaluation of path in 3D for higher dimensional robot

As depicted in fig. 19, evaluation of the collision-free path in 3D will depend on the degrees-of-freedom of the robot (i.e. whether d.o.f. =2 or >2). Nonetheless, in both the cases we need to fragment the 3D task-space in multiple slices, which may or may not be identical to one another. Thus, we will arrive at a situation wherein we have to deploy different strategies to evaluate a safe path. These models are described below.

4.5.1 Model for obtaining safe path for identical slices

The first and foremost pre-requisite of evaluating a collision-free path in this case is to have the *most significant 2D c-space slice map* for the robotic workspace under consideration, as described in 3.4.2. Once the critical c-space slice map is earmarked, the next task is to pin-point the corresponding locations for 'S' & 'G' in that map. This can be achieved by using the inverse kinematic solution for 'S' & 'G' and subsequent mapping from task space to joint space. For example, consider again the case of a seven degrees-of-freedom robot shown in fig. 9, wherein say the [θ_3 -- θ_4] map is the most significant. Thus, the corresponding visibility graph of the environment will have non-identical 'S' & 'G' signatured as, S: ($\theta_3 = \alpha^0$, $\theta_4 = \beta^0$) and G: ($\theta_3 = \gamma^0$, $\theta_4 = \delta^0$). We will assume that the set of other joint-angles, i.e. {θ_1, θ_2, θ_5,

θ_6, θ_7} to be constant throughout the process of path generation. Now, by using the developed path planning algorithm, we will finally get a collision-free optimal path between S: (α,β) and G: (γ,δ). The generalized representation of co-ordinates of any two nodes (say N_i & N_j) of the said path will be as follows,

$$N_i \equiv \{(\theta_1 = c_1,\ \theta_2 = c_2),\ \theta_3 = x_i,\ \theta_4 = y_i,\ (\theta_5 = c_5,\ \theta_6 = c_6,\ \theta_7 = c_7)\}$$

and

$$N_j \equiv \{(\theta_1 = c_1,\ \theta_2 = c_2),\ \theta_3 = x_j,\ \theta_4 = y_j,\ (\theta_5 = c_5,\ \theta_6 = c_6,\ \theta_7 = c_7)\}$$

Where [c_1 & c_2] and [c_5, c_6 & c_7] are two non-identical group of constants to be evaluated using inverse kinematics solution for 'S' and 'G' respectively.
The general lemma in this regard is stated as below,

$$N_i \equiv \{(\theta_1 = c_1,\ \theta_2 = c_2, \ldots, \theta_{p-1} = c_{p-1}),\ \theta_p = x_i,\ \theta_q = y_i,\ (\theta_{q+1} = c_{q+1},\ \theta_{q+2} = c_{q+2}, \ldots, \theta_k = c_k)\}$$

and

$$N_j \equiv \{(\theta_1 = c_1,\ \theta_2 = c_2, \ldots, \theta_{p-1} = c_{p-1}),\ \theta_p = x_j,\ \theta_q = y_j,\ (\theta_{q+1} = c_{q+1},\ \theta_{q+2} = c_{q+2}, \ldots, \theta_k = c_k)\}$$

where, k: the degrees-of-freedom of the articulated robot; θ_1, θ_2,...... θ_p, θ_q,..... ,θ_k: joint-angles of the robot of which 'p' & 'q' represent any two consequtive pair; [θ_p -- θ_q]: the most significant c-space slice map; [c_1, c_2,.....,c_{p-1}] & [c_{q+1}, c_{q+2},...,c_k]: two non-identical group of constants to be evaluated using inverse kinematics solution for 'S' and 'G' respectively.
Once this path is obtained for a particular slice, say the first one, the same procedure can be repeated for other slices too, because all the slices are identical. And, obviously the same path will be obtained in all slices, which will be designated as the final path for that robot in 3D. The kinematic inversion for 'S' & 'G' is another important facet in this regard and analytically, there can be multiple feasible positions of 'S' as well as 'G' in the c-space plot (refer fig. 25). One each from the two clusters of feasible locations can be selected for S: (α,β) and G: (γ,δ).

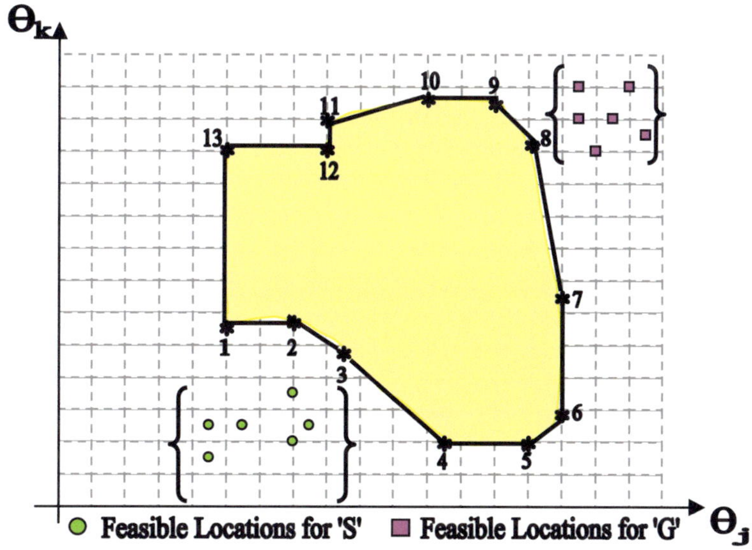

Fig. 25. Multiple feasible locations for 'S' & 'G' inside a specific c-space plot

4.5.2 Model for obtaining safe path for non-identical slices

In this case, we will get different sets of nodal points, corresponding to safe paths, for each slice. The procedure for obtaining a particular set of nodal points (nodes) for a specific slice is same as described in 4.5.1. But the challenge involved here is the most significant c-space slice is not fixed for the slices, rather in worst case it will differ. For example, let us take the case of seven d.o.f. manipulator and we assume there are five slices in the workspace. After c-space slice mapping, we find that while [θ_3 -- θ_4] is the most significant map for the first slice, [θ_1 -- θ_2] is the same for second slice. And likewise, the maps of [θ_3 -- θ_4], [θ_5 -- θ_6] & [θ_1 -- θ_2] are the significant ones for third, fourth and fifth slice respectively. Thus the hurdle becomes in unifying these varying sets of maps into one final path. This is solved considering the *union* of the available sets of nodal points.

In general, if there are 'k' non-identical slices and the sets of nodal points for each safe path are represented by, {S_k} = {N_{1k}, N_{2k},..........,N_{qk}}, where 'q' is the cardinality of the set and the value of 'q' may vary for different 'k', then the final path will be defined as,

$$\{S_{Final}\} = \bigcup_{p=1}^{p=k} \{S_p\}$$

In other words, statistical union of nodes will proceed slice-wise; i.e. to get the *safe* path complete posting all the nodes under one slice, then move on to the next slice and so on, till all the slices are exhausted. Nonetheless, the co-ordinates of the nodes in the path will be evaluated as per the lemma described in 4.5.1.

4.6 Illustrative examples

The developed path planning algorithm has been tested with two sample environments, the first one is contains a two degrees-of-freedom robot while the second one includes a seven degrees-of-freedom robot.

4.6.1 Sample workspace for two degrees-of-freedom robot

This example has a reference to the robot workspace with circular obstacles, as shown in fig. 6 and subsequently, the c-space map, vide fig. 8. Figure 26 presents the final c-space obstacles[7] with nodes numbered sequentially and the visibility graph generated there from.

Table 5 shows the output of the graph search process using our algorithm, developed with 'S' & 'G' configurations as (60^0, -120^0) and (222^0, 190^0) respectively. For comparison, the result obtained through A* search algorithm is also included.

It may be mentioned here that we can very well *benchmark* the result obtained by the Angular Deviation Algorithm, as it is representative amongst the *AI-based* heuristic algorithms. In fact, due to its logistics, the developed algorithm is having an edge over the other possible metrics of path planning, e.g. Generalized Voronoi Diagram (GVD), Cellular Automata and Potential Field. All of these three methods rely on diversification in search, which eventually leads to more computational time and complexity. Besides, the important attribute, namely, "*closeness to desired path*" is compromised in most of the non-AI based techniques. In comparison, AI-based searches are much robust and coherent; like the case

---

[7] Only obstacle 3,5 & 6, referred in figures 6 & 8, have been considered for the creation of visibility graph in order to reduce computational complexity.

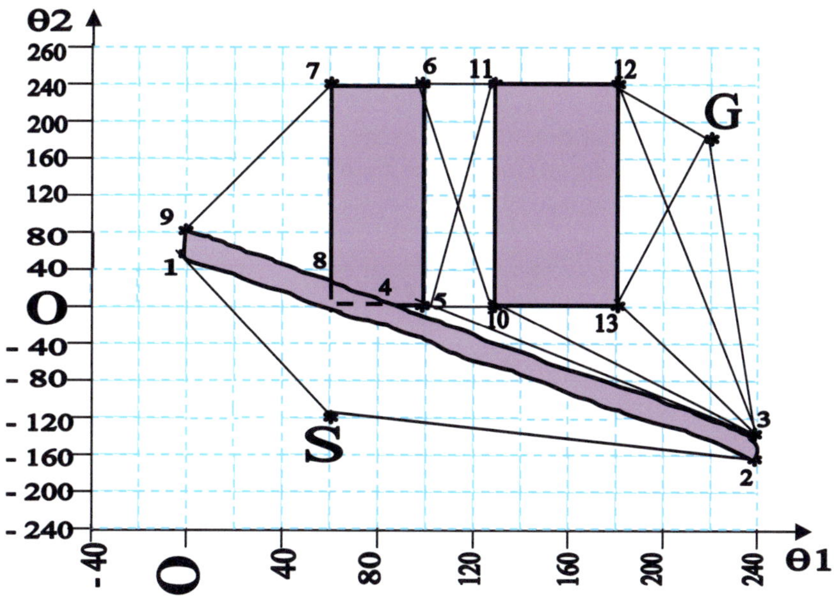

Fig. 26. Visibility graph generated out of the 2D environment, vide fig. 6

Algorithms Used	Path With Nodes	Joint-angle Combination (in degrees)
Angular Deviation Algorithm	S ⇒ 2 ⇒ 3 ⇒ G	(60,-120); (240,-166); (240,-139); (222,190)
A* Algorithm	S ⇒1⇒ 9 ⇒ 7 ⇒ 13⇒ 12 ⇒ G	(60,-120); (0,66); (0,86); (67,240); (129,240); (187,240); (222,190)

Table 5. Collision-free Near-optimal Path between 'S' & 'G' with reference to Example in fig. 26

with Angular Deviation Algorithm. The other group of search algorithms, based on mathematical programming, such as Variational Methods, Hierarchical Dynamic Programming and Tangent Graph Method, are although relatively better focused, but those are highly *memory-extensive*. Thus, in all counts, Angular Deviation Algorithm scores high amongst the various alternatives in graph-search methods.

4.6.2 Sample workspace with seven degrees-of-freedom robot

This example is in reference to the robotic environment shown in fig. 17 and subsequently the various c-space slice maps, as detailed in fig. 18. As we have declared in section 3.5 that [θ_1 -- θ_2] plot is the most significant out of the four plots, we need to obtain the v-graph for this plot. Figure 27 shows the developed v-graph for this c-space slice plot. Here the generated v-graph is relatively simpler by default as it has only four nodes, which is due to the fact that both the joint-angles in consideration, viz. θ_1 & θ_2 are plotted in their full ranges. Thus 'S' & 'G' are also located on the boundary lines, because other locations will be infeasible.

However, it is to be noted that the exact shape of the v-graph (generated out of the most significant c-space slice plot) will depend upon the joint-angle ranges of the joint-pair under consideration and we will have distinct locations for 'S' & 'G', outside the c-space zone. It is evident from fig. 27 that S⇒2⇒3⇒G is the optimal path as 'α' is the smaller angle, which guides this path as per Angular deviation algorithm.

The generalized formulation for evaluating the angular position of 'S' & 'G' in the v-graph (using inverse kinematics routine for the manipulator) is as follows,

$$\sum_{j=1}^{j=7} l_j Cos\left(\sum_{k=1}^{k=j} \theta_k^m\right) = X_m \tag{43a}$$

$$\sum_{j=1}^{j=7} l_j Sin\left(\sum_{k=1}^{k=j} \theta_k^m\right) = Y_m \tag{43b}$$

where. 'm' : positional attribute of the end-point, i.e. either 'S' or 'G'; $\{l_j\}$: link-lengths; $\{\theta_k^m\}$: joint-angles for 'S' or 'G' and (X_m, Y_m): planar Cartesian co-ordinates for 'S' or 'G'.

Now considering the Cartesian co-ordinates for 'S' as (20, 72.5) and the constant values for $\{\theta_3\ \theta_4\ \theta_5\ \theta_6\ \theta_7\}$ as $[10^0\ 5^0\ 15^0\ 6^0\ 10^0]$ we can solve for θ_1 & θ_2 using eqns. (43), which gives us $\theta_1^S \cong 60^0$ and $\theta_2^S \cong 0^0$. Similarly considering 'G' as (-30, -40) with the constant values for $\{\theta_3\ \theta_4\ \theta_5\ \theta_6\ \theta_7\}$ as $[5^0\ 8^0\ 18^0\ 4^0\ 13^0]$ we can solve for θ_1 & θ_2, which gives us $\theta_1^G \cong 108^0$ and $\theta_2^G \cong 120^0$.Thus, as proposed in section 4.5.1, the nodes, $\{N_k, \forall k=1,2,3,4\}$ of the final collision-free path of the manipulator between 'S' & 'G' will be: $N_1 \equiv$ 'S' = $(60^0, 0^0, 5^0, 8^0, 18^0, 4^0, 13^0)$; $N_2 = (140^0, 0^0, 5^0, 8^0, 18^0, 4^0, 13^0)$; $N_3 = (140^0, 120^0, 5^0, 8^0, 18^0, 4^0, 13^0)$ and $N_4 \equiv$ 'G' = $(108^0, 120^0, 5^0, 8^0, 18^0, 4^0, 13^0)$.

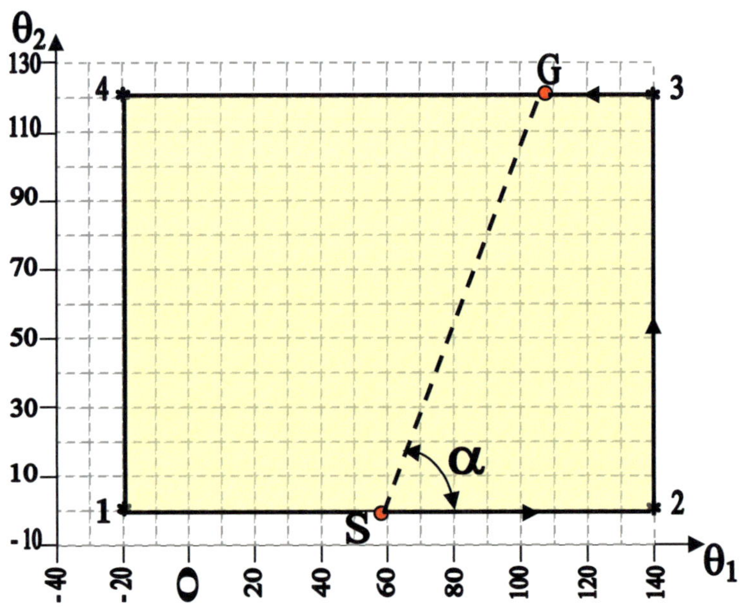

Fig. 27. Visibility graph obtained as per the most significant c-space slice plot of fig. 18

5. Case study

We have studied one real-life case of robot path planning in 3D, based on c-space modeling and v-graph searching, as delineated in the paper so far. The study was made with a five degrees-of-freedom articulated robot, RHINO-XR 3®, during its traverse between two pre-defined spatial locations through a collision-free path. The main focus was to maneuver this robot between 3D obstacles in reaching a goal location in a cluttered (laboratory) environment. Since RHINO is a low-payload robot, instead of standard pick-and-place tests, we designed our experiment such that it had to only *touch* the start ('S') and goal ('G') locations by the gripper end-point. The safe path in 3D, between the start and goal locations, was arrived using *c-space slice* mapping and *Angular Deviation Algorithm* (refer section 4.3). Figure 28 presents the photographic view of the experimental set-up, emphasizing the combined obstacle zone.

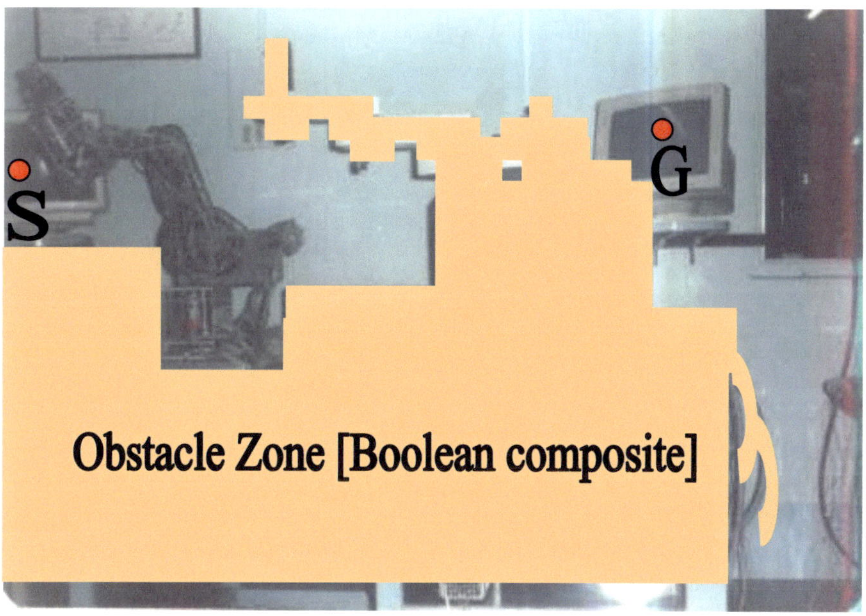

Fig. 28. Photographic view of the test set-up for spatial path planning with RHINO robot

Based on the obstacle zone map vis-à-vis waist rotation of the RHINO robot, we have discretized the workspace into three *non-identical* slices. The task-spaces, corresponding to these slices, are schematically shown in fig. 29. In all the sliced maps, the vertices of the combined obstacles are labeled alphabetically, with a numeric indication for the slice-number. For example, the vertex "A1" signifies the vertex number "A" in slice number1. It is to be noted that the vertex numbers are not *obstacle-specific*, rather those are serially numbered depending on the shape of the obstacle-zone in that very slice.

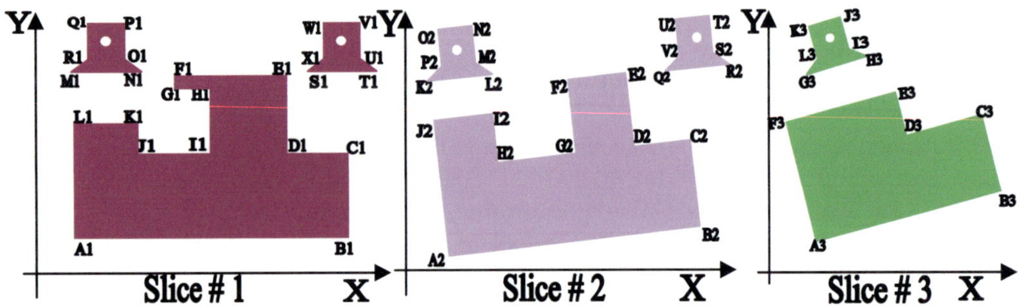

Fig. 29. Schematics of the Cartesian task-space slices for the case-study with RHINO robot

The co-ordinates of the vertices under each of the three slices were obtained by physical measurement of the task-space in 3D. In other words, first we took the measurements of the Boolean obstacle(s) in (x,y,z) form and then the planar co-ordinates of the slice-vertices were evaluated using the method of *projection geometry*. The co-ordinates of the vertices, so evaluated, under each slice, are tabulated in the matrix below.

*Slice*1 ⇒	{*A*1 : (10,20)	*B*1 : (190,20)	*C*1 : (190,68)	*D*1 : (145,68)	*E*1 : (145,98)	*F*1 : (85,98)	*G*1 : (85,80)	*H*1 : (95,80)
*I*1 : (95,68)	*J*1 : (45,68)	*K*1 : (45,78)	*L*1 : (10,78)	*M*1 : (15,128)	*N*1 : (45,128)	*O*1 : (40,135)	*P*1 : (40,155)	*Q*1 : (20,155)
*R*1 : (20,135)	*S*1 : (210,128)	*T*1 : (240,128)	*U*1 : (235,135)	*V*1 : (235,155)	*W*1 : (215,155)	*X*1 : (215,135)}		
*Slice*2 ⇒	{*A*2 : (15,25)	*B*2 : (195,35)	*C*2 : (192,54)	*D*2 : (170,58)	*E*2 : (160,88)	*F*2 : (142,68)	*G*2 : (140,58)	*I*2 : (45,68)
*J*2 : (15,68)	*K*2 : (18,130)	*L*2 : (52,132)	*M*2 : (47,138)	*N*2 : (48,142)	*O*2 : (22,150)	*P*2 : (22,132)	*Q*2 : (212,138)	*R*2 : (242,140)
*S*2 : (236,136)	*T*2 : (236,156)	*U*2 : (222,154)	*V*2 : (220,134)}					
*Slice*3 ⇒	{*A*3 : (18,28)	*B*3 : (198,38)	*C*3 : (193,56)	*D*3 : (172,58)	*E*3 : (168,88)	*F*3 : (142,88)	*G*3 : (18,134)	*H*3 : (52,134)
*I*3 : (46,138)	*J*3 : (48,144)	*K*3 : (24,148)	*L*3 : (24,128)}					

The co-ordinates of the 'S' and 'G' are measured prior to the experiment and those are (30,145,40) & (225,145,42) respectively. It may be mentioned that 'S' & 'G' will not appear in the sliced task-space(s); rather, those will be only in 3D task-space as well as in c-spaces (sliced). Now, considering the kinematics of the RHINO robot, we get a feasible set of joint-angle combinations for 'S' & 'G' though inverse kinematics as,

$$\text{'S'}: \{\theta_1=50^0, \theta_2 = -10^0, \theta_3 =15^0, \theta_4=50^0, \theta_5=15^0\}$$

and

$$\text{'G'}: \{\theta_1=60^0, \theta_2 = 120^0, \theta_3 =58^0, \theta_4=98^0, \theta_5=20^0\}.$$

As evident by now, we will have three non-identical c-space slice maps for this environment and for the clarity in comparison between these three maps, we have selected common scale for the joint-angles. For example, the scale of 'θ_1' in *slice1* map will be same as that of in *slices 2 & 3* and likewise, for other joint-angles. This universality in scaling is helpful in judging the *most critical* map of a particular slice. We will now present the details of the three c-space slice maps, in their final form, alongwith the demarcation of the most critical map(s).

Figures 30,31 & 32 illustrate the conjugate maps corresponding to slice#1, slice#2 & slice#3 respectively.

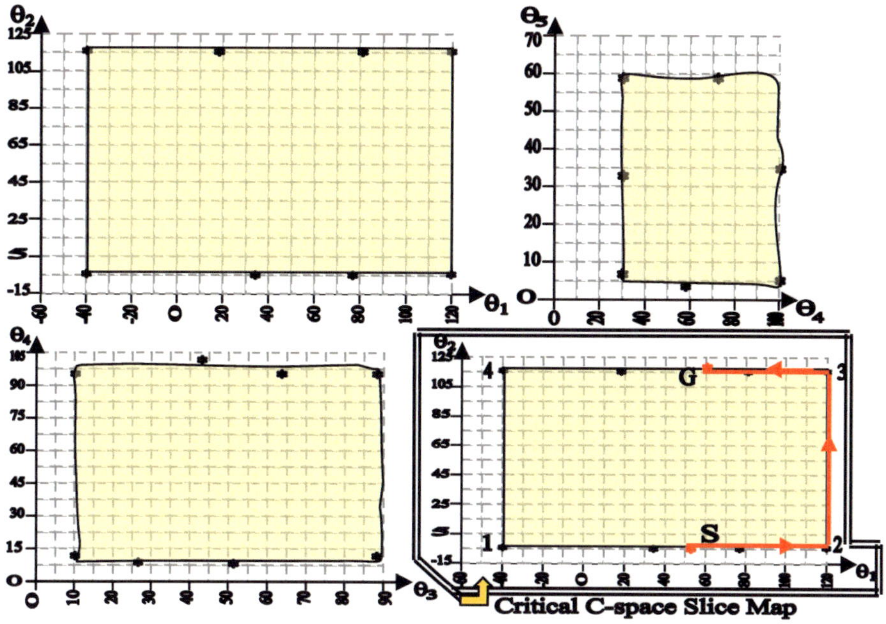

Fig. 30. C-space map for the first slice pertaining to the case- study

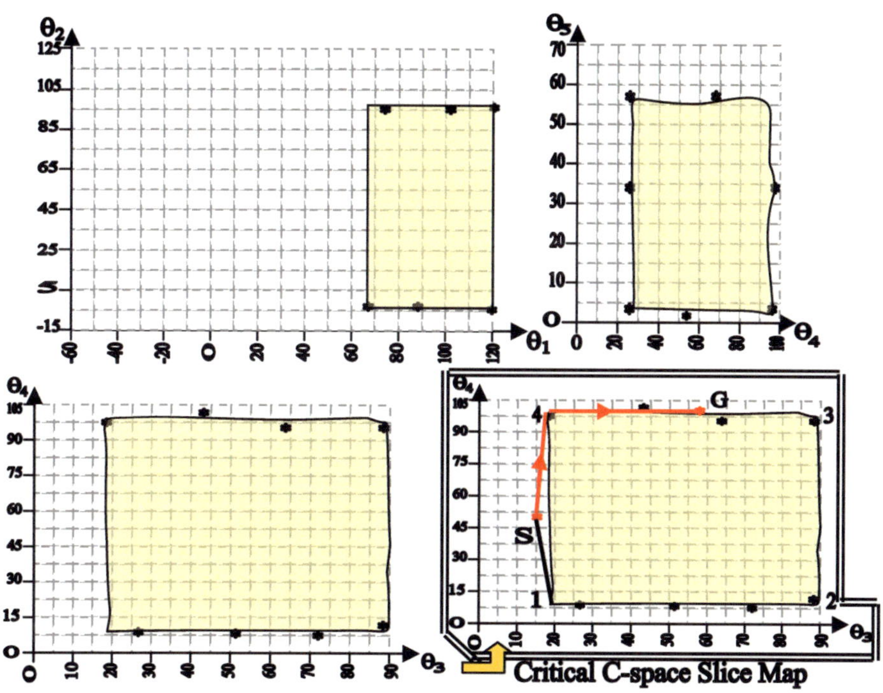

Fig. 31. C-space map for the second slice pertaining to the case – study

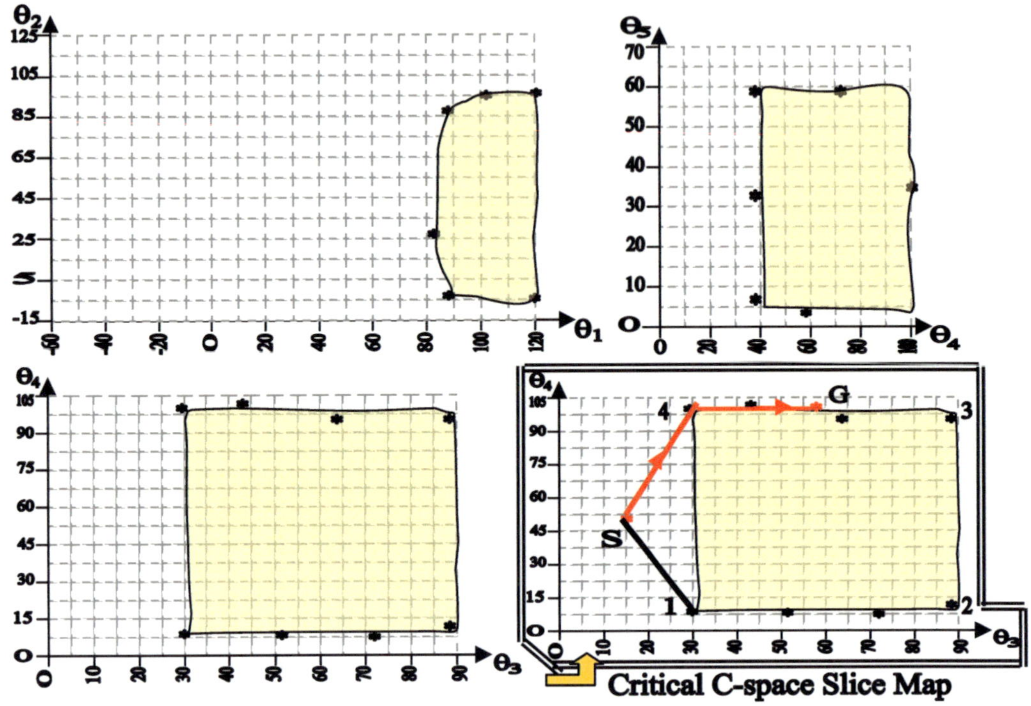

Fig. 32. C-space map for the third slice pertaining to the case - study

It is to be noted that some of the c-space slice maps in the above figures bear similarity; in fact, those maps are bounded by rectangular regions, occupying the full rotational ranges[8] of the participating joint-angles. That means, the full region is formidable, so far as the selection of safe nodes are concerned. This property is unique in the developed method, and it is helpful for obtaining the safe path in the final *go*. Now, assimilating all the three critical c-space slice maps as per figs. 30,31 & 32, we get the final safe path for the environment as the statistical *union* of the slice maps and it is represented as, $S \Rightarrow$ "2"$_{[1]} \Rightarrow$ "3"$_{[1]} \Rightarrow$ "4"$_{[2]} \Rightarrow$ "4"$_{[3]} \Rightarrow$G, where the legend "N"$_{[k]}$ symbolizes node 'N' of the k $^{th.}$ slice (refer section 4.5.2 for the formulation). Thus, the final path has got four *Intermediate Points* (IP), besides 'S' & 'G'. The joint-angle combinations for these 'IP_x', $\forall x$=1,..,4 (as labeled from 'S' onwards) are evaluated as, $IP_1 \equiv$ "2"$_{[1]} \Rightarrow \{\theta_1=120^0,\ \theta_2=-10^0,\ \theta_3=58^0,\ \theta_4=98^0\ \theta_5=20^0\}$; $IP_2 \equiv$"3"$_{[1]} \Rightarrow \{\theta_1=120^0,\ \theta_2=120^0,\ \theta_3=58^0,\ \theta_4=98^0\ \theta_5=20^0\}$; $IP_3 \equiv$"4"$_{[2]} \Rightarrow \{\theta_1=50^0,\ \theta_2=-10^0,\ \theta_3=20^0,\ \theta_4=97^0\ \theta_5=20^0\}$ and $IP_4 \equiv$"4"$_{[3]} \Rightarrow \{\theta_1=50^0,\ \theta_2=-10^0,\ \theta_3=30^0,\ \theta_4=97^0\ \theta_5=20^0\}$.

Table 6 presents a summary of the various important outputs pertaining to the case study, with details of the computational time (for PC-based evaluation). Here, *Elapsed Time* has been divided into elemental time-periods (computational) against 4 sub-heads, viz. "**A**": *Generation of slices in task-space with co-ordinates (x,y) & node numbering*; "**B**": *Generation of c-space maps, including the critical-most*; "**C**": *Development of the v-graph* and "**D**": *Graph searching & output of the Angular Deviation Algorithm.*

[8] The *effective* rotational ranges of the five joint-angles of the RHINO robot are, $\theta 1$: (-40^0 to 120^0), $\theta 2$: (-10^0 to 120^0), $\theta 3$: (10^0 to 90^0), $\theta 4$: (10^0 to 100^0) and $\theta 5$: (5^0 to 65^0), as selected on the basis of our task-space layout & experiments.

Slice	Task Space	Critical C-space & V-graph path	Elapsed Time (for computation) [sec.]				
			A	B	C	D	Total
1	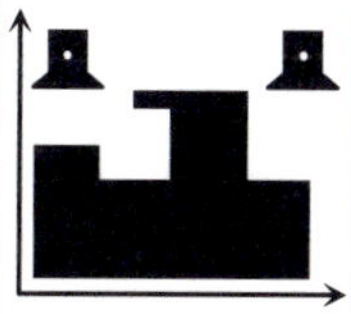	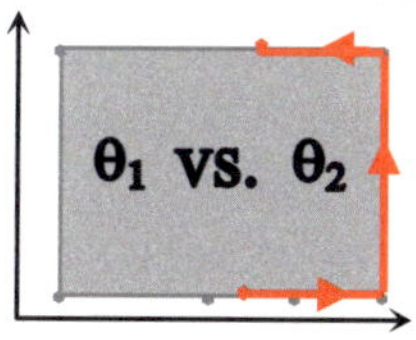	4.5869	32.3878	16.8239	3.7116	57.5102
2	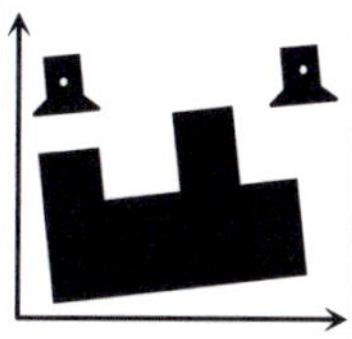	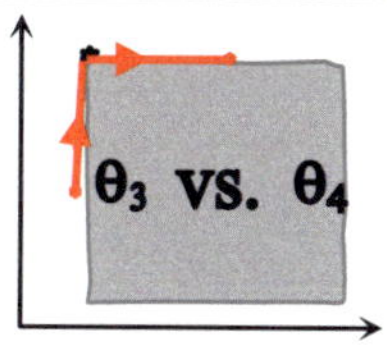	4.3758	30.9764	16.7132	3.7208	55.7862
3		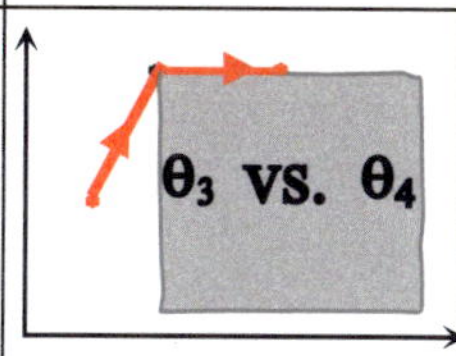	3.8916	30.3358	16.4581	3.7211	54.4066
Final (Combined Computation) ⇒			**4.7938**	**32.8832**	**16.8423**	**3.7428**	**58.2621**

Table 6. Summary Data for the Case Study with Details of the Computational Time [PC-based]

It may be noted that elemental timings for module A, B, C & D against individual slices give an apprehension regarding the relative toughness of the corresponding task-space and later on c-space & v-graphing. On the contrary, the final combined timings indicate the actual processing time (using multi-session processing of the operating system of the PC) of the problem, with usual co-processor actuations. Similar timings were observed while using *A* algorithm* for graph search.

6. Conclusions

The details of the visibility graph-based heuristic algorithm for *safe* path planning in 2D plane as well as 3D space have been discussed in the paper, backed up by the theoretical paradigms of the generation of c-space obstacles from their respective task-spaces. The outcome of the c-space and v-graph algorithms have been found effective in programming the robot in order to perform certain pre-specified tasks or a series of tasks, such as in somewhat off-the-track industrial applications. The *best* path needs to be selected out of the possible alternatives by considering the most feasible criteria, which is essentially application specific. The novelty of the developed method lies with the ease of computational burden as 2D c-space slices are being joined statistically (*union*). Also by not incorporating all obstacles in one c-space slice we are improving upon computational efficiency and thereby reducing undue technical details regarding the obstacles. However, the safe path obtained by the developed method may overrule some nearer nodes, because the corresponding c-space slices are based on maximum *safety margins*, as per the propositions of the model. In fact, the concept of *formidable zones* is introduced in our model to avert potentially dangerous joint-angle configurations and thus, at times, the entire joint-angle range-space gets selected for the c-space map. The reason for taking this lemma is to safeguard the robot's motion between 'S' & 'G' to the best extent. Thus we may end up in some joint-angle (nodal) combinations, which might have been omitted, but it is always better to select a safe & secured path, rather than risking the robot motion for potential grazing and/or full collision with the obstacle(s). As per the proposed method, c-space slices often look trivial (e.g. regular geometrical shaped obstacles), although those are quite computationally intensive. Nonetheless, the geometrical simplification in appearance makes the v-graph map easy and subsequently the graph-search process too.

7. Acknowledgment

Gratitude is due to the faculties of the robotics laboratory, department of Production Engineering, Jadavpur University, Kolkata, India for supporting with the case study. The author acknowledges useful contribution made by Shri Sovan Biswas, Infosys Ltd., India in coding the path planning algorithm used in the case study.

8. References

Acar, Ercan U., Chosel, H., Zhang, Y. & Schervish, M., "Path Planning for Robotic Demining: Robust sensor-based Coverage of Unstructured Environments and Probabilistic Methods", The International Journal of Robotics Research, vol. 22, no. 7-8, July-August 2003, pp 441-466.

Bajaj, C. & Kim, M.S., "Generation of Configuration Space Obstacles: Moving Algebraic Surfaces", The International Journal of Robotics Research, vol. 9, no. 1, February 1990, pp 92-112.

Branicky, M.S. & Newman, W.S., "Rapid Computation of Configuration Space Obstacles", Proceedings of the IEEE International Conference on Robotics & Automation, 1990, pp 304-310.

Brooks, R.A., "Solving the Find-path Problem by Good Representation of Free Space", IEEE Transactions on Systems, Man & Cybernatics, vol. SMC-13, no. 3, 1983, pp 190 - 197.

Brost, R.C., "Computing Metric and Topological Properties of Configuration Space Obstacles", Proceedings: IEEE International Conference on Robotics & Automation, 1989, pp 170-176.

Campbell, D. & Higgins, J., "Minimal Visibility Graphs", Information Processing Letters, vol. 37, no. 1, 10th. January 1991, pp 49-53.

Curto, B. & Moreno, V., "Mathematical Formalism for the Fast Evaluation of the Configuration Space", Proceedings of the IEEE International Symposium on Computational Intelligence in Robotics and Automation, Monterey, CA, U.S.A., July 1997, pp 194-199.

De Pedro, M.T. & Rosa, R.G., "Robot Path Planning in the Configuration Space with Automatic Obstacle Transformation", Cybernatics & Systems, vol. 23, no. 4, 1992, pp 367 - 378.

Erdmann, Michael, "On a Representation of Friction in Configuration Space", The International Journal of Robotics Research, vol. 13, no. 3, June 1994, pp 240-271.

Fu, Li-Chen & Liu, Dong-Yuch, "An Efficient Algorithm for Finding a Collision-free Path Among Polyhedral Obstacles", Journal of Robotics Systems, vol. 7, no.1, 1990, pp 129-137.

Gilbert, E.G. & Johnson, D.W., "Distance Functions and Their Application to Robot Path Planning in the Presence of Obstacles", IEEE Transactions on Robotics & Automation, vol. RA-1, no. 1, March 1985, pp 21-30.

Hasegawa, T. & Terasaki, H., "Collision Avoidance: Divide - and - Conquer Approach by Space Characterization and Intermediate Goals", IEEE Transactions on Systems, Man & Cybernatics, vol. SMC-18, no. 3, May-June 1988, pp 337 - 347.

Hwang, Y.K. & Ahuja, N., "Gross Motion Planning - A Survey", ACM Computing Surveys, vol. 24, no. 3, 1992, pp 219-291.

Jun, S. & Shin, K.G., "A Probabilistic Approach to Collision-free Robot Path Planning", Proceedings of the IEEE International Conference on Robotics & Automation, 1988, pp 220-225.

Keerthi, S.S. & Selvaraj, J., "A Fast Method of Collision Avoidance For An Articulated Two Link Planar Robot Using Distance Functions", Journal of the Institution of Electronics & Telecommunication Engineers, vol. 35, no. 4, 1989, pp 207-217.

Khouri, J. & Stelson, K.A., "Efficient Algorithm for Shortest Path in 3-D with Polyhedral Obstacles", Transactions of the ASME - Journal of Dynamic Systems, Measurement & Control, vol. 8, no. 3, September 1989, pp 433-436.

Kohler, M. & Spreng, M., "Fast Computation of the C-space of Convex 2D Algebraic Objects", The International Journal of Robotics Research, vol. 14, no. 6, December 1995, pp 590-608

Lozano-Perez', T., "Spatial Planning: A Configuration Space Approach", IEEE Transactions on Computers, vol. C-32, no. 2, 1983, pp 108-120.

Tomas Lozano-Perez', "A Simple Motion Planning Algorithm for General Robot Manipulators", IEEE Transactions on Robotics & Automation, vol. RA-3, no. 3, June 1987, pp 207-223.

Lumelsky, V. & Sun, K.,"A Study of the Obstacle Avoidance Problem Based on the Deformation Retract Technique", Proceedings of the 29th. IEEE Conference on Decision and Control, Honolulu, HI, U.S.A., Dec. 1990, pp 1099-1104.

Lumelsky, V. & Sun, K, "A Unified Methodology for Motion Planning with Uncertainty for 2-D and 3-D Two-link Robot Arm Manipulators", The International Journal of Robotics Research, vol. 9, no. 5, October 1990, pp 89-104.

Ralli, E. & Hirzinger, G., "Global and Resolution Complete Path Planner for up to 6 dof Robot Manipulators", Proceedings of the IEEE International Conference on Robotics & Automation, Minneapolis, MN, U.S.A., April 1996, pp 3295-3302.

Red, R.E. & Truong-Cao, H.V, "Configuration Maps for Robot Path Planning in Two Dimensions", Transactions of the ASME - Journal of Dynamic Systems, Measurement & Control, vol. 107, December 1985, pp 292-298.

Red, W.E. et al, "Robot Path Planning in Three Dimensions Using the Direct Subspace", Transactions of the ASME - Journal of Dynamic Systems, Measurement & Control, vol. 119, September 1987, pp 238-244.

Roy, D., "Study on the Configuration Space Based Algorithmic Path Planning of Industrial Robots in an Unstructured Congested 3-Dimensional Space: An Approach Using

Visibility Map", Journal of Intelligent and Robotic Systems, vol. 43, no. 2– 4, August 2005, pp 111-145.

Sacks, E. & Bajaj, C., "Sliced Configuration Spaces for Curved Planar Bodies", The International Journal of Robotics Research, vol. 17, no. 6, June 1998, pp 639-651.

Sacks, E., "Practical Sliced Configuration Spaces for Curved Planar Pairs", The International Journal of Robotics Research, vol. 18, no. 1, January 1999, pp 59-63.

Sachs, S., La Valle, S.M. & Rajko, S., "Visibility-based Pursuit - Evasion in an Unknown Planar Environment", The International Journal of Robotics Research, vol. 23, no. 1, January 2004, pp 3-26.

Schwartz, J.T. & Sharir, M., "A Survey of Motion Planning and Related Geometric Algorithms", Artificial Intelligence, vol. 37, 1988, pp 157-169.

Slotine, Jean Jacques, E. & Yang, H.S., "Improving the Efficiency of Time-optimal Path Following Algorithm", IEEE Transactions on Robotics & Automation, vol. RA-5, no. 1, 1989, pp 118-124.

Verwer, Ben J.H., "A Multi-resolution Workspace, Multi-resolution Configuration Space Approach to Solve the Path Planning Problem", Proceedings of the IEEE International Conference on Robotics & Automation, 1990, pp 2107-2112.

Welzl, E., "Constructing the Visibility Graph for n-line segments in O (n^2) Time", Information Processing Letters, vol. 20, Sept. 1985, pp 167-171.

Wise, Kevin D. & Bowyer, A., "A Survey of Global Configuration-space Mapping Techniques for a Single Robot in a Static Environment", The International Journal of Robotics Research, vol. 19, no. 8, August 2000, pp 762-779.

Yu, Y. & Gupta, K., "C-space Entropy: A Measure for View Planning and Exploration for General Robot - - Sensor Systems in Unknown Environment", The International Journal of Robotics Research, vol. 23, no. 12, December 2004, pp 1197-1223.

Zelinsky, A., "Using Path Transforms to Guide the Search for Findpath in 2D", The International Journal of Robotics Research, vol. 13, no. 4, August 1994, pp 315-325.